The firstwriter.com

Writers' Handbook

2021

The firstwriter.com

Writers' Handbook
2021

EDITOR
J. PAUL DYSON

Published in 2020 by JP&A Dyson
27 Old Gloucester Street, London WC1N 3AX, United Kingdom
Copyright JP&A Dyson

https://www.jpandadyson.com
https://www.firstwriter.com

ISBN 978-1-909935-32-7

Registered with the IP Rights Office
Copyright Registration Service
Ref: 3225986524

Foreword

The firstwriter.com Writers' Handbook returns for its 2021 edition with a brand new layout, a host of new features, and more than twice as many listings as before: over 3,000 listings of literary agents, literary agencies, publishers, and magazines that have been updated in firstwriter.com's online databases between 2018 and 2020. This includes revised and updated listings from the previous edition and over 65% new entries.

Previous editions of this handbook have been bought by writers across the United States, Canada, and Europe; and ranked in the United Kingdom as the number one bestselling writing and publishing directory on Amazon. The 2021 edition continues this international outlook, giving writers all over the English-speaking world access to the global publishing markets.

Finding the information you need is now quicker and easier than ever before, with new tables and an expanded index, and unique paragraph numbers to help you get to the listings you're looking for.

A variety of new tables help you navigate the listings in different ways, including a new Table of Authors, which lists over 3,000 authors and tells you who represents them, or who publishes them, or both.

The number of genres in the index has exploded from under 100 in the last edition to over 500 in this one. So, for example, while there was only one option for "Romance" in the previous edition, you can now narrow this down to Historical Romance, Fantasy Romance, Supernatural / Paranormal Romance, Contemporary Romance, Diverse Romance, Erotic Romance, Feminist Romance, Christian Romance, or even Amish Romance.

The handbook also provides free online access to the entire current firstwriter.com databases, including over 2,400 magazines, over 2,300 literary agents and agencies, over 2,800 book publishers that don't charge fees, and constantly updated listings of current writing competitions, with typically more than 50 added each month.

For details on how to claim your free access please see the back of this book.

Included in the subscription

A subscription to the full website is not only free with this book, but comes packed with all the following features:

Advanced search features

- Save searches and save time – set up to 15 search parameters specific to your work, save them, and then access the search results with a single click whenever you log in. You can even save multiple different searches if you have different types of work you are looking to place.
- Add personal notes to listings, visible only to you and fully searchable – helping you to organise your actions.
- Set reminders on listings to notify you when to submit your work, when to follow up, when to expect a reply, or any other custom action.
- Track which listings you've viewed and when, to help you organise your search – any listings which have changed since you last viewed them will be highlighted for your attention.

Daily email updates

As a subscriber you will be able to take advantage of our email alert service, meaning you can specify your particular interests and we'll send you automatic email updates when we change or add a listing that matches them. So if you're interested in agents dealing in romantic fiction in the United States you can have us send you emails with the latest updates about them – keeping you up to date without even having to log in.

User feedback

Our agent, publisher, and magazine databases all include a user feedback feature that allows our subscribers to leave feedback on each listing – giving you not only the chance to have your say about the markets you contact, but giving a unique authors' perspective on the listings.

Save on copyright protection fees

If you're sending your work away to publishers, competitions, or literary agents, it's vital that you first protect your copyright. As a subscriber to firstwriter.com you can do this through our site and save 10% on the copyright registration fees normally payable for protecting your work internationally through the Intellectual Property Rights Office (https://www.CopyrightRegistrationService.com).

Monthly newsletter

When you subscribe to firstwriter.com you also receive our monthly email newsletter – described by one publishing company as "the best in the business" – including articles, news, and interviews for writers. And the best part is that you can continue to receive the newsletter even after you stop your paid subscription – at no cost!

For details on how to claim your free access please see the back of this book.

Contents

*Claim your free access to **www.firstwriter.com**: See p.423*

Index

Free Access

Glossary of Terms

This section explains common terms used in this handbook, and in the publishing industry more generally.

Academic

Listings in this book will be marked as targeting the academic market only if they publish material of an academic nature; e.g. academic theses, scientific papers, etc. The term is not used to indicate publications that publish general material aimed at people who happen to be in academia, or who are described as academic by virtue of being educated.

Adult

In publishing, "adult" simply refers to books that are aimed at adults, as opposed to books that are aimed at children, or young adults, etc. It is not a euphemism for pornographic or erotic content. Nor does it necessarily refer to content which is unsuitable for children; it is just not targeted at them. In this book, most ordinary mainstream publishers will be described as "adult", unless their books are specifically targeted at other groups (such as children, professionals, etc.).

Advance

Advances are up-front payments made by traditional publishers to authors, which are off-set against future royalties.

Agented

An *agented* submission is one which is submitted by a literary agent. If a publisher accepts only *agented* submissions then you will need a literary agent to submit the work on your behalf.

Author bio

A brief description of you and your life – normally in relation to your writing activity, but if intended for publication (particularly in magazines) may be broader in scope. May be similar to *Curriculum Vitae* (CV) or résumé, depending on context.

Bio

See *Author bio*.

Curriculum Vitae

A brief description of you, your qualifications, and accomplishments – normally in this context in relation to writing (any previous publications, or awards, etc.), but in the case of nonfiction proposals may also include relevant experience that qualifies you to write on the subject. Commonly abbreviated to "CV". May

also be referred to as a résumé. May be similar to *Author bio*, depending on context.

CV

See *Curriculum Vitae*.

International Reply Coupon

When submitting material overseas you may be required to enclose *International Reply Coupons*, which will enable the recipient to send a response and/or return your material at your cost. Not applicable/available in all countries, so check with your local Post Office for more information.

IRC

See *International Reply Coupon*.

Manuscript

Your complete piece of work – be it a novel, short story, or article, etc. – will be referred to as your manuscript. Commonly abbreviated to "ms" (singular) or "mss" (plural).

MS

See *Manuscript*.

MSS

See *Manuscript*.

Professional

Listings in this book will be marked as targeting the professional market if they publish material serving a particular profession: e.g. legal journals, medical journals, etc. The term is not used to indicate publications that publish general material aimed at a notional "professional class".

Proposal

A proposal is normally requested for nonfiction projects (where the book may not yet have been completed, or even begun). Proposals can consist of a number of components, such as an outline, table of contents, CV, marketing information, etc. but the exact requirements will vary from one publisher to another.

Query

Many agents and publishers will prefer to receive a query in the first instance, rather than your full *manuscript*. A query will typically

consist of a cover letter accompanied by a *synopsis* and/or sample chapter(s). Specific requirements will vary, however, so always check on a case by case basis.

Recommendation

If an agent is only accepting approaches by recommendation this means that they will only consider your work if it comes with a recommendation from an established professional in the industry, or an existing client.

RoW

Rest of world.

SAE

See *Stamped Addressed Envelope*. Can also be referred to as SASE.

SASE

Self-Addressed Stamped Envelope. Variation of SAE. See *Stamped Addressed Envelope*.

Simultaneous submission

A simultaneous submission is one which is sent to more than one market at the same time. Normally you will be sending your work to numerous different magazines, agents, and publishers at the same time, but some demand the right to consider it exclusively – i.e. they don't accept simultaneous submissions.

Stamped Addressed Envelope

Commonly abbreviated to "SAE". Can also be referred to as Self-Addressed Stamped Envelope, or SASE. When supplying an SAE, ensure that the envelope and postage is adequate for a reply or the return of your material, as required. If you are submitting overseas, remember that postage from your own country will not be accepted, and you may need to provide an *International Reply Coupon*.

Synopsis

A short outline of your story. This should cover all the main characters and events, including the ending. It is not the kind of "teaser" found on a book's back cover. The length of synopsis required can vary, but is generally between one and three pages.

TOC

Table of Contents. These are often requested as part of nonfiction proposals.

Unagented

An unagented submission is one which is not submitted through a literary agent. If a publisher accepts unagented submissions then you can approach them directly.

Unsolicited mss

A manuscript which has not been requested. Many agents and publishers will not accept unsolicited mss, but this does not necessarily mean they are closed to approaches – many will prefer to receive a short *query* in the first instance. If they like the idea, they will request the full work, which will then be a solicited manuscript.

The Writer's Roadmap

With most objectives in life, people recognise that there is a path to follow. Whether it is career progression, developing a relationship, or chasing your dreams, we normally understand that there are foundations to lay and baby steps to take before we'll be ready for the main event.

But for some reason, with writing (perhaps because so much of the journey of a writer happens in private, behind closed doors), people often overlook the process involved. They often have a plan of action which runs something like this:

1. Write novel.
2. Get novel published.

This is a bit like having a plan for success in tennis which runs:

3. Buy tennis racket.
4. Win Wimbledon.

It misses out all the practice that is going to be required; the competing in the minor competitions and the learning of the craft that will be needed in order to succeed in the major events; the time that will need to be spent gaining reputation and experience.

In this roadmap we'll be laying out what we think is the best path to follow to try and give yourself the best shot of success in the world of writing. You don't necessarily have to jump through all the hoops, and there will always be people who, like Pop Idol or reality TV contestants, get a lucky break that propels them to stardom without laying any of the foundations laid out below, but the aim here is to limit your reliance on luck and maximise your ability to shape your destiny yourself.

1: Write short material

Writers will very often start off by writing a novel. We would advise strongly against this. It's like leaving school one day and applying for a job as a CEO of an international corporation the next. Novels are the big league. They are expensive to produce, market, and distribute. They require significant investment and pose a significant financial risk to publishers. They are not a good place for new writers to try and cut their teeth. If you've already written your novel that's great – it's great experience and you'll have learned a lot – but we'd recommend shelving it for now (you can always come back to it later) and getting stuck into writing some short form material, such as poetry and short fiction.

This is what novelist George R. R. Martin, author of *A Game of Thrones*, has to say on the subject:

> "I would also suggest that any aspiring writer begin with short stories. These days, I meet far too many young writers who try to start off with a novel right off, or a trilogy, or even a nine-book series. That's like starting in at rock climbing by tackling Mt Everest. Short stories help you learn your craft."

You will find that writing short material will improve your writing no end. Writing short fiction allows you to play with lots of different stories and characters very quickly. Because you will probably only spend a few days on any given story you will quickly gain a lot of experience with plotting stories and will learn a lot about what works, what doesn't work, and what you personally are good at. When you write a novel, by contrast, you may spend years on a single story and one set of characters, making this learning process much slower.

Your writing will also be improved by the need to stick to a word limit. Writers who start their career by writing a novel often produce huge epics, the word counts of which they wear as a badge of honour, as if they demonstrate their commitment to and enthusiasm for writing. What they actually demonstrate is a naivety about the realities of getting published. The odds are already stacked against new writers getting a novel published, because of the cost and financial risk of publishing a novel. The bigger the novel, the more it will cost to print, warehouse, and distribute. Publishers will not look at a large word count and be impressed – they will be terrified. The longer the novel, the less chance it has of getting published.

A lengthy first novel also suggests that the writer has yet to learn one of the most critical skills a writer must possess to succeed: brevity. By writing short stories that fit the limits imposed by competitions and magazines you will learn this critical skill. You will learn to remove unnecessary words and passages, and you will find that your writing becomes leaner, more engaging, and more exciting as a result. Lengthy first novels are often rambling and sometimes boring – but once you've been forced to learn how to "trim the fat" by writing short stories, the good habits you've got into will transfer across when you start writing long form works, allowing you to write novels that are pacier and better to read. They will stand a better chance of publication not just because they are shorter and cheaper to produce, but they are also likely to be better written.

2: Get a professional critique

It's a good idea to get some professional feedback on your work at some point, and it's probably better to do this sooner, rather than later. There's no point spending a long time doing something that doesn't quite work if a little advice early on could have got you on the right track sooner. It's also a lot cheaper to get a short story critiqued than a whole novel, and if you can learn the necessary lessons now it will both minimise the cost and maximise the benefit of the advice.

Should you protect the copyright of short works before showing them to anyone?

This is a matter of personal preference. We'd suggest that it certainly isn't as important to register short works as full novels, as your short works are unlikely to be of much financial value to you. Having said that, films do sometimes get made which are based on short stories, in which case you'd want to have all your rights in order. If you do choose to register your short works this can be done for a relatively small amount online at https://www.copyrightregistrationservice.com/register.

3: Submit to competitions and magazines, and build a list of writing credits

Once you have got some short works that you are happy with you can start submitting them to competitions and small magazines. You can search for competitions at https://www.firstwriter.com/competitions and magazines at https://www.firstwriter.com/magazines. Prize money may not be huge, and you probably won't be paid for having your work appear in the kind of small literary magazines you will probably be approaching at first, but the objective here is to build up a list of writing credits to give you more credibility when approaching agents and publishers. You'll be much more likely to grab their attention if you can reel off a list of places where you have already been published, or prizes you have won.

4: Finish your novel and protect your copyright

Okay – so you've built up a list of writing credits, and you've decided it's time to either write a novel, or go back to the one you had already started (in which case you'll probably find yourself cutting out large chunks and making it a lot shorter!). Once you've got your novel to the point where you're happy to start submitting it for publication you should get it registered for copyright. Unlike the registration of short works, which we think is a matter of personal preference, we'd definitely recommend registering a novel, and doing so before you show it to anybody. That *includes* family and friends. Don't worry that you might want to change it – as long as you don't rewrite it to the point where it's not recognisable it will still be protected – the important thing is to get it registered without delay. You can protect it online at https://www.copyrightregistration service.com/register.

If you've already shown it to other people then just register it as soon as you can. Proving a claim to copyright is all about proving you had a copy of the work before anyone else, so time is of the essence.

5: Editing

These days, agents and publishers increasingly seem to expect manuscripts to have been professionally edited before being submitted to them – and no, getting your husband / wife / friend / relative to do it doesn't count. Ideally, you should have the whole manuscript professionally edited, but this can be expensive. Since most agents and publishers aren't going to want to see the whole manuscript in the first instance you can probably get away with just having the first three chapters edited. It may also be worth having your query letter and synopsis edited at the same time.

6: Submit to literary agents

There will be many publishers out there who will accept your submission directly, and on the face of it that might seem like a good idea, since you won't have to pay an agent 15% of your earnings.

However, all the biggest publishers are generally closed to direct submissions from authors, meaning that if you want the chance of getting

a top publisher you're going to need a literary agent. You'll also probably find that their 15% fee is more than offset by the higher earnings you'll be likely to achieve.

To search for literary agents go to https://www.firstwriter.com/Agents. Start by being as specific in your search as possible. So if you've written a historical romance select "Fiction", "Romance", and "Historical". Once you've approached all the agents that specifically mention all three elements broaden your search to just "Fiction" and "Romance". As long as the new results don't specifically say they don't handle historical romance, these are still valid markets to approach. Finally, search for just "Fiction", as there are many agents who are willing to consider all kinds of fiction but don't specifically mention romance or historical.

Don't limit your approaches to just agents in your own country. With more and more agents accepting electronic queries it's now as easy to approach agents in other countries as in your own, and if you're ignoring either London or New York (the two main centres of English language publishing) you're cutting your chances of success in two.

7: Submit directly to publishers

Once you're certain that you've exhausted all potential agents for your work, you can start looking for publishers to submit your work directly to. You can search for publishers at https://www.firstwriter.com/publishers. Apply the same filtering as when you were searching for agents: start specific and gradually broaden, until you've exhausted all possibilities.

8: Self-publishing

In the past, once you got to the point where you'd submitted to all the publishers and agents who might be interested in your book, it would be time to pack away the manuscript in the attic, chalk it up to experience, and start writing another. However, these days writers have the option to take their book directly to market by publishing it themselves.

Before you decide to switch to self-publishing you must be sure that you've exhausted all traditional publishing possibilities – because once you've self-published your book you're unlikely to be able to submit it to agents and publishers. It will probably take a few years of exploring the world of traditional publishing to reach this point, but if you do then you've nothing to lose by giving self-publishing a shot. See our guide to self-publishing for details on how to proceed.

Why Choose Traditional Publishing

When **firstwriter.com** first started, back in 2001, there were only two games in town when it came to getting your book published: traditional publishing, and vanity publishing – and which you should pick was a no-brainer. Vanity publishing was little more than a scam that would leave you with an empty bank account and a house full of unsold books. If you were serious about being a writer, you had to follow the traditional publishing path.

Since then, there has been a self-publishing revolution, with new technologies and new printing methods giving writers a genuine opportunity to get their books into the market by themselves. So, is there still a reason for writers to choose traditional publishing?

The benefits of traditional publishing

Despite the allure and apparent ease of self-publishing, the traditional path still offers you the best chance of making a success of being a writer. There are rare cases where self-published writers make staggering fortunes and become internationally renowned on the back of their self-published books, but these cases are few and far between, and a tiny drop in the rapidly expanding ocean of self-published works. The vast majority of successful books – and the vast majority of successful writers – have their homes firmly in the established publishing houses. Even those self-published authors who find success usually end up moving to a traditional publisher in the end.

This is because the traditional publishers have the systems, the market presence, and the financial clout to *make* a book a bestseller. While successful self-published authors often owe their success in no small part to a decent dose of luck (a social media comment that goes viral; the right mention on the right media outlet at the right time), traditional publishers are in the business of engineering that success. They might not always succeed, but they have the marketing budgets and the distribution channels in place to give themselves, and the book they are promoting, the best possible chance.

And it's not just the marketing and the distribution. Getting signed with a traditional publisher brings a whole team of people with a wealth of expertise that will all work towards the success of the book. It will provide you with an editor who may have experience of working on previous bestsellers, who will not only help you get rid of mistakes in your work but may also help you refine it into a better book. They will help make sure that the quality of your content is good enough to make it in the marketplace.

The publishers will source a professional cover designer who will make your book look the part on the shelves and on the pages of the bookselling websites. They will have accountants who will handle the technicalities of tax regimes both home and abroad. They will have overseas contacts for establishing foreign publishing rights; translations; etc. They may even have contacts in the film industry, should there be a prospect of a movie adaptation. They will have experts working on every aspect of your book, right down to the printing and the warehousing and the shipping of the physical products. They will have people to manage the ebook conversion and the electronic distribution. As an author, you don't need to worry about any of this.

This means you get more time to simply be a writer. You may have to go on book tours, but even these will be organised for you by PR experts, who will also be handling all the press releases, etc.

And then there's the advances. Advances are up-front payments made by traditional publishers to authors, which are off-set against future royalties. So, an author might receive a $5,000 advance before their book is published. When the royalties start coming in, the publisher keeps the first $5,000 to off-set the advance. The good news for the author is that if the book flops and doesn't make $5,000 in royalties they still get to keep the full advance. In an uncertain profession, the security of an advance can be invaluable for an author – and of course it's not something available to self-published authors.

The drawbacks of traditional publishing

The main downside of traditional publishing is just that it's so hard to get into. If you choose to self-publish then – provided you have enough perseverance, the right help and advice, and perhaps a little bit of money – you are guaranteed to succeed and see your book in print and for sale. With traditional publishing, the cold hard fact is that most people who try will not succeed.

And for many of those people who fail it may not even be their fault. That aspect of traditional publishing which can bring so many benefits as compared to self-publishing – that of being part of a team – can also be part of its biggest drawback. It means that you have to get other people to buy into your book. It means that you have to rely on other people being competent enough to spot a bestseller. Many failed to spot the potential of the Harry Potter books. How many potential bestsellers never make it into print just because none of the professionals at the publishers' gates manage to recognise their potential?

So if you choose traditional publishing your destiny is not in your own hands – and for some writers the lack of exclusive control can also be a problem. Sometimes writers get defensive when editors try to tinker with their work, or annoyed when cover artists don't realise their vision the way they expect. But this is hardly a fair criticism of traditional publishing, as most writers (particularly when they are starting out) will benefit from advice from experienced professionals in the field, and will often only be shooting themselves in the foot if they insist on ignoring it.

The final main drawback with traditional publishing is that less of the sale price of each copy makes it to the writer. A typical royalty contract will give the writer 15%. With a self-published book, the author can expect to receive much more. So, all other things being equal, the self-published route can be more profitable – but, of course, all things are not equal. If self-publishing means lower sales (as is likely), then you will probably make less money overall. Remember, it's better to have 15% of something than 50% of nothing.

Conclusion

In conclusion, our advice to writers would be to aim for traditional publishing first. It might be a long shot, but if it works then you stand a much better chance of being successful. If you don't manage to get signed by an agent or a publisher then you still have the option of self-publishing, but make sure you don't get tempted to resort to self-publishing too soon – most agents and publishers won't consider self-published works, so this is a one-way street. Once you've self-published your work, you probably won't be able to change your mind and go back to the traditional publishers with your book unless it becomes a huge hit without them. It's therefore important that you exhaust all your traditional publishing options before making the leap to self-publishing. Be prepared for this to take perhaps a few years (lots of agents and publishers can take six months just to respond), and make sure you've submitted to everyone you can on *both* sides of the Atlantic (publishing is a global game these days, and you need to concentrate on the two main centres of English-language publishing (New York and London) equally) before you make the decision to self-publish instead.

Formatting Your Manuscript

Before submitting a manuscript to an agent, magazine, or publisher, it's important that you get the formatting right. There are industry norms covering everything from the size of your margins to the font you choose – get them wrong and you'll be marking yourself out as an amateur. Get them right, and agents and editors will be far more likely to take you seriously.

Fonts

Don't be tempted to "make your book stand out" by using fancy fonts. It *will* stand out, but not for any reason you'd want. Your entire manuscript should be in a monospaced font like Courier (not a proportional font, like Times Roman) at 12 points. (A monospaced font is one where each character takes up the same amount of space; a proportional font is where the letter "i" takes up less space than the letter "m".)

This goes for your text, your headings, your title, your name – everything. Your objective is to produce a manuscript that looks like it has been produced on a simple typewriter.

Italics / bold

Your job as the author is to indicate words that require emphasis, not to pick particular styles of font. This will be determined by the house style of the publisher in question. You indicate emphasis by underlining text; the publisher will decide whether they will use bold or italic to achieve this emphasis – you shouldn't use either in your text.

Margins

You should have a one inch (2.5 centimetre) margin around your entire page: top, bottom, left, and right.

Spacing

In terms of line spacing, your entire manuscript should be double spaced. Your word processor should provide an option for this, so you don't have to insert blank lines manually.

While line spacing should be double, spaces after punctuation should be single. If you're in the habit of putting two spaces after full stops this is the time to get out of that habit, and remove them from your manuscript. You're just creating extra work for the editor who will have to strip them all out.

Do not put blank lines between paragraphs. Start every paragraph (even those at the start of chapters) with an indent equivalent to five spaces. If you want a scene break then create a line with the "#" character centred in the middle. You don't need blank lines above or below this line.

Word count

You will need to provide an estimated word count on the front page of your manuscript. Tempting as it will be to simply use the word processor's word counting function to tell you exactly how many words there are in your manuscript, this is not what you should do. Instead, you should work out the maximum number of characters on a line, divide this number by six, and then multiply by the total number of lines in your manuscript.

Once you have got your estimated word count you need to round it to an approximate value. How you round will depend on the overall length of your manuscript:

- up to 1,500 words: round to the nearest 100;
- 1,500–10,000 words: round to the nearest 500;
- 10,000–25,000 words: round to the nearest 1,000;
- Over 25,000 words: round to the nearest 5,000.

The reason an agent or editor will need to know your word count is so that they can estimate how many pages it will make. Since actual pages include varying amounts of white space due to breaks in paragraphs, sections of speech, etc. the formula above will actually provide a better idea of how many pages will be required than an exact word count would.

And – perhaps more importantly – providing an exact word count will highlight you immediately as an amateur.

Layout of the front page

On the first page of the manuscript, place your name, address, and any other relevant contact details (such as phone number, email address, etc.) in the top left-hand corner. In the top right-hand corner write your approximate word count.

If you have registered your work for copyright protection, place the reference number two single lines (one double line) beneath your contact details. Since your manuscript will only be seen by agents or editors, not the public, this should be done as discreetly as possible, and you should refrain from using any official seal you may have been granted permissions to use. (For information on registering for copyright protection see "Protecting Your Copyright", below.)

Place your title halfway down the front page. Your title should be centred and would normally be in capital letters. You can make it bold or underlined if you want, but it should be the same size as the rest of the text.

From your title, go down two single lines (or one double line) and insert your byline. This should be centred and start with the word "By", followed by the name you are writing under. This can be your name or a pen name, but should be the name you want the work published under. However, make sure that the name in the top left-hand corner is your real, legal name.

From your byline, go down four single lines (or two double lines) and begin your manuscript.

Layout of the text

Print on only one side of the paper, even if your printer can print on both sides.

In the top right-hand corner of all pages except the first should be your running head. This should be comprised of the surname used in your byline; a keyword from your title, and the page number, e.g. "Myname / Mynovel Page 5".

Text should be left-aligned, *not* justified. This means that you should have a ragged right-hand edge to the text, with lines ending at different points. Make sure you don't have any sort of hyphenation function switched on in your word processor: if a word is too long to fit on a line it should be taken over to the next.

Start each new chapter a third of the way down the page with the centred chapter number / title, underlined. Drop down four single lines (two double lines) to the main text.

At the end of the manuscript you do not need to indicate the ending in any way: you don't need to write "The End", or "Ends", etc. The only exception to this is if your manuscript happens to end at the bottom of a page, in which case you can handwrite the word "End" at the bottom of the last page, after you have printed it out.

Protecting Your Copyright

Protecting your copyright is by no means a requirement before submitting your work, but you may feel that it is a prudent step that you would like to take before allowing strangers to see your material.

These days, you can register your work for copyright protection quickly and easily online. The Intellectual Property Rights Office operates a website called the "Copyright Registration Service" which allows you to do this:

- *https://www.CopyrightRegistrationService.com*

This website can be used for material created in any nation signed up to the Berne Convention. This includes the United States, United Kingdom, Canada, Australia, Ireland, New Zealand, and most other countries. There are around 180 countries in the world, and over 160 of them are part of the Berne Convention.

Provided you created your work in one of the Berne Convention nations, your work should be protected by copyright in all other Berne Convention nations. You can therefore protect your copyright around most of the world with a single registration, and because the process is entirely online you can have your work protected in a matter of minutes, without having to print and post a copy of your manuscript.

What is copyright?

Copyright is a form of intellectual property (often referred to as "IP"). Other forms of intellectual property include trade marks, designs, and patents. These categories refer to different kinds of ideas which may not exist in a physical form that can be owned as property in the traditional sense, but may nonetheless have value to the people who created them. These forms of intellectual property can be owned in the same way that physical property is owned, but – as with physical property – they can be subject to dispute and proper documentation is required to prove ownership.

The different types of intellectual property divide into these categories as follows:

- **Copyright:** copyright protects creative output such as books, poems, pictures, drawings, music, films, etc. Any work which can be recorded in some way can be protected by copyright, as long as it is original and of sufficient length. Copyright does not cover short phrases or names.

- **Trade marks:** trade marks cover words and/or images which distinguish the goods or services of one trader from another. Unlike copyright, trade marks can cover names and short phrases.

- **Designs:** designs cover the overall visual appearance of a product, such as its shape, etc.

- **Patents:** patents protect the technical or functional aspects of designs or inventions.

The specifics of the legal protection surrounding these various forms of intellectual property will vary from nation to nation, but there are also generally international conventions to which a lot if not most of the nations of the world subscribe. The information provided below outlines the common situation in many countries but you should be aware that this may not reflect the exact situation in every territory.

The two types of intellectual property most relevant to writers are copyright and trade marks. If a writer has written a novel, a short story, a poem, a script, or any other piece of writing then the contents themselves can be protected by copyright. The title, however, cannot be protected by copyright as it is a name. An author may therefore feel that they wish to consider protecting the title of their work by registering it as a trade mark, if they feel that it is particularly important and/or more valuable in itself than the cost of registering a trade mark.

If a writer wants to register the copyright for their work, or register the title of their work as a trade mark, there are generally registration fees to be paid. Despite the fact that copyright covers long works that could be hundreds of thousands of words long, while trade marks cover single words and short phrases, the cost for registering a trade mark is likely to be many times higher than that for registering a work for copyright protection. This is because trade marks must be unique and are checked against existing trade marks for potential conflicts. While works to be registered for copyright must also not infringe existing works, it is not practical to check the huge volume of new works to be registered for copyright against the even larger volume of all previously copyrighted works. Copyright registration therefore tends to simply archive the work in question as proof of the date at which the person registering the work was in possession of it.

In the case of both copyright and trade marks the law generally provides some protection even without any kind of registration, but registration provides the owner of the intellectual property with greater and more enforceable protection. In the case of copyright, the creator of a work usually automatically owns the copyright as soon as the work is recorded in some way (i.e. by writing it down or recording it electronically, etc.), however these rights can be difficult to prove if disputed, and therefore many countries (such as the United States) also offer an internal country-specific means of registering works. Some countries, like the United Kingdom, do not offer any such means of registration, however an international registration is available through the Intellectual Property Rights Office's Copyright Registration Service, and can be used regardless of any country-specific provisions. This can help protect copyright in all of the nations which are signatories of the Berne Convention.

In the case of trade marks, the symbol "™" can be applied to any mark which is being used as a trade mark, however greater protection is provided if this mark is registered, in which case the symbol "®" can be applied to the mark. It is often illegal to apply the "®" symbol to a trade mark which has not been registered. There are also options for international registrations of trade marks, which are administered by the World Intellectual Property Organization, however applications cannot be made to the WIPO directly – applications must be made through the relevant office of the applicant's country.

Copyright law and its history

The modern concept of copyright can be traced back to 1710 and the "Statute of Anne", which applied to England, Scotland, and Wales. Prior to this Act, governments had granted monopoly rights to publishers to produce works, but the 1710 Act was the first time that a right of ownership was acknowledged for the actual creator of a work.

From the outset, the attempt to protect the creator's rights was beset with problems due to the local nature of the laws, which applied in Britain only. This meant that lots of copyrighted works were reproduced without the permission of the author in Ireland, America, and in European countries. This not only hindered the ability of the London publishers to sell their legitimate copies of their books in these territories, but the unauthorised reproductions would also find their way into Britain, harming the home market as well.

A natural progression for copyright law was therefore its internationalisation, beginning in 1846 with a reciprocal agreement between Britain and Prussia, and culminating in a series of international treaties, the principal of which is the Berne Convention, which applies to over 160 countries.

Traditionally in the United Kingdom and the United States there has been a requirement to register a work with an official body in order to be able to claim copyright over it (Stationers Hall and the US Library of Congress respectively), however this has been changed by the Berne Convention, which requires signatory countries to grant copyright as an automatic right: i.e. the creator of a work immediately owns its copyright by virtue of creating it and recording it in some physical way (for instance by writing it down or making a recording of it, etc.). The United Kingdom and the United States have both been slow to fully adopt this approach. Though the United Kingdom signed the Berne Convention in 1887, it took 100 years for it to be fully implemented by the Copyright Designs and Patents Act 1988. The United States did not even sign the convention until 1989.

In the United States the US Library of Congress continues to provide archiving services for the purposes of copyright protection, but these are now optional. US citizens no longer need to register their work in order to be able to claim copyright over it. It is necessary, however, to be able to prove when the person who created it did so, and this is essentially the purpose of the registration today. In the United Kingdom, Stationers Hall has ceased to exist, and there is no longer any state-run means of registering the copyright to unpublished works, leaving the only available options as independent and/or international solutions such as the copyright registration service provided by the IP Rights Office.

Registering your work for copyright protection

Registering your work for copyright protection can help you protect your rights in relation to your work. Generally (particularly if you live in a Berne Convention country, as most people do) registration will not be compulsory in order to have rights over your work. Any time you create a unique original work you will in theory own the copyright over it, however you will need to be able to prove when you created it, which is the purpose of registering your work for copyright protection. There are other ways in which you might attempt to prove this, but registration provides better evidence than most other forms.

There are a range of different options for protecting your copyright that vary depending on where you live and the kind of coverage you want. Some countries, like the United States, provide internal means of registering the copyright of unpublished works, however the scope of these will tend to be restricted to the country in question. Other countries, like the United Kingdom, do not offer any specific government-sponsored system for registering the copyright of unpublished works. An international option is provided by the Intellectual Property Rights Office, which is not affiliated to any particular government or country. As long as you live in a Berne Convention country you should be able to benefit from using their Copyright Registration Service. You can register your work with the Intellectual Property Rights Office regardless of whether or not there are any specific arrangements in your home country (you may even choose to register with both to offer your work greater protection). Registration with the Intellectual Property Rights Office should provide you with protection throughout the area covered by the Berne Convention, which is most of the world.

Registering your work for copyright protection through the Intellectual Property Rights Office is an online process that can be completed in a few

minutes, provided you have your file in an accepted format and your file isn't too large (if your file is too large and cannot be reduced you may have to split it and take out two or more registrations covering it). There is a registration fee to pay ($45 / £25 / €40 at the time of writing) per file for registration, however if you are a subscriber to **firstwriter.com** you can benefit from a 10% discount when you start the registration process on our site.

When registering your work, you will need to give some consideration to what your work actually consists of. This is a straightforward question if your work is a novel, or a screenplay, but if it is a collection of poetry or short stories then the issue is more difficult. Should you register your collection as one file, or register each poem separately, which would be more expensive? Usually, you can answer this question by asking yourself what you propose to do with your collection. Do you intend to submit it to publishers as a collection only? Or do you intend to send the constituent parts separately to individual magazines? If the former is the case, then register the collection as a single work under the title of the collection. If the latter is the case then this could be unwise, as your copyright registration certificate will give the name of the collection only – which will not match the names of the individual poems or stories. If you can afford to, you should therefore register them separately. If you have so many poems and / or stories to register that you cannot afford to register them all separately, then registering them as a collection will be better than nothing.

Proper use of the copyright symbol

The first thing to note is that for copyright there is only one form of the symbol (©), unlike trade marks, where there is a symbol for registered trade marks (®) and a symbol for unregistered trade marks (™).

To qualify for use of the registered trade mark symbol (®) you must register your trade mark with the appropriate authority in your country, whereas the trade mark symbol (™) can be applied to any symbol you are using as a trade mark. Use of the copyright symbol is more similar to use of the trade mark symbol, as work does not need to be registered in order to use it.

You can place the copyright symbol on any original piece of work you have created. The normal format would be to include alongside the copyright symbol the year of first publication and the name of the copyright holder, however there are no particular legal requirements regarding this. While it has historically been a requirement in some jurisdictions to include a copyright notice on a work in order to be able to claim copyright over it, the Berne Convention does not allow such restrictions, and so any country signed up to the convention no longer has this requirement. However, in some jurisdictions failure to include such a notice can affect the damages you may be able to claim if anyone infringes your copyright.

A similar situation exists in relation to the phrase "All Rights Reserved". This phrase was a requirement in order to claim international copyright protection in countries signed up to the 1910 Buenos Aires Convention. However, since all countries signed up to the Buenos Aires Convention are now also signed up to the Berne Convention (which grants automatic copyright) this phrase has become superfluous. The phrase continues to be used frequently but is unlikely to have any legal consequences.

The Berne Convention

The Berne Convention covers 162 of the approximately 190 countries in the world, including most major nations. Countries which are signed up to the convention are compelled to offer the same protection to works created in other signatory nations as they would to works created in their own. Nations not signed up to the Berne Convention may have their own arrangements regarding copyright protection.

You can check if your country is signed up to the Berne Convention at the following website:

- *https://www.CopyrightRegistrationService.com*

The status of your country should be shown automatically on the right side of the screen. If not, you can select your country manually from the drop-down menu near the top right of the page.

Should You Self-Publish

Over recent years there has been an explosion in self-published books, as it has become easier and easier to publish your book yourself. This poses writers with a new quandary: continue to pursue publication through the traditional means, or jump into the world of self-publishing? As the rejections from traditional publishers pile up it can be tempting to reach for the control and certainty of self-publishing. Should you give into the temptation, or stick to your guns?

Isn't it just vanity publishing?

Modern self-publishing is quite different from the vanity publishing of times gone by. A vanity publisher would often pose or at least seek to appear to be a traditional publisher, inviting submissions and issuing congratulatory letters of acceptance to everyone who submitted – only slowly revealing the large fees the author would have to pay to cover the cost of printing the books.

Once the books were printed, the vanity publisher would deliver them to the author then cut and run. The author would be left with a big hole in their pocket and a mountain of boxes of books that they would be unlikely to ever sell a fraction of.

Modern self-publishing, on the other hand, is provided not by shady dealers but by some of the biggest companies involved in the publishing industry, including Penguin and Amazon. It doesn't have the large fees that vanity publishing did (depending on the path you choose and your own knowledge and technical ability it can cost almost nothing to get your book published); it *does* offer a viable means of selling your books (they can appear on the biggest bookselling websites around the world); and it *doesn't* leave you with a house full of unwanted books, because modern technology means that a copy of your book only gets printed when it's actually ordered.

That isn't to say that there aren't still shady characters out there trying to take advantage of authors' vanity by charging them enormous fees for publishing a book that stands very little chance of success, but it does mean that self-publishing – done right – can be a viable and cost effective way of an author taking their book to market.

The benefits of self-publishing

The main benefit of self-publishing, of course, is that the author gets control of whether their book is published or not. There is no need to spend years submitting to countless agents and publishers, building up countless heartbreaking rejection letters, and possibly accepting in the end that your dreams of publication will never come true – you can make them come true.

And this need not be pure vanity on the author's part. Almost every successful book – even such massive hits as *Harry Potter* – usually build up a string of rejections before someone finally accepts them. The professionals that authors rely on when going through the traditional publishing process – the literary agents and the editors – are often, it seems, just not that good at spotting what the public are going to buy. How many potential bestsellers might languish forever in the slush pile, just because agents and editors fail to spot them? What if your book is one of them? The traditional publishing process forces you to rely on the good judgment of others, but the self-publishing process enables you to sidestep

that barrier and take your book directly to the public, so that readers can decide for themselves.

Self-publishing also allows you to keep control in other areas. You won't have an editor trying to change your text, and you'll have complete control over what kind of cover your book receives.

Finally, with no publisher or team of editors and accountants taking their slice, you'll probably get to keep a lot more of the retail price of every book you sell. So if you can sell the same amount of books as if you were traditionally published, you'll stand to make a lot more money.

The drawbacks of self-publishing

While self-publishing can guarantee that your book will be available for sale, it cannot guarantee that it will actually sell. Your self-published book will probably have a much lower chance of achieving significant sales than if it had been published traditionally, because it will lack the support that a mainstream publisher could bring. You will have no marketing support, no established position in the marketplace, and no PR – unless you do it yourself. You will have to arrange your own book tours; you will have to do your own sales pitches; you will have to set your own pricing structure; and you will have to manage your own accounts and tax affairs. If you're selling through Amazon or Smashwords or Apple (and if you're not, then why did you bother self-publishing in the first place?) you're going to need to fill in the relevant forms with the IRS (the US tax office) – whether you're a US citizen or not. If you're not a US citizen then you'll have to register with the IRS and complete the necessary tax forms, and potentially other forms for claiming treaty benefits so that you don't get taxed twice (in the US and your home country). And then of course you'll also have to register for tax purposes in your home nation and complete your own tax return there (though you would also have to do this as a traditionally published author).

It can all get very complicated, very confusing, and very lonely. Instead of being able to just be a writer you can find yourself writing less and less and becoming more and more embroiled in the business of publishing a book.

And while it's great to have control over your text and your cover, you'd be ill advised to ignore the value that professionals such as editors and cover designers can bring. It's tempting to think that you don't need an editor – that you've checked the book and had a friend or family member check it too, so it's probably fine – but a professional editor brings a totally different mindset to the process and will check things that won't have even occurred to you and your reader. Without a professional editor, you will almost certainly end up publishing a book which is full of embarrassing mistakes, and trust me – there is no feeling quite as deflating as opening up the first copy of your freshly printed book to see an obvious error jump out – or, even worse, to have it pointed out in an Amazon review, for all to see.

The cover is also incredibly important. Whether for sale on the shelf or on a website, the cover is normally the first point of contact your potential reader has with your book, and will cause them to form immediate opinions about it. A good cover can help a book sell well, but a bad one can kill its chances – and all too often self-published books have amateurish covers that will have readers flicking past them without a second glance.

Claim your free access to **www.firstwriter.com**: See p.423

Finally, the financial benefits of self-publishing can often be illusory. For starters, getting a higher proportion of the retail price is pretty irrelevant if you don't sell any copies. Fifty per cent of nothing is still nothing. Far better to have 15% of something. And then there's the advances. Advances are up-front payments made by traditional publishers to authors, which are off-set against future royalties. So, an author might receive a $5,000 advance before their book is published. When the royalties start coming in, the publisher keeps the first $5,000 to off-set the advance. The good news for the author is that if the book flops and doesn't make $5,000 in royalties they still get to keep the full advance. In an uncertain profession, the security of an advance can be invaluable for an author – and of course it's not something available to self-published authors.

Conclusion

Self-publishing can seem like a tempting shortcut to publication, but in reality it has its own challenges and difficulties. For the moment at least, traditional publishing still offers you the best shot of not only financial success, but also quality of life as a writer. With other people to handle all the other elements of publishing, you get to concentrate on doing what you love.

So we think that writers should always aim for traditional publishing first. It might be a long shot, but if it works then you stand a much better chance of being successful. If you don't manage to get signed by an agent or a publisher then you still have the option of self-publishing, but make sure you don't get tempted to resort to self-publishing too soon – most agents and publishers won't consider self-published works, so this is a one-way street. Once you've self-published your work, you probably won't be able to change your mind and go back to the traditional publishers with your book unless it becomes a huge hit without them. It's therefore important that you exhaust all your traditional publishing options before making the leap to self-publishing. Be prepared for this to take perhaps a few years (lots of agents and publishers can take six months just to respond), and make sure you've submitted to everyone you can on *both* sides of the Atlantic (publishing is a global game these days, and you need to concentrate on the two main centres of English-language publishing (New York and London) equally) before you make the decision to self-publish instead.

However, once you have exhausted all options for traditional publishing, modern self-publishing does offer a genuine alternative path to success, and there are a growing number of self-published authors who have managed to sell millions of copies of their books. If you don't think traditional publishing is going to be an option, we definitely think you should give self-publishing a shot.

For directions on your path through the traditional publishing process see our Writers' Roadmap, above.

If you're sure you've already exhausted all your options for traditional publishing then see below for our quick guide to the self-publishing process.

The Self Publishing Process

Thinking about self-publishing your book? Make sure you go through all these steps first – and in the right order! Do them the wrong way round and you could find yourself wasting time and/or money.

1. Be sure you want to self-publish

You need to be 100% sure that you want to self-publish, because after you've done it there is no going back. Publishers and literary agents will not normally consider books that have been self-published, so if you wanted to get your book to print the old fashioned way you should stop now and rethink. Make absolutely sure that you've exhausted every possible opportunity for traditional publishing before you head down the self-publishing path.

For more information, see "Why choose traditional publishing?" and "Should you self-publish?", above.

2. Protect your copyright

Authors often wonder about what stage in the process they should protect their copyright – often thinking that it's best to leave it till the end so that there are no more changes to make to the book after it is registered.

However, this isn't the case. The key thing is to protect your work before you let other people see it – or, if you've already let other people see it, as soon as possible thereafter.

Don't worry about making small changes to your work after registering it – as long as the work is still recognisable as the same piece of work it will still be protected. Obviously, if you completely change everything you've written then you're going to need another registration, as it will effectively be a different book, but if you've just edited it and made minor alterations this won't affect your protection.

You can register you copyright online at https://www.copyrightregistrationservice.com.

3. Get your work edited

Editing is a vital step often overlooked by authors who self-publish. The result can often be an amateurish book littered with embarrassing mistakes. Any professionally published book will go through an editing process, and it's important that the same applies to your self-published book. It's also important to complete the editing process before beginning the layout, or you could find yourself having to start the layout again from scratch.

4. Choose your self-publishing path

Before you can go any further you are going to need to choose a size for your book, and in order to do that you are going to need to choose a self-publishing path.

There are various different ways of getting self-published, but in general these range from the expensive hands off approach, where you pay a company to do the hard work for you, to the cheap DIY approach, where you do as much as you can yourself.

At the top end, the hands off approach can cost you thousands. At the bottom end, the DIY approach allows you to publish your book for almost nothing.

5. Finalise your layout / typesetting

Before you can finalise your layout (often referred to in the industry as "typesetting") you need to be sure that you've finalised your content – which means having your full work professionally edited and all the necessary changes made. If you decide to make changes after this point it will be difficult and potentially costly, and will require you to go through many of the following steps all over again.

You also need to have selected your path to publication, so that you know what page sizes are available to you, and what page margins you are going to need to apply. If you create a layout that doesn't meet printing requirements (for instance, includes text too close to the edge of the page) then you will have to start the typesetting process all over again.

6. Organise your ISBN

Your book needs to have an ISBN. If you are using a self-publishing service then they may provide you with one of their own, but it is likely to come with restrictions, and the international record for your book will show your self-publishing service as the publisher.

You can acquire your own ISBNs directly from the ISBN issuer, but they do not sell them individually, so you will end up spending quite a lot of money buying more ISBNs than you need. You will, however, have control of the ISBN, and you will be shown as the publisher.

Alternatively, you can purchase a single ISBN at a lower price from an ISBN retailer. This should give you control over the ISBN, however the record for the book will show the ISBN retailer as the publisher, which you may not consider to be ideal.

Whatever you choose, you need to arrange your ISBN no later than this point, because it needs to appear in the preliminary pages (prelims) of your book.

7. Compile your prelims

Your prelims may include a variety of pages, but should always include a title page, a half title page, and an imprint/copyright page. You might then also include other elements, such as a foreword, table of contents, etc. You can only compile your table of contents at this stage, because you need to know your ISBN (this will be included on the copyright/imprint page) and the page numbers for your table of contents. You therefore need to make sure that you are happy with the typesetting and have no further changes to make before compiling your prelims.

8. Create your final press proof

Depending on the self-publishing path you have chosen, you may be able to use a Word file as your final document. However, you need to be careful. In order to print your book it will have to be converted into a press-ready PDF at some point. If a self-publishing service is doing this for you then you will probably find that they own the PDF file that is created, meaning you don't have control over your own press files. Some services will impose hefty charges (hundreds or even more than a thousand dollars) to release these press files.

It might also be the case that you won't get to see the final PDF, and therefore won't get chance to check it for any errors introduced by the conversion process. If it's an automated system, it may also be difficult to control the output you get from it.

We'd suggest that it's best to produce your own PDF files if possible. To do this you will need a copy of Adobe Acrobat Professional, and you will need to be familiar with the correct settings for creating print ready PDFs. Be careful to embed all fonts and make sure that all images are at 300 DPI.

9. Create your cover

Only once your press proof is finalised can you complete your cover design. That's because your cover includes not only the front cover and the back cover, but also (critically) the spine – and the width of the spine will vary according to the number of pages in your final press proof. In order to complete your cover design you therefore need to know your page size, your page count (including all prelims), and your ISBN, as this will appear on the back cover. You also need to get a barcode for your ISBN.

10. Produce your book

Once your cover and press proof are ready you can go through whichever self-publishing path you have chosen to create your book. With some pathways the production of a print proof can be an optional extra that is only available at an extra cost – but we'd recommend standing that cost and getting a print version of your book to check. You never know exactly how it's going to come out until you have a physical copy in your hand.

If you're happy with the proof you can clear your book for release. You don't need to do anything to get it on online retailers like Amazon – they will automatically pick up the ISBN and add your book to their websites themselves.

11. Create an ebook version

In the modern day, having an ebook version of your book is imperative. Ebooks account for a significant proportion of all book sales and are a particularly effective vehicle for unknown and self-published authors.

There are various different file formats used by the different platforms, but .epub is emerging as a standard, and having your book in .epub format should enable you to access all the platforms with a single file.

12. Distribute your ebook

Unlike with print books, you will need to act yourself to get your ebooks into sales channels. At a minimum, you need to ensure that you get your ebook available for sale through Amazon, Apple, and Google Play.

Table of US Literary Agencies

Table of UK Literary Agencies

Table of US Literary Agents

Table of UK Literary Agents

Table of Canadian Literary Agents

Table of US Magazines

Table of UK Magazines

Table of Canadian Magazines

Table of US Book Publishers

Table of UK Book Publishers

Table of Canadian Book Publishers

Table of Irish Book Publishers

Table of Authors

Claim your free access to **www.firstwriter.com**: *See p.423*

Claim your free access to www.firstwriter.com: *See p.423*

Literary Agents and Agencies

For the most up-to-date listings of these and hundreds of other literary agents and agencies, visit https://www.firstwriter.com/Agents

To claim your free access to the site, please see the back of this book.

L0001 3 Seas Literary Agency
Literary Agency
PO Box 444, Sun Prairie, WI 53590
United States
Tel: +1 (608) 834-9317

threeseaslit@aol.com

https://www.threeseasagency.com
https://www.facebook.com/3-Seas-Literary-Agency-75205869856/
https://twitter.com/threeseaslit?lang=en

ADULT > **Fiction** > *Novels*
  Fantasy; Romance; Science Fiction; Thrillers; Women's Fiction

CHILDREN'S > **Fiction** > *Middle Grade*

YOUNG ADULT > **Fiction** > *Novels*

How to send: Query Manager
How not to send: Email

Accepts queries through online submission system only. See website for full guidelines.

Literary Agents: Cori Deyoe (**L0363**); Stacey Graham (**L0568**); Michelle Grajkowski (**L0570**)

L0002 42 Management and Production
Literary Agency
Palladium House, 7th Floor, 1-4 Argyll Street, London, W1F 7TA
United Kingdom
Tel: +44 (0) 20 7292 0554

https://www.42mp.com

Professional Body: The Association of Authors' Agents (AAA)

A fully integrated management and production company, producing film, television and content, representing actors, writers, directors, producers, casting directors and media book rights; with offices in London and Los Angeles.

Literary Agents: Eugenie Furniss (**L0516**); Emily MacDonald (**L0898**); Marilia Savvides (**L1223**)

L0003 A for Authors
Literary Agency
73 Hurlingham Road, Bexleyheath, Kent, DA7 5PE
United Kingdom
Tel: +44 (0) 1322 463479

enquiries@aforauthors.co.uk

http://aforauthors.co.uk

Fiction > *Novels*
  Commercial; Literary

How to send: Word file email attachment; PDF file email attachment

Query by email only. Include synopsis and first three chapters (or up to 50 pages) and short author bio. All attachments must be Word format documents. No poetry, fantasy, SF, horror, erotica, or short stories. No submissions by post or by downloadable link.

Literary Agents: Annette Crossland (*L0312*); Bill Goodall (*L0564*)

L0004 A.M. Heath & Company Limited, Author's Agents
Literary Agency
6 Warwick Court, Holborn, London, WC1R 5DJ
United Kingdom
Tel: +44 (0) 20 7242 2811

enquiries@amheath.com

https://amheath.com
https://twitter.com/AMHeathLtd
https://www.instagram.com/a.m.heath

Professional Body: The Association of Authors' Agents (AAA)

Fiction > *Novels*

Nonfiction > *Nonfiction Books*

Send: Query; Synopsis; Writing sample
How to send: Online submission system
How not to send: Post

Handles general commercial and literary fiction and nonfiction. Submit work with cover letter, synopsis, and writing sample up to 10,000 words, via online submission system only. No paper submissions. Aims to respond within six weeks.

Agency Assistant: Jessica Lee

Agency Assistant / Associate Agent: Florence Rees (**L1134**)

Literary Agents: Julia Churchill (**L0271**); Bill Hamilton (**L0598**); Victoria Hobbs (**L0652**); Zoe King (**L0789**); Oli Munson (**L1009**); Rebecca Ritchie (**L1152**); Euan Thorneycroft (**L1369**)

L0005 A3 Artists Agency
Literary Agency
The Empire State Building, 350 Fifth Ave. 38th Floor, New York, NY 10118, 750 North San Vicente Blvd., East Tower, 11th Floor, Los Angeles, CA 90069
United States
Tel: +1 (646) 486-4600

contactla@a3artistsagency.com
contactny@a3artistsagency.com

https://www.a3artistsagency.com/

Scripts
  Film Scripts; *TV Scripts*

Closed to approaches.

L0006 Lisa Abellera
Literary Agent
United States

Literary Agency: Kimberley Cameron & Associates (**L0787**)

L0007 Abner Stein
Literary Agency
Suite 137, China Works, 100 Black Prince Road, London, SE1 7SJ
United Kingdom

info@abnerstein.co.uk

http://www.abnerstein.co.uk

Professional Body: The Association of Authors' Agents (AAA)

Types: Fiction; Nonfiction
Markets: Adult; Children's

Agency based in London. Handles fiction, general nonfiction, and children's.

Literary Agents: Anna Carmichael (**L0224**); Rachel Clements (**L0279**); Caspian Dennis (**L0356**); Ben Fowler (**L0486**); Vanessa Kerr (**L0781**); Sandy Violette (**L1408**)

L0008 Stephanie Abou
Literary Agent
United States

Literary Agency: Massie & McQuilkin
(**L0934**)

L0009 Above the Line Agency
Literary Agency
468 N. Camden Drive, #200, Beverly Hills,
CA 90210
United States
Tel: +1 (310) 859-6115

abovethelineagency@gmail.com

http://www.abovethelineagency.com

Professional Body: Writers Guild of America
(WGA)

Types: Scripts
Formats: Film Scripts; TV Scripts
Markets: Adult; Children's

Send: Query
Don't send: Full text

Costs: Offers services that writers have to pay
for.

Send query via online web system only.
Represents writers and directors; feature films,
movies of the week, animation. Offers
consultations at a rate of $200 per hour.

Literary Agents: Bruce Bartlett (*L0095*); Rima
Greer (*L0581*)

L0010 Lauren E. Abramo
Literary Agent
United States

Literary Agency: Dystel, Goderich & Bourret
LLC (**L0399**)

L0011 Landa Acevedo-Scott
Literary Agent
United Kingdom

http://www.tiborjones.com/about/

Literary Agency: Tibor Jones & Associates
(**L1371**)

L0012 Kwaku Acheampong
Literary Agent
United States

kwaku@carolynjenksagency.com

https://www.carolynjenksagency.com/agent/
Kwaku-Acheampong

Literary Agency: Carolyn Jenks Agency
(**L0228**)

ADULT
  Fiction > *Novels*
  Nonfiction > *Nonfiction Books*

NEW ADULT
  Fiction > *Novels*
  Nonfiction > *Nonfiction Books*

Send: Query; Writing sample
How to send: In the body of an email

Looking for fiction and nonfiction across most
genres, though he has a special passion for new
adult.

L0013 Steph Adam
Literary Agent
United Kingdom

Literary Agency: Aitken Alexander Associates
(**L0025**)

L0014 Adams Literary
Literary Agency
7845 Colony Road, C4 #215, Charlotte, NC
28226
United States
Tel: +1 (704) 542-1440
Fax: +1 (704) 542-1450

info@adamsliterary.com

http://www.adamsliterary.com

Types: Fiction
Markets: Children's; Young Adult

Closed to approaches.

**Temporarily closed to submissions as at
July 2019. Check website for current
status.** Handles books for children and young
adults, from picture books to teen novels. No
unsolicited MSS. Send query with complete ms
via webform. See website for full submission
guidelines.

Literary Agents: Josh Adams (*L0015*); Tracey
Adams (*L0016*)

L0015 Josh Adams
Literary Agent
United States

Literary Agency: Adams Literary (**L0014**)

L0016 Tracey Adams
Literary Agent
United States

Literary Agency: Adams Literary (**L0014**)

L0017 Jazz Adamson
Literary Agent
United Kingdom

Literary Agency: Micheline Steinberg
Associates (**L0976**)

L0018 Roxana Adle
Literary Agent
United Kingdom

Literary Agency: Independent Talent Group
Ltd (**L0683**)

L0019 Aevitas
Literary Agency
19 West 21st Street, Suite 501, New York, NY
10010
United States
Tel: +1 (212) 765-6900

http://aevitascreative.com

Professional Body: Association of Authors'
Representatives, Inc. (AAR)

Types: Fiction; Nonfiction
Subjects: Arts; Autobiography; Beauty;
Business; Comedy / Humour; Commercial;
Cookery; Culture; Design; Fashion; Health;
History; Lifestyle; Literary; Nature; New Age;
Personal Development; Politics; Psychology;
Religion; Science; Technology
Markets: Adult; Children's; Young Adult

Send: Query
Don't send: Full text

See website for individual agent interests and
query using online submission system.

Chief Executive Officers / Literary Agents:
David Kuhn (**L0812**); Todd Shuster (**L1273**)

Consulting Agent: Karen Brailsford (**L0171**)

Literary Agencies: Aevitas Creative
Management (ACM) UK (**L0020**); Toby
Mundy Associates Ltd (**L1373**)

Literary Agent / President: Esmond
Harmsworth (**L0608**)

Literary Agent / Senior Partner: Jennifer Gates
(**L0530**)

Literary Agents: Erica Bauman (**L0100**); Sarah
Bowlin (**L0166**); Justin Brouckaert (**L0189**);
Chris Bucci (**L0195**); Maggie Cooper (**L0297**);
Jon Michael Darga (**L0330**); Lori Galvin
(**L0525**); Georgia Frances King (**L0788**);
Danya Kukafka (**L0813**); Lauren Sharp
(**L1259**); Becky Sweren (**L1347**)

Literary Agents / Partners: Michelle Brower
(**L0190**); Bridget Wagner Matzie (**L0939**);
Jane von Mehren (**L0964**); Rick Richter
(**L1147**)

Literary Agents / Senior Partners: Laura Nolan
(**L1038**); Janet Silver (**L1278**)

L0020 Aevitas Creative Management (ACM) UK
Literary Agency
49 Greek Street, London, W1D 4EG
United Kingdom

ukenquiries@aevitascreative.com

https://aevitascreative.com/home/acm-uk/
https://twitter.com/AevitasCreative
https://www.facebook.com/AevitasCreative/

Literary Agency: Aevitas (**L0019**)

UK branch of a US agency, founded in 2019,
representing writers and brands throughout the
world.

Chief Executive Officer / Literary Agent: Toby
Mundy (**L1007**)

Literary Agents: Trevor Dolby (**L0375**); Max Edwards (**L0409**); Natalie Jerome (**L0723**); Sara O' Keeffe (**L0772**); Simon Targett (**L1356**)

L0021 The Agency (London) Ltd

Literary Agency
24 Pottery Lane, Holland Park, London, W11 4LZ
United Kingdom

submissions@theagency.co.uk

http://www.theagency.co.uk

Professional Body: The Association of Authors' Agents (AAA)

ADULT > Scripts
 Film Scripts; TV Scripts; Theatre Scripts
CHILDREN'S > Fiction
 Middle Grade; Novels; Picture Books
TEEN > Fiction > *Novels*

YOUNG ADULT > Fiction > *Novels*

Send: Query; Synopsis; Writing sample
How to send: Email

Represents writers and authors for film, television, radio and the theatre. Also represents directors, producers, composers, and film and television rights in books, as well as authors of children's books from picture books to teen fiction. For script writers, only considers unsolicited material if it has been recommended by a producer, development executive or course tutor. If this is the case send CV, covering letter and details of your referee by email. Do not email more than one agent at a time. For directors, send CV, showreel and cover letter by email. For children's authors, send query by email with synopsis and first three chapters (middle grade, teen, or Young Adult) or complete ms (picture books) to address given on website.

Literary Agents: Ian Benson (*L0117*); Nicola Biltoo (*L0134*); Simon Blakey (*L0140*); Hannah Boulton (*L0163*); Hilary Delamere (*L0351*); Stephen Durbridge (*L0398*); Bethan Evans (*L0441*); Katie Haines (*L0595*); Emily Hickman (*L0648*); Jonathan Kinnersley (*L0792*); Julia Kreitman (*L0807*); Norman North (*L1041*); Nick Quinn (*L1122*); Leah Schmidt (*L1233*); Emily Smith (*L1291*); Tanya Tillett (*L1372*)

L0022 AHA Talent Ltd

Literary Agency
2 Percy Street, London, W1T 1DD
United Kingdom
Tel: +44 (0) 20 7250 1760

mail@ahacreatives.co.uk

https://www.ahatalent.co.uk
https://twitter.com/AHAcreatives

Scripts

Film Scripts; Radio Scripts; TV Scripts; Theatre Scripts

Send: Query; Author bio; Writing sample

Handles actors and creatives. Send query with CV/bio, and examples of your work.

Literary Agent: Amanda Fitzalan Howard (*L0668*)

L0023 The Ahearn Agency, Inc

Literary Agency
3436 Magazine St., #615, New Orleans, LA 70115
United States
Tel: +1 (504) 866-6434
Fax: +1 (504) 866-6434

pahearn@aol.com

http://www.ahearnagency.com

Fiction > *Novels*
 Suspense; Women's Fiction

Send: Query; Market info; Self-Addressed Stamped Envelope (SASE)
How to send: Email; Post
How not to send: Email attachment

Send one page query with SASE, description, length, market info, and any writing credits. Accepts email queries without attachments. Response in 2-3 months.

Specialises in women's fiction and suspense. No nonfiction, poetry, juvenile material or science fiction.

Authors: Michele Albert; Rexanne Becnel; Wendy Hilton; Sabrina Jeffries; Connie Koslow; Sandra Landry; Deb Marlowe; Meagan McKinney; Kate Moore; Gerri Russell; Susan Sipal

Literary Agent: Pamela G. Ahearn

L0024 Jamilah Ahmed

Associate Agent
United Kingdom

Literary Agency: Barbara Levy Literary Agency (**L0085**)

Fiction > *Novels*

Nonfiction > *Nonfiction Books*

Briefed with developing new writers in fiction and nonfiction.

L0025 Aitken Alexander Associates

Literary Agency
291 Gray's Inn Road, Kings Cross, London, WC1X 8QJ
United Kingdom
Tel: +44 (0) 20 7373 8672

submissions@aitkenalexander.co.uk

http://www.aitkenalexander.co.uk

Professional Body: The Association of Authors' Agents (AAA)

Types: Fiction; Nonfiction
Markets: Adult

Send: Query
Don't send: Full text
How to send: Email

Send query by email, with short synopsis, and first 30 pages as a Word document. See website for list of agents and their interests and indicate in the subject line which agent you would like to query. No self-help, poetry, or picture books.

Literary Agents: Steph Adam (*L0013*); Clare Alexander (*L0028*); Lisa Baker (*L0079*); Matthew Hamilton (*L0599*); Emma Paterson (*L1070*); Gillie Russell (*L1208*); Lesley Thorne (*L1368*); Chris Wellbelove (*L1428*)

L0026 Alan Brodie Representation Ltd

Literary Agency
Paddock Suite, The Courtyard, 55 Charterhouse Street, London, EC1M 6HA
United Kingdom
Tel: +44 (0) 20 7253 6226
Fax: +44 (0) 20 7183 7999

ABR@alanbrodie.com

http://www.alanbrodie.com

Types: Scripts
Formats: Film Scripts; Radio Scripts; TV Scripts; Theatre Scripts
Markets: Adult

Send: Query
Don't send: Full text
How to send: Email

Handles scripts only. No books. Approach with preliminary letter, recommendation from industry professional, and CV. Do not send a sample of work unless requested. No fiction, nonfiction, or poetry.

Literary Agents: Alan Brodie (*L0182*); Kara Fitzpatrick (*L0472*); Victoria Williams (*L1453*)

L0027 Michael Alcock

Literary Agent; Chair
United Kingdom

michael@johnsonandalcock.co.uk

http://www.johnsonandalcock.co.uk/michael-alcock

Literary Agency: Johnson & Alcock (**L0732**)

Nonfiction > *Nonfiction Books*
 Arts; Biography; Current Affairs; Food; Health; History; Lifestyle; Popular Science

Send: Query; Writing sample; Synopsis

L0028 Clare Alexander

Literary Agent
United Kingdom

Literary Agency: Aitken Alexander Associates (**L0025**)

L0029 Julian Alexander
Literary Agent; Company Director
United Kingdom

Literary Agency: The Soho Agency (**L1297**)

L0030 Alive Literary Agency
Literary Agency
5001 Centennial Blvd #50742, Colorado Springs, CO 80908
United States

http://aliveliterary.com

Nonfiction > *Nonfiction Books*
Lifestyle; Personal Development; Religion

How to send: By referral

Accepts queries from referred authors only. Works primarily with well-established, best-selling, and career authors.

Authors: Jamie Blaine; Michael Hyatt; Karen Kingsbury

Literary Agents: Andrea Heinecke; Lisa Jackson (*L0701*); Bryan Norman (*L1039*)

L0031 Rica Allannic
Literary Agent
United States

Literary Agency: David Black Literary Agency (**L0336**)

L0032 Allen O'Shea Literary Agency
Literary Agency
United States
Tel: +1 (203) 820-5967

marilyn@allenoshea.com

https://www.allenoshea.com

Professional Body: Association of Authors' Representatives, Inc. (AAR)

Types: Nonfiction
Subjects: Business; Cookery; Crafts; Culture; Finance; Health; History; Lifestyle; Politics; Science; Sport
Markets: Adult

Send: Query
Don't send: Full text
How to send: Email

Works mainly with nonfiction writers. Send query by email, describing why your work is unique, your experience, your platform, and any awards or honours received for your writing. See website for full guidelines.

L0033 Marilyn Allen
Literary Agent
United States

L0034 The Alpern Group
Literary Agency
15645 Royal Oak Rd., Encino, California 91436
United States
Tel: +1 (818) 528 1111

http://www.alperngroup.com/
https://twitter.com/alperngroup

Scripts
Film Scripts: General
TV Scripts: Comedy / Humour; Drama

Send: Query; Pitch; Synopsis
How to send: Online submission system
How not to send: Email

Agency based in Los Angeles accepting screenplays and pilots for comedy and drama.

Literary Agents: Jeff Aghassi; Jeff Alpern; Liz Wise

L0035 Elias Altman
Literary Agent
United States

Literary Agency: Massie & McQuilkin (**L0934**)

L0036 Jessica Alvarez
Literary Agent
United States

Literary Agency: BookEnds, LLC (**L0155**)

L0037 Ambassador Speakers Bureau & Literary Agency
Literary Agency
1107 Battlewood Street, Franklin, TN 37069
United States
Tel: +1 (615) 370-4700

info@ambassadorspeakers.com

https://www.ambassadorspeakers.com

Types: Fiction; Nonfiction
Subjects: Adventure; Autobiography; Commercial; Contemporary; Culture; Current Affairs; Finance; Health; History; How To; Legal; Lifestyle; Literary; Medicine; Personal Development; Politics; Religion; Women's Interests
Markets: Adult

Send: Query
Don't send: Full text
How to send: Email

Represents select authors and writers who are published by religious and general market publishers in the US and Europe. No short stories, children's books, screenplays, or poetry. Send query by email with short description. Submit work on invitation only.

L0038 AMP Literary
Literary Agency
c/o Studio Sixty Billion, The Metal Box

Factory, 30 Great Guildford Street, London, SE1 0HS
United Kingdom

submissions@ampliterary.co.uk

https://www.ampliterary.co.uk

Types: Nonfiction
Subjects: Commercial
Markets: Adult

Specialises in commercial nonfiction. Particularly interested in bold female voices. Send query by email.

L0039 The Ampersand Agency Ltd
Literary Agency
Ryman's Cottages, Little Tew, Chipping Norton, Oxfordshire, OX7 4JJ
United Kingdom
Tel: +44 (0) 1608 683677 / 683898
Fax: +44 (0) 1608 683449

submissions@theampersandagency.co.uk

http://www.theampersandagency.co.uk

Professional Body: The Association of Authors' Agents (AAA)

Fiction > *Novels*
Contemporary; Crime; Fantasy; Historical Fiction; Literary; Science Fiction; Thrillers

Nonfiction > *Nonfiction Books*
Biography; Current Affairs; History; Popular Science

Send: Query; Synopsis; Author bio; Writing sample
How to send: Email; Post

Costs: Author covers sundry admin costs.

We handle contemporary and historical novels, literary, crime, thrillers, fantasy, science fiction; non-fiction: current affairs, history, biography, popular science. Send query by post or email with brief bio, outline, and first three chapters. If emailing material, send as attachments rather than pasted into the body of the email. Also accepts science fiction, fantasy, horror, and Young Adult material to separate email address listed on website. No scripts except those by existing clients, no poetry, self-help or illustrated children's books. No unpublished American writers, because in our experience British and European publishers aren't interested unless there is an American publisher on board. And we'd like to make it clear that American stamps are no use outside America!

Authors: Quentin Bates; Will Davis; Phillip Hunter; Vikas Swarup

Literary Agents: Peter Buckman (*L0196*); Jamie Cowen (*L0302*); Anne-Marie Doulton (*L0383*)

L0040 Betsy Amster

Literary Agent
United States

Literary Agency: Betsy Amster Literary
Enterprises (**L0125**)

L0041 Marcia Amsterdam

Literary Agent
United States

Literary Agency: Marcia Amsterdam Agency
(**L0916**)

L0042 The Anderson Literary Agency

Literary Agency
United States
Tel: +1 (917) 363-6829

giles@andersonliteraryagency.com

http://andersonliteraryagency.com

Types: Nonfiction
Subjects: Autobiography; Crime; Religion;
Science
Markets: Adult

Send: Query
Don't send: Full text
How to send: Email

Particularly interested in books that help us
understand people, ideas and the possibility of
change. Send query by email.

Literary Agent: Giles Anderson (*L0044*)

L0043 Darley Anderson

Literary Agent
United Kingdom

Literary Agency: The Darley Anderson Agency
(**L0333**)

Authors: Constance Briscoe; Chris Carter;
Cathy Cassidy; Lee Child; Martina Cole; John
Connolly; Liza Costello; Margaret Dickinson;
Clare Dowling; Jack Ford; Tana French; Paul
Hauck; Joan Jonker; Annie Murray; Abi
Oliver; Adrian Plass; Hazel Prior; David
Rhodes; Jacqui Rose; Stephen Spotswood; Erik
Storey; Lee Weeks

L0044 Giles Anderson

Literary Agent
United States

Literary Agency: The Anderson Literary
Agency (**L0042**)

L0045 Claire Anderson-Wheeler

Literary Agent
United States

Literary Agency: Regal Hoffmann &
Associates LLC (**L1136**)

L0046 Andlyn

Literary Agency
United Kingdom
Tel: +44 (0) 20 3290 5638

submissions@andlyn.co.uk

http://www.andlyn.co.uk

Types: Fiction; Nonfiction
Markets: Children's; Young Adult

Send: Query
Don't send: Full text
How to send: Email

Specialises in children's/teen fiction and
content. Handles picture books, middle-grade,
young adult, and cross-over. Send query by
email with one-page synopsis and first three
chapters (fiction) or proposal and market
analysis (nonfiction). Not accepting picture
book submissions as at December 2018. Check
website for current status.

Literary Agent: Davinia Andrew-Lynch
(*L0052*)

L0047 Andrea Brown Literary Agency, Inc.

Literary Agency
1076 Eagle Drive, Salinas, CA 93905
United States

andrea@andreabrownlit.com

http://www.andreabrownlit.com

Professional Body: Association of Authors'
Representatives, Inc. (AAR)

Types: Fiction; Nonfiction
Subjects: Anthropology; Archaeology;
Architecture; Arts; Autobiography; Comedy /
Humour; Commercial; Contemporary; Culture;
Current Affairs; Design; Drama; Fantasy;
History; How To; Literary; Mystery; Nature;
Photography; Romance; Science; Science
Fiction; Society; Sport; Technology; Thrillers;
Women's Interests
Markets: Children's; Young Adult

Send: Query
Don't send: Full text
How to send: Email

Handles children's from picture books to
young adult only. Send query by email only.
Visit website and view individual agent
profiles, then select one specific agent to send
a query to at their own specific email address
(given on website). Put the word "Query" in
the subject line and include all material in the
text of the email. No attachments. For picture
books, include full MS. For fiction send first
ten pages. For nonfiction submit proposal and
a sample chapter. For graphic novels, send
summary and 2-3 sample page spreads in .jpg
or .pdf format. Indicated which publishers, if
any, the MS has been sent to. No queries by
fax.

Associate Agent: Jemiscoe Chambers-Black
(**L0247**)

Literary Agents: Andrea Brown (*L0191*); Jamie
Weiss Chilton (*L0261*); Jennifer Laughran
(*L0830*); Jennifer Mattson (*L0938*); Lara
Perkins (*L1084*); Laura Rennert (*L1142*);
Jennifer Rofe (**L1179**); Kathleen Rushall
(*L1205*); Jennifer March Soloway (*L1300*);
Kelly Sonnack (*L1302*); Caryn Wiseman
(*L1463*)

L0048 Andrew Lownie Literary Agency Ltd

Literary Agency
36 Great Smith Street, London, SW1P 3BU
United Kingdom
Tel: +44 (0) 20 7222 7574
Fax: +44 (0) 20 7222 7576

lownie@globalnet.co.uk

http://www.andrewlownie.co.uk
https://twitter.com/andrewlownie

Nonfiction > *Nonfiction Books*

Send: Query; Synopsis; Author bio; Market
info; Writing sample
How to send: Email

This agency, founded in 1988, is now one of
the UK's leading literary agencies with some
two hundred nonfiction and fiction authors. It
prides itself on its personal attention to its
clients and specialises both in launching new
writers and taking established writers to a new
level of recognition.

Authors: Daniel Cowling; James Davies; Andy
Donaldson; Angela Findlay; Katreen Hardt;
Catherine Hewitt; Christian Jennings; David
McClure; Danny Orbach; Linda Porter; Louise
Ramsay; Dan Smith; Nicola Stow; Tim Tate;
Ian Williams; Chris Woodford

Literary Agent: Andrew Lownie (*L0880*)

L0049 Andrew Mann Ltd

Literary Agency
6 Quernmore Road, London, N4 4QU
United Kingdom
Tel: +44 (0) 20 7609 6218

tina@andrewmann.co.uk

http://www.andrewmann.co.uk

Professional Body: The Association of
Authors' Agents (AAA)

Types: Fiction
Subjects: Commercial; Crime; History;
Literary; Thrillers
Markets: Adult

Closed to approaches.

**Closed to submissions as at March 2018.
Check website for current status.** Interested
in literary and commercial fiction, historical,
and crime/thriller. Send query by email, or by
post if absolutely necessary with SAE, with

brief synopsis and first three chapters or 30 pages. See website for specific email address for crime/thriller submissions. No children's, screenplays or theatre, misery memoirs, new age philosophy, nonfiction, fantasy, science fiction, poetry, short stories, vampires, or dystopian fiction. See website for full submission guidelines.

Literary Agents: Tina Betts (*L0126*); Louise Burns (*L0200*)

L0050 Andrew Nurnberg Associates, Ltd
Literary Agency
3-11 Eyre St Hill, London, EC1R 5ET
United Kingdom
Tel: +44 (0) 20 3327 0400

info@nurnberg.co.uk
submissions@nurnberg.co.uk

http://www.andrewnurnberg.com
https://twitter.com/nurnberg_agency
https://www.instagram.com/
andrewnurnbergassociates/?hl=en

Professional Body: The Association of Authors' Agents (AAA)

ADULT
  Fiction > *Novels*
  Nonfiction > *Nonfiction Books*

CHILDREN'S > **Fiction** > *Novels*

Does not want:

> **ADULT** > **Scripts**
>   *Film Scripts*; *Radio Scripts*; *TV Scripts*;
>   *Theatre Scripts*
> **CHILDREN'S** > **Fiction** > *Picture Books*

Send: Query; Synopsis; Writing sample
How to send: Email

Handles adult fiction and nonfiction, and children's fiction. No poetry, children's picture books, or scripts for film, TV, radio or theatre. Send query by email with one-page synopsis and first three chapters or 50 pages as attachments.

Literary Agents: Sarah Nundy (*L1044*); Andrew Nurnberg (*L1045*)

L0051 Nelle Andrew
Literary Agent
United Kingdom

nelle@rmliterary.co.uk

Literary Agency: Rachel Mills Literary (**L1124**)

Fiction > *Novels*
  Book Club Fiction; Commercial Women's Fiction; Crime; Feminism; Historical Fiction; Literary; Suspense; Thrillers

Nonfiction > *Nonfiction Books*: Narrative Nonfiction

Send: Author bio; Synopsis; Writing sample
How to send: Email

Looking for fiction and nonfiction. Loves historical, literary, commercial female fiction, reading group, suspense and thrillers and intelligent crime. Particularly interested in books that shine a light on new ideas or little known histories, diverse backgrounds, and emotionally moving narratives that resonate with modern complexities.

L0052 Davinia Andrew-Lynch
Literary Agent
United Kingdom

Literary Agency: Andlyn (**L0046**)

L0053 Andy Ross Agency
Literary Agency
767 Santa Ray Avenue, Oakland, CA 94610
United States
Tel: +1 (510) 238-8965

andyrossagency@hotmail.com

http://www.andyrossagency.com

Professional Body: Association of Authors' Representatives, Inc. (AAR)

Types: Fiction; Nonfiction
Subjects: Commercial; Contemporary; Culture; Current Affairs; History; Literary; Religion; Science
Markets: Adult; Young Adult

Send: Query
Don't send: Full text
How to send: Email

We encourage queries for material in our fields of interest. No poetry, short stories, adult romance, science fiction and fantasy, adult and teen paranormal, or film scripts. The agent has worked in the book business for 36 years, all of his working life. He was owner and general manager of Cody's Books in Berkeley, California from 1977-2006. Cody's has been recognised as one of America's great independent book stores. During this period, the agent was the primary trade book buyer. This experience has given him a unique understanding of the retail book market, of publishing trends and, most importantly and uniquely, the hand selling of books to book buyers. The agent is past president of the Northern California Booksellers Association, a board member and officer of the American Booksellers Association and a national spokesperson for issues concerning independent businesses. He has had significant profiles in the Wall Street Journal, Time Magazine, and the San Francisco Chronicle. Queries by email only. See website for full guidelines.

Literary Agent: Andy Ross (*L1188*)

L0054 Anne Clark Literary Agency
Literary Agency
United Kingdom

submissions@anneclarkliteraryagency.co.uk

https://www.anneclarkliteraryagency.co.uk

CHILDREN'S
  Fiction
    Middle Grade; *Picture Books*
  Nonfiction > *Nonfiction Books*

YOUNG ADULT
  Fiction > *Novels*
  Nonfiction > *Nonfiction Books*

Send: Synopsis; Writing sample; Full text; Proposal
How to send: Email

Handles fiction and picture books for children and young adults. Send query by email only with the following pasted into the body of the email (not as an attachment): for fiction, include brief synopsis and first 3,000 words; for picture books, send complete ms; for nonfiction, send short proposal and the text of three sample pages. No submissions by post. See website for full guidelines.

Literary Agent: Anne Clark (*L0275*)

L0055 Anne Edelstein Literary Agency
Literary Agency
258 Riverside Drive #8D, New York, NY 10025
United States
Tel: +1 (212) 414-4923
Fax: +1 (212) 414-2930

info@aeliterary.com

http://www.aeliterary.com

Professional Body: Association of Authors' Representatives, Inc. (AAR)

Types: Fiction; Nonfiction
Subjects: Autobiography; Commercial; History; Literary; Psychology; Religion
Markets: Adult

Closed to approaches.

Note: Note accepting approaches as at August 2020

Send query letter with SASE and for fiction a summary of your novel plus the first 25 pages, or for nonfiction an outline of your book and one or two sample chapters. No queries by email.

Authors: Roderick Anscombe; Stephen Batchelor; Sophy Burnham; Mark Epstein; Kathleen Finneran; James Goodman; Patricia Hersch; His Holiness the Dalai Lama with Jeffrey Hopkins; Peter Levitt; Josip Novakovich; Natasha Rodijcic-Kane; James Shapiro; Jody Shields; Russell Shorto; Rachel Simon; Sasha Troyan; Phyllis Vane

Literary Agent: Anne Edelstein

L0056 Annette Green Authors' Agency
Literary Agency
5 Henwoods Mount, Pembury, Kent, TN2 4BH
United Kingdom

annette@annettegreenagency.co.uk
david@annettegreenagency.co.uk

http://www.annettegreenagency.co.uk

Types: Fiction; Nonfiction
Formats: Film Scripts; TV Scripts
Subjects: Autobiography; Comedy / Humour;
Commercial; Culture; Current Affairs; History;
Horror; Literary; Music; Politics; Science;
Sport; Thrillers
Markets: Adult; Children's; Young Adult

Send: Query
Don't send: Full text
How to send: Email

Costs: Offers services that writers have to pay for.

Send query by email with a brief synopsis (fiction) or overview (nonfiction), and the opening few chapters (up to about 10,000 words). No poetry, scripts, science fiction, or fantasy. Send Word documents rather than PDFs.

L0057 Jason Anthony
Literary Agent
United States

Literary Agency: Massie & McQuilkin
(**L0934**)

L0058 Antony Harwood Limited
Literary Agency
103 Walton Street, Oxford, OX2 6EB
United Kingdom
Tel: +44 (0) 1865 559615

mail@antonyharwood.com

http://www.antonyharwood.com

Fiction > *Novels*

Nonfiction > *Nonfiction Books*

Send: Query; Synopsis; Writing sample; Self-Addressed Stamped Envelope (SASE)
How to send: Email; Post

Handles fiction and nonfiction in every genre and category, except for screenwriting and poetry. Send brief outline and first 50 pages by email, or by post with SASE.

Authors: Alastair Bonnett; Michael Bracewell; Peter Bunzl; Amanda Craig; Candida Crewe; David Dabydeen; Tracy Darnton; Louise Doughty; Robert Edric

Literary Agents: Jonathan Gregory (**L0583**);
Antony Harwood (*L0621*); James Macdonald
Lockhart (**L0872**); Jo Williamson (**L1454**)

L0059 Zoe Apostolides
Literary Agent
United Kingdom

https://cmm.agency/about-us.php

Literary Agency: Coombs Moylett & Maclean
Literary Agency (**L0295**)

ADULT
  Fiction > *Novels*
    Coming of Age; Crime; Historical Fiction;
    Horror; Mystery

  Nonfiction > *Nonfiction Books*

CHILDREN'S > **Fiction** > *Novels*

YOUNG ADULT > **Fiction** > *Novels*

Send: Synopsis; Writing sample
How to send: Online submission system

Manages a list of crime, historical, young adult and children's authors and is also looking to build a nonfiction list. She is especially interested in original horror novels, coming-of-age stories and any sort of whodunnit.

L0060 Apple Tree Literary Ltd
Literary Agency
86-90 Paul Street, London, EC2A 4NE
United Kingdom
Tel: +44 (0) 7515 876444

max@appletreeliterary.co.uk

http://appletreeliterary.co.uk

Types: Fiction; Nonfiction
Markets: Adult; Young Adult

Send: Query
Don't send: Full text
How to send: Email

Represents a range of authors, from journalism and academic non-fiction, to genre fiction and fiction for young adults. No poetry, self-help or lifestyle books, picture books, or romance novels. See website for full guidelines.

Literary Agent: Max Edwards (**L0409**)

L0061 Arcadia
Literary Agency
31 Lake Place North, Danbury, CT 06810
United States

arcadialit@gmail.com

Types: Nonfiction
Subjects: Biography; Culture; Current Affairs;
Health; History; Medicine; Psychology;
Science
Markets: Adult

Agency handling biography, current affairs, health, history, medicine, popular culture, psychology, and science. No fiction.

Literary Agent: Victoria Gould Pryor (*L1117*)

L0062 Sophieclaire Armitage
Literary Agent
United Kingdom

Literary Agency: Noel Gay (**L1037**)

L0063 Victoria Wells Arms
Literary Agent
United States

submissions@wellsarms.com

https://www.hgliterary.com/victoria
https://twitter.com/VWArms

Literary Agencies: Wells Arms Literary
(**L1429**); HG Literary (**L0646**)

CHILDREN'S > **Fiction**
  Middle Grade: Magical Realism
  Picture Books: General

YOUNG ADULT > **Fiction** > *Novels*: Contemporary

How to send: Email

L0064 Susan Armstrong
Literary Agent
United Kingdom

Literary Agency: C+W (Conville & Walsh)
(**L0205**)

L0065 Frances Arnold
Literary Agent
United Kingdom

Literary Agency: Rochelle Stevens & Co.
(**L1172**)

L0066 Michelle Arnold
Literary Agent
United Kingdom

Literary Agency: The Dench Arnold Agency
(**L0353**)

L0067 Artellus Limited
Literary Agency
30 Dorset House, Gloucester Place, London,
NW1 5AD
United Kingdom
Tel: +44 (0) 20 7935 6972
Fax: +44 (0) 20 8609 0347

artellussubmissions@gmail.com

http://www.artellusltd.co.uk

Professional Body: The Association of
Authors' Agents (AAA)

Types: Fiction; Nonfiction
Subjects: Arts; Beauty; Biography;
Contemporary; Crime; Culture; Current
Affairs; Entertainment; Fantasy; Fashion;
History; Literary; Science; Science Fiction;
Warfare
Markets: Adult; Young Adult

Send: Full text
How to send: Email

Welcomes submissions from new fiction and nonfiction writers. Send first three chapters and synopsis in first instance, or send query by email. No film or TV scripts. If you would prefer to submit electronically send query by email in advance.

Chair: Gabriele Pantucci

Company Director: Leslie Gardner

Literary Agents: Jon Curzon (*L0321*); Darryl Samaraweera (*L1216*)

L0068 ASH Literary
Literary Agency
United Kingdom

info@ashliterary.com
submissions@ashliterary.com

https://www.ashliterary.com/
https://twitter.com/ashliterary
https://instagram.com/aliceisagenting

CHILDREN'S > **Fiction**
Graphic Novels: Contemporary; Fantasy; Magical Realism; Surreal
Middle Grade: Contemporary; Fantasy; Magical Realism
Picture Books: General

YOUNG ADULT > **Fiction**
Graphic Novels: Contemporary; Fantasy; Magical Realism; Surreal
Novels: College / University; High School; Road Trips; Romantic Comedy

Send: Synopsis; Writing sample
How to send: Email

Actively seeking creators working across picture books through to Young Adult, including graphic novels.

Authors: Kelly Allen; Zoey Allen; Ryan Crawford; Niyla Farook; Gina Gonzales; Gavin Gray; Ravena Guron; Richard Mercado; Samuel Pollen; Ryan Robinson; Elizabeth Rounding; Jessica Russak-Hoffman; Chitra Soundar

Literary Agent: Alice Sutherland-Hawes (**L1342**)

L0069 Isabel Atherton
Literary Agent
United Kingdom

Literary Agency: Creative Authors Ltd (**L0307**)

L0070 Charlotte Atyeo
Literary Agent
United Kingdom

charlotte@kingsfordcampbell.com

http://kingsfordcampbell.com/about-us/charlotte-atyeo/
https://twitter.com/EverSoBookish

Literary Agency: Kingsford Campbell Literary Agency (**L0790**)

Fiction > *Novels*: Literary

Nonfiction > *Nonfiction Books*
General, and in particular: Biography; Design; Equality; Exercise; Feminism; Fitness; Gender Issues; Gender; Memoir; Music; Nature; Sport; Travel

L0071 The August Agency LLC
Literary Agency
United States

submissions@augustagency.com

http://www.augustagency.com

Types: Fiction; Nonfiction
Subjects: Arts; Autobiography; Business; Culture; Current Affairs; Entertainment; Finance; History; Literary; Media; Politics; Society; Technology; Women's Interests
Markets: Adult

Send: Query
Don't send: Full text
How not to send: Email

Costs: Author covers sundry admin costs.

Accepts queries by referral or by request at a writers' conference only.

Literary Agent: Cricket Freeman (*L0504*)

L0072 AVAnti Productions & Management
Literary Agency
7 Parkside Mews, Hurst Road, Horsham, West Sussex, RH12 2SA
United Kingdom

avantiproductions@live.co.uk

https://www.avantiproductions.co.uk

Scripts > *Film Scripts*

Send: Full text
How to send: Email
How not to send: Post

Costs: Author covers sundry admin costs.

Talent and literary representation. Open to screenplay submissions for short films and feature films, but no theatre scripts.

Literary Agent: Veronica Lazar (**L0838**)

L0073 Ayesha Pande Literary
Literary Agency
128 West 132 Street, New York, NY 10027
United States
Tel: +1 (212) 283-5825

queries@pandeliterary.com

http://pandeliterary.com

A New York based boutique literary agency with a small and eclectic roster of clients. Submit queries via form on website. No poetry, business books, cookbooks, screenplays or illustrated children's books.

Literary Agents: Madison Smartt Bell (**L0114**); Stephany Evans (**L0443**); Serene Hakim (**L0596**); Annie Hwang (**L0679**); Luba Ostashevsky (**L1061**); Ayesha Pande (**L1065**); Anjali Singh (**L1286**)

L0074 Matilda Ayris
Literary Agent
United Kingdom

Literary Agency: C+W (Conville & Walsh) (**L0205**)

L0075 Azantian Literary Agency
Literary Agency
United States

queries@azantianlitagency.com

http://www.azantianlitagency.com

Types: Fiction
Subjects: Fantasy; Horror; Science Fiction
Markets: Adult; Children's; Young Adult

Send: Query
Don't send: Full text
How to send: Email

Currently accepting middle grade and young adult novels only. Send query via online submission system.

Literary Agents: Jennifer Azantian (*L0076*); Ben Baxter (*L0102*); Amanda Rutter (**L1211**)

L0076 Jennifer Azantian
Literary Agent
United States

Literary Agency: Azantian Literary Agency (**L0075**)

L0077 Oliver Azis
Literary Agent
United Kingdom

Literary Agency: Independent Talent Group Ltd (**L0683**)

L0078 Becky Bagnell
Literary Agent
United Kingdom

Literary Agency: Lindsay Literary Agency (**L0858**)

L0079 Lisa Baker
Literary Agent
United Kingdom

Literary Agency: Aitken Alexander Associates (**L0025**)

L0080 Natalie Ball
Literary Agent
United Kingdom

Literary Agency: Noel Gay (**L1037**)

L0081 Sarah Ballard

Literary Agent
United Kingdom

sballard@unitedagents.co.uk

https://www.unitedagents.co.uk/
sballardunitedagentscouk

Literary Agency: United Agents (**L1389**)

Fiction > *Novels*

Nonfiction > *Nonfiction Books*
Feminism; History; Memoir

Does not want:

> **Fiction** > *Novels*
> Saga; Science Fiction

Send: Synopsis; Writing sample; Pitch; Market info
How to send: Email

I have extremely broad taste in fiction and non-fiction, but the underlying quality of the work that I'm interested in is a sense of urgency, and an attempt to make a change in the world, whether that is fiction with a compelling plot or structure overlaying a set of big ideas; memoir-ish non fiction flavoured with obsession and unfolding a hidden agenda; or meticulously researched history which changes our world view. I have a particular interest in feminism and feminist approaches – but exploring ideas or angles which are completely new to me is one of the great joys of my job. I prefer to work with writers who are more-or-less based in the UK, and are aiming to deliver a book every one or two years, and for whom I can add something to every area of their creative lives.

L0082 Dan Balow

Literary Agent
United States

Literary Agency: The Steve Laube Agency (**L1318**)

L0083 Alex Barba

Literary Agent
United States

Literary Agency: The Jennifer DeChiara Literary Agency (**L0721**)

L0084 Barbara Braun Associates, Inc.

Literary Agency
7 East 14th St #19F, New York, NY 10003
United States

bbasubmissions@gmail.com

http://www.barbarabraunagency.com

Professional Body: Association of Authors' Representatives, Inc. (AAR)

Types: Fiction; Nonfiction
Formats: Film Scripts
Subjects: Architecture; Arts; Autobiography; Beauty; Commercial; Culture; Design; Entertainment; Fashion; History; Literary; Literary Criticism; Mystery; Photography; Politics; Psychology; Society; Thrillers; Women's Interests
Markets: Adult

Send: Query
Don't send: Full text
How to send: Email

Send query by email only, with "Query" in the subject line, including brief summary, word count, genre, any relevant publishing experience, and the first five pages pasted into the body of the email. No attachments. No poetry, science fiction, fantasy, horror, or screenplays. Particularly interested in stories for women, art-related fiction, historical and multicultural stories, and to a lesser extent mysteries and thrillers. Also interested in narrative nonfiction and current affairs books by journalists.

Literary Agent: Barbara Braun (*L0175*)

L0085 Barbara Levy Literary Agency

Literary Agency
64 Greenhill, Hampstead High Street, London, NW3 5TZ
United Kingdom
Tel: +44 (0) 20 7435 9046

submissions@barbaralevyagency.com

http://barbaralevyagency.com
https://twitter.com/BLLA_NW3

Professional Body: The Association of Authors' Agents (AAA)

Types: Fiction; Nonfiction
Markets: Adult

Send: Query; Synopsis; Author bio; Writing sample
How to send: Email; Post

Send query with synopsis and first three chapters (approximately 50 pages) by email or by post with SAE. No poetry, plays, original screenplays, scripts or picture books for children.

Associate Agent: Jamilah Ahmed (**L0024**)

Literary Agents: Barbara Levy (*L0852*); Vicki Salter (*L1215*)

L0086 Stephen Barbara

Literary Agent
United States

Literary Agency: InkWell Management (**L0686**)

L0087 Bruce R. Barbour

Literary Agent
United States

Literary Agency: Literary Management Group, Inc. (**L0864**)

L0088 Julie Barer

Literary Agent
United States

Literary Agency: The Book Group (**L0154**)

L0089 Kate Barker

Literary Agent
United Kingdom

Literary Agency: Kate Barker Literary, TV, & Film Agency (**L0762**)

L0090 Barone Literary Agency

Literary Agency
United States

baronelit@outlook.com

http://www.baroneliteraryagency.com

Types: Fiction
Subjects: Erotic; History; Horror; Romance; Women's Interests
Markets: Adult; Young Adult

Closed to approaches.

Closed to submissions as at September 2019. Check website for current status.

Send query online form on website. Include synopsis and first three chapters. No plays, screenplays, picture books, middle grade, science fiction, paranormal, or nonfiction.

Literary Agent: Denise Barone (**L0091**)

L0091 Denise Barone

Literary Agent
United States

Literary Agency: Barone Literary Agency (**L0090**)

Authors: Laurie Albano; Michele Barrow-Belisle; Cathy Bennett; Sarah Biglow; KateMarie Collins; Jennifer Petersen Fraser; Yvette Geer; Suzanne Hay; Richard Moore; Rebekah Purdy; Curt Rude; Wyatt Shev; Anna Snow; Sharon Sullivan-Craver; Molly Zenk

L0092 Baror International, Inc.

Literary Agency
P.O. Box 868, Armonk, NY 10504-0868
United States

Heather@Barorint.com

http://www.barorint.com

ADULT
Fiction > *Novels*
Commercial; Fantasy; Literary; Science Fiction

Nonfiction > *Nonfiction Books*

YOUNG ADULT > Fiction > *Novels*
Closed to approaches.

Specialises in the international and domestic representation of literary works in both fiction and nonfiction, including commercial fiction, literary, science fiction, fantasy, young adult and more.

Literary Agents: Danny Baror; Heather Baror-Shapiro

L0093 Nicola Barr
Literary Agent
United States

Literary Agency: The Bent Agency (**L0119**)

L0094 Barry Goldblatt Literary Agency, Inc.
Literary Agency
C/O Industrious – Brooklyn, 594 Dean Street – 2nd Floor, Brooklyn, NY 11238
United States

query@bgliterary.com

http://www.bgliterary.com

Professional Body: Association of Authors' Representatives, Inc. (AAR)

Types: Fiction
Subjects: Contemporary; Fantasy; History; Mystery; Romance; Science Fiction; Thrillers
Markets: Children's; Young Adult

Send: Query
Don't send: Full text
How to send: Email

Handles books for young people; from picture books to middle grade and young adult. Send query by email including the word "Query" in the subject line and synopsis and first five pages in the body of the email. No attachments. Emails with attachments will be ignored. See website for full details.

Literary Agents: Barry Goldblatt (*L0560*); Jennifer Udden (*L1384*)

L0095 Bruce Bartlett
Literary Agent
United States

Literary Agency: Above the Line Agency (**L0009**)

L0096 Andrea Barzvi
Literary Agent
United States

Literary Agency: Empire Literary, LLC (**L0431**)

L0097 Ethan Bassoff
Literary Agent
United States

Literary Agency: Massie & McQuilkin (**L0934**)
Professional Body: Association of Authors' Representatives, Inc. (AAR)

L0098 Matthew Bates
Literary Agent
United Kingdom

Literary Agency: Sayle Screen Ltd (**L1226**)

L0099 Bath Literary Agency
Literary Agency
5 Gloucester Road, Bath, BA1 7BH
United Kingdom

submissions@bathliteraryagency.com

http://bathliteraryagency.com

Types: Fiction; Nonfiction
Markets: Children's; Young Adult

Send: Query
Don't send: Full text
How to send: Email

Handles fiction and nonfiction for children, from picture books to Young Adult. Send query by email or by post with SAE for reply and return of materials if required, along with the first three chapters (fiction) or the full manuscript (picture books). See website for full details.

Literary Agent: Gill McLay (*L0956*)

L0100 Erica Bauman
Literary Agent
United States

https://aevitascreative.com/agents/
https://querymanager.com/query/EricaBauman

Literary Agency: Aevitas (**L0019**)

ADULT > Fiction
Graphic Novels: General
Novels: Commercial; Folklore, Myths, and Legends; Magic; Romantic Comedy; Speculative
CHILDREN'S > Fiction > *Graphic Novels*

YOUNG ADULT > Fiction > *Graphic Novels*

How to send: Query Manager

Most interested in commercial novels that feature an exciting premise and lyrical, atmospheric writing; imaginative, genre-blending tales; speculative worlds filled with haunting, quietly wondrous magic; fresh retellings of mythology, ballet, opera, and classic literature; sharply funny rom-coms; graphic novels for all ages; fearless storytellers that tackle big ideas and contemporary issues; and working with and supporting marginalized authors and stories that represent the wide range of humanity.

L0101 Jan Baumer
Literary Agent
United States

https://www.foliolit.com/agents-1/jan-baumer

Literary Agency: Folio Literary Management, LLC (**L0480**)

Fiction > *Novels*
Allegory; Literary

Nonfiction > *Nonfiction Books*
Business; Comedy / Humour; Cookery; Health; Memoir; Narrative Nonfiction; Parenting; Prescriptive Nonfiction; Religion; Self Help; Spirituality; Wellbeing

Send: Query; Writing sample; Proposal
How to send: In the body of an email

Interests as an agent are largely nonfiction, specifically spirituality, religion, self-help, health and wellness, parenting, memoir, and business with a spirituality or self-help angle. Also open to allegorical fiction, but it must have a literary voice and an author with the writing credentials to pull it off.

L0102 Ben Baxter
Literary Agent
United States

Literary Agency: Azantian Literary Agency (**L0075**)

L0103 Veronique Baxter
Literary Agent; Company Director
United Kingdom

https://www.davidhigham.co.uk/agents-dh/veronique-baxter/

Literary Agency: David Higham Associates Ltd (**L0338**)

ADULT
Fiction > *Novels*
Historical Fiction; Literary; Speculative; Upmarket Crime; Upmarket Thrillers

Nonfiction > *Nonfiction Books*
Current Affairs; Feminism; History; Memoir; Narrative Nonfiction

CHILDREN'S > Fiction > *Middle Grade*: Adventure

YOUNG ADULT > Fiction > *Novels*: Adventure

Agency Assistant: Sara Langham

L0104 Maile Beal
Literary Agent
United States

maile@carolmannagency.com

https://www.carolmannagency.com/maile-beal
https://www.instagram.com/mailebeal/
https://twitter.com/MaileBeal

Literary Agency: Carol Mann Agency (**L0225**)

ADULT
Fiction > *Novels*: Commercial

Nonfiction
Illustrated Books: Comedy / Humour
Nonfiction Books: Cookery; Crime;
Entertainment; Intersectional Feminism;
Lifestyle; Narrative Nonfiction; Popular
Culture; Social Issues
YOUNG ADULT > **Fiction** > *Novels*

Send: Query; Author bio; Writing sample
How to send: In the body of an email
How not to send: Post; Email attachment

L0105 Diana Beaumont
Literary Agent
United Kingdom

diana@marjacq.com

http://www.marjacq.com/diana-beaumont.html

Literary Agency: Marjacq Scripts Ltd (**L0921**)

Fiction > *Novels*
Commercial; Crime; High Concept; Literary;
Thrillers; Upmarket Women's Fiction

Nonfiction > *Nonfiction Books*
Cookery; Feminism; Lifestyle; Memoir

Send: Query; Writing sample; Synopsis
How to send: Email

Looking for upmarket women's commercial
fiction with depth and heart, accessible literary
fiction, high-concept crime fiction and thrillers,
memoir, smart, funny feminists, lifestyle,
cookery and anything with a strong, original
voice. Also wants to encourage submissions
from writers who have been traditionally
under-represented.

Authors: Tanya Atapattu; Holly Baxter; Daisy
Buchanan; James Campbell; Angela Clarke;
Mathew Clayton; Fiona Collins; Caroline
Corcoran; Rhiannon Lucy Cosslett; Isabel
Costello; Francesca Dorricott; Philip Connor
Finn; Eve Harris; Louise Hulland; Catriona
Innes; Kim Izzo; Amy Jones; Laura Lexx; Eve
Makis; Andrea Mara; Claire McGowan; Adam
Pearson; Alice Peterson; Das Petrou; Rachel
Phipps; Samantha Renke; Nancy Revell; Lee
Ridley; Diana Rosie; Frances Ryan; Jennifer
Savin; Lucy Vine; James Wallman; Roz
Watkins; Eva Woods

L0106 Rachel Beck
Literary Agent
United States

queryrachel@lizadawson.com

https://www.lizadawsonassociates.com/team/
rachel-beck/

Literary Agency: Liza Dawson Associates
(**L0868**)

ADULT
Fiction > *Novels*
Book Club Women's Fiction;
Contemporary Romance; Domestic

Suspense; Millennial Fiction; Upmarket
Women's Fiction

Nonfiction > *Nonfiction Books*
Career Development; Feminism; Personal
Development

YOUNG ADULT > **Fiction** > *Novels*
Contemporary; Cyberpunk; Post-Apocalyptic

Send: Query; Writing sample
How to send: In the body of an email

Believes that the right book can change or heal
a life, and she wants to find those. But she's
also interested in lighter fiction that helps you
escape or simply makes you laugh after a
tough day. Or nonfiction that teaches you
something about an obscure topic, thus
opening up a new world.

L0107 Laney Katz Becker
Literary Agent
United States

Literary Agency: Massie & McQuilkin
(**L0934**)

Closed to approaches.

L0108 Emily Van Beek
Literary Agent; Partner
United States

emily@foliolitmanagement.com

https://www.publishersmarketplace.com/
members/vanbeek/

Literary Agency: Folio Literary Management,
LLC (**L0480**)

CHILDREN'S > **Fiction**
Middle Grade; Picture Books
YOUNG ADULT > **Fiction** > *Novels*
Adventure; Comedy / Humour; Dystopian
Fiction; Fantasy; High Concept; Magical
Realism; Supernatural / Paranormal

Send: Query; Writing sample
How to send: In the body of an email

L0109 Ann Behar
Literary Agent
United States

Literary Agency: Scovil Galen Ghosh Literary
Agency, Inc. (**L1244**)

**L0110 Bell Lomax Moreton
Agency**
Literary Agency
Suite C, 131 Queensway, Petts Wood, Kent,
BR5 1DG
United Kingdom
Tel: +44 (0) 20 7930 4447
Fax: +44 (0) 1689 820061

agency@bell-lomax.co.uk

http://www.belllomaxmoreton.co.uk

Professional Body: The Association of
Authors' Agents (AAA)

Types: Fiction; Nonfiction
Subjects: Biography; Business; Sport
Markets: Adult; Children's

How to send: Email

Considers most fiction, nonfiction, and
children's book proposals. No poetry, short
stories, novellas, textbooks, film scripts, stage
plays, or science fiction. Send query by email
with details of any previous work, short
synopsis, and first three chapters (up to 50
pages). For children's picture books send
complete ms. Also accepts postal submissions.
See website for full guidelines.

Literary Agents: Eddie Bell (*L0111*); Jo Bell
(*L0112*); June Bell (*L0113*); Lauren Gardner
(*L0527*); Pat Lomax (*L0873*); Sarah
McDonnell (*L0953*); Paul Moreton (*L0997*);
Helen Mackenzie Smith (*L1292*)

L0111 Eddie Bell
Literary Agent
United Kingdom

Literary Agency: Bell Lomax Moreton Agency
(**L0110**)

L0112 Jo Bell
Literary Agent
United Kingdom

Literary Agency: Bell Lomax Moreton Agency
(**L0110**)

L0113 June Bell
Literary Agent
United Kingdom

Literary Agency: Bell Lomax Moreton Agency
(**L0110**)

L0114 Madison Smartt Bell
Literary Agent
United States

https://www.pandeliterary.com/about-
pandeliterary

Literary Agency: Ayesha Pande Literary
(**L0073**)

Fiction > *Novels*
Literary; Noir; Police Procedural

L0115 Lorella Belli
Literary Agent
United Kingdom

Literary Agency: Lorella Belli Literary Agency
(LBLA) (**L0875**)

L0116 Faye Bender
Literary Agent
United States

Literary Agency: The Book Group (**L0154**)

L0117 Ian Benson
Literary Agent
United Kingdom

Literary Agency: The Agency (London) Ltd
(**L0021**)

L0118 The Bent Agency (UK)
Literary Agency
17 Kelsall Mews, Richmond, TW9 4BP
United Kingdom

info@thebentagency.com

http://www.thebentagency.com

Professional Body: The Association of
Authors' Agents (AAA)
Literary Agency: The Bent Agency (**L0119**)

ADULT
  Fiction
    Graphic Novels; Novels
  Nonfiction > *Nonfiction Books*

CHILDREN'S > **Fiction**
  *Chapter Books; Graphic Novels; Middle
  Grade*
YOUNG ADULT
  Fiction
    Graphic Novels; Novels
  Nonfiction > *Nonfiction Books*

Send: Query
How to send: Email; Query Manager

UK office of established US agency. See
website for individual agent interests and
contact details and approach appropriate agent.
Do not send submissions to general agency
email address. See website for full submission
guidelines.

Literary Agent: Molly Ker Hawn (**L0625**)

L0119 The Bent Agency
Literary Agency
529 W 42nd St, New York, NY 10036
United States

info@thebentagency.com

http://www.thebentagency.com

ADULT
  Fiction
    Graphic Novels; Novels
  Nonfiction > *Nonfiction Books*

CHILDREN'S > **Fiction**
  *Chapter Books; Graphic Novels; Middle
  Grade*
YOUNG ADULT
  Fiction
    Graphic Novels; Novels
  Nonfiction > *Nonfiction Books*

Send: Query
How to send: Email; Query Manager

Accepts email or Query Manager queries only.
See website for agent bios and specific
interests and email addresses, then query one

agent only. See website for full submission
guidelines.

Literary Agency: The Bent Agency (UK)
(**L0118**)

Literary Agents: Nicola Barr (*L0093*); Jenny
Bent (*L0120*); Victoria Cappello (*L0217*);
Gemma Copper (**L0300**); Claire Draper
(*L0384*); Louise Fury (*L0517*); Sarah Hornsley
(*L0665*); James Mustelier (**L1019**); Zoe Plant
(*L1102*); John Silbersack (*L1276*); Laurel
Symonds (*L1351*); Desiree Wilson (**L1458**)

L0120 Jenny Bent
Literary Agent
United States

Literary Agency: The Bent Agency (**L0119**)
Professional Body: Association of Authors'
Representatives, Inc. (AAR)

L0121 Jane R. Berkey
Literary Agent
United States

Literary Agency: Jane Rotrosen Agency
(**L0709**)

L0122 Berlin Associates
Literary Agency
7 Tyers Gate, London, SE1 3HX
United Kingdom
Tel: +44 (0) 20 7836 1112
Fax: +44 (0) 20 7632 5296

submissions@berlinassociates.com

http://www.berlinassociates.com

Types: Scripts
Formats: Film Scripts; Radio Scripts; TV
Scripts; Theatre Scripts
Markets: Adult

Send: Query
Don't send: Full text
How to send: Email

Most clients through recommendation or
invitation, but accepts queries by email with
CV, experience, and outline of work you
would like to submit.

L0123 Marlo Berliner
Literary Agent
United States

Literary Agency: The Jennifer DeChiara
Literary Agency (**L0721**)

L0124 John Berlyne
Literary Agent
United Kingdom

http://zenoagency.com/about-us/

Literary Agency: Zeno Agency Ltd (**L1487**)

ADULT > **Fiction** > *Novels*

Crime; Fantasy; Historical Fiction; Horror;
Science Fiction; Space Opera; Thrillers;
Urban Fantasy

YOUNG ADULT > **Fiction** > *Novels*

Closed to approaches.

L0125 Betsy Amster Literary Enterprises
Literary Agency
607 Foothill Blvd #1061, La Canada
Flintridge, CA 91012
United States

b.amster.assistant@gmail.com

http://amsterlit.com

Professional Body: Association of Authors'
Representatives, Inc. (AAR)

Types: Fiction; Nonfiction
Subjects: Autobiography; Cookery; Culture;
Gardening; Health; History; Lifestyle;
Literary; Medicine; Mystery; Personal
Development; Psychology; Society; Thrillers;
Travel; Women's Interests
Markets: Adult

Send: Query
Don't send: Full text
How to send: Email

Send query by email only. For fiction and
narrative nonfiction include the first three
pages in the body of your email; for nonfiction
include your proposal, again in the body of the
email. See website for different email
addresses for adult and children's/YA
submissions. No unsolicited attachments or
queries by phone or fax. No romances,
screenplays, adult poetry, westerns, adult
fantasy, horror, science fiction, techno thrillers,
spy capers, apocalyptic scenarios, political or
religious arguments, or self-published books.

Authors: Amy Alkon; Dwight Allen; Will
Allen; Jess J. Araujo; Elaine N. Aron; Sandi
Ault; Lois Barr; Ariel Bernstein; Kim Boyce;
Helene Brenner; Karen Briner; Catheryn J.
Brockett; Karen Burns; Mónica Bustamante;
Joe P. Carr; Steven Carter; Lillian Castillo-
Speed; Robin Chotzinoff; Frank Clifford; Rob
Cohen; David Cundy; Leela Cyd; Margaret
Leslie Davis; Jan DeBlieu; David J. Diamond;
Martha O. Diamond; Phil Doran; Suzanne
Dunaway; Nick Dyer; J. Theron Elkins; Ruth
Andrew Ellenson; Loretta Ellsworth; James P.
Emswiler; Mary Ann Emswiler; Naomi Epel;
Alex Epstein; Karin Esterhammer; Jeannette
Faurot; Tom Fields-Meyer; Joline Godfrey;
Tanya Ward Goodman; Michael I. Goran;
Hindi Greenberg; Ellen Hawley; Marian
Henley; Charney Herst; Leigh Ann Hirschman;
Ariel Horn; Lisa Hunter; Jackie; Melissa
Jacobs; Janet Jaffe; Emily Katz; E. Barrie
Kavasch; Joy Keller; Eileen Kennedy-Moore;
Rachel Tawil Kenyon; Camille Landau; Carol
Lay; Anna Lefler; Margaret Lobenstine; Mark
Lowenthal; Paul Mandelbaum; Ivy Manning;

Melissa Martin; Domenico Minchilli; Elizabeth Helman Minchilli; Wendy Mogel; Sharon Montrose; Bonnie Frumkin Morales; Yolanda Nava; Joy Nicholson; Judith Nies; Susie Norris; Christopher Noxon; Lynette Padwa; Neela Paniz; Kishani Perera; Cash Peters; Barry Prizant; Winifred Reilly; Andrea Richards; Eileen Roth; Adam Sappington; Marjorie Barton Savage; Anthony Schmitz; M.D. Edward Schneider; Kyle Schuneman; George Shannon; Nancy Spiller; Allison Mia Starcher; Louise Steinman; Bill Stern; Terry Theise; Christina Baglivi Tinglof; Linda Venis; MPH Emily Ventura; Marisel Vera; Elizabeth Verdick; John Vorhaus; Hannah Voskuil; Diana Wells; Tiare White; Chris Witt; Karen Witynski; Steve D. Wolf; David Wollock; Dawn Young

Literary Agents: Betsy Amster (*L0040*); Mary Cummings (*L0315*)

L0126 Tina Betts
Literary Agent
United Kingdom

Literary Agency: Andrew Mann Ltd (**L0049**)

L0127 Beverley Slopen Literary Agency
Literary Agency
131 Bloor St. W., Suite 711, Toronto, M5S 1S3
Canada
Tel: +1 (416) 964-9598
Fax: +1 (416) 921-7726

beverley@slopenagency.ca

http://www.slopenagency.com

Types: Fiction; Nonfiction
Subjects: Anthropology; Biography; Commercial; Crime; History; Literary; Personal Development
Markets: Adult; Children's

Send: Query
Don't send: Full text
How to send: Email

Send query by email with a few sample pages. No hard copy submissions. Takes on few new authors. Handles very few children's books, and almost no romance, horror, or illustrated. No poetry.

Literary Agent: Beverley Slopen (*L1289*)

L0128 Elizabeth Bewley
Literary Agent
United States

ebewley@sll.com

https://www.sll.com/our-team

Literary Agency: Sterling Lord Literistic, Inc. (**L1317**)

ADULT
  Fiction > *Novels*

High Concept; Romance; Upmarket Commercial Fiction

Nonfiction > *Nonfiction Books*: Narrative Nonfiction

CHILDREN'S > **Fiction**
  Middle Grade; *Picture Books*
YOUNG ADULT > **Fiction** > *Novels*
  High Concept; Romance

Send: Query; Synopsis; Writing sample
How to send: Online submission system; Email

On the children's side of her list, she represents young adult and middle grade fiction, and the occasional picture book. On the adult side, she is eager to represent more upmarket commercial fiction and narrative nonfiction. Current submission wish list includes high-concept young adult novels, especially from underrepresented voices, accessible middle grade novels that will foster a love of reading (think: fun, funny, or both!), young adult romance, high-concept adult love stories, and any upmarket commercial fiction with a witty voice and eye for detail.

L0129 Bidnick & Company
Literary Agency
United States

bidnick@comcast.net

Types: Nonfiction
Subjects: Commercial; Cookery
Markets: Adult

Send: Query
Don't send: Full text
How to send: Email

Handles cookbooks and commercial nonfiction. Send query by email only.

Literary Agent: Carole Bidnick (*L0130*)

L0130 Carole Bidnick
Literary Agent
United States

Literary Agency: Bidnick & Company (**L0129**)

L0131 Vicky Bijur
Literary Agent
United States

Literary Agency: Vicky Bijur Literary Agency (**L1402**)

L0132 Bill McLean Personal Management Ltd
Literary Agency
23B Deodar Road, London, SW15 2NP
United Kingdom
Tel: +44 (0) 20 8789 8191

Types: Scripts
Formats: Film Scripts; Radio Scripts; TV Scripts; Theatre Scripts
Markets: Adult

Theatrical agent handling scripts for all media. No books.

Literary Agent: Bill McLean (*L0957*)

L0133 Joshua Bilmes
Literary Agent
United States

Literary Agency: Jabberwocky Literary Agency (**L0697**)

L0134 Nicola Biltoo
Literary Agent
United Kingdom

Literary Agency: The Agency (London) Ltd (**L0021**)

L0135 Victoria Birkett
Literary Agent
United Kingdom

https://milesstottagency.co.uk/representatives/victoria-birkett/

Literary Agency: Miles Stott Children's Literary Agency (**L0983**)

Author: Gill Lewis

L0136 Amy Bishop
Literary Agent
United States

Literary Agency: Dystel, Goderich & Bourret LLC (**L0399**)

L0137 David Black
Literary Agent
United States

Literary Agency: David Black Literary Agency (**L0336**)

L0138 The Blair Partnership
Literary Agency
PO Box, 7828, London, W1A 4GE
United Kingdom
Tel: +44 (0) 20 7504 2520

info@theblairpartnership.com

https://www.theblairpartnership.com

Professional Body: The Association of Authors' Agents (AAA)

ADULT
  Fiction > *Novels*
    Book Club Fiction; Commercial; Crime; Detective Fiction; Dystopian Fiction; High Concept; Historical Fiction; Literary; Speculative; Thrillers; Upmarket; Women's Fiction

  Nonfiction > *Nonfiction Books*
    Crime; Lifestyle; Personal Development

CHILDREN'S
  Fiction
    Middle Grade: Adventure

Novels: General, and in particular: Commercial
Nonfiction > *Nonfiction Books*

TEEN > **Fiction** > *Novels*

YOUNG ADULT > **Fiction** > *Novels*

Send: Query; Synopsis; Proposal; Writing sample
How to send: Word file email attachment; PDF file email attachment

We welcome all submissions and consider everything that is sent to the agency, though we are not currently accepting submissions for screenplays, short stories or poetry.

We welcome approaches from both debut writers and established authors. We're very happy to receive submissions from overseas, as long as they're written in English.

Associate Agent: Jordan Lees (**L0843**)

Authors: Michael Byrne; Chris Hoy; Frank Lampard; J.K. Rowling; Pete Townshend

Company Director / Literary Agent: Rory Scarfe (**L1228**)

Literary Agents: Hattie Grunewald (**L0587**); Josephine Hayes (**L0627**)

L0139 Blake Friedmann Literary Agency Ltd
Literary Agency
15 Highbury Place, London, N5 1QP
United Kingdom
Tel: +44 (0) 20 7387 0842

info@blakefriedmann.co.uk

http://www.blakefriedmann.co.uk

Professional Body: The Association of Authors' Agents (AAA)

Types: Fiction; Nonfiction; Scripts
Formats: Film Scripts; Radio Scripts; TV Scripts
Subjects: Autobiography; Commercial; Contemporary; Cookery; Crime; Culture; Current Affairs; Fantasy; Finance; History; Literary; Mystery; Nature; Politics; Psychology; Science; Science Fiction; Society; Suspense; Technology; Thrillers; Travel; Warfare; Women's Interests
Markets: Adult; Children's; Young Adult

Send: Query
Don't send: Full text
How to send: Email

Send query by email to a specific agent best suited to your work. See website for full submission guidelines, details of agents, and individual agent contact details. Media department currently only accepting submissions from writers with produced credits. Reply not guaranteed. If no response within 8 weeks, assume rejection.

Authors: Gilbert Adair; Tatamkhulu Afrika; Mary Akers; Ted Allbeury; Paul Ashton; MiMi Aye

Literary Agents: Isobel Dixon (*L0372*); Samuel Hodder (*L0654*); Juliet Pickering (*L1097*); Tom Witcomb (*L1464*)

L0140 Simon Blakey
Literary Agent
United Kingdom

Literary Agency: The Agency (London) Ltd (**L0021**)

L0141 Blanche Marvin, MBE
Literary Agency
21A St John's Wood High Street, London, NW8 7NG
United Kingdom
Tel: +44 (0) 20 7722 2313

blanchemarvin17@hotmail.com

http://www.blanchemarvin.com

Types: Scripts
Formats: Theatre Scripts
Markets: Adult

Handles full-length plays for theatre.

Literary Agent: Blanche Marvin (*L0932*)

L0142 Caitlin Blasdell
Literary Agent
United States

Literary Agency: Liza Dawson Associates (**L0868**)

L0143 Lyndsey Blessing
Literary Agent
United States

Literary Agency: InkWell Management (**L0686**)

L0144 Piers Blofeld
Literary Agent
United Kingdom

Literary Agency: Sheil Land Associates Ltd (**L1263**)

L0145 Brettne Bloom
Literary Agent
United States

Literary Agency: The Book Group (**L0154**)

L0146 Felicity Blunt
Literary Agent
United Kingdom

http://submissions.curtisbrown.co.uk/agents/
Literary Agency: Curtis Brown (**L0318**)

Fiction > *Novels*

Domestic Suspense; Historical Fiction; Literary Thrillers; Psychological Suspense; Speculative

Nonfiction > *Nonfiction Books*
Cookery; Food

How to send: Online submission system

"Most simply put I am looking for good stories, compellingly told. The books on my list have one thing in common, the combination of a distinctive voice and a great narrative."

L0147 Keely Boeving
Literary Agent
United States

Literary Agency: Wordserve Literary (**L1472**)

L0148 Hope Bolinger
Associate Agent
United States

Literary Agency: Cyle Young Literary Elite (**L0323**)

L0149 Camilla Bolton
Literary Agent
United Kingdom

Literary Agency: The Darley Anderson Agency (**L0333**)

L0150 Bond Literary Agency
Literary Agency
4340 E Kentucky Avenue, Suite 471, Denver, CO 80246
United States
Tel: +1 (303) 781-9305

queries@bondliteraryagency.com

https://www.bondliteraryagency.com

Types: Fiction; Nonfiction
Subjects: Business; Commercial; Crime; Fantasy; History; Horror; Literary; Mystery; Science; Science Fiction; Thrillers
Markets: Adult; Young Adult

Closed to approaches.

Temporarily closed to submissions as at November 2018 Agency based in Colorado, representing fiction and nonfiction for adults and young adults. No romance, poetry, children's picture books or screenplays. Send query by email with first five pages of your novel (if sending fiction) in the body of the email. For nonfiction, a proposal must be available before querying. No attachments. See website for full guidelines.

Literary Agents: Sandra Bond (*L0151*); Becky LeJeune (*L0845*)

L0151 Sandra Bond
Literary Agent
United States

Literary Agency: Bond Literary Agency (**L0150**)

L0152 Luigi Bonomi
Literary Agent
United Kingdom

http://www.lbabooks.com/agent/luigi-bonomi/

Literary Agency: LBA Books Ltd (**L0839**)

Fiction > *Novels*: Commercial

Nonfiction > *Nonfiction Books*: Commercial

I love commercial fiction across all genres, as well as intelligent non-fiction written for a commercial audience, and am always on the lookout for authors who aspire to hit the bestseller list.

Authors: Will Adams; Kirstie Allsopp; Lizzy Barber; James Barrington; James Becker; Diana Bretherick; Fern Britton; Dr James Cheshire; Sam Christer; Rosemary Conley; Gennaro Contaldo; Josephine Cox; Dean Crawford; Mason Cross; A.M. Dean; Dan Farnworth; Liz Fenwick; Judy Finnigan; Nick Foulkes; Tom Fox; Susan Gee; David Gibbins; Jane Gordon; Tom Grass; Mark Griffin; Michael Gustafson; Rachel Hamilton; Richard Hammond; Duncan Harding; Matt Hilton; Eva Holland; John Humphrys; Jessica Jarlvi; Graham Joyce; Annabel Kantaria; Catherine Kirwan; Alex Knight; Victoria Lamb; Dr Guy Leschziner; Susan Lewis; Amy Lloyd; Richard Madeley; Tom Marcus; Sam Masters; Gavin Menzies; Ben Miller; Michael Morley; Anthony Mosawi; Elizabeth Moss; Karen Osman; Sue Palmer; S.A. Patrick; Jeff Pearce; Andrew Pepper; Melanie Phillips; Gervase Phinn; Richard Porter; Esther Rantzen; Madeleine Reiss; Alice Roberts; Jacqueline Rohen; Simon Scarrow; Colin Shindler; Jack Steel; Lucy Strange; Joe Swift; Bryan Sykes; Rachel de Thame; Alan Titchmarsh; Jon Trace; Oliver Uberti; Phil Vickery; Tamsin Winter; Terry Wogan

L0153 The Book Bureau Literary Agency
Literary Agency
7 Duncairn Avenue, Bray, Co. Wicklow, Ireland
Tel: +353 (0) 1276 4996
Fax: +353 (0) 1276 4834

thebookbureau@oceanfree.net

Types: Fiction; Nonfiction
Subjects: Commercial; Crime; Literary; Thrillers; Women's Interests
Markets: Adult

Send: Query
Don't send: Full text
How to send: Email

Handles mainly general and literary fiction, plus some nonfiction. Particularly interested in women's, crime, Irish novels, and thrillers.

Send query by email (preferred) or by post with SAE, synopsis, and first three chapters. Prefers single line spacing. No poetry, children's, horror, or science fiction. Strong editorial support provided before submission to publishers.

Literary Agent: Geraldine Nichol (*L1033*)

L0154 The Book Group
Literary Agency
20 West 20th Street, Suite 601, New York, NY 10011
United States
Tel: +1 (212) 803-3360

submissions@thebookgroup.com
info@thebookgroup.com

http://www.thebookgroup.com
https://www.facebook.com/thebookgrp
https://twitter.com/thebookgrp
https://www.instagram.com/thebookgrp/

Fiction > *Novels*

Nonfiction > *Nonfiction Books*

Send: Query; Writing sample
How to send: In the body of an email
How not to send: Email attachment; Post; Phone

Represents a broad range of fiction and nonfiction. No poetry or screenplays. Send query by email only with ten sample pages and the first and last name of the agent you are querying in the subject line (see website for individual agent interests). No attachments. Include all material in the body of the email. See website for full guidelines. Response only if interested.

Literary Agents: Julie Barer (*L0088*); Faye Bender (*L0116*); Brettne Bloom (*L0145*); Jamie Carr (**L0230**); Dana Murphy (*L1011*); Elisabeth Weed (*L1424*)

L0155 BookEnds, LLC
Literary Agency
United States

Bookends@bookendsliterary.com

http://www.bookends-inc.com

Types: Fiction; Nonfiction
Formats: Reference
Subjects: Autobiography; Business; Contemporary; Culture; Current Affairs; Erotic; Fantasy; History; Horror; Lifestyle; Literary; Mystery; Romance; Science Fiction; Suspense; Thrillers; Women's Interests
Markets: Adult; Children's; Young Adult

Send: Query
Don't send: Full text

Send submissions through online submission system (see website). No short fiction, poetry, screenplays, or techno-thrillers.

Literary Agents: Jessica Alvarez (*L0036*); Naomi Davis (*L0345*); Jessica Faust (*L0453*);

Moe Ferrara (*L0464*); Amanda Jain (*L0703*); Kim Lionetti (*L0860*); Tracy Marchini (*L0915*); Natascha Morris (*L1000*)

L0156 Books & Such Literary Management
Literary Agency
52 Mission Circle, Suite 122, PMB 170, Santa Rosa, CA 95409-5370
United States

representation@booksandsuch.com

http://www.booksandsuch.biz

Types: Fiction; Nonfiction
Subjects: Comedy / Humour; History; Lifestyle; Religion; Romance; Women's Interests
Markets: Adult; Children's; Young Adult

Send: Query
Don't send: Full text
How to send: Email

Send query by email only. No attachments. Query should be up to one page detailing your book, your market, your experience, etc. No queries by post or phone. See website for full details.

Literary Agents: Rachelle Gardner (*L0528*); Janet Kobobel Grant (*L0571*); Rachel Kent (*L0778*); Wendy Lawton (*L0836*); Cynthia Ruchti (*L1197*)

L0157 Bookseeker Agency
Literary Agency
PO Box 7535, Perth, PH2 1AF
United Kingdom
Tel: +44 (0) 1738 620688

bookseeker@blueyonder.co.uk

https://bookseekeragency.com
https://twitter.com/BookseekerAgent

Fiction > *Novels*

Poetry > *Any Poetic Form*

Send: Query; Synopsis; Writing sample
How to send: Email; Post

Handles fiction and (under some circumstances) poetry. No nonfiction. Send query by post or email outlining what you have written and your current projects, along with synopsis and sample chapter (novels).

Literary Agent: Paul Thompson (*L1366*)

L0158 BookStop Literary Agency, LLC
Literary Agency
67 Meadow View Road, Orinda, CA 94563
United States

info@bookstopliterary.com

http://www.bookstopliterary.com
https://www.facebook.com/bookstopliterary/
https://www.instagram.com/bookstopliterary/

CHILDREN'S
Fiction
  Chapter Books; Graphic Novels; Middle Grade; Novels; Picture Books
Nonfiction > *Nonfiction Books*

YOUNG ADULT > **Fiction** > *Novels*

How to send: Conferences; By referral

Handles fiction and nonfiction for children and young adults.

Literary Agents: Minju Chang (*L0251*); Karyn Fischer (*L0471*); Kendra Marcus (*L0919*)

L0159 Anne Borchardt
Literary Agent
United States

Literary Agency: Georges Borchardt, Inc. (**L0539**)

L0160 Georges Borchardt
Literary Agent
United States

Literary Agency: Georges Borchardt, Inc. (**L0539**)

L0161 Valerie Borchardt
Literary Agent
United States

Literary Agency: Georges Borchardt, Inc. (**L0539**)

L0162 Stefanie Sanchez Von Borstel
Literary Agent
United States

https://www.fullcircleliterary.com/our-agents/stefanie-von-borstel/

Literary Agency: Full Circle Literary, LLC (**L0515**)

ADULT > **Nonfiction** > *Nonfiction Books*
  Creativity; Nature; Wellbeing

CHILDREN'S
Fiction
  Graphic Novels; Middle Grade
Nonfiction > *Middle Grade*

L0163 Hannah Boulton
Literary Agent
United Kingdom

Literary Agency: The Agency (London) Ltd (**L0021**)

L0164 Michael Bourret
Literary Agent
United States

Literary Agency: Dystel, Goderich & Bourret LLC (**L0399**)
Professional Body: Association of Authors' Representatives, Inc. (AAR)

L0165 Katie Shea Boutillier
Literary Agent
United States

Literary Agency: Donald Maass Literary Agency (**L0380**)

L0166 Sarah Bowlin
Literary Agent
Los Angeles
United States

https://aevitascreative.com/agents/

Literary Agency: Aevitas (**L0019**)

Fiction > *Novels*
  General, and in particular: Literary

Nonfiction > *Nonfiction Books*
  General, and in particular: Comedy / Humour; Dance; Food History; History; Narrative Nonfiction; Popular Culture; Wine

Send: Query; Market info; Author bio; Writing sample
How to send: Online submission system

Focused on bold, diverse voices in fiction and nonfiction. She's especially interested in stories of strong or difficult women and unexpected narratives of place, of identity, and of the shifting ways we see ourselves and each other. She's also interested in food history, wine, and dance.

L0167 Hannah Bowman
Literary Agent
United States

Literary Agency: Liza Dawson Associates (**L0868**)

L0168 Katherine Boyle
Literary Agent
United States

katherine@veritasliterary.com

http://www.veritasliterary.com

Literary Agency: Veritas Literary Agency (**L1400**)

ADULT
Fiction > *Novels*
  Historical Fiction; Literary

Nonfiction > *Nonfiction Books*
  Culture; History; Memoir; Narrative Nonfiction; Nature; Popular Culture; Women's Studies

CHILDREN'S > **Fiction**
  Middle Grade; Picture Books
YOUNG ADULT > **Fiction** > *Novels*

L0169 Bradford Literary Agency
Literary Agency
5694 Mission Center Road # 347, San Diego, CA 92108

United States
Tel: +1 (619) 521-1201

hannah@bradfordlit.com

https://bradfordlit.com

ADULT
Fiction > *Novels*
  Contemporary Romance; Erotic Romance; Historical Romance; Literary; Mystery; Romance; Romantic Suspense; Supernatural / Paranormal Romance; Thrillers; Upmarket Commercial Fiction; Urban Fantasy; Women's Fiction

Nonfiction > *Nonfiction Books*
  Biography; Business; Comedy / Humour; Cookery; Food; History; Memoir; Parenting; Popular Culture; Relationships; Self Help; Social Issues

CHILDREN'S > **Fiction**
  Novels; Picture Books

How to send: Query Manager; In the body of an email
How not to send: Email attachment

Represents a wide range of fiction and nonfiction. Send query by email with synopsis and first chapter (fiction), full ms (children's picture books), or proposal, including sample chapter (nonfiction). Select a particular agent at the agency to submit to, and submit to only one agent at a time.

Literary Agents: Laura Bradford (**L0170**); Sarah LaPolla; Natalie Lakosil (**L0817**); Kari Sutherland (**L1341**); Jennifer Chen Tran (**L1375**); Katherine Wessbecher (**L1433**)

L0170 Laura Bradford
Literary Agent
United States

queries@bradfordlit.com

https://bradfordlit.com/about/laura-bradford/

Literary Agency: Bradford Literary Agency (**L0169**)
Professional Bodies: Association of Authors' Representatives, Inc. (AAR); Romance Writers of America (RWA); Society of Children's Book Writers and Illustrators (SCBWI)

ADULT
Fiction > *Novels*
  Contemporary Romance; Erotic Romance; Historical Romance; Mystery; Romance; Romantic Suspense; Speculative; Thrillers; Women's Fiction

Nonfiction > *Nonfiction Books*

CHILDREN'S > **Fiction** > *Middle Grade*

YOUNG ADULT > **Fiction** > *Novels*

Send: Query; Synopsis; Writing sample
How to send: Email

Interested in romance (historical, romantic suspense, category, contemporary, erotic), speculative fiction, women's fiction, mystery, thrillers, young adult, upper middle grade, illustration as well as some select non-fiction.

L0171 Karen Brailsford

Consulting Agent
United States

https://aevitascreative.com/agents

Literary Agency: Aevitas (**L0019**)

Nonfiction > *Nonfiction Books*
Arts; Biography; Entertainment; Health; Memoir; Spirituality; Wellbeing

Send: Query; Author bio; Market info; Writing sample
How to send: Online submission system

Based in Los Angeles and is especially interested in arts and entertainment, memoir, biography, health and wellness, spirituality and works of non-fiction that inspire and shine a light on contemporary conditions.

L0172 Brandt & Hochman Literary Agents, Inc.

Literary Agency
1501 Broadway, Suite 2310, New York, NY 10036
United States
Tel: +1 (212) 840-5760
Fax: +1 (212) 840-5776

http://brandthochman.com

See website for full submission guidelines and for details of individual agents' interests and direct contact details, then approach one agent specifically.

Literary Agents: Emily Forland (**L0481**); Gail Hochman (**L0653**); Jody Kahn (**L0752**); Marianne Merola (**L0968**); Emma Patterson (**L1072**); Henry Thayer (**L1361**); Mitchell Waters (**L1417**)

L0173 Hannah Brattesani

Literary Agent
United States

http://www.friedrichagency.com/about-alternate-2/

Literary Agency: The Friedrich Agency LLC (**L0511**)

Fiction > *Novels*: Literary

Nonfiction > *Nonfiction Books*
Culture; Lifestyle; Narrative Nonfiction; Popular Science

Send: Query
How to send: In the body of an email

L0174 The Brattle Agency LLC

Literary Agency
PO Box 380537, Cambridge, MA 02238
United States
Tel: +1 (617) 721-5375

submissions@thebrattleagency.com

https://thebrattleagency.com

Types: Fiction; Nonfiction
Subjects: Arts; Culture; History; Literary; Politics; Sport
Markets: Academic; Adult

Closed to approaches.

Accepts submissions only during one-month reading periods. See website for details.

L0175 Barbara Braun

Literary Agent
United States

Literary Agency: Barbara Braun Associates, Inc. (**L0084**)

L0176 The Bravo Blue Agency

Literary Agency
United Kingdom

charlotte@bravoblue.co.uk

https://www.bravoblue.co.uk

Literary Agency: Tibor Jones & Associates (**L1371**)

ADULT
Fiction > *Novels*
Commercial; Historical Fiction; Literary

Nonfiction > *Nonfiction Books*
Lifestyle; Narrative Nonfiction; Nature; Popular History; Science; Wellbeing

CHILDREN'S > **Fiction**
Early Readers; *Middle Grade*; *Picture Books*
YOUNG ADULT > **Fiction** > *Novels*

Send: Query; Author bio; Synopsis; Writing sample
How to send: Email

Literary Agent: Charlotte Colwill (**L0290**)

L0177 Helen Breitwieser

Literary Agent
United States

https://twitter.com/HelenBreit
http://aaronline.org/Sys/PublicProfile/2176619/417813

Professional Body: Association of Authors' Representatives, Inc. (AAR)
Literary Agency: Cornerstone Literary Agency (**L0301**)

Authors: Jackie Ashenden; Anne Barton; Anna Bennett; Bethany Blake; Marnee Blake; Maya Blake; Katherine Center; Zara Cox; Robert Evans; Beth Fantaskey; Jane Goodger; Sherilee Gray; C.S. Harris; Nicole Helm; Lisa Hendrix; Kate Hewitt; Rachael Johns; Diane Kelly; Rachel Lee; Fiona Lowe; Mary McKinley; Annabel Monaghan; Trish Morey; Kerry O'Connor; Mary-Anne O'Connor; Michael Paraskevas; Kayla Perrin; Candice Proctor; Kay Thomas; Christine Trent; Ursula Vernon; Tracy Anne Warren; Michelle Willingham; Maisey Yates

L0178 Bret Adams Ltd

Literary Agency
448 West 44th Street, New York, NY 10036
United States
Tel: +1 (212) 765-5630
Fax: +1 (212) 265-2212

http://www.bretadamsltd.net

Types: Scripts
Formats: Film Scripts; TV Scripts; Theatre Scripts
Markets: Adult

A full service agency representing writers, directors, designers, and actors.

Literary Agents: Mark Orsini (*L1060*); Bruce Ostler (*L1062*)

L0179 M. Courtney Briggs

Literary Agent
United States

Literary Agency: Derrick & Briggs, LLP (**L0358**)

L0180 The Bright Agency

Literary Agency
103-105 St John's Hill, London, SW11 1SY
United Kingdom
Tel: +44 (0) 20 7326 9140

mail@thebrightagency.com

https://thebrightagency.com
https://thebrightagency.com/uk/submissions/new

Media Company: The Bright Group International Limited

CHILDREN'S > **Fiction**
Chapter Books; *Middle Grade*; *Picture Books*

Send: Outline; Synopsis; Writing sample
How to send: Online contact form

Welcomes submissions from illustrators and authors who are looking for representation. Interested in children's picture book texts, chapter books and middle grade fiction. Provide an outline with a synopsis and the first three chapters.

Literary Agent: Vicki Willden-Lebrecht

L0181 Bright Group US Inc.

Literary Agency
50 West Street, C12, New York, NY 10006
United States
Tel: +1 (646) 578 6542

mail@thebrightagency.com

https://thebrightagency.com
https://thebrightagency.com/us/submissions/new

Media Company: The Bright Group International Limited

CHILDREN'S > **Fiction**

Chapter Books; Middle Grade; Picture Books

Send: Outline; Synopsis; Writing sample
How to send: Online contact form

Welcomes submissions from illustrators and authors who are looking for representation. Interested in children's picture book texts, chapter books and middle grade fiction. Provide an outline with a synopsis and the first three chapters.

L0182 Alan Brodie
Literary Agent
United Kingdom

Literary Agency: Alan Brodie Representation Ltd (**L0026**)

L0183 Alicia Brooks
Literary Agent
United States

Literary Agency: The Jean V. Naggar Literary Agency (**L0716**)

L0184 Regina Brooks
Literary Agent
United States

Literary Agency: Serendipity Literary Agency LLC (**L1252**)
Professional Body: Association of Authors' Representatives, Inc. (AAR)

L0185 Savannah Brooks
Literary Agent
United States

Literary Agency: The Jennifer DeChiara Literary Agency (**L0721**)

L0186 Philippa Brophy
Literary Agent; President
United States

https://www.sll.com/our-team
http://aaronline.org/Sys/PublicProfile/4090020/417813

Literary Agency: Sterling Lord Literistic, Inc. (**L1317**)
Professional Body: Association of Authors' Representatives, Inc. (AAR)

Fiction > *Novels*

Nonfiction > *Nonfiction Books*
General, and in particular: Journalism

Closed to approaches.

L0187 Brotherstone Creative Management
Literary Agency
Mortimer House, 37–41 Mortimer Street, London, W1T 3JH
United Kingdom
Tel: +44 (0) 7908 542886

submissions@bcm-agency.com
info@bcm-agency.com

http://bcm-agency.com

Professional Body: The Association of Authors' Agents (AAA)

Types: Fiction; Nonfiction
Subjects: Commercial; Literary
Markets: Adult

Send: Query; Writing sample; Synopsis
How to send: Email

Always on the search for talented new writers. Send query by email. For fiction, include the first three chapters or 50 pages and 2-page synopsis. For nonfiction, include detailed outline and sample chapter. No children's and young adult fiction, sci-fi and fantasy novels or unsolicited short story and poetry collections, or scripts.

Literary Agent: Charlie Brotherstone (*L0188*)

L0188 Charlie Brotherstone
Literary Agent
United Kingdom

Literary Agency: Brotherstone Creative Management (**L0187**)

L0189 Justin Brouckaert
Literary Agent
New York
United States

https://aevitascreative.com/agents/

Literary Agency: Aevitas (**L0019**)

Fiction
Novels: Literary
Short Fiction: Literary

Nonfiction > *Nonfiction Books*
Current Affairs; History; Journalism; Memoir; Narrative Nonfiction; Parenting; Politics; Sport; Travel

Send: Author bio; Outline; Market info; Writing sample
How to send: Online submission system

Actively seeking character-driven and formally inventive literary fiction and memoir, as well as narrative nonfiction in the areas of sports, internet culture, politics and current affairs, parenting, travel, and history. Regardless of genre, he is most passionate about projects that shine a light on underserved and overlooked communities and/or highlight unique relationships between people and places. He is especially interested in pairing with debut authors and helping them grow their careers.

L0190 Michelle Brower
Literary Agent; Partner
United States

https://aevitascreative.com/agents/

Literary Agency: Aevitas (**L0019**)

ADULT
Fiction > *Novels*
Book Club Fiction; Commercial; Literary; Suspense; Upmarket; Women's Fiction

Nonfiction > *Nonfiction Books*
Memoir; Narrative Nonfiction

CHILDREN'S > **Fiction** > *Middle Grade*
YOUNG ADULT > **Fiction** > *Novels*

Send: Pitch; Market info; Writing sample
How to send: Online submission system

Represents fiction and narrative nonfiction. Her interests include book club fiction (a commercial concept with a literary execution), literary fiction (including with an element of genre), and smart women's fiction. She also represents select young adult, middle grade, and memoir projects.

L0191 Andrea Brown
Literary Agent
United States

Literary Agency: Andrea Brown Literary Agency, Inc. (**L0047**)
Professional Body: Association of Authors' Representatives, Inc. (AAR)

L0192 Jenny Brown
Literary Agent
United Kingdom

Literary Agency: Jenny Brown Associates (**L0722**)

L0193 Margaret Sutherland Brown
Literary Agent
United States

Literary Agency: Emma Sweeney Agency, LLC (**L0430**)
Professional Body: Association of Authors' Representatives, Inc. (AAR)

L0194 Browne & Miller Literary Associates
Literary Agency
52 Village Place, Hinsdale, IL 60521
United States
Tel: +1 (312) 922-3063

mail@browneandmiller.com

https://www.browneandmiller.com

Fiction > *Novels:* Commercial

Nonfiction > *Nonfiction Books:* Commercial

Send: Query
Don't send: Full text
How to send: Email

Handles books for the adult commercial book markets. No children's, young adult, science fiction, fantasy, horror, short stories, poetry, screenplays, or academic works. Send query only by email. No attachments.

Literary Agent: Danielle Egan-Miller (*L0413*)

L0195 Chris Bucci

Literary Agent
New York
United States

https://aevitascreative.com/agents/

Literary Agency: Aevitas (**L0019**)

Fiction > *Novels*
Commercial; Historical Fiction; History; Literary; Mystery; Popular Culture; Popular Science; Thrillers

Nonfiction > *Nonfiction Books*
Narrative Nonfiction; Politics; Sport

Send: Author bio; Outline; Market info; Writing sample
How to send: Online submission system

Based in the New York Metropolitan area. Represents a broad range of fiction and nonfiction.

L0196 Peter Buckman

Literary Agent
United Kingdom

Literary Agency: The Ampersand Agency Ltd (**L0039**)

L0197 Danielle Bukowski

Foreign Rights Manager; Associate Agent
United States

https://www.sll.com/our-team

Literary Agency: Sterling Lord Literistic, Inc. (**L1317**)

Fiction > *Novels*
Commercial; Literary; Upmarket Women's Fiction

Nonfiction > *Nonfiction Books*

Send: Query; Synopsis; Writing sample
How to send: Online submission system

L0198 Danielle Burby

Literary Agent
United States

https://nelsonagency.com/danielle-burby/
https://querymanager.com/query/1352
http://www.publishersmarketplace.com/members/dburby/
https://twitter.com/DanielleBurby
https://www.facebook.com/danielle.burby

Literary Agency: Nelson Literary Agency, LLC (**L1026**)

ADULT > **Fiction**
Graphic Novels: General
Novels: Adventure; Fairy Tales; Feminism; Folklore, Myths, and Legends; LGBTQIA; Magical Realism; Social Justice; Women's Fiction
CHILDREN'S > **Fiction**

Graphic Novels; *Middle Grade*; *Picture Books*
YOUNG ADULT > **Fiction**
Graphic Novels; *Novels*

Send: Query; Writing sample; Author bio
How to send: Query Manager

I am particularly drawn to: complex female characters, seaside novels, girls with swords, magical realism, LGBTQ+ love, sister stories, toxic friendships, feminist fairytales, social justice themes, folklore, creepy forests, complicated family dynamics, quirky adventures, protagonists who change systems and break rules, heartwarming love stories, whimsy.

Authors: Jillian Boehme; Kristen Ciccarelli; Lisa Duffy; Doug Engstrom; Reese Eschmann; Florence Gonsalves; Ausma Zehanat Khan; Maryann Jacob Macias; Rosaria Munda; Jennifer Nissley; Lynette Noni; Celesta Rimington; Laura Brooke Robson; Ehsaneh Sadr; Jeff Seymour; Jordyn Taylor

L0199 Megan Burkhart

Junior Agent
United States

megan@cyleyoung.com

https://cyleyoung.com/literary-agent/my-team/
https://meganlynneauthor.weebly.com/
https://www.facebook.com/meganlynne.13/
https://twitter.com/writemeganlynne
https://www.youtube.com/channel/UCv23mXzg0-9PuXBnGDAuqmg
https://www.linkedin.com/in/megan-burkhart-93858814a/
https://www.instagram.com/authormeganlynne

Literary Agency: Cyle Young Literary Elite (**L0323**)

YOUNG ADULT > **Fiction** > *Novels*: Fantasy

Send: Query; Synopsis; Writing sample
How to send: Email

Costs: Offers services that writers have to pay for. Also offers editorial services.

Looks for YA fantasy and children's picture books, especially those with a strong narrative voice. Closed to picture book submissions as at June 2020.

L0200 Louise Burns

Literary Agent
United Kingdom

Literary Agency: Andrew Mann Ltd (**L0049**)

L0201 Penelope Burns

Literary Agent
United States

Literary Agency: Gelfman Schneider / ICM Partners (**L0534**)

L0202 Juliet Burton

Literary Agent
United Kingdom

Literary Agency: Juliet Burton Literary Agency (**L0748**)

L0203 Kate Burton

Literary Agent
United Kingdom

Literary Agency: C+W (Conville & Walsh) (**L0205**)

L0204 Sheree Bykofsky

Literary Agent
United States

http://www.shereebee.com
http://aaronline.org/Sys/PublicProfile/2176625/417813

Literary Agency: Sheree Bykofsky Associates, Inc. (**L1268**)
Professional Body: Association of Authors' Representatives, Inc. (AAR)

L0205 C+W (Conville & Walsh)

Literary Agency
Haymarket House, 28-29 Haymarket, London, SW1Y 4SP
United Kingdom
Tel: +44 (0) 20 7393 4200

sue@cwagency.co.uk

http://cwagency.co.uk

Professional Body: The Association of Authors' Agents (AAA)

Types: Fiction; Nonfiction
Subjects: Autobiography; Comedy / Humour; Commercial; Crime; Current Affairs; Fantasy; History; Leisure; Lifestyle; Literary; Men's Interests; Mystery; Psychology; Science; Science Fiction; Sport; Suspense; Thrillers; Travel; Warfare; Women's Interests
Markets: Adult; Children's; Young Adult

Send: Query
Don't send: Full text

See website for agent profiles and submit to one particular agent only. Send submissions by email as Word .doc files only. No postal submissions. For fiction, please submit the first three sample chapters of the completed manuscript (or about 50 pages) with a one to two page synopsis. For nonfiction, send 30-page proposal. No poetry or scripts, or picture books. See website for full guidelines.

Author Estate: The Estate of Francis Bacon

Authors: Naoko Abe; Shahnaz Ahsan; Nigel Akehurst; Dolly Alderton; Keir Alexander; Piers Alexander; Robin Antalek; Ollie Aplin; Steven Appleby; Will Ashon; Stephen Baker; Damian Barr; Tony Barrell; Colin Barrett; Kevin Barry; Neil Bartlett; Brock Bastian; Sara Baume; Richard Beard; Francesca Beauman;

Matt Beaumont; Patrick Benson; Mandy Berriman; Josie Bevan; Michael Bhaskar; Vanessa Black; Emma Blackery; Immodesty Blaize; David Bodanis; Lee Bofkin; Simon van Booy; Megan Bradbury; John Bradshaw; Kevin Breathnach; Michael Brooks; Iain Broome; The Wild Swimming Brothers; Dea Brovig; Bill Browder

Literary Agents: Susan Armstrong (*L0064*); Matilda Ayris (*L0074*); Kate Burton (*L0203*); Alexander Cochran (*L0285*); Clare Conville (*L0294*); Allison DeFrees (*L0350*); Emma Finn (*L0470*); Katie Greenstreet (*L0580*); Carrie Kania (*L0756*); Sophie Lambert (*L0821*); Lucy Luck (*L0883*); Richard Pike (*L1099*); Jake Smith-Bosanquet (*L1295*)

L0206 CAA (Creative Artists Agency, LLC)
Literary Agency
2000 Avenue of the Stars, Los Angeles, CA 90067, 405 Lexington Avenue, 19th Floor, New York, NY 10174
United States
Tel: +1 (424) 288-2000
Fax: +1 (424) 288-2900

https://www.caa.com

Literary Agent: Cindy Uh (*L1385*)

L0207 Ellie Cahill-Nicholls
Literary Agent
United Kingdom

Literary Agency: Noel Gay (**L1037**)

L0208 Rachel Calder
Literary Agent
United Kingdom

Literary Agency: The Sayle Literary Agency (**L1225**)

L0209 William Callahan
Literary Agent
United States

Literary Agency: InkWell Management (**L0686**)

L0210 Linda Camacho
Literary Agent
United States

linda@galltzacker.com
QueryLinda@galltzacker.com

Literary Agency: Gallt & Zacker Literary Agency (**L0522**)

Fiction > *Novels*
Romance; Women's Fiction

How to send: Email

L0211 Kimberley Cameron
Literary Agent
United States

Literary Agency: Kimberley Cameron & Associates (**L0787**)

L0212 Charlie Campbell
Literary Agent

charlie@kingsfordcampbell.com

http://kingsfordcampbell.com/about-us/charlie-campbell/
https://twitter.com/ScapegoatCC

Literary Agency: Kingsford Campbell Literary Agency (**L0790**)

ADULT
Fiction > *Novels*
Commercial; Crime; Historical Fiction; Literary; Thrillers

Nonfiction > *Nonfiction Books*
Business; Comedy / Humour; Commercial; History; Literary; Popular Science; Sport

CHILDREN'S > **Fiction** > *Novels*

Send: Query; Synopsis; Writing sample
How to send: Email

L0213 Cynthia Cannell
Literary Agent
United States

Literary Agency: Cynthia Cannell Literary Agency (**L0324**)

L0214 Carrie Cantor
Literary Agent
United States

Literary Agency: Joelle Delbourgo Associates, Inc. (**L0729**)

L0215 Georgina Capel
Literary Agent
United Kingdom

Literary Agency: Georgina Capel Associates Ltd (**L0540**)

L0216 Capital Talent Agency
Literary Agency
419 South Washington Street, Alexandria, VA 22314
United States
Tel: +1 (703) 349-1649

literary.submissions@capitaltalentagency.com

http://capitaltalentagency.com

Types: Fiction; Nonfiction
Markets: Adult

Send: Query
Don't send: Full text
How to send: Email

Represents authors in all genres of fiction and nonfiction. Send query by email only. Response in 6 weeks, if interested. See website for full guidelines.

Literary Agents: Cynthia Kane (*L0755*); Shaheen Qureshi (*L1123*)

L0217 Victoria Cappello
Literary Agent
United States

Literary Agency: The Bent Agency (**L0119**)

L0218 Elise Capron
Literary Agent
United States

Literary Agency: Sandra Dijkstra Literary Agency (**L1218**)

L0219 Amber J. Caravéo
Literary Agent
United Kingdom

Literary Agency: Skylark Literary (**L1288**)

L0220 Moses Cardona
Literary Agent
United States

Literary Agency: John Hawkins & Associates, Inc. (**L0730**)

L0221 Michael V. Carlisle
Literary Agent
United States

Literary Agency: InkWell Management (**L0686**)

L0222 Agnes Carlowicz
Literary Agent
United States

agnes@carolmannagency.com

https://www.carolmannagency.com/agnes-carlowicz
https://twitter.com/AgnesCarlowicz
https://www.instagram.com/agnescarlowicz/

Literary Agency: Carol Mann Agency (**L0225**)

Fiction > *Novels*

Nonfiction > *Nonfiction Books*
Comedy / Humour; Crime; Intersectional Feminism; Memoir; Popular Culture; Wellbeing

Send: Query; Author bio; Writing sample; Synopsis
How to send: In the body of an email

Her interests include both fiction and non-fiction, with a special passion for literature that amplifies underrepresented voices and subverts the status quo. Among others, she enjoys: intersectional feminism, millennial self-care, female-driven memoir, true-crime, and humorous pop culture.

L0223 Jennifer Carlson
Literary Agent
United States

Literary Agency: Dunow, Carlson & Lerner Agency (**L0395**)

L0224 Anna Carmichael
Literary Agent
United Kingdom

anna@abnerstein.co.uk

Literary Agency: Abner Stein (**L0007**)

L0225 Carol Mann Agency
Literary Agency
55 Fifth Avenue, New York, NY 10003
United States
Tel: +1 (212) 206-5635

submissions@carolmannagency.com

https://www.carolmannagency.com

Send: Query; Author bio; Writing sample
How to send: In the body of an email
How not to send: Email attachment; Post; Phone

Send query by email only, including synopsis, brief bio, and first 25 pages, all pasted into the body of your email. No attachments. No submissions by post, or phone calls. Allow 3-4 weeks for response.

Authors: Jane Alexander; Clifton Hoodl Maria Goodavage; Rachel Kelly

Literary Agents: Maile Beal (**L0104**); Agnes Carlowicz (**L0222**); Gareth Esersky (**L0435**); Iris Blasi (**L0693**); Carol Mann (**L0911**); Myrsini Stephanides (**L1314**); Joanne Wyckoff (**L1476**); Laura Yorke (**L1480**)

L0226 Caroline Davidson Literary Agency
Literary Agency
5 Queen Anne's Gardens, London, W4 1TU
United Kingdom
Tel: +44 (0) 20 8995 5768

enquiries@cdla.co.uk

https://www.cdla.co.uk

Professional Body: The Association of Authors' Agents (AAA)

Types: Fiction; Nonfiction
Formats: Reference
Subjects: Archaeology; Architecture; Arts; Biography; Cookery; Culture; Design; Gardening; Health; History; Lifestyle; Medicine; Nature; Politics; Psychology; Science
Markets: Adult

Send: Query
Don't send: Full text
How not to send: Email

Send query by post only. See website for full guidelines.

Authors: Emma Donoghue; John Phibbs

Literary Agent: Caroline Davidson (*L0341*)

L0227 Caroline Sheldon Literary Agency
Literary Agency
71 Hillgate Place, London, W8 7SS
United Kingdom
Tel: +44 (0) 20 7727 9102

carolinesheldon@carolinesheldon.co.uk

http://www.carolinesheldon.co.uk

Professional Body: The Association of Authors' Agents (AAA)

Types: Fiction; Nonfiction
Subjects: Autobiography; Comedy / Humour; Commercial; Contemporary; Fantasy; History; Literary; Suspense; Women's Interests
Markets: Adult; Children's; Young Adult

Send: Query
Don't send: Full text
How to send: Email

Send query by email only. Do not query both agents. See website for both email addresses and appropriate subject line to include. Handles fiction and human-interest nonfiction for adults, and fiction for children, including full-length and picture books.

Literary Agents: Caroline Sheldon (*L1265*); Felicity Trew (*L1376*)

L0228 Carolyn Jenks Agency
Literary Agency
30 Cambridge Park Drive, #3140, Cambridge, MA 02140
United States

https://www.carolynjenksagency.com
https://www.facebook.com/carolynjenksagency
https://twitter.com/TheJenksAgency

Company Director / Literary Agent: Carolyn Jenks (**L0720**)

Literary Agents: Kwaku Acheampong (**L0012**); Becca Crandall (**L0306**); Brenna Girard (**L0547**); Molly McQuade

L0229 Heather Carr
Literary Agent
United States

Literary Agency: The Friedrich Agency LLC (**L0511**)

L0230 Jamie Carr
Literary Agent
United States

http://www.thebookgroup.com/jamie-carr

Literary Agency: The Book Group (**L0154**)

Fiction
Novels: Literary; Upmarket Commercial Fiction
Short Fiction: General

Nonfiction > *Nonfiction Books*

Culture; Food; Journalism; Narrative Nonfiction

Send: Query; Writing sample
How to send: In the body of an email

Represents novelists, short story writers, journalists, activists, and food and culture writers. Most interested in adult literary and upmarket commercial fiction and narrative nonfiction, she is drawn to writing that is voice-driven, highly transporting, from unique perspectives and marginalized voices, and that seeks to disrupt or reframe what appears to be known.

L0231 Michael Carr
Literary Agent
United States

http://www.veritasliterary.com

Literary Agency: Veritas Literary Agency (**L1400**)

Fiction > *Novels*
Fantasy; Historical Fiction; Science Fiction; Women's Fiction

Nonfiction > *Nonfiction Books*

L0232 Megan Carroll
Literary Agent
United Kingdom

Literary Agency: Watson, Little Ltd (**L1419**)

L0233 Lucy Carson
Literary Agent
United States

Literary Agency: The Friedrich Agency LLC (**L0511**)

L0234 Rebecca Carter
Literary Agent
United Kingdom

http://www.janklowandnesbit.co.uk/node/404
https://rebeccacarterliteraryagent.wordpress.com/
https://twitter.com/RebeccasBooks

Literary Agency: Janklow & Nesbit UK Ltd (**L0712**)

ADULT
Fiction > *Novels*
Literary; Thrillers; Upmarket Crime

Nonfiction > *Nonfiction Books*
Cultural Commentary; Design; Environment; History; Memoir; Politics; Social Commentary; Technology; Travel

CHILDREN'S > **Fiction** > *Novels*

YOUNG ADULT > **Fiction** > *Novels*

Send: Query; Synopsis; Writing sample
How to send: Email

L0235 Claire Cartey
Literary Agent
United Kingdom

claire@holroydecartey.com

https://www.holroydecartey.com/about.html
https://www.holroydecartey.com/submissions.
html

Literary Agency: Holroyde Cartey (**L0661**)

CHILDREN'S > Fiction
  Novels; Picture Books

Send: Synopsis; Full text
How to send: Email attachment

L0236 Casarotto Ramsay and Associates Ltd
Literary Agency
3rd Floor, 7 Savoy Court, Strand, London,
WC2R 0EX
United Kingdom
Tel: +44 (0) 20 7287 4450

info@casarotto.co.uk

https://www.casarotto.co.uk

Types: Scripts
Formats: Film Scripts; Radio Scripts; TV
Scripts; Theatre Scripts
Markets: Adult

Closed to approaches.

Handles scripts only – no books. Any
unsolicited scripts, treatments or other reading
materials will be deleted unread.

Authors: Alan Ayckbourn; Howard Brenton;
Caryl Churchill; Christopher Hampton; David
Hare; Nick Hornby; Amy Jephta; Sadie Jones;
Neil Jordan

Literary Agent: Jenne Casarotto (*L0237*)

L0237 Jenne Casarotto
Literary Agent
United Kingdom

Literary Agency: Casarotto Ramsay and
Associates Ltd (**L0236**)

L0238 Erin Casey
Literary Agent
United States

erin@galltzacker.com

Literary Agency: Gallt & Zacker Literary
Agency (**L0522**)

CHILDREN'S > Fiction
  Middle Grade; Picture Books
YOUNG ADULT
  Fiction
    Graphic Novels; Novels
  Nonfiction > *Nonfiction Books*

How to send: Email

L0239 Robert Caskie
Literary Agent
United Kingdom

robert@robertcaskie.com
submissions@robertcaskie.com

https://www.robertcaskie.com
https://twitter.com/rcaskie1

Literary Agency: Robert Caskie Ltd (**L1159**)

Fiction > *Novels*
  Book Club Fiction; Commercial; Literary

Nonfiction > *Nonfiction Books*
  Memoir; Narrative Nonfiction; Nature;
  Politics; Social Issues

Send: Query; Writing sample; Proposal
How to send: Email

Keen to receive fiction and nonfiction writing
that stimulates debate, comments on the world
around us, and invokes an emotional response.

L0240 The Catchpole Agency
Literary Agency
53 Cranham Street, Oxford, OX2 6DD
United Kingdom
Tel: +44 (0) 7789 588070

submissions@thecatchpoleagency.co.uk

http://www.thecatchpoleagency.co.uk

Types: Fiction
Markets: Children's

Closed to approaches.

**Closed to submissions as at March 2019.
Check website for current status.** Works on
children's books with both artists and writers.
Send query by email with sample pasted
directly into the body of the email (the whole
text of a picture book or a couple of chapters of
a novel). No attachments. See website for full
guidelines.

Literary Agents: Celia Catchpole (*L0241*);
James Catchpole (*L0242*); Lucy Catchpole
(*L0243*)

L0241 Celia Catchpole
Literary Agent
United Kingdom

Literary Agency: The Catchpole Agency
(**L0240**)

L0242 James Catchpole
Literary Agent
United Kingdom

Literary Agency: The Catchpole Agency
(**L0240**)

L0243 Lucy Catchpole
Literary Agent
United Kingdom

Literary Agency: The Catchpole Agency
(**L0240**)

L0244 Cecily Ware Literary Agents
Literary Agency
19C John Spencer Square, London, N1 2LZ
United Kingdom
Tel: +44 (0) 20 7359 3787

info@cecilyware.com

http://www.cecilyware.com

Types: Scripts
Formats: Film Scripts; TV Scripts
Subjects: Comedy / Humour; Drama
Markets: Adult; Children's

Send: Full text
How not to send: Email

Handles film and TV scripts only. No books or
theatre scripts. Submit complete script with
covering letter, CV, and SAE. No email
submissions or return of material without SAE
and correct postage.

Literary Agents: Carol Reyes (*L1144*); Gilly
Schuster (*L1240*); Warren Sherman (*L1269*)

L0245 Chalberg & Sussman
Literary Agency
115 West 29th St, Third Floor, New York, NY
10001
United States
Tel: +1 (917) 261-7550

rachel@chalbergsussman.com

http://www.chalbergsussman.com

Professional Body: Association of Authors'
Representatives, Inc. (AAR)

Types: Fiction; Nonfiction
Subjects: Autobiography; Commercial;
Culture; Fantasy; History; Horror; Literary;
Personal Development; Psychology; Romance;
Science; Science Fiction; Suspense; Thrillers;
Women's Interests
Markets: Adult; Children's; Young Adult

Send: Query
Don't send: Full text
How to send: Email

Send query by email. See website for specific
agent interests and email addresses.

Literary Agents: Terra Chalberg (*L0246*);
Jennifer Grimaldi (*L0585*); Nicole James
(*L0706*); Rachel Sussman (*L1340*)

L0246 Terra Chalberg
Literary Agent
United States

Literary Agency: Chalberg & Sussman
(**L0245**)

L0247 Jemiscoe Chambers-Black
Associate Agent
Los Angeles
United States

jemiscoe@andreabrownlit.com

https://www.andreabrownlit.com/agents.html
https://twitter.com/Jemiscoe
https://querymanager.com/query/Jemiscoe

Literary Agency: Andrea Brown Literary Agency, Inc. (**L0047**)

ADULT > **Fiction** > *Novels*
Comedy / Humour; Cozy Mysteries; Crime; LGBTQIA; Literary; Low Fantasy; Psychological Thrillers; Romance; Urban Fantasy

CHILDREN'S > **Fiction**
Graphic Novels: General
Middle Grade: Adventure; Comedy / Humour; Contemporary; Culture; Fantasy; Folklore, Myths, and Legends; Ghost Stories; Horror; LGBTQIA; Magical Realism; Mystery; Supernatural / Paranormal
YOUNG ADULT > **Fiction** > *Novels*
Contemporary; Fantasy; Ghost Stories; Horror; LGBTQIA; Mystery; Romance; Romantic Comedy; Supernatural / Paranormal

Send: Author bio; Query; Synopsis; Writing sample; Pitch; Market info
How to send: Query Manager

Currently building her client list in the middle grade, YA, and adult categories. She is also interested in considering illustrators and author-illustrators.

L0248 Jamie Chambliss
Literary Agent
United States

jamie@foliolitmanagement.com

https://www.foliolit.com/agents-1/jamie-chambliss
https://twitter.com/JChambliss1

Literary Agency: Folio Literary Management, LLC (**L0480**)

Fiction > *Novels*
Book Club Fiction; Literary; Upmarket

Nonfiction > *Nonfiction Books*
Food; History; Memoir; Narrative Nonfiction; Popular Culture; Prescriptive Nonfiction; Science; Sport

Closed to approaches.

L0249 Sonali Chanchani
Literary Agent
United States

sonali@foliolit.com

https://www.foliolit.com/agents-1/sonali-chanchani

Literary Agency: Folio Literary Management, LLC (**L0480**)

Fiction > *Novels*
Book Club Fiction; Crime; Folklore, Myths, and Legends; Historical Fiction; Literary;

Magical Realism; Mystery; Psychological Suspense; Thrillers; Upmarket Women's Fiction

Nonfiction > *Nonfiction Books*
Culture; Narrative Nonfiction; Politics; Social Justice; Society

Send: Query; Writing sample
How to send: In the body of an email

L0250 Anish Chandy
Literary Agent
India

Literary Agency: The Labyrinth Literary Agency (**L0816**)

L0251 Minju Chang
Literary Agent
United States

Literary Agency: BookStop Literary Agency, LLC (**L0158**)

L0252 Nicola Chang
Literary Agent
United Kingdom

nicolachang@davidhigham.co.uk

https://www.davidhigham.co.uk/agents-dh/nicola-chang/

Literary Agency: David Higham Associates Ltd (**L0338**)

Fiction > *Novels*
Caribbean; Contemporary; Historical Fiction; International; Literary; South America; South-East Asia

Nonfiction > *Nonfiction Books*
Cookery; Cultural Criticism; Culture; Food; Journalism; Mainstream; Memoir; Narrative Nonfiction; Philosophy; Politics; Psychology; Revisionist History; Society

Poetry > *Any Poetic Form*

Represents writers of fiction and nonfiction as well as a small list of poets. Currently accepting submissions and is primarily looking for literary fiction and nonfiction of all kinds.

Authors: Rosanna Amaka; Iman Amrani; Raymond Antrobus; Yemisí Aríbisálà; Amman Brar; Symeon Brown; Judith Bryan; Stephen Buoro; Jacqueline Crooks; Subhadra Das; Olivia Dunnett; Orit Gat; Nikita Gill; Emma Glass; Helen Goh; Will Harris; Alex Holder; Angela Hui; Sara Jafari; Bhanu Kapil; Lara Lee; Huw Lemmey; Momtaza Mehri; Mark Mukasa; Sri Owen; Riaz Phillips; Sarah Raphael; Leone Ross; Saba Sams; Varaidzo; Christian Weaver; Bryony White; Mandy Yin

L0253 Chapman & Vincent
Literary Agency
21 Ellis Street, London, SW1X 9AL
United Kingdom

chapmanvincent@hotmail.co.uk

Professional Body: The Association of Authors' Agents (AAA)

Types: Nonfiction
Subjects: Cookery; Gardening; History
Markets: Adult

Send: Query
Don't send: Full text
How to send: Email

Small agency handling illustrated nonfiction only. Not actively seeking clients but will consider queries by email. No attachments or postal submissions.

Authors: George Carter; Leslie Geddes-Brown; Lucinda Lambton; Eve Pollard

Literary Agents: Jennifer Chapman (*L0254*); Gilly Vincent (*L1405*)

L0254 Jennifer Chapman
Literary Agent
United Kingdom

Literary Agency: Chapman & Vincent (**L0253**)

L0255 Mic Cheetham
Literary Agent
United Kingdom

mic@miccheetham.com

Literary Agency: Mic Cheetham Literary Agency (**L0971**)

L0256 The Cheney Agency
Literary Agency
39 West 14th Street, Suite 403, New York, NY 10011
United States
Tel: +1 (212) 277-8007
Fax: +1 (212) 614-0728

submissions@cheneyagency.com

http://cheneyassoc.com

Types: Fiction; Nonfiction
Subjects: Autobiography; Business; Commercial; Contemporary; Culture; Current Affairs; Finance; History; Horror; Literary; Literature; Politics; Romance; Science; Sport; Suspense; Thrillers; Women's Interests
Markets: Adult

Send: Query
Don't send: Full text
How to send: Email

Send query with up to three chapters of sample material by post with SASE, or by email. Response not guaranteed.

Literary Agents: Elyse Cheney (*L0257*); Allison Devereux (*L0361*); Adam Eaglin (*L0401*); Alice Whitwham (*L1446*)

L0257 Elyse Cheney
Literary Agent
United States

Literary Agency: The Cheney Agency (**L0256**)

L0258 Anwar Chentoufi
Literary Agent
United Kingdom

Literary Agency: Independent Talent Group Ltd (**L0683**)

L0259 Cherry Weiner Literary Agency
Literary Agency
925 Oak Bluff Ct, Dacula, GA 30019-6660
United States
Tel: +1 (732) 446-2096
Fax: +1 (732) 792-0506

Cherry8486@aol.com

Types: Fiction; Nonfiction
Subjects: Adventure; Commercial; Crime;
Fantasy; History; Lifestyle; Mystery; Personal
Development; Romance; Science Fiction;
Suspense; Thrillers; Westerns
Markets: Adult

Closed to approaches.

Costs: Author covers sundry admin costs.

Only considers submissions by referral or
personal contact at writers' conferences.

Literary Agent: Cherry Weiner (*L1426*)

L0260 Jennifer De Chiara
Literary Agent
United States

Literary Agency: The Jennifer DeChiara
Literary Agency (**L0721**)

L0261 Jamie Weiss Chilton
Literary Agent
United States

Literary Agency: Andrea Brown Literary
Agency, Inc. (**L0047**)

L0262 Danielle Chiotti
Literary Agent
United States

Literary Agency: Upstart Crow Literary
(**L1394**)

L0263 Catherine Cho
Literary Agent
United Kingdom

http://madeleinemilburn.co.uk/team-member/
catherine-cho/

Literary Agency: Madeleine Milburn Literary,
TV & Film Agency (**L0907**)

Fiction > *Novels*
Family Saga; High Concept; Literary;
Magical Realism; Psychological Suspense;
Romance; Speculative; Thrillers; Upmarket

Nonfiction > *Nonfiction Books*

History; Lifestyle; Memoir; Narrative
Nonfiction; Psychology; Science; Social
Issues

L0264 Jennifer Christie
Literary Agent
United Kingdom

Literary Agency: Graham Maw Christie
Literary Agency (**L0567**)

L0265 Christine Green Authors' Agent
Literary Agency
PO Box 70098, London, SE15 5AU
United Kingdom

info@christinegreen.co.uk

http://www.christinegreen.co.uk
http://twitter.com/#!/whitehorsemews

Professional Body: The Association of
Authors' Agents (AAA)

Types: Fiction; Nonfiction
Subjects: Commercial; Literary
Markets: Adult; Young Adult

Send: Query
Don't send: Full text
How to send: Email

Focusses on fiction for adult and young adult,
and also considers narrative nonfiction. No
children's books, genre science-fiction/fantasy,
poetry or scripts. Send query by email
(preferred) or by post with SAE. No
submissions by fax or CD. See website for full
submission guidelines.

L0266 The Christopher Little Literary Agency
Literary Agency
48 Walham Grove, London, SW6 1QR
United Kingdom
Tel: +44 (0) 20 7736 4455
Fax: +44 (0) 20 7736 4490

submissions@christopherlittle.net

http://www.christopherlittle.net

Professional Body: The Association of
Authors' Agents (AAA)

Fiction > *Novels*
Commercial; Literary

Closed to approaches.

Closed to submissions as at March 2020.

Handles commercial and literary full-length
fiction and nonfiction. Film scripts handled for
existing clients only (no submissions of film
scripts). No poetry, short stories, illustrated
books or children's picture books.

Literary Agent: Christopher Little (*L0866*)

L0267 Adam Chromy
Literary Agent
United States

Literary Agency: Movable Type Management
(**L1002**)

L0268 Lynn Chu
Literary Agent
United States

L0269 The Chudney Agency
Literary Agency
72 North State Road, Suite 501, Briarcliff
Manor, NY 10510
United States
Tel: +1 (201) 758-8739
Fax: +1 (201) 758-8739

steven@thechudneyagency.com

http://www.thechudneyagency.com

ADULT > **Fiction** > *Novels*
General, and in particular: Comedy /
Humour; Gender; Historical Fiction;
LGBTQIA; Middle East; Mystery; Sexuality;
Thrillers; Women's Fiction

CHILDREN'S > **Fiction**
Chapter Books: General, and in
particular: Comedy / Humour; Coming of
Age; Contemporary; Culture; Gender;
Historical Fiction; Literary; Mystery;
Spirituality
Middle Grade: General, and in
particular: Comedy / Humour; Coming of
Age; Contemporary; Culture; Gender;
Historical Fiction; Literary; Mystery;
Spirituality
Picture Books: General

TEEN > **Fiction** > *Novels*
General, and in particular: Comedy /
Humour; Coming of Age; Contemporary;
Culture; Gender; Historical Fiction; Literary;
Mystery; Spirituality

Send: Query
How to send: Email
How not to send: Post

Specialises in children's and teen books, but
will also consider adult fiction. Send query
only in first instance. Happy to accept queries
by email. Submit material upon invitation only.
No fantasy, science fiction, early readers, or
scripts. See website for full guidelines.

Authors: Jessica Alexander; Mary Jane
Beaufrand; Tess Hilmo; Kristen Landon

Literary Agent: Steven Chudney (*L0270*)

L0270 Steven Chudney
Literary Agent
United States

Literary Agency: The Chudney Agency
(**L0269**)

L0271 Julia Churchill
Literary Agent
United Kingdom

https://amheath.com/agents/julia-churchill/
https://twitter.com/juliachurchill

Literary Agency: A.M. Heath & Company Limited, Author's Agents (**L0004**)

CHILDREN'S > **Fiction**
Novels; *Picture Books*
YOUNG ADULT > **Fiction** > *Novels*

L0272 Kayla Cichello
Literary Agent
United States

kayla.submission@gmail.com

http://www.upstartcrowliterary.com/agent/
kayla-cichello/
https://twitter.com/SeriousKayla

Literary Agency: Upstart Crow Literary (**L1394**)

CHILDREN'S > **Fiction**
Middle Grade: General
Picture Books: Comedy / Humour

YOUNG ADULT > **Fiction** > *Novels*
Commercial; Dark Humour; Literary;
Magical Realism; Mystery; Romance;
Romantic Comedy; Suspense

How to send: Email

Seeking everything from heartfelt or humorous picture books (she has a soft spot for animal protagonists) to dynamic, unpredictable YA (she loves a good murder mystery or a clever rom-com).

L0273 Andrea Cirillo
Literary Agent
United States

Literary Agency: Jane Rotrosen Agency (**L0709**)

L0274 Clare Hulton Literary Agency
Literary Agency
United Kingdom

info@clarehulton.co.uk

https://www.clarehulton.com

Professional Body: The Association of Authors' Agents (AAA)

Fiction > *Novels*

Nonfiction > *Nonfiction Books*
General, and in particular: Business;
Cookery; Health; History; Lifestyle;
Parenting; Philosophy; Pregnancy; Self Help

Send: Query
How to send: In the body of an email

Specialises in nonfiction, but also has a small commercial fiction list. Finds most authors through recommendation, but open to brief queries by email, explaining what your book is about. No attachments. If no response within two weeks, assume rejection.

Literary Agent: Clare Hulton

L0275 Anne Clark
Literary Agent
United Kingdom

Literary Agency: Anne Clark Literary Agency (**L0054**)

L0276 Ben Clark
Literary Agent
United Kingdom

Literary Agency: The Soho Agency (**L1297**)

L0277 William Clark
Literary Agent
United States

Literary Agency: Wm Clark Associates (**L1468**)
Professional Body: Association of Authors' Representatives, Inc. (AAR)

L0278 Lucy Cleland
Literary Agent
United States

Literary Agency: Kneerim & Williams (**L0796**)

L0279 Rachel Clements
Literary Agent
United Kingdom

rachel@abnerstein.co.uk

Literary Agency: Abner Stein (**L0007**)

L0280 Mary Clemmey
Literary Agent
United Kingdom

Literary Agency: Mary Clemmey Literary Agency (**L0933**)

L0281 Alexandra Cliff
Literary Agent
United Kingdom

Literary Agency: Peters Fraser + Dunlop (**L1091**)

L0282 Christina Clifford
Literary Agent
United States

Literary Agency: Union Literary (**L1388**)

L0283 Amy Cloughley
Literary Agent
United States

Literary Agency: Kimberley Cameron & Associates (**L0787**)

L0284 Jon Cobb
Associate Agent
United States

jon@hgliterary.com

https://www.hgliterary.com/jon
http://queryme.online/Cobb

Literary Agency: HG Literary (**L0646**)

ADULT > **Fiction** > *Novels*
African American; Fantasy; Literary;
Mystery; Science Fiction; Thrillers

CHILDREN'S > **Fiction** > *Middle Grade*: Contemporary

YOUNG ADULT > **Fiction** > *Novels*

How to send: Query Manager

L0285 Alexander Cochran
Literary Agent
United Kingdom

Literary Agency: C+W (Conville & Walsh) (**L0205**)

L0286 Susan Lee Cohen
Literary Agent
United States

Literary Agency: Riverside Literary Agency (**L1154**)
Professional Body: Association of Authors' Representatives, Inc. (AAR)

L0287 Gill Coleridge
Literary Agent
United Kingdom

Literary Agency: Rogers, Coleridge & White Ltd (**L1181**)

L0288 Ann Collette
Literary Agent
United States

Literary Agency: Rees Literary Agency (**L1133**)

L0289 Frances Collin
Literary Agent
United States

Literary Agency: Frances Collin Literary Agent (**L0491**)

L0290 Charlotte Colwill
Literary Agent
United Kingdom

charlotte@bravoblue.co.uk

Literary Agencies: The Bravo Blue Agency (**L0176**); Tibor Jones & Associates (**L1371**)

L0291 Cristina Concepcion
Literary Agent
United States

Literary Agency: Don Congdon Associates, Inc. (**L0378**)

L0292 Concord Theatricals
Literary Agency
235 Park Avenue South, Fifth Floor, New York, NY 10003
United States
Tel: +1 (866) 979-0447

info@concordtheatricals.com

https://www.concordtheatricals.com/

Scripts > *Theatre Scripts*

Closed to approaches.

Publishes plays and represents writers of plays. Deals in well-known plays from Broadway and London's West End.

L0293 Michael Congdon
Literary Agent
United States

Literary Agency: Don Congdon Associates, Inc. (**L0378**)

L0294 Clare Conville
Literary Agent
United Kingdom

Literary Agency: C+W (Conville & Walsh) (**L0205**)

L0295 Coombs Moylett & Maclean Literary Agency
Literary Agency
120 New Kings Road, London, SW6 4LZ
United Kingdom

info@cmm.agency

https://cmm.agency
https://www.instagram.com/cmmlitagency/
https://www.facebook.com/cmmlitagency/

ADULT
Fiction > *Novels*
Chick Lit; Commercial; Contemporary; Crime; Historical Fiction; Horror; Literary; Mystery; Suspense; Thrillers; Women's Fiction

Nonfiction > *Nonfiction Books*
General, and in particular: Biography; Crime; Current Affairs; Environment; Food; History; How To; Lifestyle; Narrative Nonfiction; Politics; Popular Science; Self Help

YOUNG ADULT > **Fiction** > *Novels*

Closed to approaches.

Send query with synopsis and first three chapters via online form. No submissions by email, fax or by post. No poetry, plays or scripts for film and TV. Whole books and postal submissions will not be read.

Editor / Literary Agent: Jamie Maclean (**L0903**)

Literary Agents: Zoe Apostolides (**L0059**); Elena Langtry (**L0827**); Lisa Moylett (**L1003**)

L0296 Brandie Coonis
Literary Agent
United States

Literary Agency: Rebecca Friedman Literary Agency (**L1128**)

L0297 Maggie Cooper
Literary Agent
Boston, MA
United States

https://aevitascreative.com/agents/

Literary Agency: Aevitas (**L0019**)

Fiction > *Novels*
Feminist Romance; Historical Fiction; LGBTQIA; Literary

Nonfiction > *Nonfiction Books*
Cookery; Food

Closed to approaches.

Represents imaginative, genre-bending literary fiction; capacious historical novels; beautifully told queer stories; and smart, feminist romance. Her other loves include unclassifiable book projects, food and cookbooks, and work by writers traditionally underrepresented in mainstream publishing.

L0298 Doe Coover
Literary Agent
United States

Literary Agency: The Doe Coover Agency (**L0373**)

L0299 Sam Copeland
Literary Agent
United Kingdom

Literary Agency: Rogers, Coleridge & White Ltd (**L1181**)

L0300 Gemma Copper
Literary Agent
United States

http://www.thebentagency.com/gemma-copper

Literary Agency: The Bent Agency (**L0119**)

Closed to approaches.

L0301 Cornerstone Literary Agency
Literary Agency
United States

info@cornerstoneliterary.com

http://www.cornerstoneliterary.com

Fiction > *Novels*

Commercial; Literary

Nonfiction > *Nonfiction Books*: Narrative Nonfiction

Send: Query; Author bio; Writing sample; Self-Addressed Stamped Envelope (SASE)
How to send: Post; Email

Send query by post or by email. No business, how-to, photography books, poetry, screenplays, self-help or Westerns.

Literary Agent: Helen Breitwieser (**L0177**)

L0302 Jamie Cowen
Literary Agent
United Kingdom

Literary Agency: The Ampersand Agency Ltd (**L0039**)

L0303 The Cowles Agency
Literary Agency
United States

katherine@cowlesagency.com

http://www.cowlesagency.com
https://twitter.com/cowlesagency
https://www.instagram.com/cowlesagency/

Nonfiction > *Nonfiction Books*
Business; Cookery; Design; Health; Memoir; Narrative Nonfiction; Photography

Authors: Bryant Austin; Catherine Bailey; Andy Baraghani; Nils Bernstein; Taylor Boetticher; Jon Bonne; Carrie Brown; Chris Burkhard; Courtney Burns; Gabriela Camara; Henry Carroll; Josef Centeno; Baylor Chapman; Andrew Chau; Bin Chen; Mark Cushing; Sohla El-Waylly; Renee Erickson; Susan Fisher; Camille Fourmont; Andrea Gentl; Monica Khemsurov; Eric Kim; George King; Jessica Koslow; Lauri Krantz; Jeff Krasno; Chris Kronner; Travis Lett; Peter Liem; Kermit Lynch; Rick Martinez; Ignacio Mattos; Margarita Matzke; Emeran Mayer; Amy Merrick; Toponia Miller; Serena Mitnik-Miller; Sam Mogannam; Carla Lalli Music; Ivan Orkin; Rafael Pelayo; Mason St. Peter; Robin Petravic; Charles Phan; Natasha Pickowicz; Paulson Fontaine Press; Elisabeth Prueitt; Christian Puglisi; Chad Robertson; Sharon Robinson; Besha Rodell; Julia Sherman; Sheldon Simeon; Jill Singer; Garrett Snyder; David Tanis; Erica Tanov; Andrew Tarlow; Thaddeus Vogler; Eric Werner; Kris Yenbamroong; Chris Ying; Maria Zizka

Literary Agent: Katherine Cowles (**L0304**)

L0304 Katherine Cowles
Literary Agent
United States

katherine@cowlesagency.com

Literary Agency: The Cowles Agency (**L0303**)
Professional Bodies: Association of Authors'

Representatives, Inc. (AAR); The Authors Guild

L0305 Peter Cox
Literary Agent
United Kingdom

Literary Agency: Redhammer (**L1131**)

L0306 Becca Crandall
Literary Agent
United States

becca@carolynjenksagency.com

https://www.carolynjenksagency.com/agent/BECCA-CRANDALL

Literary Agency: Carolyn Jenks Agency (**L0228**)

ADULT
  Fiction
    Graphic Novels; *Novels*
  Nonfiction > *Nonfiction Books*

CHILDREN'S > **Fiction**
  Middle Grade; *Picture Books*
YOUNG ADULT > **Fiction** > *Novels*

Send: Query; Writing sample
How to send: In the body of an email

L0307 Creative Authors Ltd
Literary Agency
United Kingdom

write@creativeauthors.co.uk

https://www.creativeauthors.co.uk

Types: Fiction; Nonfiction
Subjects: Arts; Autobiography; Business; Comedy / Humour; Commercial; Cookery; Crafts; Crime; Culture; Health; History; Literary; Nature; Women's Interests
Markets: Adult; Children's

How to send: Email

As at April 2019, not accepting new fiction clients. See website for current situation. We are a dynamic literary agency – established to provide an attentive and unique platform for writers and scriptwriters and representing a growing list of clients. We're on the lookout for fresh talent and books with strong commercial potential. No unsolicited MSS, but considers queries by email. No paper submissions. Do not telephone regarding submissions.

Literary Agent: Isabel Atherton (*L0069*)

L0308 Creative Media Agency
Literary Agency
United States

paige@cmalit.com

http://cmalit.com

Types: Fiction; Nonfiction
Subjects: Business; Commercial; Contemporary; History; Lifestyle; Mystery; Psychology; Religion; Romance; Thrillers; Women's Interests
Markets: Adult

Send: Query
Don't send: Full text
How to send: Email

Handles fiction and nonfiction, but no children's, science fiction, or fantasy, and no academic nonfiction. Send query by email only. No submissions by post. See website for full submission guidelines.

Literary Agent: Paige Wheeler (*L1436*)

L0309 The Creative Rights Agency
Literary Agency
United Kingdom
Tel: +44 (0) 20 3371 7673

info@creativerightsagency.co.uk

http://www.creativerightsagency.co.uk

Fiction > *Novels*

Nonfiction > *Nonfiction Books*

Publishing, Licensing, Film/TV. Based in London.

Literary Agent: Richard Scrivener

L0310 Creative Trust, Inc.
Literary Agency
210 Jamestown Park Drive, Suite 200, Brentwood, TN 37027
United States
Tel: +1 (615) 297-5010
Fax: +1 (615) 297-5020

info@creativetrust.com

http://www.creativetrust.com
https://twitter.com/Creative_Trust
https://www.facebook.com/creativetrust/
https://www.linkedin.com/company/creative-trust-media

Fiction > *Novels*

Nonfiction > *Nonfiction Books*

Scripts > *Film Scripts*

Send: Query
Don't send: Full text
How to send: Email

Literary division founded in 2001 to handle authors with particular potential in cross-media development, including movie scripts, graphic novels, etc. Accepts queries by email from previously published authors only. No attachments.

L0311 Claudia Cross
Literary Agent; Partner
United States

https://www.foliolit.com/agents-1/claudia-cross

http://aaronline.org/Sys/PublicProfile/2176647/417813

Literary Agency: Folio Literary Management, LLC (**L0480**)
Professional Body: Association of Authors' Representatives, Inc. (AAR)

Closed to approaches.

L0312 Annette Crossland
Literary Agent
United Kingdom

Literary Agency: A for Authors (**L0003**)

L0313 Sara Crowe
Literary Agent
United States

Literary Agency: Pippin Properties, Inc (**L1101**)

L0314 Sheila Crowley
Literary Agent
United Kingdom

http://submissions.curtisbrown.co.uk/agents/

Literary Agency: Curtis Brown (**L0318**)

Fiction > *Novels*
  Contemporary; Historical Fiction; Psychological Suspense Thrillers

Nonfiction > *Nonfiction Books*
  How To; Inspirational; Memoir; Personal Development

How to send: Online submission system

"My list is primarily quality fiction, psychological suspense thrillers and books in the personal development and mindfulness area. Narrative memoir, especially Irish ones, are also on my wish list."

L0315 Mary Cummings
Literary Agent
United States

Literary Agency: Betsy Amster Literary Enterprises (**L0125**)

L0316 Michael Curry
Literary Agent
United States

Literary Agency: Donald Maass Literary Agency (**L0380**)

L0317 Taylor Curtin
Literary Agent
United States

Literary Agency: Union Literary (**L1388**)

L0318 Curtis Brown
Literary Agency
Haymarket House, 28/29 Haymarket, London, SW1Y 4SP

United Kingdom
Tel: +44 (0) 20 7393 4400

info@curtisbrown.co.uk

http://www.curtisbrowncreative.co.uk

Professional Body: The Association of Authors' Agents (AAA)

Types: Fiction; Nonfiction; Scripts
Formats: Film Scripts; Radio Scripts; TV Scripts; Theatre Scripts
Subjects: Biography; Commercial; Crime; Fantasy; History; Literary; Science; Suspense; Thrillers
Markets: Adult; Children's; Young Adult

Send: Query
Don't send: Full text

Costs: Offers services that writers have to pay for.

Renowned and long established London agency. Handles general fiction and nonfiction, and scripts. Also represents directors, designers, and presenters. No longer accepts submissions by post or email – all submissions must be made using online submissions manager. Also offers services such as writing courses for which authors are charged.

Associate Agent: Viola Hayden (**L0626**)

Literary Agents: Felicity Blunt (**L0146**); Sheila Crowley (**L0314**); Jonny Geller (**L0536**); Jonathan Lloyd (*L0870*); Alice Lutyens (*L0888*); Lucy Morris (*L0999*); Cathryn Summerhayes (*L1335*); Gordon Wise (*L1462*)

L0319 Curtis Brown (Australia) Pty Ltd

Literary Agency
PO Box 19, Paddington, NSW, 2021
Australia

submission@curtisbrown.com.au

http://www.curtisbrown.com.au

Professional Body: Australian Literary Agents' Association (ALAA)

Fiction > *Novels*

Nonfiction > *Nonfiction Books*

How to send: Email

Accepts submission from within Australia and New Zealand only, during February, June, and October. No fantasy, sci-fi, stage/screenplays, poetry, self-help books, children's picture books, early reader books, young adult books, comic books, short stories, cookbooks, educational, corporate books or translations. Send query by email with synopsis up to two pages and first three chapters. See website for full guidelines.

Literary Agents: Clare Forster (*L0484*); Grace Heifetz (*L0633*); Fiona Inglis (*L0684*); Pippa Masson (*L0936*); Tara Wynne (*L1479*)

L0320 Richard Curtis

Literary Agent
United States

Literary Agency: Richard Curtis Associates, Inc. (**L1145**)

L0321 Jon Curzon

Literary Agent
United Kingdom

Literary Agency: Artellus Limited (**L0067**)

L0322 John Cusick

Literary Agent; Vice President
United States

https://www.publishersmarketplace.com/members/JohnC/
https://twitter.com/johnmcusick

Literary Agencies: Folio Literary Management, LLC (**L0480**); Folio Jr. (**L0479**)

ADULT > **Fiction** > *Novels*
Fantasy; Horror; Science Fiction; Suspense; Thrillers

CHILDREN'S > **Fiction** > *Middle Grade*
Comedy / Humour; Contemporary; Fantasy; Science Fiction; Speculative

YOUNG ADULT > **Fiction** > *Novels*
Comedy / Humour; Contemporary; Fantasy; Science Fiction; Speculative

Send: Query; Writing sample
How to send: Email

Authors: Courtney Alameda; Kayla Cagan; Josephine Cameron; Anna Carey; Marina Cohen; Paula Garner; Joan He; Christian McKay Heidicker; Sailor J; Jeramey Kraatz; Kristen Lippert-Martin; Julie Murphy; Abdi Nazemian; Jordan Reeves; Laura Sebastian; Quinn Sosna-Spear; Sharon Biggs Waller; Don Zolidis

L0323 Cyle Young Literary Elite

Literary Agency
United States

submissions@cyleyoung.com

https://cyleyoung.com
https://www.facebook.com/cyle61?fref=ts
https://twitter.com/cyleyoung

Associate Agents: Hope Bolinger (*L0148*); Caroline George (*L0538*); Alyssa Roat (*L1156*)

Author / Junior Agent: Del Duduit (**L0391**)

Author / Literary Agent: Cyle Young (**L1482**)

Junior Agents: Megan Burkhart (**L0199**); Jori Hanna (*L0604*); Chrysa Keenon (**L0774**); Kenzi Nevins (**L1030**)

Literary Agent: Tessa Emily Hall (*L0597*)

L0324 Cynthia Cannell Literary Agency

Literary Agency
54 West 40th Street, New York, NY 10018
United States
Tel: +1 (212) 396-9595

info@cannellagency.com

http://cannellagency.com

Professional Body: Association of Authors' Representatives, Inc. (AAR)

Types: Fiction; Nonfiction
Subjects: Autobiography; Contemporary; Current Affairs; Health; Literary; Personal Development; Religion
Markets: Adult

Send: Query
Don't send: Full text
How to send: Email

Full-service literary agency based in New York. Represents fiction, memoir, biography, self-improvement, spirituality, and nonfiction on contemporary issues. No screenplays, children's books, illustrated books, cookbooks, romance, category mystery, or science fiction. Send query by email only, including brief description of the project, relevant biographical information, and any publishing credits. No attachments or submissions by post. Response not guaranteed.

Literary Agent: Cynthia Cannell (*L0213*)

L0325 D4EO Literary Agency

Literary Agency
7 Indian Valley Road, Weston, CT 06883
United States
Tel: +1 (203) 544-7180
Fax: +1 (203) 544-7160

bob@d4eo.com

http://www.d4eoliteraryagency.com

Types: Fiction; Nonfiction
Formats: Reference
Subjects: Adventure; Architecture; Arts; Biography; Business; Comedy / Humour; Commercial; Contemporary; Cookery; Crime; Current Affairs; Design; Erotic; Fantasy; Finance; Health; History; Horror; How To; Lifestyle; Literary; Mystery; Personal Development; Psychology; Romance; Science; Science Fiction; Spirituality; Sport; Technology; Thrillers; Warfare; Westerns; Women's Interests
Markets: Adult; Children's; Young Adult

Send: Query
Don't send: Full text
How to send: Email

Costs: Author covers sundry admin costs.

See website for individual agent preferences and submission guidelines, then submit directly to one agent only.

Literary Agents: Jessie Devine (*L0362*); Bob Diforio (*L0367*); Julie Dinneen (*L0371*); Joyce Holland (*L0660*); Kelly Van Sant (*L1219*); Pam Victorio (*L1403*)

L0326 Laura Dail

Literary Agent; President
United States

http://www.ldlainc.com/about
http://twitter.com/lcdail
http://aaronline.org/Sys/PublicProfile/2176649/417813

Literary Agency: Laura Dail Literary Agency (**L0831**)
Professional Body: Association of Authors' Representatives, Inc. (AAR)

Closed to approaches.

L0327 Judy Daish

Literary Agent
United Kingdom

Literary Agency: Judy Daish Associates Ltd (**L0746**)

L0328 Dana Newman Literary, LLC

Literary Agency
1800 Avenue of the Stars, 12th Floor, Los Angeles, CA 90067
United States

dananewmanliterary@gmail.com

https://www.dananewman.com

Types: Fiction; Nonfiction
Subjects: Autobiography; Business; Culture; Current Affairs; Health; History; Lifestyle; Literary; Psychology; Society; Sport; Technology; Women's Interests
Markets: Adult

Send: Query
Don't send: Full text
How to send: Email

Send query by email only. Include "QUERY" in the subject line, and a one-page query letter, which identifies the category of your work, the title, the word count, and provides a brief overview of your project, credentials and previous publishing history, if any. Complete book proposals on request only.

Literary Agent: Dana Newman (*L1031*)

L0329 Melissa Danaczko

Literary Agent
United States

Literary Agency: Stuart Krichevsky Literary Agency, Inc.

Closed to approaches.

L0330 Jon Michael Darga

Literary Agent
New York
United States

https://aevitascreative.com/agents/

Literary Agency: Aevitas (**L0019**)

ADULT
  Fiction > *Novels*
    Fantasy; Literary; Science Fiction

  Nonfiction > *Nonfiction Books*
    History; Memoir; Narrative Nonfiction; Popular Culture

YOUNG ADULT > **Fiction** > *Novels*

Send: Author bio; Outline; Pitch; Market info; Writing sample
How to send: Online submission system

Represents both nonfiction and fiction. He is most interested in voice-driven pop culture writing and histories that re-cast the narrative by emphasizing unexpected or unheard voices.

L0331 Darhansoff & Verrill Literary Agents

Literary Agency
133 West 72nd Street, Room 304, New York, NY 10023
United States
Tel: +1 (917) 305-1300
Fax: +1 (917) 305-1400

submissions@dvagency.com

http://www.dvagency.com

Types: Fiction; Nonfiction
Subjects: Autobiography; Literary; Mystery; Suspense
Markets: Adult; Children's; Young Adult

Send: Query
Don't send: Full text
How to send: Email

Particularly interested in literary fiction, narrative nonfiction, memoir, sophisticated suspense, and fiction and nonfiction for younger readers. No theatrical plays or film scripts. Send queries by email. See website for full submission guidelines.

Literary Agents: Liz Darhansoff (*L0332*); Charles Verrill (*L1401*)

L0332 Liz Darhansoff

Literary Agent
United States

Literary Agency: Darhansoff & Verrill Literary Agents (**L0331**)

L0333 The Darley Anderson Agency

Literary Agency
Estelle House, 11 Eustace Road, London, SW6 1JB

United Kingdom
Tel: +44 (0) 20 7386 2674

camilla@darleyanderson.com

http://www.darleyanderson.com

Professional Body: The Association of Authors' Agents (AAA)

Types: Fiction
Subjects: Comedy / Humour; Commercial; Crime; Fantasy; History; Horror; Literary; Mystery; Romance; Suspense; Thrillers; Women's Interests
Markets: Adult; Children's; Young Adult

Send: Query
Don't send: Full text
How to send: Email

Accepts submissions by email and by post. See website for individual agent requirements, submission guidelines, and contact details. No poetry, short stories, screenplays, radio plays, or theatre scripts.

Assistant Agent: Chloe Davis (**L0343**)

Authors: Mandy Baggot; Tom Bale; Rosie Blake; Tara Bond; Constance Briscoe; James Carol; Paul Carson; Chris Carter; Lee Child; Martina Cole; John Connolly; Gloria Cook; Sophie Cousens; A J Cross; Jason Dean; Margaret Dickinson; Clare Dowling; Patrick Dunne; Kerry Fisher; Jack Ford; Tana French; Helen Grant; G.R. Halliday; Egan Hughes; Tara Hyland; Sandie Jones; Emma Kavanagh; Patrick Lennon; T M Logan; Imran Mahmood; Cesca Major; Rani Manicka; Gillian McAllister; Phoebe Morgan; Annie Murray; Lauren North; Abi Oliver; B.A. Paris; Phaedra Patrick; Jo Platt; Hazel Prior; David Rhodes; Jacqui Rose; Rob Sinclair; KL Slater; Sean Slater; Catherine Steadman; Erik Storey; G X Todd; Samantha Tonge; Elizabeth Waite; Tim Weaver; David Wishart

Literary Agents: Darley Anderson (**L0043**); Camilla Bolton (*L0149*); Lydia Silver (*L1279*); Tanera Simons (*L1281*); Clare Wallace (**L1414**)

L0334 Darley Anderson Children's

Literary Agency
Suite LG4, New Kings House, 136-144 New Kings Road, London, SW6 4LZ
United Kingdom
Tel: +44 (0) 20 7386 2674

childrens@darleyanderson.com

http://www.darleyandersonchildrens.com
http://twitter.com/DA_Childrens

Professional Body: The Association of Authors' Agents (AAA)

CHILDREN'S > **Fiction**
  Middle Grade; Picture Books
YOUNG ADULT > **Fiction** > *Novels*

Send: Query; Synopsis; Writing sample
How to send: Email
How not to send: Post

Always on the look out for exciting, inspiring and original novels for both Young Adult and Middle-Grade readers. Send query by email with synopsis and first three consecutive chapters or a maximum of 5,000 words.

L0335 Arielle Datz

Literary Agent
United States

Literary Agency: Dunow, Carlson & Lerner Agency (**L0395**)

L0336 David Black Literary Agency

Literary Agency
335 Adams Street, Suite 2707, Brooklyn, NY 11201
United States
Tel: +1 (718) 852-5500
Fax: +1 (718) 852-5539

dblack@dblackagency.com

http://www.davidblackagency.com

Professional Body: Association of Authors' Representatives, Inc. (AAR)

Types: Fiction; Nonfiction
Subjects: Arts; Autobiography; Business; Comedy / Humour; Commercial; Cookery; Crafts; Culture; Current Affairs; Entertainment; Finance; Health; History; How To; Lifestyle; Literary; Music; Nature; Philosophy; Politics; Psychology; Science; Society; Sport; Thrillers; Travel; Women's Interests
Markets: Adult; Children's; Young Adult

Send: Query
Don't send: Full text
How to send: Email

Costs: Author covers sundry admin costs.

See website for details of different agents, and specific interests and submission guidelines of each. Otherwise, query the agency generally by post only and allow 8 weeks for a response. See website for full details.

Literary Agents: Rica Allannic (*L0031*); David Black (*L0137*); Jenny Herrera (*L0642*); Deborah Hofmann (*L0657*); Gary Morris (*L0998*); Susan Raihofer (*L1125*); Sarah Smith (*L1294*); Joy Tutela (*L1382*)

L0337 David Godwin Associates

Literary Agency
2nd Floor, 40 Rosebery Avenue, Clerkenwell, London, EC1R 4RX
United Kingdom
Tel: +44 (0) 20 7240 9992

sebastiangodwin@davidgodwinassociates.co.uk

http://www.davidgodwinassociates.com

Types: Fiction; Nonfiction
Subjects: Literary
Markets: Adult

Send: Query
Don't send: Full text
How to send: Email

Handles a range of nonfiction and fiction. Send query by email with synopsis and first 30 pages. No poetry. No picture books, except for existing clients.

Literary Agent: David Godwin (*L0558*)

L0338 David Higham Associates Ltd

Literary Agency
6th Floor, Waverley House, 7-12 Noel Street, London, W1F 8GQ
United Kingdom
Tel: +44 (0) 20 7434 5900
Fax: +44 (0) 20 7437 1072

dha@davidhigham.co.uk
submissions@davidhigham.co.uk
childrenssubmissions@davidhigham.co.uk

http://www.davidhigham.co.uk

Professional Body: The Association of Authors' Agents (AAA)

Agency Assistant: Sara Langham

Authors: Rachel Abbott; J. R. Ackerley; Richard Adams; Katie Agnew; Naomi Alderman; Tracy Alexander; Geraint Anderson; Michael Arditti

Company Director / Literary Agent: Veronique Baxter (**L0103**)

Literary Agents: Olivia Barber; Nicola Chang (**L0252**); Elise Dillsworth (**L0369**); David Evans; Jemima Forrester (**L0483**); Georgia Glover; Anthony Goff; Andrew Gordon; Lizzy Kremer; Harriet Moore; Caroline Walsh; Laura West; Alice Williams; Jessica Woollard

L0339 David Luxton Associates

Literary Agency
United Kingdom

https://www.davidluxtonassociates.co.uk
https://twitter.com/DLuxAssociates
www.instagram.com/davidluxtonassociates/

Professional Body: The Association of Authors' Agents (AAA)

Nonfiction > *Nonfiction Books*
General, and in particular: Sport

Send: Query; Synopsis; Writing sample; Author bio
How to send: Email
How not to send: Post

Specialises in nonfiction, including sports, memoir, history, popular reference and politics. No scripts or screenplays. Most clients by recommendation, but will consider email queries. See website for correct email addresses for different subjects. No submissions by post.

Literary Agents: David Luxton (**L0890**); Nick Walters (**L1416**); Rebecca Winfield (**L1461**)

L0340 Tessa David

Literary Agent
United Kingdom

Literary Agency: Peters Fraser + Dunlop (**L1091**)

L0341 Caroline Davidson

Literary Agent
United Kingdom

Literary Agency: Caroline Davidson Literary Agency (**L0226**)

L0342 Sarah Davies

Literary Agent
United States

https://www.greenhouseliterary.com/the-team/sarah-davies
http://aaronline.org/Sys/PublicProfile/2715608/417813
https://querymanager.com/query/SarahDavies

Literary Agency: The Greenhouse Literary Agency (**L0579**)
Professional Body: Association of Authors' Representatives, Inc. (AAR)

ADULT > **Fiction** > *Novels*
Suspense; Women's Fiction

CHILDREN'S
Fiction
Graphic Novels: General
Middle Grade: Adventure; Magic; Magical Realism
Nonfiction > *Nonfiction Books*

YOUNG ADULT > **Fiction** > *Novels*
Contemporary Romance; Fantasy; France; Historical Fiction; Magical Realism; Middle East; Mystery; Romantic Comedy; Science; Thrillers; World War I; World War II

Does not want:

YOUNG ADULT > **Fiction** > *Novels*
American Civil War; American Revolution

Send: Query; Author bio; Writing sample; Market info
How to send: Query Manager

Seeking Fiction from Middle Grade through Young Adult and across all genres (note: she is currently closed to debut Picturebooks but does rep PBs by clients whom she's initially taken on for older fiction). She loves strong, hooky, layered plots, writing that is gorgeous but also conceptually strong, and stories that are really moving but make you think too. She is particularly seeking authors from under-represented backgrounds and stories with diverse settings and perspectives. She is also open, by referral, to women's fiction — especially in the suspense genre.

L0343 Chloe Davis
Assistant Agent
United Kingdom

http://www.darleyanderson.com/our-team

Literary Agent: Clare Wallace (**L1414**)
Literary Agency: The Darley Anderson Agency (**L0333**)

CHILDREN'S > Fiction > *Middle Grade*: Adventure

YOUNG ADULT > Fiction > *Novels*: Contemporary Romance

Particularly enjoys reading submissions, especially middle grade adventures and contemporary YA love stories.

L0344 Meg Davis
Literary Agent
United Kingdom

meg@ki-agency.co.uk

https://ki-agency.co.uk/contact

Literary Agency: Ki Agency Ltd (**L0782**)

Fiction > *Novels*

Scripts
  Film Scripts; *TV Scripts*; *Theatre Scripts*

Happy to consider scripts in all genres, and books in some genres, especially genre fiction. Not a good bet for fiction that might be considered to be wearing a cardigan, or which is narrated by an animal.

L0345 Naomi Davis
Literary Agent
United States

Literary Agency: BookEnds, LLC (**L0155**)

L0346 Caroline Dawnay
Literary Agent
United Kingdom
Tel: +44 (0) 20 3214 0931

kaitken@unitedagents.co.uk

https://www.unitedagents.co.uk/cdawnayunitedagentscouk

Literary Agency: United Agents (**L1389**)

Fiction > *Novels*: Literary

Nonfiction > *Nonfiction Books*

Send: Query; Author bio; Writing sample
How to send: Email

Interested in serious nonfiction and literary fiction. For submissions please email a short cover letter, biographical note and the first 10,000 words of your text.

Authors: Rennie Airth; Laura Beatty; Stephen Bernard; Alain de Botton; Susie Boyt; Christopher Brookmyre; James Buchan; Eleanor Catton; Charles Chadwick; Catherine Chidgey; Rupert Christiansen; Charles Clover; Peter Conrad; Jill Dawson; Guy Deutscher; Minoo Dinshaw; Gaston Dorren; Philip Eade; James Le Fanu; Tim Finch; Tom Fort; Richard Francis; John Fuller; James Grant; Thomas Grant; Tessa Hadley; James Hall; Christopher de Hamel; Lynsey Hanley; Alexandra Harris; Jane Hasell-McCosh; David Hendy; Richard Holloway; Sheena Joughin; Adam Forrest Kay; Martin Kemp; Nick Lane; Richard Layard; Hermione Lee; Margaret MacMillan; Jan Morris; Chris Mullin; James Mylet; Jeremy Mynott; Virginia Nicholson; Constantine Phipps; Edward Platt; Jennifer Potter; Matthew Rice; Jane Ridley; Posy Simmonds; Helen Smith; Dan Snow; Donald Sturrock; Sasha Swire; Stephen Taylor; Tony Thompson; Francesca Wade; Nadia Wassef; Philip Ziegler; Sofka Zinovieff

L0347 Liza Dawson
Literary Agent
United States

Literary Agency: Liza Dawson Associates (**L0868**)

L0348 Deborah Owen Ltd
Literary Agency
78 Narrow Street, Limehouse, London, E14 8BP
United Kingdom
Tel: +44 (0) 20 7987 5119 / 5441

Types: Fiction; Nonfiction

Closed to approaches.

Represents only two authors worldwide. Not accepting any new authors.

Authors: David Owen; Delia Smith

Literary Agent: Deborah Owen (*L1063*)

L0349 Stacia Decker
Literary Agent
United States

Literary Agency: Dunow, Carlson & Lerner Agency (**L0395**)

Closed to approaches.

L0350 Allison DeFrees
Literary Agent
United Kingdom

Literary Agency: C+W (Conville & Walsh) (**L0205**)

L0351 Hilary Delamere
Literary Agent
United Kingdom

Literary Agency: The Agency (London) Ltd (**L0021**)

L0352 Joelle Delbourgo
Literary Agent
United States

Literary Agency: Joelle Delbourgo Associates, Inc. (**L0729**)
Professional Body: Association of Authors' Representatives, Inc. (AAR)

L0353 The Dench Arnold Agency
Literary Agency
10 Newburgh Street, London, W1F 7RN
United Kingdom
Tel: +44 (0) 20 7437 4551

fiona@dencharnold.com

http://www.dencharnold.co.uk

Types: Scripts
Formats: Film Scripts; TV Scripts
Markets: Adult

Send: Query
Don't send: Full text
How to send: Email

Send query with CV and synopsis by email only. Represents writers, directors and heads of department (directors of photography, production designers, costume designers, editors and make-up designers).

Authors: Joe Ainsworth; Maurice Bessman; Giles Borg; William Borthwick; Peter Briggs; Karen Brown; Peter Chelsom; Rob Churchill; David Conolly; Hannah Davies; Jim Davies; Eric Deacon; Adrian Dunbar; Chris Fallon; Susanne Farrell; Matthew Faulk; Lucy Flannery; Ellis Freeman; Liam Gavin; Nicholas Gibbs; Steve Gough; Robert Hammond; James Handel; Michael Harvey; Jo Ho; David Lg Hughes; Julian Kemp; Malcolm Kohll; Anna Kythreotis; Sarah Lambert; Dominic Macdonald; Steve Mcateer; Alan Mcdonald; Kevin Molony; Courttia Newland; Matthew Newman; Omid Nooshin; Paul Parkes; Junior Rhone; Dave Simpson; Mark Skeet; Mark Stay; Francesca Tatini; Stewart Thomson; Alan Whiting; Terry Winsor; Kate Wood

Literary Agents: Michelle Arnold (*L0066*); Elizabeth Dench (*L0354*); Matthew Dench (*L0355*)

L0354 Elizabeth Dench
Literary Agent
United Kingdom

Literary Agency: The Dench Arnold Agency (**L0353**)

L0355 **Matthew Dench**
Literary Agent
United Kingdom

Literary Agency: The Dench Arnold Agency
(**L0353**)

L0356 **Caspian Dennis**
Literary Agent
United Kingdom

caspian@abnerstein.co.uk

Literary Agency: Abner Stein (**L0007**)

L0357 **Liz Dennis**
Literary Agent
United Kingdom

http://www.johnsonandalcock.co.uk/liz-dennis

Literary Agency: Johnson & Alcock (**L0732**)

CHILDREN'S > **Fiction** > *Middle Grade*

YOUNG ADULT > **Fiction** > *Novels*

Closed to approaches.

L0358 **Derrick & Briggs, LLP**
Literary Agency
BancFirst Tower, Suite 2700, 100 North
Broadway Avenue, Oklahoma City, OK 73102
United States
Tel: +1 (405) 235-1900
Fax: +1 (405) 235-1995

briggs@derrickandbriggs.com

http://derrickandbriggs.com

Types: Fiction; Nonfiction
Subjects: Autobiography; Commercial;
Contemporary; Health; Medicine; Nature;
Personal Development
Markets: Adult; Children's; Young Adult

Combines her primary work as a literary agent
with expertise in intellectual property,
entertainment law and estates and probate. Her
clients are published authors (exclusively),
theatres, and a variety of small businesses and
individuals.

Literary Agent: M. Courtney Briggs (*L0179*)

L0359 **Dado Derviskadic**
Literary Agent
United States
Tel: +1 (212) 400-1494

dado@foliolit.com

http://foliolit.com/dado-derviskadic

Literary Agency: Folio Literary Management,
LLC (**L0480**)

Fiction > *Novels*

Nonfiction > *Nonfiction Books*
Biography; Cookery; Cultural History; Food;
Health; Language; Memoir; Motivational
Self-Help; Nutrition; Popular Culture;
Popular Science

Send: Query; Writing sample; Proposal
How to send: In the body of an email

L0360 **Francesca Devas**
Literary Agent
United Kingdom

Literary Agency: Independent Talent Group
Ltd (**L0683**)

L0361 **Allison Devereux**
Literary Agent
United States

Literary Agency: The Cheney Agency (**L0256**)

L0362 **Jessie Devine**
Literary Agent
United States

Literary Agency: D4EO Literary Agency
(**L0325**)

L0363 **Cori Deyoe**
Literary Agent
United States

cori@threeseaslit.com

https://www.threeseasagency.com/cori-deyoe
https://querymanager.com/query/Cori3Seas

Literary Agency: 3 Seas Literary Agency
(**L0001**)

ADULT > **Fiction** > *Novels*
Mystery; Romance; Thrillers; Women's
Fiction

CHILDREN'S > **Fiction**
Middle Grade; *Picture Books*
YOUNG ADULT > **Fiction** > *Novels*

Send: Query; Synopsis; Writing sample; Pitch;
Market info
How to send: Query Manager

Actively looking to expand her list of clients.
She represents all sub-genres of romance,
women's fiction, young adult, middle grade,
picture books, thrillers, mysteries and select
non-fiction.

L0364 **DHH Literary Agency**
Ltd
Literary Agency
23-27 Cecil Court, London, WC2N 4EZ
United Kingdom
Tel: +44 (0) 20 7836 7376

enquiries@dhhliteraryagency.com

http://www.dhhliteraryagency.com

Professional Body: The Association of
Authors' Agents (AAA)

Types: Fiction; Nonfiction; Scripts
Formats: Film Scripts; TV Scripts; Theatre
Scripts
Subjects: Adventure; Archaeology;
Autobiography; Crime; Fantasy; History;

Literary; Science Fiction; Thrillers; Women's
Interests
Markets: Adult; Children's; Young Adult

Send: Query
Don't send: Full text

Accepts submissions by email only. No postal
submissions. See website for specific agent
interests and email addresses and approach one
agent only. Do not send submissions to generic
"enquiries" email address.

Associate Agent: Emily Glenister (**L0553**)

Literary Agent / Managing Director: David H.
Headley (**L0628**)

Literary Agents: Broo Doherty (*L0374*);
Natalie Galustian (*L0524*); Harry Illingworth
(*L0682*); Hannah Sheppard (*L1267*)

L0365 **Diamond Kahn and**
Woods (DKW) Literary Agency
Ltd
Literary Agency
United Kingdom
Tel: +44 (0) 20 3514 6544

info@dkwlitagency.co.uk

http://dkwlitagency.co.uk

Professional Body: The Association of
Authors' Agents (AAA)

Types: Fiction; Nonfiction
Subjects: Adventure; Archaeology; Biography;
Comedy / Humour; Commercial;
Contemporary; Crime; Culture; Fantasy;
Gothic; History; Literary; Politics; Science
Fiction; Society; Suspense; Thrillers
Markets: Adult; Children's; Young Adult

Closed to approaches.

Closed to submissions as at September 2019.
Check website for current status.

Send submissions by email. See website for
specific agent interests and contact details. Do
not send submissions to general agency email
address.

Literary Agents: Ella Diamond Kahn (**L0751**);
Bryony Woods (**L1471**)

L0366 **Diana Finch Literary**
Agency
Literary Agency
116 West 23rd Street, Suite 500, New York,
NY 10011
United States
Tel: +1 (917) 544-4470

diana.finch@verizon.net

http://dianafinchliteraryagency.blogspot.com

Professional Body: Association of Authors'
Representatives, Inc. (AAR)

Types: Fiction; Nonfiction
Subjects: Autobiography; Business; Fantasy;
History; Literary; Nature; Politics; Science;

Science Fiction
Markets: Adult; Children's; Young Adult

Send: Query
Don't send: Full text

Costs: Author covers sundry admin costs.

Approach using online submission system – see website for link. No romance, but will consider other genres, especially science fiction and fantasy.

Literary Agent: Diana Finch (*L0468*)

L0367 Bob Diforio
Literary Agent
United States

Literary Agency: D4EO Literary Agency (**L0325**)

L0368 Sandra Dijkstra
Literary Agent
United States

Literary Agency: Sandra Dijkstra Literary Agency (**L1218**)

L0369 Elise Dillsworth
Literary Agent
United Kingdom

elise@elisedillsworthagency.com

https://www.davidhigham.co.uk/agents-dh/elise-dillsworth/

Literary Agencies: Elise Dillsworth Agency (EDA) (**L0422**); David Higham Associates Ltd (**L0338**)

Fiction > *Novels*
  Commercial; International; Literary

Nonfiction > *Nonfiction Books*
  Commercial; International; Literary

Represents literary and commercial fiction and nonfiction, with a keen aim to reflect writing that is international.

L0370 Dinah Wiener Ltd
Literary Agency
12 Cornwall Grove, Chiswick, London, W4 2LB
United Kingdom
Tel: +44 (0) 20 8994 6011

dinah@dwla.co.uk

Professional Body: The Association of Authors' Agents (AAA)

Types: Fiction; Nonfiction
Subjects: Autobiography; Cookery; Science
Markets: Adult

Closed to approaches.

Not taking on new clients as at October 2018. Send preliminary query letter with SAE. No poetry, short stories, scripts, or children's books.

Authors: Valerie-Anne Baglietto; Malcolm Billings; Guy Burt; David Deutsch; Wendy K. Harris; Jenny Hobbs; Mark Jeffery; Michael Lockwood; Daniel Snowman; Rachel Trethewey; Marcia Willett

Literary Agent: Dinah Wiener (*L1447*)

L0371 Julie Dinneen
Literary Agent
United States

Literary Agency: D4EO Literary Agency (**L0325**)

L0372 Isobel Dixon
Literary Agent
United Kingdom

Literary Agency: Blake Friedmann Literary Agency Ltd (**L0139**)

L0373 The Doe Coover Agency
Literary Agency
PO Box 668, Winchester, MA 01890
United States
Tel: +1 (781) 721-6000
Fax: +1 (781) 721-6727

info@doecooveragency.com

http://doecooveragency.com

Types: Fiction; Nonfiction
Formats: Reference
Subjects: Autobiography; Business; Comedy / Humour; Commercial; Cookery; Current Affairs; Finance; Gardening; Health; History; Literary; Music; Politics; Psychology; Science; Society; Sport; Technology
Markets: Adult

Handles nonfiction, popular reference, literary fiction and narrative nonfiction.

Literary Agents: Doe Coover (*L0298*); Colleen Mohyde (*L0993*)

L0374 Broo Doherty
Literary Agent
United Kingdom

Literary Agency: DHH Literary Agency Ltd (**L0364**)

L0375 Trevor Dolby
Literary Agent
United Kingdom

https://aevitascreative.com/agents/#agent-7410

Literary Agency: Aevitas Creative Management (ACM) UK (**L0020**)

Nonfiction > *Nonfiction Books*
  Biography; Comedy / Humour; Memoir; Military History; Narrative History; Nature; Popular Culture; Popular Science

Send: Query; Writing sample
How to send: Online submission system

Looking for popular science with a clear relevance to everyday life, narrative history, military history, humour, biography, popular culture, natural history and great memoirs by passionate people whose lives have been well lived.

L0376 Adriana Dominguez
Literary Agent
United States

https://www.fullcircleliterary.com/our-agents/adriana-dominguez/

Literary Agency: Full Circle Literary, LLC (**L0515**)

Closed to approaches.

L0377 Don Buchwald and Associates
Literary Agency
5900 Wilshire Boulevard, 31st floor, Los Angeles, CA 90036
United States
Tel: +1 (323) 655-7400

info@buchwald.com

https://www.buchwald.com

Professional Body: Writers Guild of America (WGA)

Types: Scripts
Formats: Film Scripts; TV Scripts; Theatre Scripts
Markets: Adult

Send query by post with SASE or by fax. No unsolicited MSS. Finds most new clients by combing the NY and LA theatre scenes, and by attending film festivals, entertainment symposiums and other industry gatherings.

L0378 Don Congdon Associates, Inc.
Literary Agency
110 William St. Suite 2202, New York, NY 10038
United States
Tel: +1 (212) 645-1229
Fax: +1 (212) 727-2688

dca@doncongdon.com

http://doncongdon.com

Professional Body: Association of Authors' Representatives, Inc. (AAR)

Types: Fiction; Nonfiction
Formats: Film Scripts; Theatre Scripts
Subjects: Adventure; Anthropology; Archaeology; Arts; Autobiography; Comedy / Humour; Commercial; Cookery; Crime; Culture; Current Affairs; Fantasy; Health; History; Legal; Lifestyle; Literary; Literary Criticism; Medicine; Music; Mystery; Nature; Politics; Psychology; Science; Sport; Suspense; Technology; Thrillers; Travel;

Warfare; Women's Interests
Markets: Adult; Children's; Young Adult

Send: Query
Don't send: Full text
How to send: Email

Costs: Author covers sundry admin costs.

Send query by email (no attachments) only. Include one-page synopsis, relevant background info, and first chapter, all within the body of the email if submitting by email. Include the word "Query" in the subject line. See website for full guidelines. No unsolicited MSS.

Literary Agents: Cristina Concepcion (*L0291*); Michael Congdon (*L0293*); Katie Grimm (*L0586*); Katie Kotchman (*L0804*); Maura Kye-Casella (*L0814*); Susan Ramer (*L1126*)

L0379 Donaghy Literary Group
Literary Agency
United States

stacey@donaghyliterary.com

http://www.donaghyliterary.com

ADULT > **Fiction** > *Novels*
Fantasy; Historical Fantasy; Historical Fiction; Mystery; Romance; Science Fiction; Suspense; Thrillers; Women's Fiction

YOUNG ADULT > **Fiction** > *Novels*
Fantasy; Historical Fantasy; Historical Fiction; Mystery; Romance; Science Fiction; Suspense; Thrillers; Women's Fiction

Send: Query
How to send: Online submission system

See website for individual agent interests, and submit using online submission system.

Literary Agents: Amanda Ayers Barnett; Stacey Donaghy; Liis McKinstry; Sue Miller; Valerie Noble; Susan Spann

L0380 Donald Maass Literary Agency
Literary Agency
1000 Dean Street, Suite 252, Brooklyn, NY 11238
United States
Tel: +1 (212) 727-8383
Fax: +1 (212) 727-3271

info@maassagency.com

http://www.maassagency.com

Professional Body: Association of Authors' Representatives, Inc. (AAR)

Types: Fiction
Subjects: Comedy / Humour; Commercial; Crime; Fantasy; History; Horror; Literary; Mystery; Romance; Science Fiction; Suspense; Thrillers; Westerns; Women's Interests
Markets: Adult; Young Adult

Send: Query
Don't send: Full text
How to send: Email

Welcomes all genres, in particular science fiction, fantasy, mystery, suspense, horror, romance, historical, literary and mainstream novels. Send query to a specific agent, by email, with "query" in the subject line. No queries by post. See website for individual agent interests and email addresses.

Authors: Saladin Ahmed; Sonya Bateman; Jim Butcher

Literary Agents: Katie Shea Boutillier (*L0165*); Michael Curry (*L0316*); Jennifer Goloboy (*L0561*); Jennifer Jackson (*L0700*); Kat Kerr (*L0780*); Donald Maass (*L0897*); Cameron McClure (*L0947*); Caitlin McDonald (*L0952*); Kiana Nguyen (*L1032*); Paul Stevens

L0381 Priya Doraswamy
Literary Agent
United States

Literary Agency: Lotus Lane Literary (**L0876**)

L0382 Dorie Simmonds Agency
Literary Agency
United Kingdom
Tel: +44 (0) 20 7736 0002

info@doriesimmonds.com

https://doriesimmonds.com/

Professional Body: The Association of Authors' Agents (AAA)

ADULT
Fiction > *Novels*: Commercial

Nonfiction > *Nonfiction Books*

CHILDREN'S > **Fiction** > *Novels*

Send: Query; Writing sample; Author bio
How to send: PDF file email attachment; Word file email attachment

Send query by email as Word or PDF attachments. Include details on your background and relevant writing experience, and first three chapters or fifty pages. See website for full details.

Literary Agents: Pearl Baxter; Dorie Simmonds (**L1280**)

L0383 Anne-Marie Doulton
Literary Agent
United Kingdom

Literary Agency: The Ampersand Agency Ltd (**L0039**)

L0384 Claire Draper
Literary Agent
United States

Literary Agency: The Bent Agency (**L0119**)

L0385 Catherine Drayton
Literary Agent
United States

Literary Agency: InkWell Management (**L0686**)

L0386 The Drummond Agency
Literary Agency
PO Box 572, Woodend, Vic, 3442
Australia
Tel: +61 (0) 3 5427 3644

sheila@drummondagency.com.au

http://www.drummondagency.com.au

Professional Body: Australian Literary Agents' Association (ALAA)

Types: Fiction; Nonfiction
Formats: Film Scripts; Radio Scripts; TV Scripts; Theatre Scripts
Subjects: Adventure; Anthropology; Antiques; Archaeology; Architecture; Arts; Autobiography; Business; Comedy / Humour; Commercial; Cookery; Crime; Culture; Current Affairs; Design; Drama; Entertainment; Finance; Gardening; Health; History; Horror; How To; Legal; Leisure; Lifestyle; Literary Criticism; Media; Medicine; Men's Interests; Music; Mystery; Nature; Personal Development; Philosophy; Photography; Politics; Psychology; Romance; Satire; Science; Society; Spirituality; Suspense; Technology; Travel; Warfare; Women's Interests
Markets: Academic; Adult; Children's; Professional; Young Adult

Closed to approaches.

Costs: Author covers sundry admin costs.

Closed to submissions as at January 2019. Check website for current status. A small personalised agency with contacts with all major houses and a good network of sub agents in most territories.

Authors: Randa Abdel-Fattah; Alexandra Alt; Meredith Appleyard; Kate Belle; Deborah Burrows; Liz Byrski; Anne Connor; Janita Cunnington; Neil Curtis; Catherine DeVrye; Barbara Gaskell Denvil; Jill Dobson; Cath Ferla; Lee Fox; Ian Gow; Joan Grant; Carmen Gray; Susan Green; Des Guilfoyle; Sue Gunningham; Nicholas Hasluck; GS Johnston; Chantal Kayem; Stuart Kells; Elizabeth Kleinhenz; Veronicah Larkin; David Lawrence; Wenn Lawson; Kathryn Ledson; Casey Lever; Dianne Maguire; Jo McGahey; Tom McGill; Wilson McOrist; KB Mcgavin; Margaret Merrilees; Jane Messer; David Middleton; Phillip Middleton; Marianne Musgrove; Margareta Osborn; Ida Di Pastena; Kate Richards; A D Scott; Tom Skinner; Jennifer Smart; Jurgen Tampke; Glenna Thomson; Vikki Wakefield; Yvette Walker; Felicity Young; Claire Zorn

Literary Agent: Sheila Drummond (*L0387*)

L0387 Sheila Drummond

Literary Agent
Australia

Literary Agency: The Drummond Agency
(L0386)

L0388 Ian Drury

Literary Agent
United Kingdom

Literary Agency: Sheil Land Associates Ltd
(L1263)

L0389 Alec Drysdale

Literary Agent
United Kingdom

Literary Agency: Independent Talent Group
Ltd **(L0683)**

L0390 Robert Dudley

Literary Agent
United Kingdom

Literary Agency: Robert Dudley Agency
(L1160)

L0391 Del Duduit

Junior Agent; Author
United States

https://cyleyoung.com/literary-agent/my-team/

Literary Agency: Cyle Young Literary Elite
(L0323)
Literary Agent / Author: Cyle Young **(L1482)**

Nonfiction > *Nonfiction Books*
Christian Living; Cookery; Health;
Inspirational; Leadership; Leisure; Lifestyle;
Motivational Self-Help; Sport; Travel

L0392 Duncan McAra

Literary Agency
3 Viewfield Avenue, Bishopbriggs, Glasgow,
Scotland, G64 2AG
United Kingdom
Tel: +44 (0) 1417 721067

duncanmcara@mac.com

Types: Fiction; Nonfiction
Subjects: Archaeology; Architecture; Arts;
Biography; History; Literary; Travel; Warfare
Markets: Adult

Send: Query
Don't send: Full text

Also interested in books of Scottish interest.
Send query letter with SAE in first instance.

L0393 Dunham Literary, Inc.

Literary Agency
United States

query@dunhamlit.com
dunhamlit@gmail.com

https://www.dunhamlit.com

ADULT
Fiction > *Novels*

Nonfiction > *Nonfiction Books*: Narrative
Nonfiction

CHILDREN'S > Fiction
Novels; *Picture Books*

Send: Query; Writing sample
Don't send: Full text
How to send: In the body of an email
How not to send: Post; Fax; Phone; Email
attachment

Handles quality fiction and nonfiction for
adults and children. Send query by email only.
See website for full guidelines. No approaches
by post, phone or fax. No email attachments.

Literary Agents: Jennie Dunham **(L0394)**;
Bridget Smith; Leslie Zampetti **(L1485)**

L0394 Jennie Dunham

Literary Agent
United States

https://www.dunhamlit.com/jennie-dunham.
html
http://aaronline.org/Sys/PublicProfile/2176658/
417813

Literary Agency: Dunham Literary, Inc.
(L0393)
Professional Bodies: Association of Authors'
Representatives, Inc. (AAR); Society of
Children's Book Writers and Illustrators
(SCBWI)

ADULT
Fiction
Graphic Novels: General
Novels: Comedy / Humour; Historical
Fiction; LGBTQIA; Literary; Mystery;
Thrillers; Women's Fiction
Nonfiction > *Nonfiction Books*
Biography; Current Affairs; Family;
History; Memoir; Narrative Nonfiction;
Parenting; Politics; Relationships; Science;
Technology

CHILDREN'S > Fiction
Middle Grade; *Picture Books*
NEW ADULT
Fiction > *Novels*
Nonfiction > *Nonfiction Books*
YOUNG ADULT > **Fiction** > *Novels*

Send: Query; Writing sample
Don't send: Full text
How to send: In the body of an email
How not to send: Post; Fax; Phone; Email
attachment

Represents literary fiction and non-fiction for
adults and children.

L0395 Dunow, Carlson & Lerner Agency

Literary Agency
27 West 20th Street, Suite 1107, New York,
NY 10011
United States
Tel: +1 (212) 645-7606

mail@dclagency.com

http://www.dclagency.com

Professional Body: Association of Authors'
Representatives, Inc. (AAR)

Types: Fiction; Nonfiction
Subjects: Arts; Autobiography; Comedy /
Humour; Commercial; Culture; Current
Affairs; Health; History; Literary; Literary
Criticism; Music; Mystery; Science; Sport;
Suspense; Thrillers; Women's Interests
Markets: Adult; Children's; Young Adult

Send: Query
Don't send: Full text
How to send: Email

Prefers queries by email, but will also accept
queries by post with SASE. No attachments.
Does not respond to all email queries.

Author Estates: The Estate of Donald J. Sobol;
The Estate of Jim Carroll; The Estate of John
Steptoe; The Estate of Joseph Mitchell; The
Estate of William Lee Miller

Authors: Nathaniel Adams; Siobhan Adcock;
Cameron Alborzian; Preston Allen; Mara
Altman; Stephen Amidon; Cynthia Anderson;
Jessica Applestone; Josh Applestone; Heather
Armstrong; Ali Bahrampour; Kevin Baker;
Nancy Balbirer; Wilton Barnhardt; Jackie
Battenfield; Douglas Bauer; Richard Bausch;
Aimee Bender; Martellus Bennett; Frank Bill;
Brandon Bird; George Black; Lea Black;
Robin Black; Francesca Lia Block; Michael
Bobelian; Lorraine Boissoneault; Amy
Bonnaffons; Sheri Booker; Shira Boss; Patricia
Bosworth; Svetlana Boym; G.B. Bragg;
Benjamin Breen; Elise Broach; Kevin
Brockmeier; Mikita Brottman; David W.
Brown; Stacia Brown; David Browne; Lucy
Buffett; Mónica Bustamante; Clay Byars;
Hamilton Cain; Katrina Carrasco; Bill Carter;
Erika Carter; Climate Central; Bryn
Chancellor; Joelle Charbonneau; Noah
Charney; Paula Chase; Emily Chenoweth; K
Chess; Mark Childress; Christina Chiu; Adam
Christopher; Mimi Chubb; Cassandra Rose
Clarke; Nigel Cliff; Esme Raji Codell; Nancy
Coffelt; Jaed Coffin; Cole Cohen; Jaimee
Wriston Colbert; Deborah Joy Corey; Paul
Cornell; Jeremy Craig; Katherine Crowley;
Dave Cullen; Mark Dapin; Dame Darcy; Alice
Elliott Dark; Michael Dart; Elizabeth Davis;
Elaine Dimopoulos; Heather Dixon; Allyson
Downey; Alice Dreger; Mike Duncan; Damien
Echols; Daniel Ehrenhaft; Rhian Ellis; Kathy
Elster; Marion Ettlinger; Howard Falco; Boris
Fishman; Pia Frey; Seth Fried; Steven
Galloway; John Gartner; Amina Gautier;
Joshua Gaylord; Valerie Geary; Poppy Gee;
Michael Gerber; Alfred Gingold; Owen
Gleiberman; Brandt Goldstein; Gary Golio;
Matthew Goodman; Eli Gottlieb; Temple

Grandin; Elizabeth Graver; Casey Gray; Seth Greenland; Gwendolen Gross; Rudy Gutierrez; Sam Gwynne; Kathleen Hale; Lisa Hale; Mary Ellen Hannibal; Karen Harrington; Ethan Hauser; Robert Hellenga; Steve Hendricks; Joe Henry; Becky Hepinstall; George Hodgman; Stacy Horn; Ilze Hugo; Josie Iselin; Jeremy Jackson; John Hornor Jacobs; Matthew Jobin; Daron Joffe; T. Geronimo Johnson; Noah Z. Jones; David Joy; Juris Jurjevics; Karen Kane; Hester Kaplan; Brad Kessler; Christian Kiefer; Andrea Kleine; Chrissy Kolaya; Amanda Korman; Nik Korpon; J. Kasper Kramer; Andrew Krivak; Johanna Lane; Sarah Langan; Richard Lange; Sarah Laskow; Owen Laukkanen; Holly LeCraw; Theodora Lee; Edan Lepucki; Elizabeth Lesser; Jerry Lee Lewis; Robin Lewis; David Lida; Natalie Lindeman; Brad Listi; William Bryant Logan; Jenny Lombard; Leil Lowndes; Joshua Lyon; Fiona Maazel; Robin MacArthur; David Stuart MacLean; Rosemary Mahoney; Tanya Marquardt; Debra Marquart; Alex Marshall; Cate Marvin; Suzanne Matson; Abi Maxwell; Matthew McBride; Mary McCluskey; Jill McCorkle; Elizabeth McCracken; Patrick McDonnell; Sean McGinty; Jon McGoran; Will McGrath; Adam McOmber; Bob Mehr; June Melby; Susan Scarf Merrell; Deborah Meyler; Jenny Milchman; Barnabas Miller; Daphne Miller; Leslie F. Miller; Paul Miller; Denise Mina; T. T. Monday; Gregory Mone; Amanda Montell; Carrie Morey; Amelia Morris; Bradford Morrow; Brian Morton; Layne Mosler; Sarah Moss; Debbie Nathan; Ed Nawotka; Greg Neri; Robert Neuwirth; Alana Newhouse; Jay Baron Nicorvo; Aline Ohanesian; Elizabeth Oness; Mark Oppenheimer; David Orr; Chad Orzel; Tom Paine; Richard Panek; Michel Paradis; Debra Pascali-Bonaro; Rachel Pastan; Justin Peacock; Jamie Pearlberg; Catherine Pelonero; Tony Perrottet; Linda Vigen Phillips; Max Phillips; Melissa Holbrook Pierson; Nic Pizzolatto; Daria Polichetti; Richard Polt; Maggie Pouncey; Mark Powell; Jessica Powers; Caroline Preston; Susan Puckett; D. M. Pulley; Carol Purington; Joan Quigley; Mark Rader; Susanna Reich; Nelly Reifler; James Renner; Paul Reyes; Robert Riesman; Nicholas Rinaldi; M. L. Rio; Todd Robinson; Marisa Robinson-Textor; Annie Rogers; Stuart Rojstaczer; Jane Roper; Rebecca Rotert; Shannan Rouss; Katherine Rowland; Lena Roy; David Rubel; Joan Ryan; Richard Sandoval; Marisa de los Santos; Steven Satterfield; Shya Scanlon; Alexis Schaitkin; Gary Schanbacher; Kodi Scheer; Patty Schemel; David Schickler; Molly Schiot; Heidi Jon Schmidt; Pat Schories; William Todd Schultz; Paul Selig; Kieran Shea; Hugh Sheehy; Jeff Shelby; Joshua Wolf Shenk; Jessica Shortall; Jenefer Shute; Marisa Silver; Patti Smith; Tatjana Soli; Lily Sparks; Kelli Stanley; Leigh Stein; Javaka Steptoe; Jude Stewart; Susan Straight; Jay Stringer; Vivian Swift; Liara Tamani; Nick Taylor;

David Teague; Tori Telfer; Melanie Thernstrom; Jean Thompson; Richard Todd; Susan Todd; David Tomlinson; Lara Tupper; Lawrence Turman; James Twitchell; Neil deGrasse Tyson; Karen Valby; Katherine Vaz; Sarah St. Vincent; Christine Wade; Laura Waldon; Casey Walker; Mark Van de Walle; Margaret Wappler; Steve Weddle; Jillian Weise; Jan Merete Weiss; Chuck Wendig; Frank Wheeler; Kamy Wicoff; Matt Wiegle; Marianne Wiggins; David Wilcock; Corban Wilkinson; Adam Wilson; Tim Wirkus; Mishna Wolff; Hilma Wolitzer; Alisson Wood; Kim Wozencraft; Ronald Wright; David Wroblewski; David Yoo; Kenji Yoshino; Alia Yunis; Alan Ziegler; Jean Zimmerman; Jennifer duBois

Literary Agents: Jennifer Carlson (*L0223*); Arielle Datz (*L0335*); Stacia Decker (*L0349*); Henry Dunow (*L0396*); Erin Hosier (*L0666*); Amy Hughes (*L0671*); Eleanor Jackson (*L0699*); Julia Kenny (*L0777*); Betsy Lerner (*L0846*); Edward Necarsulmer (*L1024*); Yishai Seidman (*L1250*)

L0396 Henry Dunow
Literary Agent
United States

Literary Agency: Dunow, Carlson & Lerner Agency (**L0395**)

L0397 David Dunton
Literary Agent
United States

Literary Agency: Harvey Klinger, Inc (**L0619**)

L0398 Stephen Durbridge
Literary Agent
United Kingdom

Literary Agency: The Agency (London) Ltd (**L0021**)

L0399 Dystel, Goderich & Bourret LLC
Literary Agency
One Union Square West, Suite 904, New York, NY 10003
United States
Tel: +1 (212) 627-9100
Fax: +1 (212) 627-9313

miriam@dystel.com

http://www.dystel.com

Professional Body: Association of Authors' Representatives, Inc. (AAR)

Types: Fiction; Nonfiction
Subjects: Adventure; Anthropology; Archaeology; Autobiography; Business; Comedy / Humour; Commercial; Contemporary; Cookery; Crime; Culture; Current Affairs; Fantasy; Finance; Health; History; Lifestyle; Literary; Mystery; New

Age; Politics; Psychology; Religion; Romance; Science; Science Fiction; Suspense; Technology; Thrillers; Warfare; Women's Interests
Markets: Adult; Children's; Young Adult

Send: Query
Don't send: Full text
How to send: Email

See website for individual agent interests and contact details and approach one agent only. Send query by email with brief synopsis and sample chapter in the body of the email. Attachments to blank emails will not be opened. Queries should be brief, devoid of gimmicks, and professionally presented, including author details and any writing credits. See website for more details.

Literary Agents: Lauren E. Abramo (*L0010*); Amy Bishop (*L0136*); Michael Bourret (*L0164*); Jane Dystel (*L0400*); Kemi Faderin (*L0448*); Stacey Glick (*L0554*); Miriam Goderich (*L0556*); Mike Hoogland (*L0663*); Jim McCarthy (*L0945*); Jessica Papin (*L1066*); Sharon Pelletier (*L1080*); John Rudolph (*L1198*); Ann Leslie Tuttle (*L1383*); Kieryn Ziegler (*L1489*)

L0400 Jane Dystel
Literary Agent
United States

Literary Agency: Dystel, Goderich & Bourret LLC (**L0399**)

L0401 Adam Eaglin
Literary Agent
United States

Literary Agency: The Cheney Agency (**L0256**)

L0402 Ebeling & Associates
Literary Agency
United States

michael@ebelingagency.com

http://www.ebelingagency.com

Types: Nonfiction
Subjects: Business; Commercial; Health; New Age; Personal Development
Markets: Adult

Send: Query
Don't send: Full text
How to send: Email

Costs: Offers services that writers have to pay for.

Offers literary representation, coaching, and platform development. Handles nonfiction only. Send query by email with proposal.

Literary Agent: Michael Ebeling (*L0403*)

L0403 Michael Ebeling
Literary Agent
United States

Literary Agency: Ebeling & Associates (**L0402**)

L0404 Chelsea Eberly
Literary Agent
United States

https://www.greenhouseliterary.com/the-team/chelsea-eberly/
https://twitter.com/chelseberly
https://www.publishersmarketplace.com/members/ChelseaEberly/
https://querymanager.com/query/ChelseaEberly

Literary Agency: The Greenhouse Literary Agency (**L0579**)

ADULT
  Fiction > *Novels*
    Comedy / Humour; Commercial; Contemporary; Domestic Mystery; Domestic Thriller; Fantasy; Feminism; High Concept; Literary; Magical Realism; Romance; Social Justice; Thrillers; Upmarket; Women's Fiction

  Nonfiction > *Nonfiction Books*

CHILDREN'S
  Fiction
    Graphic Novels: Comedy / Humour; Contemporary; Fantasy; Historical Fiction
    Middle Grade: General
    Picture Books: General, and in particular: Comedy / Humour
  Nonfiction > *Picture Books*: Contemporary

YOUNG ADULT > **Fiction**
    Graphic Novels: Comedy / Humour; Contemporary; Fantasy; Historical Fiction
    Novels: Feminism; Mystery; Romance; Thrillers

Send: Query; Author bio; Writing sample; Proposal
How to send: Query Manager

Represents authors of middle grade, young adult, graphic novels, and women's fiction, as well as writer-illustrators of picture books. Seeks high-concept, commercial reads that will stand out in a crowded market with depth and heart. She is actively building her list and is primarily interested in fantasy, magical realism, contemporary fiction (particularly romance, thrillers, and humor), and graphic novels.

L0405 Eddie Kritzer Productions
Literary Agency
1112 Montana Avenue, Suite 449, Santa Monica, CA 90403
United States
Tel: +1 (310) 702-5356

eddiekritzer@gmail.com

http://www.eddiekritzer.com

Fiction > *Novels*

Nonfiction > *Nonfiction Books*
Scripts
  Film Scripts; *TV Scripts*

Send: Query; Full text
How to send: Email

Agency is seeking writers or individuals that have a compelling story to tell. If you have a story that you believe in, and you can't believe it's not at your local Barnes & Noble or in Theaters, email a synopsis of your story in one or two paragraphs for review

Editor: Ms Larisa Wain

L0406 Eddison Pearson Ltd
Literary Agency
West Hill House, 6 Swains Lane, London, N6 6QS
United Kingdom
Tel: +44 (0) 20 7700 7763

enquiries@eddisonpearson.com

https://www.eddisonpearson.com
https://eddisonpearson.tumblr.com/
https://www.linkedin.com/in/clare-pearson-epla
https://twitter.com/ClarePearson_EP

Professional Body: The Association of Authors' Agents (AAA)

CHILDREN'S
  Fiction
    Novels: Contemporary; Historical Fiction
    Picture Books: General

  Poetry > *Any Poetic Form*

YOUNG ADULT > **Fiction** > *Novels*

Send: Query; Writing sample
How to send: Email

A London-based literary agency providing a personal service to a small stable of talented authors, mainly of books for children and young adults. Send query by email only for auto-response containing up-to-date submission guidelines and email address for submissions. No submissions or enquiries by post.

Authors: Valerie Bloom; Michael Catchpool; Sue Heap; Caroline Lawrence; Robert Muchamore; Mary Murphy; Megan Rix

Literary Agent: Clare Pearson (*L1076*)

L0407 Sam Edenborough
Literary Agent
United Kingdom

Literary Agency: ILA (Intercontinental Literary Agency) (**L0681**)

L0408 Edwards Fuglewicz
Literary Agency
49 Great Ormond Street, London, WC1N 3HZ
United Kingdom
Tel: +44 (0) 20 7405 6725

jill@efla.co.uk

Professional Body: The Association of Authors' Agents (AAA)

Types: Fiction; Nonfiction
Subjects: Biography; Commercial; History; Literary
Markets: Adult

Handles literary and commercial fiction, and nonfiction. No children's, science fiction, horror, or email submissions.

Literary Agents: Ros Edwards (*L0410*); Helenka Fuglewicz (*L0514*)

L0409 Max Edwards
Literary Agent
United Kingdom

max@appletreeliterary.co.uk

https://aevitascreative.com/agents/#agent-7412
http://appletreeliterary.co.uk/about/

Literary Agencies: Apple Tree Literary Ltd (**L0060**); Aevitas Creative Management (ACM) UK (**L0020**)

Fiction > *Novels*
    Commercial; Crime; Fantasy; High Concept; Science Fiction

Nonfiction > *Nonfiction Books*
    Arts; Football / Soccer; Journalism; Science; Sport

Send: Author bio; Query; Writing sample; Synopsis
How to send: Email; Online submission system

Looking for commercial and genre novels, and is a fan of novels that mix genres in a unique way. Keen on high concepts, smart plots and unique characters – twists and turns, good (and bad) guys with depth and life. Also looking for great stories that can be told through nonfiction; either unique or surprising takes on a subject, or something wildly original. Would like to hear from academics mixing the arts and science in a new way, journalists wanting to take their writing beyond the article, sports writers with a new way of exploring what we play (particularly football/soccer), or writers with an untold history to tell.

L0410 Ros Edwards
Literary Agent
United Kingdom

Literary Agency: Edwards Fuglewicz (**L0408**)

L0411 Silé Edwards
Literary Agent
United Kingdom

sesubmissions@mushens-entertainment.com

https://www.mushens-entertainment.com/submissions
https://twitter.com/sileloquies

Literary Agency: Mushens Entertainment (**L1017**)

Fiction > *Novels*
Crime Thrilllers; Romantic Comedy; Upmarket

Nonfiction > *Nonfiction Books*
Cookery; Food

Poetry > *Poetry Collections*

Send: Query; Proposal; Writing sample
How to send: Email

Looking for books that inform our understanding of the world, society and the ways we live. Interested in a range of Non-Fiction from emotive life writing to topical essay-like writing to projects on cookery and food. She is particularly keen on finding experts in their field who want to write about what they know in a way that everyone can understand, appreciate and enjoy.

Also accepts fiction submissions. She is open to all genres, but especially interested in crime thrillers, romantic comedies, poetry and upmarket fiction.

L0412 Stephen Edwards
Literary Agent
United Kingdom

Literary Agency: Rogers, Coleridge & White Ltd (**L1181**)

L0413 Danielle Egan-Miller
Literary Agent
United States

Literary Agency: Browne & Miller Literary Associates (**L0194**)

L0414 Ryan Eichenwald
Literary Agent
United States

Literary Agency: The Jennifer DeChiara Literary Agency (**L0721**)

L0415 Einstein Literary Management
Literary Agency
United States
Tel: +1 (212) 221-8797

submissions@einsteinliterary.com

https://www.einsteinliterary.com
https://twitter.com/Einstein_Lit

ADULT
Fiction > *Novels*
Commercial; Literary

Nonfiction > *Nonfiction Books*
Cookery; Memoir; Narrative Nonfiction

CHILDREN'S > **Fiction** > *Novels*

YOUNG ADULT > **Fiction** > *Novels*

Send: Query; Writing sample
How to send: In the body of an email

Send query by email with first ten double-spaced pages pasted into the body of the email. No attachments. See website for details of individual agents and their interests and include the name of specific agent you are submitting to in the subject line. No poetry, textbooks, or screenplays. No queries by post or by phone. Response only if interested.

Literary Agents: Susanna Einstein (**L0416**); Susan Graham (**L0569**); Shana Kelly

L0416 Susanna Einstein
Literary Agent
United States

https://www.einsteinliterary.com/staff/
http://aaronline.org/Sys/PublicProfile/4557347/417813

Literary Agency: Einstein Literary Management (**L0415**)
Professional Body: Association of Authors' Representatives, Inc. (AAR)

ADULT
Fiction > *Novels*
Commercial Women's Fiction; Crime; Upmarket Women's Fiction

Nonfiction > *Nonfiction Books*: Narrative Nonfiction

CHILDREN'S > **Fiction** > *Middle Grade*

YOUNG ADULT > **Fiction** > *Novels*

Has a particular fondness for crime fiction, upmarket commercial women's fiction, MG and YA fiction, and narrative non-fiction. She likes a good story well told.

L0417 Naomi Eisenbeiss
Literary Agent
United States

http://www.inkwellmanagement.com/staff/
naomi-eisenbeiss

Literary Agency: InkWell Management (**L0686**)

Fiction > *Novels*: Literary

Nonfiction > *Nonfiction Books*
Memoir; Narrative Nonfiction

L0418 Caroline Eisenmann
Literary Agent
United States

Literary Agency: Frances Goldin Literary Agency, Inc. (**L0492**)
Professional Body: Association of Authors' Representatives, Inc. (AAR)

Authors: Kyle Chayka; Ye Chun; Linda Rui Feng; Amanda Goldblatt; James Gregor; Peter Kispert; Theresa Levitt; Micah Nemerever; Jenny Odell; Kate Wagner; Michelle Webster-Hein

L0419 Rachel Ekstrom
Literary Agent
United States
Tel: +1 (212) 400-1494

rekstrom@foliolitmanagement.com
rachel@foliolit.com

https://www.publishersmarketplace.com/
members/ekstrach/
http://www.twitter.com/ekstromrachel

Literary Agency: Folio Literary Management, LLC (**L0480**)

ADULT
Fiction > *Novels*
General, and in particular: Dystopian Fiction; Health; Historical Fiction; Lifestyle; Literary; Mind, Body, Spirit; Mystery; Speculative; Suspense; Thrillers; Upmarket

Nonfiction > *Nonfiction Books*
Animals; Mental Health; Nature; Parenting; Psychology; Social Issues

CHILDREN'S
Fiction > *Middle Grade*
Nonfiction > *Nonfiction Books*

YOUNG ADULT
Fiction > *Novels*
Nonfiction > *Nonfiction Books*

Does not want:

ADULT
Fiction > *Novels*
Cozy Mysteries; Hard Science Fiction; High / Epic Fantasy; Political Thrillers; Romance; Supernatural / Paranormal; Urban Fantasy

Nonfiction > *Nonfiction Books*: Memoir

CHILDREN'S > **Fiction** > *Picture Books*

Send: Query; Writing sample
How to send: In the body of an email

L0420 Lisa Ekus
Literary Agent
United States

Literary Agency: The Lisa Ekus Group, LLC (**L0861**)

L0421 Elaine Steel
Literary Agency
49 Greek Street, London, W1D 4EG
United Kingdom
Tel: +44 (0) 1273 739022

info@elainesteel.com

http://www.elainesteel.com

Professional Body: The Association of Authors' Agents (AAA)

Types: Fiction; Nonfiction; Scripts
Formats: Film Scripts; Radio Scripts; TV Scripts
Markets: Adult

Send: Query
Don't send: Full text

Send query by email with CV and outline, along with details of experience. No unsolicited mss.

Authors: Gwyneth Hughes; James Lovelock; Ben Steiner

L0422 Elise Dillsworth Agency (EDA)

Literary Agency
United Kingdom

submissions@elisedillsworthagency.com

http://elisedillsworthagency.com

Types: Fiction; Nonfiction
Subjects: Autobiography; Commercial; Cookery; Literary; Travel
Markets: Adult

Send: Query
Don't send: Full text

Represents writers from around the world. Looking for literary and commercial fiction, and nonfiction (especially memoir, autobiography, biography, cookery and travel writing). No science fiction, fantasy, poetry, film scripts, or plays. No young adult, or children's, except for existing authors. Send query by email only (postal submissions no longer accepted). For fiction, include synopsis up to two pages and first three chapters, up to about 50 pages, as Word or PDF attachments. For nonfiction, send details of expertise / credentials, proposal, chapter outline, and writing sample of around 30 pages as a Word file attachment. See website for full guidelines. Allow eight weeks for response.

Literary Agent: Elise Dillsworth (**L0369**)

L0423 Elizabeth Roy Literary Agency

Literary Agency
White Cottage, Greatford, Stamford, Lincolnshire, PE9 4PR
United Kingdom
Tel: +44 (0) 1778 560672

http://www.elizabethroy.co.uk

Types: Fiction; Nonfiction
Subjects: Comedy / Humour; Romance
Markets: Children's

Send: Query
Don't send: Full text

Handles fiction and nonfiction for children. Particularly interested in funny fiction, gentle romance for young teens, picture book texts for pre-school children, and books with international market appeal. Send query by

post with return postage, synopsis, and sample chapters. No science fiction, poetry, plays or adult books.

Literary Agent: Elizabeth Roy (*L1195*)

L0424 Ethan Ellenberg

Literary Agent; President
United States

agent@ethanellenberg.com

https://ethanellenberg.com
http://aaronline.org/Sys/PublicProfile/2176663/417813

Literary Agency: Ethan Ellenberg Literary Agency (**L0437**)
Professional Body: Association of Authors' Representatives, Inc. (AAR)

ADULT
  Fiction > *Novels*
    Commercial; Romance

  Nonfiction > *Nonfiction Books*

CHILDREN'S > **Fiction**
  Novels; Picture Books

L0425 Humphrey Elles-Hill

Literary Agent
United Kingdom

Literary Agency: Independent Talent Group Ltd (**L0683**)

L0426 Tracey Elliston

Literary Agent
United Kingdom

Literary Agency: Judy Daish Associates Ltd (**L0746**)

L0427 Zabé Ellor

Literary Agent
United States

https://www.jdlit.com/zabe-ellor
https://querymanager.com/query/ZabeEllor

Literary Agency: The Jennifer DeChiara Literary Agency (**L0721**)

ADULT
  Fiction
    Graphic Novels: General
    Novels: Commercial; Fantasy; Mystery; Science Fiction; Thrillers; Upmarket Contemporary Fiction
  Nonfiction > *Nonfiction Books*
    History; Science

CHILDREN'S > **Fiction**
  Graphic Novels: General
  Middle Grade: Adventure; Comedy / Humour; Speculative
YOUNG ADULT > **Fiction**
  Graphic Novels: General
  Novels: General, and in particular: Contemporary; Fantasy; Mystery; Romance; Science Fiction; Thrillers

Send: Query; Synopsis; Writing sample
How to send: Query Manager

For fiction, send a query, a 1-2 page synopsis, and the first 25 pages of your project. For nonfiction, send a query and a sample chapter. For graphic novels, send a query with a link to your portfolio website. I strive to respond to all queries in 4-6 weeks.

L0428 Emerald City Literary Agency

Literary Agency
718 Griffin Avenue, #195, Enumclaw, WA 98022
United States

Mandy@EmeraldCityLiterary.com

https://emeraldcityliterary.com

Types: Fiction; Nonfiction
Subjects: Contemporary; Horror; Romance
Markets: Adult; Children's; Young Adult

Send: Query
Don't send: Full text
How to send: Email

See website for individual agent interests, contact details, and submission guidelines. Welcomes submissions about LGBTQ themes and diverse characters and by traditionally underrepresented authors. All queries must be sent by email – no snail mail submissions. No screenplays, poetry, short stories, adult nonfiction, or fiction for adults that does not fall into the romance genre.

Literary Agents: Linda Epstein (*L0432*); Mandy Hubbard (*L0670*); Lindsay Mealing (*L0962*)

L0429 Emily Sweet Associates

Literary Agency
United Kingdom

http://www.emilysweetassociates.com

Types: Fiction; Nonfiction
Subjects: Biography; Commercial; Cookery; Current Affairs; History; Literary
Markets: Adult

Send: Query
Don't send: Full text

No Young Adult or children's. Query through form on website in first instance.

Literary Agent: Emily Sweet (*L1346*)

L0430 Emma Sweeney Agency, LLC

Literary Agency
245 East 80th Street, Suite 7E, New York, NY 10075-0506
United States

queries@emmasweeneyagency.com

http://emmasweeneyagency.com

Professional Body: Association of Authors' Representatives, Inc. (AAR)

Types: Fiction; Nonfiction
Subjects: Autobiography; History; Literary; Mystery; Religion; Science; Thrillers; Women's Interests
Markets: Adult

Send: Query
Don't send: Full text
How to send: Email

Send query by email with cover letter and first 10 pages of MS pasted into body of email. No attachments, unsolicited MSS, screenplays, romances, or westerns.

Literary Agents: Margaret Sutherland Brown (*L0193*); Emma Sweeney (*L1344*)

L0431 Empire Literary, LLC
Literary Agency
115 West 29th Street, 3rd Floor, New York, NY 10001
United States
Tel: +1 (917) 213-7082

Queries@empireliterary.com

http://www.empireliterary.com

Types: Fiction; Nonfiction
Subjects: Autobiography; Culture; Health; Lifestyle; Literary; Women's Interests
Markets: Adult; Children's; Young Adult

Send: Query
Don't send: Full text
How to send: Email

See website for specific agent guidelines and contact details, and query one agent at a time. Response not guaranteed unless interested.

Literary Agent: Andrea Barzvi (*L0096*)

L0432 Linda Epstein
Literary Agent
United States

Literary Agency: Emerald City Literary Agency (**L0428**)

L0433 Erin Murphy Literary Agency, Inc.
Literary Agency
824 Roosevelt Trail #290, Windham, ME 04062
United States

https://emliterary.com

Types: Fiction; Nonfiction
Subjects: Adventure; Contemporary; Fantasy; History; Literary
Markets: Children's; Young Adult

Considers approaches only by referral or through contact at a conference.

Literary Agents: Tara Gonzalez (*L0562*); Tricia Lawrence (*L0834*); Kevin Lewis (*L0854*); Erin

Murphy (*L1012*); Ammi-Joan Paquette (*L1067*)

L0434 Jessica Errera
Literary Agent
United States

https://www.janerotrosen.com/agents
https://www.janerotrosen.com/contact-jessica-errera

Literary Agency: Jane Rotrosen Agency (**L0709**)

ADULT > **Fiction** > *Novels*
Commercial Women's Fiction; Contemporary Romance; Historical Fiction; Suspense; Thrillers

YOUNG ADULT > **Fiction** > *Novels*

Looking for commercial women's fiction with a fresh and fun hook, all genres of YA (especially diverse stories), contemporary romance, thrillers and suspense, the occasional historical fiction, and anything that might be read in a day on the beach.

L0435 Gareth Esersky
Literary Agent
United States

gesersky@verizon.net

https://www.carolmannagency.com/gareth-esersky

Literary Agency: Carol Mann Agency (**L0225**)

Nonfiction > *Nonfiction Books*
Health; Jewish Culture; Literary; Memoir; Narrative Nonfiction; Nutrition; Parenting; Psychology; Spirituality

Send: Query; Author bio; Writing sample
How to send: In the body of an email

Represents nonfiction authors whose work falls into the following categories: health, nutrition, psychology, parenting, spirituality, Judaica, and literary and narrative nonfiction and memoir.

L0436 Felicia Eth
Literary Agent
United States

Literary Agency: Felicia Eth Literary Representation (**L0459**)

L0437 Ethan Ellenberg Literary Agency
Literary Agency
155 Suffolk Street, #2R, New York, NY 10002
United States
Tel: +1 (212) 431-4554

agent@ethanellenberg.com

https://ethanellenberg.com

Professional Bodies: Science Fiction and Fantasy Writers of America (SFWA); Society

of Children's Book Writers and Illustrators (SCBWI); Romance Writers of America (RWA); Mystery Writers of America (MWA)

ADULT
Fiction > *Novels*
General, and in particular: Commercial; Ethnic; Fantasy; Literary; Mystery; Romance; Science Fiction; Thrillers; Women's Fiction

Nonfiction > *Nonfiction Books*
Adventure; Biography; Cookery; Crime; Current Affairs; Health; History; Memoir; New Age; Popular Culture; Psychology; Science; Spirituality

CHILDREN'S > **Fiction** > *Novels*

Send: Query; Synopsis; Writing sample; Self-Addressed Stamped Envelope (SASE); Proposal
How to send: Email; Post

Send query by email (no attachments; paste material into the body of the email) or by post with SASE. For fiction send synopsis and first 50 pages. For nonfiction send proposal, author bio, and sample chapters. For picture books send complete MS. No poetry, short stories, scripts, or queries by fax.

We have been in business for over 17 years. We are a member of the AAR. We accept unsolicited submissions and, of course, do not charge reading fees.

Author Estates: The Estate of Bertrice Small; The Estate of Johnny Quarles

Authors: G.A. Aiken; Jay Allan; Carac Allison; Amanda Ashley; Claire Avery; Madeline Baker; Sarah Banks; Jon Bergeron; Patty Blount; Pat Bowne; Robin Bridges; Leah Marie Brown; James Cambias; Elaine Coffman; MaryJanice Davidson; Delilah Devlin; John Domagalski; Ian Douglas; Bill Ferris; Candace Fleming; Whitney Gaskell; Susan Grant; James Hider; Ben Hillman; Marthe Jocelyn; Aer-ki Jyr; William H. Keith; Kay Kenyon; Marko Kloos; Travis Langley; Shelly Laurenston; Georgie Lee; Michael Livingston; Kevin Luthardt; Gail Z. Martin; Lt. Col. Matt Martin; Thersa Matsuura; John McCormack; Karen Miller; Lucy Monroe; Helen Myers; J. Madison Newsome; Andre Norton; Christopher Nuttall; Mel Odoam; Melissa F. Olson; Tim Owens; Cindy Spencer Pape; Thomas Philpott; Steven Popkes; Paladin Press; Riptide Publishing; Clay Reynolds; Matthew Rivett; Eric Rohmann; Peter Sasgen; Charles Sasser; John Scalzi; Eric Schnabel; Sharon Shinn; Susan Sizemore; Oz Spies; Ferret Steinmetz; James Tabor; Dennis E. Taylor; Kimberly Kaye Terry; Kate Tietje; Judd Trichter; Margaret Vellez; Wendy Wagner; Christine Warren; Jennifer Wilde; Edward Willett; Robert Wolke; Rebecca York

Literary Agent / President: Ethan Ellenberg (**L0424**)

Literary Agents: Evan Gregory (**L0582**); Bibi Lewis (**L0853**)

L0438 Eunice McMullen Children's Literary Agent Ltd

Literary Agency
Low Ibbotsholme Cottage, Off Bridge Lane, Troutbeck Bridge, Windermere, Cumbria, LA23 1HU
United Kingdom
Tel: +44 (0) 1539 448551

eunice@eunicemcmullen.co.uk

http://www.eunicemcmullen.co.uk

CHILDREN'S > Fiction
   Middle Grade; Novels; Picture Books
TEEN > Fiction > Novels

Send: Query; Synopsis; Writing sample; Full text
How to send: Email

Enquire by email, including details about yourself, the opening chapters and synopsis, or two or three full texts for picture books. All types of material for children, particularly for those 9 and over. Strong list of authors and illustrators of picture books.

L0439 The Evan Marshall Agency

Literary Agency
1 Pacio Court, Roseland, NJ 07068-1121
United States
Tel: +1 (973) 287-6216

evan@evanmarshallagency.com

https://www.evanmarshallagency.com

Professional Body: Association of Authors' Representatives, Inc. (AAR)

Types: Fiction; Nonfiction
Markets: Adult; Young Adult

Send: Query
Don't send: Full text

Represents all genres of adult and young-adult full-length fiction. New clients by referral only.

Literary Agent: Evan Marshall (*L0928*)

L0440 Ann Evans

Literary Agent
United Kingdom

Literary Agency: Jonathan Clowes Ltd (**L0734**)

L0441 Bethan Evans

Literary Agent
United Kingdom

Literary Agency: The Agency (London) Ltd (**L0021**)

L0442 Kate Evans

Literary Agent
United Kingdom

Literary Agency: Peters Fraser + Dunlop (**L1091**)

L0443 Stephany Evans

Literary Agent
United States

https://www.pandeliterary.com/about-pandeliterary
https://twitter.com/firerooster
http://aaronline.org/Sys/PublicProfile/2176670/417813

Literary Agency: Ayesha Pande Literary (**L0073**)
Professional Bodies: Association of Authors' Representatives, Inc. (AAR); Romance Writers of America (RWA); Mystery Writers of America (MWA); The Agents Round Table (ART)

Fiction > Novels
   Commercial; Crime; Literary; Mystery; Romance; Thrillers; Upmarket Women's Fiction; Women's Fiction

Nonfiction > Nonfiction Books
   Fitness; Food and Drink; Health; Lifestyle; Memoir; Narrative Nonfiction; Running; Spirituality; Sustainable Living; Wellbeing

Send: Pitch; Author bio; Synopsis; Writing sample
How to send: Online submission system

L0444 Suzy Evans

Literary Agent
United States

Literary Agency: Sandra Dijkstra Literary Agency (**L1218**)

L0445 Eve White: Literary Agent

Literary Agency
54 Gloucester Street, London, SW1V 4EG
United Kingdom
Tel: +44 (0) 20 7630 1155

fiction@evewhite.co.uk

http://www.evewhite.co.uk

Professional Body: The Association of Authors' Agents (AAA)

Types: Fiction; Nonfiction
Subjects: Commercial; Literary
Markets: Adult; Children's; Young Adult

Send: Full text

Important! Check and follow website submission guidelines before contacting! DO NOT send nonfiction or children's submissions to email address listed on this page – see website for specific submission email addresses for different

areas. FICTION SUBMISSIONS ONLY to the email address on this page. This agency requests that you go to their website for up-to-date submission procedure. Commercial and literary fiction, nonfiction and children's fiction. Not currently accepting picture books as at October 2018 (check website for current status). No reading fee. See website for detailed submission guidelines. Submission by email only.

Authors: Christine Hamill; Sarah J Naughton; Jane Shemilt; Andy Stanton

Literary Agent: Eve White (*L1440*)

L0446 Lisa Eveleigh

Literary Agent
United Kingdom

Literary Agency: Richford Becklow Literary Agency (**L1146**)

L0447 Samantha Fabien

Literary Agent
United States

http://www.ldlainc.com/about
http://twitter.com/samanthashnh
http://aaronline.org/Sys/PublicProfile/48927898/417813
https://querymanager.com/query/samanthafabien

Literary Agency: Laura Dail Literary Agency (**L0831**)
Professional Body: Association of Authors' Representatives, Inc. (AAR)

ADULT > Fiction
   Graphic Novels: General
   Novels: Book Club Fiction; Commercial; Fantasy; High Concept; Historical Fiction; Horror; Mystery; Psychological Thrillers; Romantic Comedy; Speculative; Suspense; Thrillers; Upmarket Women's Fiction
CHILDREN'S > Fiction
   Graphic Novels: General
   Middle Grade: Contemporary; Grounded Fantasy; Horror; Mystery; Romance; Romantic Comedy; Speculative; Suspense; Thrillers
YOUNG ADULT > Fiction
   Graphic Novels: General
   Novels: Contemporary; Grounded Fantasy; Horror; Mystery; Romance; Romantic Comedy; Speculative; Suspense; Thrillers

Send: Query; Synopsis; Writing sample
How to send: Query Manager

Across genres, I'm looking for high-concept, commercial fiction for adults and children that feature diverse, marginalized, and/or underrepresented voices with all-or-nothing stakes.

L0448 Kemi Faderin

Literary Agent
United States

Literary Agency: Dystel, Goderich & Bourret LLC (**L0399**)

L0449 Fairbank Literary Representation

Literary Agency
P.O. Box 6, Hudson, NY 12534-0006
United States
Tel: +1 (617) 576-0030

queries@fairbankliterary.com

http://www.fairbankliterary.com

Professional Body: Association of Authors' Representatives, Inc. (AAR)

Types: Fiction
Subjects: Autobiography; Comedy / Humour; Culture; Design; Lifestyle; Literary; Mystery; Thrillers; Women's Interests
Markets: Adult; Children's

Send: Query
Don't send: Full text
How to send: Email

Send query by email with the first three to five pages pasted below your query (no attachments), or by post with SASE and up to the first 10 pages. Unlikely to consider work over 120,000 words. No genre romance, sci-fi, fantasy, sports fiction, YA, screenplays, or children's works unless by an illustrator / artist. No queries by phone.

Literary Agent: Sorche Elizabeth Fairbank (*L0450*)

L0450 Sorche Elizabeth Fairbank

Literary Agent
United States

Literary Agency: Fairbank Literary Representation (**L0449**)
Professional Bodies: The Agents Round Table (ART); Association of Authors' Representatives, Inc. (AAR)

L0451 Natasha Fairweather

Literary Agent
United Kingdom

Literary Agency: Rogers, Coleridge & White Ltd (**L1181**)

L0452 Holly Faulks

Literary Agent
United Kingdom

http://greeneheaton.co.uk/agents/holly-faulks/
https://twitter.com/hollycfaulks

Literary Agency: Greene & Heaton Ltd (**L0578**)

Fiction > *Novels*
  Literary; Upmarket Commercial Fiction

Nonfiction > *Nonfiction Books*

Current Affairs; Language; Lifestyle; Memoir; Popular Science

Send: Synopsis; Writing sample
How to send: Email

Authors: Joseph Coward; Emma Garland; Lily Hackett; Juliet Jacques; Iggy LDN; Sara-Ella Ozbek; Julie Reverb; Ella Frances Sanders

L0453 Jessica Faust

Literary Agent
United States

Literary Agency: BookEnds, LLC (**L0155**)

L0454 Lucy Fawcett

Literary Agent
United Kingdom

Literary Agency: Sheil Land Associates Ltd (**L1263**)

L0455 Ariella Feiner

Literary Agent
United Kingdom

afeiner@unitedagents.co.uk

https://www.unitedagents.co.uk/afeinerunitedagentscouk
https://twitter.com/ariellafeiner

Literary Agency: United Agents (**L1389**)

Fiction > *Novels*
  Book Club Fiction; Crime; High Concept; Historical Fiction; Thrillers

Nonfiction > *Nonfiction Books*
  Cookery; Memoir

Send: Synopsis; Writing sample; Proposal
How to send: Email

Always open to submissions. In fiction, would like to see crime and thrillers, issue-led books, plot-driven stories, reading group books, high-concept tales, a great elevator pitch, novels with strong female characters, and historical fiction with a twist. In nonfiction, is interested in topics which feel untouched before now or are inspiring, expert-led ideas, mouth-watering cook books, narrative memoir, and empowering female tales.

Authors: Francesca Armour-Chelu; Holly Bell; Nargisse Benkabbou; Vicky Bennison; Mark Bostridge; Robert Bryndza; Beth Cartwright; Jane Casey; Alice Clark-Platts; John Coldstream; Elle Croft; Laura Dockrill; Mike Gayle; Paul Grzegorzek; Olia Hercules; Mina Holland; Laura Jarratt; Lora Jones; Dean Lomax; Emily Midorikawa; Robert Nicholls; Selina Periampillai; Sarah Peverley; Natasha Preston; Jane Riley; Nick Spalding; Danny Wallace; Lucy Watson; Julie Welch; Kate Williams; Louisa Young

L0456 The Feldstein Agency

Literary Agency; Editorial Service; Consultancy

54 Abbey Street, Bangor, Northern Ireland, BT20 4JB
United Kingdom
Tel: +44 (0) 2891 472823

submissions@thefeldsteinagency.co.uk

https://www.thefeldsteinagency.co.uk
https://twitter.com/feldsteinagency

Fiction > *Novels*

Nonfiction > *Nonfiction Books*

Does not want:

> **Fiction** > *Novels*
>   Fantasy; Historical Fiction; Romance; Science Fiction

Send: Query; Synopsis; Author bio
How to send: Email

Costs: Offers services that writers have to pay for. Offers editing, ghostwriting, and consultancy services.

Handles adult fiction and nonfiction only. No children's, young adult, romance, science fiction, fantasy, poetry, scripts, or short stories. Send query by email with 1-2 pages synopsis. No reading fees or evaluation fees. The only instance in which an author would be charged a fee is for ghost-writing.

Consultant / Literary Agent: Paul Feldstein (**L0457**)

Editor / Literary Agent: Susan Feldstein (**L0458**)

L0457 Paul Feldstein

Literary Agent; Consultant
United Kingdom

paul@thefeldsteinagency.co.uk

Literary Agency / Editorial Service / Consultancy: The Feldstein Agency (**L0456**)

L0458 Susan Feldstein

Literary Agent; Editor
United Kingdom

susan@thefeldsteinagency.co.uk

http://www.susanfeldstein.co.uk

Literary Agency / Editorial Service / Consultancy: The Feldstein Agency (**L0456**)

L0459 Felicia Eth Literary Representation

Literary Agency
555 Bryant Street, Suite 350, Palo Alto, CA 94301
United States

feliciaeth.literary@gmail.com

https://ethliterary.com

Professional Body: Association of Authors' Representatives, Inc. (AAR)

Types: Fiction; Nonfiction
Formats: Short Fiction
Subjects: Business; Cookery; Culture; History; Lifestyle; Literary; Literature; Psychology; Science; Sport; Suspense; Travel; Women's Interests
Markets: Adult; Young Adult

Send: Query
Don't send: Full text
How to send: Email

Costs: Author covers sundry admin costs.

Send query by email or by post with SASE, including details about yourself and your project. Send sample pages upon invitation only.

Literary Agent: Felicia Eth (*L0436*)

L0460 Felicity Bryan Associates

Literary Agency
2a North Parade Avenue, Banbury Road, Oxford, OX2 6LX
United Kingdom
Tel: +44 (0) 1865 513816

submissions@felicitybryan.com

https://felicitybryan.com

Professional Body: The Association of Authors' Agents (AAA)

ADULT
 Fiction > *Novels*
  Book Club Fiction; Literary

 Nonfiction > *Nonfiction Books:* Upmarket

 CHILDREN'S > **Fiction** > *Middle Grade*
  Contemporary; Realistic

Send: Query; Synopsis; Proposal; Writing sample
How to send: Online submission system

Looking for exciting, original 'bookclub' and literary debut fiction; contemporary, realistic middle-grade fiction (i.e. 8-12) with a memorable and highly distinctive voice

accessible; upmarket non-fiction, written by an author with clear and demonstrable expertise (in practice, this means many years of professional work or PhD level study within the topic).

No young adult, fantasy, science-fiction, horror, dystopia or satire, romance or erotica, self-help, religion or philosophy (this includes fiction), scripts or poetry, picture books or graphic novels, books with animals as the main protagonists, anything aimed at children under the age of 8, pamphlets or articles.

L0461 Felix de Wolfe

Literary Agency
20 Old Compton Street, London, W1D 4TW
United Kingdom

Tel: +44 (0) 20 7242 5066
Fax: +44 (0) 20 7242 8119

info@felixdewolfe.com

http://www.felixdewolfe.com

Types: Fiction; Scripts
Formats: Film Scripts; Radio Scripts; TV Scripts; Theatre Scripts
Markets: Adult

Send: Query
Don't send: Full text
How not to send: Email

Send query letter with SAE, short synopsis, and CV by post only, unless alternative arrangements have been made with the agency in advance. Quality fiction and scripts only. No nonfiction, children's books, or unsolicited MSS.

Authors: Kris Akabussi; Aileen Gonsalves; Bill MacIlwraith; Paul Todd

Literary Agents: Wendy Scozzaro (*L1246*); Caroline de Wolfe (*L1469*)

L0462 Hannah Fergesen

Literary Agent
United States

Literary Agency: KT Literary (**L0811**)
Professional Body: Association of Authors' Representatives, Inc. (AAR)

L0463 Julie Fergusson

Literary Agent
United Kingdom

http://thenorthlitagency.com/our-friends-in-the-north/
https://twitter.com/julie_fergusson

Literary Agency: The North Literary Agency (**L1040**)

Fiction > *Novels*
  Book Club Fiction; Domestic Suspense; Literary; Psychological Thrillers; Romantic Comedy; Science Fiction; Speculative

Nonfiction > *Nonfiction Books*
  Popular Science; Social Justice

Send: Query; Synopsis; Writing sample; Proposal
How to send: Email

Looking for fiction across a range of genres, particularly psychological thrillers, domestic suspense, sci-fi, near-future speculative, romcoms, reading group and literary fiction. She is interested in nonfiction that explores big ideas in the areas of popular science and social justice.

L0464 Moe Ferrara

Literary Agent
United States

Literary Agency: BookEnds, LLC (**L0155**)

L0465 Samantha Ferris

Literary Agent
United Kingdom

Literary Agency: Knight Features (**L0798**)

L0466 Janet Fillingham

Literary Agent
United Kingdom

Literary Agency: Janet Fillingham Associates (**L0711**)

L0467 Film Rights Ltd in association with Laurence Fitch Ltd

Literary Agency
11 Pandora Road, London, NW6 1TS
United Kingdom
Tel: +44 (0) 20 8001 3040
Fax: +44 (0) 20 8711 3171

information@filmrights.ltd.uk

http://filmrights.ltd.uk

Types: Fiction; Scripts
Formats: Film Scripts; Radio Scripts; TV Scripts; Theatre Scripts
Subjects: Horror
Markets: Adult; Children's

Represents films, plays, and novels, for adults and children.

L0468 Diana Finch

Literary Agent
United States

Literary Agency: Diana Finch Literary Agency (**L0366**)

L0469 Stevie Finegan

Junior Agent
United Kingdom

finegan@zenoagency.com

http://zenoagency.com/news/stevie-finegan/
https://twitter.com/StevieFinegan

Literary Agency: Zeno Agency Ltd (**L1487**)

ADULT
 Fiction
  Graphic Novels: Feminism; LGBTQIA
  Novels: High / Epic Fantasy; Soft Science Fiction
 Nonfiction > *Nonfiction Books*
  Feminism; Mental Health; Politics; Social Issues

CHILDREN'S > **Fiction**
  Early Readers; Middle Grade; Picture Books

Closed to approaches.

L0470 Emma Finn

Literary Agent
United Kingdom

Literary Agency: C+W (Conville & Walsh) (**L0205**)

L0471 Karyn Fischer
Literary Agent
United States

Literary Agency: BookStop Literary Agency, LLC (**L0158**)

L0472 Kara Fitzpatrick
Literary Agent
United Kingdom

Literary Agency: Alan Brodie Representation Ltd (**L0026**)

L0473 Flannery Literary
Literary Agency
1140 Wickfield Court, Naperville, IL 60563-3300
United States
Tel: +1 (630) 428-2682
Fax: +1 (630) 428-2683

jennifer@flanneryliterary.com

http://flanneryliterary.com

Types: Fiction; Nonfiction
Markets: Children's; Young Adult

Send: Query
Don't send: Full text
How to send: Email

Send query by email, with the word "Query" in the subject line. Deals exclusively in children's and young adults' fiction and nonfiction, including picture books. See website for full guidelines.

Literary Agent: Jennifer Flannery (*L0474*)

L0474 Jennifer Flannery
Literary Agent
United States

Literary Agency: Flannery Literary (**L0473**)

L0475 Diana Flegal
Literary Agent
United States

http://hartlineagency.com/agentsandauthors/

Literary Agency: Hartline Literary Agency (**L0618**)

Fiction > *Novels*
Inspirational; Mainstream

How to send: Conferences; By referral

Represents mainstream and inspirational titles. Accepts submissions only from writers she has met face to face at writers conferences or from industry referral.

Authors: Robin Bayne; Robert Cook; Jody Bailey Day; Jamie R. Forth; Ryan Fraser; Barton Goldsmith; Kathy Ide; Danielle Ayers Jones; Eddie Jones; Jayme Mansfield; Linda

Massucci; Karen McSpadden; Elaine W. Miller; Ava Pennington; Cheryl Plato; Mike Plato; Jill Richardson; Sara Sadik; Susan Walley Schlesman; Laurel Shaler; David Stearman; Kimberly Rae Thigpen; Cynthia Watkins; Angela Williams

Authors / Literary Agents: Linda S. Glaz (**L0551**); Patricia Riddle-Gaddis (**L1149**)

L0476 Caitie Flum
Literary Agent
United States

Literary Agency: Liza Dawson Associates (**L0868**)

L0477 Jacqueline Flynn
Literary Agent
United States

Literary Agency: Joelle Delbourgo Associates, Inc. (**L0729**)

L0478 Katherine Flynn
Literary Agent
United States

Literary Agency: Kneerim & Williams (**L0796**)

L0479 Folio Jr.
Literary Agency
United States

https://www.foliojr.com
https://twitter.com/FolioJr
https://www.instagram.com/foliojr/
https://www.facebook.com/FolioJr/

Literary Agency: Folio Literary Management, LLC (**L0480**)

Literary Agent / Vice President: John Cusick (**L0322**)

L0480 Folio Literary Management, LLC
Literary Agency
630 9th Avenue, Suite 1101, New York, NY 10036
United States
Tel: +1 (212) 400-1494
Fax: +1 (212) 967-0977

http://www.foliolit.com
https://www.facebook.com/folio.literary
https://twitter.com/FolioLiterary

Fiction > *Novels*
Commercial; Literary; Upmarket

Nonfiction > *Nonfiction Books*
Memoir; Narrative Nonfiction

Read agent bios on website and decide which agent to approach. Do not submit to multiple agents simultaneously. Each agent has different submission requirements: consult website for details. No unsolicited MSS or multiple submissions.

Affiliated Agents: Ruth Pomerance (**L1106**); Jeff Silberman (**L1275**)

Literary Agencies: Folio Jr. (**L0479**); Harold Ober Associates, Inc. (**L0609**)

Literary Agents: Jan Baumer (**L0101**); Jamie Chambliss (**L0248**); Sonali Chanchani (**L0249**); Dado Derviskadic (**L0359**); Rachel Ekstrom (**L0419**); Michael Harriot (**L0610**); Melissa White (**L1442**)

Literary Agents / Partners: Emily Van Beek (**L0108**); Claudia Cross (**L0311**); Scott Hoffman (**L0655**); Jeff Kleinman (**L0793**); Steve Troha (**L1378**); Frank Weimann (**L1425**)

Literary Agents / Senior Vice Presidents: Erin Niumata (**L1036**); Marcy Posner (**L1109**)

Literary Agents / Vice Presidents: John Cusick (**L0322**); Erin Harris (**L0611**); Katherine Latshaw (**L0828**)

L0481 Emily Forland
Literary Agent
United States

eforland@bromasite.com

Literary Agency: Brandt & Hochman Literary Agents, Inc. (**L0172**)
Professional Body: Association of Authors' Representatives, Inc. (AAR)

ADULT
Fiction
Graphic Novels: General
Novels: Comedy / Humour; Literary
Nonfiction > *Nonfiction Books*
General, and in particular: Biography; Cultural Criticism; Food; History; Memoir; Narrative Nonfiction

YOUNG ADULT > **Fiction** > *Novels*

Send: Query
How to send: Email

L0482 David Forrer
Literary Agent
United States

Literary Agency: InkWell Management (**L0686**)

L0483 Jemima Forrester
Literary Agent
United Kingdom

jemimaforrester@davidhigham.co.uk

https://www.davidhigham.co.uk/agents-dh/jemima-forrester/

Literary Agency: David Higham Associates Ltd (**L0338**)

Fiction > *Novels*
Commercial; Crime; Feminism; High Concept; Historical Fiction; Literary; Psychological Suspense; Speculative; Thrillers; Upmarket; Women's Fiction

Nonfiction > *Nonfiction Books*
Comedy / Humour; Cookery; Feminism;
Lifestyle; Popular Culture

Send: Query; Synopsis; Writing sample
How to send: Email

Authors: Tessa Bickers; Lauren Bravo; Seerut
K. Chawla; Lizzie Daykin; Sarah Daykin;
Sophie Draper; Kat French; Jessica George;
Sarah J. Harris; Deborah Hewitt; Alex
Hutchinson; Beth Lewis; Richard Lumsden;
Deborah O'Donoghue; Alison Percival;
Christina Pishiris; Kohinoor Sahota; Josie
Silver; Michael Stewart; Rose Stokes; Adam
Zmith

L0484 Clare Forster
Literary Agent
Australia

Literary Agency: Curtis Brown (Australia) Pty
Ltd (**L0319**)

L0485 Roz Foster
Literary Agent
United States

Literary Agency: Frances Goldin Literary
Agency, Inc. (**L0492**)

Fiction > *Novels*
Commercial; Contemporary; Historical
Fantasy; Historical Fiction; Literary;
Multicultural; Science Fiction; Speculative;
Upmarket

Nonfiction > *Nonfiction Books*
Current Affairs; Design; History; Memoir;
Politics; Science; Technology

L0486 Ben Fowler
Literary Agent
United Kingdom

ben@abnerstein.co.uk

Literary Agency: Abner Stein (**L0007**)

L0487 Jon Fowler
Literary Agent
United Kingdom

Literary Agency: Peters Fraser + Dunlop
(**L1091**)

L0488 Fox & Howard Literary Agency
Literary Agency
39 Eland Road, London, SW11 5JX
United Kingdom
Tel: +44 (0) 20 7223 9452

enquiries@foxandhoward.co.uk

http://www.foxandhoward.co.uk

Professional Body: The Association of
Authors' Agents (AAA)

Types: Nonfiction
Formats: Reference

Subjects: Biography; Business; Culture;
Health; History; Lifestyle; Personal
Development; Psychology; Spirituality
Markets: Adult

Closed to approaches.

Closed to submissions as at June 2019.
Please check website for current status. Send
query with synopsis and SAE for response.
Small agency specialising in nonfiction that
works closely with its authors. No unsolicited
MSS.

Literary Agents: Chelsey Fox (*L0489*);
Charlotte Howard (*L0669*)

L0489 Chelsey Fox
Literary Agent
United Kingdom

Literary Agency: Fox & Howard Literary
Agency (**L0488**)

L0490 FRA (Futerman, Rose, & Associates)
Literary Agency
91 St Leonards Road, London, SW14 7BL
United Kingdom
Tel: +44 (0) 20 8255 7755

guy@futermanrose.co.uk

http://www.futermanrose.co.uk

Professional Body: The Association of
Authors' Agents (AAA)

Types: Nonfiction; Scripts
Formats: Film Scripts; TV Scripts
Subjects: Business; Entertainment; Music;
Politics; Sport
Markets: Adult

Send: Query
Don't send: Full text
How to send: Email

Handles nonfiction on practically any subject,
but particularly interested in politics, sport,
show business and the music industry. Also
handles scripts for film and television. No
educational textbooks. For nonfiction, send
proposal including chapter breakdown, two or
three sample chapters, and any relevant
biographical detail. For scripts, send sample
episode or section of the script. Accepts
submissions by post (include SAE of return of
work required) or by email with attachments.
See website for full guidelines.

Authors: Jill Anderson; Larry Barker; Nick
Battle; Christian Piers Betley; Tracey
Cheetham; Chengde Chen; Kevin Clarke;
Lesley Crewe; Richard Digance; Peter Dobbie;
Bobby Elliott; Paul Ferris; John French; Susan
George; Keith Gillespie; Stephen Griffin; Paul
Hendy; Terry Ilott; Sara Khan; Jerry Leider;
Sue Lenier; Keith R. Lindsay; Stephen Lowe;
Eric MacInnes; Paul Marsden; Paul Marx;
Tony McAndrew; Tony McMahon; Sir Vartan
Melkonian; Michael Misick; Max Morgan-

Witts; Sir Derek Morris; Peter Murphy; Judge
Chris Nicholson; Antonia Owen; Tom Owen;
Mary O'Hara; Ciarán O'Keeffe; Miriam
O'Reilly; Zoe Paphitis; Liz Rettig; Kenneth G.
Ross; Robin Callender Smith; Rt. Hon Iain
Duncan Smith; Paul Stinchcombe; Felicity Fair
Thompson; Bill Tidy; Mark White; Toyah
Willcox; Simon Woodham; Tappy Wright;
Allen Zeleski

Literary Agents: James Jacob (**L0702**); Guy
Rose (*L1184*)

L0491 Frances Collin Literary Agent
Literary Agency
PO Box 33, Wayne, PA 19087-0033
United States
Tel: +1 (610) 254-0555
Fax: +1 (610) 254-5029

queries@francescollin.com

http://www.francescollin.com

Professional Body: Association of Authors'
Representatives, Inc. (AAR)

Types: Fiction; Nonfiction
Subjects: Autobiography; Culture; Fantasy;
History; Literary; Nature; Science Fiction;
Travel; Women's Interests
Markets: Adult

Send: Query
Don't send: Full text
How to send: Email

Send query by email (no attachments) or by
post with SASE, or IRCs if outside the US. No
queries by phone or fax.

Literary Agent: Frances Collin (*L0289*)

L0492 Frances Goldin Literary Agency, Inc.
Literary Agency
214 W 29th St., Suite 1006, New York, NY
10001
United States

agency@goldinlit.com

http://www.goldinlit.com

Professional Body: Association of Authors'
Representatives, Inc. (AAR)

Types: Fiction; Nonfiction; Poetry;
Translations
Formats: Film Scripts
Subjects: Arts; Autobiography; Commercial;
Crime; Culture; Current Affairs;
Entertainment; History; Legal; Literary;
Nature; Philosophy; Politics; Science; Society;
Sport; Technology; Thrillers; Travel
Markets: Adult; Children's; Young Adult

Send: Query
Don't send: Full text
How to send: Email

Submit to one agent only. See website for specific agent interests and preferred method of approach. No screenplays, romances (or most other genre fiction), and only rarely poetry. No work that is racist, sexist, ageist, homophobic, or pornographic.

Literary Agents: Caroline Eisenmann (**L0418**); Roz Foster (**L0485**); Frances Goldin; Ria Julien (*L0747*); Matt McGowan (**L0955**)

President / Senior Agent: Sam Stoloff (**L1324**)

Senior Agent / Vice President: Ellen Geiger (**L0532**)

L0493 Frances Kelly Agency
Literary Agency
111 Clifton Road, Kingston upon Thames, Surrey, KT2 6PL
United Kingdom
Tel: +44 (0) 20 8549 7830

Professional Body: The Association of Authors' Agents (AAA)

ACADEMIC > **Nonfiction**
Nonfiction Books; *Reference*
ADULT > **Nonfiction**
Nonfiction Books; *Reference*
PROFESSIONAL > **Nonfiction**
Nonfiction Books; *Reference*

Send: Query; Synopsis; Author bio; Self-Addressed Stamped Envelope (SASE)
Don't send: Full text
How to send: Post

Send query with SAE, CV, and synopsis or brief description of work. Scripts handled for existing clients only. No unsolicited MSS.

Literary Agent: Frances Kelly

L0494 Will Francis
Literary Agent
United Kingdom

http://www.janklowandnesbit.co.uk/people/will-francis
https://twitter.com/zcosini

Literary Agency: Janklow & Nesbit UK Ltd (**L0712**)

Fiction > *Novels*: Literary

Nonfiction > *Nonfiction Books*
History; Investigative Journalism; Popular Science

Send: Query; Synopsis; Writing sample
How to send: Email

L0495 Carol Franco
Literary Agent
United States

Literary Agency: Kneerim & Williams (**L0796**)

L0496 Frank Fahy
Literary Agency
5 Barna Village Centre, Seapoint, Galway,

H91 DF24
Ireland
Tel: +353 (0) 86 226 9330

submissions@frank-fahy.com

http://www.frank-fahy.com

Types: Fiction
Markets: Adult; Young Adult

Send: Query
Don't send: Full text
How to send: Email

Costs: Offers services that writers have to pay for.

Handles adult and young adult fiction. No picture books, poetry, or nonfiction. Send query by email with author profile, synopsis, and first three chapters by email. No hard copy submissions.

L0497 Alexandra Franklin
Literary Agent
United States

Literary Agency: Vicky Bijur Literary Agency (**L1402**)

L0498 Fraser Ross Associates
Literary Agency
6/2 Wellington Place, Edinburgh, Scotland, EH6 7EQ
United Kingdom
Tel: +44 (0) 1315 532759

fraserrossassociates@gmail.com

http://www.fraserross.co.uk

Types: Fiction; Nonfiction
Subjects: Commercial; Literary
Markets: Adult; Children's

Send: Query
Don't send: Full text
How to send: Email

Send query by email or by post, including CV, the first three chapters and synopsis for fiction, or a one page proposal and the opening and a further two chapters for nonfiction. For picture books, send complete MS, without illustrations. No poetry, playscripts, screenplays, or individual short stories.

Authors: Jo Allan; Sorrel Anderson; Gill Arbuthnott; Tim Archbold; Alice Balfour; Barroux; Jason Beresford; Thomas Bloor; Ella Burfoot; Jill Calder; Simon Chapman; Judy Cumberbatch; Caroline Deacon; Emily Dodd; Lari Don; Christiane Dorion; Nicole Dryburgh; Jane Eagland; Teresa Flavin; Ciara Flood; Hannah Foley; Vivian French; Joe Friedman; Darren Gate; Roy Gill; Edward Hardy; Diana Hendry; Chris Higgins; Barry Hutchison; J D (Julie) Irwin; Cate James; Ann Kelley; Louise Kelly; Tanya Landman; Kate Leiper; Joan Lennon; Joan Lingard; Janis Mackay; L J Macwhirter; Kasia Matyjaszek; Eilidh Muldoon; Erica Mary Orchard; Judy Paterson;

Helena Pielichaty; Sue Purkiss; Lynne Rickards; Jamie Rix; Karen Saunders; Dugald Steer; Chae Strathie; Kate Wakeling; Rosie Wallace

Literary Agents: Lindsey Fraser (*L0499*); Kathryn Ross (*L1190*)

L0499 Lindsey Fraser
Literary Agent
United Kingdom

Literary Agency: Fraser Ross Associates (**L0498**)

L0500 Stephen Fraser
Literary Agent
United States

Literary Agency: The Jennifer DeChiara Literary Agency (**L0721**)

L0501 Warren Frazier
Literary Agent
United States

Literary Agency: John Hawkins & Associates, Inc. (**L0730**)

L0502 Dawn Frederick
Literary Agent
United States

Literary Agency: Red Sofa Literary (**L1129**)

L0503 Robert Freedman
Literary Agent; President
United States

http://aaronline.org/Sys/PublicProfile/2176681/417813

Literary Agency: Robert A. Freedman Dramatic Agency, Inc. (**L1158**)
Professional Body: Association of Authors' Representatives, Inc. (AAR)

Scripts > *Theatre Scripts*

L0504 Cricket Freeman
Literary Agent
United States

Literary Agency: The August Agency LLC (**L0071**)

L0505 Sarah Joy Freese
Literary Agent
United States

Literary Agency: Wordserve Literary (**L1472**)

L0506 Fresh Books Literary Agency
Literary Agency
United States

matt@fresh-books.com

http://www.fresh-books.com

Types: Nonfiction
Formats: Reference
Subjects: Business; Comedy / Humour;
Design; Finance; Health; How To; Lifestyle;
Personal Development; Photography; Science;
Technology
Markets: Adult

Send: Query
Don't send: Full text
How to send: Email

Handles narrative non-fiction, lifestyle and
reference titles on subjects such as popular
science, technology, health, fitness,
photography, design, computing, gadgets,
social media, career development, education,
business, leadership, personal finance, how-to,
and humour. No fiction, children's books,
screenplays, or poetry. Send query by email.
No attachments. Send further material upon
request only.

Authors: Silviu Angelescu; John Arnold;
Edward Baig; Matt Barton; Gary David
Bouton; Ted Coombs; Dave Crenshaw; Harold
Davis; Michele Davis; Phyllis Davis; Holly
Day; Stephanie Diamond; Kevin Epstein; Mike
Fine; Dan Gookin; Sue Jenkins; Ron Kay;
Rene Kratz; Bill Loguidice; Ajay Malik;
Richard Mansfield; John Mueller; Stephen P.
Olejniczak; Roger C. Parker; Ronda Racha
Penrice; C.P.A. Gail Perry; Jon Phillips; Janet
Rae-Dupree; Meri Raffetto; Andy Rathbone;
Alison Rogers; Swain Scheps; Barry
Schoenborn; Cameron Smith; Barrie Sosinsky;
Christopher Matthew Spencer; Taz Tally; Cliff
Truesdell; Lee Varis; Rich Wagner; Michelle
Waitzman; Tamar Weinberg

Literary Agent: Matt Wagner (*L1411*)

L0507 Claire Friedman

Literary Agent
United States

http://www.inkwellmanagement.com/staff/
claire-friedman

Literary Agency: InkWell Management
(**L0686**)

ADULT
   Fiction > *Novels*: Commercial

   Nonfiction > *Nonfiction Books*: Narrative
   Nonfiction

CHILDREN'S > **Fiction** > *Novels*

YOUNG ADULT > **Fiction** > *Novels*

Send: Query; Writing sample
How to send: In the body of an email

L0508 Fredrica Friedman

Literary Agent

Professional Body: The Agents Round Table
(ART)
Literary Agency: Fredrica S. Friedman and Co.
Inc.

L0509 Jessica Friedman

Literary Agent
United States

https://www.sll.com/our-team

Literary Agency: Sterling Lord Literistic, Inc.
(**L1317**)

Fiction > *Novels*: Literary

Nonfiction > *Nonfiction Books*

Represents literary fiction and nonfiction.
Interested in distinctive voices and writing that
challenges the expected -- stylistically,
formally, or otherwise. Particularly drawn to
incisive, voice-driven writing and
underrepresented narratives.

L0510 Rebecca Friedman

Literary Agent
United States

Literary Agency: Rebecca Friedman Literary
Agency (**L1128**)

L0511 The Friedrich Agency LLC

Literary Agency
United States

mfriedrich@friedrichagency.com

http://www.friedrichagency.com

Types: Fiction; Nonfiction
Subjects: Commercial; Literary
Markets: Adult

Send: Query
Don't send: Full text
How to send: Email

See website for agent bios and individual
contact details, then submit to one by email
only. See website for full guidelines.

Literary Agents: Hannah Brattesani (**L0173**);
Heather Carr (*L0229*); Lucy Carson (*L0233*);
Molly Friedrich (*L0512*)

L0512 Molly Friedrich

Literary Agent
United States

Literary Agency: The Friedrich Agency LLC
(**L0511**)

L0513 Autumn Frisse

Literary Agent
United States

Literary Agency: Prentis Literary (**L1114**)

L0514 Helenka Fuglewicz

Literary Agent
United Kingdom

Literary Agency: Edwards Fuglewicz (**L0408**)

L0515 Full Circle Literary, LLC

Literary Agency
3268 Governor Drive #323, San Diego, CA
92122
United States

info@fullcircleliterary.com

http://www.fullcircleliterary.com

Types: Fiction; Nonfiction
Subjects: Biography; Comedy / Humour;
Contemporary; Crafts; Culture; Current
Affairs; Design; Fantasy; History; How To;
Lifestyle; Literary; Nature; Science Fiction;
Women's Interests
Markets: Adult; Children's; Young Adult

Send: Query
Don't send: Full text

See website for individual agent interests and
submit using online submission system.

Literary Agents: Stefanie Sanchez Von Borstel
(**L0162**); Adriana Dominguez (**L0376**); Nicole
Geiger (**L0533**); Lilly Ghahremani (**L0543**);
Taylor Martindale Kean (**L0768**)

L0516 Eugenie Furniss

Literary Agent

eugeniefurniss@42mp.com

https://www.42mp.com/agents
https://twitter.com/Furniss

Literary Agency: 42 Management and
Production (**L0002**)

Fiction > *Novels*
   Comedy / Humour; Crime; Historical Fiction

Nonfiction > *Nonfiction Books*
   Biography; Finance; Memoir; Politics;
   Popular History

How to send: Email

Drawn to crime in all its guises and historical
fiction. On the nonfiction front seeks
biography and popular history, and politics.

L0517 Louise Fury

Literary Agent
United States

Literary Agency: The Bent Agency (**L0119**)

L0518 The G Agency, LLC

Literary Agency
116 West 23rd Street, 5th floor, New York,
NY 10011
United States
Tel: +1 (718) 664-4505

Literary Agent: Jeff Gerecke (**L0541**)

L0519 Clementine Gaisman

Literary Agent
United Kingdom

Literary Agency: ILA (Intercontinental
Literary Agency) (**L0681**)

L0520 Russell Galen
Literary Agent
United States

Literary Agency: Scovil Galen Ghosh Literary Agency, Inc. (**L1244**)

L0521 Lauren Galit
Literary Agent
United States

Literary Agency: The LKG Agency (**L0869**)

L0522 Gallt & Zacker Literary Agency
Literary Agency
273 Charlton Avenue, South Orange, NJ 07079
United States
Tel: +1 (973) 761-6358

http://www.galltzacker.com

Handles fiction and nonfiction for children, young adults, and adults. See website for submission guidelines and specific agent interests / contact details and approach relevant agent by email.

Literary Agents: Linda Camacho (**L0210**); Erin Casey (**L0238**); Nancy Gallt (**L0523**); Beth Phelan (**L1095**); Marietta B. Zacker (**L1484**)

L0523 Nancy Gallt
Literary Agent
United States

nancy@galltzacker.com

Literary Agency: Gallt & Zacker Literary Agency (**L0522**)

CHILDREN'S > *Fiction*
Middle Grade; Picture Books
YOUNG ADULT
Fiction > *Novels*
Nonfiction > *Nonfiction Books*

How to send: Email

L0524 Natalie Galustian
Literary Agent
United Kingdom

Literary Agency: DHH Literary Agency Ltd (**L0364**)

L0525 Lori Galvin
Literary Agent
Boston
United States

https://aevitascreative.com/agents/
https://querymanager.com/query/QueryLoriGalvin

Literary Agency: Aevitas (**L0019**)

Fiction > *Novels*
General, and in particular: Thrillers; Women's Fiction

Nonfiction > *Nonfiction Books*

Cookery; Personal Development

Send: Author bio; Query; Synopsis; Writing sample; Pitch; Market info
How to send: Query Manager

Represents both adult fiction (especially women's fiction and thrillers) and nonfiction (personal development and cookbooks).

L0526 Karen Gantz
Literary Agent
United States

Literary Agency: Karen Gantz Literary Management (**L0759**)

L0527 Lauren Gardner
Literary Agent
United Kingdom

Literary Agency: Bell Lomax Moreton Agency (**L0110**)

L0528 Rachelle Gardner
Literary Agent
United States

Literary Agency: Books & Such Literary Management (**L0156**)

L0529 Georgia Garrett
Literary Agent
United Kingdom

Literary Agency: Rogers, Coleridge & White Ltd (**L1181**)

L0530 Jennifer Gates
Senior Partner; Literary Agent
United States

https://aevitascreative.com/agents/

Literary Agency: Aevitas (**L0019**)

ADULT
Fiction > *Novels*: Literary

Nonfiction > *Nonfiction Books*
Current Affairs; Memoir; Narrative Nonfiction; Popular Culture

CHILDREN'S > *Fiction* > *Novels*

Send: Author bio; Pitch; Market info; Writing sample
How to send: Online submission system

Represents a range of nonfiction, including narrative and expert-driven works, memoir, current affairs, pop culture, as well as literary fiction and children's books.

L0531 Adam Gauntlett
Literary Agent
United Kingdom

Literary Agency: Peters Fraser + Dunlop (**L1091**)

L0532 Ellen Geiger
Senior Agent; Vice President
United States

https://goldinlit.com/agents/

Literary Agency: Frances Goldin Literary Agency, Inc. (**L0492**)

Fiction > *Novels*
Culture; Historical Fiction; Literary Thrillers; Multicultural

Nonfiction > *Nonfiction Books*
Biography; History; Investigative Journalism; Multicultural; Politics; Psychology; Religion; Social Issues; Women's Issues

Send: Query; Writing sample
How to send: Submittable

Represents a broad range of fiction and non-fiction. She has a lifelong interest in multicultural and social issues embracing change. History, biography, progressive politics, psychology, women's issues, religion and serious investigative journalism are special interests.

In fiction, she loves a good literary thriller, and novels in general that provoke and challenge the status quo, as well as historical and multicultural works. She is drawn to big themes which make a larger point about the culture and times we live in, such as Barbara Kingsolver's Poisonwood Bible. She is not the right agent for New Age, romance, how-to or right-wing politics.

L0533 Nicole Geiger
Literary Agent
United States

https://www.fullcircleliterary.com/submissions/
https://querymanager.com/query/NicoleFCL

Literary Agency: Full Circle Literary, LLC (**L0515**)

CHILDREN'S > *Fiction* > *Graphic Novels*

Represents graphic novels for middle grade and younger only.

L0534 Gelfman Schneider / ICM Partners
Literary Agency
850 Seventh Avenue, Suite 903, New York, NY 10019
United States

mail@gelfmanschneider.com

http://www.gelfmanschneider.com

Professional Body: Association of Authors' Representatives, Inc. (AAR)

Types: Fiction; Nonfiction
Subjects: Autobiography; Commercial; Culture; Current Affairs; History; Literary; Mystery; Politics; Science; Suspense; Thrillers;

Women's Interests
Markets: Adult; Young Adult

Send: Query
Don't send: Full text
How to send: Email

Costs: Author covers sundry admin costs.

Different agents within the agency have different submission guidelines. See website for full details. No screenplays, or poetry.

Literary Agents: Penelope Burns (*L0201*); Jane Gelfman (*L0535*); Heather Mitchell (*L0990*); Deborah Schneider (*L1234*)

L0535 Jane Gelfman
Literary Agent
United States

Literary Agency: Gelfman Schneider / ICM Partners (**L0534**)

L0536 Jonny Geller
Literary Agent
United Kingdom

http://submissions.curtisbrown.co.uk/agents/

Literary Agency: Curtis Brown (**L0318**)

Fiction > *Novels*
  Commercial Women's Fiction; Literary; Thrillers

Nonfiction > *Nonfiction Books*: Journalism

Send: Query; Synopsis; Writing sample
How to send: Online submission system

"I am lucky enough to work with a fantastic range of writers – from authors of first class literary fiction to best selling thriller writers, from ground-breaking journalists to the very best writers in the field of women's commercial fiction – my focus is original fiction from writers who have a distinctive voice."

Associate Agent: Viola Hayden (**L0626**)

L0537 Tara Gelsomino
Literary Agent
United States

Literary Agency: One Track Literary Agency, Inc. (**L1057**)

L0538 Caroline George
Associate Agent
United States

Literary Agency: Cyle Young Literary Elite (**L0323**)

L0539 Georges Borchardt, Inc.
Literary Agency
136 East 57th Street, New York, NY 10022
United States
Tel: +1 (212) 753-5785

anne@gbagency.com

http://www.gbagency.com

Types: Fiction; Nonfiction
Formats: Short Fiction
Subjects: Arts; Biography; Commercial; Current Affairs; History; Literary; Literature; Philosophy; Politics; Religion; Science
Markets: Adult; Young Adult

New York based literary agency founded in 1967. No unsolicited MSS or screenplays.

Literary Agents: Anne Borchardt (*L0159*); Georges Borchardt (*L0160*); Valerie Borchardt (*L0161*); Samantha Shea (*L1262*)

L0540 Georgina Capel Associates Ltd
Literary Agency
29 Wardour Street, London, W1D 6PS
United Kingdom
Tel: +44 (0) 20 7734 2414

georgina@georginacapel.com

http://www.georginacapel.com

Professional Body: The Association of Authors' Agents (AAA)

Types: Fiction; Nonfiction
Formats: Film Scripts; Radio Scripts; TV Scripts
Subjects: Biography; Commercial; History; Literary
Markets: Adult

Send: Query
Don't send: Full text
How to send: Email

Handles general fiction and nonfiction. Send query outlining writing history (for nonfiction, what qualifies you to write your book), with synopsis around 500 words and first three chapters, plus SAE or email address for reply. Submissions are not returned. Mark envelope for the attention of the Submissions Department. Accepts submissions by email, but prefers them by post. Response only if interested, normally within 6 weeks. Film and TV scripts handled for established clients only.

Authors: John Bew; Vince Cable; Daisy Dunn; Lauren Johnson

Literary Agent: Georgina Capel (*L0215*)

L0541 Jeff Gerecke
Literary Agent
United States

gagencyquery@gmail.com
jeff@gagencylit.com

https://www.publishersmarketplace.com/members/jeffg/
http://aaronline.org/Sys/PublicProfile/2176689/417813

Literary Agency: The G Agency, LLC (**L0518**)
Professional Body: Association of Authors' Representatives, Inc. (AAR)

Fiction > *Novels*
  General, and in particular: Commercial; Literary; Mystery

Nonfiction > *Nonfiction Books*
  Biography; Business; Computers; Finance; History; Military History; Popular Culture; Sport; Technology

Send: Query; Writing sample
How to send: Email attachment

I am interested in commercial and literary fiction, as well as serious non-fiction and pop culture. My focus as an agent has always been on working with writers to shape their work for its greatest commercial potential. I provide lots of editorial advice in sharpening manuscripts and proposals before submission.

L0542 Josh Getzler
Literary Agent; Partner
United States

josh@hgliterary.com

https://www.hgliterary.com/josh
https://twitter.com/jgetzler
http://www.publishersmarketplace.com/members/jgetzler/
http://aaronline.org/Sys/PublicProfile/2902758/417813
http://queryme.online/Getzler

Literary Agency: HG Literary (**L0646**)
Professional Body: Association of Authors' Representatives, Inc. (AAR)

ADULT
  Fiction > *Novels*
    Historical Fiction; Mystery; Thrillers; Women's Fiction

  Nonfiction > *Nonfiction Books*
    Business; History; Politics

CHILDREN'S > **Fiction** > *Middle Grade*
  Comedy / Humour; Contemporary

Send: Query; Writing sample
How to send: Query Manager
How not to send: Email

L0543 Lilly Ghahremani
Literary Agent
United States

https://www.fullcircleliterary.com/our-agents/lilly-ghahremani/
https://twitter.com/Wonderlilly

Literary Agency: Full Circle Literary, LLC (**L0515**)

Closed to approaches.

L0544 Anna Ghosh
Literary Agent
United States

Literary Agency: Scovil Galen Ghosh Literary Agency, Inc. (**L1244**)

L0545 Jim Gill
Literary Agent
United Kingdom

jgill@unitedagents.co.uk

https://www.unitedagents.co.uk

Literary Agency: United Agents (**L1389**)

Fiction > *Novels*

Nonfiction > *Nonfiction Books*

Acts for a broad range of both fiction and non-fiction authors writing for the general-trade market, and is always on the look-out for the original and the excellent.

Authors: Ishbel Addyman; Dr Elizabeth Archibald; Joe Bennett; Mark Binelli; Jonathan Blyth; Lawrence Booth; Pete Brown; Christopher Bryant; Barnabas Calder; Justin Cartwright; Tom Chatfield; John Henry Clay; Sean Conway; Nicholas Crane; Emma Dibdin; Dominick Donald; Margaret Drabble; David Hart Dyke; Giles Foden; Tom Gregory; Sudhir Hazareesingh; Eleanor Henderson; Patrick Hennessey; Mark Keating; Yasmin Khan; Jamie Kornegay; Robert Lautner; Thomas Leveritt; Joshua Levine; Matt Lewis; Rebecca Loncraine; Robert Low; Kevin Maher; Liam McIlvanney; Ciarán McMenamin; Steven Merritt Miner; Jonny Owen; Justin Pollard; Tony Pollard; Oliver Poole; James Rebanks; Jasper Rees; Harry Sidebottom; Ian Thomson; Joanna Trollope; Teddy Wayne; James Yorkston

L0546 Elena Giovinazzo
Literary Agent
United States

Literary Agency: Pippin Properties, Inc (**L1101**)

L0547 Brenna Girard
Literary Agent
United States

brenna@carolynjenksagency.com

https://www.carolynjenksagency.com/agent/BRENNA-GIRARD

Literary Agency: Carolyn Jenks Agency (**L0228**)

Nonfiction > *Nonfiction Books*
General, and in particular: Business; Cookery

L0548 The Gislason Agency
Literary Agency
7362 University Avenue NE Ste 120, Fridley, MN 55432
United States
Tel: +1 (763) 220-2983
Fax: +1 (763) 571-1576

http://www.thegislasonagency.com

Fiction > *Novels*

Closed to approaches.

Costs: Offers services that writers have to pay for.

Represented fiction writers, including a mystery author who received critical acclaim in Publishers Weekly. Currently, she will only consider solicited authors. In some instances, she is willing to give people feedback on a writing project for a fee.

Authors: Linda Cook; Terence Faherty; Deborah Woodworth

Literary Agent: Barbara J. Gislason (*L0549*)

L0549 Barbara J. Gislason
Literary Agent
United States

Literary Agency: The Gislason Agency (**L0548**)

L0550 Bill Gladstone
Literary Agent
United States

Literary Agency: Waterside Productions, Inc (**L1418**)

L0551 Linda S. Glaz
Author; Literary Agent
United States

linda@hartlineliterary.com

http://hartlineagency.com/agentsandauthors/
https://www.facebook.com/linda.glaz
https://twitter.com/LindaGlaz

Literary Agency: Hartline Literary Agency (**L0618**)
Professional Body: Advanced Writers and Speakers Association (AWSA)
Literary Agent: Diana Flegal (**L0475**)

Fiction > *Novels*
General, and in particular: Contemporary Romance; Historical Romance; Romance; Romantic Suspense

Nonfiction > *Nonfiction Books*

How to send: Email
How not to send: Post

Looking for nonfiction by experts in their field. In fiction, will consider anything well written, particularly romance, either contemporary, suspense, or historic. No children's or works that include graphic sexuality or profanity.

Authors: Karla Akins; Cindy Amos; Rick Barry; Kate Breslin; Lance Brown; Raquel Byrnes; J'nell Ciesielski; Ben Conlon; Angela Couch; Susan F. Craft; Barbara Ellin Fox; Linda Gilden; Janet Grunst; Hilary Hamblin; Voni Harris; Ann Clark Van Hines; K Denise Holmberg; Dennis Lambert; A. D. Lawrence; Delores Liesner; Chuck Locklear; Ashley Ludwig; Linda Maran; Cheryl Linn Martin; Joy Massenburge; Dale McElhinney; Naomi Musch; Kathleen Neely; Tiffany Nicole; Candice Brooks Patterson; Karen Campbell

Prough; Cindy Regnier; Kathleen Rouser; Colleen Scott; Laura Smith; Patti Stockdale; Elizabeth Summitt; Ken Swarner; Donn Taylor; Evelyn Taylor; Pegg Thomas; Tom Threadgill; Kari Trumbo; Susan L. Tuttle; Jennifer Hough Uhlarik; Hannah Vanderpool; Barbara Warren; Denise Weimer; Karen Wingate; Amie Winningham; Frank V. Yates

L0552 Kerry Glencorse
Literary Agent
United Kingdom

https://www.susannalea.com/team-member/kerry-glencorse/

Literary Agency: Susanna Lea Associates (UK) (**L1337**)

Fiction > *Novels*
Crime; Historical Fiction; Literary; Thrillers; Upmarket Commercial Fiction; Women's Fiction

Nonfiction > *Nonfiction Books*
Cultural History; Memoir; Narrative Nonfiction; Nature; Popular Science; Social History

Send: Query; Synopsis; Writing sample
How to send: Email

Always on the lookout for new talent, especially in the areas of literary and upmarket commercial fiction; well-written genre fiction, including crime, thrillers, women's fiction, and historical. And on the non-fiction side: memoir, narrative non-fiction, popular science, natural science, social and cultural history.

L0553 Emily Glenister
Associate Agent
United Kingdom

eg.submission@dhhliteraryagency.com

http://www.dhhliteraryagency.com/emily-glenister.html
http://www.twitter.com/emily_glenister

Literary Agency: DHH Literary Agency Ltd (**L0364**)

Fiction > *Novels*
Book Club Fiction; Commercial; Crime; Ghost Stories; Gothic; Historical Fiction; Thrillers; Upmarket Women's Fiction

Send: Synopsis; Writing sample
How to send: Email

Looking for reading group and commercial novels, as well as diverse / own voices, with an emphasis on crime / thriller, upmarket women's fiction with a unique hook, post-eighteenth century history, and gothic novels / ghost stories.

Authors: S.V. Leonard; Reagan Lee Ray

L0554 Stacey Glick
Literary Agent
United States

Literary Agency: Dystel, Goderich & Bourret LLC (**L0399**)

L0555 Global Lion Intellectual Property Management, Inc.

Literary Agency
PO BOX 669238, Pompano Beach, FL 33066
United States
Tel: +1 (754) 222-6948

queriesgloballionmgt@gmail.com

http://www.globallionmanagement.com

Types: Fiction; Nonfiction
Subjects: Spirituality
Markets: Adult

Send: Query
Don't send: Full text
How to send: Email

Specialises in nonfiction, spirituality, and generally anything that "improvement" for the world and human race. Looks for cutting-edge authors of both fiction and nonfiction with global marketing and motion picture/television production potential. Authors must not only have a great book and future, but also a specific game-plan of how to use social media to grow their fan base. Send query by email only with synopsis, up to 20 pages if available (otherwise, chapter synopsis), author bio, and any social media outlets. See website for full details.

L0556 Miriam Goderich

Literary Agent
United States

Literary Agency: Dystel, Goderich & Bourret LLC (**L0399**)

L0557 Susannah Godman

Literary Agent
United Kingdom

Literary Agency: Lutyens and Rubinstein (**L0887**)

L0558 David Godwin

Literary Agent
United Kingdom

Literary Agency: David Godwin Associates (**L0337**)

L0559 Ellen Goff

Associate Agent
United States

ellen@hgliterary.com

https://www.hgliterary.com/ellen

Literary Agency: HG Literary (**L0646**)

YOUNG ADULT > Fiction
  Graphic Novels: General
  Novels: General, and in particular: Ghost Stories; Gothic; Historical Fiction

Interested in all genres and formats of YA, especially anything spooky, historical fiction, and graphic novels. She has a soft spot for Shakespeare as well as southern gothic stories that remind her of her home state of Kentucky.

L0560 Barry Goldblatt

Literary Agent
United States

Literary Agency: Barry Goldblatt Literary Agency, Inc. (**L0094**)

L0561 Jennifer Goloboy

Literary Agent
United States

Literary Agency: Donald Maass Literary Agency (**L0380**)

L0562 Tara Gonzalez

Literary Agent
United States

Literary Agency: Erin Murphy Literary Agency, Inc. (**L0433**)

L0563 The Good Literary Agency

Literary Agency
United Kingdom

info@thegoodliteraryagency.org

https://www.thegoodliteraryagency.org

Types: Fiction; Nonfiction
Markets: Adult; Children's; Young Adult

Send: Query
Don't send: Full text

Focused on discovering, developing and launching the careers of writers of colour, disability, working class, LGBTQ+ and anyone who feels their story is not being told in the mainstream. Writers must be born or resident in Britain. No poetry, plays, or screenplays. See website for full guidelines and to submit via online form.

L0564 Bill Goodall

Literary Agent
United Kingdom

Literary Agency: A for Authors (**L0003**)

L0565 Howard Gooding

Literary Agent
United Kingdom

Literary Agency: Judy Daish Associates Ltd (**L0746**)

L0566 Irene Goodman

Literary Agent
United States

Literary Agency: Irene Goodman Literary Agency (IGLA) (**L0688**)

L0567 Graham Maw Christie Literary Agency

Literary Agency
37 Highbury Place, London, N5 1QP
United Kingdom
Tel: +44 (0) 7971 268342

submissions@grahammawchristie.com

http://www.grahammawchristie.com

Professional Body: The Association of Authors' Agents (AAA)

Types: Nonfiction
Formats: Reference
Subjects: Autobiography; Business; Comedy / Humour; Cookery; Crafts; Gardening; Health; History; Lifestyle; Personal Development; Philosophy; Science
Markets: Adult; Children's

Send: Query
Don't send: Full text
How to send: Email

No fiction, poetry, or scripts. Send query with one-page summary, a paragraph on the contents of each chapter, your qualifications for writing it, details of your online presence, market analysis, what you could do to help promote your book, and a sample chapter or two. Prefers approaches by email.

Literary Agents: Jennifer Christie (*L0264*); Jane Graham Maw (*L0941*)

L0568 Stacey Graham

Literary Agent
United States

stacey@threeseaslit.com

https://www.threeseasagency.com/copy-of-michelle-grajkowski
http://querymanager.com/Stacey3Seas

Literary Agency: 3 Seas Literary Agency (**L0001**)

ADULT
  Fiction > *Novels*: Romantic Comedy

  Nonfiction > *Nonfiction Books*

CHILDREN'S > Fiction > *Middle Grade*
  Comedy / Humour; Ghost Stories

How to send: Query Manager

Currently looking to expand her list with snappy Rom-Coms, hilarious/spooky middle grade, and weird nonfiction.

L0569 Susan Graham

Literary Agent
United States

https://www.einsteinliterary.com/staff/
http://aaronline.org/Sys/PublicProfile/52451502/417813

Literary Agency: Einstein Literary Management (**L0415**)

Professional Body: Association of Authors' Representatives, Inc. (AAR)

ADULT > **Fiction** > *Novels*
General, and in particular: Fantasy; LGBTQIA; Science Fiction

CHILDREN'S > **Fiction** > *Novels*
General, and in particular: Fantasy; LGBTQIA; Science Fiction

YOUNG ADULT
Fiction > *Novels*
General, and in particular: Fantasy; LGBTQIA; Science Fiction

Nonfiction > *Nonfiction Books*

Looking for children's and young adult fiction in all genres, but their favorite books are often science fiction and fantasy, especially written with a queer lens. They also enjoy picture books and represent graphic novels in all age categories and in all genres. They're particularly interested in friendships and sibling narratives, and monster protagonists are always a plus. They're looking for a good nonfiction or two for children or teens but don't know about what. For adult prose, they prefer genre fiction, and monster protagonists are still a plus. Works by and about marginalized voices are welcome and encouraged.

L0570 Michelle Grajkowski
Literary Agent
United States

michelle@threeseaslit.com

https://www.threeseasagency.com/michelle-grajkowski
http://querymanager.com/Michelle3Seas
http://aaronline.org/Sys/PublicProfile/2176701/417813

Literary Agency: 3 Seas Literary Agency (**L0001**)
Professional Body: Association of Authors' Representatives, Inc. (AAR)

ADULT
Fiction > *Novels*
Romance; Women's Fiction

Nonfiction > *Nonfiction Books*

CHILDREN'S > **Fiction** > *Middle Grade*

How to send: Query Manager

Primarily represents romance, women's fiction, young adult and middle grade fiction along with select nonfiction projects with a terrific message. She is currently looking for fantastic writers with a voice of their own.

Authors: Katie MacAlister; Cathy McDavid; Kerrelyn Sparks; C.L. Wilson

L0571 Janet Kobobel Grant
Literary Agent
United States

Literary Agency: Books & Such Literary Management (**L0156**)

L0572 Olivia Gray
Literary Agent
United Kingdom

Literary Agency: Independent Talent Group Ltd (**L0683**)

L0573 Donna Greaves
Literary Agent
United Kingdom

Literary Agency: Jo Unwin Literary Agency (**L0728**)

Closed to approaches.

L0574 Christine Green
Literary Agent
United Kingdom

L0575 Kathryn Green
Literary Agent
United States

Literary Agency: Kathryn Green Literary Agency, LLC (**L0766**)

L0576 Vivien Green
Literary Agent
United Kingdom

Literary Agency: Sheil Land Associates Ltd (**L1263**)

L0577 Louise Greenberg
Literary Agent
United Kingdom

Literary Agency: Louise Greenberg Books Ltd (**L0877**)

L0578 Greene & Heaton Ltd
Literary Agency
37 Goldhawk Road, London, W12 8QQ
United Kingdom
Tel: +44 (0) 20 8749 0315

submissions@greeneheaton.co.uk
info@greeneheaton.co.uk

http://www.greeneheaton.co.uk
https://twitter.com/greeneandheaton

Professional Body: The Association of Authors' Agents (AAA)

Does not want:

> **CHILDREN'S** > **Fiction** > *Picture Books*

Send: Query; Synopsis; Writing sample
Don't send: Full text
How to send: Email
How not to send: Post

Send query by email only, including synopsis and three chapters or approximately 50 pages. No submissions by post. No response unless interested. Handles all types of fiction and nonfiction, but no scripts or children's picture books.

Author Estates: The Estate of Julia Darling; The Estate of Sarah Gainham

Authors: Anthony Anaxagorou; Bridget; Lily Dunn; Helen Giltrow; Beatrice Hitchman; David Howard; Charles Jennings; Joan; Gabrielle Kimm; Sonya Kudei; Eric Lindstrom; Paul Keers: Sediment; Sarai Walker

Literary Agents: Holly Faulks (**L0452**); Carol Heaton (**L0631**); Judith Murray (**L1015**); Antony Topping (**L1374**); Laura Williams (**L1451**); Claudia Young (**L1481**)

L0579 The Greenhouse Literary Agency
Literary Agency

https://www.greenhouseliterary.com
https://www.facebook.com/The-Greenhouse-Literary-Agency-359292813053/?ref=nf

CHILDREN'S > **Fiction**
Chapter Books; *Graphic Novels*; *Middle Grade*; *Picture Books*
YOUNG ADULT > **Fiction** > *Novels*

How to send: Query Manager

Transatlantic literary agency with agents in the US and UK. See individual agent details for more info.

Literary Agents: Sarah Davies (**L0342**); Chelsea Eberly (**L0404**); Polly Nolan

L0580 Katie Greenstreet
Literary Agent
United Kingdom

Literary Agency: C+W (Conville & Walsh) (**L0205**)

L0581 Rima Greer
Literary Agent
United States

Literary Agency: Above the Line Agency (**L0009**)

L0582 Evan Gregory
Literary Agent
United States

agent@ethanellenberg.com

https://ethanellenberg.com
https://twitter.com/#!/EvanJGregory
http://aaronline.org/Sys/PublicProfile/2309906/417813

Literary Agency: Ethan Ellenberg Literary Agency (**L0437**)

Professional Body: Association of Authors' Representatives, Inc. (AAR)

ADULT
  Fiction > *Novels*
    Fantasy; Horror; Mystery; Science Fiction; Thrillers; Women's Fiction

  Nonfiction > *Nonfiction Books*
    Arts; Biography; Business; Cookery; Culture; Current Affairs; Entertainment; Family; Films; Food and Drink; Health; History; Memoir; Nature; Parenting; Photography; Politics; Popular Culture; Science; Sport; Technology; Travel

CHILDREN'S > **Fiction**
  Middle Grade; Picture Books
YOUNG ADULT > **Fiction** > *Novels*

Send: Query; Synopsis; Writing sample
How to send: Email
How not to send: Post

L0583 Jonathan Gregory
Literary Agent
United Kingdom

jonathan@antonyharwood.com

http://antonyharwood.com/jonathan-gregory/

Literary Agency: Antony Harwood Limited (**L0058**)

Nonfiction > *Nonfiction Books*
  Biography; History; Medicine; Philosophy; Politics; Science

L0584 Alexandra Grese
Literary Agent
United States

Literary Agency: Freak Unleashed

L0585 Jennifer Grimaldi
Literary Agent
United States

Literary Agency: Chalberg & Sussman (**L0245**)

L0586 Katie Grimm
Literary Agent
United States

Literary Agency: Don Congdon Associates, Inc. (**L0378**)

L0587 Hattie Grunewald
Literary Agent
United Kingdom

https://www.theblairpartnership.com/our_people/hattie-grunewald-literary-agent/

Literary Agency: The Blair Partnership (**L0138**)

Fiction > *Novels*
  Book Club Fiction; Commercial; Crime; Historical Fiction; Thrillers; Upmarket; Women's Fiction

Nonfiction > *Nonfiction Books*
  Lifestyle; Personal Development

L0588 Robbie Guillory
Junior Agent; Editor; Proofreader
United Kingdom

https://katenashlit.co.uk/people/
https://twitter.com/RobbieGuillory

Literary Agency: Kate Nash Literary Agency (**L0764**)

Fiction > *Novels*
  Commercial; Crime; Historical Fiction; Psychological Thrillers; Science Fiction

Nonfiction > *Nonfiction Books*: Nature

Send: Query; Synopsis; Writing sample
How to send: In the body of an email

Looking for outstanding writing across a number of genres: stand-out commercial fiction, science fiction that focuses on communities and relationships whilst the galaxy looks after itself, crime and psychological thrillers with a difference, gripping historical dramas, and beautiful nonfiction with roots in the natural world.

L0589 Robert Guinsler
Senior Agent
United States

https://www.sll.com/our-team

Literary Agency: Sterling Lord Literistic, Inc. (**L1317**)

Nonfiction > *Nonfiction Books*

Send: Query; Synopsis; Writing sample
How to send: Online submission system

L0590 Kanishka Gupta
Literary Agent
India

kanishka@writersside.com
kanishka500@gmail.com

https://www.facebook.com/kanishka.gupta.754?fref=ts
https://twitter.com/kan_writersside

Literary Agency / Editorial Service: Writer's Side (**L1473**)

L0591 Gurman Agency, LLC
Literary Agency
United States
Tel: +1 (212) 749-4618

assistant@gurmanagency.com

http://www.gurmanagency.com

Professional Body: Writers Guild of America (WGA)

Scripts > *Theatre Scripts*

How to send: By referral

Represents playwrights, directors, choreographers, composers and lyricists. New clients by referral only, so prospective clients should seek a referral rather than querying. No queries accepted.

Literary Agent: Susan Gurman (*L0592*)

L0592 Susan Gurman
Literary Agent
United States

Literary Agency: Gurman Agency, LLC (**L0591**)

L0593 Allan Guthrie
Literary Agent
United Kingdom

http://thenorthlitagency.com/our-friends-in-the-north/

Literary Agency: The North Literary Agency (**L1040**)

Fiction > *Novels*: Crime

Send: Query; Synopsis; Writing sample; Proposal
How to send: Email

Has worked in the book trade since 1996 and has been a literary agent since 2005. He is also an award-winning novelist, freelance editor and former publisher. His main area of interest is crime fiction.

L0594 Julie Gwinn
Literary Agent
United States

Literary Agency: The Seymour Agency (**L1254**)

L0595 Katie Haines
Literary Agent
United Kingdom

Literary Agency: The Agency (London) Ltd (**L0021**)

L0596 Serene Hakim
Literary Agent
United States

https://www.pandeliterary.com/about-pandeliterary
https://twitter.com/serenemaria
http://aaronline.org/Sys/PublicProfile/52119398/417813

Literary Agency: Ayesha Pande Literary (**L0073**)
Professional Body: Association of Authors' Representatives, Inc. (AAR)

ADULT
  Fiction > *Novels*
    Feminism; International; LGBTQIA; Middle East

  Nonfiction > *Nonfiction Books*

Feminism; International; LGBTQIA;
Middle East

YOUNG ADULT
Fiction > *Novels*
Fantasy; Feminism; International;
LGBTQIA; Middle East; Realistic; Science
Fiction

Nonfiction > *Nonfiction Books*
Feminism; International; LGBTQIA;
Middle East

Closed to approaches.

L0597 Tessa Emily Hall
Literary Agent
United States

Literary Agency: Cyle Young Literary Elite
(**L0323**)

L0598 Bill Hamilton
Literary Agent
United Kingdom

https://amheath.com/agents/bill-hamilton/

Literary Agency: A.M. Heath & Company
Limited, Author's Agents (**L0004**)

Fiction > *Novels*

Nonfiction > *Nonfiction Books*

Agency Assistant / Associate Agent: Florence
Rees (**L1134**)

L0599 Matthew Hamilton
Literary Agent
United Kingdom

Literary Agency: Aitken Alexander Associates
(**L0025**)

L0600 Samar Hammam
Literary Agent
United Kingdom

Literary Agency: Rocking Chair Books
(**L1173**)

L0601 The Hanbury Agency
Literary Agency
Suite 103, 88 Lower Marsh, London, SE1 7AB
United Kingdom

enquiries@hanburyagency.com

http://www.hanburyagency.com
https://www.facebook.com/HanburyAgency/
https://twitter.com/hanburyagency
https://www.instagram.com/
the_hanbury_agency/

Professional Body: The Association of
Authors' Agents (AAA)

Fiction > *Novels*

Nonfiction > *Nonfiction Books*
Current Affairs; History; Popular Culture

Closed to approaches.

Closed to submissions as at August 2019.
Check website for current status.

No film scripts, plays, poetry, books for
children, self-help. Not accepting fantasy,
science fiction, or misery memoirs. Send query
by post with brief synopsis, first 30 pages
(roughly), and your email address and phone
number. No submissions by email. Do not
include SAE, as no material is returned.
Response not guaranteed, so assume rejection
if no reply after 8 weeks.

Authors: George Alagiah; Simon Callow; Jane
Glover; Bernard Hare; Imran Khan; Judith
Lennox; Katie Price

Literary Agent: Margaret Hanbury (*L0602*)

L0602 Margaret Hanbury
Literary Agent
United Kingdom

Literary Agency: The Hanbury Agency
(**L0601**)

L0603 Erik Hane
Literary Agent
United States

Literary Agency: Red Sofa Literary (**L1129**)

L0604 Jori Hanna
Junior Agent
United States

Literary Agency: Cyle Young Literary Elite
(**L0323**)

L0605 Carrie Hannigan
Literary Agent; Partner
United States

carrie@hgliterary.com

https://www.hgliterary.com/carrie
http://queryme.online/Hannigan

Literary Agency: HG Literary (**L0646**)
Professional Body: Association of Authors'
Representatives, Inc. (AAR)

ADULT > **Nonfiction** > *Nonfiction Books*

CHILDREN'S
Fiction
Graphic Novels: General
Novels: Comedy / Humour; Contemporary;
Fantasy
Nonfiction > *Nonfiction Books*

How to send: Query Manager

L0606 Hardman & Swainson
Literary Agency
S86, New Wing, Somerset House, Strand,
London, WC2R 1LA
United Kingdom
Tel: +44 (0) 20 3701 7449

submissions@hardmanswainson.com

http://www.hardmanswainson.com
https://twitter.com/HardmanSwainson

Professional Body: The Association of
Authors' Agents (AAA)

Send: Full text; Synopsis
How to send: Email
How not to send: Post

Agency launched June 2012 by former
colleagues at an established agency. Welcomes
submissions of fiction and nonfiction, but no
submissions by post. See website for full
submission guidelines.

Authors: Jennifer Barclay; Lilly Bartlett; Jackie
Bateman; Alex Bell; Anna Bell; Jon Bounds;
Oggy Boytchev; Cathy Bramley; Matt Brolly;
Elizabeth Brooks; Isabelle Broom; Tracy
Buchanan; Meg Cabot; Ellie Campbell;
Elisabeth Carpenter; Simon Cheshire; Abby
Clements; Helen Cox; Joshua Cunningham;
Stuart David; Daniel M. Davis; Lisa
Dickenson; Miranda Dickinson; Carol
Donaldson; Charlotte Duckworth; Simon
David Eden; Rachel Edwards; Miranda
Emmerson; Miguel Farias; Helen Fields; Rosie
Fiore; Carrie Hope Fletcher; Giovanna
Fletcher; Harry Freedman; Michele Gorman;
Vanessa Greene; Kirsty Greenwood; Alastair
Gunn; Caroline Hulse; Cass Hunter; Dinah
Jefferies; Ishani Kar-Purkayastha; Beth
Kempton; Holly Kingston; Lucy Lawrie; Peter
Laws; Christine Lehnen; Malinda Lo; Kevin
Macneil; Katie Marsh; S R Masters; Cressida
Mclaughlin; Ali Mcnamara; Susy Mcphee;
Siobhan Miller; Kr Moorhead; Ann Morgan;
Julien Musolino; Nigel Packer; Lauren Price;
Martina Reilly; Caroline Roberts; Nick
Russell-Pavier; Nikola Scott; Catherine
Simpson; Emma Slade; Danny Smith; Gareth
Southwell; Fiona Sussman; Sarah Tierney; Liz
Trenow; Sarah Turner; Rebecca Wait; Louise
Walters; Victoria Walters; Sue Watson; Alison
White; Catherine Wikholm; Samantha Wilson;
Laura Ziepe

Literary Agents: Therese Coen; Hannah
Ferguson; Caroline Hardman (*L0607*); Joanna
Swainson (**L1343**)

L0607 Caroline Hardman
Literary Agent
United Kingdom

submissions@hardmanswainson.com
caroline@hardmanswainson.com

http://www.hardmanswainson.com/agents/
caroline-hardman/
https://twitter.com/LittleHardman

Literary Agency: Hardman & Swainson
(**L0606**)

Fiction > *Novels*
Commercial; Crime; Historical Fiction;
Literary; Suspense; Thrillers; Upmarket
Commercial Fiction

Nonfiction > *Nonfiction Books*

Current Affairs; Environment; Feminism; Food; Health; Human Biology; Lifestyle; Medicine; Memoir; Narrative Nonfiction; Popular Psychology; Popular Science; Wellbeing

Send: Synopsis; Full text
How to send: Email
How not to send: Post

Authors: Katie Allen; Jennifer Barclay; Tracy Buchanan; Ellie Campbell; Elisabeth Carpenter; HS Chandler; Emma Christie; Daniel M. Davis; Andrew Doig; Charlotte Duckworth; Miranda Emmerson; Miguel Farias; Louise Fein; Helen Fields; Eliese Colette Goldbach; Michele Gorman; Paula Greenlees; Alastair Gunn; Caroline Hulse; Cass Hunter; Dinah Jefferies; Helen Joyce; Ishani Kar-Purkayastha; Beth Kempton; Ann Morgan; Jenni Nuttall; Elisabeth Parry; Julia Parry; Laura Pashby; Vanessa Potter; Martina Reilly; Nikola Scott; Joanne Sefton; Miss South; Kathleen Stock; John Tregoning; Liz Trenow; Rebecca Wait; Alison White; Catherine Wikholm; Ryan Wilson; Eleanor Wood

L0608 Esmond Harmsworth

Literary Agent; President
United States

https://aevitascreative.com/agents/

Literary Agency: Aevitas (**L0019**)

Fiction > *Novels*
Crime; Historical Fiction; Horror; Literary; Mystery; Suspense; Thrillers

Nonfiction > *Nonfiction Books*
Business; Culture; History; Politics; Psychology; Science

How to send: Online submission system

Represents serious nonfiction books on topics such as politics, psychology, culture, business, history and science. For fiction, he represents literary fiction, mystery and crime, thriller, suspense and horror, and historical novels.

L0609 Harold Ober Associates, Inc.

Literary Agency
United States

http://www.foliolit.com/harold-ober-associates

Literary Agency: Folio Literary Management, LLC (**L0480**)

Types: Fiction; Nonfiction
Markets: Adult; Children's

L0610 Michael Harriot

Literary Agent
United States

michael@foliolit.com

http://foliolit.com/michael-harriot

Literary Agency: Folio Literary Management, LLC (**L0480**)

Fiction > *Novels*
Fantasy; Science Fiction

Nonfiction > *Nonfiction Books*
Comic Books; Commercial; Films; Music; Narrative Nonfiction; Popular Culture; Prescriptive Nonfiction; Sport

Send: Proposal; Writing sample
How to send: Email attachment

L0611 Erin Harris

Literary Agent; Vice President
United States

eharris@foliolitmanagement.com

https://www.publishersmarketplace.com/members/eharris/
https://twitter.com/ErinHarrisFolio

Literary Agency: Folio Literary Management, LLC (**L0480**)

ADULT
Fiction
Novels: Book Club Fiction; Family Saga; Folklore, Myths, and Legends; Historical Fiction; Literary Mystery; Literary; Speculative; Suspense
Short Fiction: General

Nonfiction
Essays: General
Nonfiction Books: Feminism; High Concept; Memoir; Narrative Nonfiction; Social Issues
YOUNG ADULT > **Fiction** > *Novels*
Contemporary; Fantasy; Speculative; Suspense

Send: Query; Writing sample
How to send: In the body of an email

L0612 Joy Harris

Literary Agent
United States

Literary Agency: Joy Harris Literary Agency, Inc. (**L0742**)

L0613 Samara Harris

Literary Agent
United States

Literary Agency: Robert A. Freedman Dramatic Agency, Inc. (**L1158**)

L0614 Nick Harrison

Literary Agent
United States

Literary Agency: Wordserve Literary (**L1472**)

L0615 Jim Hart

Literary Agent
United States

jim@hartlineliterary.com

http://hartlineagency.com/agentsandauthors/

Literary Agency: Hartline Literary Agency (**L0618**)

Fiction > *Novels*
Contemporary Romance; Historical Romance; Romantic Suspense; Science Fiction; Speculative; Suspense; Thrillers; Women's Fiction

Nonfiction > *Nonfiction Books*
Business; Christian Living; Leadership; Parenting; Self Help; Social Issues

Send: Query; Proposal
How to send: Email attachment

Interested in nonfiction on the topics of Christian living, church growth, leadership, business, social issues, parenting, and some self-help. Nonfiction writers will need to show a strong platform in their area of expertise. Not looking at memoirs or devotionals at this time.

Looking at select fiction in these categories: suspense/thrillers, romance (contemporary, historical, suspense, Amish), women's fiction, and some speculative and sci-fi. Fiction writers should possess a strong and growing platform. He is not looking at children's or middle-grade fiction at this time.

Not looking at proposals for books that have been previously self-published. Please do not send proposals for books that include graphic language and sex.

Authors: David Awbrey; Diane Awbrey; David Awbrey Matt Aynes; Diane Awbrey Matt Aynes; Matt Aynes; Bethany Baker; Mark Baker; Sandra Barnes; Chaim Bentorah; Robin Bertram; Amy C. Blake; Laura C. Brandenberg; Suzanne Bratcher; Shanna Brickell; Kristi Burton Brown; Terri Clark; Hope Toler Dougherty; F.R. D'Onofrio; Jacqueline Gillam Fairchild; Huey Freeman; Justin Gabriel; Anna Elizabeth Gant; Heidi Gaul; Chandler Gerber; PJ Gover; John Gray; Glenn Haggerty; Brandy Heineman; Chaka Heinz; Kim Taylor Henry; Bill Higgs; Dena Hobbs; Jason Hobbs; Angela M. Hutchinson; Dalton Jantzen; Vicki Jantzen; Gary Keel; Troy M. Kennedy; Ken Koopman; Anita Knight Kuhnley; R.J. Larson; Joseph Max Lewis; Marco Lupis; Kathi Macias; Paul Marshall; Vicki McCollum; Stephenia McGee; Jairo de Oliveira; Kevin Ott; Ava Pennington; R.K. Pillai; Leigh Powers; Daniel Rhee; Penny Richards; Dominic Rivera; Mary Selzer; James Shupp; Neil Silverberg; Greg Singleton; Martha Singleton; Adam Smith; Richard Spillman; Buck Storm; Robert C. Stroud; Jill Thomas; C Kevin Thompson; Mary Kay Tuberty; Hope Welborn; Beth E. Wescott; Karol Whaley; Jessica White; Zillah Williams; Beth Ann Ziarnik

L0616 Joyce A. Hart

Literary Agent; President
United States

joyce@hartlineliterary.com

http://hartlineliteraryagency.blogspot.com

Literary Agency: Hartline Literary Agency (**L0618**)

Fiction > *Novels*: Inspirational

Over 35 years of experience marketing and promoting books. A pioneer of selling high quality fiction to the inspirational market.

Authors: Christy Barritt; Lorraine Beatty; Molly Noble Bull; Peggy Byers; Daniel Carl; Michael Carl; Dorothy Clark; David Clarke; Ace Collins; Dawn Crandall; Charles Dodgen; Lena Nelson Dooley; Birdie Etchison; Suzanne Fisher; Suzanne Woods Fisher; Lisa Godfrees; Jeenie Gordon; Anne Greene; Pamela Griffin; Eleanor Gustafson; Ann Guyer; Lisa Harris; Sandra M. Hart; Rebecca Jepson; Melanie M. Jeschke; Mary Johnson; Jane Kirkpatrick; Zoe M. McCarthy; Rebekah Montgomery; Pola Marie Muzyka; Darrel Nelson; Melissa Ohden; Susan Titus Osborne; Carrie Fancett Pagels; Sam D. Pakan; Susan J. Reinhardt; Beverly Rodgers; Tom Rodgers; Rita A. Schulte; Stacie Ruth Stoelting; Ward Tanneberg; Diana Taylor; Dorothy Valcarcel; Margorie Vawter; Jacqueline Wheelock; Nancy Willich; Linda Winn; Courtney Young

L0617 Glen Hartley

Literary Agent
United States

L0618 Hartline Literary Agency

Literary Agency
123 Queenston Drive, Pittsburgh, PA 15235-5429
United States
Tel: +1 (412) 829-2483

http://www.hartlineliterary.com

Fiction > *Novels*

Nonfiction > *Nonfiction Books*

Costs: Offers services that writers have to pay for.

Specialises in Christian bookseller market, and particularly interested in adult fiction, nutritional, business, devotional, and self-help. No short fiction, screenplays, scripts, poetry, magazine articles, science fiction, fantasy, extraordinary violence, unnecessary profanity, gratuitous sexuality, or material that conflicts with the Christian worldview. Probably not the right agency for literary fiction, either. See website for detailed submission guidelines.

Note that this agency also offers literary services, which may be considered a conflict of interests.

Author: David E. Clarke

Author / Literary Agent: Cyle Young (**L1482**)

Authors / Literary Agents: Linda S. Glaz (**L0551**); Patricia Riddle-Gaddis (**L1149**)

Literary Agent / President: Joyce A. Hart (**L0616**)

Literary Agents: Diana Flegal (**L0475**); Jim Hart (**L0615**)

L0619 Harvey Klinger, Inc

Literary Agency
300 West 55th Street, Suite 11V, New York, NY 10019
United States
Tel: +1 (212) 581-7068

queries@harveyklinger.com

http://www.harveyklinger.com

Professional Body: Association of Authors' Representatives, Inc. (AAR)

Types: Fiction; Nonfiction
Formats: Film Scripts; TV Scripts
Subjects: Adventure; Autobiography; Business; Comedy / Humour; Commercial; Contemporary; Cookery; Crafts; Crime; Culture; Current Affairs; Design; Fantasy; Health; History; Horror; How To; Lifestyle; Literary; Literature; Media; Medicine; Music; Mystery; Personal Development; Politics; Psychology; Romance; Science; Science Fiction; Spirituality; Sport; Suspense; Technology; Thrillers; Travel; Westerns; Women's Interests
Markets: Adult; Children's; Young Adult

Send: Query
Don't send: Full text
How to send: Email

Costs: Author covers sundry admin costs.

Send query by email. No submissions by post. Do not query more than one agent at the agency at a time. See website for individual agent interests and email addresses. No screenplays, or queries by phone or fax. See website for full submission guidelines.

Literary Agents: David Dunton (**L0397**); Harvey Klinger (**L0794**); Wendy Levinson (**L0851**); Rachel Ridout (**L1150**); Andrew Somberg (**L1301**)

L0620 Hilary Harwell

Literary Agent
United States

Literary Agency: KT Literary (**L0811**)

L0621 Antony Harwood

Literary Agent
United Kingdom

Literary Agency: Antony Harwood Limited (**L0058**)

L0622 Shannon Hassan

Literary Agent
United States

Literary Agency: Marsal Lyon Literary Agency LLC (**L0925**)

L0623 Susan Hawk

Literary Agent
United States

http://www.upstartcrowliterary.com/agent/susan-hawk/
https://twitter.com/@susanhawk

Literary Agency: Upstart Crow Literary (**L1394**)

CHILDREN'S
   Fiction
      Chapter Books; *Middle Grade*; *Picture Books*
   Nonfiction > *Nonfiction Books*

TEEN > **Fiction** > *Novels*

YOUNG ADULT > **Fiction** > *Novels*

L0624 Anne Hawkins

Literary Agent
United States

Literary Agency: John Hawkins & Associates, Inc. (**L0730**)

L0625 Molly Ker Hawn

Literary Agent
United Kingdom

http://www.thebentagency.com/molly-ker-hawn
http://www.twitter.com/mollykh
https://www.publishersmarketplace.com/members/mkhawn

Literary Agency: The Bent Agency (UK) (**L0118**)

ADULT > **Nonfiction** > *Nonfiction Books*
Intersectional Feminism; Modern History; Popular Culture

CHILDREN'S
   Fiction > *Middle Grade*
   Nonfiction > *Nonfiction Books*

YOUNG ADULT > **Fiction** > *Novels*

Closed to approaches.

I'm looking for middle grade and young adult fiction that's inventive, well-crafted, and rich with emotion. I'm also interested in non-fiction for readers ages 8–18. I like wit, but not snark; I prefer books that lean more toward literary than commercial, but of course, my perfect book neatly bridges the two. The fiction on my list all has a strong sense of authentic place, whether real or imaginary; I'm not the right agent for books with animal protagonists.

I also represent select non-fiction projects for adults. I'm interested in intersectional feminism, popular culture, and accessible modern history.

L0626 Viola Hayden

Associate Agent
United Kingdom

http://submissions.curtisbrown.co.uk/agents/

Literary Agency: Curtis Brown (**L0318**)
Literary Agent: Jonny Geller (**L0536**)

Fiction > *Novels*

Nonfiction > *Nonfiction Books*

Send: Query; Synopsis; Writing sample
How to send: Online submission system

I am looking for confident writing that puts me at ease from the first page; a captivating voice or character, an exciting style, an unusual structure, an original premise or fresh take. A book that can't be replicated. If you have written a book like that – fiction or non-fiction – then it's on my wish list.

L0627 Josephine Hayes
Literary Agent
United Kingdom

josephinesubmissions@
theblairpartnership.com

https://www.theblairpartnership.com/
our_people/josephine-hayes/
https://twitter.com/josephine_hayes

Literary Agency: The Blair Partnership
(**L0138**)

CHILDREN'S > **Fiction**
Chapbook: Comedy / Humour
Middle Grade: General, and in particular: Adventure; Comedy / Humour; Low Fantasy; Mystery
Novels: Commercial
Picture Books: General

YOUNG ADULT > **Fiction**
Chapbook: Comedy / Humour
Novels: General, and in particular: Romance

How to send: Email

Naturally gravitates towards quality middle-grade fiction, especially a good mystery or adventure with a dash of light fantasy (nothing high fantasy), or something whacky with a great sense of humour. In teen and YA fiction she loves an anti-hero, and is always keen to see strong young female characters taking centre stage. She's after a standout YA romance or something with strong relationships and characters who you fall in love with and think about even when you're not reading. Across 7+ to YA she's looking for humorous chapter books with series potential, particularly for readers at the younger end. She's also searching for children's author/illustrators for 2-7+ with a contemporary, quirky style and non-rhyming picture book texts.

L0628 David H. Headley
Literary Agent; Managing Director
United Kingdom

http://www.dhhliteraryagency.com/david-h-headley.html
https://twitter.com/davidhheadley

Literary Agency: DHH Literary Agency Ltd
(**L0364**)

Fiction > *Novels*
General, and in particular: Crime; Romance; Thrillers

L0629 Duncan Heath
Literary Agent
United Kingdom

Literary Agency: Independent Talent Group Ltd (**L0683**)

L0630 Rupert Heath
Literary Agent
United Kingdom

Literary Agency: Rupert Heath Literary Agency (**L1202**)

L0631 Carol Heaton
Literary Agent
United Kingdom

http://greeneheaton.co.uk/agents/carol-heaton/

Literary Agency: Greene & Heaton Ltd
(**L0578**)

Fiction > *Novels*

Nonfiction > *Nonfiction Books*
Biography; Current Affairs; Gardening; Health; History; Travel

Closed to approaches.

Author Estate: The Estate of P.D. James

Authors: Stephen Anderton; Lewis Chester; Helen Craig; Charles Elliott; Michael Frayn; Richard Jenkyns

L0632 Catherine Hedrick
Literary Agent
United States

Literary Agency: The Purcell Agency, LLC
(**L1118**)

L0633 Grace Heifetz
Literary Agent
Australia

Literary Agency: Curtis Brown (Australia) Pty Ltd (**L0319**)

L0634 Helen Zimmermann Literary Agency
Literary Agency
55 Riverwalk Place, New York, NY 07093
United States

Submit@ZimmAgency.com

http://www.zimmagency.com

Professional Body: Association of Authors' Representatives, Inc. (AAR)

Types: Fiction; Nonfiction
Subjects: Autobiography; Comedy / Humour;

Cookery; Culture; Health; History; How To; Lifestyle; Literary; Music; Mystery; Nature; Science; Spirituality; Sport; Suspense; Technology; Thrillers; Women's Interests
Markets: Adult

Send: Query
Don't send: Full text
How to send: Email

Particularly interested in health and wellness, relationships, popular culture, women's issues, lifestyle, sports, and music. No poetry, science fiction, horror, or romance. Prefers email queries, but no attachments unless requested. Send pitch letter – for fiction include summary, bio, and first chapter in the body of the email.

Literary Agent: Helen Zimmermann (*L1490*)

L0635 Jenny Heller
Literary Agent
United Kingdom

Literary Agency: Robertson Murray Literary Agency (**L1163**)

L0636 Herman Agency Inc.
Literary Agency
350 Central Park West, New York, NY 10025
United States
Tel: +1 (212) 749-4907

ronnie@hermanagencyinc.com

https://www.hermanagencyinc.com

Types: Fiction; Nonfiction
Markets: Children's; Young Adult

Closed to approaches.

Costs: Offers services that writers have to pay for.

Represents fiction and nonfiction for children and young adults, including picture books and middle grade books, educational books and supplementary materials, children's toys, magazines, cartoons, licensed characters, stationery, advertising, and editorial illustrations. Not taking on any new clients.

Literary Agents: Katia Herman (*L0639*);
Ronnie Ann Herman (*L0640*)

L0637 Deborah Levine Herman
Literary Agent
United States

Literary Agency: The Jeff Herman Agency, LLC (**L0717**)

L0638 Jeff Herman
Literary Agent
United States

Literary Agency: The Jeff Herman Agency, LLC (**L0717**)

L0639 **Katia Herman**
Literary Agent
United States

Literary Agency: Herman Agency Inc. (**L0636**)

L0640 **Ronnie Ann Herman**
Literary Agent
United States

Literary Agency: Herman Agency Inc. (**L0636**)

L0641 **Saritza Hernandez**
Literary Agent
United States

Literary Agency: Corvisiero Literary Agency

Closed to approaches.

L0642 **Jenny Herrera**
Literary Agent
United States

Literary Agency: David Black Literary Agency
(**L0336**)

L0643 **Dan Herron**
Literary Agent
United Kingdom

Literary Agency: Peters Fraser + Dunlop
(**L1091**)

L0644 **Andrew Hewson**
Literary Agent; Company Director
United Kingdom

http://www.johnsonandalcock.co.uk/andrew-hewson

Literary Agency: Johnson & Alcock (**L0732**)

Closed to approaches.

L0645 **Jenny Hewson**
Literary Agent
United Kingdom

Literary Agency: Rogers, Coleridge & White
Ltd (**L1181**)

L0646 **HG Literary**
Literary Agency
United States

https://www.hgliterary.com

Associate Agents: Jon Cobb (**L0284**); Ellen
Goff (**L0559**)

Literary Agent / Vice President: Soumeya
Bendimerad Roberts (**L1162**)

Literary Agents: Victoria Wells Arms (**L0063**);
Julia Kardon (**L0758**); Rhea Lyons (**L0894**)

Literary Agents / Partners: Josh Getzler
(**L0542**); Carrie Hannigan (**L0605**)

L0647 **hhb agency ltd**
Literary Agency
62 Grafton Way, London, W1T 5DW
United Kingdom
Tel: +44 (0) 20 7405 5525

http://www.hhbagency.com
https://twitter.com/hhbagencyltd

Professional Body: The Association of
Authors' Agents (AAA)

Fiction > *Novels*

Nonfiction
Illustrated Books: General
Nonfiction Books: Biography; Comedy /
Humour; Cookery; Crafts; Current Affairs;
Entertainment; Food; History; Memoir;
Politics; Popular Culture; Science; Sport

Closed to approaches.

Represents nonfiction writers, particularly in
the areas of journalism, history and politics,
travel and adventure, contemporary
autobiography and biography, books about
words and numbers, popular culture and quirky
humour, entertainment and television,
business, family memoir, food and cookery.
Also handles commercial fiction. Not
accepting unsolicited submissions as at
September 2019.

Literary Agents: Heather Holden-Brown
(**L0659**); Elly James (**L0705**)

L0648 **Emily Hickman**
Literary Agent
United Kingdom

Literary Agency: The Agency (London) Ltd
(**L0021**)

L0649 **Sophie Hicks**
Literary Agent
United Kingdom

sophie@sophiehicksagency.com

http://www.sophiehicksagency.com/
sophiehicks

Literary Agency: Sophie Hicks Agency
(**L1303**)

ADULT
Fiction > *Novels*
Nonfiction > *Nonfiction Books*

CHILDREN'S > **Fiction** > *Middle Grade*

YOUNG ADULT > **Fiction** > *Novels*

Does not want:

Fiction > *Novels*: Women's Fiction

L0650 **Hill Nadell Literary
Agency**
Literary Agency
6442 Santa Monica Blvd, Suite 201, Los

Angeles, CA 90038
United States
Tel: +1 (310) 860-9605
Fax: +1 (323) 380-5206

queries@hillnadell.com

http://www.hillnadell.com

Types: Fiction; Nonfiction
Subjects: Autobiography; Commercial;
Cookery; Culture; Current Affairs; Health;
History; Legal; Literary; Nature; Politics;
Science; Thrillers; Women's Interests
Markets: Adult; Young Adult

Send: Query
Don't send: Full text
How to send: Email

Costs: Author covers sundry admin costs.

Handles current affairs, food, memoirs and
other narrative nonfiction, fiction, thrillers,
upmarket women's fiction, literary fiction,
genre fiction, graphic novels, and occasional
young adult novels. No scripts or screenplays.
Accepts queries both by post and by email. See
website for full submission guidelines.

Literary Agent: Dara Hyde (*L0680*)

President: Bonnie Nadell

L0651 **Sam Hiyate**
*Literary Agent; President; Chief Executive
Officer*
Canada

Literary Agency: The Rights Factory (**L1151**)

Associate Agent / Author: Cecilia Lyra
(**L0895**)

Authors: Oscar Allueva; Ho Che Anderson;
Michel Basilières; Margot Berwin; Varda
Burstyn; Dave Butler; Lila Cecil; Timothy
Christian; Elaine Dewar; Oonagh Duncan;
Norine Dworkin-McDaniel; Benjamin Errett;
John Farndon; Sara Flemington; Debbie Fox;
Patricia Fulton; Pat Giles; Rupinder Gill; Jesse
Gilmour; Peter Goddard; Lee Matthew
Goldberg; Shinan Govani; Lee Gowan;
Alexandra Grigorescu; Kamal Gupta; Nicole
Hackett; Denise Hearn; Alex Huntley; Cole
Imperi; Chris Johns; Sam Juric; Andrew
Kaufman; Charlotte Joyce Kidd; Michelle
Kim; Sohan Koonar; Arkadi Kuhlmann; David
Layton; David Leach; Barbra Leslie; Claire
Letemendia; Emily Lipinski; Anneke Lucas;
Kiirsten May; Maureen Medved; Mark Milke;
Elana Millman; Nathaniel G Moore; Sally
Moore; Hal Niedzviecki; Rebecca Nison; Brad
Orsted; Kathryn Paulsen; Nick Pengelley;
Katie Peyton; Bruce Philp; Barbara Radecki;
Greg Rhyno; Alexandra Risen; Lynne
Schmidt; John Semley; Leslie Shimotakahara;
David Skuy; Robert Earl Stewart; Stephen
Stohn; Jonathan Tepper; Diane Terrana; Chris
Turner; Joanne Vannicola; Alex Varricchio;
Maurice Vellekoop; Willow Verkerk; Cory
Vitiello; Andy Walker; Kay Walker; Imogen

Lloyd Webber; Jessica Westhead; John Windsor; Showey Yazdanian; E. Paul Zehr; Yvette d'Entremont

L0652 Victoria Hobbs
Literary Agent
United Kingdom

https://amheath.com/agents/victoria-hobbs/
http://twitter.com/victoriajhobbs

Literary Agency: A.M. Heath & Company Limited, Author's Agents (**L0004**)

Fiction > *Novels*
General, and in particular: Crime; Post-Apocalyptic; Thrillers

Nonfiction > *Nonfiction Books*
General, and in particular: Food; Health; Narrative Nonfiction; Nature; Politics

Agency Assistant: Jessica Lee

L0653 Gail Hochman
Literary Agent
Brandt & Hochman Literary Agents, Inc., 1501 Broadway, Suite 2310, New York, NY 10036
United States

ghochman@bromasite.com

Literary Agency: Brandt & Hochman Literary Agents, Inc. (**L0172**)
Professional Body: Association of Authors' Representatives, Inc. (AAR)

ADULT
Fiction > *Novels*: Literary

Nonfiction > *Nonfiction Books*
General, and in particular: Literary Memoir

CHILDREN'S > **Fiction** > *Novels*

Send: Query
How to send: Email

L0654 Samuel Hodder
Literary Agent
United Kingdom

Literary Agency: Blake Friedmann Literary Agency Ltd (**L0139**)

L0655 Scott Hoffman
Literary Agent; Partner
United States

shoffman@foliolitmanagement.com

https://www.foliolit.com/agents-1/scott-hoffman

Literary Agency: Folio Literary Management, LLC (**L0480**)

Nonfiction > *Nonfiction Books*
Business; Fitness; Health; History; Psychology; Social Issues; Wellbeing

Send: Query; Writing sample
How to send: In the body of an email
How not to send: Email attachment

Send query by email with first ten pages. Assume rejection if no response within six weeks.

L0656 Markus Hoffmann
Literary Agent
United States

Literary Agency: Regal Hoffmann & Associates LLC (**L1136**)

L0657 Deborah Hofmann
Literary Agent
United States

Literary Agency: David Black Literary Agency (**L0336**)

L0658 Christina Hogrebe
Literary Agent
United States

Literary Agency: Jane Rotrosen Agency (**L0709**)

L0659 Heather Holden-Brown
Literary Agent
United Kingdom

heather@hhbagency.com

Literary Agency: hhb agency ltd (**L0647**)

L0660 Joyce Holland
Literary Agent
United States

Literary Agency: D4EO Literary Agency (**L0325**)

L0661 Holroyde Cartey
Literary Agency
United Kingdom

http://www.holroydecartey.com

Professional Body: The Association of Authors' Agents (AAA)

Handles fiction and nonfiction for children of all ages, including picture books. Also represents illustrators. Welcomes submissions from debut and established authors and illustrators. Send query by email only, with cover letter, synopsis, and full ms as separate Word file attachments. See website for individual agent details and interests and approach one agent only. Aims to respond to every submission, within six weeks.

Literary Agents: Claire Cartey (**L0235**); Penny Holroyde (**L0662**)

L0662 Penny Holroyde
Literary Agent
United Kingdom

penny@holroydecartey.com

https://www.holroydecartey.com/about.html
https://www.holroydecartey.com/submissions.html

Literary Agency: Holroyde Cartey (**L0661**)

ADULT > **Fiction** > *Novels*

CHILDREN'S > **Fiction** > *Novels*

NEW ADULT > **Fiction** > *Novels*

YOUNG ADULT > **Fiction** > *Novels*

Send: Synopsis; Full text
How to send: Email attachment

L0663 Mike Hoogland
Literary Agent
United States

Literary Agency: Dystel, Goderich & Bourret LLC (**L0399**)

L0664 Kate Hordern
Literary Agent
United Kingdom

kate@khla.co.uk

https://twitter.com/katehordern

Literary Agency: Kate Hordern Literary Agency (**L0763**)

ADULT
Fiction > *Novels*
General, and in particular: Commercial; Crime; Historical Fiction; Literary; Psychological Suspense; Speculative; Upmarket Women's Fiction

Nonfiction > *Nonfiction Books*
History; Memoir

CHILDREN'S > **Fiction** > *Middle Grade*

L0665 Sarah Hornsley
Literary Agent
United States

Literary Agency: The Bent Agency (**L0119**)

L0666 Erin Hosier
Literary Agent
United States

Literary Agency: Dunow, Carlson & Lerner Agency (**L0395**)

L0667 Bob Hostetler
Literary Agent
United States

Literary Agency: The Steve Laube Agency (**L1318**)

L0668 Amanda Fitzalan Howard
Literary Agent
United Kingdom

Literary Agency: AHA Talent Ltd (**L0022**)

L0669 Charlotte Howard
Literary Agent
United Kingdom

Literary Agency: Fox & Howard Literary Agency (**L0488**)

L0670 Mandy Hubbard
Literary Agent
United States

Literary Agency: Emerald City Literary Agency (**L0428**)

L0671 Amy Hughes
Literary Agent
United States

Literary Agency: Dunow, Carlson & Lerner Agency (**L0395**)

L0672 Edward Hughes
Literary Agent
United Kingdom

Literary Agency: Linda Seifert Management (**L0857**)

L0673 Greg Hunt
Literary Agent
United Kingdom

Literary Agency: Independent Talent Group Ltd (**L0683**)

L0674 Jemima Hunt
Literary Agent
United Kingdom

L0675 Hunter Profiles
Literary Agency
London
United Kingdom

info@hunterprofiles.com

http://www.hunterprofiles.com

Fiction > *Novels*: Commercial

Nonfiction > *Nonfiction Books*: Commercial

Send: Query; Author bio; Synopsis; Writing sample
How to send: Email
How not to send: Post

We specialise in commercial and narrative fiction and nonfiction. We only accept proposals by email. See website for submission guidelines.

Author / Literary Agent / Publisher: Humfrey Hunter (**L0676**)

L0676 Humfrey Hunter
Literary Agent; Publisher; Author
United Kingdom

https://www.silvertailbooks.com/author/humfrey-hunter/

Literary Agency: Hunter Profiles (**L0675**)
Book Publisher: Silvertail Books (**P0812**)

A former journalist and public relations consultant who is now a publisher and literary agent.

L0677 Alexis Hurley
Literary Agent
United States

Literary Agency: InkWell Management (**L0686**)

L0678 Margot Maley Hutchison
Literary Agent
United States

Literary Agency: Waterside Productions, Inc (**L1418**)

L0679 Annie Hwang
Literary Agent
United States

https://twitter.com/AnnieAHwang
https://www.publishersmarketplace.com/members/hwangan/

Literary Agency: Ayesha Pande Literary (**L0073**)

Fiction > *Novels*: Literary

Nonfiction > *Nonfiction Books*: Narrative Nonfiction

Send: Pitch; Author bio; Synopsis; Writing sample
How to send: Online submission system

Represents voice-driven literary fiction and select nonfiction. In particular, she gravitates toward subversive, genre-inflected literary fiction and impactful mission-driven narrative nonfiction that explores and grapples with the complex, fundamental truths of our world.

L0680 Dara Hyde
Literary Agent
United States

Literary Agency: Hill Nadell Literary Agency (**L0650**)

L0681 ILA (Intercontinental Literary Agency)
Literary Agency
5 New Concordia Wharf, Mill Street, London, SE1 2BB
United Kingdom
Tel: +44 (0) 20 7379 6611

ila@ila-agency.co.uk

http://www.ila-agency.co.uk

Professional Body: The Association of Authors' Agents (AAA)

ADULT
   Fiction in Translation > *Novels*

Nonfiction in Translation > *Nonfiction Books*

CHILDREN'S > **Fiction in Translation** > *Novels*
   Closed to approaches.

Handles translation rights only for, among others, the authors of LAW Ltd, London; Harold Matson Co. Inc., New York; PFD, London. Submissions accepted via client agencies and publishers only – no submissions from writers seeking agents.

Literary Agents: Sam Edenborough (*L0407*); Clementine Gaisman (*L0519*); Nicki Kennedy (*L0776*); Jenny Robson (*L1171*); Katherine West (*L1434*)

L0682 Harry Illingworth
Literary Agent
United Kingdom

Literary Agency: DHH Literary Agency Ltd (**L0364**)

L0683 Independent Talent Group Ltd
Literary Agency
40 Whitfield Street, London, W1T 2RH
United Kingdom
Tel: +44 (0) 20 7636 6565

writersubmissions@independenttalent.com

http://www.independenttalent.com

Scripts
   Film Scripts; Radio Scripts; TV Scripts; Theatre Scripts

Send: Full text
How to send: Email

Specialises in scripts and works in association with agencies in Los Angeles and New York. No submissions from North America.

Literary Agents: Roxana Adle (*L0018*); Oliver Azis (*L0077*); Anwar Chentoufi (*L0258*); Francesca Devas (*L0360*); Alec Drysdale (*L0389*); Humphrey Elles-Hill (*L0425*); Olivia Gray (*L0572*); Duncan Heath (*L0629*); Greg Hunt (*L0673*); Jago Irwin (*L0694*); Georgia Kanner (*L0757*); Paul Lyon-Maris (*L0892*); Michael McCoy (*L0951*); Jennie Miller (*L0986*); Ikenna Obiekwe (*L1051*); Will Peterson (*L1092*); Lyndsey Posner (*L1108*); Sue Rodgers (*L1178*); Laura Rourke (*L1194*); Alex Rusher (*L1207*); Paul Stevens (*L1319*); Jessica Stewart (*L1323*); Jessica Sykes (*L1350*); Jack Thomas (*L1363*); Sarah Williams (*L1452*); Hugo Young (*L1483*)

L0684 Fiona Inglis
Literary Agent
Australia

Literary Agency: Curtis Brown (Australia) Pty Ltd (**L0319**)

L0685 Ink and Colors Ltd

Literary Agency
Casella postale 10947, Cpd Milano Isola,
20110 Milano
Italy
Tel: +44 (0) 20 7558 8374

http://www.inkandcolors.com

ADULT

Fiction > *Novels*
General, and in particular: Commercial;
Ethnic; Fantasy; Mystery; Romance;
Science Fiction; Thrillers; Women's
Fiction

Nonfiction > *Nonfiction Books*
General, and in particular: Adventure;
Biography; Cookery; Crime; Current
Affairs; Health; Memoir; New Age;
Popular Culture; Psychology; Science;
Spirituality

CHILDREN'S > **Fiction**
Novels; *Picture Books*

Send: Query; Full text; Self-Addressed
Stamped Envelope (SASE)
How to send: Post; Email
How not to send: Email attachment

Costs: Offers services that writers have to pay
for.

International agency with offices in UK and
Italy, representing Publishing Houses, Authors
and Illustrators all over the world. On our
website you'll find the submission guide and
all information.

Accepts submissions by post with SASE or
queries by email (no attachments).

firstwriter.com note: This agency submitted
their details for inclusion in our database in
January 2007. Upon receiving a negative
feedback comment in June 2007 they have
made demands that we remove the negative
comment and have also made threats of legal
action. We have offered to post their response
to the negative comment, but this has only
been met by further threats of legal action.

Literary Agent: Andrea Sabbadini

L0686 InkWell Management

Literary Agency
521 Fifth Avenue, 26th Floor, New York, NY
10175
United States
Tel: +1 (212) 922-3500
Fax: +1 (212) 922-0535

submissions@inkwellmanagement.com

http://www.inkwellmanagement.com

Types: Fiction; Nonfiction
Subjects: Business; Comedy / Humour;
Commercial; Contemporary; Crime; Current
Affairs; Finance; Health; History; Literary;
Medicine; Mystery; Personal Development;
Psychology; Thrillers
Markets: Adult

Send: Query
Don't send: Full text
How to send: Email

Accepts submissions in all genres, but no
screenplays. Send query by email with up to
two sample chapters. No large attachments.
Response not guaranteed. Response within two
months if interested. See website for full
guidelines.

Literary Agents: Stephen Barbara (*L0086*);
Lyndsey Blessing (*L0143*); William Callahan
(*L0209*); Michael V. Carlisle (*L0221*); Sharon
Chudnow; Catherine Drayton (*L0385*); Naomi
Eisenbeiss (**L0417**); David Forrer (*L0482*);
Claire Friedman (**L0507**); Emma Gougeon;
Alexis Hurley (*L0677*); Nathaniel Jacks
(*L0698*); Phoebe Low; George Lucas (*L0881*);
Jessica Mileo (*L0982*); Christina Miller
(**L0985**); Michael Mungiello (*L1008*);
Jacqueline Murphy (*L1013*); Kristin van
Ogtrop (*L1053*); Charlie Olsen (*L1054*);
Richard Pine (*L1100*); Eliza Rothstein
(**L1192**); Jessie Thorsted (*L1370*); Maria
Whelan (**L1437**); Jenny Witherell (*L1465*);
Kimberly Witherspoon (*L1466*)

L0687 InterSaga

Literary Agency
237 St Helier Avenue, Morden, Surrey, SM4
6JH
United Kingdom
Tel: +44 (0) 7534 013597

anna@intersaga.co.uk

http://www.intersaga.co.uk

Types: Fiction; Nonfiction; Poetry; Scripts
Formats: Reference
Subjects: Adventure; Autobiography;
Commercial; Contemporary; Drama;
Experimental; Fantasy; Literary; Literary
Criticism; Romance; Satire; Science Fiction;
Suspense; Thrillers; Traditional; Women's
Interests
Markets: Adult; Children's; Young Adult

Send: Full text
How to send: Email

A literary agency that started in the heart of
Chiswick. The managing director is a former
bookseller and bookshop manager. You can
read more on the website. All genres are
welcome. We look forward to hearing from
you!

Authors: Jane Clamp; Susan Lee Kerr; Kate
Vick

L0688 Irene Goodman Literary Agency (IGLA)

Literary Agency
27 West 24th St., Suite 804, New York, NY
10010
United States

irene.queries@irenegoodman.com

http://www.irenegoodman.com

Professional Body: Association of Authors'
Representatives, Inc. (AAR)

Types: Fiction; Nonfiction
Subjects: Autobiography; Beauty;
Commercial; Contemporary; Cookery; Culture;
Design; Fantasy; Fashion; History; Horror;
Lifestyle; Literary; Mystery; Politics;
Romance; Science; Science Fiction; Society;
Suspense; Thrillers; Women's Interests
Markets: Adult; Children's; Young Adult

Send: Query
Don't send: Full text
How to send: Email

Select specific agent to approach based on
details given on website (specific agent email
addresses on website). Send query by email
only with synopsis, bio, and first ten pages in
the body of the email. No poetry, inspirational
fiction, screenplays, or children's picture
books. Response only if interested. See website
for further details.

Literary Agents: Irene Goodman (*L0566*);
Miriam Kriss (*L0809*); Victoria Marini
(*L0920*); Kim Perel (*L1082*); Barbara Poelle
(*L1105*); Whitney Ross (*L1191*)

L0689 Amy Ireson

Literary Agent
United Kingdom

Literary Agency: The Narrow Road Company
(**L1021**)

L0690 Dan Ireson

Literary Agent
United Kingdom

Literary Agency: The Narrow Road Company
(**L1021**)

L0691 James Ireson

Literary Agent
United Kingdom

Literary Agency: The Narrow Road Company
(**L1021**)

L0692 Richard Ireson

Literary Agent
United Kingdom

richardireson@narrowroad.co.uk

Literary Agency: The Narrow Road Company
(**L1021**)

Closed to approaches.

Do not approach directly. Approaches should
be sent to the agency rather than individual
agents.

L0693 Iris Blasi

Literary Agent
United States

iris@carolmannagency.com

https://www.carolmannagency.com/iris-blasi
https://twitter.com/IrisBlasi
https://www.instagram.com/irisblasi

Literary Agency: Carol Mann Agency (**L0225**)

Nonfiction > *Nonfiction Books*
  Biography; Cultural Criticism; Current
  Affairs; Environment; Feminism; History;
  Intersectional Feminism; Memoir; Narrative
  Nonfiction; Nature; Politics; Popular Culture;
  Science; Social Justice; Sustainable Living

Send: Query; Author bio; Synopsis; Writing
sample
How to send: In the body of an email
How not to send: Post

L0694 Jago Irwin

Literary Agent
United Kingdom

Literary Agency: Independent Talent Group
Ltd (**L0683**)

L0695 Isabel White Literary Agent

Literary Agency
United Kingdom
Tel: +44 (0) 20 3070 1602

query.isabelwhite@googlemail.com

http://www.isabelwhite.co.uk

Types: Fiction; Nonfiction
Markets: Adult

Closed to approaches.

Selective one-woman agency, not taking on
new clients as at October 2018.

Literary Agent: Isabel White (*L1441*)

L0696 J. de S. Associates, Inc.

Literary Agency
9 Shagbark Road, South Norwalk, CT 06854
United States
Tel: +1 (203) 838-7571
Fax: +1 (203) 866-2713

jdespoel@aol.com

http://www.jdesassociates.com

Types: Fiction; Nonfiction
Subjects: Commercial; Literary
Markets: Adult

Send: Query
Don't send: Full text
How to send: Email

Welcomes brief queries by post and by email,
but no samples or other material unless
requested.

Literary Agent: Jacques de Spoelberch (*L1307*)

L0697 Jabberwocky Literary Agency

Literary Agency
49 West 45th Street, 12th Floor North, New
York, NY 10036
United States
Tel: +1 (917) 388-3010
Fax: +1 (917) 388-2998

queryeddie@awfulagent.com

http://awfulagent.com

Types: Fiction; Nonfiction
Subjects: Fantasy; History; Literary; Science;
Science Fiction
Markets: Adult; Children's; Young Adult

Send: Query
Don't send: Full text
How to send: Email

Handles a broad range of fiction and nonfiction
intended for general audiences, but no series
romance or poetry. Book-length material only.
Also considers graphic novels and comics.
Send query by post with SASE or IRC, or by
email. No queries by phone or by fax. See
website for full guidelines.

Authors: Tim Akers; K. C. Alexander; Dave
Bara; Edo Van Belkom; Marie Brennan;
Mayer Alan Brenner; Peter V. Brett; Jack
Campbell; Adam-Troy Castro; A. Bertram
Chandler; Louis Charbonneau; Myke Cole;
Jason Denzel; William C. Dietz; Frederic S.
Durbin; K. Eason; David Louis Edelman;
Mickey Eisenberg; Brenda English; Alex
Erickson; V. M. Escalada; Nancy Farmer;
Michael Garrett; Randall Garrett; Jeff Gelb;
Michael Ghiglieri; Simon R. Green; Gil
Griffin; Mike Grosso; Auston Habershaw;
Charlaine Harris; Jason Heller; John Hemry;
Grady Hendrix; Jim C. Hines; Mark Hodder;
Del Howison; Tanya Huff; Sylvia Izzo Hunter;
Gregory Scott Katsoulis; Marjorie Kellogg;
Toni L. P. Kelner; Kathleen Kimmel; R.A.
Lafferty; Keith Laumer; Mary Soon Lee;
Meyer Levin; Erin Lindsey; Scott Mackay;
Violette Malan; Michael Mammay; Ari
Marmell; Kate Alice Marshall; Nick Martell;
Michael Mccollum; Scott Meyer; Elizabeth
Moon; Bryce Moore; John Moore; Sharon
Moore; Dan Moren; Silvia Moreno-Garcia;
E.C. Myers; Daniel José Older; Joshua
Palmatier; Stuart Palmer; Suzanne Palmer;
Janci Patterson; Leigh Perry; Chen Qiufan;
Ellery Queen; Lilliam Rivera; Brandon
Sanderson; Michael Schiefelbein; Rick
Shelley; Julie Dean Smith; Jon Sprunk;
Rochelle Staab; Eric James Stone; Michael J.
Sullivan; Denise Grover Swank; Benjamin
Tate; E.L. Tettensor; Elaine Viets; Judy
Wearing; Jeri Westerson; Alison Wilgus;
Walter Jon Williams

Literary Agents: Joshua Bilmes (*L0133*); Lisa
Rodgers (*L1177*); Eddie Schneider (*L1235*)

L0698 Nathaniel Jacks

Literary Agent
United States

Literary Agency: InkWell Management
(**L0686**)

L0699 Eleanor Jackson

Literary Agent
United States

Literary Agency: Dunow, Carlson & Lerner
Agency (**L0395**)

L0700 Jennifer Jackson

Literary Agent
United States

Literary Agency: Donald Maass Literary
Agency (**L0380**)

L0701 Lisa Jackson

Literary Agent
United States

Literary Agency: Alive Literary Agency
(**L0030**)

L0702 James Jacob

Literary Agent
United Kingdom

james@futermanrose.co.uk

http://www.futermanrose.co.uk/aboutus.html

Literary Agency: FRA (Futerman, Rose, &
Associates) (**L0490**)

Scripts
  Film Scripts; TV Scripts

Send: Writing sample
How to send: Post; Email attachment

Handles drama script submissions for film and
television.

L0703 Amanda Jain

Literary Agent
United States

Literary Agency: BookEnds, LLC (**L0155**)

L0704 The James Fitzgerald Agency

Literary Agency
PO Box 940, 70 Irish Road, Ranchos de Taos,
NM 87557
United States
Tel: +1 (575) 758-2687

submissions@jfitzagency.com

https://jfitzagency.com

ADULT
Fiction > *Novels*
  Crime; Popular Culture

Nonfiction
  Illustrated Books: Popular Culture

Nonfiction Books: Adventure; Biography; Crime; Films; Food; History; Memoir; Music; Popular Culture; Religion; Socio-Political; Spirituality; Sport; TV
CHILDREN'S > **Fiction** > *Novels*

YOUNG ADULT > **Fiction** > *Novels*

Send: Full text; Synopsis; Author bio; Market info
How to send: Email attachment

Primarily represents books reflecting the popular culture of the day, in fiction, nonfiction, graphic and packaged books. No poetry or screenplays. All information must be submitted in English, even if the manuscript is in another language. See website for detailed submission guidelines.

Editorial Assistant: Anna Tatelman

Literary Agent: Dylan Lowy

Literary Agent / President: James Fitzgerald

L0705 Elly James
Literary Agent
United Kingdom

elly@hhbagency.com

Literary Agency: hhb agency ltd (**L0647**)

L0706 Nicole James
Literary Agent
United States

Literary Agency: Chalberg & Sussman (**L0245**)

L0707 Jane Dowary Agency
Literary Agency
9B Little Street, Hawthorne, NJ 07506
United States

jane.dowary@gmail.com

http://www.janedowaryagency.mozello.com
https://accrispin.blogspot.com/2014/02/alert-jane-dowary-agency.html

Types: Fiction
Subjects: Adventure; Commercial; Contemporary; Crime; Drama; Fantasy; History; Horror; Literary; Mystery; Romance; Satire; Science; Science Fiction; Suspense; Thrillers
Markets: Adult; Children's; Young Adult

Send: Query
Don't send: Full text
How to send: Email

I only accept email queries. No queries by regular mail, please. Please include a full synopsis of the novel, first sample chapter, and please let me know if the novel is complete and if any other agent/Editor/Publisher/Movie Producer has read the book (This will not stop me from reading a project I am interested in).

Author: Gary B. Maier

Literary Agent: Julia Levin (**L0849**)

L0708 Jane Judd Literary Agency
Literary Agency
18 Belitha Villas, London, N1 1PD
United Kingdom
Tel: +44 (0) 20 7607 0273

https://www.janejudd.com
https://twitter.com/@Janelitagent

Professional Body: The Association of Authors' Agents (AAA)

Fiction > *Novels*
    Commercial; Literary

Nonfiction > *Nonfiction Books*
    Cookery; Films; Sport

Closed to approaches.

Closed to submissions as at December 2019. Check website for current status.

For fiction, send query with synopsis, first two or three chapters, and SAE. For nonfiction send first and/or other sample chapter, synopsis, market info, chapter breakdown, and any supporting evidence or articles. You may telephone in advance to save time for both parties. Also option of submitting online using contact form on website. Particularly interested in self-help, health, biography, popular history and narrative nonfiction, general and historical fiction and literary fiction.

Authors: Lynne Barrett-Lee; Michelle Birkby; Andy Dougan; Quentin Falk; Cliff Goodwin; Kathleen Griffin; Jill Mansell; David Winner

Literary Agent: Jane Judd (*L0744*)

L0709 Jane Rotrosen Agency
Literary Agency
318 East 51st Street, New York, NY 10022
United States
Tel: +1 (212) 593-4330
Fax: +1 (212) 935-6985

acirillo@janerotrosen.com

http://www.janerotrosen.com

Types: Fiction; Nonfiction
Subjects: Autobiography; Business; Comedy / Humour; Commercial; Crime; Culture; Health; History; Literary; Mystery; Psychology; Romance; Suspense; Thrillers; Women's Interests
Markets: Adult; Young Adult

Send: Query
Don't send: Full text
How to send: Email

Costs: Author covers sundry admin costs.

Send query by email to one of the agent email addresses provided on the agency bios page of the website, or by post with SASE, describing your work and giving relevant biographical details and publishing history, along with

synopsis and the first three chapters in the case of fiction, or proposal in the case of nonfiction. Submissions without an SASE will be recycled without response. Attachments to a blank email will not be opened. See website for full guidelines and individual agent details.

Literary Agents: Jane R. Berkey (*L0121*); Andrea Cirillo (*L0273*); Jessica Errera (**L0434**); Christina Hogrebe (*L0658*); Annelise Robey (*L1165*); Meg Ruley (*L1200*); Rebecca Scherer (*L1230*); Kathy Schneider (**L1236**); Amy Tannenbaum (**L1355**)

L0710 Jane Turnbull
Literary Agency
Barn Cottage, Veryan, Truro, TR2 5QA
United Kingdom
Tel: +44 (0) 20 7727 9409 / +44 (0) 1872 501317

jane@janeturnbull.co.uk

http://www.janeturnbull.co.uk

Professional Body: The Association of Authors' Agents (AAA)

Types: Fiction; Nonfiction
Formats: TV Scripts
Subjects: Biography; Comedy / Humour; Commercial; Current Affairs; Entertainment; Gardening; History; Lifestyle; Literary; Nature
Markets: Adult; Young Adult

Send: Query
Don't send: Full text
How not to send: Email

Agency with offices in London and Cornwall. New clients always welcome and a few taken on every year. Will occasionally take on fiction for older children, but no science fiction, fantasy, or "misery memoirs". Send query by post to Cornwall office with short description of your book or idea. No unsolicited MSS, or queries by email.

Authors: Denis Avey; Barney Bardsley; Harold Carlton; Lisa Comfort; Mike Dilger; Sue Elliott; Roger Garfitt; Tessa Hainsworth; Joanna Hodgkin; Simon Hoggart

L0711 Janet Fillingham Associates
Literary Agency
52 Lowther Road, London, SW13 9NU
United Kingdom
Tel: +44 (0) 20 8748 5594

info@janetfillingham.com

https://www.janetfillingham.com

Types: Scripts
Formats: Film Scripts; TV Scripts; Theatre Scripts
Markets: Adult; Children's; Young Adult

Send: Query
Don't send: Full text
How to send: Email

Represents writers and directors for stage, film and TV, as well as librettists, lyricists and composers in musical theatre. Does not represent books. See website for full submission guidelines.

Literary Agents: Janet Fillingham (*L0466*); Kate Weston (*L1435*)

L0712 Janklow & Nesbit UK Ltd
Literary Agency
13a Hillgate Street, London, W8 7SP
United Kingdom
Tel: +44 (0) 20 7243 2975

submissions@janklow.co.uk

http://www.janklowandnesbit.co.uk
https://twitter.com/JanklowUK

Professional Body: The Association of Authors' Agents (AAA)

ADULT
  Fiction > *Novels*
    General, and in particular: Commercial; Literary

  Nonfiction > *Nonfiction Books*

CHILDREN'S > **Fiction** > *Novels*

YOUNG ADULT > **Fiction** > *Novels*

Send: Query; Synopsis; Writing sample
How to send: Email

Send query by email, including informative covering letter providing background about yourself and your writing; first three chapters / approx. 50 pages; a brief synopsis for fiction, or a full outline for nonfiction.

Literary Agents: Rebecca Carter (**L0234**); Claire Paterson Conrad; Will Francis (**L0494**); Hellie Ogden

L0713 Oscar Janson-Smith
Literary Agent
United Kingdom

Literary Agency: Kruger Cowne (**L0810**)

L0714 John Jarrold
Literary Agent
United Kingdom

Literary Agency: John Jarrold Literary Agency (**L0731**)

L0715 Javelin
Literary Agency
203 South Union Street, Alexandria, VA 22314
United States
Tel: +1 (703) 490-8845

submissions@javelindc.com
hello@javelindc.com

http://javelindc.com

Nonfiction > *Nonfiction Books*

History; Journalism; Politics; Science

Send: Proposal
How to send: Email

Represents presidential contenders, diplomats, journalists, historians, scientists – and others with a unique and compelling story to share.

L0716 The Jean V. Naggar Literary Agency
Literary Agency
216 East 75th Street, Suite 1E, New York, NY 10021
United States
Tel: +1 (212) 794-1082

jvnla@jvnla.com

http://www.jvnla.com

Professional Body: Association of Authors' Representatives, Inc. (AAR)

Types: Fiction; Nonfiction
Subjects: Adventure; Autobiography; Comedy / Humour; Commercial; Cookery; Crime; Culture; Current Affairs; Fantasy; Gothic; Health; History; Lifestyle; Literary; Music; Mystery; Personal Development; Psychology; Romance; Science; Sport; Suspense; Thrillers; Women's Interests
Markets: Adult; Children's; Young Adult

Send: Query
Don't send: Full text

Accepts queries via online submission system only. See website for more details.

Literary Agents: Alicia Brooks (*L0183*); Jean Naggar (*L1020*); Ariana Philips (*L1096*); Alice Tasman (*L1357*); Jennifer Weltz (*L1431*)

L0717 The Jeff Herman Agency, LLC
Literary Agency
PO Box 1522, Stockbridge, MA 01262
United States
Tel: +1 (413) 298-0077

submissions@jeffherman.com

http://www.jeffherman.com

Types: Nonfiction
Formats: Reference
Subjects: Autobiography; Business; Crime; Culture; Health; History; How To; Lifestyle; Personal Development; Psychology; Spirituality
Markets: Academic; Adult; Professional

Send: Query
Don't send: Full text
How to send: Email

Costs: Author covers sundry admin costs.

Send query by post with SASE, or by email. With few exceptions, handles nonfiction only, with particular interest in the genres given above. No scripts or unsolicited MSS.

Literary Agents: Deborah Levine Herman (*L0637*); Jeff Herman (*L0638*)

L0718 Jeffrey Simmons
Literary Agency
15 Penn House, Mallory Street, London, NW8 8SX
United Kingdom
Tel: +44 (0) 20 7224 8917

jasimmons@unicombox.co.uk

Types: Fiction; Nonfiction
Formats: Film Scripts; Theatre Scripts
Subjects: Autobiography; Commercial; Crime; Current Affairs; Entertainment; History; Legal; Literary; Politics; Psychology; Sport
Markets: Adult

Send: Query
Don't send: Full text

Send query with brief bio, synopsis, history of any prior publication, and list of any publishers or agents to have already seen the MSS. Particularly interested in personality books of all kinds and fiction from young writers (under 40) with a future. No children's books, science fiction, fantasy, cookery, crafts, gardening, or hobbies. Film scripts handled for existing book clients only.

L0719 Carole Jelen
Literary Agent
United States

Literary Agency: Waterside Productions, Inc (**L1418**)

L0720 Carolyn Jenks
Literary Agent; Company Director
United States

carolyn@carolynjenksagency.com

https://www.carolynjenksagency.com/agent/CAROLYN-JENKS

Literary Agency: Carolyn Jenks Agency (**L0228**)

Fiction > *Novels*

Nonfiction > *Nonfiction Books*

Send: Author bio; Writing sample; Pitch
How to send: In the body of an email

L0721 The Jennifer DeChiara Literary Agency
Literary Agency
245 Park Avenue, 39th Floor, New York, NY 10167
United States
Tel: +1 (212) 372-8989

jenndec@aol.com

http://www.jdlit.com

Types: Fiction; Nonfiction
Formats: Film Scripts; Theatre Scripts
Subjects: Adventure; Arts; Autobiography;

Comedy / Humour; Commercial; Contemporary; Cookery; Culture; Fantasy; Health; History; Horror; How To; Lifestyle; Literary; Literature; Mystery; Personal Development; Romance; Science; Society; Sport; Suspense; Thrillers; Travel; Women's Interests
Markets: Adult; Children's; Young Adult

Send: Query
Don't send: Full text
How to send: Email

Costs: Offers services that writers have to pay for.

Send query online only. Posted submissions will be discarded. See website for full guidelines and for specific agent interests and email addresses.

Literary Agents: Alex Barba (*L0083*); Marlo Berliner (*L0123*); Savannah Brooks (*L0185*); Jennifer De Chiara (*L0260*); Ryan Eichenwald (*L0414*); Zabé Ellor (**L0427**); Stephen Fraser (*L0500*); Cari Lamba (*L0819*); Marie Lamba (*L0820*); Damian McNicoll (*L0960*); Colleen Oefelein (*L1052*); Alex Weiss (*L1427*); Roseanne Wells (*L1430*)

L0722 Jenny Brown Associates
Literary Agency
31 Marchmont Road, Edinburgh, Scotland, EH9 1HU
United Kingdom
Tel: +44 (0) 1312 295334

submissions@jennybrownassociates.com

https://www.jennybrownassociates.com

Professional Body: The Association of Authors' Agents (AAA)

Types: Fiction; Nonfiction
Subjects: Autobiography; Comedy / Humour; Commercial; Crime; Culture; Finance; History; Literary; Music; Romance; Science; Sport; Thrillers; Women's Interests
Markets: Adult; Children's

Send: Query
Don't send: Full text

Submissions by email only. Accepts submissions only during specific reading periods. See website for details.

Literary Agents: Jenny Brown (*L0192*); Lucy Juckes (*L0743*)

L0723 Natalie Jerome
Literary Agent
United Kingdom

https://aevitascreative.com/agents/#agent-7411

Literary Agency: Aevitas Creative Management (ACM) UK (**L0020**)

ADULT > **Nonfiction** > *Nonfiction Books*

Commercial; Culture; Current Affairs; Entertainment; Food; Health; Music; Wellbeing

CHILDREN'S > **Fiction** > *Novels*

Send: Query; Writing sample
How to send: Online submission system

Has a specific interest in commercial nonfiction across areas of health and wellness, food, current events, culture, music and entertainment as well as looking for vibrant new authors in children's fiction.

L0724 JET Literary Associates, Inc.
Literary Agency
941 Calle Mejia, #507, Santa Fe, NM 87501
United States
Tel: +1 (505) 780-0721

etp@jetliterary.com

http://jetliterary.com

Types: Fiction; Nonfiction
Subjects: Business; Comedy / Humour; Cookery; Crime; Gardening; History; How To; Lifestyle; Literary; Politics; Romance; Suspense; Thrillers
Markets: Adult

Send: Query
Don't send: Full text
How to send: Email

Send query by email only, including a brief description of your work and your background. Do not send attachments, sample chapters, or proposals in first instance. No poetry, plays, film scripts, science fiction, fantasy, YA or books for young children.

Literary Agent: Elizabeth Trupin-Pulli (*L1379*)

L0725 JetReid Literary Agency
Literary Agency
PO Box 1385, New York, NY 10009
United States

http://www.jetreidliterary.com

Authors: Robin Becker; Bill Cameron; Gary Corby; Phillip DePoy; Stephanie Evans; Kennedy Foster; Lee Goodman; Dana Haynes; Patrick Lee; Thomas Lippman; Jeff Marks; Warren Richey; Terry Shames; Jeff Somers; Robert Stubblefield; Deb Vlock

Literary Agent: Janet Reid (**L1139**)

L0726 JFL Agency
Literary Agency
48 Charlotte Street, London, W1T 2NS
United Kingdom
Tel: +44 (0) 20 3137 8182

agents@jflagency.com

http://www.jflagency.com

Scripts

Film Scripts; *Radio Scripts*; *TV Scripts*; *Theatre Scripts*

Send: Query
How to send: Email

Handles scripts only (for television, film, theatre and radio). Considers approaches from established writers with broadcast experience, but only accepts submissions from new writers during specific periods – consult website for details.

Authors: Humphrey Barclay; Liam Beirne; Adam Bostock-Smith; Tim Brooke-Taylor; Ian Brown; Grant Cathro; Paul Charlton; Gabby Hutchinson Crouch; Bill Dare; Tim Dawson; Martin Day; Ed Dyson; Polly Eden; Jan Etherington; Sinéad Fagan; Anji Loman Field; Phil Ford; Patrick Gallagher; Ted Gannon; Lisa Gifford; Rob Gittins; Ben Harris; James Hendrie; Wayne Jackman; Tony Lee; Richard Leslie Lewis; Jane Marlow; Jonathan Morris; Cardy O'Donnell; Jim Pullin; Jackie Robb; Graeme Rooney; Gary Russell; David Semple; James Serafinowicz; Pete Sinclair; Paul Smith; Fraser Steele

Literary Agents: Alison Finch; Dominic Lord; Gary Wild

L0727 Jim Donovan Literary
Literary Agency
5635 SMU Boulevard, Suite 201, Dallas, TX 75206
United States
Tel: +1 (214) 696-9411

jdliterary@sbcglobal.net

https://www.jimdonovanliterary.com

Fiction > *Novels*
Commercial; Literary; Mystery; Thrillers

Nonfiction > *Nonfiction Books*
American History; Biography; Military; Narrative Nonfiction; Popular Culture

Send: Query; Writing sample; Synopsis
How to send: Email; Post

Literary Agent: Melissa Shultz (*L1272*)

President: Jim Donovan

L0728 Jo Unwin Literary Agency
Literary Agency
West Wing, Somerset House, London, WC2R 1LA
United Kingdom
Tel: +44 (0) 20 7257 9599

submissions@jounwin.co.uk

http://www.jounwin.co.uk

Professional Body: The Association of Authors' Agents (AAA)

Types: Fiction; Nonfiction; Translations
Subjects: Anthropology; Autobiography; Comedy / Humour; Commercial; Literary;

Medicine; Politics; Psychology; Women's Interests
Markets: Adult; Children's; Young Adult

How to send: Email

Handles literary fiction, commercial women's fiction, comic writing, narrative nonfiction, Young Adult fiction and fiction for children aged 9+. No poetry, picture books, or screenplays, except for existing clients. Accepts submissions by email. Mainly represents authors from the UK and Ireland, and sometimes Australia and New Zealand. Only represents US authors in very exceptional circumstances. See website for full guidelines.

Literary Agents: Donna Greaves (*L0573*); Rachel Mann (**L0912**); Milly Reilly (*L1140*); Jo Unwin (*L1393*)

L0729 Joelle Delbourgo Associates, Inc.

Literary Agency
101 Park St., Montclair, Montclair, NJ 07042
United States
Tel: +1 (973) 773-0836

joelle@delbourgo.com

http://www.delbourgo.com

Professional Body: Association of Authors' Representatives, Inc. (AAR)

Types: Fiction; Nonfiction
Subjects: Autobiography; Comedy / Humour; Cookery; Current Affairs; History; Lifestyle; Politics; Psychology; Science
Markets: Adult

Send: Query
Don't send: Full text

Costs: Author covers sundry admin costs.

We are a highly selective agency, broad in our interests. No category romance, Westerns, early readers, or picture books. Send query by email to specific agent (see website for interests and email addresses). Submissions must include the word "QUERY" in the subject line. See website for full guidelines.

Authors: Tanya Acker; Jennifer Lynn Alvarez; Heather Anastasiu; Lisa Anselmo; Thomas Armstrong; Sara Au; Frances Bartkowski; Suzanne Bohan; Lynn Kiele Bonasia; Michele Borba; Robert Bornstein; Elizabeth Reid Boyd; Nora Bradbury-Haehl; Anne Greenwood Brown; Gay Browne; Ariel Burger; Craig Carlson; Debbie Cenziper; John Christianson; Gay Courter; Nancy Cowan; Nancy Dreyfus; Chris Farrell; Marilyn Fedewa; Laura Berman Fortgang; Susan Forward; Philip Freeman; Terry Gaspard; John Gaudet; Susan Gilbert-Collins; Ann E. Grant; Jonathon Grayson; Brenda Greene; Beth A. Grosshans; Julie L. Hall; Kate Harding; Laura Hartema; Kristi Hedges; Holly Herrick; Helaina Hovitz; Erik Forrest Jackson; Theresa Kaminski; Rachelle Katz; Joseph Kelly; Stephen Kelly; Brynne S.

Kennedy; Nancy Kennedy; Willem Kuyken; Mary Languirand; Missy Chase Lapine; Irene S. Levine; Alexandra Levitt; Geralyn Lucas; Lauren Mackler; Juliet Madison; Kerstin March; David J. Marsh; Chuck Martin; Lama Marut; Carol Masciola; Colleen O'Grady; Jim Obergefell; Elaine Neil Orr; Lindsey J. Palmer; Theresa Payton; Michelle Pearce; Gleb Raygorodetsky; Eliza Redgold; Michael Reichert; Ashley Rhodes-Courter; Paige Rien; Jillian Roberts; Tatsha Robertson; Lisa Romeo; Marilyn Simon Rothstein; Dale Russakoff; Roberta Sandenbergh; Sue Scheff; Melissa Schorr; Ellen E. Schultz; Robert Sher; Heather Shumaker; Alexandra Silber; Pamela Slim; Laura Sobiech; Peter L. Stavinoha; Maryon Stewart; Nancy Rubin Stuart; Rachel Sulivan; Deborah J. Swiss; Jeff Sypeck; John Temple; Christopher Van Tilburg; Julie Valerie; Michael Volpatt; Caroline Welch; Kristin M. White; Barrie Wilson; Ben H. Winters; Jon Wuebben; Gabra Zackman; Peter Zheutlin; Gabe Zichermann

Literary Agents: Carrie Cantor (*L0214*); Joelle Delbourgo (*L0352*); Jacqueline Flynn (*L0477*)

L0730 John Hawkins & Associates, Inc.

Literary Agency
80 Maiden Lane, STE 1503, New York, NY 10038
United States
Tel: +1 (212) 807-7040
Fax: +1 (212) 807-9555

jha@jhalit.com

http://www.jhalit.com

Professional Body: Association of Authors' Representatives, Inc. (AAR)

Types: Fiction; Nonfiction
Formats: Short Fiction
Subjects: Autobiography; Business; Crime; Current Affairs; Fantasy; Gardening; Health; History; Lifestyle; Mystery; Nature; Politics; Psychology; Science; Science Fiction; Technology; Thrillers; Travel; Women's Interests
Markets: Adult

Send query by email with details about you and your writing, and for fiction the first three chapters as a single Word attachment, or for nonfiction include proposal as a single attachment. Include the word "Query" in the subject line. See website for full guidelines.

Literary Agents: Moses Cardona (*L0220*); Warren Frazier (*L0501*); Anne Hawkins (*L0624*); William Reiss (*L1141*)

L0731 John Jarrold Literary Agency

Literary Agency
Lincoln,
United Kingdom

j.jarrold@btinternet.com

http://www.johnjarrold.co.uk

Types: Fiction
Subjects: Commercial; Fantasy; Horror; Science Fiction
Markets: Adult

Send: Query
Don't send: Full text
How to send: Email

Costs: Offers services that writers have to pay for.

The agency specialises in SF and Fantasy, but also deals with horror. No other types of material are accepted. After fifteen years in the UK publishing industry as editorial director of three imprints, I am aware of the market on both sides of the Atlantic, and the editors to approach. Handles adult books in the fields of science fiction, fantasy, and horror only. No nonfiction, children's, or young adult. Contact by email in first instance – see website for full submission guidelines. Also offers editorial services which are "completely separate from the literary agency".

Authors: David Barnett; Chris Beckett; Chaz Brenchley; Eric Brown; Saxon Bullock; Ramsey Campbell; Cory Daniells; Rjurik Davidson; Christopher Evans; Toby Frost; Eric Furey; Debbie Gallagher; Jon George; Justine Hopkins; Stephen Hunt; Curtis Jobling; Leigh Kennedy; Jasper Kent; John Marshall; Suzanne McLeod; Mark Morris; Helen-Rose Owen; Philip Palmer; Ruaridh Pringle; Harvey Raines; Hannu Rajaniemi; Rod Rees; Ian Sales; Gaie Sebold; Jeremy Szal; Martyn Taylor; Richard Webb; John Whitbourn; Neil Williamson

Literary Agent: John Jarrold (*L0714*)

L0732 Johnson & Alcock

Literary Agency
Bloomsbury House, 74-77 Great Russell Street, London, WC1B 3DA
United Kingdom
Tel: +44 (0) 20 7251 0125

http://www.johnsonandalcock.co.uk

Professional Body: The Association of Authors' Agents (AAA)

Send: Query; Synopsis; Writing sample
How to send: Email attachment; Post

Send query by email (response only if interested), or by post with SASE. Include synopsis and first three chapters (approximately 50 pages). Email submissions should go to specific agents. See website for list of agents and full submission guidelines.

Chair / Literary Agent: Michael Alcock (**L0027**)

Company Director / Literary Agent: Andrew Hewson (**L0644**)

Literary Agent / Managing Director: Anna Power (**L1111**)

Literary Agents: Liz Dennis (**L0357**); Becky Thomas (**L1362**); Ed Wilson (**L1459**)

L0733 Greg Johnson
Literary Agent
United States

Literary Agency: Wordserve Literary (**L1472**)

L0734 Jonathan Clowes Ltd
Literary Agency
10 Iron Bridge House, Bridge Approach, London, NW1 8BD
United Kingdom
Tel: +44 (0) 20 7722 7674
Fax: +44 (0) 20 7722 7677

cara@jonathanclowes.co.uk

https://www.jonathanclowes.co.uk

Professional Body: The Association of Authors' Agents (AAA)

Types: Fiction; Nonfiction; Scripts
Formats: Film Scripts; Radio Scripts; TV Scripts; Theatre Scripts
Subjects: Commercial; Literary
Markets: Adult

Send: Query
Don't send: Full text
How to send: Email

Send query with synopsis and three chapters (or equivalent sample) by email. No science fiction, poetry, short stories, academic. Only considers film/TV clients with previous success in TV/film/theatre. If no response within six weeks, assume rejection.

Authors: Michael Baigent; David Bellamy; Oscar Brodkin; Angela Chadwick; Simon Critchley; Len Deighton; Maureen Duffy; Brian Freemantle; Miles Gibson; Victoria Glass; Rana Haddad; Francesca Hornak; Elizabeth Jane Howard; Ruqaya Izzidien; Richard Leigh; Doris Lessing; Mario Matassa; Clive McAlpin; Claire Miles; Teresa Forcades i Vila

Literary Agents: Ann Evans (*L0440*); Nemonie Craven Roderick (*L1176*); Cara Lee Simpson (**L1282**)

L0735 Jonathan Pegg Literary Agency
Literary Agency
67 Wingate Square, London, SW4 OAF
United Kingdom
Tel: +44 (0) 20 7603 6830

submissions@jonathanpegg.com

http://www.jonathanpegg.com

Professional Body: The Association of Authors' Agents (AAA)

Types: Fiction; Nonfiction
Subjects: Arts; Autobiography; Commercial; Culture; Current Affairs; History; Lifestyle; Literary; Nature; Psychology; Science; Thrillers
Markets: Adult

Send: Query
Don't send: Full text
How to send: Email

Established by the agent after twelve years at Curtis Brown. The agency's main areas of interest are: Fiction: literary fiction, thrillers and quality commercial in general Non-Fiction: current affairs, memoir and biography, history, popular science, nature, arts and culture, lifestyle, popular psychology Rights: Aside from the UK market, the agency will work in association with translation, US, TV & film agents according to each client's best interests. If you're looking for an agent: I accept submissions by email. See website for full submission guidelines.

Literary Agent: Jonathan Pegg (*L1077*)

L0736 Jonathan Williams Literary Agency
Literary Agency
1 Urban Villas, Tivoli Terrace North, Dun Laoghaire, County Dublin, A96 YC95
Ireland
Tel: +353 (0) 1-280-3482
Fax: +353 (0) 1-280-3482

Types: Fiction; Nonfiction
Subjects: Literary
Markets: Adult

Costs: Offers services that writers have to pay for.

Agency also has agents in Holland, Italy, France, Spain, and Japan. Send SASE with IRCs if outside of Ireland. Charges a reading fee if a very fast decision is required.

Literary Agent: Rosney Mews

L0737 Cara Jones
Literary Agent
United Kingdom

Literary Agency: Rogers, Coleridge & White Ltd (**L1181**)

L0738 Mary Jones
Literary Agent
United Kingdom

L0739 Rebecca Jones
Literary Agent
United Kingdom

Literary Agency: Rogers, Coleridge & White Ltd (**L1181**)

L0740 Robin Jones
Literary Agent
United Kingdom

https://twitter.com/AgentRobinJones

Literary Agency: Robin Jones Literary Agency (**L1166**)

L0741 Lawrence Jordan
Literary Agent
United States

Literary Agency: Lawrence Jordan Literary Agency (**L0833**)

L0742 Joy Harris Literary Agency, Inc.
Literary Agency
1501 Broadway, Suite 2310, New York, NY 10036
United States
Tel: +1 (212) 924-6269
Fax: +1 (212) 840-5776

submissions@joyharrisliterary.com

http://www.joyharrisliterary.com

Professional Body: Association of Authors' Representatives, Inc. (AAR)

Types: Fiction; Nonfiction; Translations
Formats: Short Fiction
Subjects: Autobiography; Comedy / Humour; Commercial; Culture; Experimental; History; Literary; Media; Mystery; Satire; Spirituality; Suspense; Women's Interests
Markets: Adult; Young Adult

Closed to approaches.

Costs: Author covers sundry admin costs.

Closed to submissions as at October 2019. Check website for current status.

Send query by email, including sample chapter or outline. No poetry, screenplays, genre fiction, self-help, or unsolicited mss. See website for full guidelines.

Literary Agents: Joy Harris (*L0612*); Adam Reed (*L1132*)

L0743 Lucy Juckes
Literary Agent
United Kingdom

Literary Agency: Jenny Brown Associates (**L0722**)

L0744 Jane Judd
Literary Agent
United Kingdom

Literary Agency: Jane Judd Literary Agency (**L0708**)

L0745 Judith Murdoch Literary Agency

Literary Agency
19 Chalcot Square, London, NW1 8YA
United Kingdom
Tel: +44 (0) 20 7722 4197

jmlitag@btinternet.com

http://www.judithmurdoch.co.uk

Professional Body: The Association of Authors' Agents (AAA)

Types: Fiction
Subjects: Commercial; Crime; Literary; Women's Interests
Markets: Adult

Send: Query
Don't send: Full text
How not to send: Email

Send query by post with SAE or email address for response, brief synopsis, and and first three chapters. Provides editorial advice. No science fiction, fantasy, children's stories, email submissions, or unsolicited MSS.

Author Estates: The Estate of Catherine King; The Estate of Meg Hutchinson

Authors: Diane Allen; Trisha Ashley; Anne Bennett; Maggie Bennett; Anne Berry; Frances Brody; Rosie Clarke; Howard Coombs; Dincy Costeloe; Norma Curtis; Anne Doughty; Kate Eastham; Leah Fleming; Sarah Flint; Caro Fraser; Emma Fraser; Elizabeth Gill; Gracie Hart; Faith Hogan; Maggie Hope; Emma Hornby; Alex Howard; Minna Howard; Alrene Hughes; Lindsey Hutchinson; Lola Jaye; Sheila Jeffries; Sophie Jenkins; Carol Jones; Pamela Jooste; Mary de Laszlo; Catherine Law; Jill McGivering; Alison Mercer; Beth Miller; Jaishree Misra; Barbara Mutch; Kitty Neale; Sheila Newberry; Della Parker; Carol Rivers; Cathy Sharp; Alison Sherlock; Linda Sole; June Tate; Annie Wilkinson; Mary Wood

Literary Agent: Judith Murdoch (*L1010*)

L0746 Judy Daish Associates Ltd

Literary Agency
2 St Charles Place, London, W10 6EG
United Kingdom
Tel: +44 (0) 20 8964 8811
Fax: +44 (0) 20 8964 8966

judy@judydaish.com

http://www.judydaish.com

Types: Scripts
Formats: Film Scripts; Radio Scripts; TV Scripts; Theatre Scripts
Markets: Adult

Represents writers, directors, designers and choreographers for theatre, film, television, radio and opera. No books or unsolicited mss.

Literary Agents: Judy Daish (*L0327*); Tracey Elliston (*L0426*); Howard Gooding (*L0565*)

L0747 Ria Julien

Literary Agent
United States

Literary Agency: Frances Goldin Literary Agency, Inc. (**L0492**)

L0748 Juliet Burton Literary Agency

Literary Agency
2 Clifton Avenue, London, W12 9DR
United Kingdom
Tel: +44 (0) 20 8762 0148

juliet.burton@julietburton.com

Professional Body: The Association of Authors' Agents (AAA)

Types: Fiction; Nonfiction
Subjects: Crime; Women's Interests
Markets: Adult

Send: Query
Don't send: Full text

Particularly interested in crime and women's fiction. Send query with SAE, synopsis, and two sample chapters. No poetry, plays, film scripts, children's, articles, academic material, science fiction, fantasy, or unsolicited MSS.

Literary Agent: Juliet Burton (*L0202*)

L0749 Juri Gabriel

Literary Agency
35 Camberwell Grove, London, SE5 8JA
United Kingdom
Tel: +44 (0) 20 7703 6186

juri@jurigabriel.com

Types: Fiction; Nonfiction
Markets: Adult

Send: Query
Don't send: Full text

Send query with 1-2 page synopsis and three sample chapters. Include SAE if submitting by post. No short stories, verse, articles, or books for children.

Authors: Nick Bradbury; Paul Genney; Robert Irwin; David Miller

L0750 K2 Literary

Literary Agency
Canada

https://k2literary.com
https://www.facebook.com/k2literary/
https://twitter.com/k2literary
https://instagram.com/k2literary

ADULT > **Fiction** > *Novels*

CHILDREN'S > **Fiction** > *Novels*

Closed to approaches.

Literary Agent: Kelvin Kong (*L0803*)

L0751 Ella Diamond Kahn

Literary Agent
United Kingdom

http://dkwlitagency.co.uk/agents/
https://twitter.com/elladkahn

Literary Agency: Diamond Kahn and Woods (DKW) Literary Agency Ltd (**L0365**)

Closed to approaches.

L0752 Jody Kahn

Literary Agent
United States

jkahn@bromasite.com

http://brandthochman.com/agents
http://aaronline.org/Sys/PublicProfile/7225167/417813

Literary Agency: Brandt & Hochman Literary Agents, Inc. (**L0172**)
Professional Body: Association of Authors' Representatives, Inc. (AAR)

Fiction > *Novels*
Comedy / Humour; Culture; Literary; Upmarket

Nonfiction > *Nonfiction Books*
Culture; Food; History; Journalism; Literary Memoir; Narrative Nonfiction; Social Justice; Sport

Send: Query
How to send: Email

L0753 Elianna Kan

Literary Agent
United States

Literary Agency: Regal Hoffmann & Associates LLC (**L1136**)

L0754 Kane Literary Agency

Literary Agency
United Kingdom

submissions@kaneliteraryagency.com
submissions@standenliteraryagency.com

https://www.kaneliteraryagency.com
https://www.facebook.com/Kane-Literary-Agency-326069577432096/

Fiction > *Novels*

Nonfiction > *Nonfiction Books*
Cookery; Lifestyle; Spirituality

Send: Query; Synopsis; Writing sample
How to send: Email

Send one-page synopsis and first three chapters by email only. No picture books. Responds if interested only. If no response in 6 weeks assume rejection.

Authors: Simon Arrowsmith; J Y Bee; Isabelle Brizec; Louise Cliffe-Minns; Sarah Harris;

Vicki Howie; Zoe Marriott; Andrew Murray; Emily Nagle; Marisa Noelle

Literary Agent: Yasmin Standen (*L1308*)

L0755 Cynthia Kane
Literary Agent
United States

Literary Agency: Capital Talent Agency (**L0216**)

L0756 Carrie Kania
Literary Agent
United Kingdom

Literary Agency: C+W (Conville & Walsh) (**L0205**)

L0757 Georgia Kanner
Literary Agent
United Kingdom

Literary Agency: Independent Talent Group Ltd (**L0683**)

L0758 Julia Kardon
Literary Agent
United States

julia@hgliterary.com

https://www.hgliterary.com/julia
https://twitter.com/jlkardon

Literary Agency: HG Literary (**L0646**)

Fiction > *Novels*
 Literary; Upmarket

Nonfiction > *Nonfiction Books*
 History; Journalism; Memoir; Narrative Nonfiction

L0759 Karen Gantz Literary Management
Literary Agency
United States

kgzahler@aol.com

https://karengantzliterarymanagement.com
https://www.facebook.com/
Karengantzliterarymanagement/
https://twitter.com/karengantz
https://www.instagram.com/karen_gantz/

Fiction > *Novels*

Nonfiction > *Nonfiction Books*
 Cookery; Current Affairs; History; Lifestyle; Memoir; Narrative Nonfiction; Politics; Psychology; Religion

Send: Query; Synopsis
How to send: Email

Considers all genres but specialises in nonfiction. Send query and summary by email only.

Assistant Agent: Hester Malin (**L0910**)

Literary Agent: Karen Gantz (*L0526*)

L0760 Maryann Karinch
Literary Agent
United States

mak@rudyagency.com

http://rudyagency.com

Literary Agency: The Rudy Agency (**L1199**)

Fiction > *Novels*

Nonfiction > *Nonfiction Books*
 Business; Health; History; Investigative Journalism; Medicine; Sport

Send: Query
How to send: Email

L0761 Kiran Kataria
Literary Agent
United Kingdom

https://www.keanekataria.co.uk/agents/

Literary Agency: Keane Kataria Literary Agency (**L0769**)

L0762 Kate Barker Literary, TV, & Film Agency
Literary Agency
London,
United Kingdom
Tel: +44 (0) 20 7688 1638

kate@katebarker.net

https://www.katebarker.net

Fiction > *Novels*
 Book Club Fiction; Crime; Family Saga; High Concept; Historical Fiction; Literary; Thrillers; Women's Fiction

Nonfiction > *Nonfiction Books*
 Economics; History; Lifestyle; Memoir; Narrative Nonfiction; Popular Psychology; Science; Wellbeing

Send: Query; Writing sample
How to send: Online submission system

No science fiction (unless literary) and no fantasy or children's. Submit via website submission form.

Literary Agent: Kate Barker (*L0089*)

L0763 Kate Hordern Literary Agency
Literary Agency
18 Mortimer Road, Clifton, Bristol, BS8 4EY
United Kingdom
Tel: +44 (0) 1179 239368

kate@khla.co.uk
anne@khla.co.uk

https://khla.co.uk

Professional Body: The Association of Authors' Agents (AAA)

Send: Query; Writing sample; Synopsis
How to send: Email
How not to send: Post

Send query by email only with pitch, an outline or synopsis and the first three chapters. If no response within six weeks, assume rejection.

Authors: Garry Abson; Merryn Allingham; Lyn Andrews; Richard Bassett; Helen Carey; Sam Carrington; Jane Corry; Jeff Dawson; Rosemary Dun; Kylie Fitzpatrick; Leona Francombe; Mary Gibson; Catherine Hanley; Sven Hassel; David Helton; Duncan Hewitt; Julie Houston; Kathryn Hughes; Victoria Jenkins; Ewa Jozefkowicz; Julian Lees; Denzil Meyrick; P.J.Brackston; Will Randall; Dave Roberts; Abbie Ross; John Sadler; Alastair Sawday; Dominic Selwood; Genevieve Taylor; Sandy Taylor

Literary Agents: Kate Hordern (**L0664**); Anne Williams (*L1449*)

L0764 Kate Nash Literary Agency
Literary Agency
United Kingdom

justin@katenashlit.co.uk
submissions@katenashlit.co.uk

https://katenashlit.co.uk
https://www.facebook.com/
KateNashLiteraryAgency/
https://twitter.com/katenashagent
https://www.youtube.com/channel/
UCAugaYbUoZXD7wldntZ8DwQ

Professional Body: The Association of Authors' Agents (AAA)

ADULT
 Fiction > *Novels*

  Nonfiction > *Nonfiction Books*: Commercial

CHILDREN'S > **Fiction** > *Middle Grade*

YOUNG ADULT > **Fiction** > *Novels*

Closed to approaches.

Open to approaches from both new and established authors. Represents general and genre fiction and popular nonfiction. No poetry, drama, or genre SFF. Send query by email with synopsis and first chapter (fiction) or up to three chapters (nonfiction) pasted into the body of the email (no attachments).

Editor / Junior Agent / Proofreader: Robbie Guillory (**L0588**)

Literary Agent: Kate Nash (*L1022*)

L0765 Kathi J. Paton Literary Agency
Literary Agency
United States
Tel: +1 (212) 265-6586

kjplitbiz@optonline.net

http://www.PatonLiterary.com

Types: Fiction; Nonfiction
Subjects: Biography; Business; Comedy / Humour; Commercial; Culture; Current Affairs; Finance; Health; History; Lifestyle; Literary; Politics; Religion; Science; Sport; Technology
Markets: Adult

Send: Query
Don't send: Full text
How to send: Email

Costs: Offers services that writers have to pay for.

Send query with brief description by email only. No attachments or referrals to websites. Specialises in adult nonfiction. No science fiction, fantasy, horror, category romance, juvenile, young adult or self-published books. Response only if interested. Also offers editorial services.

Literary Agent: Kathi Paton (*L1071*)

L0766 Kathryn Green Literary Agency, LLC
Literary Agency
157 Columbus Avenue, Suite 510, New York, NY 10023
United States
Tel: +1 (212) 245-4225

query@kgreenagency.com
kathy@kgreenagency.com

https://www.kathryngreenliteraryagency.com
https://twitter.com/kathygreenlit

ADULT
Fiction > *Novels*
General, and in particular: Cozy Mysteries; Historical Fiction

Nonfiction > *Nonfiction Books*
General, and in particular: Comedy / Humour; History; Memoir; Parenting; Popular Culture

CHILDREN'S > **Fiction** > *Middle Grade*

YOUNG ADULT > **Fiction** > *Novels*

Does not want:

ADULT > **Fiction** > *Novels*
Fantasy; Science Fiction

CHILDREN'S > **Fiction**
Middle Grade: Fantasy; Science Fiction
Picture Books: General

YOUNG ADULT > **Fiction** > *Novels*
Fantasy; Science Fiction

Send: Query
How to send: Email
How not to send: Post; Email attachment

Send query by email. Do not send samples unless requested. No science fiction, fantasy,

children's picture books, screenplays, or poetry.
Literary Agent: Kathryn Green (*L0575*)

L0767 Simon Kavanagh
Literary Agent
United Kingdom

simon@miccheetham.com

Literary Agency: Mic Cheetham Literary Agency (**L0971**)

L0768 Taylor Martindale Kean
Literary Agent
United States

https://www.fullcircleliterary.com/our-agents/taylor-martindale-kean/

Literary Agency: Full Circle Literary, LLC (**L0515**)

Closed to approaches.

L0769 Keane Kataria Literary Agency
Literary Agency
United Kingdom

info@keanekataria.co.uk

https://www.keanekataria.co.uk/submissions/

Fiction > *Novels*
Book Club Fiction; Crime; Historical Fiction; Women's Fiction

Send: Query; Synopsis; Writing sample
How to send: PDF file email attachment
How not to send: Word file email attachment

Currently accepting submissions in the crime, domestic noir and women's fiction genres. No thrillers, science fiction, fantasy or children's books. Send query by email only with synopsis and first three chapters. Attachments in PDF format only.

Literary Agents: Kiran Kataria (**L0761**); Sara Keane (**L0770**)

L0770 Sara Keane
Literary Agent
United Kingdom

https://www.keanekataria.co.uk/agents/

Literary Agency: Keane Kataria Literary Agency (**L0769**)

L0771 Trena Keating
Literary Agent
United States

Literary Agency: Union Literary (**L1388**)

L0772 Sara O' Keeffe
Literary Agent
United Kingdom

sokeeffe@aevitascreative.com

https://www.saraokeeffe.co.uk
https://aevitascreative.com/agents/#agent-7942
https://www.instagram.com/sarabookcrazy/
https://twitter.com/okeeffe05

Literary Agency: Aevitas Creative Management (ACM) UK (**L0020**)

Fiction > *Novels*
Crime; Ireland; Science Fiction; Women's Fiction

Send: Writing sample; Query
How to send: Email

Has worked with major brand names in crime, science fiction and has a passion for Irish writing.

L0773 Mariam Keen
Literary Agent
United Kingdom

Literary Agency: Whispering Buffalo Literary Agency Ltd (**L1439**)

L0774 Chrysa Keenon
Junior Agent
United States

chrysa@cyleyoung.com

https://www.chrysakeenon.com
https://cyleyoung.com/literary-agent/my-team/
https://www.instagram.com/chrysakeenonwriting/
https://www.linkedin.com/in/chrysa-keenon-4a617177/
https://twitter.com/Chrysa_Keenon

Literary Agency: Cyle Young Literary Elite (**L0323**)

ADULT > **Fiction** > *Novels*
Low Fantasy; Magical Realism; Romance; Urban Fantasy

CHILDREN'S
Fiction > *Middle Grade*
Horror; Low Fantasy; Magical Realism; Urban Fantasy

Nonfiction > *Picture Books*

YOUNG ADULT > **Fiction** > *Novels*
Comedy / Humour; Contemporary Romance; Diverse Romance; Low Fantasy; Magical Realism; Urban Fantasy

How to send: Email

Currently seeking Adult: Romance, Low-Fantasy; YA: Humorous/lighthearted Contemporary Romance, Diverse Romance, Low-Fantasy, Magical Realism, and characters from marginalized backgrounds. Actively taking on submissions.

L0775 Tristan Kendrick
Literary Agent
United Kingdom

Literary Agency: Rogers, Coleridge & White Ltd (**L1181**)

L0776 Nicki Kennedy

Literary Agent
United Kingdom

Literary Agency: ILA (Intercontinental Literary Agency) (**L0681**)

L0777 Julia Kenny

Literary Agent
United States

Literary Agency: Dunow, Carlson & Lerner Agency (**L0395**)

L0778 Rachel Kent

Literary Agent
United States

Literary Agency: Books & Such Literary Management (**L0156**)

L0779 Eli Keren

Literary Agent
United Kingdom
Tel: +44 (0) 20 3214 0775

ekeren@unitedagents.co.uk

https://www.unitedagents.co.uk/
sballardunitedagentscouk

Literary Agency: United Agents (**L1389**)

Fiction > *Novels*
Commercial; Literary

Nonfiction > *Nonfiction Books*: Popular Science

Send: Synopsis; Writing sample; Pitch; Market info
How to send: Email

I am particularly interested in smart and engaging popular science, as well as literary and commercial fiction. I do not represent authors for children's and YA literature.

L0780 Kat Kerr

Literary Agent
United States

Literary Agency: Donald Maass Literary Agency (**L0380**)

L0781 Vanessa Kerr

Literary Agent
United Kingdom

vanessa@abnerstein.co.uk

Literary Agency: Abner Stein (**L0007**)

L0782 Ki Agency Ltd

Literary Agency
Studio 315, Screenworks, 22 Highbury Grove, London, N5 2ER
United Kingdom
Tel: +44 (0) 20 3214 8287

https://ki-agency.co.uk

Professional Bodies: The Association of Authors' Agents (AAA); Personal Managers' Association (PMA); Writers' Guild of Great Britain (WGGB)

Fiction > *Novels*

Nonfiction > *Nonfiction Books*
Coaching; Leadership; Personal Development

Scripts
Film Scripts; *TV Scripts*; *Theatre Scripts*

Send: Synopsis; Writing sample
How to send: Email attachment

Represents novelists and scriptwriters in all media. No children's or poetry. Send synopsis and first three chapters / first 50 pages by email. See website for individual agent interests.

Literary Agents: Meg Davis (**L0344**); Roz Kidd (**L0783**); Ruth Needham; Anne C. Perry (**L1087**)

L0783 Roz Kidd

Literary Agent
United Kingdom

roz@ki-agency.co.uk

https://ki-agency.co.uk/contact

Literary Agency: Ki Agency Ltd (**L0782**)

Scripts
Film Scripts; *TV Scripts*; *Theatre Scripts*

Accepts submissions of scripts for film, TV or theatre in any genre.

L0784 Emily Sylvan Kim

Literary Agent
United States

Literary Agency: Prospect Agency (**L1116**)

L0785 Jennifer Kim

Literary Agent
United States

Literary Agency: Sandra Dijkstra Literary Agency (**L1218**)

L0786 Natalie Kimber

Literary Agent
Canada

Literary Agency: The Rights Factory (**L1151**)

ADULT
Fiction
Graphic Novels: General
Novels: Adventure; Commercial; Cookery; Historical Fiction; Literary; Science Fiction
Nonfiction > *Nonfiction Books*
Creative Nonfiction; Memoir; Popular Culture; Science; Spirituality; Sustainable Living

YOUNG ADULT > **Fiction** > *Novels*: Boy Books

Send: Query; Author bio; Writing sample
How to send: Email

L0787 Kimberley Cameron & Associates

Literary Agency
1550 Tiburon Blvd #704, Tiberon, CA 94920
United States
Tel: +1 (415) 789-9191

info@kimberleycameron.com

http://www.kimberleycameron.com

Professional Body: Association of Authors' Representatives, Inc. (AAR)

Types: Fiction; Nonfiction
Subjects: Autobiography; Commercial; Contemporary; Cookery; Culture; Current Affairs; Fantasy; Health; History; Horror; Lifestyle; Literary; Mystery; Personal Development; Politics; Religion; Science; Science Fiction; Technology; Thrillers; Travel; Women's Interests
Markets: Adult; Young Adult

Send: Query
Don't send: Full text

See website for specific agent interests and submit to most suitable agent through their online submission system.

Literary Agents: Lisa Abellera (*L0006*); Kimberley Cameron (*L0211*); Amy Cloughley (*L0283*); Elizabeth Kracht (*L0805*); Dorian Maffei (*L0908*); Mary C. Moore (*L0996*)

L0788 Georgia Frances King

Literary Agent
United States

https://aevitascreative.com/agents/

Literary Agency: Aevitas (**L0019**)

Nonfiction > *Nonfiction Books*
Arts; Culture; Design; Futurism; Science; Technology

Send: Query; Market info; Writing sample
How to send: Online submission system

Interested in nonfiction books about emerging science and technology, futurism, design, culture, and the arts, and supporting underrepresented voices.

L0789 Zoe King

Literary Agent
United Kingdom

https://amheath.com/agents/zoe-king/
https://twitter.com/ZoeKingAgent

Literary Agency: A.M. Heath & Company Limited, Author's Agents (**L0004**)

Nonfiction > *Nonfiction Books*
Business; Health; Science; Spirituality

L0790 Kingsford Campbell Literary Agency

Literary Agency
United Kingdom

info@kingsfordcampbell.com

http://kingsfordcampbell.com

Fiction > *Novels*

Nonfiction > *Nonfiction Books*

Send: Query; Synopsis; Writing sample
How to send: Email

Chair: Patrick Janson-Smith

Literary Agents: Charlotte Atyeo (**L0070**);
Charlie Campbell (**L0212**); Julia Kingsford
(**L0791**); Julia Silk (**L1277**)

L0791 Julia Kingsford

Literary Agent

http://kingsfordcampbell.com/about-us/julia-kingsford/
https://twitter.com/juliakingsford

Literary Agency: Kingsford Campbell Literary
Agency (**L0790**)

Fiction > *Novels*

Nonfiction > *Nonfiction Books*

Closed to approaches.

L0792 Jonathan Kinnersley

Literary Agent
United Kingdom

Literary Agency: The Agency (London) Ltd
(**L0021**)

L0793 Jeff Kleinman

Literary Agent; Partner
United States

jeff@foliolit.com

https://www.publishersmarketplace.com/
members/jkleinman/

Literary Agency: Folio Literary Management,
LLC (**L0480**)
Professional Body: Association of Authors'
Representatives, Inc. (AAR)

Fiction > *Novels*
   Book Club Fiction; Literary; Suspense;
   Thrillers; Upmarket

Nonfiction > *Nonfiction Books*
   Animals; History; Memoir; Narrative
   Nonfiction

Send: Query; Writing sample; Synopsis
How to send: In the body of an email

L0794 Harvey Klinger

Literary Agent
United States

Literary Agency: Harvey Klinger, Inc (**L0619**)

L0795 Kelly Knatchbull

Literary Agent
United Kingdom

Literary Agency: Sayle Screen Ltd (**L1226**)

L0796 Kneerim & Williams

Literary Agency
90 Canal Street, Boston, MA 02114
United States
Tel: +1 (617) 303-1650
Fax: +1 (617) 542-1660

submissions@kwlit.com

https://kwlit.com

Professional Body: Association of Authors'
Representatives, Inc. (AAR)

Types: Fiction; Nonfiction
Subjects: Adventure; Anthropology;
Archaeology; Autobiography; Business;
Commercial; Crime; Culture; Current Affairs;
Finance; Health; History; Legal; Lifestyle;
Literary; Literature; Medicine; Nature;
Politics; Psychology; Religion; Science;
Society; Sport; Technology; Women's
Interests
Markets: Adult

Send: Query
Don't send: Full text

Send query by email with synopsis, brief bio,
and 10-20 pages of initial sample material in
the body of the email. No attachments or
queries by post or by phone. See website for
full guidelines.

Literary Agents: Lucy Cleland (*L0278*);
Katherine Flynn (*L0478*); Carol Franco
(*L0495*); Jill Kneerim (*L0797*); Elaine Rogers
(*L1182*); Carolyn Savarese (*L1222*); Matthew
Valentinas (*L1395*); Ike Williams (*L1450*)

L0797 Jill Kneerim

Literary Agent
United States

Literary Agency: Kneerim & Williams (**L0796**)

L0798 Knight Features

Literary Agency
Trident Business Centre, 89 Bickersteth Road,
London, SW17 9SH
United Kingdom
Tel: +44 (0) 20 7622 1467

http://www.knightfeatures.com

Nonfiction > *Nonfiction Books*
   Business; Military

Send: Proposal; Query; Self-Addressed
Stamped Envelope (SASE)
How to send: Phone; Post; Online submission
system

Make initial contact by phone or proposal
through online submission system. If sending
work by post, include SAE. Main areas of
interest are: Motorsports, Graphic Novels,

Business, History, Factual and
Biographical/Autobiographical. Closed to
fiction submissions as at February 2020.

Literary Agents: Samantha Ferris (*L0465*);
Gaby Martin (*L0931*)

L0799 Knight Hall Agency

Literary Agency
Lower Ground Floor, 7 Mallow Street,
London, EC1Y 8RQ
United Kingdom
Tel: +44 (0) 20 3397 2901

office@knighthallagency.com

http://www.knighthallagency.com

Types: Scripts
Formats: Film Scripts; TV Scripts; Theatre
Scripts
Subjects: Drama
Markets: Adult

Closed to approaches.

**Note: Closed to submissions as at February
2020. Check website for current status.**

Send query by post or email (no attachments).
Only send sample if requested. Represents
playwrights, screenwriters and writer-directors.
Handles adaptation rights for novels, but does
not handle books directly.

Authors: Simon Beaufoy; Jeremy Brock; Liz
Lochhead; Martin McDonagh; Simon Nye

Literary Agent: Charlotte Knight (*L0800*)

L0800 Charlotte Knight

Literary Agent
United Kingdom

Literary Agency: Knight Hall Agency (**L0799**)

L0801 Kohner Agency

Literary Agency
9300 Wilshire Boulevard, Suite 555, Beverly
Hills, CA 90212
United States
Tel: +1 (310) 550-1060

http://paulkohner.com

Closed to approaches.

The second oldest talent agency in Los
Angeles, with a literary department boasting
representation of 24 major publishing houses.
No unsolicited submissions, ideas, or
suggestions.

Literary Agents: Stephen Moore; Deborah
Obad; Pearl Wexler

L0802 Stacey Kondla

Literary Agent
Canada

Literary Agency: The Rights Factory (**L1151**)

L0803 **Kelvin Kong**
Literary Agent
Canada

Literary Agency: K2 Literary (**L0750**)

L0804 **Katie Kotchman**
Literary Agent
United States

Literary Agency: Don Congdon Associates, Inc. (**L0378**)

L0805 **Elizabeth Kracht**
Literary Agent
United States

Literary Agency: Kimberley Cameron & Associates (**L0787**)

L0806 **Jill Kramer**
Literary Agent
United States

Literary Agency: Waterside Productions, Inc (**L1418**)

L0807 **Julia Kreitman**
Literary Agent
United Kingdom

Literary Agency: The Agency (London) Ltd (**L0021**)

L0808 **Mary Krienke**
Associate Agent
United States

https://www.sll.com/our-team

Literary Agency: Sterling Lord Literistic, Inc. (**L1317**)

Fiction > *Novels*
Literary; Upmarket

Nonfiction > *Nonfiction Books*
Culture; Health; Sexuality

Send: Query; Synopsis; Writing sample
How to send: Online submission system

Represents literary and upmarket fiction, voice-driven nonfiction, and memoir. She is particularly drawn to nonfiction that speaks to something essential and of-the-moment, especially work that engages with themes of culture, identity, sexuality, and health.

L0809 **Miriam Kriss**
Literary Agent
United States

Literary Agency: Irene Goodman Literary Agency (IGLA) (**L0688**)

L0810 **Kruger Cowne**
Literary Agency
Unit 7C, Chelsea Wharf, 15 Lots Road, London, SW10 0QJ

United Kingdom
Tel: +44 (0) 20 7352 2277

oscar@krugercowne.com

https://www.krugercowne.com
https://twitter.com/krugercowne
https://www.instagram.com/krugercowne/
https://www.facebook.com/krugercowne
https://www.linkedin.com/company/kruger-cowne
https://www.youtube.com/user/KrugerCowneTalent

Professional Body: The Association of Authors' Agents (AAA)

Types: Fiction; Nonfiction
Subjects: Adventure; Anthropology; Arts; Autobiography; Beauty; Business; Comedy / Humour; Commercial; Contemporary; Crime; Culture; Current Affairs; Erotic; Experimental; Fashion; Gothic; Health; History; Hobbies; How To; Lifestyle; Literary; Men's Interests; Music; Nature; New Age; Personal Development; Philosophy; Psychology; Satire; Science; Sport; Suspense; Thrillers; Warfare; Westerns; Women's Interests
Markets: Adult; Children's; Young Adult

Send: Full text
How to send: Email

A talent management agency, with an extremely strong literary arm.

The majority of the works handled by the agency fall into the category of celebrity nonfiction. However, also regularly work with journalists, entrepreneurs and influencers on projects, with a speciality in polemics, and speculative works on the future.

Occasionally take on exceptional fiction authors.

Authors: Akala; Bruce Dickinson; Bob Geldof; Kelly Holmes; Gail Porter

Literary Agent: Oscar Janson-Smith (*L0713*)

L0811 **KT Literary**
Literary Agency
9249 S. Broadway #200-543, Highlands Ranch, CO 80129
United States
Tel: +1 (720) 344-4728
Fax: +1 (720) 344-4728

contact@ktliterary.com

http://ktliterary.com

Types: Fiction
Subjects: Contemporary; Erotic; Fantasy; Romance; Science Fiction
Markets: Adult; Children's; Young Adult

Send: Query
Don't send: Full text
How to send: Email

Actively seeking new clients for middle grade, young adult, and adult categories. See website for individual agent interests and contact

details and query one agent at a time. See website for full details.

Literary Agents: Hannah Fergesen (*L0462*); Hilary Harwell (*L0620*); Sara Megibow (*L0963*); Renee Nyen (*L1048*); Kate Testerman (*L1360*)

L0812 **David Kuhn**
Literary Agent; Chief Executive Officer
United States

https://aevitascreative.com/agents/

Literary Agency: Aevitas (**L0019**)

Nonfiction > *Nonfiction Books*
Culture; Current Affairs; Entertainment; Food; History; Memoir; Music; Politics

Closed to approaches.

Represents nonfiction books that will educate, entertain, and enlighten in the areas of memoir, current events, history, politics, culture, style, food, music, and entertainment.

L0813 **Danya Kukafka**
Literary Agent
United States

https://aevitascreative.com/agents/

Literary Agency: Aevitas (**L0019**)

Fiction > *Novels*
Experimental; Literary; Speculative; Suspense; Thrillers; Upmarket

Nonfiction > *Nonfiction Books*
Crime; Culture

Send: Query; Writing sample
How to send: Online submission system

She is interested literary fiction with particularly propulsive storylines. She is seeking literary suspense, sophisticated thrillers, speculative fiction, and experimental fiction—she also loves true crime that feels attuned to today's cultural conversations, as well as upmarket literary fiction you can read in one gulp.

L0814 **Maura Kye-Casella**
Literary Agent
United States

Literary Agency: Don Congdon Associates, Inc. (**L0378**)

L0815 **The LA Literary Agency**
Literary Agency
United States

ann@laliteraryagency.com

https://www.laliteraryagency.com

Fiction > *Novels*
Commercial; Literary

Nonfiction > *Nonfiction Books*
Biography; Business; Cookery; Health; History; Lifestyle; Memoir; Narrative

Nonfiction; Parenting; Psychology; Science; Sport

Send: Query; Proposal; Full text
How to send: Email attachment

Costs: Offers services that writers have to pay for. Sister company provides editorial services.

Send query with proposal (nonfiction) or full ms (fiction) by email. Response only if interested.

Literary Agents: Eric Lasher; Maureen Lasher

L0816 The Labyrinth Literary Agency
Literary Agency
2nd Floor, 141A, Shahpur Jat, Siri Fort, Delhi 110049
India

ac@labyrinthagency.com

http://www.labyrinthagency.com
https://www.instagram.com/labyrinthagency/
https://twitter.com/LabyrinthAgency
https://twitter.com/LabyrinthAgency

Fiction > *Novels*

Nonfiction > *Nonfiction Books*

Send: Synopsis; Writing sample; Author bio
How to send: Email

Costs: Offers services that writers have to pay for. Offers editorial and advice services to authors with whom they do not have a business relationship.

Literary Agent: Anish Chandy (*L0250*)

L0817 Natalie Lakosil
Literary Agent
United States

https://bradfordlit.com/about/natalie-lakosil/
https://twitter.com/Natalie_Lakosil
http://www.manuscriptwishlist.com/mswl-post/natalie-lakosil/

Literary Agency: Bradford Literary Agency (**L0169**)

ADULT
Fiction > *Novels*
Comedy / Humour; Cozy Mysteries; Crime; Diversity; Women's Fiction

Nonfiction > *Nonfiction Books*
Business; Comedy / Humour; New Age; Prescriptive Nonfiction; Psychology; Science; Self Help

CHILDREN'S
Fiction
Chapter Books: General, and in particular: Diversity
Middle Grade: Commercial; Contemporary; Dark; Diversity; Fantasy; Historical Fiction; Horror; LGBTQIA; Magical Realism; Science Fiction; Thrillers
Picture Books: General

Nonfiction
Nonfiction Books: Biography; Feminism; Social Issues
Picture Books: Biography

YOUNG ADULT
Fiction > *Novels*
Commercial; Contemporary; Dark; Diversity; Fantasy; Historical Fiction; Horror; LGBTQIA; Magical Realism; Science Fiction; Thrillers

Nonfiction > *Nonfiction Books*

Closed to approaches.

Specialties are all ages (PB, chapter book, MG, YA) of children's literature (fiction and nonfiction), adult cozy mystery/crime, female-driven thrillers, and upmarket women's/general fiction. She also represents illustrators and select adult nonfiction.

L0818 Laurence Laluyaux
Literary Agent
United Kingdom

Literary Agency: Rogers, Coleridge & White Ltd (**L1181**)

L0819 Cari Lamba
Literary Agent
United States

Literary Agency: The Jennifer DeChiara Literary Agency (**L0721**)

L0820 Marie Lamba
Literary Agent
United States

Literary Agency: The Jennifer DeChiara Literary Agency (**L0721**)

L0821 Sophie Lambert
Literary Agent
United Kingdom

Literary Agency: C+W (Conville & Walsh) (**L0205**)

L0822 Louise Lamont
Literary Agent
United Kingdom

louisesubmissions@lbabooks.com

http://www.lbabooks.com/agent/louise-lamont/

Literary Agency: LBA Books Ltd (**L0839**)

CHILDREN'S > **Fiction** > *Novels*
Adventure; Comedy / Humour

Does not want:

> **CHILDREN'S** > **Fiction** > *Picture Books*

How to send: Email

L0823 Andrew Lampack
Literary Agent
United States

Literary Agency: Peter Lampack Agency, Inc (**L1090**)

L0824 Sonia Land
Literary Agent
United Kingdom

Literary Agency: Sheil Land Associates Ltd (**L1263**)

L0825 Sarah Landis
Literary Agent
United States

https://www.sll.com/our-team

Literary Agency: Sterling Lord Literistic, Inc. (**L1317**)

CHILDREN'S > **Fiction** > *Middle Grade*
Comedy / Humour; Contemporary; Fantasy

YOUNG ADULT > **Fiction** > *Novels*
Contemporary; Fantasy; High Concept; Historical Fiction; Mystery; Science Fiction; Thrillers

Send: Query; Synopsis; Writing sample
How to send: Online submission system

This agent is looking for middle grade and young adult books across all genres. She is particularly drawn to middle grade fantasy and contemporary with heart, humor, and magic. In the young adult space, she has an affinity for southern voices, high-concept plots, grounded sci-fi/fantasy, historical, mysteries and thrillers, and emotionally compelling contemporary.

L0826 Lina Langlee
Literary Agent
United Kingdom

http://thenorthlitagency.com/our-friends-in-the-north/
https://twitter.com/LinaLanglee

Literary Agency: The North Literary Agency (**L1040**)

ADULT
Fiction > *Novels*
Commercial; Crime; High Concept; Literary; Speculative; Thrillers

Nonfiction > *Nonfiction Books*

CHILDREN'S > **Fiction** > *Middle Grade*

YOUNG ADULT > **Fiction** > *Novels*

Closed to approaches.

Looking for books across genres: commercial fiction with a great hook, literary fiction, speculative or high concept books that remain very readable, crime fiction that stands out, fun and moving Middle Grade, and any genre of Young Adult. In terms of nonfiction, interested either in 'the small made big' or 'the big made small': specialists that can make really niche subjects accessible and interesting to a wider market, or deeply personal accounts of the big issues we might all one day tackle.

L0827 Elena Langtry
Literary Agent
United Kingdom

https://cmm.agency/about-us.php

Literary Agency: Coombs Moylett & Maclean Literary Agency (**L0295**)

Fiction > *Novels*
Commercial Women's Fiction; Psychological Thrillers

Nonfiction > *Nonfiction Books*
Popular Science; Self Help

How to send: Online submission system

L0828 Katherine Latshaw
Literary Agent; Vice President
United States

klatshaw@foliolitmanagement.com

https://www.foliolit.com/agents-1/katherine-latshaw

Literary Agency: Folio Literary Management, LLC (**L0480**)

ADULT
  Fiction > *Novels*

  Nonfiction
    Essays: General
    Illustrated Books: General
    Nonfiction Books: Commercial; Cookery; Feminism; Health; Lifestyle; Memoir; Narrative Nonfiction; Popular Culture; Prescriptive Nonfiction; Wellbeing
CHILDREN'S > **Fiction** > *Middle Grade*

YOUNG ADULT > **Fiction** > *Novels*

How to send: Email

L0829 Steve Laube
Literary Agent
United States

Literary Agency: The Steve Laube Agency (**L1318**)

L0830 Jennifer Laughran
Literary Agent
United States

Literary Agency: Andrea Brown Literary Agency, Inc. (**L0047**)
Professional Body: Association of Authors' Representatives, Inc. (AAR)

L0831 Laura Dail Literary Agency
Literary Agency
121 West 27th Street, Suite 1201, New York,

NY 10001
United States
Tel: +1 (212) 239-7477

queries@ldlainc.com

http://www.ldlainc.com
https://twitter.com/LDLiterary
https://www.instagram.com/lauradaillit/

How to send: Query Manager

Send query through online submission system only. Query one agent at a time with one project at a time.

Literary Agent / President: Laura Dail (**L0326**)

Literary Agents: Samantha Fabien (**L0447**); Elana Roth Parker (**L1068**); Carrie Pestritto (**L1089**)

L0832 Sophie Laurimore
Literary Agent
United Kingdom

sohoagencysubmissions@gmail.com

https://thesohoagency.co.uk/agent/sophie-laurimore

Literary Agency: The Soho Agency (**L1297**)

Nonfiction > *Nonfiction Books*

Send: Writing sample; Synopsis; Query
How to send: Email attachment

L0833 Lawrence Jordan Literary Agency
Literary Agency
231 Lenox Avenue, Suite One, New York, NY 10027
United States
Tel: +1 (212) 662-7871
Fax: +1 (212) 865-7171

ljlagency@aol.com

Types: Fiction; Nonfiction
Subjects: Autobiography; Mystery; Religion; Suspense; Thrillers
Markets: Adult

Send: Query
Don't send: Full text
How to send: Email

Costs: Author covers sundry admin costs.

Send query by email only. Particularly interested in spiritual / religion; biographies, autobiographies and celebrity books; mysteries, suspense, and thrillers. No poetry, movie or stage scripts, juvenile, fantasy, or science fiction.

Literary Agent: Lawrence Jordan (*L0741*)

L0834 Tricia Lawrence
Literary Agent
United States

Literary Agency: Erin Murphy Literary Agency, Inc. (**L0433**)

L0835 Rowan Lawton
Company Director; Literary Agent
United Kingdom

https://twitter.com/Rowan_Lawton

Literary Agency: The Soho Agency (**L1297**)

Fiction > *Novels*
Book Club Fiction; Commercial Women's Fiction; Contemporary Romance; Crime; Domestic Suspense; Literary; Memoir; Romantic Comedy; Women's Fiction

L0836 Wendy Lawton
Literary Agent
United States

Literary Agency: Books & Such Literary Management (**L0156**)

L0837 Laxfield Literary Associates
Literary Agency
United Kingdom

https://laxfieldliterary.com

Fiction > *Novels*
Commercial; Literary

Nonfiction > *Nonfiction Books*
Creative Nonfiction; Nature; Travel

Send: Query; Synopsis; Writing sample; Author bio; Outline
How to send: Word file email attachment

We are looking for fiction and non-fiction of the highest quality. We are keen to receive literary and commercial fiction. We are also looking for non-fiction, particularly creative non-fiction, travel writing and nature writing. We do not represent poetry, plays or children's books.

L0838 Veronica Lazar
Literary Agent
United Kingdom

https://www.imdb.com/name/nm4400468/

Literary Agency: AVAnti Productions & Management (**L0072**)

L0839 LBA Books Ltd
Literary Agency
91 Great Russell Street, London, WC1B 3PS
United Kingdom
Tel: +44 (0) 20 7637 1234

info@lbabooks.com

http://www.lbabooks.com

Professional Body: The Association of Authors' Agents (AAA)

Send query with synopsis and first three chapters to specific agent by email only. See website for specific agents' interests and email addresses. No scripts, short stories, or poetry.

Authors: Ellie Adams; Will Adams; Nazneen Ahmed; Sarah Alderson; Kirstie Allsopp; Laura Archer; Helen Arney; Melissa Bailey; James Barrington; Chris Beardshaw; James Becker; Lucy Beresford-Knox; Virginia Bergin; A.L. Bird; Kate Beal Blyth; Darcie Boleyn; Katie Bonna; Joanna Boyle; Diana Bretherick; Fern Britton; Amanda Brooke; Julie Brunelle; Charlotte Butterfield; Alex Caan; Jo Carnegie; Lucie Cave; Roland Chambers; Rebecca Chance; James Cheshire; Sam Christer; Katie Clapham; George Clarke; Hannah Coates; Rebecca Cobb; Daniel A. Cohen; Megan Cole; Rosemary Conley; Gennaro Contaldo; Ping Coombes; Emma Cooper; Josephine Cox; Dean Crawford; Mason Cross; Tricia Cusden; A.M. Dean; Hannah Doyle; Matthew Dunn; Matt Edmondson; Joey Essex; Kate Faithfull-Williams; Liz Fenwick; Cal Finnigan; Judy Finnigan; Rosheen Finnigan; Clare Foges; Nick Foulkes; Tom Fox; Rosie French; David Gibbins; Ellie Grace; Tom Grass; Julia Gray; Mila Gray; Christian Guiltenane; Abigail Haas; Kate Hackworthy; Rachel Hamilton; Richard Hammond; Helen Hancocks; Charlotte Haptie; Isabella Harcourt; Fiona Harper; Zinnie Harris; Matt Hilton; Eva Holland; Jane Holland; Restoration Home; Joanne Hull; John Humphrys; Jessica Jarlvi; Jessica Johnson; Graham Joyce; Miranda Kane; Annabel Kantaria; Lesley Kara; Eva Katzler; Simon Kernick; Margaret Kirk; Victoria Lamb; Lauren Libbert; Agnes Light; Freda Lightfoot; Jane Linfoot; Amy Lloyd; Rachael Lucas; Dee MacDonald; Richard Madeley; Lucy Mangan; Ian Marber; Tom Marcus; Sam Masters; James May; Julie Mayhew; Colin McDowell; Ross McGovern; David Meikle; Gavin Menzies; Nicole Mones; Marcia Moody; Michael Morley; Elizabeth Moss; Steve Mould; Faya Nilsson; Jen Offord; Karen Osman; Sue Palmer; Angelique Panagos; Seth Patrick; Andrew Pepper; Ivor Peters; Hannah Phillips; Melanie Phillips; Gervase Phinn; Anna Pointer; Richard Porter; Jem Poster; Esther Rantzen; Louisa Reid; Madeleine Reiss; Alice Roberts; Bernadette Robinson; Amber Rose; Mike Rossiter; Cate Sampson; Super Scrimpers; Colin Shindler; Fleur Sinclair; Jack Steel; Zara Stoneley; Lucy Strange; Heidi Swain; Karen Swan; Joe Swift; Bryan Sykes; Sophie Tanner; Rachel de Thame; Alan Titchmarsh; Andy Torbet; Jon Trace; Jonathan Trigell; Oliver Uberti; Phil Vickery; Ria Voros; Jennifer Wells; Kate Winter; Tamsin Winter; Terry Wogan; Peter Wood; Katherine Woodfine; Sally Worboyes; Emma Yarlett

Junior Agent: Hannah Schofield (**L1237**)

Literary Agents: Luigi Bonomi (**L0152**); Louise Lamont (**L0822**); Amanda Preston (**L1115**)

L0840 Thao Le

Literary Agent
United States

Literary Agency: Sandra Dijkstra Literary Agency (**L1218**)

L0841 Ned Leavitt

Literary Agent
United States

Literary Agency: The Ned Leavitt Agency (**L1025**)

L0842 Lee Sobel Literary Agency

Literary Agency
9 Church Street, Middletown, NJ 07748
United States
Tel: +1 (917) 553-4991

LeeSobel15@gmail.com

https://www.facebook.com/
leesobelliteraryagency/

Types: Fiction; Nonfiction
Formats: Film Scripts
Subjects: Autobiography; Comedy / Humour; Commercial; Contemporary; Crime; Culture; Current Affairs; Entertainment; Erotic; Fantasy; Horror; Literary; Music; Mystery; Satire; Science Fiction; Suspense; Thrillers; Traditional
Markets: Adult; Young Adult

Send: Full text
How to send: Email

Currently selling a lot of nonfiction books but more focused on finding commercial novels now. Seeking ambitious epic books with attractive characters to lend themselves for movie adaptations. Think big! Check out the detailed Q&A with me on my agency Facebook site as it will give you a lot of info about why I might be the right agent for you.

Authors: Peter Aaron; Peter Benjaminson; Steve Bergsman; Laura Davis-Chanin; Dave Thompson

Literary Agent: Lee Sobel (*L1296*)

L0843 Jordan Lees

Associate Agent
United Kingdom

jordansubmissions@theblairpartnership.com

https://www.theblairpartnership.com/
our_people/jordan-lees/

Literary Agency: The Blair Partnership (**L0138**)

Fiction > *Novels*
   Commercial; Crime; Detective Fiction; Dystopian Fiction; High Concept; Historical Fiction; International; Literary; Speculative; Thrillers

Nonfiction > *Nonfiction Books*

Crime; International

Send: Synopsis; Proposal; Writing sample
How to send: Word file email attachment; PDF file email attachment
How not to send: WeTransfer; Dropbox; Google Docs email attachment; Google Docs shared document

Represents commercial and literary crime/thrillers, detective fiction, historical fiction, dystopian/speculative fiction, literary fiction, true crime and smart non-fiction.

L0844 Lindsay Leggett

Associate Agent
Canada

Literary Agency: The Rights Factory (**L1151**)

ADULT > **Fiction**
   Graphic Novels: General
   Novels: Horror; LGBTQIA; Romance; Thrillers
CHILDREN'S > **Fiction** > *Middle Grade*

YOUNG ADULT > **Fiction** > *Novels*

Closed to approaches.

L0845 Becky LeJeune

Literary Agent
United States

Literary Agency: Bond Literary Agency (**L0150**)

L0846 Betsy Lerner

Literary Agent
United States

Literary Agency: Dunow, Carlson & Lerner Agency (**L0395**)

L0847 The Leshne Agency

Literary Agency
590 West End Avenue, Suite 11D, New York, NY 10024
United States

Submissions@LeshneAgency.com

http://leshneagency.com

Types: Fiction; Nonfiction
Formats: Film Scripts
Subjects: Arts; Autobiography; Business; Comedy / Humour; Commercial; Cookery; Crafts; Culture; Gardening; Health; History; Literary; Personal Development; Photography; Science; Spirituality; Sport; Technology; Travel; Women's Interests
Markets: Adult; Children's; Young Adult

Send: Query
Don't send: Full text
How to send: Email

Seeking new and existing authors across all genres. Particularly interested in narrative, memoir, prescriptive nonfiction (including sports, health, wellness, business, political and parenting topics), commercial fiction, young adult and middle grade books. No screenplays, scripts, poetry, or picture books. Submit online through online submissions system or by email. See website for full details.

Literary Agent: Lisa Leshne (*L0848*)

L0848 Lisa Leshne
Literary Agent
United States

Literary Agency: The Leshne Agency (**L0847**)

L0849 Julia Levin
Literary Agent
United States

https://accrispin.blogspot.com/2014/02/alert-jane-dowary-agency.html

Literary Agency: Jane Dowary Agency (**L0707**)

L0850 Paul S. Levine
Literary Agent
United States

Literary Agency: Paul S. Levine Literary Agency (**L1074**)

L0851 Wendy Levinson
Literary Agent
United States

Literary Agency: Harvey Klinger, Inc (**L0619**)

L0852 Barbara Levy
Literary Agent
United Kingdom

Literary Agency: Barbara Levy Literary Agency (**L0085**)

L0853 Bibi Lewis
Literary Agent
United States

https://ethanellenberg.com/our-agents/

Literary Agency: Ethan Ellenberg Literary Agency (**L0437**)

ADULT > **Fiction** > *Novels*
  Mystery; Romance; Thrillers; Women's Fiction

CHILDREN'S
  Fiction > *Picture Books*
  Nonfiction > *Picture Books*

YOUNG ADULT
  Fiction > *Novels*
  Nonfiction > *Nonfiction Books*

L0854 Kevin Lewis
Literary Agent
United States

Literary Agency: Erin Murphy Literary Agency, Inc. (**L0433**)

L0855 Limelight Management
Literary Agency
10 Filmer Mews, 75 Filmer Road, London, SW6 7JF
United Kingdom
Tel: +44 (0) 20 7384 9950

mail@limelightmanagement.com

https://www.limelightmanagement.com
https://www.facebook.com/pages/Limelight-Celebrity-Management-Ltd/399328580099859?fref=ts
https://twitter.com/Fionalimelight
https://www.youtube.com/channel/UCCmxquRk_blKqjR8jKRryFA
https://instagram.com/limelightcelebritymanagement/
https://www.linkedin.com/company-beta/11219861/

Professional Body: The Association of Authors' Agents (AAA)

Fiction > *Novels*
  Commercial Women's Fiction; Crime; Historical Fiction; Mystery; Suspense; Thrillers

Nonfiction > *Nonfiction Books*
  Arts; Autobiography; Biography; Business; Cookery; Crafts; Health; Nature; Popular Science; Sport; Travel

Send: Query; Synopsis; Writing sample; Author bio
How to send: Email

Always looking for exciting new authors. Send query by email with the word "Submission" in the subject line and synopsis and first three chapters as Word or Open Document attachments. Also include market info, and details of your professional life and writing ambitions. Film and TV scripts for existing clients only. See website for full guidelines.

Literary Agent: Fiona Lindsay (*L0859*)

L0856 Linda Konner Literary Agency
Literary Agency
10 West 15 Street, Suite 1918, New York, NY 10011
United States

ldkonner@cs.com

http://www.lindakonnerliteraryagency.com

Types: Nonfiction
Formats: Reference
Subjects: Biography; Business; Cookery; Culture; Entertainment; Finance; Health; How To; Lifestyle; Personal Development; Psychology; Science; Women's Interests
Markets: Adult

Send: Query
Don't send: Full text
How to send: Email

Costs: Author covers sundry admin costs.

Send one to two page query by email only. Attachments from unknown senders will be deleted unread. Nonfiction only. Books must be written by or with established experts in their field. No Fiction, Memoir, Religion, Spiritual/Christian, Children's/young adult, Games/puzzles, Humour, History, Politics, or unsolicited MSS. See website for full guidelines.

Literary Agent: Linda Konner

L0857 Linda Seifert Management
Literary Agency
Screenworks, Room 315, 22 Highbury Grove, Islington, London, N5 2ER
United Kingdom
Tel: +44 (0) 20 3214 8293

contact@lindaseifert.com

http://www.lindaseifert.com

Professional Body: Personal Managers' Association (PMA)

ADULT > **Scripts**
  Film Scripts; *TV Scripts*
CHILDREN'S > **Scripts**
  Film Scripts; *TV Scripts*
Closed to approaches.

Costs: Author covers sundry admin costs.

A London-based management company representing screenwriters and directors for film and television. Our outstanding client list ranges from the highly established to the new and exciting emerging talent of tomorrow. Represents UK-based writers and directors only.

Literary Agent: Edward Hughes (*L0672*)

L0858 Lindsay Literary Agency
Literary Agency
United Kingdom
Tel: +44 (0) 1420 831430

info@lindsayliteraryagency.co.uk

http://www.lindsayliteraryagency.co.uk
https://twitter.com/lindsaylit?lang=en

CHILDREN'S > **Fiction**
  Middle Grade; *Picture Books*
YOUNG ADULT > **Fiction** > *Novels*

Send: Query; Author bio; Pitch; Synopsis; Writing sample
How to send: Email

No submissions from white people.

Send query by email only, including single-page synopsis and first three chapters. For picture books send complete ms. No submissions by post.

Authors: Gina Blaxill; Helen Brandom; Pamela Butchart; Christina Collins; Donna David; Sam

Gayton; Ruth Hatfield; Peter Jones; Jay Joseph; Titania Krimpas; Mike Lancaster; Giles Paley-Phillips; Sharon Tregenza; Rachel Valentine; Sue Wallman; Jacqueline Whitehart; Joe Wilson

Literary Agent: Becky Bagnell (*L0078*)

L0859 Fiona Lindsay
Literary Agent
United Kingdom

Literary Agency: Limelight Management (**L0855**)

L0860 Kim Lionetti
Literary Agent
United States

Literary Agency: BookEnds, LLC (**L0155**)

L0861 The Lisa Ekus Group, LLC
Literary Agency
57 North Street, Hatfield, MA 01038
United States
Tel: +1 (413) 247-9325

info@lisaekus.com

http://www.lisaekus.com

Types: Nonfiction
Subjects: Cookery
Markets: Adult

Send: Query
Don't send: Full text

Handles cookery books only. Submit proposal through submission system on website.

Literary Agent: Lisa Ekus (*L0420*)

L0862 The Lisa Richards Agency
Literary Agency
108 Upper Leeson Street, Dublin, 4
Ireland
Tel: +353 1 637 5000
Fax: +353 1 667 1256

info@lisarichards.ie

http://www.lisarichards.ie

Types: Fiction; Nonfiction; Scripts
Formats: Theatre Scripts
Subjects: Autobiography; Comedy / Humour; Commercial; Culture; History; Lifestyle; Literary; Personal Development; Sport
Markets: Adult; Children's

Send: Query
Don't send: Full text
How to send: Email

Send query by email or by post with SASE, including three or four sample chapters in the case of fiction, or proposal and sample chapter for nonfiction. No horror, science fiction, screenplays, or children's picture books.

L0863 Laurie Liss
Literary Agent; Executive Vice President
United States

https://www.sll.com/our-team
http://aaronline.org/Sys/PublicProfile/2176754/417813

Literary Agency: Sterling Lord Literistic, Inc. (**L1317**)
Professional Body: Association of Authors' Representatives, Inc. (AAR)

Fiction > *Novels*
   Commercial; Literary

Nonfiction > *Nonfiction Books:* Commercial

Send: Query; Synopsis; Writing sample
How to send: Online submission system

L0864 Literary Management Group, Inc.
Literary Agency
8530 Calistoga Way, Brentwood, TN 37027
United States
Tel: +1 (615) 812-4445

BruceBarbour@
LiteraryManagementGroup.com

https://literarymanagementgroup.com/

Nonfiction > *Nonfiction Books*
   Biography; Business; Lifestyle; Religion

Send: Query; Writing sample
How to send: Word file email attachment
How not to send: PDF file email attachment

Handles Christian books (defined as books which are consistent with the historical, orthodox teachings of the Christian fathers). Handles adult nonfiction only. No children's or illustrated books, poetry, memoirs, YA Fiction or text/academic books. Download proposal from website then complete and send with sample chapters.

Literary Agent: Bruce R. Barbour (*L0087*)

L0865 Literary Services, Inc.
Literary Agency
PO Box 888, Barnegat, NJ 08005
United States

jwlitagent@msn.com

http://literaryservicesinc.com

Types: Fiction; Nonfiction
Formats: Reference
Subjects: Business; Commercial; Crime; Finance; Health; History; Lifestyle; Literary; Politics; Psychology; Science; Spirituality; Sport; Technology
Markets: Adult

Send: Query
Don't send: Full text
How to send: Email

Costs: Offers services that writers have to pay for.

Send one-page synopsis by email only. particularly interested in business and management; business narratives; careers; gift and reference books; health, fitness and aging; history and politics; literary nonfiction and historical fiction; mind, body, spirit; personal finance, investing and trading; personal growth and psychology; science; sports; technology and trends; true crime.

L0866 Christopher Little
Literary Agent
United Kingdom

Literary Agency: The Christopher Little Literary Agency (**L0266**)

L0867 Mandy Little
Literary Agent
United Kingdom

Literary Agency: Watson, Little Ltd (**L1419**)

L0868 Liza Dawson Associates
Literary Agency
121 West 27th Street, Suite 1201, New York, NY 10001
United States
Tel: +1 (973) 743-2535

queryliza@LizaDawsonAssociates.com

http://www.lizadawsonassociates.com

Professional Body: Association of Authors' Representatives, Inc. (AAR)

Types: Fiction; Nonfiction
Formats: Theatre Scripts
Subjects: Autobiography; Business; Comedy / Humour; Commercial; Culture; Current Affairs; Fantasy; History; Lifestyle; Literary; Medicine; Mystery; Personal Development; Politics; Psychology; Religion; Romance; Science; Science Fiction; Society; Suspense; Thrillers; Warfare; Women's Interests
Markets: Academic; Adult; Children's; Young Adult

See website for specific agent interests and query appropriate agent directly. Specific agent submission guidelines and contact details are available on website.

Authors: Marie Bostwick; Robyn Carr; Scott Hawkins; Marybeth Whalen

Literary Agents: Rachel Beck (**L0106**); Caitlin Blasdell (*L0142*); Hannah Bowman (*L0167*); Liza Dawson (*L0347*); Caitie Flum (*L0476*); Kayla Lightner; Tom Miller (*L0987*)

L0869 The LKG Agency
Literary Agency
60 Riverside Blvd, #1101, New York, NY 10069
United States

query@LKGAgency.com

http://lkgagency.com

Types: Fiction; Nonfiction
Subjects: Autobiography; Beauty; Design;
Entertainment; Fashion; Health; Lifestyle;
Psychology; Women's Interests
Markets: Adult; Children's; Young Adult

Send: Query
Don't send: Full text
How to send: Email

Specialises in nonfiction, but will also consider
middle grade and young adult fiction. No
history, spirituality, biography, screenplays,
true crime, poetry, religion, picture books, or
any other fiction besides middle grade and
young adult. See website for full submission
guidelines.

Literary Agents: Lauren Galit (*L0521*); Caitlen
Rubino-Bradway (*L1196*)

L0870 Jonathan Lloyd
Literary Agent
United Kingdom

Literary Agency: Curtis Brown (**L0318**)

L0871 Rozzy Lloyd
Literary Agent
United Kingdom

Literary Agency: The Narrow Road Company
(**L1021**)

L0872 James Macdonald Lockhart
Literary Agent
United Kingdom

james@antonyharwood.com

http://antonyharwood.com/james-macdonald-
lockhart/

Literary Agency: Antony Harwood Limited
(**L0058**)

Nonfiction > *Nonfiction Books*
   History; Nature; Politics; Science; Travel

L0873 Pat Lomax
Literary Agent
United Kingdom

Literary Agency: Bell Lomax Moreton Agency
(**L0110**)

L0874 Rupert Lord
Literary Agent
United Kingdom

Literary Agency: Macnaughton Lord
Representation (**L0905**)

L0875 Lorella Belli Literary Agency (LBLA)
Literary Agency
54 Hartford House, 35 Tavistock Crescent,
Notting Hill, London, W11 1AY

United Kingdom
Tel: +44 (0) 20 7727 8547
Fax: +44 (0) 870 787 4194

info@lorellabelliagency.com

http://www.lorellabelliagency.com

Professional Body: The Association of
Authors' Agents (AAA)

Types: Fiction; Nonfiction
Subjects: Literary
Markets: Adult

Send: Query
Don't send: Full text
How to send: Email

Send query by post or by email in first
instance. No attachments. Particularly
interested in multicultural / international
writing, and books relating to Italy, or written
in Italian; first novelists, and journalists;
successful sel-published authors. Welcomes
queries from new authors and will suggest
revisions where appropriate. No poetry,
children's, original scripts, academic, SF, or
fantasy.

Authors: Shahena Ali; Zoe Bran; Emily Giffin;
Nisha Minhas; Alanna Mitchell; Rick Mofina;
Dave Singleton; Diana Winston; Carol Wright

Literary Agent: Lorella Belli (*L0115*)

L0876 Lotus Lane Literary
Literary Agency
United States

contact@lotuslit.com

https://lotuslit.com

Fiction > *Novels*

Nonfiction > *Nonfiction Books*

Send: Query; Author bio; Synopsis; Writing
sample
How to send: Email

Independent literary agency based in New
Jersey, representing a diverse list of debut and
seasoned authors. Handles adult fiction and
nonfiction, and sells rights to the US, UK,
Europe, and India.

Literary Agent: Priya Doraswamy (*L0381*)

L0877 Louise Greenberg Books Ltd
Literary Agency
The End House, Church Crescent, London, N3
1BG
United Kingdom
Tel: +44 (0) 20 8349 1179

louisegreenberg@btinternet.com

http://louisegreenbergbooks.co.uk

Professional Body: The Association of
Authors' Agents (AAA)

Types: Fiction; Nonfiction
Subjects: Literary
Markets: Adult

Closed to approaches.

**Not accepting new writers as at July 2019.
Check website for current status.** Handles
full-length literary fiction and serious
nonfiction only. Only considers new writers by
recommendation.

Literary Agent: Louise Greenberg (*L0577*)

L0878 Lowenstein Associates, Inc.
Literary Agency
115 East 23rd Street, 4th Floor, New York, NY
10010
United States
Tel: +1 (212) 206-1630

assistant@bookhaven.com

http://www.lowensteinassociates.com

Professional Body: Association of Authors'
Representatives, Inc. (AAR)

Types: Fiction; Nonfiction
Subjects: Autobiography; Business;
Commercial; Contemporary; Crime; Culture;
Health; Literary; Medicine; Mystery;
Psychology; Science; Society; Thrillers;
Women's Interests
Markets: Adult; Children's; Young Adult

Send: Query
Don't send: Full text
How to send: Email

Send query by email with one-page query letter
and first ten pages pasted into the body of the
email (fiction) or table of contents and (if
available) proposal. See website for full
guidelines. No Westerns, textbooks, children's
picture books, or books in need of translation.

Literary Agents: Barbara Lowenstein (*L0879*);
Mary South (*L1304*)

L0879 Barbara Lowenstein
Literary Agent
United States

Literary Agency: Lowenstein Associates, Inc.
(**L0878**)

L0880 Andrew Lownie
Literary Agent
United Kingdom

Literary Agency: Andrew Lownie Literary
Agency Ltd (**L0048**)

L0881 George Lucas
Literary Agent
United States

Literary Agency: InkWell Management
(**L0686**)

L0882 Mark Lucas
Literary Agent; Chair
United Kingdom

Literary Agency: The Soho Agency (**L1297**)

L0883 Lucy Luck
Literary Agent
United Kingdom

Literary Agency: C+W (Conville & Walsh) (**L0205**)

L0884 Amanda Luedeke
Literary Agent; Vice President
United States

http://www.macgregorandluedeke.com/about/agents/amanda-luedeke/

Literary Agency: MacGregor & Luedeke (**L0899**)

L0885 Luithlen Agency
Literary Agency
United Kingdom

penny@luithlenagency.co.uk

http://www.luithlenagency.com

CHILDREN'S > **Fiction**
  Early Readers; *Middle Grade*; *Novels*
YOUNG ADULT > **Fiction** > *Novels*
Closed to approaches.

Closed to submissions as at March 2020. Check website for current status.

Authors: David Belbin; Jennifer Bell; Caroline Clough; Harry Edge; John Hickman; Stuart Hill; Pete Johnson; Maxine Linnell; Clive Mantle; Gary Morecombe; Alison Prince; Bali Rai; James Riordan; Jamie Scallion; Joe Standerline; Robert Swindells; Gareth Thompson; John Townsend; Dan Tunstall

Literary Agent: Jennifer Luithlen (*L0886*)

L0886 Jennifer Luithlen
Literary Agent
United Kingdom

Literary Agency: Luithlen Agency (**L0885**)

L0887 Lutyens and Rubinstein
Literary Agency
21 Kensington Park Road, London, W11 2EU
United Kingdom
Tel: +44 (0) 20 7792 4855

submissions@lutyensrubinstein.co.uk

https://www.lutyensrubinstein.co.uk
https://twitter.com/LandRAgency
https://instagram.com/LandRAgency

Professional Body: The Association of Authors' Agents (AAA)

Fiction > *Novels*
  Commercial; Literary

Nonfiction > *Nonfiction Books*

Send: Query; Synopsis; Writing sample
How to send: Email
How not to send: Post

Send up to 5,000 words or first three chapters by email with covering letter and short synopsis. No film or TV scripts, or unsolicited submissions by hand or by post.

Literary Agent: Susannah Godman (*L0557*)

L0888 Alice Lutyens
Literary Agent
United Kingdom

Literary Agency: Curtis Brown (**L0318**)

L0889 Reggie Lutz
Literary Agent
United States

Literary Agency: Prentis Literary (**L1114**)

L0890 David Luxton
Literary Agent
United Kingdom

https://www.davidluxtonassociates.co.uk/the-agency/

Literary Agency: David Luxton Associates (**L0339**)

Nonfiction > *Nonfiction Books*
  History; Music; Politics; Sport

Principal interests are in the fields of sport, music, history and politics and represents a diverse range of authors including countless high-profile sports personalities.

L0891 Kevan Lyon
Literary Agent
United States

Literary Agency: Marsal Lyon Literary Agency LLC (**L0925**)

L0892 Paul Lyon-Maris
Literary Agent
United Kingdom

Literary Agency: Independent Talent Group Ltd (**L0683**)

L0893 Jennifer Lyons
Literary Agent; President
United States

jenniferlyonsagency@gmail.com

https://www.jenniferlyonsliteraryagency.com/who-we-are/

Literary Agency: The Jennifer Lyons Literary Agency, LLC

ADULT
  Fiction > *Novels*
    Commercial Women's Fiction; Literary; Upmarket

Nonfiction > *Nonfiction Books*: Narrative Nonfiction

CHILDREN'S > **Fiction** > *Middle Grade*
YOUNG ADULT > **Fiction** > *Novels*

Send: Query
How to send: Post; Email

Seeking: Literary fiction and upmarket, commercial women's fiction. Narrative nonfiction. Children's books, especially middle grade and young adult. Prefers hard copy queries, but can also be queried by email.

L0894 Rhea Lyons
Literary Agent
United States

rhea@hgliterary.com

https://www.hgliterary.com/rhea

Literary Agency: HG Literary (**L0646**)

Closed to approaches.

L0895 Cecilia Lyra
Associate Agent; Author
Canada

https://www.therightsfactory.com/Agents/Cecilia-Lyra
https://twitter.com/ceciliaclyra
https://querymanager.com/query/1464

Literary Agency: The Rights Factory (**L1151**)
Literary Agent / President / Chief Executive Officer: Sam Hiyate (**L0651**)

Fiction > *Novels*: Women's Fiction

Nonfiction > *Nonfiction Books*
  Business; Feminism; Lifestyle; Memoir; Narrative Nonfiction; Popular Culture; Psychology; Science

Send: Query
How to send: Query Manager

Specializes in both fiction and nonfiction on the adult side. In terms of fiction, she is looking for stories that feature diverse, layered characters and unexpected plot twists. She adores stories involving moral or ethical dilemmas and is especially drawn to novels about dysfunctional families. In terms of nonfiction, Cecilia is seeking Psychology, Pop Culture, Science, Business, and Lifestyle from experts in their fields with an original angle, as well as compelling memoirs.

L0896 Johanna Maaghul
Literary Agent
United States

Literary Agency: Waterside Productions, Inc (**L1418**)

L0897 Donald Maass
Literary Agent
United States

Literary Agency: Donald Maass Literary
Agency (**L0380**)

L0898 Emily MacDonald
Literary Agent
United Kingdom

emilymacdonald@42mp.com

https://www.42mp.com/agents
https://twitter.com/Ebh_mac

Literary Agency: 42 Management and
Production (**L0002**)

Fiction > *Novels*: Literary

Nonfiction > *Nonfiction Books*
  History; Narrative Nonfiction; Regional;
  Scotland

How to send: Email

Looking for literary fiction, narrative
nonfiction with an investigative twist, and
untold true stories, either personal or historical.
Also interested in Scottish and regional voices
with stories to tell.

L0899 MacGregor & Luedeke
Literary Agency
PO Box 1316, Manzanita, OR 97130
United States
Tel: +1 (503) 389-4803

submissions@macgregorliterary.com

http://www.macgregorandluedeke.com
https://twitter.com/MacGregorLit

Types: Fiction; Nonfiction
Formats: Short Fiction
Subjects: Autobiography; Business; Comedy /
Humour; Commercial; Contemporary; Crime;
Culture; Current Affairs; Finance; History;
How To; Lifestyle; Mystery; Personal
Development; Religion; Romance; Sport;
Suspense; Thrillers; Women's Interests
Markets: Academic; Adult

Send: Query
Don't send: Full text
How to send: Email

Costs: Author covers sundry admin costs.

Handles work in a variety of genres, but all
from a Christian perspective. Currently closed
to fiction submissions, but still accepting
nonfiction. Send query with proposal /
synopsis and first three chapters
(approximately 50 pages). See website for full
guidelines.

Authors: Don Brown; Davis Bunn; Rashawn
Copeland; Sheila Gregoire; Rachel Hauck;
James Byron Huggins; Steve Jackson; Jessica
Kate; Rachel Linden; Holly Lorincz; Evelyn
Lozada; Scott Parazynski; Jay Payleitner; Tom
Satterly; Kimberly Stuart; David Thomas;
Vincent Zandri

Literary Agent / President: Chip MacGregor
(**L0900**)

Literary Agent / Vice President: Amanda
Luedeke (**L0884**)

L0900 Chip MacGregor
Literary Agent; President
United States

http://www.macgregorandluedeke.com/about/
agents/chip-macgregor/
http://aaronline.org/Sys/PublicProfile/2176764/
417813

Literary Agency: MacGregor & Luedeke
(**L0899**)
Professional Body: Association of Authors'
Representatives, Inc. (AAR)

L0901 Joanna MacKenzie
Literary Agent
United States

https://nelsonagency.com/joanna-mackenzie/
https://www.publishersmarketplace.com/
members/JoannaMacKenzie/
https://twitter.com/joannamackenzie
https://www.facebook.com/joanna.topor.
mackenzie

Literary Agency: Nelson Literary Agency,
LLC (**L1026**)

ADULT > **Fiction** > *Novels*
  High Concept; Mystery; Speculative;
  Thrillers; Women's Fiction

YOUNG ADULT > **Fiction** > *Novels*

Send: Author bio; Query; Writing sample
How to send: Query Manager

I'm looking for that epic adult or YA read that,
at its center, beats with a universal heart.
Anything set on a creepy island;
mysteries/thrillers set in close-knit
communities (if those communities happen to
be in the Midwest, all the better); high concept
stories with a strong voice in the areas of
women's fiction, mystery/thriller, and
speculative; anything featuring fierce female
heroines who will do whatever it takes to
protect their brood; Smart and timely women's
fiction where the personal intersects with the
world at large; Narratives about reinvention or
the second and third acts of women's lives;
Stories about the immigrant experience both
adult and YA; Anything dealing with the
relationships that make us who we are for both
the YA and adult market.

Authors: Brooke Abrams; Kate Baer; Shana
Galen; John Galligan; Alison Hammer; Robin
Huber; Sarah Zachrich Jeng; Sierra Kincade;
Amanda Marbais; Jonathan Messinger;
Meghan Scott Molin; Katrina Monroe; Kristen
Simmons; Jennifer Springsteen; Stacy Stokes;
Ben Tanzer; Kathleen West

L0902 Robert Mackwood
Literary Agent
Canada

Literary Agency: Seventh Avenue Literary
Agency (**L1253**)

L0903 Jamie Maclean
Literary Agent; Editor
United Kingdom

https://cmm.agency/about-us.php

Literary Agency: Coombs Moylett & Maclean
Literary Agency (**L0295**)
Magazine: Erotic Review (**M0209**)

Fiction > *Novels*
  Erotic; Historical Crime; Mystery; Thrillers

Nonfiction > *Nonfiction Books*
  Gender Politics; How To; Lifestyle;
  Relationships

Send: Synopsis; Writing sample
How to send: Online submission system

Specialises in both fiction and nonfiction and is
particularly interested in sexual politics,
relationship, lifestyle how-to's, erotica,
thrillers, whodunit and historical crime.

L0904 Lauren MacLeod
Literary Agent
United States

https://www.strothmanagency.com/about
https://twitter.com/Lauren_MacLeod
http://aaronline.org/Sys/PublicProfile/
12259463/417813

Literary Agency: The Strothman Agency
(**L1331**)
Professional Body: Association of Authors'
Representatives, Inc. (AAR)

ADULT
  Fiction > *Novels*: Literary

  Nonfiction > *Nonfiction Books*
    Crime; Feminism; Food; History; Narrative
    Nonfiction; Popular Culture; Science

CHILDREN'S > **Fiction** > *Middle Grade*

YOUNG ADULT
  Fiction > *Novels*
    General, and in particular: Environment;
    Politics; Social Issues

  Nonfiction > *Nonfiction Books*
    General, and in particular: Environment;
    Politics; Social Issues

Not accepting queries for adult novels, picture
books, or chapter books for early readers at this
time. She does not represent adult romance,
adult SFF, or adult mysteries and thrillers.

L0905 Macnaughton Lord Representation
Literary Agency
United Kingdom
Tel: +44 (0) 20 7407 9201

info@mlrep.com

http://www.mlrep.com

Scripts
Film Scripts; *TV Scripts*; *Theatre Scripts*
Closed to approaches.

Theatrical and literary agency representing established names and emerging talent in theatre, film, tv and the performing arts. No unsolicited mss.

Literary Agents: Rupert Lord (*L0874*); Helen Mumby (*L1006*); Davina Shah (*L1255*)

L0906 **Neeti Madan**
Senior Agent
United States

https://www.sll.com/our-team

Literary Agency: Sterling Lord Literistic, Inc. (**L1317**)

Nonfiction > *Nonfiction Books*
  Journalism; Lifestyle; Memoir; Multicultural; Popular Culture; Women's Issues

Send: Query; Synopsis; Writing sample
How to send: Online submission system

L0907 **Madeleine Milburn Literary, TV & Film Agency**
Literary Agency
The Factory, 1 Park Hill, London, SW4 9NS
United Kingdom
Tel: +44 (0) 20 7499 7550

submissions@madeleinemilburn.com
childrens@madeleinemilburn.com

http://madeleinemilburn.co.uk

Professional Body: The Association of Authors' Agents (AAA)

Types: Fiction; Nonfiction; Scripts; Translations
Formats: Film Scripts; TV Scripts
Subjects: Autobiography; Comedy / Humour; Commercial; Crime; Fantasy; History; Horror; Lifestyle; Literary; Mystery; Nature; Personal Development; Psychology; Romance; Science; Science Fiction; Sport; Suspense; Thrillers; Women's Interests
Markets: Adult; Children's; Young Adult

Send: Query
Don't send: Full text
How to send: Email

Send query by email only, with one-page synopsis and first three chapters for fiction, or proposal and 30-page writing sample for nonfiction. Send material for children and young adults to "childrens" email address. See website for full submission guidelines. Film and TV scripts for established clients only.

Literary Agents: Catherine Cho (**L0263**); Giles Milburn (*L0979*); Madeleine Milburn (*L0980*); Chloe Seager (*L1247*); Hayley Steed (*L1310*)

L0908 **Dorian Maffei**
Literary Agent
United States

Literary Agency: Kimberley Cameron & Associates (**L0787**)

L0909 **Maggie Pearlstine Associates Ltd**
Literary Agency
31 Ashley Gardens, Ambrosden Avenue, London, SW1P 1QE
United Kingdom
Tel: +44 (0) 20 7828 4212
Fax: +44 (0) 20 7834 5546

maggie@pearlstine.co.uk

Professional Body: The Association of Authors' Agents (AAA)

Types: Fiction; Nonfiction
Subjects: Biography; Current Affairs; Health; History
Markets: Adult

Closed to approaches.

Small, selective agency, not currently taking on new clients.

Authors: Matthew Baylis; Roy Hattersley; Lesley Regan; Christopher Ward

Literary Agent: Maggie Pearlstine (*L1075*)

L0910 **Hester Malin**
Assistant Agent
United States

https://karengantzliterarymanagement.com/about-1

Literary Agency: Karen Gantz Literary Management (**L0759**)

L0911 **Carol Mann**
Literary Agent
United States

https://www.carolmannagency.com/our-team

Literary Agency: Carol Mann Agency (**L0225**)
Professional Body: Association of Authors' Representatives, Inc. (AAR)

Fiction > *Novels*

Nonfiction > *Nonfiction Books*
  Current Affairs; Health; History; Medicine; Narrative Nonfiction; Parenting; Religion; Self Help; Spirituality

Send: Query; Author bio; Writing sample
How to send: In the body of an email

Specialises in nonfiction (health/medical, religion, spirituality, self-help, parenting, current affairs, history, narrative non-fiction) while also taking on the occasional fiction writer.

L0912 **Rachel Mann**
Literary Agent
United Kingdom

http://www.jounwin.co.uk/rachel-mann/

Literary Agency: Jo Unwin Literary Agency (**L0728**)

ADULT
  Fiction > *Novels*
  Nonfiction > *Nonfiction Books*

CHILDREN'S
  Fiction
    Middle Grade: Commercial
    Novels: General

  Nonfiction > *Nonfiction Books*

YOUNG ADULT
  Fiction > *Novels*
  Nonfiction > *Nonfiction Books*

Does not want:

CHILDREN'S > **Fiction** > *Picture Books*

L0913 **Lauren Manoy**
Literary Agent
United States

Laurenm@rudyagency.com

http://rudyagency.com/

Literary Agency: The Rudy Agency (**L1199**)

Nonfiction > *Nonfiction Books*
  Entrepreneurship; Memoir; Regional Cooking; Sustainable Living; Women in Business

Send: Query
How to send: Email

L0914 **Mansion Street Literary Management**
Literary Agency
United States

jean@mansionstreet.com

http://mansionstreet.com

Types: Fiction; Nonfiction
Subjects: Arts; Cookery; Culture; Design; Lifestyle
Markets: Adult; Children's; Young Adult

Send query via online submission system. See website for full details and individual agent interests.

Literary Agents: Jean Sagendorph (*L1214*); Michelle Witte (*L1467*)

L0915 **Tracy Marchini**
Literary Agent
United States

Literary Agency: BookEnds, LLC (**L0155**)

L0916 Marcia Amsterdam Agency
Literary Agency
41 W. 82nd St., New York, NY 10024-5613
United States

Types: Fiction; Scripts
Formats: Film Scripts; TV Scripts
Subjects: Adventure; Comedy / Humour; Commercial; Contemporary; Crime; History; Horror; Mystery; Romance; Science; Thrillers
Markets: Adult; Young Adult

Closed to approaches.

Costs: Author covers sundry admin costs.

Not taking on new clients as at June 2018. Send query with SASE. No poetry, how-to, books for the 8-10 age-group, or unsolicited MSS. Response to queries usually in one month.

Authors: Jonathan Canter; Isaac Millman

Literary Agent: Marcia Amsterdam (*L0041*)

L0917 Marcil O'Farrell Literary, LLC and Denise Marcil Literary Agency, LLC
Literary Agency
86 Dennis Street, Manhasset, NY 11030
United States
Tel: +1 (212) 337-3402

annemarie@marcilofarrellagency.com

https://www.marcilofarrellagency.com

Professional Body: Association of Authors' Representatives, Inc. (AAR)

Types: Nonfiction
Subjects: Business; Cookery; Health; Personal Development; Spirituality; Sport; Travel
Markets: Adult

Send: Query
Don't send: Full text
How to send: Email

Costs: Author covers sundry admin costs.

No fiction, memoirs, or screenplays. Send query up to 200 words by email.

Literary Agent: Denise Marcil (*L0918*)

L0918 Denise Marcil
Literary Agent
United States

Literary Agency: Marcil O'Farrell Literary, LLC and Denise Marcil Literary Agency, LLC (**L0917**)
Professional Body: The Agents Round Table (ART)

L0919 Kendra Marcus
Literary Agent
United States

Literary Agency: BookStop Literary Agency, LLC (**L0158**)

L0920 Victoria Marini
Literary Agent
United States

Literary Agency: Irene Goodman Literary Agency (IGLA) (**L0688**)
Professional Body: Association of Authors' Representatives, Inc. (AAR)

L0921 Marjacq Scripts Ltd
Literary Agency
The Space, 235 High Holborn, London, WC1V 7LE
United Kingdom
Tel: +44 (0) 20 7935 9499

enquiries@marjacq.com

http://www.marjacq.com
https://twitter.com/marjacqscripts

Professional Body: The Association of Authors' Agents (AAA)

Types: Fiction; Nonfiction; Scripts
Formats: Film Scripts; Radio Scripts; TV Scripts
Subjects: Biography; Commercial; Crime; Health; History; Literary; Science Fiction; Sport; Thrillers; Travel; Women's Interests
Markets: Adult; Children's; Young Adult

Send: Query
Don't send: Full text
How to send: Email
How not to send: Post

Accepts submissions by email only. For books, send query with synopsis and first 50 pages. For scripts, send short treatment and entire screenplay. Send only Word or PDF documents less than 2MB. Do not paste work into the body of the email. See website for full details. No children's picture books, poetry, plays or musical theatre.

Literary Agents: Diana Beaumont (**L0105**); Leah Middleton (**L0978**); Philip Patterson (*L1073*); Imogen Pelham (*L1078*); Catherine Pellegrino (*L1079*); Sandra Sawicka (*L1224*)

L0922 Matthew Marland
Literary Agent
United Kingdom

Literary Agency: Rogers, Coleridge & White Ltd (**L1181**)

L0923 Mildred Marmur
Literary Agent
United States

Literary Agency: Mildred Marmur Associates, Ltd. (**L0981**)
Professional Body: Association of Authors' Representatives, Inc. (AAR)

L0924 Jill Marr
Literary Agent
United States

Literary Agency: Sandra Dijkstra Literary Agency (**L1218**)

Closed to approaches.

L0925 Marsal Lyon Literary Agency LLC
Literary Agency
PMB 121, 665 San Rodolfo Dr. 124, Solana Beach, CA 92075
United States

Kevan@MarsalLyonLiteraryAgency.com

http://www.marsallyonliteraryagency.com

Types: Fiction; Nonfiction
Subjects: Autobiography; Business; Commercial; Cookery; Culture; Current Affairs; Finance; Health; History; Lifestyle; Music; Mystery; Personal Development; Politics; Psychology; Romance; Sport; Suspense; Thrillers; Women's Interests
Markets: Adult; Children's; Young Adult

Send: Query
Don't send: Full text
How to send: Email

Send query by email only to one agent only. See website for individual agent interests and email addresses. No submissions by post.

Literary Agents: Shannon Hassan (*L0622*); Kevan Lyon (*L0891*); Jill Marsal (*L0926*); Patricia Nelson (*L1028*); Deborah Ritchken (*L1153*)

L0926 Jill Marsal
Literary Agent
United States

Literary Agency: Marsal Lyon Literary Agency LLC (**L0925**)

L0927 The Marsh Agency
Literary Agency
50 Albemarle Street, London, W1S 4BD
United Kingdom
Tel: +44 (0) 20 7493 4361
Fax: +44 (0) 20 7495 8961

english.language@marsh-agency.co.uk

http://www.marsh-agency.co.uk

Professional Body: The Association of Authors' Agents (AAA)

Types: Fiction; Nonfiction
Subjects: Literary
Markets: Adult; Young Adult

Closed to approaches.

Not currently accepting unsolicited mss as at March 2018. Most new clients come through recommendations.

Authors: Jill Bays; Tsitsi Dangarembga; Ian Dear; Ed Halliwell; Tendai Huchu; Sam Kriss; Anita Nair; Alan Palmer; Allyson Pollock; Alfred Price; Gillian Riley; Richard Seymour; Christine Shaw

Literary Agent: Susie Nicklin (*L1035*)

L0928 Evan Marshall
Literary Agent
United States

Literary Agency: The Evan Marshall Agency (**L0439**)

L0929 Joanna Marston
Literary Agent
United Kingdom

Literary Agency: Rosica Colin Ltd (**L1187**)

L0930 Sylvie Marston
Literary Agent
United Kingdom

Literary Agency: Rosica Colin Ltd (**L1187**)

L0931 Gaby Martin
Literary Agent
United Kingdom

Literary Agency: Knight Features (**L0798**)

L0932 Blanche Marvin
Literary Agent
United Kingdom

Literary Agency: Blanche Marvin, MBE (**L0141**)

L0933 Mary Clemmey Literary Agency
Literary Agency
6 Dunollie Road, London, NW5 2XP
United Kingdom
Tel: +44 (0) 20 7267 1290

mcwords@googlemail.com

Professional Body: The Association of Authors' Agents (AAA)

Types: Fiction; Nonfiction; Scripts
Formats: Film Scripts; Radio Scripts; TV Scripts; Theatre Scripts
Markets: Adult

Send: Query
Don't send: Full text
How not to send: Email

Send query with SAE and description of work only. Handles high-quality work with an international market. No children's books, science fiction, fantasy, or unsolicited MSS or submissions by email. Scripts handled for existing clients only. Do not submit a script or idea for a script unless you are already a client.

Literary Agent: Mary Clemmey (*L0280*)

L0934 Massie & McQuilkin
Literary Agency
27 West 20th Street, Suite 305, New York, NY 10011
United States
Tel: +1 (212) 352-2055
Fax: +1 (212) 352-2059

info@lmqlit.com

http://www.mmqlit.com

Types: Fiction; Nonfiction
Subjects: Autobiography; Comedy / Humour; Commercial; Crime; Culture; Current Affairs; Fantasy; Health; History; Literary; Politics; Psychology; Science; Society; Sport; Suspense; Thrillers; Women's Interests
Markets: Adult; Children's; Young Adult

Send: Query
Don't send: Full text
How to send: Email

Costs: Author covers sundry admin costs.

See website for specific agent interests and contact details. Query only one agent at a time.

Literary Agents: Stephanie Abou (*L0008*); Elias Altman (*L0035*); Jason Anthony (*L0057*); Ethan Bassoff (*L0097*); Laney Katz Becker (*L0107*); Maria Massie (*L0935*); Rob McQuilkin (*L0961*); Neil Olson (**L1055**); Rayhane Sanders (*L1217*); Julie Stevenson (*L1321*); Jade Wong-Baxter (**L1470**); Renee Zuckerbrot (*L1491*)

L0935 Maria Massie
Literary Agent
United States

Literary Agency: Massie & McQuilkin (**L0934**)

L0936 Pippa Masson
Literary Agent
Australia

Literary Agency: Curtis Brown (Australia) Pty Ltd (**L0319**)

L0937 Peter Matson
Literary Agent; Chair
United States

https://www.sll.com/our-team

Literary Agency: Sterling Lord Literistic, Inc. (**L1317**)

Fiction > *Novels*

Nonfiction > *Nonfiction Books*
History; Science

Send: Query; Synopsis; Writing sample
How to send: Online submission system

L0938 Jennifer Mattson
Literary Agent
United States

Literary Agency: Andrea Brown Literary Agency, Inc. (**L0047**)

L0939 Bridget Wagner Matzie
Literary Agent; Partner
United States

https://aevitascreative.com/agents/

Literary Agency: Aevitas (**L0019**)

Fiction > *Novels*: Commercial

Nonfiction > *Nonfiction Books*

Closed to approaches.

Represents nonfiction and commercial fiction.

L0940 Shari Maurer
Literary Agent
United States

https://querymanager.com/query/1434

Literary Agency: The Stringer Literary Agency LLC (**L1329**)

ADULT
Fiction > *Novels*
Crime; Fantasy; Suspense; Thrillers; Upmarket Women's Fiction

Nonfiction > *Nonfiction Books*
Memoir; Narrative Nonfiction; Parenting; Popular Science

CHILDREN'S
Fiction
Middle Grade: Contemporary; Historical Fiction; Literary; Mystery
Picture Books: General

Nonfiction > *Middle Grade*

YOUNG ADULT
Fiction > *Novels*
Contemporary; Historical Fiction; Literary; Mystery

Nonfiction > *Nonfiction Books*

Does not want:

ADULT > **Fiction** > *Novels*: Erotic Romance

CHILDREN'S > **Fiction** > *Middle Grade*: Fantasy

Send: Query; Synopsis; Writing sample; Pitch
How to send: Query Manager

L0941 Jane Graham Maw
Literary Agent
United Kingdom

Literary Agency: Graham Maw Christie Literary Agency (**L0567**)

L0942 MBA Literary Agents Ltd
Literary Agency
62 Grafton Way, London, W1T 5DW

United Kingdom
Tel: +44 (0) 20 7387 2076

submissions@mbalit.co.uk

http://www.mbalit.co.uk

Professional Bodies: The Association of Authors' Agents (AAA); Personal Managers' Association (PMA); Writers' Guild of Great Britain (WGGB)

Types: Fiction; Nonfiction; Scripts
Formats: Film Scripts; Radio Scripts; TV Scripts; Theatre Scripts
Subjects: Arts; Biography; Commercial; Crafts; Health; History; Lifestyle; Literary; Personal Development
Markets: Adult; Children's; Young Adult

How to send: Email

For books, send query with CV, synopsis and first three chapters. Not currently accepting unsolicited film and television submissions. Submissions by email only, in Word, PDF or Final Draft format. No submissions by post. See website for full submission guidelines. Works in conjunction with agents in most countries.

L0943 Donna McCafferty
Literary Agent
United Kingdom

Literary Agency: Sheil Land Associates Ltd (**L1263**)

Scripts
  Film Scripts; *TV Scripts*; *Theatre Scripts*

L0944 Bridget McCarthy
Literary Agent
United States

Literary Agency: McCormick Literary (**L0949**)

L0945 Jim McCarthy
Literary Agent
United States

Literary Agency: Dystel, Goderich & Bourret LLC (**L0399**)

L0946 Sean McCarthy
Literary Agent
United States

Literary Agency: Sean McCarthy Literary Agency (**L1248**)

L0947 Cameron McClure
Literary Agent
United States

Literary Agency: Donald Maass Literary Agency (**L0380**)

L0948 Kim Blair McCollum
Literary Agent
United States

Literary Agency: The Purcell Agency, LLC (**L1118**)

L0949 McCormick Literary
Literary Agency
150 West 28th Street, Suite 903, New York, NY 10001
United States

queries@mccormicklit.com

http://mccormicklit.com

Types: Fiction; Nonfiction
Subjects: Arts; Autobiography; Comedy / Humour; Commercial; Cookery; Culture; History; Lifestyle; Literary; Personal Development; Politics; Science; Sport; Women's Interests
Markets: Adult; Young Adult

Send: Query
Don't send: Full text
How to send: Email

Send queries by email with short bio and ten sample pages, indicating in the subject line which agent you are querying (see website for individual agent interests). No attachments. Will also consider submissions by post, but these will not be returned. Response only if interested.

Literary Agents: Bridget McCarthy (*L0944*); David McCormick (*L0950*); Daniel Menaker; Edward Orloff (*L1058*); Pilar Queen (*L1121*)

L0950 David McCormick
Literary Agent
United States

Literary Agency: McCormick Literary (**L0949**)

L0951 Michael McCoy
Literary Agent
United Kingdom

Literary Agency: Independent Talent Group Ltd (**L0683**)

L0952 Caitlin McDonald
Literary Agent
United States

Literary Agency: Donald Maass Literary Agency (**L0380**)

L0953 Sarah McDonnell
Literary Agent
United Kingdom

Literary Agency: Bell Lomax Moreton Agency (**L0110**)

L0954 Holly McGhee
Literary Agent
United States

Literary Agency: Pippin Properties, Inc (**L1101**)

L0955 Matt McGowan
Literary Agent
United States

Literary Agency: Frances Goldin Literary Agency, Inc. (**L0492**)

Fiction > *Novels:* Literary

Nonfiction
  Essays: General
  Nonfiction Books: Biography; Crime; Culture; Food; Football / Soccer; History; Journalism; Memoir; Narrative Nonfiction; Politics; Popular Culture; Popular Science; Sport; Sub-Culture; Travel

L0956 Gill McLay
Literary Agent
United Kingdom

Literary Agency: Bath Literary Agency (**L0099**)

L0957 Bill McLean
Literary Agent
United Kingdom

Literary Agency: Bill McLean Personal Management Ltd (**L0132**)

L0958 Eunice McMullen
Literary Agent
United Kingdom

L0959 Laura McNeill
Literary Agent
United Kingdom

Literary Agency: Peters Fraser + Dunlop (**L1091**)

L0960 Damian McNicoll
Literary Agent
United States

Literary Agency: The Jennifer DeChiara Literary Agency (**L0721**)

L0961 Rob McQuilkin
Literary Agent
United States

Literary Agency: Massie & McQuilkin (**L0934**)

L0962 Lindsay Mealing
Literary Agent
United States

Literary Agency: Emerald City Literary Agency (**L0428**)

L0963 Sara Megibow
Literary Agent
United States

Literary Agency: KT Literary (**L0811**)

L0964 Jane von Mehren

Literary Agent; Partner
United States

https://aevitascreative.com/agents/

Literary Agency: Aevitas (**L0019**)

Fiction > *Novels*
Book Club Fiction; Historical Fiction; Literary

Nonfiction > *Nonfiction Books*
Business; History; Memoir; Popular Culture; Science

Send: Query; Author bio; Market info; Writing sample
How to send: Online submission system

Interested in narratives in the areas of business, history, memoir, popular culture and science, books that help us live our best lives, literary, book club, and historical fiction.

L0965 Mendel Media Group, LLC

Literary Agency
115 West 30th Street, Suite 209, New York, NY 10001
United States
Tel: +1 (646) 239-9896

scott@mendelmedia.com

http://www.mendelmedia.com

Professional Body: Association of Authors' Representatives, Inc. (AAR)

Types: Fiction; Nonfiction
Subjects: Autobiography; Comedy / Humour; Commercial; Contemporary; Culture; Current Affairs; Entertainment; Finance; History; How To; Literary; Literature; Media; Mystery; Personal Development; Politics; Religion; Science; Thrillers; Women's Interests
Markets: Adult; Children's; Young Adult

Send: Query
Don't send: Full text
How to send: Email

Send query by email only. No longer accepts submissions by post. For fiction, send synopsis and first 20 pages. For nonfiction, send proposal and sample chapters. See website for full guidelines.

Literary Agent: Scott Mendel (*L0966*)

L0966 Scott Mendel

Literary Agent
United States

Literary Agency: Mendel Media Group, LLC (**L0965**)

L0967 Adam Mendlesohn

Literary Agent
United Kingdom

Literary Agency: The Narrow Road Company (**L1021**)

L0968 Marianne Merola

Literary Agent
United States

mmerola@bromasite.com

Literary Agency: Brandt & Hochman Literary Agents, Inc. (**L0172**)
Professional Body: Association of Authors' Representatives, Inc. (AAR)

ADULT
Fiction > *Novels*
Nonfiction > *Nonfiction Books*

CHILDREN'S > **Fiction** > *Novels*

Send: Query
How to send: Email

L0969 Annabel Merullo

Literary Agent
United Kingdom

Literary Agency: Peters Fraser + Dunlop (**L1091**)

L0970 Jackie Meyer

Literary Agent
United States

Literary Agency: Whimsy Literary Agency, LLC (**L1438**)

L0971 Mic Cheetham Literary Agency

Literary Agency
62 Grafton Way, London, W1T 5DW
United Kingdom

submissions@miccheetham.com

http://www.miccheetham.com

Fiction > *Novels*

Nonfiction > *Nonfiction Books*

Send: Query; Outline; Writing sample; Author bio
How to send: Email

Agency with a deliberately small list. Only takes on two or three new writers each year. New writers are advised to acquaint themselves with the work of the writers currently represented by the agency before submitting their own work.

Authors: Carol Birch; Nm Browne; Pat Cadigan; Alan Campbell; Gregory Doran; Barbara Ewing; Ian Green; M John Harrison; Alice James; Ken MacLeod; Paul Mcauley; China Miéville; Sharon Penman; Antony Sher; Adrian Tchaikovsky

Literary Agents: Mic Cheetham (**L0255**); Simon Kavanagh (**L0767**)

L0972 The Michael Greer Literary Agency

Literary Agency
United Kingdom

melanie@michaelgreerliteraryagency.co.uk

http://www.michaelgreerliteraryagency.co.uk
https://twitter.com/SportLitAgent

ADULT
Fiction > *Novels*: Urban

Nonfiction > *Nonfiction Books*: Sport

YOUNG ADULT > **Fiction** > *Novels*

Send: Synopsis; Writing sample
How to send: Email

Costs: Author covers sundry admin costs.

Handles books in three areas: sport; City Fiction; and Young Adult. Send synopsis and three chapters by email.

Literary Agent: Melanie Michael-Greer (*L0974*)

L0973 Michael Snell Literary Agency

Literary Agency
PO Box 1206, Truro, MA 02666-1206
United States
Tel: +1 (508) 349-3718

query@michaelsnellagency.com

http://michaelsnellagency.com

Types: Fiction; Nonfiction
Subjects: Business; Health; How To; Lifestyle; Personal Development; Psychology; Science; Suspense; Thrillers; Travel; Women's Interests
Markets: Adult

Costs: Offers services that writers have to pay for.

Send query by post or by email. Specialises in business, how-to and self-help. No unsolicited MSS. Additional writing services available for a fee.

L0974 Melanie Michael-Greer

Literary Agent
United Kingdom

Literary Agency: The Michael Greer Literary Agency (**L0972**)

L0975 Caroline Michel

Literary Agent
United Kingdom

Literary Agency: Peters Fraser + Dunlop (**L1091**)

L0976 Micheline Steinberg Associates

Literary Agency
Suite 315, ScreenWorks, 22 Highbury Grove, London, N5 2ER

United Kingdom
Tel: +44 (0) 20 3214 8292

info@steinplays.com

http://www.steinplays.com

Types: Scripts
Formats: Film Scripts; Radio Scripts; TV Scripts; Theatre Scripts
Markets: Adult

Send: Query
Don't send: Full text

We're a mid-size agency in which all the agents have background in theatre and related media. We work closely with writers and the industry, developing writers work, managing their careers, and negotiating all rights. We also have affiliations with book agents and agents overseas including in the USA. Send query with your CV and brief outline of your work through online form, available on website. No unsolicited submissions. Does not consider books.

Literary Agents: Jazz Adamson (*L0017*); Micheline Steinberg (*L1312*)

L0977 Michelle Kass Associates
Literary Agency
85 Charing Cross Road, London, WC2H 0AA
United Kingdom
Tel: +44 (0) 20 7439 1624

office@michellekass.co.uk

http://www.michellekass.co.uk

Professional Body: The Association of Authors' Agents (AAA)

Fiction > *Novels*
Commercial; Literary

Scripts
Film Scripts; TV Scripts

How to send: Phone

Represents authors, dramatists/screenwriters, and screenwriters based in the UK and Ireland. Call before submitting.

Literary Agent: Michelle Kass

L0978 Leah Middleton
Literary Agent
United Kingdom

leah@marjacq.com

http://www.marjacq.com/leah-middleton.html

Literary Agency: Marjacq Scripts Ltd (**L0921**)

Scripts
Film Scripts: General, and in particular: Comedy / Humour
TV Scripts: General, and in particular: Comedy / Humour

Send: Full text; Synopsis; Author bio
How to send: Email

Considers scripts across all formats and genres, but is particularly interested in comedy and returnable TV. No book submissions, or submissions from US screenwriters.

L0979 Giles Milburn
Literary Agent
United Kingdom

Literary Agency: Madeleine Milburn Literary, TV & Film Agency (**L0907**)

L0980 Madeleine Milburn
Literary Agent
United Kingdom

Literary Agency: Madeleine Milburn Literary, TV & Film Agency (**L0907**)

L0981 Mildred Marmur Associates, Ltd.
Literary Agency
2005 Palmer Avenue, Suite 127, Larchmont, NY 10538
United States

http://aaronline.org/Sys/PublicProfile/2176773/417813

Fiction > *Novels*

Nonfiction > *Nonfiction Books*

Literary agent based in Larchmont, New York.

Literary Agent: Mildred Marmur (*L0923*)

L0982 Jessica Mileo
Literary Agent
United States

Literary Agency: InkWell Management (**L0686**)

L0983 Miles Stott Children's Literary Agency
Literary Agency
East Hook Farm, Lower Quay Road, Hook, Haverfordwest, Pembrokeshire, SA62 4LR
United Kingdom
Tel: +44 (0) 7855 252043

fictionsubs@milesstottagency.co.uk
picturebooksubs@milesstottagency.co.uk

https://www.milesstottagency.co.uk
https://www.facebook.com/pages/Miles-Stott-Childrens-Literary-Agency/311096870669
https://twitter.com/MilesStott
https://www.instagram.com/milesstottagency/

Professional Body: The Association of Authors' Agents (AAA)

CHILDREN'S
Fiction
Middle Grade; Novels; Picture Books
Nonfiction > *Nonfiction Books*

YOUNG ADULT > **Fiction** > *Novels*

Send: Query; Synopsis; Writing sample; Full text
How to send: Email

Handles Board books, Picture books, Novelty Books, Young fiction, Middle grade fiction, YA fiction, and Non-fiction. No poetry, musical works, or educational texts. For fiction send query with synopsis and first three chapters. For picture book submissions, send query by email only, with short covering letter, details about you and your background, and up to three stories. See website for full guidelines.

Authors: Kate Alizadeh; Kirsty Applebaum; Atinuke; Dominic Barker; Jane Bartlett; Helen Baugh; Adam Beer; Rachel Bright; Mark Burgess; Rachel Carter; Ali Clack; Ruth Doyle; Jan Fearnley; Lu Fraser; Annelise Gray; Stacy Gregg; Frances Hardinge; Caryl Hart; Sophie Kirtley; Gill Lewis; Zoë Marriott; Julia Miranda; Tom Percival; Gareth Peter; Tom Pollock; Mark Sperring; Amber Stewart; Daniel Whelan

Literary Agents: Victoria Birkett (**L0135**); Caroline Hill-Trevor; Nancy Miles (**L0984**); Mandy Suhr (**L1334**)

L0984 Nancy Miles
Literary Agent
United Kingdom

nancy@milesstottagency.co.uk

https://www.milesstottagency.co.uk/about-nancy-miles.php

Literary Agency: Miles Stott Children's Literary Agency (**L0983**)

CHILDREN'S > **Fiction** > *Novels*
Comedy / Humour; Contemporary; Fantasy; Historical Fiction; Science Fiction

YOUNG ADULT > **Fiction** > *Novels*
Comedy / Humour; Contemporary; Fantasy; Historical Fiction; Science Fiction

"Whatever the book – funny, fantasy, sci-fi, contemporary, historical – and for whichever age, a strong voice, great characters and an engaging plot will be the first things to reel me in."

L0985 Christina Miller
Literary Agent
United States

http://www.inkwellmanagement.com/staff/christina-miller

Literary Agency: InkWell Management (**L0686**)

Fiction > *Novels*
Historical Fiction; Mystery; Romance; Thrillers

L0986 Jennie Miller
Literary Agent
United Kingdom

Literary Agency: Independent Talent Group Ltd (**L0683**)

L0987 Tom Miller
Literary Agent
United States

Literary Agency: Liza Dawson Associates (**L0868**)

L0988 Rachel Mills
Literary Agent; Company Director
United Kingdom

rachel@rmliterary.co.uk

https://twitter.com/bookishyogini

Literary Agency: Rachel Mills Literary (**L1124**)

Nonfiction > *Nonfiction Books*
Biography; Current Affairs; Feminism; Food; Health; Memoir; Narrative Nonfiction; Nature; Popular Science; Psychology; Social Media; Sustainable Living; Wellbeing

Send: Query; Writing sample
How to send: Email

Looking for nonfiction on subjects including current affairs, feminism, psychology, popular science, well-being, narrative nonfiction, memoir, biography, food, nature, sustainability, health, social media and platform led projects.

Send email with as much detail about yourself and the project as possible, ideally with at least one sample chapter.

L0989 Philippa Milnes-Smith
Literary Agent; Managing Director
United Kingdom

https://www.facebook.com/philippa.milnessmith

Literary Agency: The Soho Agency (**L1297**)

L0990 Heather Mitchell
Literary Agent
United States

Literary Agency: Gelfman Schneider / ICM Partners (**L0534**)

L0991 Jamie Mitchell
Literary Agent
United Kingdom

Literary Agency: The Soho Agency (**L1297**)

L0992 Kristen Moeller
Literary Agent
United States

Literary Agency: Waterside Productions, Inc (**L1418**)

L0993 Colleen Mohyde
Literary Agent
United States

Literary Agency: The Doe Coover Agency (**L0373**)

L0994 Silvia Molteni
Literary Agent
United Kingdom

Literary Agency: Peters Fraser + Dunlop (**L1091**)

L0995 Caroline Montgomery
Literary Agent
United Kingdom

Literary Agency: Rupert Crew Ltd (**L1201**)

L0996 Mary C. Moore
Literary Agent
United States

Literary Agency: Kimberley Cameron & Associates (**L0787**)

L0997 Paul Moreton
Literary Agent
United Kingdom

Literary Agency: Bell Lomax Moreton Agency (**L0110**)

L0998 Gary Morris
Literary Agent
United States

Literary Agency: David Black Literary Agency (**L0336**)

L0999 Lucy Morris
Literary Agent
United Kingdom

Literary Agency: Curtis Brown (**L0318**)

L1000 Natascha Morris
Literary Agent
United States

Literary Agency: BookEnds, LLC (**L0155**)

L1001 Joanna Moult
Literary Agent
United Kingdom

Literary Agency: Skylark Literary (**L1288**)

L1002 Movable Type Management
Literary Agency
244 Madison Avenue, Suite 334, New York, NY 10016
United States
Tel: +1 (646) 431-6134

AChromy@MovableTM.com

http://www.mtmgmt.net

Types: Fiction; Nonfiction
Subjects: Commercial
Markets: Adult

Send: Query
Don't send: Full text
How to send: Email

Looking for authors of high quality commercial fiction and nonfiction with archetypal themes, stories, and characters, especially if they have strong film/TV potential. Send queries by email only. For nonfiction send query describing topic, approach, and bio. For fiction send query with first 10 pages. Include "Query" in the subject line. No attachments or approaches by post. Response only if interested.

Literary Agent: Adam Chromy (*L0267*)

L1003 Lisa Moylett
Literary Agent
United Kingdom

https://cmm.agency/about-us.php
http://twitter.com/MoylettLisa

Literary Agency: Coombs Moylett & Maclean Literary Agency (**L0295**)

Fiction > *Novels*: Commercial Women's Fiction

Send: Synopsis; Writing sample
How to send: Online submission system
How not to send: Email

Represents an eclectic list of authors and writers and is currently looking for well-written, commercial women's fiction.

L1004 Mulcahy Associates (Part of MMB Creative)
Literary Agency
The Old Truman Brewery, 91 Brick Lane, London, E1 6QL
United Kingdom
Tel: +44 (0) 20 3582 9370
Fax: +44 (0) 20 3582 9377

talent@mmbcreative.com

https://mmbcreative.com

Professional Body: The Association of Authors' Agents (AAA)

Types: Fiction; Nonfiction
Subjects: Biography; Commercial; Crime; Finance; History; Lifestyle; Literary; Sport; Thrillers; Women's Interests
Markets: Adult; Children's; Young Adult

Closed to approaches.

See books pages of website to get an idea of the kind of material represented, and submit via online form.

Literary Agents: Ivan Mulcahy (*L1005*); Sallyanne Sweeney (*L1345*)

L1005 Ivan Mulcahy
Literary Agent
United Kingdom

Literary Agency: Mulcahy Associates (Part of MMB Creative) (**L1004**)

L1006 Helen Mumby
Literary Agent
United Kingdom

Literary Agency: Macnaughton Lord Representation (**L0905**)

L1007 Toby Mundy
Literary Agent; Chief Executive Officer
United Kingdom

https://aevitascreative.com/agents/#agent-7413

Literary Agencies: Toby Mundy Associates Ltd (**L1373**); Aevitas Creative Management (ACM) UK (**L0020**)

Fiction > *Novels*
Literary; Thrillers

Nonfiction > *Nonfiction Books*
Biography; Current Affairs; History; Memoir; Narrative Nonfiction; Popular Culture; Popular Science; Sport

Send: Query; Writing sample
How to send: Online submission system

Looking for gripping narrative nonfiction, and well written, mind-expanding works in the areas of history, biography, memoir, current affairs, sport, popular culture and popular science. Also represents a small number of thriller writers and literary novelists.

Authors: James Aldred; Michael Dine; Armand D'Angour; Jonathan Hillman; Graham Lawton; Mark Leonard; Isabel Losada; Kenan Malik; Peter Mead; Christopher Miller; Richard V. Reeves; Peter Ricketts; Donald Sassoon; Mark Sedgwick; Jeevan Vasagar; Owen Walker; Justin Webb; Christian Wolmar

L1008 Michael Mungiello
Literary Agent
United States

Literary Agency: InkWell Management (**L0686**)

L1009 Oli Munson
Literary Agent
United Kingdom

https://amheath.com/agents/oli-munson/
http://twitter.com/oliagent

Literary Agency: A.M. Heath & Company Limited, Author's Agents (**L0004**)

Fiction > *Novels*
Commercial; Crime; High Concept; Speculative; Suspense; Thrillers

Nonfiction > *Nonfiction Books*
Narrative Nonfiction; Social Issues; Sport

Agency Assistant / Associate Agent: Florence Rees (**L1134**)

L1010 Judith Murdoch
Literary Agent
United Kingdom

Literary Agency: Judith Murdoch Literary Agency (**L0745**)

L1011 Dana Murphy
Literary Agent
United States

Literary Agency: The Book Group (**L0154**)

L1012 Erin Murphy
Literary Agent
United States

Literary Agency: Erin Murphy Literary Agency, Inc. (**L0433**)

L1013 Jacqueline Murphy
Literary Agent
United States

Literary Agency: InkWell Management (**L0686**)

L1014 Hilary Murray
Literary Agent
United Kingdom

Literary Agency: Robertson Murray Literary Agency (**L1163**)

L1015 Judith Murray
Literary Agent
United Kingdom

Literary Agency: Greene & Heaton Ltd (**L0578**)

Fiction > *Novels*
Crime; Historical Fiction; Literary; Thrillers; Women's Fiction

Nonfiction > *Nonfiction Books*
Biography; Cookery; History; Literary; Memoir; Travel

Authors: Poppy Adams; Mark Alder; Lucy Atkins; Laura Barnett; Mark Barrowcliffe; Darcey Bell; Caroline Bond; Elizabeth Buchan; P. Kearney Byrne; Helen Callaghan; Clare Chambers; Lucy Clarke; Emma Cook; Kate Davies; Lydia Davis; Sabine Durrant; Samantha Ellis; Helen Fisher; Susanna Forrest; L. R. Fredericks; Martin J. Gilbert; Andrea Gillies; Paula Gosling; Victoria Gosling; Stella Grey; Joanna Hall; Maeve Haran; Belinda Harley; Anjali Joseph; M.D. Lachlan; Reif Larsen; Jardine Libaire; Rebecca Mackenzie; Ben Marcus; Ian McGuire; Laura McHugh; Ben McPherson; Kamin Mohammadi; Kate Morrison; Joanna Nadin; Jenny Offill; Temi Oh; Sean O'Connor; Helen Paris; Miranda Popkey; Jonathan Ray; Maria Realf; Karen Russell; Steven Savile; Clare Swatman;

Susannah Walker; Jacqueline Ward; Patricia Wastvedt; Sarah Waters; Benjamin Wood; Anne Youngson

L1016 Tamela Hancock Murray
Literary Agent
United States

Literary Agency: The Steve Laube Agency (**L1318**)

L1017 Mushens Entertainment
Literary Agency
London
United Kingdom

https://www.mushens-entertainment.com
https://twitter.com/MushensEnt

Professional Body: The Association of Authors' Agents (AAA)

London literary agency with a boutique feel. Represents a diverse range of Sunday Times and New York Times bestsellers, authors, actors, brands, and more.

Literary Agents: Silé Edwards (**L0411**); Juliet Mushens (**L1018**)

L1018 Juliet Mushens
Literary Agent
United Kingdom

jmsubmissions@mushens-entertainment.com

Literary Agency: Mushens Entertainment (**L1017**)

ADULT > **Fiction** > *Novels*
Book Club Fiction; Crime; Fantasy; Ghost Stories; High Concept; Historical Fiction; Romantic Comedy; Science Fiction; Thrillers

YOUNG ADULT > **Fiction** > *Novels*

Does not want:

> **ADULT**
> **Fiction**
> *Illustrated Books*: General
> *Novellas*: General
> *Novels*: Erotic; Politics; Satire
> *Short Fiction*: General
>
> **Nonfiction** > *Nonfiction Books*
>
> **Poetry** > *Poetry Collections*
>
> **CHILDREN'S** > **Fiction** > *Novels*

Closed to approaches.

Looking for adult fiction and YA only. She is looking for crime, thriller, YA, reading group fiction, ghost stories, historical fiction, SFF, romcoms, high concept novels, and books which fall a little bit in between.

L1019 James Mustelier
Literary Agent
United States

---

http://www.thebentagency.com/james-mustelier
https://querymanager.com/query/1908

Literary Agency: The Bent Agency (**L0119**)

ADULT > Fiction
  Novels: Comedy / Humour; Commercial;
  Crime; Horror; Literary; Mystery; Suspense;
  Thrillers
  Short Fiction: General

YOUNG ADULT > Fiction > *Novels*

How to send: Query Manager

L1020 Jean Naggar
Literary Agent
United States

Literary Agency: The Jean V. Naggar Literary
Agency (**L0716**)

L1021 The Narrow Road Company
Literary Agency
1st Floor, 37 Great Queen Street, Covent
Garden, London, WC2B 5AA
United Kingdom
Tel: +44 (0) 20 7831 4450

creatives@narrowroad.co.uk

https://narrowroad.co.uk/

Scripts
  Film Scripts: General
  Radio Scripts: General
  TV Scripts: General
  Theatre Scripts: Theatre

Send: Query
Don't send: Full text
How to send: Email
How not to send: Email attachment

Send query by email. Seeks writers with some
experience and original ideas. Handles scripts
only. No novels, poetry, unsolicited MSS, or
email attachments.

Authors: Joe Graham; Richard Groves; Lincoln
Hudson; Simon Macallum

Literary Agents: Amy Ireson (*L0689*); Dan
Ireson (*L0690*); James Ireson (*L0691*); Richard
Ireson (**L0692**); Rozzy Lloyd (*L0871*); Adam
Mendlesohn (*L0967*); Sarah Veecock (*L1399*)

L1022 Kate Nash
Literary Agent
United Kingdom

Literary Agency: Kate Nash Literary Agency
(**L0764**)

L1023 Natasha Kern Literary Agency
Literary Agency
United States

http://natashakernliterary.com

Fiction > *Novels*

How to send: By referral; Conferences

Closed to queries from unpublished writers.
Focusses on developing the careers of
established writers. Will continue to accept
referrals through current clients or editors, and
through conferences.

Authors: Tamera Alexander; Nikki Arana;
Nina Bangs; Angela Benson; Cheryl Bolen;
Maggie Brendan

Literary Agent: Natasha Kern

L1024 Edward Necarsulmer
Literary Agent
United States

Literary Agency: Dunow, Carlson & Lerner
Agency (**L0395**)

L1025 The Ned Leavitt Agency
Literary Agency
70 Wooster Street, Suite 4F, New York, NY
10012
United States
Tel: +1 (212) 334-0999

http://www.nedleavittagency.com

Professional Body: Association of Authors'
Representatives, Inc. (AAR)

Types: Fiction; Nonfiction
Formats: Short Fiction
Subjects: Autobiography; Commercial; Health;
Literary; Mystery; Science Fiction; Spirituality
Markets: Adult

Send: Query
Don't send: Full text

Accepts approaches by recommendation only.

Literary Agent: Ned Leavitt (*L0841*)

L1026 Nelson Literary Agency, LLC
Literary Agency
1732 Wazee Street, Suite 207, Denver, CO
80202
United States
Tel: +1 (303) 292-2805

info@nelsonagency.com

http://www.nelsonagency.com

Professional Body: Association of Authors'
Representatives, Inc. (AAR)

Types: Fiction
Subjects: Commercial; Fantasy; History;
Literary; Mystery; Romance; Science Fiction;
Thrillers; Women's Interests
Markets: Adult; Children's; Young Adult

Send: Query
Don't send: Full text

Handles young adult, upper-level middle
grade, "big crossover novels with one foot
squarely in genre", literary commercial novels,

upmarket women's fiction, single-title
romances (especially historicals), and lead title
or hardcover science fiction and fantasy. No
nonfiction, memoirs, screenplays, short story
collections, poetry, children's picture books or
chapter books, or material for the
Christian/inspirational market. Submit through
online submission system. No queries by post,
phone, in person, or through Facebook. No
email attachments. See website for full
submission guidelines.

Literary Agents: Danielle Burby (**L0198**);
Joanna MacKenzie (**L0901**); Kristin Nelson
(**L1027**); Quressa Robinson (*L1170*)

L1027 Kristin Nelson
Literary Agent
United States

https://nelsonagency.com/kristin-nelson/
https://twitter.com/agentkristinNLA

Literary Agency: Nelson Literary Agency,
LLC (**L1026**)
Professional Body: Association of Authors'
Representatives, Inc. (AAR)

ADULT > Fiction > *Novels*
  Commercial; Fantasy; High Concept;
  Historical Fiction; Literary; Science Fiction;
  Speculative; Thrillers

CHILDREN'S > Fiction > *Middle Grade*

YOUNG ADULT > Fiction > *Novels*

Send: Author bio; Query; Writing sample
How to send: Query Manager

Query via online form.

L1028 Patricia Nelson
Literary Agent
United States

Literary Agency: Marsal Lyon Literary Agency
LLC (**L0925**)

L1029 Zoe Nelson
Literary Agent
United Kingdom

Literary Agency: Rogers, Coleridge & White
Ltd (**L1181**)

L1030 Kenzi Nevins
Junior Agent
United States

kenzi@cyleyoung.com

http://www.kenzimelody.com
https://cyleyoung.com/literary-agent/my-team/
https://www.facebook.com/kenzimelody/
https://www.linkedin.com/in/mckenzie-nevins-063681116/
https://www.pinterest.com/kenzinevins/
https://twitter.com/Kenzi_Melody
https://www.instagram.com/
kenzimelodyauthor/

Literary Agency: Cyle Young Literary Elite (**L0323**)

CHILDREN'S > **Fiction**
Graphic Novels: Fairy Tales; Fantasy; Folklore, Myths, and Legends; Historical Fiction; Magical Realism; Urban Fantasy; Vikings Fiction
Middle Grade: Fairy Tales; Fantasy; Folklore, Myths, and Legends; Historical Fiction; Magical Realism; Urban Fantasy; Vikings Fiction
Picture Books: Environment; Fairy Tales; Folklore, Myths, and Legends; Magic; Nature
YOUNG ADULT > **Fiction**
Graphic Novels: Fairy Tales; Fantasy; Folklore, Myths, and Legends; Historical Fiction; Magical Realism; Urban Fantasy; Vikings Fiction
Novels: Fairy Tales; Fantasy; Folklore, Myths, and Legends; Historical Fiction; Magical Realism; Urban Fantasy; Vikings Fiction

Closed to approaches.

Represents both illustrators and writers for children's picture books, middle grade, and young adult. Interested in magic realism and mythology.

L1031 Dana Newman
Literary Agent
United States

Literary Agency: Dana Newman Literary, LLC (**L0328**)

L1032 Kiana Nguyen
Literary Agent
United States

Literary Agency: Donald Maass Literary Agency (**L0380**)

L1033 Geraldine Nichol
Literary Agent
Ireland

Literary Agency: The Book Bureau Literary Agency (**L0153**)

L1034 Nick Turner Management Ltd
Literary Agency
32 Tavistock Street, London, WC2E 7PB
United Kingdom
Tel: +44 (0) 20 7450 3355

nick@nickturnermanagement.com

http://nickturnermanagement.com

Types: Scripts
Formats: Film Scripts; Radio Scripts; TV Scripts
Subjects: Comedy / Humour; Drama
Markets: Adult; Children's

Closed to approaches.

London-based creative talent agency representing a broad mix of writers, directors and producers working across feature-film, television drama, comedy, children's, continuing-drama and radio. No unsolicited submissions. New clients come through producer or personal recommendations only.

Literary Agent: Nick Turner (*L1381*)

L1035 Susie Nicklin
Literary Agent
United Kingdom

Literary Agency: The Marsh Agency (**L0927**)

L1036 Erin Niumata
Literary Agent; Senior Vice President
United States
Tel: +1 (212) 400-1494

erin@foliolit.com

https://www.foliolit.com/agents-1/erin-niumata
https://www.instagram.com/ecniumata/?hl=en
https://twitter.com/ecniumata?ref_src=twsrc%5Egoogle%7Ctwcamp%5Eserp%7Ctwgr%5Eauthor

Literary Agency: Folio Literary Management, LLC (**L0480**)

Fiction > *Novels*
Book Club Fiction; Commercial Women's Fiction; Mystery; Psychological Thrillers; Romance

Nonfiction > *Nonfiction Books*
Commercial; Cookery; Memoir; Narrative Nonfiction; Prescriptive Nonfiction

Closed to approaches.

L1037 Noel Gay
Literary Agency
1st Floor, 2 Stephen Street, Fitzrovia, London, W1T 1AN
United Kingdom
Tel: +44 (0) 20 7836 3941

info@noelgay.com

https://www.noelgay.com
https://twitter.com/NoelGay19

Scripts
Film Scripts; Radio Scripts; TV Scripts; Theatre Scripts

Agency representing writers, directors, performers, presenters, comedians, etc.

Literary Agents: Sophieclaire Armitage (*L0062*); Natalie Ball (*L0080*); Philip Bell; Ellie Cahill-Nicholls (*L0207*)

L1038 Laura Nolan
Literary Agent; Senior Partner
United States

https://aevitascreative.com/agents/

Literary Agency: Aevitas (**L0019**)
Professional Body: Association of Authors' Representatives, Inc. (AAR)

Fiction > *Novels*: Upmarket Commercial Fiction

Nonfiction > *Nonfiction Books*
Alternative Health; Celebrity; Cookery; Food; Investigative Journalism; Lifestyle; Music; Politics; Science; Women's Issues

Send: Query; Writing sample
How to send: Online submission system

Represents platform-driven narrative nonfiction in the areas of celebrity, music, investigative journalism, women's issues, alternative health, and lifestyle. She is passionate about cookbooks and food narrative informed by politics or science. She is seeking challenging ideas, incisive writing that asks "big" questions, and artists who are successful in one medium but whose talents and passion translate into narrative.

L1039 Bryan Norman
Literary Agent
United States

Literary Agency: Alive Literary Agency (**L0030**)

L1040 The North Literary Agency
Literary Agency
The Chapel, Market Place, Corbridge, Northumberland, NE45 5AW
United Kingdom

hello@thenorthlitagency.com

http://thenorthlitagency.com

Fiction > *Novels*

Nonfiction > *Nonfiction Books*: Narrative Nonfiction

Send: Query; Synopsis; Proposal; Writing sample
How to send: Email

Looking for all types of fiction and narrative nonfiction. No academic writing, poetry, self-help, picture books or screenplays. No submissions by post.

Literary Agents: Julie Fergusson (**L0463**); Allan Guthrie (**L0593**); Lina Langlee (**L0826**); Kevin Pocklington (**L1103**); Mark "Stan" Stanton (**L1309**)

L1041 Norman North
Literary Agent
United Kingdom

Literary Agency: The Agency (London) Ltd (**L0021**)

L1042 Northbank Talent Management
Literary Agency
United Kingdom
Tel: +44 (0) 20 3973 0837

info@northbanktalent.com

http://www.northbanktalent.com

Professional Body: The Association of Authors' Agents (AAA)

Types: Fiction; Nonfiction
Subjects: Autobiography; Business; Commercial; Crime; Current Affairs; Drama; Fantasy; Health; History; Lifestyle; Personal Development; Politics; Psychology; Science; Science Fiction; Suspense; Thrillers; Women's Interests
Markets: Adult; Children's; Young Adult

Send: Query
Don't send: Full text
How to send: Email

Literary and talent agency based in central London. Actively seeking new clients. Send query by email with synopsis and first three chapters as Word or Open Document attachments. See website for specific email addresses to use for different types of material.

Literary Agents: Martin Redfern (*L1130*); Hannah Weatherill (*L1423*)

L1043 Trodayne Northern
Literary Agent; President
United States

Literary Agency: Prentis Literary (**L1114**)

L1044 Sarah Nundy
Literary Agent
United Kingdom

Literary Agency: Andrew Nurnberg Associates, Ltd (**L0050**)

L1045 Andrew Nurnberg
Literary Agent
United Kingdom

Literary Agency: Andrew Nurnberg Associates, Ltd (**L0050**)

L1046 Haskell Nussbaum
Associate Agent
Canada

Literary Agency: The Rights Factory (**L1151**)

L1047 NY Creative Management
Literary Agency
United States

http://www.nycreative.com

Types: Fiction; Nonfiction
Markets: Children's

Send: Synopsis

Send one-page synopsis by email, giving a brief, informative paragraph about your novel, non-fiction book, screenplay or magazine-length article, giving the main idea and basic structure of your project.

Literary Agent: Jeff Schmidt (**L1232**)

L1048 Renee Nyen
Literary Agent
United States

Literary Agency: KT Literary (**L0811**)

L1049 Niamh O'Grady
Associate Agent
United Kingdom

https://www.thesohoagency.co.uk/agent/niamh-ogrady

Literary Agency: The Soho Agency (**L1297**)

Fiction > *Novels*
  Book Club Fiction; Comedy / Humour; Family; Literary; Relationships

Nonfiction > *Nonfiction Books*
  Comedy / Humour; Narrative Nonfiction

Send: Query; Synopsis; Writing sample
How to send: Email attachment

Actively looking for accessible literary and reading-group fiction, and narrative non-fiction. She is drawn to books with heart and humour, thought-provoking writing and distinctive, compelling voices. She particularly loves novels that explore family and relationships and wants to read stories that leave an emotional impact, with characters that stay with her long after the final page. She is keen to find new Irish and Northern writing talent.

L1050 Coleen O'Shea
Literary Agent
United States

Professional Body: Association of Authors' Representatives, Inc. (AAR)

L1051 Ikenna Obiekwe
Literary Agent
United Kingdom

Literary Agency: Independent Talent Group Ltd (**L0683**)

L1052 Colleen Oefelein
Literary Agent
United States

Literary Agency: The Jennifer DeChiara Literary Agency (**L0721**)

L1053 Kristin van Ogtrop
Literary Agent
United States

Literary Agency: InkWell Management (**L0686**)

L1054 Charlie Olsen
Literary Agent
United States

Literary Agency: InkWell Management (**L0686**)

L1055 Neil Olson
Literary Agent
United States

neil@mmqlit.com

Literary Agency: Massie & McQuilkin (**L0934**)

Fiction > *Novels*

Nonfiction > *Nonfiction Books*
  Biography; Environment; History; Travel

How to send: Email

L1056 One Piece Agency
Literary Agency
Beijing, 100026
China

onepieceagency@163.com

Types: Fiction; Nonfiction
Subjects: Adventure; Architecture; Arts; Business; Comedy / Humour; Commercial; Contemporary; Crafts; Crime; Culture; Design; Experimental; Fantasy; Gardening; Health; Horror; How To; Leisure; Lifestyle; Literary; Literature; Mystery; Nature; Personal Development; Photography; Romance; Science Fiction; Suspense; Technology; Thrillers; Travel
Markets: Adult; Children's; Young Adult

Send: Full text
How to send: Email

A boutique agency founded in July 2016. Desires to engage itself to discover those talents with the fresh, original and creative ideas and stories. The agency's diverse interest cover from fiction to nonfiction, in addition to the children book and those illustrated books with the wonderful images.

L1057 One Track Literary Agency, Inc.
Literary Agency
United States
Tel: +1 (401) 595-1949

tara@onetrackliterary.com

http://www.onetrackliterary.com

Types: Fiction
Subjects: Commercial; Contemporary; Mystery; Romance; Satire; Thrillers; Traditional; Women's Interests
Markets: Adult

Send: Full text
How to send: Email

A full-service boutique agency providing hands-on guidance throughout each and every part of the publishing pursuit. OTLA is single-minded and fully dedicated to getting you on the right track to launch your career or progress to the next level. From honing manuscripts to be their very best, to identifying the right market for placement, through contract advisement and negotiation, to crafting promotional campaigns to help grow your audience, the prime objective is to help you achieve your goals. Currently seeking completed works with vibrant, fresh voices in these genres: romance, women's fiction, mysteries, and young adult.

Authors: Elley Arden; Elizabeth Boyce; Pema Donyo; Licie Laine; Ruby Lang; Julie LeMense; Becky Lower; Robyn Neeley; Alicia Hunter Pace; Micah Persell; Dana Volney

Literary Agent: Tara Gelsomino (*L0537*)

L1058 Edward Orloff
Literary Agent
United States

Literary Agency: McCormick Literary (**L0949**)

L1059 Rachel Orr
Literary Agent
United States

Literary Agency: Prospect Agency (**L1116**)

L1060 Mark Orsini
Literary Agent
United States

Literary Agency: Bret Adams Ltd (**L0178**)

L1061 Luba Ostashevsky
Literary Agent
United States

https://www.pandeliterary.com/about-pandeliterary

Literary Agency: Ayesha Pande Literary (**L0073**)

Nonfiction > *Nonfiction Books*
Health; History; Popular Science

Send: Pitch; Author bio; Synopsis; Writing sample
How to send: Online submission system

Interested in nonfiction popular science projects, written by either research scientists, medical or mental health professionals, or journalists. Not comfortable representing fiction, cookbooks, YA, self help, nor business or politics (unless directly about science).

L1062 Bruce Ostler
Literary Agent
United States

Literary Agency: Bret Adams Ltd (**L0178**)

L1063 Deborah Owen
Literary Agent
United Kingdom

Literary Agency: Deborah Owen Ltd (**L0348**)

L1064 Anne Marie O'Farrell
Literary Agent

Professional Body: The Agents Round Table (ART)

L1065 Ayesha Pande
Literary Agent
United States

https://www.pandeliterary.com/about-pandeliterary
https://twitter.com/agent_ayesha
http://aaronline.org/Sys/PublicProfile/2455085/417813

Literary Agency: Ayesha Pande Literary (**L0073**)
Professional Bodies: Association of Authors' Representatives, Inc. (AAR); The Agents Round Table (ART)

Fiction > *Novels*
African American; International; Literary; Popular; Women's Fiction

Nonfiction > *Nonfiction Books*
Biography; Cultural Commentary; History; Memoir; Narrative Nonfiction; Popular Culture

Closed to approaches.

L1066 Jessica Papin
Literary Agent
United States

Literary Agency: Dystel, Goderich & Bourret LLC (**L0399**)

L1067 Ammi-Joan Paquette
Literary Agent
United States

Literary Agency: Erin Murphy Literary Agency, Inc. (**L0433**)

L1068 Elana Roth Parker
Literary Agent
United States

http://www.ldlainc.com/submissions/
http://www.manuscriptwishlist.com/mswl-post/elana-roth-parker/
https://querymanager.com/query/queryelana
http://aaronline.org/Sys/PublicProfile/43775067/417813

Literary Agency: Laura Dail Literary Agency (**L0831**)
Professional Body: Association of Authors' Representatives, Inc. (AAR)

CHILDREN'S
Fiction
Graphic Novels: Commercial
Middle Grade: Commercial; High Concept
Nonfiction > *Nonfiction Books:* Narrative Nonfiction

TEEN > **Nonfiction** > *Nonfiction Books:* Narrative Nonfiction

YOUNG ADULT > **Fiction**
Graphic Novels: Commercial
Novels: Commercial; High Concept

Send: Query; Pitch; Synopsis; Author bio
How to send: Query Manager

Commercial and high-concept middle-grade and young adult fiction (all genres, but maybe avoid Christmas, talking animal books, or anything nightmare-inducing); commercial or fanciful graphic novels for middle-grade and young adult audiences (author/illustrators preferred); narrative non-fiction for children and teens; picture books by referral only.

L1069 Marina De Pass
Associate Agent
United Kingdom

https://www.thesohoagency.co.uk/agent/marina-de-pass
https://twitter.com/marinadepass

Literary Agency: The Soho Agency (**L1297**)

Fiction > *Novels*
Crime; Historical Fiction; Literary; Romantic Comedy; Thrillers; Upmarket Commercial Fiction

Send: Query; Synopsis; Writing sample
How to send: Email attachment

Loves commercial and book-club fiction in all its forms – from police procedurals and twisty, domestic noir to smart rom-coms and big, sweeping love stories – and is actively looking to take on clients in this area.

L1070 Emma Paterson
Literary Agent
United Kingdom

Literary Agency: Aitken Alexander Associates (**L0025**)

L1071 Kathi Paton
Literary Agent
United States

Literary Agency: Kathi J. Paton Literary Agency (**L0765**)

L1072 Emma Patterson
Literary Agent
United States

epatterson@bromasite.com

Literary Agency: Brandt & Hochman Literary Agents, Inc. (**L0172**)

Professional Body: Association of Authors' Representatives, Inc. (AAR)

ADULT

Fiction > *Novels*
Historical Fiction; Literary; Upmarket

Nonfiction > *Nonfiction Books*
Investigative Journalism; Memoir; Narrative Nonfiction; Popular History

YOUNG ADULT > **Fiction** > *Novels*
Historical Fiction; Literary; Upmarket

Send: Query
How to send: Email

L1073 Philip Patterson
Literary Agent
United Kingdom

Literary Agency: Marjacq Scripts Ltd (**L0921**)

L1074 Paul S. Levine Literary Agency
Literary Agency
1054 Superba Avenue, Venice, CA 90291-3940
United States
Tel: +1 (310) 450-6711
Fax: +1 (310) 450-0181

paul@paulslevinelit.com

http://www.paulslevinelit.com

Types: Fiction; Nonfiction
Subjects: Adventure; Business; Commercial; Contemporary; Culture; How To; Legal; Lifestyle; Mystery; Personal Development; Politics; Romance; Sport; Thrillers; Women's Interests
Markets: Adult; Children's; Young Adult

Send: Query
Don't send: Full text

Send query by email, or by post with SASE. No phone calls.

Literary Agent: Paul S. Levine (*L0850*)

L1075 Maggie Pearlstine
Literary Agent
United Kingdom

Literary Agency: Maggie Pearlstine Associates Ltd (**L0909**)

L1076 Clare Pearson
Literary Agent
United Kingdom

Literary Agency: Eddison Pearson Ltd (**L0406**)

L1077 Jonathan Pegg
Literary Agent
United Kingdom

Literary Agency: Jonathan Pegg Literary Agency (**L0735**)

L1078 Imogen Pelham
Literary Agent
United Kingdom

Literary Agency: Marjacq Scripts Ltd (**L0921**)

L1079 Catherine Pellegrino
Literary Agent
United Kingdom

Literary Agency: Marjacq Scripts Ltd (**L0921**)

L1080 Sharon Pelletier
Literary Agent
United States

Literary Agency: Dystel, Goderich & Bourret LLC (**L0399**)

L1081 Peregrine Whittlesey Agency
Literary Agency
United States

https://www.linkedin.com/in/peregrine-whittlesey-33423830

Types: Scripts
Formats: Film Scripts; TV Scripts; Theatre Scripts
Markets: Adult

Handles mainly theatre scripts, plus a small number of film/TV scripts by playwrights who also write for screen.

Literary Agent: Peregrine Whittlesey (*L1445*)

L1082 Kim Perel
Literary Agent
United States

Literary Agency: Irene Goodman Literary Agency (IGLA) (**L0688**)

L1083 Kristina Perez
Associate Agent
United Kingdom

perez@zenoagency.com

http://zenoagency.com/agents/kristina-perez/
https://twitter.com/kperezagent

Literary Agency: Zeno Agency Ltd (**L1487**)

ADULT

Fiction > *Novels*
Dystopian Fiction; Fantasy; Feminism; Historical Fantasy; Historical Romance; Magical Realism; Retellings; Romance; Science Fiction; Space Opera; Supernatural / Paranormal Romance; Witches

Nonfiction > *Nonfiction Books*

CHILDREN'S
Fiction > *Middle Grade*
Fantasy; Historical Fiction

Poetry > *Novels in Verse*

YOUNG ADULT

Fiction > *Novels*
Coming of Age; Contemporary; Fantasy; Folklore, Myths, and Legends; Ghost Stories; Historical Fiction; LGBTQIA; Retellings; Romantic Comedy; Soft Science Fiction; Theatre; Vampires

Nonfiction > *Nonfiction Books*

Poetry > *Novels in Verse*

Does not want:

Fiction > *Novels*
Contemporary Romance; Hard Science Fiction

Closed to approaches.

Accepts submissions only from BAME and other marginalised creators.

Authors: Alexia Casale; Sharon Emmerichs; Erin Rose Kim; Vincent Tirado; Khadija L. VanBrakle; Stephen Vines; Cristin Williams; Joshua Winning; Yuchi Zhang

L1084 Lara Perkins
Literary Agent
United States

Literary Agency: Andrea Brown Literary Agency, Inc. (**L0047**)
Professional Body: Association of Authors' Representatives, Inc. (AAR)

L1085 Martha Perotto-Wills
Literary Agent
United Kingdom

http://www.thebentagency.com/martha-perotto-wills

Fiction > *Novels*

Closed to approaches.

Particularly enjoys self-aware spookiness, joyful radicalism, eccentric glamour, and anything that could be described as 'an intelligent romp'.

L1086 Perry Literary, Inc.
Literary Agency
211 South Ridge Street, Suite 2, Rye Brook, NY 10573
United States

jperry@perryliterary.com

https://www.perryliterary.com

Types: Fiction; Nonfiction
Formats: Film Scripts; TV Scripts
Subjects: Biography; Business; Cookery; Crime; Culture; Current Affairs; Finance; History; Legal; Lifestyle; Literary; Medicine; Music; Personal Development; Philosophy; Politics; Psychology; Science; Society; Sport; Technology; Travel
Markets: Adult; Children's

How to send: Email

Send query by email with first ten pages in the body of the email (or full manuscript for picture books). No attachments. See website for full guidelines.

Literary Agent: Joseph Perry (*L1088*)

L1087 Anne C. Perry
Literary Agent
United Kingdom

anne@ki-agency.co.uk

https://ki-agency.co.uk/contact

Literary Agency: Ki Agency Ltd (**L0782**)

Fiction > *Novels*

Nonfiction > *Nonfiction Books*
Dinosaurs; Dorset; Memoir; Nature; Popular History; Popular Science; Robots

Happy to accept fiction submissions in all genres. In non-fiction, she is looking for popular science, natural history, popular history and memoirs. She loves dinosaurs, robots, the Dorset coast, and Oxford commas.

L1088 Joseph Perry
Literary Agent
United States

Literary Agency: Perry Literary, Inc. (**L1086**)

L1089 Carrie Pestritto
Literary Agent
United States

http://www.ldlainc.com/about
http://aaronline.org/Sys/PublicProfile/
53765008/417813
http://twitter.com/literarycarrie
https://literarycarrie.wixsite.com/blog
http://www.manuscriptwishlist.com/mswl-post/carrie-pestritto/

Literary Agency: Laura Dail Literary Agency (**L0831**)
Professional Body: Association of Authors' Representatives, Inc. (AAR)

ADULT
Fiction > *Novels*
Comedy / Humour; Commercial; Cozy Mysteries; Historical Fiction; LGBTQIA; Relationships; Romance; Romantic Comedy; Suspense; Thrillers; Upmarket Women's Fiction

Nonfiction > *Nonfiction Books*
Biography; Commercial; History; LGBTQIA; Memoir; Narrative Nonfiction; Popular Science; Prescriptive Nonfiction

CHILDREN'S > **Fiction**
Chapter Books: Adventure; Fantasy; High Concept; Mystery; Science Fiction; Thrillers
Middle Grade: Adventure; Fantasy; High Concept; Mystery; Science Fiction; Thrillers
YOUNG ADULT > *Fiction* > *Novels*
Adventure; Fantasy; High Concept; Mystery; Science Fiction; Thrillers

How to send: Query Manager

Loves the thrill of finding new authors with strong, unique voices and working closely with her clients. Always strives to help create books that will introduce readers to new worlds and is drawn in by relatable characters, meticulous world-building, and unusual, compelling premises.

L1090 Peter Lampack Agency, Inc
Literary Agency
The Empire State Building, 350 Fifth Avenue, Suite 5300, New York, NY 10118
United States
Tel: +1 (212) 687-9106
Fax: +1 (212) 687-9109

andrew@peterlampackagency.com

https://www.peterlampackagency.com

Types: Fiction; Nonfiction
Subjects: Commercial; Literary
Markets: Adult

Send: Query
Don't send: Full text
How to send: Email

Specialises in commercial and literary fiction as well as nonfiction by recognised experts in a given field. Send query by email only, with cover letter, author bio, sample chapter, and 1-2 page synopsis. No children's books, horror, romance, westerns, science fiction or screenplays.

Authors: Russell Blake; Sandra Burton; Thomas Caplan; Linda Cirino; J.M. Coetzee; Clive Cussler; Stephen Horn; Judith Kelman; Paul Kemprecos; Brian Lysaght; Gerry Spence; Fred Mustard Stewart

Literary Agent: Andrew Lampack (*L0823*)

L1091 Peters Fraser + Dunlop
Literary Agency
55 New Oxford Street, London, WC1A 1BS
United Kingdom
Tel: +44 (0) 20 7344 1000
Fax: +44 (0) 20 7836 9539

info@pfd.co.uk

http://www.pfd.co.uk

Professional Body: The Association of Authors' Agents (AAA)

Types: Fiction; Nonfiction; Scripts
Formats: Film Scripts; Radio Scripts; TV Scripts; Theatre Scripts
Subjects: Autobiography; Comedy / Humour; Commercial; Cookery; Crime; Culture; Finance; Gothic; History; Literary; Nature; Psychology; Science; Sport; Suspense; Thrillers; Women's Interests
Markets: Adult; Children's; Young Adult

Send: Query
Don't send: Full text
How to send: Email

See website for individual agent interests and submission guidelines.

Book Publisher: Agora Books (**P0025**)

Literary Agents: Alexandra Cliff (*L0281*); Tessa David (*L0340*); Kate Evans (*L0442*); Jon Fowler (*L0487*); Adam Gauntlett (*L0531*); Dan Herron (*L0643*); Laura McNeill (*L0959*); Annabel Merullo (*L0969*); Caroline Michel (*L0975*); Silvia Molteni (*L0994*); Michael Sissons and Fiona Petheram (*L1093*); Elizabeth Sheinkman (*L1264*); Camilla Shestopal (*L1270*); Jonathan Sissons (*L1287*); Rebecca Wearmouth (*L1422*)

L1092 Will Peterson
Literary Agent
United Kingdom

Literary Agency: Independent Talent Group Ltd (**L0683**)

L1093 Michael Sissons and Fiona Petheram
Literary Agent
United Kingdom

Literary Agency: Peters Fraser + Dunlop (**L1091**)

L1094 PEW Literary
Literary Agency
46 Lexington Street, London, W1F 0LP
United Kingdom
Tel: +44 (0) 20 7734 4464

submissions@pewliterary.com

http://www.pewliterary.com

Types: Fiction; Nonfiction
Subjects: Crime; Literary; Thrillers
Markets: Adult

Send: Query
Don't send: Full text
How to send: Email

Send query by post or by email, with synopsis and first three chapters (or fifty pages) (fiction); or proposal (nonfiction). If submitting by email, send material in Word or PDF attachment. If submitting by post, do not include SAE as material will be recycled once read. Include email address for response. Aims to respond within six weeks.

Literary Agent: Patrick Walsh (*L1415*)

L1095 Beth Phelan
Literary Agent
United States

beth@galltzacker.com

Literary Agency: Gallt & Zacker Literary Agency (**L0522**)

CHILDREN'S
  Fiction > *Middle Grade*
  Nonfiction > *Middle Grade*
YOUNG ADULT
  Fiction > *Novels*
  Nonfiction > *Nonfiction Books*

Closed to approaches.

L1096 **Ariana Philips**
Literary Agent
United States

Literary Agency: The Jean V. Naggar Literary Agency (**L0716**)

L1097 **Juliet Pickering**
Literary Agent
United Kingdom

Literary Agency: Blake Friedmann Literary Agency Ltd (**L0139**)

L1098 **Nell Pierce**
Associate Agent
United States

https://www.sll.com/our-team

Literary Agency: Sterling Lord Literistic, Inc. (**L1317**)

Fiction > *Novels*
  Commercial; Literary

Nonfiction > *Nonfiction Books*
  Language; Narrative Nonfiction

Send: Query; Synopsis; Writing sample
How to send: Online submission system

Looking for literary and commercial fiction, narrative nonfiction, character-driven young adult novels, and books about language and linguistics.

L1099 **Richard Pike**
Literary Agent
United Kingdom

Literary Agency: C+W (Conville & Walsh) (**L0205**)

L1100 **Richard Pine**
Literary Agent
United States

Literary Agency: InkWell Management (**L0686**)

L1101 **Pippin Properties, Inc**
Literary Agency
110 West 40th Street, Suite 1704, New York, NY 10016
United States
Tel: +1 (212) 338-9310
Fax: +1 (212) 338-9579

info@pippinproperties.com

http://www.pippinproperties.com

Professional Body: Association of Authors' Representatives, Inc. (AAR)

Types: Fiction
Markets: Adult; Children's; Young Adult

Send: Query
Don't send: Full text
How to send: Email

Costs: Author covers sundry admin costs.

Devoted primarily to picture books, middle-grade, and young adult novels, but also represents adult projects on occasion. Send query by email with synopsis, first chapter, or entire picture book manuscript in the body of your email. No attachments. See website for full guidelines.

Literary Agents: Sara Crowe (*L0313*); Elena Giovinazzo (*L0546*); Holly McGhee (*L0954*)

L1102 **Zoe Plant**
Literary Agent
United States

Literary Agency: The Bent Agency (**L0119**)

L1103 **Kevin Pocklington**
Literary Agent
United Kingdom

http://thenorthlitagency.com/our-friends-in-the-north/

Literary Agency: The North Literary Agency (**L1040**)

Fiction > *Novels*
  Crime; Literary

Nonfiction > *Nonfiction Books*

Send: Query; Synopsis; Writing sample; Proposal
How to send: Email

Looking for a wide range of nonfiction submissions and would like to develop a fiction list with new authors, including accessible literary fiction and crime titles.

L1104 **Rebecca Podos**
Literary Agent
United States

Literary Agency: Rees Literary Agency (**L1133**)

L1105 **Barbara Poelle**
Literary Agent
United States

Literary Agency: Irene Goodman Literary Agency (IGLA) (**L0688**)

L1106 **Ruth Pomerance**
Affiliated Agent
United States

http://foliolit.com/ruth-pomerance

Literary Agency: Folio Literary Management, LLC (**L0480**)

Fiction > *Novels*: Commercial

Nonfiction > *Nonfiction Books*: Narrative Nonfiction

Does not want:

Nonfiction > *Nonfiction Books*: Prescriptive Nonfiction

Closed to approaches.

L1107 **Pontas Copyright Agency, S.L.**
Literary Agency
P.O. Box / Apartat postal # 11, E-08183 Castellterçol (Barcelona)
Spain
Tel: (+34) 93 218 22 12

info@pontas-agency.com

http://www.pontas-agency.com

Fiction > *Novels*

Send: Author bio; Writing sample
How to send: Email

International literary and film agency accepting submissions of adult fiction in English and French by email only. Include at least the first five chapters and the author's biography.

L1108 **Lyndsey Posner**
Literary Agent
United Kingdom

Literary Agency: Independent Talent Group Ltd (**L0683**)

L1109 **Marcy Posner**
Literary Agent; Senior Vice President
United States

marcy@foliolit.com

https://www.foliolit.com/agents-1/marcy-posner

Literary Agency: Folio Literary Management, LLC (**L0480**)

ADULT
  Fiction > *Novels*
    Book Club Fiction; Commercial; Historical Fiction; Literary; Mystery; Thrillers; Women's Fiction

  Nonfiction > *Nonfiction Books*
    Cookery; History; Narrative Nonfiction; Prescriptive Nonfiction; Psychology

CHILDREN'S
  Fiction > *Middle Grade*
  Nonfiction > *Middle Grade*

YOUNG ADULT
  Fiction > *Novels*
  Nonfiction > *Nonfiction Books*

Does not want:

> **ADULT > Fiction >** *Novels*
> Fantasy; Science Fiction
>
> **CHILDREN'S > Fiction >** *Middle Grade*
> Fantasy; Science Fiction
>
> **YOUNG ADULT > Fiction >** *Novels*
> Fantasy; Science Fiction

Closed to approaches.

L1110 Elizabeth Poteet

Literary Agent
United States

Literary Agency: The Seymour Agency (**L1254**)

L1111 Anna Power

Literary Agent; Managing Director
Bloomsbury House, 74-77 Great Russell Street, London, WC1B 3DA
United Kingdom

anna@johnsonandalcock.co.uk

http://www.johnsonandalcock.co.uk/anna-power
https://twitter.com/APowerAgent

Literary Agency: Johnson & Alcock (**L0732**)

ADULT
  Fiction > *Novels*
    Commercial; Historical Fiction; Literary; Psychological Suspense; Thrillers; Women's Fiction

  Nonfiction > *Nonfiction Books*
    Biography; Food; History

CHILDREN'S > Fiction > *Middle Grade*

YOUNG ADULT > Fiction > *Novels*

Send: Query; Synopsis; Writing sample
How to send: Email attachment; Post

L1112 Shelley Power

Literary Agent
United Kingdom

Literary Agency: Shelley Power Literary Agency Ltd (**L1266**)

L1113 Marta Praeger

Literary Agent
United States

http://aaronline.org/Sys/PublicProfile/1715282/417813

Literary Agency: Robert A. Freedman Dramatic Agency, Inc. (**L1158**)
Professional Body: Association of Authors' Representatives, Inc. (AAR)

Scripts > *Theatre Scripts*

L1114 Prentis Literary

Literary Agency
PMB 496, 6830 NE Bothell Way, Suite C, Kenmore, WA 98028
United States

info@prentisliterary.com

https://www.prentisliterary.com

ADULT
  Fiction > *Novels*
    Fantasy; Horror; LGBTQIA; Literary; Mystery; Romance; Science Fiction; Suspense; Thrillers; Women's Fiction

  Nonfiction > *Nonfiction Books*: Memoir

CHILDREN'S > Fiction
  Chapter Books; *Early Readers*; *Middle Grade*; *Picture Books*
YOUNG ADULT > Fiction > *Novels*

Closed to approaches.

Agency with a historic focus on science fiction and fantasy, but now working with well crafted stories in a variety of genres.

Literary Agents: Autumn Frisse (*L0513*); Reggie Lutz (*L0889*)

Literary Agents / Presidents: Trodayne Northern (*L1043*); Leslie Varney (*L1398*)

L1115 Amanda Preston

Literary Agent
United Kingdom

amandasubmissions@lbabooks.com

http://www.lbabooks.com/agent/amanda-preston/

Literary Agency: LBA Books Ltd (**L0839**)

Fiction > *Novels*
  Book Club Fiction; Commercial; Crime Thrillers; Psychological Suspense; Women's Fiction

Nonfiction > *Nonfiction Books*

L1116 Prospect Agency

Literary Agency
551 Valley Rd., PMB 377, Upper Montclair, NJ 07043
United States
Tel: +1 (718) 788-3217
Fax: +1 (718) 360-9582

esk@prospectagency.com

http://www.prospectagency.com

Professional Body: Association of Authors' Representatives, Inc. (AAR)

Types: Fiction; Nonfiction
Subjects: Adventure; Autobiography; Commercial; Contemporary; Crime; Erotic; Fantasy; History; Literary; Mystery; Romance; Science; Science Fiction; Suspense; Thrillers; Westerns; Women's Interests
Markets: Adult; Children's; Young Adult

Send: Query
Don't send: Full text

Handles very little nonfiction. Specialises in romance, women's fiction, literary fiction, young adult/children's literature, and science fiction. Send submissions via website submission system **only** (no email queries – **email queries are not accepted or responded to** – or queries by post (these will be recycled). No poetry, short stories, text books, screenplays, or most nonfiction.

Literary Agents: Emily Sylvan Kim (*L0784*); Rachel Orr (*L1059*); Ann Rose (*L1183*); Emma Sector (*L1249*)

L1117 Victoria Gould Pryor

Literary Agent
United States

Literary Agency: Arcadia (**L0061**)

L1118 The Purcell Agency, LLC

Literary Agency
United States

TPAqueries@gmail.com

http://thepurcellagency.com

Types: Fiction; Nonfiction
Subjects: Culture; Romance; Sport; Women's Interests
Markets: Adult; Children's; Young Adult

Closed to approaches.

Closed to submissions as at May 2018. Check website for current status. Handles middle grade, young adult, women's fiction, and some new adult. No science fiction or fantasy, or picture book manuscripts. See website for full submission guidelines.

Literary Agents: Catherine Hedrick (*L0632*); Kim Blair McCollum (*L0948*); Tina P. Schwartz (*L1241*)

L1119 Queen Literary Agency, Inc.

Literary Agency
30 East 60th Street, Suite 1004, New York, NY 10024
United States
Tel: +1 (212) 974-8333
Fax: +1 (212) 974-8347

submissions@queenliterary.com

http://www.queenliterary.com

Types: Fiction; Nonfiction
Subjects: Business; Commercial; Cookery; History; Literary; Mystery; Psychology; Science; Sport; Thrillers
Markets: Adult

Send: Query
Don't send: Full text
How to send: Email

Founded by a former publishing executive, most recently head of IMG WORLDWIDE'S literary division. Handles a wide range of nonfiction titles, with a particular interest in business books, food writing, science and popular psychology, as well as books by well-known chefs, radio and television personalities and sports figures. Also handles commercial and literary fiction, including historical fiction, mysteries, and thrillers.

Literary Agent: Lisa Queen (*L1120*)

L1120 Lisa Queen
Literary Agent
United States

Literary Agency: Queen Literary Agency, Inc. (**L1119**)

L1121 Pilar Queen
Literary Agent
United States

Literary Agency: McCormick Literary (**L0949**)

L1122 Nick Quinn
Literary Agent
United Kingdom

Literary Agency: The Agency (London) Ltd (**L0021**)

L1123 Shaheen Qureshi
Literary Agent
United States

Literary Agency: Capital Talent Agency (**L0216**)

L1124 Rachel Mills Literary
Literary Agency
3rd Floor, 86-90 Paul Street, London, EC2A 4NE
United Kingdom

submissions@rmliterary.co.uk

https://www.rachelmillsliterary.co.uk
https://twitter.com/bookishyogini
https://www.instagram.com/rachelmillsliterary/

Professional Body: The Association of Authors' Agents (AAA)

How to send: Email

Company Director / Literary Agent: Rachel Mills (**L0988**)

Literary Agent: Nelle Andrew (**L0051**)

L1125 Susan Raihofer
Literary Agent
United States

Literary Agency: David Black Literary Agency (**L0336**)

L1126 Susan Ramer
Literary Agent
United States

Literary Agency: Don Congdon Associates, Inc. (**L0378**)

L1127 Kiele Raymond
Literary Agent
United States

Literary Agency: Thompson Literary Agency (**L1364**)

L1128 Rebecca Friedman Literary Agency
Literary Agency
United States

queries@rfliterary.com

https://rfliterary.com

Types: Fiction; Nonfiction
Subjects: Autobiography; Commercial; Contemporary; Cookery; Lifestyle; Literary; Romance; Suspense; Women's Interests
Markets: Adult; Young Adult

Send: Query
Don't send: Full text
How to send: Email

See website for full submission guidelines and specific agent interests and contact details. Aims to respond in 6-8 weeks, but may take longer.

Literary Agents: Brandie Coonis (*L0296*); Rebecca Friedman (*L0510*); Abby Schulman (**L1238**)

L1129 Red Sofa Literary
Literary Agency
United States

dawn@redsofaliterary.com

https://redsofaliterary.com

Types: Fiction; Nonfiction
Subjects: Biography; Comedy / Humour; Contemporary; Culture; Current Affairs; Erotic; Fantasy; History; Literary Criticism; Mystery; Politics; Romance; Science; Science Fiction; Society; Spirituality; Sport; Westerns; Women's Interests
Markets: Adult; Children's; Young Adult

Send: Query
Don't send: Full text

Send query by email in first instance. See website for individual agent contact details and interests.

Literary Agents: Dawn Frederick (*L0502*); Erik Hane (*L0603*); Laura Zats (*L1486*)

L1130 Martin Redfern
Literary Agent
United Kingdom

Literary Agency: Northbank Talent Management (**L1042**)

L1131 Redhammer
Literary Agency
United Kingdom

http://redhammer.info

Types: Fiction; Nonfiction
Subjects: Autobiography; Crime; Entertainment; Mystery; Thrillers
Markets: Adult

Closed to approaches.

Generally too busy to consider approaches from writers, unless they already have some experience of the publishing industry. However does offer occasional pop-up submission opportunities. Check website for details.

Literary Agent: Peter Cox (*L0305*)

L1132 Adam Reed
Literary Agent
United States

Literary Agency: Joy Harris Literary Agency, Inc. (**L0742**)

L1133 Rees Literary Agency
Literary Agency
One Westinghouse Plaza, Suite A203, Boston, MA 02136-2075
United States
Tel: +1 (617) 227-9014

lorin@reesagency.com

http://www.reesagency.com

Professional Body: Association of Authors' Representatives, Inc. (AAR)

Types: Fiction; Nonfiction
Formats: Film Scripts
Subjects: Autobiography; Business; Comedy / Humour; Commercial; Contemporary; Culture; Fantasy; History; Horror; Literary; Mystery; Personal Development; Psychology; Romance; Science; Science Fiction; Suspense; Thrillers; Warfare; Westerns; Women's Interests
Markets: Adult; Children's; Young Adult

Send: Query
Don't send: Full text
How to send: Email

See website for specific agents' interests and submission requirements.

Authors: Tom Cooper; Siobhan Fallon; S.M. Hulse; Nicco Mele

Literary Agents: Ann Collette (*L0288*); Rebecca Podos (*L1104*); Lorin Rees (*L1135*)

L1134 Florence Rees
Agency Assistant; Associate Agent
United Kingdom

florence.rees@amheath.com

https://amheath.com/agents/florence-rees/
https://twitter.com/florencerees93

Literary Agency: A.M. Heath & Company Limited, Author's Agents (**L0004**)
Literary Agents: Bill Hamilton (**L0598**); Oli Munson (**L1009**)

Fiction > *Novels*
Fantasy; Science Fiction

Nonfiction > *Nonfiction Books*
Environment; Memoir; Sustainable Living

L1135 Lorin Rees
Literary Agent
United States

Literary Agency: Rees Literary Agency (**L1133**)

L1136 Regal Hoffmann & Associates LLC
Literary Agency
143 West 29th Street, Suite 901, New York, NY 10001
United States
Tel: +1 (212) 684-7900
Fax: +1 (212) 684-7906

submissions@rhaliterary.com

http://www.rhaliterary.com

Types: Fiction; Nonfiction
Formats: Short Fiction
Subjects: Autobiography; History; Literary; Science; Thrillers
Markets: Adult; Children's; Young Adult

Send: Query
Don't send: Full text
How to send: Email

Send one-page query by email or by post with SASE, outline, and author bio/qualifications. For fiction, include first ten pages or one story from a collection. No response unless interested.

Literary Agents: Claire Anderson-Wheeler (*L0045*); Markus Hoffmann (*L0656*); Elianna Kan (*L0753*); Joseph Regal (*L1137*); Grace A. Ross (*L1189*); Stephanie Steiker (*L1311*)

L1137 Joseph Regal
Literary Agent
United States

Literary Agency: Regal Hoffmann & Associates LLC (**L1136**)

L1138 Regina Ryan Publishing Enterprises
Literary Agency
251 Central Park West, #7D, New York, NY 10024
United States
Tel: +1 (212) 787-5589

queries@reginaryanbooks.com

http://www.reginaryanbooks.com

Professional Body: Association of Authors' Representatives, Inc. (AAR)

Types: Nonfiction
Formats: Reference
Subjects: Adventure; Architecture; Autobiography; Business; Cookery; Gardening; Health; History; Legal; Leisure; Lifestyle; Nature; Politics; Psychology; Science; Spirituality; Sport; Travel; Women's Interests
Markets: Adult

Send: Full text
How to send: Email

Costs: Author covers sundry admin costs.

Send submissions through email. See website for full guidelines.

Authors: Ben Austro; Randi Minetor; Doug Whynott

Literary Agent: Regina Ryan (*L1212*)

L1139 Janet Reid
Literary Agent
United States

Janet@JetReidLiterary.com

http://www.jetreidliterary.com
http://jetreidliterary.blogspot.com/
https://queryshark.blogspot.com/
http://aaronline.org/Sys/PublicProfile/2176820/417813
https://www.publishersmarketplace.com/members/JanetReid/

Literary Agency: JetReid Literary Agency (**L0725**)
Professional Bodies: Association of Authors' Representatives, Inc. (AAR); Mystery Writers of America (MWA); Society of Children's Book Writers and Illustrators (SCBWI)

ADULT
Fiction > *Novels*
Commercial; Crime; Domestic Suspense; Literary; Mystery; Thrillers

Nonfiction > *Nonfiction Books*
Biography; History; Memoir; Narrative Nonfiction; Science

CHILDREN'S > **Nonfiction**
Middle Grade: Biography; History
Picture Books: Biography; History

Send: Query; Writing sample; Author bio; Proposal
How to send: In the body of an email
How not to send: Email attachment

New York literary agent with a list consisting mainly of crime novels and thrillers, and narrative nonfiction in history and biography.

Authors: Robin Becker; Bill Cameron; Gary Corby; Phillip DePoy; Stephanie Evans; Kennedy Foster; Lee Goodman; Dana Haynes; Patrick Lee; Thomas Lippman; Jeff Marks;

Warren Richey; Terry Shames; Jeff Somers; Robert Stubblefield; Deb Vlock

L1140 Milly Reilly
Literary Agent
United Kingdom

Literary Agency: Jo Unwin Literary Agency (**L0728**)

L1141 William Reiss
Literary Agent
United States

Literary Agency: John Hawkins & Associates, Inc. (**L0730**)

L1142 Laura Rennert
Literary Agent
United States

Literary Agency: Andrea Brown Literary Agency, Inc. (**L0047**)

L1143 Nicole Resciniti
Literary Agent
United States

Literary Agency: The Seymour Agency (**L1254**)

L1144 Carol Reyes
Literary Agent
United Kingdom

Literary Agency: Cecily Ware Literary Agents (**L0244**)

L1145 Richard Curtis Associates, Inc.
Literary Agency
200 East 72nd Street, Suite 28J, New York, NY 10021
United States

info@curtisagency.com

http://www.curtisagency.com

Professional Body: Association of Authors' Representatives, Inc. (AAR)

Types: Fiction; Nonfiction
Subjects: Autobiography; Business; Fantasy; Finance; Health; History; Medicine; Mystery; Romance; Science; Science Fiction; Technology; Thrillers; Westerns
Markets: Adult; Children's; Young Adult

Send: Query
Don't send: Full text

Costs: Author covers sundry admin costs.

Send query with sample chapter via online submission form on website. No screenplays, stage scripts, playwrights, or screenwriters.

Literary Agent: Richard Curtis (*L0320*)

L1146 Richford Becklow Literary Agency

Literary Agency
United Kingdom
Tel: +44 (0) 1728 660879 / + 44 (0) 7510 023823

lisa.eveleigh@richfordbecklow.co.uk

https://www.richfordbecklow.com
https://www.facebook.com/
RichfordBecklowLiteraryAgency/
https://twitter.com/richfordbecklow

Fiction > *Novels*
Crime; Fantasy; Historical Fiction; Literary; Romance; Saga

Nonfiction > *Nonfiction Books*
Biography; Memoir

Closed to approaches.

Company founded in 2012 by an experienced agent, previously at the longest established literary agency in the world. Interested in fiction and nonfiction. See website for full submission guidelines.

Authors: Caroline Ashton; Amanda Austen; Hugo Barnacle; Stephen Buck; Anne Corlett; Iestyn Edwards; Sam Giles; Jane Gordon-Cumming; R P Marshall; Carol McGrath; Madalyn Morgan; Sophie Parkin; Robert Ross; Lakshmi Raj Sharma; Tony Slattery; Jonathan Socrates; Adrienne Vaughan; Grace Wynne-Jones

Literary Agent: Lisa Eveleigh (*L0446*)

L1147 Rick Richter

Literary Agent; Partner
United States

https://aevitascreative.com/agents/

Literary Agency: Aevitas (**L0019**)

ADULT
Fiction > *Novels*
Men's Fiction; Thrillers

Nonfiction > *Nonfiction Books*
Business; Celebrity; History; Memoir; Military History; Music; Popular Culture; Religion; Self Help; Sports Celebrity

CHILDREN'S > **Fiction** > *Novels*

Send: Author bio; Market info; Writing sample
How to send: Online submission system

Areas of interest include self-help, music and pop culture, military history and memoir, history, thriller, men's fiction, business, celebrity, sports celebrity and faith. He has deep experience and interest in children's books.

L1148 Rick Broadhead & Associates Literary Agency

Literary Agency
47 St. Clair Avenue West, Suite 501, Toronto, Ontario, M4V 3A5

Canada
Tel: +1 (416) 929-0516

submissions@rbaliterary.com

http://www.rbaliterary.com

Professional Body: The Authors Guild

Nonfiction > *Nonfiction Books*
Biography; Business; Comedy / Humour; Crime; Current Affairs; Environment; Health; History; Investigative Journalism; Medicine; National Security; Nature; Politics; Popular Culture; Science; Secret Intelligence; Self Help

Send: Query
How to send: Email

Welcomes queries by email. Send brief query outlining your project and your credentials. Responds only if interested. No screenplays, poetry, children's books, or fiction.

Literary Agent: Rick Broadhead

L1149 Patricia Riddle-Gaddis

Author; Literary Agent
United States

patricia@hartlineliterary.com

http://hartlineagency.com/agentsandauthors/

Literary Agent: Diana Flegal (**L0475**)
Literary Agency: Hartline Literary Agency (**L0618**)

ADULT
Fiction > *Novels*
Cozy Mysteries; Romance

Nonfiction > *Nonfiction Books*

YOUNG ADULT > **Fiction** > *Novels*

Interested in obtaining sweet romance, cozy mysteries, and young adult categories. (think Princess Diaries and a modern Nancy Drew.) She will also consider a range of nonfiction.

Authors: Amy Indech; Maria Jacobs; Marlys Johnson; Jody Lebel; Rabbi Elchanan Poupko; Karl A. Schultz; Norma F. Swanson; Ashley Thompson

L1150 Rachel Ridout

Literary Agent
United States

Literary Agency: Harvey Klinger, Inc (**L0619**)

L1151 The Rights Factory

Literary Agency
PO Box 499, Station C, Toronto, Ontario, M6J 3P6
Canada

http://therightsfactory.com

Types: Fiction; Nonfiction
Subjects: Adventure; Autobiography; Business; Commercial; Contemporary; Cookery; Crime; Culture; Fantasy; Health; History; Lifestyle; Literary; Mystery; Politics;

Romance; Science; Science Fiction; Spirituality; Sport; Thrillers; Travel; Women's Interests
Markets: Adult; Children's; Young Adult

Send first three chapters (fiction), proposal (nonfiction), or complete ms (picture books) via online submission form on website.

Associate Agent / Author: Cecilia Lyra (**L0895**)

Associate Agents: Olga Filina; Lindsay Leggett (**L0844**); Haskell Nussbaum (*L1046*)

Chief Executive Officer / Literary Agent / President: Sam Hiyate (**L0651**)

Literary Agents: Natalie Kimber (**L0786**); Stacey Kondla (*L0802*); Ali McDonald; Cassandra Rodgers

L1152 Rebecca Ritchie

Literary Agent
United Kingdom

https://amheath.com/agents/rebecca-ritchie/
https://twitter.com/Becky_Ritchie1

Literary Agency: A.M. Heath & Company Limited, Author's Agents (**L0004**)

Fiction > *Novels*
Book Club Fiction; Comedy / Humour; Commercial; Contemporary Women's Fiction; Crime; Historical Fiction; Police Procedural; Psychological Suspense; Romance; Saga; Thrillers

Nonfiction > *Nonfiction Books*
Cookery; Health; Travel; Wellbeing

L1153 Deborah Ritchken

Literary Agent
United States

Literary Agency: Marsal Lyon Literary Agency LLC (**L0925**)

L1154 Riverside Literary Agency

Literary Agency
41 Simon Keets Road, Leyden, MA 01337
United States
Tel: +1 (413) 772-0067
Fax: +1 (413) 772-0969

rivlit@sover.net

http://www.riversideliteraryagency.com

Types: Fiction; Nonfiction
Markets: Adult

Costs: Author covers sundry admin costs.

Agency based in Leyden, Massachusetts.

Literary Agent: Susan Lee Cohen (*L0286*)

L1155 Carina Rizvi

Literary Agent
United Kingdom

Literary Agency: The Soho Agency (**L1297**)

L1156 Alyssa Roat

Associate Agent
United States

Literary Agency: Cyle Young Literary Elite
(**L0323**)

L1157 The Robbins Office, Inc.

Literary Agency
405 Park Avenue, New York, NY 10022
United States
Tel: +1 (212) 223-0720
Fax: +1 (212) 223-2535

translation@robbinsoffice.com

http://robbinsoffice.com

Types: Fiction; Nonfiction
Subjects: Commercial; Literary
Markets: Adult

Closed to approaches.

Costs: Author covers sundry admin costs.

Literary agency based in New York. Does not
accept submissions of unsolicited material.

L1158 Robert A. Freedman Dramatic Agency, Inc.

Literary Agency
1501 Broadway, Suite 2310, New York, NY
10036
United States
Tel: +1 (212) 840-5760

info@robertfreedmanagency.com
mprfda@gmail.com
mp@bromasite.com

https://www.robertfreedmanagency.com
https://www.facebook.com/RAFagency/
https://twitter.com/RFreedmanAgency
https://www.linkedin.com/company/robert-a-
freedman-dramatic-agency-inc/

Professional Body: Writers Guild of America
(WGA)

Scripts
  Film Scripts; *TV Scripts*; *Theatre Scripts*

Dramatic literary agency based in New York
City representing playwrights and film and
television writers.

Literary Agent / President: Robert Freedman
(**L0503**)

Literary Agents: Samara Harris (*L0613*); Marta
Praeger (**L1113**)

L1159 Robert Caskie Ltd

Literary Agency
United Kingdom

submissions@robertcaskie.com

https://www.robertcaskie.com/
https://twitter.com/rcaskie1

Literary Agent: Robert Caskie (**L0239**)

L1160 Robert Dudley Agency

Literary Agency
135A Bridge Street, Ashford, Kent, TN25 5DP
United Kingdom

info@robertdudleyagency.co.uk

http://www.robertdudleyagency.co.uk

Types: Nonfiction
Subjects: Adventure; Biography; Business;
Current Affairs; History; Medicine; Personal
Development; Sport; Technology; Travel;
Warfare
Markets: Adult

Send: Full text
How to send: Email

Specialises in nonfiction. No fiction
submissions. Send submissions by email,
preferably in Word format, as opposed to PDF.

Literary Agent: Robert Dudley (*L0390*)

L1161 Robert Smith Literary Agency Ltd

Literary Agency
12 Bridge Wharf, 156 Caledonian Road,
London, N1 9UU
United Kingdom
Tel: +44 (0) 20 7278 2444
Fax: +44 (0) 20 7833 5680

robert@robertsmithliteraryagency.com

http://www.robertsmithliteraryagency.com

Professional Body: The Association of
Authors' Agents (AAA)

Types: Nonfiction
Subjects: Autobiography; Comedy / Humour;
Commercial; Crime; Culture; Current Affairs;
Health; History; Lifestyle; Personal
Development; Warfare
Markets: Adult

Send: Query
Don't send: Full text

Send query with synopsis initially and sample
chapter if available, by post or by email. No
poetry, fiction, scripts, children's books,
academic, or unsolicited MSS. See website for
full guidelines.

Authors: Arthur Aldridge; Sarbjit Kaur
Athwal; Richard Anthony Baker; Delia
Balmer; Juliet Barnes; Amanda Barrie; John
Baxter; William Beadle; Robert Beasley; Peta
Bee; Paul Begg; John Bennett; Kevin Booth;
Ralph Bulger; James Carnac; John Casson;
Gary Chapman; Shirley Charters; John Clarke;
Robert Clarke; Carol Clerk; Martyn Compton;
Michelle Compton; Judy Cook; Les
Cummings; Clive Driscoll; Rosie Dunn;
Georgie Edwards; Russell Edwards; Kate
Elysia; Stewart P. Evans; Penny Farmer;
Martin Fido; Sarah Flower; Freddie Foreman;
Helen Foster; Becci Fox; Astrid Franse;

Stephen Fulcher; Alison Goldie; Charlotte
Green; Christopher Green; Allan Grice;
Christine Hamilton; Andrew Hansford; James
Haspiel; Chris Hutchins; Rosalinda Hutton;
Albert Jack; Naomi Jacobs; Muriel Jakubait;
Nikola James; Sarah Jones; Christine Keeler;
Anita Kelsey; Siobhan Kennedy-McGuinness;
Heidi Kingstone; Brian Kirby; Tim Kirby;
John Knight; Ronnie Knight; Reg Kray;
Roberta Kray; Tony Lambrianou; Carol Ann
Lee; John Lee; Angela Levin; Chris
Lightbown; Seth Linder; David R. L.
Litchfield; Mary Long; Tony Long; Jean
MacColl; Gretel Mahoney; Maurice Mayne;
Lenny McLean; Ann Ming; Paddy Monaghan;
James Moore; Michelle Morgan; Caroline
Morris; Zana Morris; Rochelle Morton; Alan
Moss; Bobbie Neate; Paul Nero; Kim Noble;
Laurie O'Leary; Marnie Palmer; Theo
Paphitas; Gordon Rayner; Mike Reid; Frances
Reilly; Lyn Rigby; William D. Rubinstein;
Mark Ryan; Sarah Schenker; Nathan Shapow;
Alexander Sinclair; Keith Skinner; David
Slattery-Christy; Len Smith; Rita Smith; Allan
Starkie; Jayne Sterne; Cameron Stewart; Neil
R. Storey; Claudia Strachan; Bob Taylor;
Christopher Warwick; Monica Weller; Natalie
Welsh; Wynne Weston-Davies; Karl Williams;
Peter Wilton; Robert Winnett; Joanne Zorian-
Lynn

Literary Agents: Anne Smith (*L1290*); Robert
Smith (*L1293*)

L1162 Soumeya Bendimerad Roberts

Literary Agent; Vice President
United States

soumeya@hgliterary.com

https://www.hgliterary.com/soumeya
https://querymanager.com/query/SBR
https://www.publishersmarketplace.com/
members/SoumeyaRoberts/

Literary Agency: HG Literary (**L0646**)

ADULT
  Fiction > *Novels*
    Literary; Upmarket

  Nonfiction > *Nonfiction Books*
    Adventure; Business; Comedy / Humour;
    Cookery; Crafts; Current Affairs; Design;
    Gardening; Health; Memoir; Narrative
    Nonfiction; Parenting; Personal Essays;
    Politics; Popular Culture; Popular Science;
    Psychology; Travel

CHILDREN'S > **Fiction** > *Middle Grade*

YOUNG ADULT > **Fiction** > *Novels*

Send: Query; Synopsis; Writing sample
How to send: Query Manager

Seeking literary and upmarket novels and
collections, and also represents realistic young-
adult and middle-grade. She likes books with
vivid voices and compelling, well-developed
story-telling, and is particularly interested in

fiction that reflects on the post-colonial world and narratives by people of color. A lover of craft, she is drawn to observant writing that illuminates dynamic relationships between complex but sympathetic characters, intelligent experiments with form, and stories that enchant and transport the reader in inventive ways.

In non-fiction, she is primarily looking for idea-driven or voice-forward memoirs, personal essay collections, and approachable narrative non-fiction of all stripes: politics, current events; popular culture, especially anything that deals with subcultures (the more minute the better); unconventional business; popular science; adventure; psychology; and more. She also represents a select list of practical nonfiction in cooking, design, craft, gardening, travel and the outdoors, humor, health, and parenting.

L1163 Robertson Murray Literary Agency

Literary Agency
3rd Floor, 37 Great Portland Street, London, W1W 8QH
United Kingdom
Tel: +44 (0) 20 7580 0702

info@robertsonmurray.com

https://robertsonmurray.com

Types: Fiction; Nonfiction
Subjects: Autobiography; Comedy / Humour; Commercial; Cookery; Current Affairs; History; Lifestyle; Literary; Science; Society; Sport
Markets: Adult; Children's; Young Adult

Send: Query
Don't send: Full text

No science fiction, academic books, scripts, or poetry. Submit online through form on website. No postal submissions. Currently closed to submissions of children's books as at April 2019. See website current status and for full guidelines.

Literary Agents: Jenny Heller (*L0635*); Hilary Murray (*L1014*); Charlotte Robertson (*L1164*)

L1164 Charlotte Robertson
Literary Agent
United Kingdom

Literary Agency: Robertson Murray Literary Agency (**L1163**)

L1165 Annelise Robey
Literary Agent
United States

Literary Agency: Jane Rotrosen Agency (**L0709**)

L1166 Robin Jones Literary Agency

Literary Agency
66 High Street, Dorchester on Thames, OX10 7HN
United Kingdom
Tel: +44 (0) 1865 341486

robijones@gmail.com

https://twitter.com/AgentRobinJones

Fiction > *Novels*
   Commercial; Literary; Russia

Nonfiction > *Nonfiction Books*
   Commercial; Russia

Send: Query; Synopsis; Writing sample

Costs: Offers services that writers have to pay for.

Literary agency founded in 2007 by an agent who has previously worked at four other agencies, and was the UK scout for international publishers in 11 countries. Handles commercial and literary fiction and nonfiction for adults. Welcomes Russian language fiction and nonfiction. No children's, poetry, young adult, or original scripts. Send query with synopsis and 50-page sample. Also editorial services.

Literary Agent: Robin Jones (**L0740**)

L1167 Eva Robinson
Literary Agent
United Kingdom

Literary Agency: Sayle Screen Ltd (**L1226**)

L1168 Lloyd Robinson
Literary Agent
United States

Literary Agency: Suite A Management

L1169 Peter Robinson
Literary Agent
United Kingdom

Literary Agency: Rogers, Coleridge & White Ltd (**L1181**)

L1170 Quressa Robinson
Literary Agent
United States

Literary Agency: Nelson Literary Agency, LLC (**L1026**)

Closed to approaches.

L1171 Jenny Robson
Literary Agent
United Kingdom

Literary Agency: ILA (Intercontinental Literary Agency) (**L0681**)

L1172 Rochelle Stevens & Co.
Literary Agency
2 Terretts Place, Upper Street, London, N1 1QZ
United Kingdom
Tel: +44 (0) 20 7359 3900

info@rochellestevens.com

http://www.rochellestevens.com

Types: Scripts
Formats: Film Scripts; Radio Scripts; TV Scripts; Theatre Scripts
Markets: Adult

Send: Query
Don't send: Full text
How not to send: Email

Handles script writers for film, television, theatre, and radio. No longer handles writers of fiction, nonfiction, or children's books. Submit by post only. See website for full submission guidelines.

Literary Agents: Frances Arnold (*L0065*); Rochelle Stevens (*L1320*)

L1173 Rocking Chair Books
Literary Agency
2 Rudgwick Terrace, St Stephens Close, London, NW8 6BR
United Kingdom
Tel: +44 (0) 7809 461342

representme@rockingchairbooks.com

http://www.rockingchairbooks.com

Professional Body: The Association of Authors' Agents (AAA)

Types: Fiction; Nonfiction; Translations
Subjects: Adventure; Arts; Commercial; Contemporary; Crime; Culture; Current Affairs; Entertainment; Experimental; History; Horror; Lifestyle; Literary; Literature; Mystery; Nature; Romance; Satire; Thrillers; Traditional; Travel; Women's Interests
Markets: Adult

Send: Full text
How to send: Email

Founded in 2011 after the founder worked for five years as a Director at an established London literary agency. Send complete ms or a few chapters by email only. No Children's, YA or Science Fiction / Fantasy.

Authors: Mike Medaglia; John Rensten; Lakimbini Sitoy; Brian Turner

Literary Agent: Samar Hammam (*L0600*)

L1174 Rodeen Literary Management
Literary Agency
3501 N. Southport #497, Chicago, IL 60657
United States

submissions@rodeenliterary.com

http://www.rodeenliterary.com

Types: Fiction; Nonfiction
Markets: Children's; Young Adult

Send: Query
Don't send: Full text
How to send: Email

Independent literary agency providing career management for experienced and aspiring authors and illustrators of children's literature. Open to submissions from writers and illustrators of all genres of children's literature including picture books, early readers, middle-grade fiction and nonfiction, graphic novels and comic books as well as young adult fiction and nonfiction. See website for full submission guidelines.

Literary Agent: Paul Rodeen (*L1175*)

L1175 Paul Rodeen
Literary Agent
United States

Literary Agency: Rodeen Literary Management (**L1174**)

L1176 Nemonie Craven Roderick
Literary Agent
United Kingdom

Literary Agency: Jonathan Clowes Ltd (**L0734**)

L1177 Lisa Rodgers
Literary Agent
United States

Literary Agency: Jabberwocky Literary Agency (**L0697**)

L1178 Sue Rodgers
Literary Agent
United Kingdom

Literary Agency: Independent Talent Group Ltd (**L0683**)

L1179 Jennifer Rofe
Literary Agent
United States

jennifer@andreabrownlit.com

https://www.andreabrownlit.com/agents.html
http://queryme.online/jenrofe

Literary Agency: Andrea Brown Literary Agency, Inc. (**L0047**)

CHILDREN'S > Fiction
Middle Grade: General, and in particular: Commercial; Contemporary; Fantasy; Historical Fiction; Literary; Magic
Picture Books: General

Send: Query; Author bio; Writing sample
How to send: Query Manager

Seeks masterful writing, distinct voices and perspectives, and richly developed characters (if she is completely consumed by your characters, she will follow them anywhere). Middle grade has always been her soft spot and she's open to all genres in this category – literary, commercial, contemporary, magical, fantastical, historical, and everything in between. She especially appreciates stories that make her both laugh and cry, and that offer an unexpected view into the pre-teen/teen experience. In picture books, she likes funny, character-driven projects; beautifully imagined and written stories; and milestone moments with a twist. She longs to have an emotional response to the ending of a picture book – be it a guffaw, hurrah!, or a heart-tug. In illustration, she seeks unique voices and perspectives that have a voice so strong that it's immediately recognizable as belonging to the creator.

L1180 Roger Hancock Ltd
Literary Agency
4th Floor, 7-10 Chandos Street, Cavendish Square, London, W1G 9DQ
United Kingdom
Tel: +44 (0) 20 8341 7243

enquiries@rogerhancock.com

http://www.rogerhancock.com

Types: Scripts
Subjects: Comedy / Humour; Drama; Entertainment
Markets: Adult

Handles scripts only. Interested in comedy dramas and light entertainment. No books or unsolicited MSS.

L1181 Rogers, Coleridge & White Ltd
Literary Agency
20 Powis Mews, London, W11 1JN
United Kingdom
Tel: +44 (0) 20 7221 3717
Fax: +44 (0) 20 7229 9084

info@rcwlitagency.com

http://www.rcwlitagency.com

Professional Body: The Association of Authors' Agents (AAA)

Types: Fiction; Nonfiction
Markets: Adult; Children's; Young Adult

Send: Query
Don't send: Full text
How to send: Email

Send query providing info about yourself and the background of the book. For fiction include first three chapters or approximately 50 pages up to a natural break with a brief synopsis; for nonfiction include proposal up to about 20 pages. Return only with SAE. No plays, poetry, technical books, unsolicited MSS, or fax submissions. Check website for individual agent preferences and whether or not they accept submissions by email. Children's and young adult fiction should be submitted by email to the address provided on the website.

Literary Agents: Gill Coleridge (*L0287*); Sam Copeland (*L0299*); Stephen Edwards (*L0412*); Natasha Fairweather (*L0451*); Georgia Garrett (*L0529*); Jenny Hewson (*L0645*); Cara Jones (*L0737*); Rebecca Jones (*L0739*); Tristan Kendrick (*L0775*); Laurence Laluyaux (*L0818*); Matthew Marland (*L0922*); Zoe Nelson (*L1029*); Peter Robinson (*L1169*); Peter Straus (*L1328*); Matthew Turner (*L1380*); Zoe Waldie (*L1413*); Pat White (*L1443*); Claire Wilson (*L1457*)

L1182 Elaine Rogers
Literary Agent
United States

Literary Agency: Kneerim & Williams (**L0796**)

L1183 Ann Rose
Literary Agent
United States

Literary Agency: Prospect Agency (**L1116**)

L1184 Guy Rose
Literary Agent
United Kingdom

Literary Agency: FRA (Futerman, Rose, & Associates) (**L0490**)

L1185 The Rosenberg Group
Literary Agency
23 Lincoln Avenue, Marblehead, MA 01945
United States

rosenberglitsubmit@icloud.com

http://www.rosenberggroup.com

Professional Body: Association of Authors' Representatives, Inc. (AAR)

Types: Nonfiction
Formats: Film Scripts; Reference; Theatre Scripts
Subjects: Arts; Biography; Contemporary; Culture; Current Affairs; Finance; Health; History; How To; Media; Music; Personal Development; Philosophy; Politics; Psychology; Romance; Science; Society; Sport; Suspense; Women's Interests
Markets: Adult

Send: Query
Don't send: Full text
How to send: Email

Send query letter up to one page by email. Specialises in romance, women's, young adult, new adult, and college textbooks.

Literary Agent: Barbara Collins Rosenberg (*L1186*)

L1186 **Barbara Collins Rosenberg**
Literary Agent
United States

Literary Agency: The Rosenberg Group (**L1185**)

L1187 **Rosica Colin Ltd**
Literary Agency
1 Clareville Grove Mews, London, SW7 5AH
United Kingdom
Tel: +44 (0) 20 7370 1080

Types: Fiction; Nonfiction; Scripts
Formats: Film Scripts; Radio Scripts; TV Scripts; Theatre Scripts
Subjects: Autobiography; Beauty; Comedy / Humour; Cookery; Crime; Current Affairs; Erotic; Fantasy; Fashion; Gardening; Health; History; Horror; Leisure; Lifestyle; Literary; Men's Interests; Mystery; Nature; Psychology; Religion; Romance; Science; Sport; Suspense; Thrillers; Travel; Warfare; Women's Interests
Markets: Academic; Adult; Children's

Send: Query
Don't send: Full text

Send query with SAE, CV, synopsis, and list of other agents and publishers where MS has already been sent. Considers any full-length mss (except science fiction and poetry), but send synopsis only in initial query.

Literary Agents: Joanna Marston (*L0929*); Sylvie Marston (*L0930*)

L1188 **Andy Ross**
Literary Agent
United States

Literary Agency: Andy Ross Agency (**L0053**)

L1189 **Grace A. Ross**
Literary Agent
United States

Literary Agency: Regal Hoffmann & Associates LLC (**L1136**)

L1190 **Kathryn Ross**
Literary Agent
United Kingdom

Literary Agency: Fraser Ross Associates (**L0498**)

L1191 **Whitney Ross**
Literary Agent
United States

Literary Agency: Irene Goodman Literary Agency (IGLA) (**L0688**)

L1192 **Eliza Rothstein**
Literary Agent
United States

http://www.inkwellmanagement.com/staff/eliza-rothstein
https://twitter.com/elizaloren

Literary Agency: InkWell Management (**L0686**)

Fiction > *Novels*
Commercial; Literary

Nonfiction > *Nonfiction Books*
Business; Comedy / Humour; Food; Journalism; Medicine; Memoir; Narrative Nonfiction; Popular Culture; Psychology; Science; Technology

Send: Query; Writing sample
How to send: In the body of an email

Represents memoir, literary and commercial fiction, and a wide range of journalists and nonfiction authors who seek to generate deep conversations, inspire social and systemic change, or advance our understanding of our minds and bodies. In addition to finding publishers for their books, she helps writers expand their reach by placing essays and journalism in publications ranging from The New York Times and The Atlantic to National Geographic and Sports Illustrated. She is particularly interested in the intersection of narrative writing with topics of psychology, medicine, science, food, technology, business, humor and pop culture. She is also drawn to literary fiction that explores diverse communities or intergenerational stories, commercial fiction that crosses genre borders, and fiction from Latinx and Spanish-speaking writers.

L1193 **Steph Roundsmith**
Literary Agent; Editor
United Kingdom

Literary Agency / Editorial Service: Steph Roundsmith Agent and Editor (**L1313**)

L1194 **Laura Rourke**
Literary Agent
United Kingdom

Literary Agency: Independent Talent Group Ltd (**L0683**)

L1195 **Elizabeth Roy**
Literary Agent
United Kingdom

Literary Agency: Elizabeth Roy Literary Agency (**L0423**)

L1196 **Caitlen Rubino-Bradway**
Literary Agent
United States

Literary Agency: The LKG Agency (**L0869**)

L1197 **Cynthia Ruchti**
Literary Agent
United States

Literary Agency: Books & Such Literary Management (**L0156**)

L1198 **John Rudolph**
Literary Agent
United States

Literary Agency: Dystel, Goderich & Bourret LLC (**L0399**)

L1199 **The Rudy Agency**
Literary Agency
Estes Park, CO
United States
Tel: +1 (970) 577-8500

http://www.rudyagency.com

Fiction > *Novels*
Adventure; Crime; Historical Fiction; Mystery; Thrillers

Nonfiction > *Nonfiction Books*
Biography; Business; Career Development; Cookery; Culture; Current Affairs; Health; History; Lifestyle; Medicine; Memoir; Politics; Relationships; Science; Self Help; Society; Sport; Technology; Women's Issues

Send: Query
Don't send: Full text
How to send: Email
How not to send: Post

Concentrates on adult nonfiction in the areas listed above. Handles a very limited amount of fiction. See individual agent details for specific interests and contact details.

Literary Agents: Hilary Claggett; Maryann Karinch (**L0760**); Lauren Manoy (*L0913*); Geoffrey Stone (**L1325**)

L1200 **Meg Ruley**
Literary Agent
United States

Literary Agency: Jane Rotrosen Agency (**L0709**)

L1201 **Rupert Crew Ltd**
Literary Agency
Southgate, 7 Linden Avenue, Dorchester, Dorset, DT1 1EJ
United Kingdom
Tel: +44 (0) 1305 260335

info@rupertcrew.co.uk

http://www.rupertcrew.co.uk

Professional Body: The Association of Authors' Agents (AAA)

Types: Fiction; Nonfiction
Markets: Adult

Closed to approaches.

Closed to submissions as at August 2019. Check website for current status.

Send query with SAE, synopsis, and first two or three consecutive chapters. International representation, handling volume and subsidiary rights in fiction and nonfiction properties. No Short Stories, Science Fiction, Fantasy, Horror, Poetry or original scripts for Theatre, Television and Film. Email address for correspondence only. No response by post and no return of material with insufficient return postage.

Literary Agent: Caroline Montgomery (*L0995*)

L1202 Rupert Heath Literary Agency
Literary Agency
United Kingdom

emailagency@rupertheath.com

http://www.rupertheath.com
https://twitter.com/RupertHeathLit
https://www.facebook.com/RupertHeathLit/
https://www.pinterest.com/rupertheathlit/
https://www.youtube.com/user/RupertHeathLit
http://www.linkedin.com/company/rupert-heath-literary-agency

Professional Body: The Association of Authors' Agents (AAA)

Fiction > *Novels*
Commercial; Crime; Historical Fiction; Literary; Science Fiction; Thrillers

Nonfiction > *Nonfiction Books*
Arts; Autobiography; Biography; Comedy / Humour; Current Affairs; History; Nature; Politics; Popular Culture; Popular Science

Send: Query; Author bio; Outline
How to send: Email

Send query giving some information about yourself and the work you would like to submit by email. Response only if interested.

Authors: Michael Arnold; Mark Blake; Andy Bull; Paddy Docherty; Peter Doggett; Nina Lyon; Lorna Martin; Christopher Moore

Literary Agent: Rupert Heath (*L0630*)

L1203 The Ruppin Agency
Literary Agency
London,
United Kingdom

submissions@ruppinagency.com

https://www.ruppinagency.com/
https://twitter.com/ruppinagency

Fiction > *Novels*
Commercial; Crime; Historical Fiction; Literary; Mystery; Thrillers

Nonfiction > *Nonfiction Books*
Memoir; Narrative Nonfiction; Nature; Science; Social Issues

Send: Synopsis; Writing sample
How to send: Email

Literary agency set up by a former bookseller, offering writers a new perspective on finding the right publisher for their work. Keen to find

writers with something to say about society today and particularly looking for storylines that showcase voices and communities that have tended to be overlooked by the publishing world, although that should deter no-one from sending their writing. No poetry, children's, young adult, graphic novels, plays and film scripts, self-help or lifestyle (including cookery, gardening, or interiors), religious or other esoteric titles, illustrated, academic, business or professional titles.

Literary Agent: Jonathan Ruppin (*L1204*)

L1204 Jonathan Ruppin
Literary Agent
United Kingdom

Literary Agency: The Ruppin Agency (**L1203**)

L1205 Kathleen Rushall
Literary Agent
United States

Literary Agency: Andrea Brown Literary Agency, Inc. (**L0047**)

L1206 Uli Rushby-Smith
Literary Agent
United Kingdom

Literary Agency: Uli Rushby-Smith Literary Agency (**L1386**)

L1207 Alex Rusher
Literary Agent
United Kingdom

Literary Agency: Independent Talent Group Ltd (**L0683**)

L1208 Gillie Russell
Literary Agent
United Kingdom

Literary Agency: Aitken Alexander Associates (**L0025**)

L1209 Laetitia Rutherford
Literary Agent
United Kingdom

https://www.watsonlittle.com/agent/laetitia-rutherford/
http://www.twitter.com/laetitialit

Literary Agency: Watson, Little Ltd (**L1419**)

Fiction > *Novels*
Crime; Literary

Nonfiction > *Nonfiction Books*
Contemporary; Culture; Environment; Gender; Nature; Parenting; Sexuality

Send: Query; Synopsis; Writing sample
How to send: Email

I represent a broad and diverse list of authors, ranging across Fiction and contemporary Non Fiction, and including literary prizewinners

and commercial bestsellers. In Fiction, my special areas are Literary and Crime.

Authors: R.G. Adams; Lucy Ayrton; Petrina Banfield; Jenny Blackhurst; Andrew Brown; Clare Brown; Ursula Brunetti; Emile Chabal; Ajay Chowdhury; Cynthia Clark; Vivianne Crowley; Jeremy Daldry; Rebecca Elliott; Christine Evans; Robin Harvie; JM Hewitt; Samson Kambalu; Hiba Noor Khan; Rosie Lewis; Holan Liang; Chrissie Manby; Lindiwe Maqhubela; Alex Marwood; Thabi Moeketsi; Tamsin Omond; Matt Rendell; Amos Ruiz; Anika Scott; Zoe Somerville; Shane Spall; Akemi Tanaka; Geeta Vara; Vincent Vincent

L1210 Jim Rutman
Senior Agent
United States

https://www.sll.com/our-team
http://aaronline.org/Sys/PublicProfile/4090054/417813

Literary Agency: Sterling Lord Literistic, Inc. (**L1317**)
Professional Body: Association of Authors' Representatives, Inc. (AAR)

Fiction > *Novels*

Nonfiction > *Nonfiction Books*
Culture; History

Send: Query; Synopsis; Writing sample
How to send: Online submission system

Represents formally adventurous and stylistically diverse authors of fiction as well as a variety of journalists and critics whose nonfiction work examines an array of cultural and historical subjects.

L1211 Amanda Rutter
Literary Agent
United States

http://www.azantianlitagency.com/pages/team-ar.html

Literary Agency: Azantian Literary Agency (**L0075**)

ADULT > **Fiction** > *Novels*
Fantasy; Science Fiction

CHILDREN'S > **Fiction** > *Middle Grade*
Fantasy; Science Fiction

YOUNG ADULT > **Fiction** > *Novels*
Fantasy; Science Fiction

Send: Query; Synopsis; Writing sample
How to send: Query Manager

Looking for adult, YA and MG fantasy and science fiction. She is particularly keen to find hopeful science fiction, political fantasy and fresh takes on familiar tropes. Stories that definitely agree with her include: enemy to friend dynamics, women in STEM environments, antagonists with realistic motivations, and characters that overcome challenges in surprising ways. Stories that don't appeal include steampunk and zombie fiction! She would like to see witty dialogue, strong world building, and tales about characters from diverse backgrounds that don't concentrate on issues, but explore all facets of life.

L1212 Regina Ryan
Literary Agent
United States

Literary Agency: Regina Ryan Publishing Enterprises (**L1138**)
Professional Body: The Agents Round Table (ART)

L1213 Lesley Sabga
Literary Agent
United States

Literary Agency: The Seymour Agency (**L1254**)

L1214 Jean Sagendorph
Literary Agent
United States

Literary Agency: Mansion Street Literary Management (**L0914**)

L1215 Vicki Salter
Literary Agent
United Kingdom

Literary Agency: Barbara Levy Literary Agency (**L0085**)

L1216 Darryl Samaraweera
Literary Agent
United Kingdom

Literary Agency: Artellus Limited (**L0067**)

L1217 Rayhane Sanders
Literary Agent
United States

Literary Agency: Massie & McQuilkin (**L0934**)

L1218 Sandra Dijkstra Literary Agency
Literary Agency
PMB 515, 1155 Camino Del Mar, Del Mar, CA 92014
United States
Tel: +1 (858) 755-3115
Fax: +1 (858) 794-2822

queries@dijkstraagency.com

http://www.dijkstraagency.com

Types: Fiction; Nonfiction
Formats: Short Fiction
Subjects: Autobiography; Business; Comedy / Humour; Commercial; Contemporary; Cookery; Crime; Culture; Current Affairs; Design; Fantasy; Health; History; Lifestyle;

Literary; Music; Mystery; Nature; Personal Development; Philosophy; Politics; Religion; Romance; Science; Science Fiction; Society; Sport; Suspense; Thrillers; Travel; Women's Interests
Markets: Adult; Children's; Young Adult

Send: Query
Don't send: Full text
How to send: Email

Check author bios on website and submit query by email to one agent only. For fiction, include a one-page synopsis, brief bio, and first 10-15 pages. For nonfiction, include overview, chapter outline, brief bio, and first 10-15 pages. All material must be in the body of the email. No attachments. See website for full submission guidelines.

Literary Agents: Elise Capron (*L0218*); Sandra Dijkstra (*L0368*); Suzy Evans (*L0444*); Jennifer Kim (*L0785*); Thao Le (*L0840*); Jill Marr (*L0924*); Jessica Watterson (**L1421**)

L1219 Kelly Van Sant
Literary Agent
United States

Literary Agency: D4EO Literary Agency (**L0325**)

L1220 Sarah Such Literary Agency
Literary Agency
81 Arabella Drive, London, SW15 5LL
United Kingdom
Tel: +44 (0) 20 8876 4228

info@sarah-such.com

https://sarahsuchliteraryagency.tumblr.com

Types: Fiction; Nonfiction
Subjects: Autobiography; Comedy / Humour; Commercial; Culture; History; Literary
Markets: Adult; Children's; Young Adult

Send: Query
Don't send: Full text
How to send: Email

Handles literary and commercial nonfiction and fiction for adults, young adults and children. Particularly interested in debut novels, biography, memoir, history, popular culture and humour. Works mainly by recommendation, but does also accept unsolicited approaches, by email only. Send synopsis, author bio, and sample chapter as Word attachment. No unsolicited mss or queries by phone. Handles TV and film scripts for existing clients, but no radio or theatre scripts. No poetry, fantasy, self-help or short stories.

Literary Agent: Sarah Such (*L1333*)

L1221 Alice Saunders
Literary Agent
United Kingdom

Literary Agency: The Soho Agency (**L1297**)

L1222 Carolyn Savarese
Literary Agent
United States

Literary Agency: Kneerim & Williams (**L0796**)

L1223 Marilia Savvides
Literary Agent
United Kingdom

mariliasavvides@42mp.com

https://www.42mp.com/agents
https://twitter.com/MariliaSavvides

Literary Agency: 42 Management and Production (**L0002**)

Fiction > *Novels*
Book Club Fiction; Crime; Dark; High Concept Thrillers; Horror; Legal Thrillers; Psychological Suspense; Speculative

Nonfiction > *Nonfiction Books*
Crime; Investigative Journalism; Memoir; Narrative History; Popular Psychology; Popular Science

How to send: Email

On the hunt for high-concept thrillers, crime, psychological suspense, horror and speculative, genre-bending fiction, reading group fiction in the vein of Jodi Picoult or Liane Moriarty; pop science / psychology, narrative history, true crime and investigative journalism.

L1224 Sandra Sawicka
Literary Agent
United Kingdom

Literary Agency: Marjacq Scripts Ltd (**L0921**)

L1225 The Sayle Literary Agency
Literary Agency
1 Petersfield, Cambridge, CB1 1BB
United Kingdom
Tel: +44 (0) 1223 303035

info@sayleliteraryagency.com

http://www.sayleliteraryagency.com

Professional Body: The Association of Authors' Agents (AAA)

Types: Fiction; Nonfiction
Subjects: Biography; Crime; Current Affairs; History; Literary; Music; Science; Travel
Markets: Adult

Closed to approaches.

Note: Not accepting new manuscripts as at July 2018. See website for current status. Send query with CV, synopsis, and three sample chapters. No text books, technical, legal, medical, children's, plays, poetry, unsolicited MSS, or approaches by email. Do not include SAE as all material submitted is recycled. If no response after three months assume rejection.

Literary Agent: Rachel Calder (*L0208*)

L1226 Sayle Screen Ltd

Literary Agency
11 Jubilee Place, London, SW3 3TD
United Kingdom
Tel: +44 (0) 20 7823 3883

info@saylescreen.com

http://www.saylescreen.com

Types: Scripts
Formats: Film Scripts; Radio Scripts; TV Scripts; Theatre Scripts
Markets: Adult

Send: Full text
How to send: Email

Only considers material which has been recommended by a producer, development executive or course tutor. In this case send query by email with cover letter and details of your referee to the relevant agent. Query only one agent at a time.

Authors: Fateme Ahmadi; Josh Appignanesi; Fred Armesto; Andrea Arnold; Iain Banks; Clio Barnard; Maria Martínez Bayona; Jules Bishop; Fyzal Boulifa; Sue Bourne; Orhan Boztas; NG Bristow; Simon Brooke; David Joss Buckley; Victor Buhler; Chanya Button; Maurice Caldera; Owen Calvert-Lyons; Oliver Cheetham; Jethro Compton; William Corlett; Shelagh Delaney; Gaëlle Denis; Greg Dinner; Jeannine Dominy; Jim Doyle; Mali Evans; Marc Evans; Siân Evans; Daniel Fajemisin-Duncan; Paul Farrell; Toby Fell-Holden; Efthimis Filippou; Jeanie Finlay; Jon Finn; John Fitzpatrick; Margaret Forster; John Forte; Nicki Frei; Bruce Goodison; Scott Graham; Adam Gyngell; Kate Hardie; Damian Harris; Joanne Harris; Timothy Harris; Cat Hepburn; Stuart Hepburn; David Hilton; Sally El Hosaini; Allegra Huston; Mark Illis; Mark Jagasia; Annabel Jankel; Will Jewell; Jenna Jovi; Dominic Keavey; Aleem Khan; Clare Kilner; Chris King; Gideon Koppel; Steven Lally; Yorgos Lanthimos; Steve Lewis; Harry Lighton; Joan Littlewood; Billy Lumby; George Mann; Brian Martin; Rachel Mathews; James Mavor; Edward McGown; Geoff McQueen; Richie Mehta; Christopher Monger; Mongiwekhaya; Carol Morley; Paul Morrison; Rungano Nyoni; Alex Oates; Tony Owen; Dean O'Loughlin; Thordur Palsson; Vinay Patel; Diana Patrick; Tommaso Pitta; Tim Prager; Ian Rankin; Seth Resnik; Healah Riazi; James Rogan; Alex Rose; Jerry Rothwell; C.J. Sansom; Jonathan Schey; Ronald Searle; Jon Sen; Gitta Sereny; Owen Sheers; Eva Sigurdardottir; Marlon Smith; Peter Stanley-Ward; Josephine Starte; Martin Stellman; Eddie Sternberg; Sarah Swords; Jeremy Thomas; Sue Townsend; Paul Trewartha; Paul

Unwin; Kit de Waal; Mike Walden; Stephen Walker; Brian Ward; Anoushka Warden; Angela Workman

Literary Agents: Matthew Bates (*L0098*); Kelly Knatchbull (*L0795*); Eva Robinson (*L1167*); Jane Villiers (*L1404*)

L1227 Eva Scalzo

Literary Agent
United States

Literary Agency: Speilburg Literary Agency (**L1305**)

L1228 Rory Scarfe

Literary Agent; Company Director
United Kingdom

https://www.theblairpartnership.com/our_people/rory-scarfe/

Literary Agency: The Blair Partnership (**L0138**)

ADULT

   Fiction > *Novels:* Commercial

   Nonfiction > *Nonfiction Books:* Commercial

   Scripts
     Film Scripts; TV Scripts
CHILDREN'S > **Fiction** > *Novels*

L1229 Christopher Schelling

Literary Agent
United States

Literary Agency: Selectric Artists (**L1251**)

L1230 Rebecca Scherer

Literary Agent
United States

Literary Agency: Jane Rotrosen Agency (**L0709**)

L1231 Wendy Schmalz

Literary Agent
United States

Literary Agency: Wendy Schmalz Agency (**L1432**)

L1232 Jeff Schmidt

Literary Agent

jschmidt@nycreative.com

http://www.nycreative.com/contact.html

Literary Agency: NY Creative Management (**L1047**)

L1233 Leah Schmidt

Literary Agent
United Kingdom

Literary Agency: The Agency (London) Ltd (**L0021**)

L1234 Deborah Schneider

Literary Agent
United States

Literary Agency: Gelfman Schneider / ICM Partners (**L0534**)
Professional Body: Association of Authors' Representatives, Inc. (AAR)

L1235 Eddie Schneider

Literary Agent
United States

Literary Agency: Jabberwocky Literary Agency (**L0697**)

L1236 Kathy Schneider

Literary Agent
United States

Literary Agency: Jane Rotrosen Agency (**L0709**)

Fiction > *Novels*
   Literary; Upmarket

Nonfiction > *Nonfiction Books*
   Business; Current Affairs; Health; Narrative Nonfiction; Personal Development; Popular Culture; Women's Interests

L1237 Hannah Schofield

Junior Agent
United Kingdom

http://www.lbabooks.com/agent/hannah-schofield/

Literary Agency: LBA Books Ltd (**L0839**)

Fiction > *Novels*
   Historical Fiction; Women's Fiction

Closed to approaches.

Interested in smart women's fiction, sumptuous historical, and heartrending YA.

Authors: Emad Ahmed; Amanda Brooke; Charlotte Butterfield; Isabella Harcourt; Amy Lavelle

L1238 Abby Schulman

Literary Agent
United States

Abby@rfliterary.com

Literary Agency: Rebecca Friedman Literary Agency (**L1128**)

YOUNG ADULT > **Fiction** > *Novels:* Fantasy

Closed to approaches.

L1239 Susan Schulman

Literary Agent
United States

Literary Agency: Susan Schulman Literary Agency LLC (**L1336**)

L1240 Gilly Schuster
Literary Agent
United Kingdom

Literary Agency: Cecily Ware Literary Agents
(**L0244**)

L1241 Tina P. Schwartz
Literary Agent
United States

Literary Agency: The Purcell Agency, LLC
(**L1118**)

L1242 The Science Factory
Literary Agency
Scheideweg 34C, Hamburg, 20253
Germany
Tel: + 49 40 4327 4959; +44 (0) 20 7193 7296
(Skype)

info@sciencefactory.co.uk

https://www.sciencefactory.co.uk

Types: Fiction; Nonfiction
Subjects: Autobiography; Current Affairs;
History; Medicine; Music; Politics; Science;
Technology; Travel
Markets: Adult

Send: Query; Writing sample
Don't send: Full text
How to send: Email

Specialises in science, technology, medicine,
and natural history, but will also consider other
areas of nonfiction. Novelists handled only
occasionally, and if there is some special
relevance to the agency (e.g. a thriller about
scientists, or a novel of ideas). See website for
full submission guidelines.

Literary Agents: Jeff Shreve (**L1271**); Tisse
Takagi (*L1353*); Peter Tallack (*L1354*)

L1243 Kevin Conroy Scott
Literary Agent
United Kingdom

http://www.tiborjones.com/about/

Literary Agency: Tibor Jones & Associates
(**L1371**)

L1244 Scovil Galen Ghosh Literary Agency, Inc.
Literary Agency
276 Fifth Avenue, Suite 708, New York, NY
10001
United States
Tel: +1 (212) 679-8686
Fax: +1 (212) 679-6710

russellgalen@sgglit.com

http://www.sgglit.com

Professional Body: Association of Authors'
Representatives, Inc. (AAR)

Types: Fiction; Nonfiction
Subjects: Adventure; Arts; Autobiography;

Business; Commercial; Contemporary;
Cookery; Culture; Health; History; Literary;
Nature; Politics; Psychology; Religion;
Science; Society; Sport; Women's Interests
Markets: Adult; Children's; Young Adult

Send: Query
Don't send: Full text

Send query letter only in first instance. Prefers
contact by email, but no attachments. If
contacting by post include letter only, with
email address for response rather than an
SASE.

Literary Agents: Ann Behar (*L0109*); Russell
Galen (*L0520*); Anna Ghosh (*L0544*); Jack
Scovil (*L1245*)

L1245 Jack Scovil
Literary Agent
United States

Literary Agency: Scovil Galen Ghosh Literary
Agency, Inc. (**L1244**)

L1246 Wendy Scozzaro
Literary Agent
United Kingdom

Literary Agency: Felix de Wolfe (**L0461**)

L1247 Chloe Seager
Literary Agent
United Kingdom

Literary Agency: Madeleine Milburn Literary,
TV & Film Agency (**L0907**)

L1248 Sean McCarthy Literary Agency
Literary Agency
United States

submissions@mccarthylit.com

http://www.mccarthylit.com

Types: Fiction
Subjects: Adventure; Comedy / Humour;
Mystery
Markets: Children's; Young Adult

How to send: Email

Accepts submissions across all genres and age
ranges in children's books. Send query by
email with a description of your book, author
bio, and literary or relevant professional
credits, and first three chapters (or roughly 25
pages) for novels, or complete ms if your work
is a picture book. No picture books over 1,000
words. Response in 6-8 weeks.

Literary Agent: Sean McCarthy (*L0946*)

L1249 Emma Sector
Literary Agent
United States

Literary Agency: Prospect Agency (**L1116**)

L1250 Yishai Seidman
Literary Agent
United States

Literary Agency: Dunow, Carlson & Lerner
Agency (**L0395**)

L1251 Selectric Artists
Literary Agency
9 Union Square #123, Southbury, CT 06488
United States
Tel: +1 (347) 668-5426

query@selectricartists.com

https://www.selectricartists.com

ADULT
  Fiction
    Graphic Novels: General
    Novels: Commercial; Science Fiction;
    Thrillers
  Nonfiction
    Graphic Nonfiction: General
    Nonfiction Books: Memoir; Narrative
    Nonfiction
YOUNG ADULT > **Fiction** > *Novels*
  Fantasy; Science Fiction

Closed to approaches.

Send query by email with your manuscript
attached as a .doc, .pdf, or .pages file. Put the
word "query" in the subject line. No queries by
phone. Response only if interested.

Literary Agent: Christopher Schelling (*L1229*)

L1252 Serendipity Literary Agency LLC
Literary Agency
305 Gates Avenue, Brooklyn, NY 11216
United States

info@serendipitylit.com

http://www.serendipitylit.com

Professional Body: Association of Authors'
Representatives, Inc. (AAR)

Types: Fiction; Nonfiction
Subjects: Biography; Crime; History;
Lifestyle; Literary; Mystery; Psychology;
Religion; Romance; Science; Sport; Suspense;
Thrillers; Women's Interests
Markets: Adult; Children's

Send: Query
Don't send: Full text

Not accepting submissions of adult fiction as at
January 2018. Check website for current status.
For nonfiction and children's fiction, approach
using submission forms on website.

Literary Agent: Regina Brooks (*L0184*)

L1253 Seventh Avenue Literary Agency
Literary Agency
Canada

info@seventhavenuelit.com

http://www.seventhavenuelit.com

Types: Nonfiction
Markets: Adult

Describes itself as one of Canada's largest nonfiction and personal management agencies.

Literary Agent: Robert Mackwood (*L0902*)

L1254 The Seymour Agency
Literary Agency
475 Miner Street Road, Canton, NY 13617
United States

nicole@theseymouragency.com

https://www.theseymouragency.com

Professional Body: Association of Authors' Representatives, Inc. (AAR)

Types: Fiction; Nonfiction
Subjects: Adventure; Autobiography; Comedy / Humour; Contemporary; Cookery; Fantasy; History; Horror; Mystery; Personal Development; Religion; Romance; Science Fiction; Suspense; Thrillers; Warfare; Women's Interests
Markets: Adult; Children's; Young Adult

Send: Query
Don't send: Full text
How to send: Email

Brief email queries accepted (no attachments), including first five pages pasted into the bottom of your email. All agents prefer queries by email. See website for full submission guidelines and specific interests of each agent.

Literary Agents: Julie Gwinn (*L0594*); Elizabeth Poteet (*L1110*); Nicole Resciniti (*L1143*); Lesley Sabga (*L1213*); Tina Wainscott (*L1412*); Jennifer Wills (*L1456*)

L1255 Davina Shah
Literary Agent
United Kingdom

Literary Agency: Macnaughton Lord Representation (**L0905**)

L1256 The Sharland Organisation Ltd
Literary Agency
The Manor House, Manor Street, Raunds, Northamptonshire, NN9 6JW
United Kingdom
Tel: +44 (0) 1933 626600

tso@btconnect.com

http://www.sharlandorganisation.co.uk

Types: Scripts
Formats: Film Scripts; Radio Scripts; TV Scripts; Theatre Scripts
Markets: Adult

Send: Query
Don't send: Full text

Query by post with SAE in first instance. No technical, scientific, poetry, or unsolicited MSS. Specialises in national and international film and TV negotiations, as well as negotiations for multimedia, interactive TV, and video games. Markets books for films and handles stage, radio, film and TV rights for authors.

Literary Agents: Alice Sharland (*L1257*); Mike Sharland (*L1258*)

L1257 Alice Sharland
Literary Agent
United Kingdom

Literary Agency: The Sharland Organisation Ltd (**L1256**)

L1258 Mike Sharland
Literary Agent
United Kingdom

Literary Agency: The Sharland Organisation Ltd (**L1256**)

L1259 Lauren Sharp
Literary Agent
United States

https://aevitascreative.com/agents/

Literary Agency: Aevitas (**L0019**)

Nonfiction > *Nonfiction Books*
Current Affairs; History; Narrative Nonfiction; Politics; Science

Closed to approaches.

Represents nonfiction in the areas of politics, history, current affairs, narrative nonfiction, and science.

L1260 The Shaw Agency
Literary Agency
United Kingdom

https://www.theshawagency.co.uk

ADULT
Fiction > *Novels*
Commercial; Literary

Nonfiction > *Nonfiction Books*
Lifestyle; Narrative Nonfiction; Wellbeing

CHILDREN'S > **Fiction** > *Novels*

TEEN > **Fiction** > *Novels*

Send: Query; Pitch; Synopsis; Writing sample
Don't send: Full text
How to send: Online contact form

Handles literary and commercial fiction, crime fiction, powerful and quirky nonfiction, teen and children's books. Send query through online form with one-page synopsis, first 10 pages, and email address for response. See website for full guidelines.

Literary Agent: Kate Shaw (*L1261*)

L1261 Kate Shaw
Literary Agent
United Kingdom

Literary Agency: The Shaw Agency (**L1260**)

L1262 Samantha Shea
Literary Agent
United States

Literary Agency: Georges Borchardt, Inc. (**L0539**)

L1263 Sheil Land Associates Ltd
Literary Agency
52 Doughty Street, London, WC1N 2LS
United Kingdom
Tel: +44 (0) 20 7405 9351
Fax: +44 (0) 20 7831 2127

info@sheilland.co.uk

http://www.sheilland.co.uk

ADULT
Fiction > *Novels*
Book Club Fiction; Commercial Women's Fiction; Contemporary; Crime; Family Saga; Fantasy; Ghost Stories; Historical Fiction; Horror; Literary; Mystery; Romance; Science Fiction; Thrillers

Nonfiction
Gift Books: Comedy / Humour
Nonfiction Books: Biography; Cookery; Gardening; Lifestyle; Memoir; Mind, Body, Spirit; Personal Development; Politics; Popular Science; Psychology; Travel
Scripts
Film Scripts; TV Scripts; Theatre Scripts
CHILDREN'S
Fiction > *Novels*

Scripts
Animation Scripts; TV Scripts
YOUNG ADULT > **Fiction** > *Novels*

Send: Query
Don't send: Full text
How to send: Email

Send query with synopsis, CV, and first three chapters (or around 50 pages), by post addressed to "The Submissions Dept", or by email. If posting mss, do not send only copy as submissions are recycled and responses sent by email. If you require response by post, include SAE.

Authors: Peter Ackroyd; Melvyn Bragg; Susan Hill; David Lister; Catherine Robertson; Jonathan Steele

Literary Agents: Piers Blofeld (*L0144*); Ian Drury (*L0388*); Lucy Fawcett (*L0454*); Vivien Green (*L0576*); Sonia Land (*L0824*); Donna McCafferty (**L0943**)

L1264 **Elizabeth Sheinkman**
Literary Agent
United Kingdom

Literary Agency: Peters Fraser + Dunlop
(**L1091**)

L1265 **Caroline Sheldon**
Literary Agent
United Kingdom

Literary Agency: Caroline Sheldon Literary
Agency (**L0227**)

L1266 **Shelley Power Literary Agency Ltd**
Literary Agency
33 Dumbrells Court, North End, Ditchling,
East Sussex, BN6 8TG
United Kingdom
Tel: +44 (0) 1273 844467

sp@shelleypower.co.uk

Professional Body: The Association of
Authors' Agents (AAA)

Types: Fiction; Nonfiction
Markets: Adult

Send: Query
Don't send: Full text
How to send: Email

Send query by email or by post with return
postage. No attachments. No poetry, scripts,
science fiction, fantasy, young adult, or
children's books.

Literary Agent: Shelley Power (*L1112*)

L1267 **Hannah Sheppard**
Literary Agent
United Kingdom

Literary Agency: DHH Literary Agency Ltd
(**L0364**)

L1268 **Sheree Bykofsky Associates, Inc.**
Literary Agency
4326 Harbor Beach Boulevard, PO Box 706,
Brigantine, NJ 08203
United States

submitbee@aol.com
shereebee@aol.com

http://www.shereebee.com

Fiction > *Novels*
Commercial; Literary; Mystery

Nonfiction > *Nonfiction Books*
Biography; Business; Comedy / Humour;
Cookery; Current Affairs; Films; Games;
Health; Multicultural; Music; Parenting;
Personal Development; Psychology;
Spirituality; Women's Interests

Send: Query; Synopsis; Writing sample
Don't send: Full text

How to send: Email
How not to send: Fax; Post

Send query by email only. Include one page
query, and for fiction a one page synopsis, and
first page of manuscript, all in the body of the
email. No attachments. Always looking for a
bestseller in any category, but generally not
interested in horror, westerns, occult, picture
books, or fantasy.

Authors: Jeffrey Fox; Sue Hitzmann; Jason
Kelly

Literary Agent: Sheree Bykofsky (**L0204**)

L1269 **Warren Sherman**
Literary Agent
United Kingdom

Literary Agency: Cecily Ware Literary Agents
(**L0244**)

L1270 **Camilla Shestopal**
Literary Agent
United Kingdom

Literary Agency: Peters Fraser + Dunlop
(**L1091**)

L1271 **Jeff Shreve**
Literary Agent
United States

https://www.sciencefactory.co.uk/agents

Literary Agency: The Science Factory (**L1242**)

Nonfiction > *Nonfiction Books*
Astronomy; Biology; Business; Genetics;
Health; Neuroscience; Personal
Development; Physics; Technology

L1272 **Melissa Shultz**
Literary Agent
United States

Literary Agency: Jim Donovan Literary
(**L0727**)

L1273 **Todd Shuster**
Literary Agent; Chief Executive Officer
United States

Literary Agency: Aevitas (**L0019**)

Fiction > *Novels*
Commercial; Literary; Mystery; Thrillers

Nonfiction > *Nonfiction Books*
Business; Current Affairs; Health; History;
Memoir; Politics; Wellbeing

Closed to approaches.

Represents both fiction and nonfiction. His
nonfiction list primarily focuses on current
affairs, politics and civil rights, health and
wellness, memoir, business, and history. His
fiction list includes both literary and
commercial novels, including mysteries and
thrillers.

L1274 **Signature Literary Agency**
Literary Agency
4200 Wisconsin Ave, NW #106-233,
Washington, DC 20016
United States

gary@signaturelit.com

http://www.signaturelit.com

ADULT
Fiction
Graphic Novels: General
Novels: Commercial; Historical Fiction;
Literary; Mystery; Thrillers
Nonfiction > *Nonfiction Books*
Biography; Comedy / Humour; Current
Affairs; Entertainment; History; How To;
Memoir; Narrative Nonfiction; Popular
Culture; Science

YOUNG ADULT > **Fiction** > *Novels*

Send: Query
How to send: Email

Costs: Author covers sundry admin costs.

Agency with agents based in Washington DC
and North Carolina. Send all queries by email
only.

Literary Agents: Gary Heidt; Ellen Pepus;
Amy Tipton

L1275 **Jeff Silberman**
Affiliated Agent
United States

jsilberman@foliolitmanagement.com

https://www.publishersmarketplace.com/
members/silberjeff/

Literary Agency: Folio Literary Management,
LLC (**L0480**)
Professional Body: Association of Authors'
Representatives, Inc. (AAR)

Fiction > *Novels*
Book Club Fiction; Literary

Nonfiction > *Nonfiction Books*
Biography; Comedy / Humour; Cookery;
Current Affairs; Food; Health; History;
Lifestyle; Memoir; Politics; Popular Culture;
Science; Sport; Technology

Send: Query; Writing sample
How to send: In the body of an email

L1276 **John Silbersack**
Literary Agent
United States

Literary Agency: The Bent Agency (**L0119**)

L1277 **Julia Silk**
Literary Agent
United Kingdom

julia.silk@kingsfordcampbell.com

http://kingsfordcampbell.com/about-us/julia-silk/
https://twitter.com/juliasreading
https://www.instagram.com/juliasreading/
https://www.pinterest.co.uk/juliasreadingbo/my-favourite-books/

Literary Agency: Kingsford Campbell Literary Agency (**L0790**)

Fiction > *Novels*
Book Club Fiction; Upmarket Crime; Upmarket Thrillers

Nonfiction > *Nonfiction Books*
Memoir; Narrative Nonfiction

Send: Query; Writing sample
How to send: Email

L1278 Janet Silver
Literary Agent; Senior Partner
United States

https://aevitascreative.com/agents/

Literary Agency: Aevitas (**L0019**)

Fiction > *Novels*: Literary

Nonfiction > *Nonfiction Books*
Biography; Creative Nonfiction; History; Memoir; Narrative Nonfiction; Philosophy; Women's Studies

Send: Query; Writing sample
How to send: Online submission system

Represents literary fiction, memoir, and creative/narrative nonfiction with a compelling storyline. In both fiction and nonfiction, she seeks diverse, singular voices, and unique perspectives.

L1279 Lydia Silver
Literary Agent
United Kingdom

Literary Agency: The Darley Anderson Agency (**L0333**)

L1280 Dorie Simmonds
Literary Agent
United Kingdom

https://doriesimmonds.com/about-us/
https://twitter.com/Dorie_Simmonds

Literary Agency: Dorie Simmonds Agency (**L0382**)

Will consider material from any genre except reference books and children's picture books.

L1281 Tanera Simons
Literary Agent
United Kingdom

Literary Agency: The Darley Anderson Agency (**L0333**)

L1282 Cara Lee Simpson
Literary Agent
United Kingdom

cara@jonathanclowes.co.uk

Literary Agency: Jonathan Clowes Ltd (**L0734**)

Fiction > *Novels*
Literary; Upmarket

Nonfiction > *Nonfiction Books*
Feminism; Gender Politics; Memoir; Mental Health; Nature; Popular Science; Psychology; Sexuality

Send: Synopsis; Writing sample
How to send: Email

Authors: Jacqueline Bublitz; Angela Chadwick; Bethany Clift; Ben Halls; Okechukwu Nzelu

L1283 Sinclair-Stevenson
Literary Agency
3 South Terrace, London, SW7 2TB
United Kingdom
Tel: +44 (0) 20 7581 2550

Types: Fiction; Nonfiction
Subjects: Arts; Biography; Current Affairs; History; Travel
Markets: Adult

Send: Query
Don't send: Full text

Send query with synopsis and SAE. No children's books, scripts, academic, science fiction, or fantasy.

Author Estates: The Estate of Alec Guiness; The Estate of John Cowper Powys; The Estate of John Galsworthy

Authors: Jennifer Johnston; J.D.F. Jones; Ross King; Christopher Lee; Andrew Sinclair

Literary Agents: Christopher Sinclair-Stevenson (*L1284*); Deborah Sinclair-Stevenson (*L1285*)

L1284 Christopher Sinclair-Stevenson
Literary Agent
United Kingdom

Literary Agency: Sinclair-Stevenson (**L1283**)

L1285 Deborah Sinclair-Stevenson
Literary Agent
United Kingdom

Literary Agency: Sinclair-Stevenson (**L1283**)

L1286 Anjali Singh
Literary Agent
United States

https://www.pandeliterary.com/about-pandeliterary
https://twitter.com/agent_anjali

http://aaronline.org/Sys/PublicProfile/52119428/417813

Literary Agency: Ayesha Pande Literary (**L0073**)
Professional Body: Association of Authors' Representatives, Inc. (AAR)

ADULT
Fiction > *Novels*
Literary Thrillers; Literary; Memoir

Nonfiction > *Nonfiction Books*: Narrative Nonfiction

YOUNG ADULT > **Fiction**
Graphic Novels; *Novels*

Closed to approaches.

Looking for new voices, character-driven fiction or nonfiction works that reflect an engagement with the world around us, literary thrillers, memoirs, YA literature and graphic novels.

L1287 Jonathan Sissons
Literary Agent
United Kingdom

Literary Agency: Peters Fraser + Dunlop (**L1091**)

L1288 Skylark Literary
Literary Agency
19 Parkway, Weybridge, Surrey, KT13 9HD
United Kingdom
Tel: +44 (0) 20 8144 7440

submissions@skylark-literary.com

http://www.skylark-literary.com

Types: Fiction
Markets: Children's; Young Adult

Send: Full text
How to send: Email

Handles fiction for children, from chapter books for emerging readers up to young adult / crossover titles. No picture books. Send query by email with one-page synopsis and full ms. No postal submissions.

Literary Agents: Amber J. Caravéo (*L0219*); Joanna Moult (*L1001*)

L1289 Beverley Slopen
Literary Agent
Canada

Literary Agency: Beverley Slopen Literary Agency (**L0127**)

L1290 Anne Smith
Literary Agent
United Kingdom

Literary Agency: Robert Smith Literary Agency Ltd (**L1161**)

L1291 Emily Smith
Literary Agent
United Kingdom

Literary Agency: The Agency (London) Ltd
(**L0021**)

L1292 Helen Mackenzie Smith
Literary Agent
United Kingdom

Literary Agency: Bell Lomax Moreton Agency
(**L0110**)

L1293 Robert Smith
Literary Agent
United Kingdom

Literary Agency: Robert Smith Literary
Agency Ltd (**L1161**)

L1294 Sarah Smith
Literary Agent
United States

Literary Agency: David Black Literary Agency
(**L0336**)

L1295 Jake Smith-Bosanquet
Literary Agent
United Kingdom

Literary Agency: C+W (Conville & Walsh)
(**L0205**)

L1296 Lee Sobel
Literary Agent
United States

Literary Agency: Lee Sobel Literary Agency
(**L0842**)

L1297 The Soho Agency
Literary Agency
16–17 Wardour Mews, London, W1F 8AT
United Kingdom
Tel: +44 (0) 20 7471 7900

sohoagencysubmissions@gmail.com
sohoagencychildrenssubmissions@gmail.com

http://www.thesohoagency.co.uk
https://twitter.com/TheSohoAgencyUK
https://www.instagram.com/thesohoagencyuk/

Professional Bodies: The Association of
Authors' Agents (AAA); Personal Managers'
Association (PMA); Association of Illustrators
(AOI)

Fiction > *Novels*

Nonfiction > *Nonfiction Books*

Send: Query; Synopsis; Writing sample
How to send: Email attachment

Send query by email only. Include short
synopsis and the first three chapters or up to 30
pages. For children's books under 1,000 words,
submit complete ms. See website for separate
email address for children's submissions. No

plays, poetry, or textbooks. Film and TV
scripts handled for existing clients only.

Associate Agents: Niamh O'Grady (**L1049**);
Marina De Pass (**L1069**)

Chair / Literary Agent: Mark Lucas (*L0882*)

Company Director / Literary Agent: Rowan
Lawton (**L0835**)

Company Directors / Literary Agents: Julian
Alexander (*L0029*); Araminta Whitley (*L1444*)

Literary Agent / Managing Director: Philippa
Milnes-Smith (**L0989**)

Literary Agents: Ben Clark (*L0276*); Sophie
Laurimore (**L0832**); Jamie Mitchell (*L0991*);
Carina Rizvi (*L1155*); Alice Saunders (*L1221*)

L1298 Solow Literary Enterprises, Inc.
Literary Agency
United States

info@solowliterary.com

http://www.solowliterary.com
https://www.facebook.com/SolowLiterary
https://twitter.com/SolowLiterary

Nonfiction > *Nonfiction Books*
Business; Culture; Education; Health;
Memoir; Narrative Nonfiction; Nature;
Psychology; Science; Wellbeing

Send: Query
Don't send: Full text
How to send: Email

Handles nonfiction in the stated areas only.
Send single-page query by email, providing
information on what your book is about; why
you think it has to be written; and why you are
the best person to write it. Response only if
interested.

Foreign Rights Manager: Taryn Fagerness

Literary Agent: Bonnie Solow (*L1299*)

L1299 Bonnie Solow
Literary Agent
United States

Literary Agency: Solow Literary Enterprises,
Inc. (**L1298**)
Professional Bodies: Association of Authors'
Representatives, Inc. (AAR); The Authors
Guild

L1300 Jennifer March Soloway
Literary Agent
United States

Literary Agency: Andrea Brown Literary
Agency, Inc. (**L0047**)

L1301 Andrew Somberg
Literary Agent
United States

Literary Agency: Harvey Klinger, Inc (**L0619**)

L1302 Kelly Sonnack
Literary Agent
United States

Literary Agency: Andrea Brown Literary
Agency, Inc. (**L0047**)

L1303 Sophie Hicks Agency
Literary Agency
60 Gray's Inn Road, London, WC1X 8LU
United Kingdom
Tel: +44 (0) 20 3735 8870

info@sophiehicksagency.com

http://www.sophiehicksagency.com
https://twitter.com/SophieHicksAg
https://www.instagram.com/
sophiehicksagency/

Professional Body: The Association of
Authors' Agents (AAA)

ADULT
Fiction > *Novels*
Nonfiction > *Nonfiction Books*

CHILDREN'S > **Fiction** > *Novels*

Send: Query; Writing sample; Synopsis
How to send: Email

Welcomes submissions. Send query by email
with sample pages attached as Word or PDF
documents. See website for full guidelines and
specific submissions email addresses. No
poetry or scripts for theatre, film or television,
and not currently accepting illustrated books
for children.

Literary Agents: Sophie Hicks (**L0649**); Sarah
Williams

L1304 Mary South
Literary Agent
United States

Literary Agency: Lowenstein Associates, Inc.
(**L0878**)

L1305 Speilburg Literary Agency
Literary Agency
United States

speilburgliterary@gmail.com

https://speilburgliterary.com

Types: Fiction; Nonfiction
Subjects: Commercial; Culture; Fantasy;
History; Horror; Mystery; Romance; Science;
Suspense
Markets: Adult; Young Adult

Closed to approaches.

**Closed to submissions between July 4 and
September 3, 2018.** Send query by email with
first three chapters (fiction), or proposal,
including table of contents and sample chapter
(nonfiction). No picture books, poetry, or

screenplays. See website for full guidelines and individual agent interests.

Literary Agents: Eva Scalzo (*L1227*); Alice Speilburg (*L1306*)

L1306 Alice Speilburg
Literary Agent
United States

Literary Agency: Speilburg Literary Agency (**L1305**)

L1307 Jacques de Spoelberch
Literary Agent
United States

Literary Agency: J. de S. Associates, Inc. (**L0696**)

L1308 Yasmin Standen
Literary Agent
United Kingdom

Literary Agency: Kane Literary Agency (**L0754**)

L1309 Mark "Stan" Stanton
Literary Agent
United Kingdom

http://thenorthlitagency.com/our-friends-in-the-north/
https://twitter.com/litagent007

Literary Agency: The North Literary Agency (**L1040**)

Fiction > *Novels*
Book Club Fiction; Crime; High Concept; Historical Fiction; Politics; Romantic Comedy; Satire; Thrillers

Nonfiction > *Nonfiction Books*
Biography; Politics; Popular Culture; Popular Science; Sport

Send: Query; Synopsis; Writing sample; Proposal
How to send: Email

Actively searching for new novelists and nonfiction projects, particularly in the areas of sport, culture and politics.

L1310 Hayley Steed
Literary Agent
United Kingdom

Literary Agency: Madeleine Milburn Literary, TV & Film Agency (**L0907**)

L1311 Stephanie Steiker
Literary Agent
United States

Literary Agency: Regal Hoffmann & Associates LLC (**L1136**)

L1312 Micheline Steinberg
Literary Agent
United Kingdom

Literary Agency: Micheline Steinberg Associates (**L0976**)

L1313 Steph Roundsmith Agent and Editor
Literary Agency; Editorial Service
United Kingdom

agent@stephroundsmith.co.uk

http://www.stephroundsmith.co.uk
https://twitter.com/StephRoundsmith

CHILDREN'S
    Fiction > *Novels*
    Nonfiction > *Nonfiction Books*

Closed to approaches.

Costs: Offers services that writers have to pay for.

Interested in any genre for children under 12. Also offers proofreading and editorial services.

Authors: Paul Adshead; Greg Dobbins; Jen Dodds; Sara Fellows; Julian Green; Diana Shaw

Editor / Literary Agent: Steph Roundsmith (*L1193*)

L1314 Myrsini Stephanides
Literary Agent
United States

myrsini@carolmannagency.com

https://www.carolmannagency.com/myrsini-stephanides
https://twitter.com/myrrr
https://www.instagram.com/myrsini_s/
https://www.goodreads.com/author/show/2512266.Myrsini_Stephanides

Literary Agency: Carol Mann Agency (**L0225**)

ADULT > **Nonfiction** > *Nonfiction Books*
General, and in particular: Activism; Business; Comedy / Humour; Inspirational; Memoir; Mind, Body, Spirit; Music; Narrative Nonfiction; Politics; Popular Culture; Popular Science; Science Journalism; Self Help; Social Justice

CHILDREN'S > **Nonfiction** > *Nonfiction Books*

Send: Query
How to send: Email
How not to send: Post

Handles adult and children's nonfiction (illustrated or narrative) in the following areas: pop culture and music; humor of all kinds, popular science and science journalism, narrative nonfiction, memoir, business, self-help and self-care; inspiration; mind, body, spirit; politics; social justice and activism.

Authors: Huda Al-Marashi; Claire Belton; Kelsey Crowe; John Doerr; Cyndy Etler; Laura Garnett; Matthew Inman; Jarrett Lerner; Emily McDowell; Martine Rothblatt; Hannah Shaw; Jen Waite

L1315 Stephanie Tade Literary Agency
Literary Agency
United States

submissions@stephanietadeagency.com

http://www.stephanietadeagency.com

Professional Body: Association of Authors' Representatives, Inc. (AAR)

Types: Nonfiction
Subjects: Autobiography; Culture; Health; Philosophy; Politics; Psychology; Spirituality
Markets: Adult

Send: Query
Don't send: Full text
How to send: Email

Send single-page query by email with information about your proposed book, your publishing history, and any media or online platform you have developed. Response only if interested.

Literary Agent: Stephanie Tade (*L1352*)

L1316 Jenny Stephens
Literary Agent
United States

https://www.sll.com/our-team

Literary Agency: Sterling Lord Literistic, Inc. (**L1317**)

Nonfiction > *Nonfiction Books*
Cookery; Cultural Criticism; Economics; Environment; Food; History; Lifestyle; Nature; Science; Social Justice

Send: Query; Synopsis; Writing sample
How to send: Online submission system

L1317 Sterling Lord Literistic, Inc.
Literary Agency
115 Broadway, New York, NY 10006
United States
Tel: +1 (212) 780-6050
Fax: +1 (212) 780-6095

info@sll.com

https://www.sll.com

Send: Query; Synopsis; Writing sample
How to send: Online submission system

Select one agent to query and approach via online form on website.

Associate Agent / Foreign Rights Manager: Danielle Bukowski (**L0197**)

Associate Agents: Mary Krienke (**L0808**); Nell Pierce (**L1098**)

Chair / Literary Agent: Peter Matson (**L0937**)

Executive Vice President / Literary Agent: Laurie Liss (**L0863**)

Foreign Rights Director: Szilvia Molnar

Literary Agent / President: Philippa Brophy (**L0186**)

Literary Agent / Vice President: Douglas Stewart (**L1322**)

Literary Agents: Elizabeth Bewley (**L0128**); Brian Egan; Celeste Fine; Jessica Friedman (**L0509**); Sarah Landis (**L0825**); Sterling Lord; John Maas; Alison MacKeen; Martha Millard; George Nicholson; Sarah Passick; Jenny Stephens (**L1316**)

Senior Agents: Robert Guinsler (**L0589**); Neeti Madan (**L0906**); Jim Rutman (**L1210**)

L1318 The Steve Laube Agency

Literary Agency
24 W. Camelback Rd. A-635, Phoenix, AZ 85013
United States

krichards@stevelaube.com

http://www.stevelaube.com

Types: Fiction; Nonfiction
Subjects: Religion
Markets: Adult; Young Adult

Send: Query
Don't send: Full text
How to send: Email

Handles quality Christian fiction and nonfiction in all genres, except poetry, personal biographies, personal stories, end-times literature (either fiction or nonfiction), and children's picture books. Accepts submissions by post or by email. See website for extensive information on making submissions.

Literary Agents: Dan Balow (*L0082*); Bob Hostetler (*L0667*); Steve Laube (*L0829*); Tamela Hancock Murray (*L1016*); Thomas Umstattd (*L1387*)

L1319 Paul Stevens

Literary Agent
United Kingdom

Literary Agency: Independent Talent Group Ltd (**L0683**)

L1320 Rochelle Stevens

Literary Agent
United Kingdom

Literary Agency: Rochelle Stevens & Co. (**L1172**)

L1321 Julie Stevenson

Literary Agent
United States

Literary Agency: Massie & McQuilkin (**L0934**)

L1322 Douglas Stewart

Literary Agent; Vice President
United States

https://www.sll.com/our-team

Literary Agency: Sterling Lord Literistic, Inc. (**L1317**)

ADULT > **Fiction** > *Novels*
  Commercial; Literary

CHILDREN'S > **Fiction** > *Novels*

YOUNG ADULT > **Fiction** > *Novels*

Send: Query; Synopsis; Writing sample
How to send: Online submission system

L1323 Jessica Stewart

Literary Agent
United Kingdom

Literary Agency: Independent Talent Group Ltd (**L0683**)

L1324 Sam Stoloff

President; Senior Agent
United States

https://goldinlit.com/agents/

Literary Agency: Frances Goldin Literary Agency, Inc. (**L0492**)

Fiction
  Graphic Novels: Literary
  Novels: Literary; Speculative
Nonfiction
  Graphic Nonfiction: General
  Nonfiction Books: Culture; Current Affairs; Environment; Food; History; Journalism; Legal; Memoir; Narrative Nonfiction; Philosophy; Politics; Science; Sociology; Sustainable Living; Technology

Send: Query; Writing sample
How to send: Submittable

Interested in books that advance the public conversation on crucial issues and groundbreaking work of all kinds, including literary fiction, memoir, history, accessible sociology and philosophy, cultural studies, serious journalism on contemporary and international affairs, and narrative and topical nonfiction with a progressive orientation. Among his particular interests are literary graphic fiction and nonfiction, works on environmental sustainability, books on legal affairs and the justice system, works that dissect the right wing and American imperialism, the history of race in America, the history of science and technology, and books on food culture and history. His taste in fiction ranges from the psychologically realistic to first-rate speculative literature.

L1325 Geoffrey Stone

Literary Agent
United States

gstone@rudyagency.com

http://rudyagency.com/

Literary Agency: The Rudy Agency (**L1199**)

Nonfiction > *Nonfiction Books*
  Christian Living; Cookery; History; Sport

Send: Proposal; Full text
How to send: Email

L1326 Strachan Literary Agency

Literary Agency
P.O. Box 2091, Annapolis, MD 21404
United States

Query@StrachanLit.com

http://www.strachanlit.com

Types: Fiction; Nonfiction
Subjects: Autobiography; Comedy / Humour; Commercial; Cookery; Crime; Gardening; Health; Lifestyle; Literary; Mystery; Personal Development; Religion; Suspense; Thrillers; Travel; Women's Interests
Markets: Adult; Children's; Young Adult

Send: Query
Don't send: Full text

Send query through online form on website, providing a brief description of your book as well as your biographical information and writing credits or professional experience. No samples or mss unless requested. No picture books, genre fiction, poetry, or screenplays.

Literary Agents: Laura Strachan (*L1327*); Marisa Zeppieri (*L1488*)

L1327 Laura Strachan

Literary Agent
United States

Literary Agency: Strachan Literary Agency (**L1326**)

L1328 Peter Straus

Literary Agent
United Kingdom

Literary Agency: Rogers, Coleridge & White Ltd (**L1181**)

L1329 The Stringer Literary Agency LLC

Literary Agency
PO Box 111255, Naples, FL 34108
United States

https://www.stringerlit.com
https://www.instagram.com/stringerlit/
https://www.pinterest.com/stringerlit/
https://www.facebook.com/StringerLit
https://twitter.com/MarleneStringer

Professional Bodies: Association of Authors' Representatives, Inc. (AAR); Mystery Writers of America (MWA); Society of Children's Book Writers and Illustrators (SCBWI); The Authors Guild; Women's Fiction Writers Association (WFWA)

ADULT > Fiction > *Novels*

CHILDREN'S > **Fiction**
  Middle Grade; Picture Books
YOUNG ADULT > **Fiction** > *Novels*

A full-service literary agency specializing in commercial fiction since 2008.

Literary Agents: Shari Maurer (**L0940**); Marlene Stringer (**L1330**)

L1330 Marlene Stringer
Literary Agent
United States

http://aaronline.org/Sys/PublicProfile/5108942/417813
https://querymanager.com/query/StringerLit

Literary Agency: The Stringer Literary Agency LLC (**L1329**)

ADULT
  Fiction > *Novels*
    Book Club Fiction; Commercial; Contemporary Crime; Contemporary Fantasy; Contemporary Women's Fiction; Crime; Fantasy; Historical Crime; Historical Fiction; Literary; Magical Realism; Mystery; Romance; Science Fiction; Suspense; Thrillers; Upmarket Women's Fiction; Women's Fiction

  Nonfiction > *Nonfiction Books*: Narrative Nonfiction

CHILDREN'S > **Fiction** > *Middle Grade*

YOUNG ADULT > **Fiction** > *Novels*
  Contemporary; Fantasy

Does not want:

> **Fiction** > *Novels*
>   Alien Fiction; Erotic Romance; Space

Send: Author bio; Query; Synopsis; Writing sample; Pitch; Market info
How to send: Query Manager

L1331 The Strothman Agency
Literary Agency
63 East 9th Street, 10X, New York, NY 10003
United States

strothmanagency@gmail.com
info@strothmanagency.com

https://www.strothmanagency.com/
https://twitter.com/StrothmanAgency
https://www.facebook.com/StrothmanAgency/

Send: Query
How to send: Email
How not to send: Post; Email attachment

Only accepts electronic submissions. Physical query letters will be recycled unopened. Do not send entire manuscripts or attachments unless requested. All unrequested attachments will be deleted unread. Does not accept or respond to queries via fax or telephone.

Literary Agents: Lauren MacLeod (**L0904**); Wendy Strothman (**L1332**)

L1332 Wendy Strothman
Literary Agent
United States

https://www.strothmanagency.com/about
http://aaronline.org/Sys/PublicProfile/2176866/417813

Literary Agency: The Strothman Agency (**L1331**)
Professional Body: Association of Authors' Representatives, Inc. (AAR)

Nonfiction > *Nonfiction Books*
  Current Affairs; History; Narrative Journalism; Narrative Nonfiction; Nature; Science

Send: Query
Don't send: Full text
How to send: Email
How not to send: Email attachment; Fax; Phone

Looking for books that matter, books that change the way we think about things we take for granted, that tell stories that readers can't forget, and advance scholarship and knowledge. History, narrative nonfiction, narrative journalism, science and nature, and current affairs.

L1333 Sarah Such
Literary Agent
United Kingdom

Literary Agency: Sarah Such Literary Agency (**L1220**)

L1334 Mandy Suhr
Literary Agent
United Kingdom

https://milesstottagency.co.uk/representatives/mandy-suhr/

Literary Agency: Miles Stott Children's Literary Agency (**L0983**)

CHILDREN'S > **Fiction** > *Picture Books*

"I offer an experienced guiding hand to authors and illustrators, new and established, keen to work within this exciting genre. As well as editorial development of a style or story, I'll also help navigate through the business of publishing and that all important contract, ensuring each of my clients gets the best possible deal."

Authors: Rachel Bright; Lu Fraser

L1335 Cathryn Summerhayes
Literary Agent
United Kingdom

Literary Agency: Curtis Brown (**L0318**)

L1336 Susan Schulman Literary Agency LLC
Literary Agency
454 West 44th Street, New York, NY 10036
United States
Tel: +1 (212) 713-1633

queries@schulmanagency.com

https://twitter.com/SusanSchulman

Professional Body: Association of Authors' Representatives, Inc. (AAR)

Types: Fiction; Nonfiction; Scripts
Formats: Film Scripts; Theatre Scripts
Subjects: Adventure; Anthropology; Archaeology; Arts; Autobiography; Business; Comedy / Humour; Commercial; Cookery; Crafts; Crime; Culture; Current Affairs; Entertainment; Finance; Health; History; Hobbies; How To; Legal; Lifestyle; Literary; Literature; Medicine; Music; Mystery; Nature; Personal Development; Photography; Politics; Psychology; Religion; Science; Society; Sport; Suspense; Technology; Thrillers; Travel; Women's Interests
Markets: Adult; Children's; Young Adult

Send: Query
Don't send: Full text
How to send: Email

Send query with synopsis and SASE by post; or with synopsis and first three chapters in the body of an email. No Christian, Erotica, Horror, Poetry, Puzzles, Games, Romance, Science-fiction, Fantasy, Western, Professional, Reference, or Screenplays.

Literary Agent: Susan Schulman (*L1239*)

L1337 Susanna Lea Associates (UK)
Literary Agency
South Wing, Somerset House, Strand, London, WC2R 1LA
United Kingdom
Tel: +44 (0) 20 7287 7757

london@susannalea.com

https://www.susannalea.com

Professional Body: The Association of Authors' Agents (AAA)

Fiction > *Novels*

Nonfiction > *Nonfiction Books*

Send: Query; Synopsis; Writing sample
How to send: Email

Literary agency with offices in Paris, London, and New York. Always on the lookout for exciting new talent. No poetry, plays, screen plays, science fiction, educational text books, short stories or illustrated works. No queries by fax or post. Accepts queries by email only. Include cover letter, synopsis, and first three chapters or proposal. Response not guaranteed.

Literary Agent: Kerry Glencorse (**L0552**)

L1338 The Susijn Agency

Literary Agency
820 Harrow Road, London, NW10 5JU
United Kingdom
Tel: +44 (0) 20 8968 7435

submissions@thesusijnagency.com

http://www.thesusijnagency.com

Types: Fiction; Nonfiction
Subjects: Literary
Markets: Adult

Send: Query
Don't send: Full text
How to send: Email

Send query with synopsis and three sample chapters only by post or by email. Include SASE if return of material required. Response in 8-10 weeks. Specialises in selling rights worldwide and also represents non-English language authors and publishers for US, UK, and translation rights worldwide. No self-help, science-fiction, fantasy, romance, children's, illustrated, business, screenplays, or theatre plays.

Authors: Saud Al-Sanousi; Robin Baker; Conny Braam; Pauline Butcher; Ottavio Cappellani; Ciaran Carson; Robert Craig; Gwynne Dyer; Olivia Fane; Radhika Jha; Sophia Khan; Uzma Aslam Khan; Rik Kuiper; Kolton Lee; Christine Leunens; Helen Lewis; Yan Lianke; Tessa De Loo; Karel Glastra Van Loon; Peter Loveday; Mazen Maarouf; Jeffrey Moore; Tonie Mudde; Mark Mulholland; Tor Norretranders; Annette Pas; John Richardson; Rose Rouse; Mario Sabino; Parinoush Saniee; Mineke Schipper; Philibert Schogt; Karl Shaw; Rowan Simons; Darren Simpson; Sunny Singh; Hwang Sok-yong; Bogdan Stanescu; Paul Sussman; Shimon Tzabar; Edith Velmans; Simone Van Der Vlugt; Alex Wheatle; David Whitehouse; Henk Van Woerden; Ramsay Wood; Adam Zameenzad

Literary Agent: Laura Susijn (*L1339*)

L1339 Laura Susijn

Literary Agent
United Kingdom

Literary Agency: The Susijn Agency (**L1338**)

L1340 Rachel Sussman

Literary Agent
United States

Literary Agency: Chalberg & Sussman (**L0245**)

L1341 Kari Sutherland

Literary Agent
United States

https://bradfordlit.com/about/kari-sutherland/
https://querymanager.com/query/
Kari_Sutherland_Query_Form
https://twitter.com/KariSutherland

Literary Agency: Bradford Literary Agency (**L0169**)

ADULT
  Fiction > *Novels*
    General, and in particular: Contemporary; Historical Fiction; Magical Realism; Upmarket Women's Fiction

  Nonfiction > *Nonfiction Books*
    Biography; Comedy / Humour; History; Parenting; Popular Science; Psychology

CHILDREN'S > **Fiction**
  Novels: Comedy / Humour; High / Epic Fantasy; Magical Realism
  Picture Books: General

YOUNG ADULT > **Fiction** > *Novels*

Closed to approaches.

Open to genres from picture books through adult. Most interested in finding stories full of heart; ones that carry readers to faraway places or deep into a character's mind; action-packed page-turners that surprise her; dark dramas with touches of humor; and, above all, a voice that leaps off the page. She is actively seeking diverse voices across all genres.

L1342 Alice Sutherland-Hawes

Literary Agent
United Kingdom

https://www.ashliterary.com/#about

Literary Agency: ASH Literary (**L0068**)

L1343 Joanna Swainson

Literary Agent
United Kingdom

submissions@hardmanswainson.com

http://www.hardmanswainson.com/agents/joanna-swainson/
https://twitter.com/JoannaSwainson

Literary Agency: Hardman & Swainson (**L0606**)

ADULT
  Fiction > *Novels*
    Comedy / Humour; Commercial; Contemporary; Crime; Folk Horror; Ghost Stories; Historical Fiction; Horror; Literary; Speculative; Thrillers

  Nonfiction > *Nonfiction Books*
    Folklore, Myths, and Legends; Memoir; Narrative Nonfiction; Nature; Popular History; Science

CHILDREN'S > **Fiction** > *Novels*

Send: Synopsis; Full text
How to send: Email
How not to send: Post

L1344 Emma Sweeney

Literary Agent
United States

Literary Agency: Emma Sweeney Agency, LLC (**L0430**)

L1345 Sallyanne Sweeney

Literary Agent
United Kingdom

Literary Agency: Mulcahy Associates (Part of MMB Creative) (**L1004**)

L1346 Emily Sweet

Literary Agent
United Kingdom

Literary Agency: Emily Sweet Associates (**L0429**)

L1347 Becky Sweren

Literary Agent
United States

https://aevitascreative.com/agents/#agent-7413

Literary Agency: Aevitas (**L0019**)

Nonfiction > *Nonfiction Books*
  Culture; History; Investigative Journalism; Memoir

Closed to approaches.

Authors: Jesse Ball; Mark Braude; Adin Dobkin; Beck Dorey-Stein; Renee Dudley; Penina Eilberg-Schwartz; Valerie Fridland; Nicholas Griffin; Lawrence Jackson; Mohamad Jebara; Faith Jones; Jillian Keenan; Jake Keiser; Sulaiman Khatib; Ali Kriegsman; Daniel Levin; Eric M. O'Neill; Matteson Perry; Pen Rhodeen; Mohammed Al Samawi; Laurie Segall; Shabtai Shavit; Gabourey Sidibe; Judith E. Stein; Noa Tishby; Steven Ujifusa; Jack Viertel; Lijia Zhang

L1348 Swetky Literary Agency

Literary Agency
929 W. Sunset Blvd #21-285, St. George, UT 84770
United States
Tel: +1 (719) 859-2211
Fax: +1 (435) 579-5000

swetkyagency@amsaw.org

http://www.swetkyagency.com

Types: Fiction; Nonfiction
Markets: Adult

Send: Query
Don't send: Full text

Submit query using submission form on website.

Literary Agent: Faye Swetky (*L1349*)

L1349 Faye Swetky
Literary Agent
United States

Literary Agency: Swetky Literary Agency
(**L1348**)

L1350 Jessica Sykes
Literary Agent
United Kingdom

Literary Agency: Independent Talent Group
Ltd (**L0683**)

L1351 Laurel Symonds
Literary Agent
United States

Literary Agency: The Bent Agency (**L0119**)

L1352 Stephanie Tade
Literary Agent
United States

Literary Agency: Stephanie Tade Literary
Agency (**L1315**)

L1353 Tisse Takagi
Literary Agent
Germany

Literary Agency: The Science Factory (**L1242**)

L1354 Peter Tallack
Literary Agent
Germany

Literary Agency: The Science Factory (**L1242**)

L1355 Amy Tannenbaum
Literary Agent
United States

atannenbaum@janerotrosen.com

https://www.janerotrosen.com/agents
https://www.janerotrosen.com/contact-amy-
tannenbaum

Literary Agency: Jane Rotrosen Agency
(**L0709**)

Fiction > *Novels*
   Commercial; Contemporary Romance;
   Literary; Psychological Suspense; Thrillers;
   Women's Fiction

Send: Query
How to send: In the body of an email
How not to send: Email attachment

Represents clients who write across a variety
of genres including women's fiction,
contemporary romance, thriller and
psychological suspense. She is particularly
interested in those categories, as well as fiction
that falls into the sweet spot between literary
and commercial, and works by diverse voices.

L1356 Simon Targett
Literary Agent
United Kingdom

https://aevitascreative.com/agents/#agent-7409

Literary Agency: Aevitas Creative
Management (ACM) UK (**L0020**)

Fiction > *Novels*: Historical Fiction

Nonfiction > *Nonfiction Books*
   Biography; Business; Current Affairs;
   Genealogy; History; Journalism; Leadership;
   Music; Nature; Popular Science; Sport;
   Travel

Send: Market info; Writing sample
How to send: Online submission system

Interested in a wide range of nonfiction,
including business and leadership, history,
journalism, current affairs, biography, sport,
music, popular science, nature, travel,
genealogy. Will also consider historical fiction.
The common factor is an emphasis on big
ideas, great stories, and fine writing.

L1357 Alice Tasman
Literary Agent
United States

Literary Agency: The Jean V. Naggar Literary
Agency (**L0716**)

L1358 The Tennyson Agency
Literary Agency
109 Tennyson Avenue, New Malden, Surrey,
KT3 6NA
United Kingdom
Tel: +44 (0) 20 8543 5939

agency@tenagy.co.uk

http://www.tenagy.co.uk

Types: Scripts
Formats: Film Scripts; Radio Scripts; TV
Scripts; Theatre Scripts
Subjects: Drama
Markets: Adult

Send: Query
Don't send: Full text

Mainly deals in scripts for film, TV, theatre,
and radio, along with related material on an ad-
hoc basis. Handles writers in the European
Union only. Send query with CV and outline of
work. Prefers queries by email. No nonfiction,
poetry, short stories, science fiction and
fantasy or children's writing, or unsolicited
MSS.

L1359 Teresa Chris Literary
Agency Ltd
Literary Agency
43 Musard Road, London, W6 8NR
United Kingdom
Tel: +44 (0) 20 7386 0633

teresachris@litagency.co.uk

http://www.teresachrisliteraryagency.co.uk

Professional Body: The Association of
Authors' Agents (AAA)

Fiction > *Novels*
   Commercial Women's Fiction; Commercial;
   Crime; Literary

Does not want:

> **Fiction** > *Novels*
>   Fantasy; Horror; Science Fiction

Send: Query; Synopsis; Writing sample; Self-
Addressed Stamped Envelope (SASE)
How to send: Domestic Post; Email if overseas

Welcomes submissions. Overseas authors must
approach by email, otherwise submit by post.
Send query with SAE, first three chapters, and
one-page synopsis. Specialises in crime fiction
and commercial women's fiction. No poetry,
short stories, fantasy, science fiction, horror,
children's fiction or young adult.

Authors: Stephanie Austin; Lily Baxter; Ginny
Bell; M A Bennett; Victoria Blake; Stephen
Booth; Benita Brown; Rory Clements; Julie
Cohen; Dilly Court; Martin Davies; Ellie
Dean; Linda Finlay; Marina Fiorato; Emily
Freud; Kate Furnivall; Annie Groves; Clare
Harvey; Debby Holt; Hunter; Corrie Jackson;
Jim Kelly; Danuta Kot; Linscott; Tamara
McKinley; Jane McMorland; Charlotte
Parsons; Stuart Pawson; Caro Peacock/Gillian;
Nicola Pryce; Eileen Ramsay; Kate Rhodes;
Mary-Jane Riley; Caroline Scott; Marsali
Taylor; Jane Wenham-Jones

L1360 Kate Testerman
Literary Agent
United States

Literary Agency: KT Literary (**L0811**)

L1361 Henry Thayer
Literary Agent
United States

hthayer@bromasite.com

Literary Agency: Brandt & Hochman Literary
Agents, Inc. (**L0172**)
Professional Body: Association of Authors'
Representatives, Inc. (AAR)

Fiction > *Novels*
   General, and in particular: Literary

Nonfiction > *Nonfiction Books*
   General, and in particular: American History;
   Popular Music; Sport

Send: Query
How to send: Email

L1362 Becky Thomas
Literary Agent
United Kingdom

becky@johnsonandalcock.co.uk

http://www.johnsonandalcock.co.uk/becky-thomas
https://twitter.com/iambeckish

Literary Agency: Johnson & Alcock (**L0732**)

Fiction > *Novels*
Book Club Fiction; Literary

Nonfiction > *Nonfiction Books*
Feminism; Films; Food; Memoir; Music; Narrative Nonfiction; Nature; Popular Culture; Sport

Send: Query; Synopsis; Writing sample
How to send: Email attachment; Post

L1363 Jack Thomas
Literary Agent
United Kingdom

Literary Agency: Independent Talent Group Ltd (**L0683**)

L1364 Thompson Literary Agency
Literary Agency
115 West 29th St, Third Floor, New York, NY 10001
United States
Tel: +1 (347) 281-7685

submissions@thompsonliterary.com

https://thompsonliterary.com

Professional Body: Association of Authors' Representatives, Inc. (AAR)

Types: Fiction; Nonfiction
Subjects: Arts; Autobiography; Beauty; Commercial; Cookery; Culture; Fashion; Health; History; Literary; Music; Politics; Science; Spirituality; Sport
Markets: Adult; Children's; Young Adult

Send: Query
Don't send: Full text
How to send: Email

Accepts commercial and literary fiction, but specialises in nonfiction. See website for list of agent interests and address submission by email to specific agent.

Literary Agents: Kiele Raymond (*L1127*); Meg Thompson (*L1365*); John Thorn (*L1367*)

L1365 Meg Thompson
Literary Agent
United States

Literary Agency: Thompson Literary Agency (**L1364**)

L1366 Paul Thompson
Literary Agent
United Kingdom

Literary Agency: Bookseeker Agency (**L0157**)

L1367 John Thorn
Literary Agent
United States

Literary Agency: Thompson Literary Agency (**L1364**)

L1368 Lesley Thorne
Literary Agent
United Kingdom

Literary Agency: Aitken Alexander Associates (**L0025**)

L1369 Euan Thorneycroft
Literary Agent
United Kingdom

https://amheath.com/agents/euan-thorneycroft/
http://twitter.com/EuanThorneycrof

Literary Agency: A.M. Heath & Company Limited, Author's Agents (**L0004**)

Fiction > *Novels*
Crime; Historical Fiction; Literary; Thrillers

Nonfiction > *Nonfiction Books*
History; Memoir; Nature; Politics; Science; Technology

Agency Assistant: Jessica Lee

L1370 Jessie Thorsted
Literary Agent
United States

Literary Agency: InkWell Management (**L0686**)

L1371 Tibor Jones & Associates
Literary Agency
PO Box 74604, London, SW2 9NH
United Kingdom

enquiries@tiborjones.com

http://www.tiborjones.com
https://twitter.com/TiborJones

Fiction > *Novels*

Nonfiction > *Nonfiction Books*

Send: Query; Synopsis; Author bio; Writing sample
How to send: Email

Welcomes fiction and nonfiction proposals from writers who are looking to publish something different. Send query by email giving details about you and your writing background, with one-page synopsis and first five pages of the novel/proposal.

Literary Agency: The Bravo Blue Agency (**L0176**)

Literary Agents: Landa Acevedo-Scott (**L0011**); Charlotte Colwill (**L0290**); Kevin Conroy Scott (**L1243**)

L1372 Tanya Tillett
Literary Agent
United Kingdom

Literary Agency: The Agency (London) Ltd (**L0021**)

L1373 Toby Mundy Associates Ltd
Literary Agency
38 Berkeley Square, London, W1J 5AE
United Kingdom
Tel: +44 (0) 20 3713 0067

submissions@tma-agency.com

http://tma-agency.com
https://twitter.com/tma_agency
https://facebook.com/tobymundyassociates
https://flipboard.com/@tobymundy/publishing-futures-rkd4uodqy

Literary Agency: Aevitas (**L0019**)

Fiction > *Novels*

Nonfiction > *Nonfiction Books*

Send: Query; Synopsis; Writing sample
How to send: Email; By referral

Accepts submissions upon recommendation only. Send query by email with brief synopsis, first chapter, and a note about yourself, all pasted into the body of the email.

Chief Executive Officer / Literary Agent: Toby Mundy (**L1007**)

L1374 Antony Topping
Literary Agent
United Kingdom

http://greeneheaton.co.uk/agents/antony-topping/

Literary Agency: Greene & Heaton Ltd (**L0578**)

Fiction > *Novels*
Contemporary; Historical Literary; Historical Thrillers

Nonfiction > *Nonfiction Books*
Comedy / Humour; Food; Science

Authors: Amen Alonge; Meg Arroll; Louise Atkinson; Helena Attlee; Michael Booth; James Bridle; Jason Byrne; Tom Campbell; Emma Chapman; Charles Cockell; Pam Corbin; Andrew Davidson; Russell Davies; Anna Davis; Patrick Drake; Nikki Duffy; Suzannah Dunn; Jeremy Duns; Olaf Falafel; Hugh Fearnley-Whittingstall; Jane Fearnley-Whittingstall; Nick Fisher; Christopher Fitz-Simon; Christophe Galfard; Stuart Heritage; Julian Hitch; Andrew Holmes; Alex Hourston; D.B. John; Max Kinnings; David Kirk; Rikke Schmidt Kjærgaard; Joseph Knox; William Leith; Dan Lepard; Robert Lewis; Kieran Long; Dorian Lynskey; Jolyon Maugham; James McGee; Gill Meller; Thomasina Miers; Lottie Moggach; Cathy Newman; Mary-Ann

Ochota; Christopher Osborn; Iain Overton; John O'Connell; Pete Paphides; Tom Phillips; Shivi Ramoutar; Richard Reed; Sam Rice; C. J. Sansom; Marcus du Sautoy; Rebecca Seal; Laura Shepherd-Robinson; Mimi Spencer; Count Arthur Strong; Andrew Taylor; Ian Vince; John Vincent; Jennie Walker; Andrew Webb; Mark Wernham; Robyn Wilder; Will Wiles; Robyn Young; Andrew Ziminski.

L1375 Jennifer Chen Tran
Literary Agent
United States

http://bradfordlit.com/about/jennifer-chen-tran-agent/

Literary Agency: Bradford Literary Agency (**L0169**)

Closed to submissions from August 20, 2019 to October 15, 2019.

L1376 Felicity Trew
Literary Agent
United Kingdom

Literary Agency: Caroline Sheldon Literary Agency (**L0227**)

L1377 Simon Trewin
Literary Agent
United Kingdom

Literary Agency: William Morris Endeavor (WME) London (**L1448**)

L1378 Steve Troha
Literary Agent; Partner
United States

https://www.publishersmarketplace.com/members/stroha/
http://aaronline.org/Sys/PublicProfile/5633367/417813

Literary Agency: Folio Literary Management, LLC (**L0480**)
Professional Body: Association of Authors' Representatives, Inc. (AAR)

L1379 Elizabeth Trupin-Pulli
Literary Agent
United States

Literary Agency: JET Literary Associates, Inc. (**L0724**)

L1380 Matthew Turner
Literary Agent
United Kingdom

Literary Agency: Rogers, Coleridge & White Ltd (**L1181**)

L1381 Nick Turner
Literary Agent
United Kingdom

Literary Agency: Nick Turner Management Ltd (**L1034**)

L1382 Joy Tutela
Literary Agent
United States

Literary Agency: David Black Literary Agency (**L0336**)
Professional Body: Association of Authors' Representatives, Inc. (AAR)

L1383 Ann Leslie Tuttle
Literary Agent
United States

Literary Agency: Dystel, Goderich & Bourret LLC (**L0399**)

L1384 Jennifer Udden
Literary Agent
United States

Literary Agency: Barry Goldblatt Literary Agency, Inc. (**L0094**)

L1385 Cindy Uh
Literary Agent
United States

Literary Agency: CAA (Creative Artists Agency, LLC) (**L0206**)

L1386 Uli Rushby-Smith Literary Agency
Literary Agency
72 Plimsoll Road, London, N4 2EE
United Kingdom
Tel: +44 (0) 20 7354 2718

uli.rushby-smith@btconnect.com

Types: Fiction; Nonfiction
Subjects: Commercial; Literary
Markets: Adult

Send: Query
Don't send: Full text

Send query with SAE, outline, and two or three sample chapters. Film and TV rights handled in conjunction with a sub-agent. No disks, poetry, picture books, films, or plays.

Literary Agent: Uli Rushby-Smith (*L1206*)

L1387 Thomas Umstattd
Literary Agent
United States

Literary Agency: The Steve Laube Agency (**L1318**)

L1388 Union Literary
Literary Agency
30 Vandam Street, Suite 5A, New York, NY 10013
United States
Tel: +1 (212) 255-2112

queries@threeseaslit.com

https://www.unionliterary.com

Professional Body: Association of Authors' Representatives, Inc. (AAR)

Types: Fiction; Nonfiction
Subjects: Autobiography; Business; Cookery; History; Literary; Science; Society
Markets: Adult

Send: Query
Don't send: Full text
How to send: Email

Prefers queries by email. Include a proposal and sample chapter for nonfiction, or a synopsis and sample pages for fiction. See website for specific agent interests and contact details, and approach one agent only. Response only if interested.

Literary Agents: Christina Clifford (*L0282*); Taylor Curtin (*L0317*); Trena Keating (*L0771*)

L1389 United Agents
Literary Agency
12-26 Lexington Street, London, W1F 0LE
United Kingdom
Tel: +44 (0) 20 3214 0800
Fax: +44 (0) 20 3214 0801

info@unitedagents.co.uk

http://unitedagents.co.uk

Professional Body: The Association of Authors' Agents (AAA)

Types: Fiction; Nonfiction; Scripts
Formats: Film Scripts; Radio Scripts; TV Scripts; Theatre Scripts
Subjects: Biography
Markets: Adult; Children's; Young Adult

Send: Query
Don't send: Full text
How to send: Email

Do not approach the book department generally. Consult website and view details of each agent before selecting a specific agent to approach personally. Accepts submissions by email only. Submissions by post will not be returned or responded to.

Literary Agents: Sarah Ballard (**L0081**); Caroline Dawnay (**L0346**); Ariella Feiner (**L0455**); Jim Gill (**L0545**); Eli Keren (**L0779**)

L1390 United Talent Agency (UTA)
Literary Agency
888 Seventh Avenue, Seventh Floor, New York, NY 10106
United States
Tel: +1 (212) 659-2600

https://www.unitedtalent.com

Types: Fiction; Nonfiction
Subjects: Business; History; Literary; Science;

Science Fiction
Markets: Adult

Send: Query
Don't send: Full text

Multimedia agency representing recording artists, celebrities, and with a literary agency operating out of the New York and London offices. Accepts queries by referral only.

L1391 The Unter Agency
Literary Agency
23 West 73rd Street, Suite 100, New York, NY 10023
United States
Tel: +1 (212) 401-4068

Jennifer@theunteragency.com

http://www.theunteragency.com

Types: Fiction; Nonfiction
Subjects: Adventure; Autobiography; Cookery; Crime; Culture; Health; Nature; Politics; Travel
Markets: Adult; Children's; Young Adult

Send: Query
Don't send: Full text
How to send: Email

Interested in quality fiction and general nonfiction, particularly memoir, food/cooking, nature/environment, biography, pop culture, travel/adventure, true crime, politics and health/fitness. Also all types of children's literature (picture books, middle grade, and young adult). Send query letter by email or via online form on website. If no response within three months, assume rejection.

Literary Agent: Jennifer Unter (*L1392*)

L1392 Jennifer Unter
Literary Agent
United States

Literary Agency: The Unter Agency (**L1391**)

L1393 Jo Unwin
Literary Agent
United Kingdom

Literary Agency: Jo Unwin Literary Agency (**L0728**)

L1394 Upstart Crow Literary
Literary Agency
244 Fifth Avenue, 11th Floor, New York, NY 10001
United States

danielle.submission@gmail.com

http://www.upstartcrowliterary.com

Types: Fiction; Nonfiction
Subjects: Autobiography; Comedy / Humour; Commercial; Contemporary; Cookery; Current Affairs; Fantasy; History; Lifestyle; Mystery;

Science Fiction
Markets: Adult; Children's; Young Adult

Send: Query
Don't send: Full text
How to send: Email

Send query by email with 20 pages of your ms, in the body of an email. No attachments or hard copy submissions. See website for more details, and specific agent interests and contact details.

Literary Agents: Danielle Chiotti (*L0262*); Kayla Cichello (**L0272**); Susan Hawk (**L0623**)

L1395 Matthew Valentinas
Literary Agent
United States

Literary Agency: Kneerim & Williams (**L0796**)

L1396 Valerie Hoskins Associates
Literary Agency
20 Charlotte Street, London, W1T 2NA
United Kingdom
Tel: +44 (0) 20 7637 4490

info@vhassociates.co.uk

http://www.vhassociates.co.uk

Scripts
  Film Scripts; *Radio Scripts*; *TV Scripts*

Send: Query; Self-Addressed Stamped Envelope (SASE)
Don't send: Full text

Small agency extremely limited as to the number of new clients that can be taken on. Allow up to eight weeks for response to submissions.

Literary Agents: Valerie Hoskins; Rebecca Watson

L1397 Vanessa Holt Ltd
Literary Agency
59 Crescent Road, Leigh-on-Sea, Essex, SS9 2PF
United Kingdom
Tel: +44 (0) 1702 473787

v.holt791@btinternet.com

Professional Body: The Association of Authors' Agents (AAA)

Fiction > *Novels*

Nonfiction > *Nonfiction Books*

Send: Query
Don't send: Full text

General fiction and nonfiction. No unsolicited mss or overseas approaches.

Literary Agent: Vanessa Holt

L1398 Leslie Varney
Literary Agent; President
United States

Literary Agency: Prentis Literary (**L1114**)

L1399 Sarah Veecock
Literary Agent
United Kingdom

Literary Agency: The Narrow Road Company (**L1021**)

L1400 Veritas Literary Agency
Literary Agency
601 Van Ness Avenue, Opera Plaza Suite E, San Francisco, CA 94102
United States

submissions@veritasliterary.com

http://www.veritasliterary.com
https://www.twitter.com/verlit

Professional Body: Association of Authors' Representatives, Inc. (AAR)

ADULT
  Fiction > *Novels*
    Commercial; Fantasy; Historical Fiction; Speculative; Women's Fiction

  Nonfiction > *Nonfiction Books*
    Biography; Cultural History; History; Memoir; Narrative Nonfiction; Nature; Popular Culture; Popular Science; Women's Studies

CHILDREN'S > **Fiction** > *Middle Grade*

YOUNG ADULT > **Fiction** > *Novels*

Send: Query; Writing sample
How to send: In the body of an email
How not to send: Post

Send query or proposal by email only. Submit further information on request only. For fiction, include cover letter listing previously published work, one-page summary and first five pages. For nonfiction, include author bio, overview, chapter-by-chapter summary, sample chapters or text, and analysis of competing titles.

Literary Agents: Katherine Boyle (**L0168**); Michael Carr (**L0231**)

Literary Scout: Chiara Rosati

L1401 Charles Verrill
Literary Agent
United States

Literary Agency: Darhansoff & Verrill Literary Agents (**L0331**)

L1402 Vicky Bijur Literary Agency
Literary Agency
27 West 20th Street, Suite 1003, New York, NY 10011
United States

queries@vickybijuragency.com

http://www.vickybijuragency.com

Types: Fiction; Nonfiction
Subjects: Autobiography; Commercial;
Literary; Thrillers; Women's Interests
Markets: Adult

Send: Query
Don't send: Full text
How to send: Email

Send query by email or by post with SASE.
For fiction include synopsis and first ten pages
(pasted into the body of the email if submitting
electronically). For nonfiction include proposal
and first ten pages. No attachments or queries
by phone or fax. No picture books, poetry, self-
help, science fiction, fantasy, horror, or
romance.

Literary Agents: Vicky Bijur (*L0131*);
Alexandra Franklin (*L0497*)

L1403 Pam Victorio
Literary Agent
United States

Literary Agency: D4EO Literary Agency
(**L0325**)

L1404 Jane Villiers
Literary Agent
United Kingdom

Literary Agency: Sayle Screen Ltd (**L1226**)

L1405 Gilly Vincent
Literary Agent
United Kingdom

Literary Agency: Chapman & Vincent (**L0253**)

L1406 The Viney Agency
Literary Agency
21, Dartmouth Park Ave, London, NW5 IJL
United Kingdom

charlie@thevineyagency.com

http://thevineyagency.com

Professional Body: The Association of
Authors' Agents (AAA)

ADULT
  Fiction > *Novels*

  Nonfiction > *Nonfiction Books*
  Biography; History; Journalism

CHILDREN'S > **Fiction** > *Novels*

Send: Query
Don't send: Full text
How not to send: Email

Handles high quality nonfiction, and adult and
children's fiction. See website for examples of
the kinds of books represented. Send query by
first or second class post.

Literary Agent: Charlie Viney (*L1407*)

L1407 Charlie Viney
Literary Agent
United Kingdom

Literary Agency: The Viney Agency (**L1406**)

L1408 Sandy Violette
Literary Agent
United Kingdom

sandy@abnerstein.co.uk

Literary Agency: Abner Stein (**L0007**)

L1409 Wade & Co Literary Agency
Literary Agency
33 Cormorant Lodge, Thomas More Street,
London, E1W 1AU
United Kingdom
Tel: +44 (0) 20 7488 4171
Fax: +44 (0) 20 7488 4172

rw@rwla.com

http://www.rwla.com

Types: Fiction; Nonfiction
Markets: Adult; Young Adult

Send: Query
Don't send: Full text
How to send: Email

New full-length proposals for adult and young
adult fiction and nonfiction always welcome.
Send query with detailed 1- 6 page synopsis,
brief biography, and first 10,000 words via
email as Word documents (.doc) or PDF; or by
post with SAE if return required. We much
prefer to correspond by email. Actively
seeking new writers across the literary
spectrum. No poetry, children's, short stories,
scripts or plays.

Author Estate: The Estate of Louise Cooper

Authors: Darrell Alden; Steve Alton; Steuart
Campbell; Ed Davey; Jack Dixon; Kimberly
Greene; Nick Griffiths; Adam Guillain;
Matthew Harffy; Brenda James; Jackie Kabler;
Chris Kissling; Chris Luttichau; Andy
McDermott; Mike McInnes; Richard Newman;
Stephen Norman; Nigel Perrin; Lorna Read;
Anthony Riches; Jos Sharrer; Andrea Shavick;
Ewen Southby-Tailyour; Colin Sutton; Ayowa
Taylor; John Tiffin; Russell Whitfield; Stuart
Wyatt

Literary Agent: Robin Wade (*L1410*)

L1410 Robin Wade
Literary Agent
United Kingdom

Literary Agency: Wade & Co Literary Agency
(**L1409**)

L1411 Matt Wagner
Literary Agent
United States

Literary Agency: Fresh Books Literary Agency
(**L0506**)

L1412 Tina Wainscott
Literary Agent
United States

Literary Agency: The Seymour Agency
(**L1254**)

L1413 Zoe Waldie
Literary Agent
United Kingdom

Literary Agency: Rogers, Coleridge & White
Ltd (**L1181**)

L1414 Clare Wallace
Literary Agent
United Kingdom

Literary Agency: The Darley Anderson Agency
(**L0333**)

Assistant Agent: Chloe Davis (**L0343**)

L1415 Patrick Walsh
Literary Agent
United Kingdom

Literary Agency: PEW Literary (**L1094**)

L1416 Nick Walters
Literary Agent
United Kingdom

nick@davidluxtonassociates.co.uk

https://www.davidluxtonassociates.co.uk/the-
agency/

Literary Agency: David Luxton Associates
(**L0339**)

Nonfiction > *Nonfiction Books*
  Crime; Current Affairs; Lifestyle; Self Help;
  Sport

Send: Synopsis; Writing sample; Author bio
How to send: Email

Agent and Rights Manager. Principle interests
are in the fields of sport, true crime, current
affairs, lifestyle and self-help.

L1417 Mitchell Waters
Literary Agent
United States

mwaters@bromasite.com

https://brandthochman.com/agents
http://aaronline.org/Sys/PublicProfile/1681270/
417813

Literary Agency: Brandt & Hochman Literary
Agents, Inc. (**L0172**)
Professional Body: Association of Authors'
Representatives, Inc. (AAR)

ADULT
  Fiction > *Novels*

Comedy / Humour; Commercial; Historical Fiction; Literary; Mystery

Nonfiction > *Nonfiction Books*
Biography; History; Memoir

YOUNG
ADULT > **Fiction** > *Novels*: Realistic

How to send: Email

L1418 Waterside Productions, Inc

Literary Agency
2055 Oxford Avenue, Cardiff, CA 92007
United States
Tel: +1 (760) 632-9190
Fax: +1 (760) 632-9295

admin@waterside.com

http://www.waterside.com

Types: Fiction; Nonfiction
Subjects: Business; Cookery; Culture; Health; Hobbies; How To; Lifestyle; Personal Development; Psychology; Society; Spirituality; Sport; Technology; Women's Interests
Markets: Adult

Send: Query
Don't send: Full text

Read each agent bio on website and approach appropriate agent by email with query letter in the body of your email, and proposal or sample material as an attached Word document.

Literary Agents: Bill Gladstone (*L0550*); Margot Maley Hutchison (*L0678*); Carole Jelen (*L0719*); Jill Kramer (*L0806*); Johanna Maaghul (*L0896*); Kristen Moeller (*L0992*)

L1419 Watson, Little Ltd

Literary Agency
Suite 315, ScreenWorks, 22 Highbury Grove, London, N5 2ER
United Kingdom
Tel: +44 (0) 20 7388 7529

submissions@watsonlittle.com

http://www.watsonlittle.com

Professional Body: The Association of Authors' Agents (AAA)

Types: Fiction; Nonfiction
Formats: Film Scripts
Subjects: Business; Comedy / Humour; Commercial; Crime; History; Leisure; Literary; Music; Personal Development; Psychology; Science; Sport; Technology; Women's Interests
Markets: Adult; Children's; Young Adult

Send: Query
Don't send: Full text
How to send: Email

Send query by email only with synopsis and sample material, addressed to a specific agent. See website for full guidelines and details of specific agents. No scripts, poetry, or unsolicited MSS.

Literary Agents: Megan Carroll (*L0232*); Mandy Little (*L0867*); Laetitia Rutherford (**L1209**); James Wills (**L1455**); Donald Winchester (*L1460*)

L1420 Mackenzie Brady Watson

Literary Agent
United States

Literary Agency: Stuart Krichevsky Literary Agency, Inc.

Closed to approaches.

L1421 Jessica Watterson

Literary Agent
United States

https://www.dijkstraagency.com/agent-page. php?agent_id=Watterson
https://querymanager.com/query/ jessicawatterson

Literary Agency: Sandra Dijkstra Literary Agency (**L1218**)

ADULT > **Fiction** > *Novels*
Cozy Mysteries; Romance; Women's Fiction

CHILDREN'S
Fiction > *Picture Books*

Nonfiction > *Nonfiction Books*: Popular Culture

YOUNG ADULT > **Fiction** > *Novels*
Contemporary; Romance

Closed to approaches.

Most interested in all genres of romance. Also loves women's fiction and is open to select Cozy Mysteries. In Young Adult, will consider just about anything in the contemporary sphere, particularly with some romance. Will also consider author-illustrated books and nonfiction on Pop Culture by authors who have established platforms.

L1422 Rebecca Wearmouth

Literary Agent
United Kingdom

Literary Agency: Peters Fraser + Dunlop (**L1091**)

L1423 Hannah Weatherill

Literary Agent
United Kingdom

Literary Agency: Northbank Talent Management (**L1042**)

L1424 Elisabeth Weed

Literary Agent
United States

Literary Agency: The Book Group (*L0154*)

L1425 Frank Weimann

Literary Agent; Partner
United States
Tel: +1 (212) 400-1494

fweimann@foliolit.com

https://www.publishersmarketplace.com/ members/weimann/

Literary Agency: Folio Literary Management, LLC (**L0480**)

Nonfiction > *Nonfiction Books*
General, and in particular: African American; Biography; Business; CIA; Celebrity; Comedy / Humour; Finance; Health; History; Mafia; Memoir; Military; Narrative Nonfiction; Pets; Prescriptive Nonfiction; Religion; Science; Special Forces; Sport

Send: Query; Writing sample
How to send: In the body of an email

Authors: Kareem Abdul-Jabbar; Dan Abrams; Gregg Allman; George Anastasia; Mario Andretti; Michael Baden; Joe Bonanno; Terry Bradshaw; Charles Brandt; John Douglas; Tamer Elnoury; Rickson Gracie; John Gray; Homer Hickam; Harry Markopolos; Kevin Maurer; Maria Menounos; Mark Olshaker; Joe Pistone; Laura Prepon; Bill Russell

L1426 Cherry Weiner

Literary Agent
United States

Literary Agency: Cherry Weiner Literary Agency (**L0259**)

L1427 Alex Weiss

Literary Agent
United States

Literary Agency: The Jennifer DeChiara Literary Agency (**L0721**)

L1428 Chris Wellbelove

Literary Agent
United Kingdom

Literary Agency: Aitken Alexander Associates (**L0025**)

L1429 Wells Arms Literary

Literary Agency
United States

victoria@wellsarms.com

https://www.wellsarms.com

Professional Body: Association of Authors' Representatives, Inc. (AAR)

Types: Fiction
Markets: Children's; Young Adult

Closed to approaches.

Represents authors and illustrators of books for children of all ages, including picture books, middle grade, early readers, and young adult.

Closed to submissions as at February 2018. Check website for current status.

Literary Agent: Victoria Wells Arms (**L0063**)

L1430 Roseanne Wells
Literary Agent
United States

Literary Agency: The Jennifer DeChiara Literary Agency (**L0721**)

L1431 Jennifer Weltz
Literary Agent
United States

Literary Agency: The Jean V. Naggar Literary Agency (**L0716**)

L1432 Wendy Schmalz Agency
Literary Agency
402 Union St. #831, Hudson, NY 12534
United States
Tel: +1 (518) 672-7697

wendy@schmalzagency.com

http://www.schmalzagency.com

CHILDREN'S
  Fiction > *Middle Grade*
  Nonfiction > *Middle Grade*

YOUNG ADULT
  Fiction > *Novels*
  Nonfiction > *Nonfiction Books*

Send: Query; Synopsis
Don't send: Full text; Writing sample
How to send: Email

Handles books for middle grade and young adults. No science fiction, fantasy, or picture books. Send query by email. No unsolicited mss or sample chapters. If no response after two weeks, assume no interest.

Literary Agent: Wendy Schmalz (*L1231*)

L1433 Katherine Wessbecher
Literary Agent
United States

https://bradfordlit.com/about/katherine-wessbecher/
https://twitter.com/KatWessbecher

Literary Agency: Bradford Literary Agency (**L0169**)

ADULT
  Fiction > *Novels*
    Commercial; Literary; Upmarket

  Nonfiction
    Graphic Nonfiction: General
    Nonfiction Books: Narrative Nonfiction

CHILDREN'S
  Fiction
    Middle Grade: Epistolary; Fantasy; Historical Fiction
    Picture Books: General

  Nonfiction
    Graphic Nonfiction: General
    Nonfiction Books: Narrative Nonfiction

YOUNG ADULT
  Fiction > *Novels*
    Epistolary; Fantasy; Historical Fiction

  Nonfiction
    Graphic Nonfiction: General
    Nonfiction Books: Narrative Nonfiction

Does not want:

> **Fiction** > *Novels*
>   High / Epic Fantasy; Romance; Science Fiction; Thrillers
>
> **Nonfiction** > *Nonfiction Books*
>   Business; Memoir
>
> **Poetry** > *Any Poetic Form*
>
> **Scripts**
>   *Film Scripts; TV Scripts*

Send: Query; Synopsis; Proposal; Writing sample
How to send: Email

Looking for children's books (picture books through YA), upmarket adult fiction, and narrative nonfiction for all ages.

L1434 Katherine West
Literary Agent
United Kingdom

Literary Agency: ILA (Intercontinental Literary Agency) (**L0681**)

L1435 Kate Weston
Literary Agent
United Kingdom

Literary Agency: Janet Fillingham Associates (**L0711**)

L1436 Paige Wheeler
Literary Agent
United States

Literary Agency: Creative Media Agency (**L0308**)
Professional Body: The Agents Round Table (ART)

L1437 Maria Whelan
Literary Agent
United States

http://www.inkwellmanagement.com/staff/maria-whelan

Literary Agency: InkWell Management (**L0686**)

Fiction > *Novels*
  Comedy / Humour; Literary; Magical Realism; Upmarket Women's Fiction

Nonfiction > *Nonfiction Books*
  General, and in particular: Society

Send: Query; Writing sample
How to send: In the body of an email

Enjoys literary fiction, magical realism, upmarket women's fiction and humor, as well as non-fiction, revolving around peculiar topics especially overlooked facets of society.

L1438 Whimsy Literary Agency, LLC
Literary Agency
49 North 8th Street, 6G, Brooklyn, NY 11249
United States
Tel: +1 (212) 674-7162

whimsynyc@aol.com

http://whimsyliteraryagency.com

Types: Nonfiction
Subjects: Arts; Autobiography; Business; Comedy / Humour; Cookery; Current Affairs; Design; Finance; Health; History; How To; Lifestyle; Literature; New Age; Personal Development; Photography; Psychology; Technology; Women's Interests
Markets: Adult

Send: Query
Don't send: Full text

No unsolicited mss. Send query in first instance. Response only if interested.

Literary Agent: Jackie Meyer (*L0970*)

L1439 Whispering Buffalo Literary Agency Ltd
Literary Agency
97 Chesson Road, London, W14 9QS
United Kingdom
Tel: +44 (0) 20 7565 4737

info@whisperingbuffalo.com

http://www.whisperingbuffalo.com

Types: Fiction; Nonfiction
Formats: Film Scripts
Subjects: Adventure; Anthropology; Arts; Autobiography; Beauty; Comedy / Humour; Commercial; Design; Entertainment; Fashion; Health; Lifestyle; Literary; Music; Nature; Personal Development; Politics; Romance; Science Fiction; Thrillers
Markets: Adult; Children's; Young Adult

Send: Query
Don't send: Full text
How to send: Email

Handles commercial/literary fiction/nonfiction and children's/YA fiction with special interest in book to film adaptations. No TV, film, radio or theatre scripts, or poetry or academic. Accepts submissions by email only. For fiction, send query with CV, synopsis, and first three chapters. For nonfiction, send proposal and sample chapter. Response only if interested. Aims to respond within 6-8 weeks.

Literary Agent: Mariam Keen (*L0773*)

L1440 Eve White
Literary Agent
United Kingdom

Literary Agency: Eve White: Literary Agent (**L0445**)

L1441 Isabel White
Literary Agent
United Kingdom

Literary Agency: Isabel White Literary Agent (**L0695**)

L1442 Melissa White
Literary Agent
United States

melissa@foliolit.com

https://www.publishersmarketplace.com/members/sarverm/

Literary Agency: Folio Literary Management, LLC (**L0480**)

ADULT
Fiction > *Novels*

Nonfiction > *Nonfiction Books*
Business; Cookery; Health; Memoir; Narrative Nonfiction; Parenting; Wellbeing

CHILDREN'S > **Fiction**
Chapter Books: Contemporary
Middle Grade: Contemporary

YOUNG ADULT > **Fiction** > *Novels*
Contemporary; Fantasy; Historical Fiction; Magical Realism; Science Fiction; Thrillers

Does not want:

CHILDREN'S > **Fiction** > *Middle Grade*: Adventure

Closed to approaches.

L1443 Pat White
Literary Agent
United Kingdom

Literary Agency: Rogers, Coleridge & White Ltd (**L1181**)

L1444 Araminta Whitley
Literary Agent; Company Director
United Kingdom

Literary Agency: The Soho Agency (**L1297**)

L1445 Peregrine Whittlesey
Literary Agent
United States

Literary Agency: Peregrine Whittlesey Agency (**L1081**)

L1446 Alice Whitwham
Literary Agent
United States

Literary Agency: The Cheney Agency (**L0256**)

L1447 Dinah Wiener
Literary Agent
United Kingdom

Literary Agency: Dinah Wiener Ltd (**L0370**)

L1448 William Morris Endeavor (WME) London
Literary Agency
100 New Oxford Street, London, WC1A 1HB
United Kingdom
Tel: +44 (0) 20 7534 6800
Fax: +44 (0) 20 7534 6900

ldnsubmissions@wmeentertainment.com

http://www.wmeentertainment.com

Professional Body: The Association of Authors' Agents (AAA)

Types: Fiction; Nonfiction
Subjects: Autobiography; Commercial; Crime; Culture; History; Literary; Thrillers
Markets: Adult; Young Adult

London office of a worldwide theatrical and literary agency, with offices in New York, Beverly Hills, Nashville, Miami, and Shanghai, as well as associates in Sydney.

Literary Agent: Simon Trewin (*L1377*)

L1449 Anne Williams
Literary Agent
United Kingdom

Literary Agency: Kate Hordern Literary Agency (**L0763**)

L1450 Ike Williams
Literary Agent
United States

Literary Agency: Kneerim & Williams (**L0796**)

Closed to approaches.

L1451 Laura Williams
Literary Agent
United Kingdom

lwilliams@greeneheaton.co.uk

http://greeneheaton.co.uk/agents/laura-williams/
https://twitter.com/laurabirdland

Literary Agency: Greene & Heaton Ltd (**L0578**)

ADULT > **Fiction** > *Novels*
Commercial; Ghost Stories; Gothic; Horror; Literary; Psychological Thrillers

YOUNG ADULT
Fiction > *Novels*
Contemporary; High Concept

Nonfiction > *Nonfiction Books*: Narrative Nonfiction

Authors: Eve Ainsworth; Catherine Barter; Anna Day; Sue Divin; John Donoghue; Helen Dring; Maggy Van Eijk; Zoe Feeney; Gabrielle Fernie; Lindsay Galvin; Sarah Goodwin; Oliver Grant; Maria Hummer; Jem Lester; Claire McGlasson; Gemma Milne; Barney Norris; Nina De Pass; Richard Roper; Zuzana Ruzickova; Nancy Springer; John Sutherland; Alyssa Warren; Gill Wyness; Bella Younger

L1452 Sarah Williams
Literary Agent
United Kingdom

Literary Agency: Independent Talent Group Ltd (**L0683**)

L1453 Victoria Williams
Literary Agent
United Kingdom

Literary Agency: Alan Brodie Representation Ltd (**L0026**)

L1454 Jo Williamson
Literary Agent
United Kingdom

jo@antonyharwood.com

http://antonyharwood.com/jo-williamson/

Literary Agency: Antony Harwood Limited (**L0058**)

CHILDREN'S > **Fiction**
Middle Grade: Adventure
Picture Books: General

YOUNG ADULT > **Fiction** > *Novels*

L1455 James Wills
Literary Agent
United Kingdom

Literary Agency: Watson, Little Ltd (**L1419**)

L1456 Jennifer Wills
Literary Agent
United States

Literary Agency: The Seymour Agency (**L1254**)
Professional Body: Association of Authors' Representatives, Inc. (AAR)

L1457 Claire Wilson
Literary Agent
United Kingdom

Literary Agency: Rogers, Coleridge & White Ltd (**L1181**)

L1458 Desiree Wilson
Literary Agent
United States

http://www.thebentagency.com/desiree-wilson
https://twitter.com/swindlesoiree

Literary Agency: The Bent Agency (**L0119**)

ADULT
Fiction
Novels: Contemporary; Experimental; Fantasy; Horror; Magic; Science Fiction; Speculative; Urban Fantasy
Short Fiction: LGBTQIA

Nonfiction > *Nonfiction Books*: Memoir

CHILDREN'S > *Fiction*
Graphic Novels; *Middle Grade*
YOUNG ADULT > *Fiction*
Graphic Novels: General
Novels: Fantasy; Science Fiction

Closed to approaches.

I am currently looking for middle-grade, young adult, and adult horror novels; narrative memoirs, especially from BIPOC communities; lush, dark, speculative science fiction and fantasy for young adult and adult readers; YA fantasy, especially adaptations of non-Western folklore and mythos, or interpretations of Western folklore/mythos centering nontraditional protagonists; and short story collections of LGBTQ+ fiction. I am also accepting graphic novel pitches that fall within the above genres, as well as graphic narratives meant to teach complex skills and/or practical information.

L1459 Ed Wilson
Literary Agent
United Kingdom
Tel: +44 (0) 20 7251 0125

ed@johnsonandalcock.co.uk

http://www.johnsonandalcock.co.uk/ed-wilson
https://twitter.com/literarywhore

Literary Agency: Johnson & Alcock (**L0732**)

ADULT
Fiction > *Novels*
Commercial; Crime; Fantasy; High Concept; Literary; Science Fiction; Thrillers

Nonfiction > *Nonfiction Books*
Nature; Popular Culture; Sport

YOUNG ADULT > *Fiction* > *Novels*

Send: Query; Synopsis; Writing sample
How to send: Email attachment; Post

L1460 Donald Winchester
Literary Agent
United Kingdom

Literary Agency: Watson, Little Ltd (**L1419**)

L1461 Rebecca Winfield
Literary Agent
United Kingdom

https://www.davidluxtonassociates.co.uk/the-agency/

Literary Agency: David Luxton Associates (**L0339**)

Nonfiction
Nonfiction Books: History; Memoir; Nature; Travel
Reference: Popular Reference

Send: Synopsis; Writing sample; Author bio
How to send: Email
How not to send: Post

L1462 Gordon Wise
Literary Agent
United Kingdom

Literary Agency: Curtis Brown (**L0318**)

L1463 Caryn Wiseman
Literary Agent
United States

Literary Agency: Andrea Brown Literary Agency, Inc. (**L0047**)

L1464 Tom Witcomb
Literary Agent
United Kingdom

Literary Agency: Blake Friedmann Literary Agency Ltd (**L0139**)

L1465 Jenny Witherell
Literary Agent
United States

Literary Agency: InkWell Management (**L0686**)

L1466 Kimberly Witherspoon
Literary Agent
United States

Literary Agency: InkWell Management (**L0686**)

L1467 Michelle Witte
Literary Agent
United States

Literary Agency: Mansion Street Literary Management (**L0914**)

L1468 Wm Clark Associates
Literary Agency
United States
Tel: +1 (212) 675-2784

general@wmclark.com

http://www.wmclark.com

Types: Fiction; Nonfiction; Translations
Formats: Film Scripts; Theatre Scripts
Subjects: Architecture; Arts; Autobiography; Commercial; Contemporary; Culture; Current Affairs; Design; History; Literary; Music; Philosophy; Religion; Science; Society; Technology
Markets: Adult

Send: Query
Don't send: Full text

Query through online form on website only. No simultaneous submissions or screenplays.

Author Estates: The Estate of John Diamond; The Estate of Mark Hampton; The Estate of Steven Martin

Authors: Kim Adelman; Jake Adelstein; Ibrahim Amin; Mark Anderson; Jake Austen; Cornelia Bailey; Lois Banner; Hugh Barker; James Barrat; Brian Bates; Jennifer Boles; Tristan Carrasco; Paula Champa; C.J. Dellatore; Brian Doherty; Sarah Erdman; Ann Fensterstock; Barbara Fisher; Will Friedwald; Jessa Gamble; James Gardner; Heather Gautney; Gan Golan; Vivien Goldman; Tristan Gooley; Pat Graham; George Gurley; Deena Guzder; Peter Gwin; Dayle Haddon; Alexa Hampton; Duane Hampton; Lee Hanson; Charlie Hess; Peter Hessler; Feng-hsiung Hsu; Jack Huberman; Nicholas L. Johnson; Keith Kachtick; Stephane Kirkland; Chad Kushins; Bob van Laerhoven; Michelle Lee; Cory MacLauchlin; Eric Maddox; Joanie McDonell; James McGuane; Dan McMillan; Keith McNally; Alex Moazed; Susan Morgan; Stephen Murdoch; Reggie Nadelson; Riad Nasr; Juliet Nicolson; Erich Origen; Zak Pelaccio; Joel Pickett; Claire Prentice; Nick Prueher; Dzogchen Ponlop Rinpoche; Tara Rodgers; Joseph Rosenbloom; Chris Ruen; Charlie Scheips; Rick Shenkman; Lady Anne Somerset; Guy Spier; Erich Stonestreet; Bill Talen; David Taylor; Yuval Taylor; Cullen Thomas; Franklin Toker; Ellen Wald; Nicholas Fox Weber; Bryant Welch; Carolin Young; Erin Zammett

Literary Agent: William Clark (*L0277*)

L1469 Caroline de Wolfe
Literary Agent
United Kingdom

Literary Agency: Felix de Wolfe (**L0461**)

L1470 Jade Wong-Baxter
Literary Agent
United States

jade@mmqlit.com

http://www.mmqlit.com/contact/

Literary Agency: Massie & McQuilkin (**L0934**)

Fiction > *Novels*
Literary; Magical Realism; Upmarket

Nonfiction > *Nonfiction Books*
Cultural Criticism; History; Memoir; Narrative Nonfiction; Popular Culture

Send: Query; Writing sample
How to send: Email

L1471 Bryony Woods
Literary Agent
United Kingdom

http://dkwlitagency.co.uk/agents/
https://twitter.com/BryonyWoods

Literary Agency: Diamond Kahn and Woods
(DKW) Literary Agency Ltd (**L0365**)

L1472 Wordserve Literary

Literary Agency
United States

admin@wordserveliterary.com

http://www.wordserveliterary.com

Types: Fiction; Nonfiction
Subjects: Autobiography; Commercial;
Culture; Current Affairs; Fantasy; Finance;
Health; History; Legal; Literary; Personal
Development; Psychology; Religion;
Romance; Science Fiction; Suspense; Thrillers;
Warfare; Women's Interests
Markets: Adult; Children's; Young Adult

Send: Query
Don't send: Full text
How to send: Email

Represents books for the general and Christian
markets. Nonfiction 40,000 – 100,000 words;
fiction 60,000-120,000 words. No gift books,
poetry, short stories, screenplays, graphic
novels, children's picture books, science
fiction or fantasy for any age. Email
approaches only. See website for detailed
submission guidelines. Submissions that
disregard the submission guidelines may
themselves be disregarded.

Literary Agents: Keely Boeving (*L0147*);
Sarah Joy Freese (*L0505*); Nick Harrison
(*L0614*); Greg Johnson (*L0733*)

L1473 Writer's Side

Literary Agency; Editorial Service
8 Chanan Singh Park, Delhi Cantt, New Delhi,
110010
India

kanishka500@gmail.com
kanishka@writersside.com

http://www.writersside.com

Fiction > *Novels*
Commercial; Contemporary; Experimental;
Literary; Mystery; Satire; Thrillers

Nonfiction > *Nonfiction Books*
Biography; Business; History; Travel

Send: Synopsis; Author bio; Writing sample
How to send: Word file email attachment
How not to send: PDF file email attachment

Costs: Offers services that writers have to pay
for.

Describes itself as the number one literary
agency in South Asia. Represents authors from
India and abroad. Particularly interested in
debut writing from India, Pakistan, Sri Lanka
and Bangladesh. Also offers editorial services,
but this is held separate from the literary

agency and customers of the editorial service
will not be represented by the agency.

Literary Agent: Kanishka Gupta (**L0590**)

L1474 The Writers' Practice

Literary Agency
United Kingdom
Tel: +44 (0) 7940 533243

jemima@thewriterspractice.com

http://www.thewriterspractice.com

Types: Fiction; Nonfiction
Subjects: Commercial; Literary
Markets: Adult

Send: Query
Don't send: Full text
How to send: Email

Costs: Offers services that writers have to pay
for.

Send query by email with for fiction a
synopsis, brief bio, and first three chapters; and
for nonfiction a pitch, brief bio, chapter
outline, and at least one sample chapter. Also
offers consultancy services to writers.

L1475 Writers' Representatives, LLC

Literary Agency
116 W. 14th St., 11th Fl., New York, NY
10011-7305
United States
Tel: +1 (212) 620-0023
Fax: +1 (212) 620-0023

transom@writersreps.com

http://www.writersreps.com

Types: Fiction; Nonfiction; Poetry
Formats: Reference
Subjects: Autobiography; Business; Comedy /
Humour; Cookery; Current Affairs; Finance;
History; Legal; Literary; Literary Criticism;
Mystery; Personal Development; Philosophy;
Politics; Science; Thrillers
Markets: Adult

Send: Full text
How to send: Email

Costs: Author covers sundry admin costs.

Send email describing your project and
yourself, or send proposal, outline, CV, and
sample chapters, or complete unsolicited MS,
with SASE. See website for submission
requirements in FAQ section. Specialises in
serious and literary fiction and nonfiction. No
screenplays. No science fiction or children's or
young adult fiction unless it aspires to serious
literature.

L1476 Joanne Wyckoff

Literary Agent
United States

joanne@carolmannagency.com

https://www.carolmannagency.com/joanne-
wyckoff

Literary Agency: Carol Mann Agency (**L0225**)

Nonfiction > *Nonfiction Books*
General, and in particular: African American
Issues; Animals; Comedy / Humour; Culture;
Education; Food; Health; History; Memoir;
Narrative Journalism; Narrative Nonfiction;
Nature; Psychology; Religion; Science;
Spirituality; Sport; Wellbeing; Women's
Issues

Send: Query
How to send: Email

Represents a wide array of nonfiction. Has vast
experience working with academics and
experts in diverse fields, helping them develop
and write books for a broad market. She also
has a particular love of the memoir, narrative
nonfiction, the personal narrative, and narrative
journalism. She is always looking for writers
with strong, original voices who explore a
subject in new and surprising ways. Her list
includes books in psychology, women's issues,
history, education, science, health and
wellness, sports, humour, food and culture,
natural history and anything about animals,
religion and spirituality, and African American
issues.

L1477 The Wylie Agency (UK) Ltd

Literary Agency
17 Bedford Square, London, WC2B 3JA
United Kingdom
Tel: +44 (0) 20 7908 5900
Fax: +44 (0) 20 7908 5901

mail@wylieagency.co.uk

http://www.wylieagency.co.uk

Types: Fiction; Nonfiction
Markets: Adult

Closed to approaches.

**Note: Not accepting unsolicited mss as at
October 2018** Send query by post or email
before submitting. All submissions must
include adequate return postage. No scripts,
children's books, or unsolicited MSS.

L1478 The Wylie Agency

Literary Agency
250 West 57th Street, Suite 2114, New York,
NY 10107
United States

mail@wylieagency.com

http://www.wylieagency.com

Types: Fiction
Markets: Adult

Closed to approaches.

Agency with offices in New York and London. Not accepting submissions as at February 2018.

L1479 Tara Wynne
Literary Agent
Australia

Literary Agency: Curtis Brown (Australia) Pty Ltd (**L0319**)

L1480 Laura Yorke
Literary Agent
United States

https://www.carolmannagency.com/laura-yorke

Literary Agency: Carol Mann Agency (**L0225**)

L1481 Claudia Young
Literary Agent
United Kingdom

http://greeneheaton.co.uk/agents/claudia-young/
https://twitter.com/ClaudiaL_Young

Literary Agency: Greene & Heaton Ltd (**L0578**)

Fiction > *Novels*
Contemporary; Crime; Historical Fiction; Literary; Thrillers

Nonfiction > *Nonfiction Books*
Comedy / Humour; Cookery; Food Journalism; Travel

Closed to approaches.

Currently on maternity leave as at May 2020.

Authors: Sam Akbar; Anthony Anaxagorou; Ros Atkinson; Jordan Bourke; Matt Chapple; Martha Collison; Jack Cooke; Kevan Davis; Ella Frears; Lewis Goodall; Peter Harper; Alice Hart; Lizzie King; Vanessa King; Jenny Lee; Eleanor Maidment; Janina Matthewson; Val Payne; Alice Procter; Rejina Pyo; James Ramsden; Rosie Ramsden; Ryan Riley; Charlie Ryrie; Kat Sadler; Viviane Schwarz; Tim Sebastian; Dale Shaw; Rachel de Thample; Regina Wong

L1482 Cyle Young
Literary Agent; Author
United States

cyle@hartlineliterary.com
submissions@cyleyoung.com

https://cyleyoung.com
http://hartlineagency.com/agentsandauthors/
https://www.facebook.com/cyleyoung

Literary Agencies: Hartline Literary Agency (**L0618**); Cyle Young Literary Elite (**L0323**)

ADULT
Fiction > *Novels*
Amish Romance; Christianity; Fantasy; Romance; Science Fiction; Speculative

Nonfiction > *Nonfiction Books*
Christianity; Leadership; Parenting; Self Help

Scripts
Film Scripts; *TV Scripts*
CHILDREN'S > **Fiction**
Chapter Books; *Early Readers*; *Middle Grade*; *Picture Books*
YOUNG ADULT > **Fiction** > *Novels*

How to send: Conferences; Online pitch events
How not to send: Email

Represents work in both the General and Christian markets.

Author / Junior Agent: Del Duduit (**L0391**)

Authors: Dreama Archibald; Starr Ayers; Deborah Bailey; Marie E. Bast; Del Bates; Don Best; Lisa E. Betz; Cherrilynn Bisbano; Adam Blumer; Catherine Brakefield; Clare Campbell; George Cargill; Andy Clapp; Ray Comfort; Karen Condit; Elaine Marie Cooper; Jacy Corral; Shelley Cummings; Robin Currie; Callie Daruk; Bryan Davis; Melody Delgado; Rene Dick; Joyce K. Ellis; Diana Estell; Ryan Farr; C. Hope Flinchbaugh; Jennifer Froelich; Mary Gardner; Carla Gasser; Darlo Gemeinhardt; Annette Griffin; P.K. Hallinan; Jennifer Hallmark; Ruth Hartman; Cindy Huff; Carlton Hughes; Nancy L. Hull; Pauline Hylton; Kathy Ide; Ashley Kirby Jones; Jeff Jones; Stephanie Kehr; Marcie Keithley; Lisa Kibler; Victoria Kimble; Cary Knox; D.L. Koontz; Julie Lavender; Sarah Limardo; Beckie Lindsey; Jan Lis; Robin Luftig; Jayme Mansfield; Lori Marett; Jann Martin; Jake McCandless; Britt Mooney; Kay Mortimer; Susan Neal; Shelley Pierce; Dana Romanin; Andrew Roth; Patty Schell; Nicole Schrader; Olivia Schwab; Tim Shoemaker; Susan Holt Simpson; Donna L. H. Smith; John Snyder; Debbie Sprinkle; Kendra Stanton-Lee; Bruce A. Stewart; Cecil Stokes; Melissa Stroh; Janet Surette; Rachel Swanson; Elaine Tomski; John Turney; Bill Watkins; Molly White; Y.K. Willemse; Jean Wilund; Jean Wise

L1483 Hugo Young
Literary Agent
United Kingdom

Literary Agency: Independent Talent Group Ltd (**L0683**)

L1484 Marietta B. Zacker
Literary Agent
United States

marietta@galltzacker.com

Literary Agency: Gallt & Zacker Literary Agency (**L0522**)

CHILDREN'S > **Fiction**
Middle Grade; *Picture Books*
YOUNG ADULT
Fiction
Graphic Novels; *Novels*

Nonfiction > *Nonfiction Books*

How to send: By referral

L1485 Leslie Zampetti
Literary Agent
United States

https://www.dunhamlit.com/leslie-zampetti.html
http://aaronline.org/Sys/PublicProfile/46970641/417813
https://twitter.com/leslie_zampetti

Literary Agency: Dunham Literary, Inc. (**L0393**)
Professional Bodies: Association of Authors' Representatives, Inc. (AAR); Society of Children's Book Writers and Illustrators (SCBWI)

ADULT
Fiction > *Novels*
Historical Fiction; Literary Mystery; Upmarket Romance

Nonfiction > *Nonfiction Books*
Crime; Literature; Memoir

CHILDREN'S
Fiction > *Middle Grade*
Baseball; Contemporary; Florida; Historical Fiction; Mystery; Romance

Nonfiction > *Picture Books*
Comedy / Humour; Diversity; Florida

Poetry > *Novels in Verse*

YOUNG ADULT > **Fiction** > *Novels*
Baseball; Contemporary; Florida; Historical Fiction; Mystery; Romance

Send: Query
Don't send: Full text
How to send: Email
How not to send: Phone; Fax; Email attachment; Post

Seeks middle grade and young adult novels, especially mysteries and contemporary fiction. Historical fiction with a specific hook to the time and place, novels in verse, and off-the-beaten-path romances are on her wish list. For picture books, she prefers nonfiction that tells a story almost too good to be true, stories that show everyday diversity to mirror under-represented readers and open windows to others (per Dr. Rudine Sims Bishop), witty wordplay, and dry, sly humor. Drawn to books about Florida, odd homes, and kids with book smarts and big hearts.

For adult fiction, she is interested in literary mysteries, upmarket romance with interfaith or marginalized couples, and historical fiction set in regions other than Europe and North America. For nonfiction, she finds narrative nonfiction that straddles the boundaries between crime, memoir, and literature especially appealing. An armchair adventurer, she enjoys experiencing wild places and extreme challenges from the comfort of her chair. Though she reads widely, she's not a fit for political thrillers, inspirational Christian fiction, memoirs about violence against women, or hard sci-fi.

L1486 Laura Zats

Literary Agent
United States

Literary Agency: Red Sofa Literary (**L1129**)

L1487 Zeno Agency Ltd

Literary Agency
Primrose Hill Business Centre, 110 Gloucester Avenue, London, NW1 8HX
United Kingdom
Tel: +44 (0) 20 7096 0927

louisebuckleyagent@gmail.com

http://zenoagency.com

Professional Body: The Association of Authors' Agents (AAA)

Types: Fiction; Nonfiction
Subjects: Autobiography; Commercial; Cookery; Crime; Fantasy; Health; History; Horror; Lifestyle; Literary; Nature; Science Fiction; Society; Suspense; Thrillers; Women's Interests
Markets: Adult; Children's; Young Adult

London-based literary agency specialising in Science Fiction, Fantasy, and Horror, but expanding into other areas such as crime, thrillers, women's fiction, and young adult fiction. Adult fiction must be at least 75,000 words and children's fiction should be at least 50,000 words. Send query by email with synopsis up to two pages, and first three chapters (or approximately 50 double-spaced pages) as attachments in .docx or .pdf format. No submissions by post.

Associate Agent: Kristina Perez (**L1083**)

Junior Agent: Stevie Finegan (**L0469**)

Literary Agents: John Berlyne (**L0124**); Louise Buckley

L1488 Marisa Zeppieri

Literary Agent
United States

Literary Agency: Strachan Literary Agency (**L1326**)

L1489 Kieryn Ziegler

Literary Agent
United States

Literary Agency: Dystel, Goderich & Bourret LLC (**L0399**)

L1490 Helen Zimmermann

Literary Agent
United States

Literary Agency: Helen Zimmermann Literary Agency (**L0634**)

L1491 Renee Zuckerbrot

Literary Agent
United States

Literary Agency: Massie & McQuilkin (**L0934**)

Magazines

For the most up-to-date listings of these and hundreds of other magazines, visit https://www.firstwriter.com/magazines

To claim your free access to the site, please see the back of this book.

M0001 110% Gaming

Magazine
United Kingdom

Newspaper Publisher / Magazine Publisher:
DC Thomson Media

M0002 30 North

Magazine
United States

https://30northliterarymagazine.com

Fiction > *Short Fiction*: Literary

Nonfiction > *Short Nonfiction*: Creative Nonfiction

Poetry > *Any Poetic Form*

Send: Full text
How to send: Submittable

Publishes previously unpublished poetry, fiction, creative non-fiction, and art by undergraduate writers and artists. Submit via online submission system.

M0003 32 Poems

Magazine
Washington & Jefferson College, Department of English, 60 S. Lincoln Street, Washington, PA 15301
United States

submissions@32poems.com

http://32poems.com

Nonfiction > *Reviews*: Poetry as a Subject

Poetry > *Any Poetic Form*

Send: Full text
How to send: Online submission system; Post

Costs: A fee is charged for online submissions. $3 fee for online submissions. Postal submissions are free.

Publishes poems and reviews of recent poetry collections. Submit by post or via online submission system.

Editor: George David Clark

Managing Editor: Elisabeth Clark

M0004 34th Parallel

Magazine
United States

editorial@34thparallel.net

https://34thparallel.net

Fiction > *Short Fiction*: Literary

Nonfiction
  Articles: Journalism
  Essays: Creative Nonfiction

Poetry > *Any Poetic Form*

Send: Full text

Costs: A fee is charged upon submission. $14.50 fee includes download of latest digital edition.

Publishes fiction, creative nonfiction, essays, scripts, poetry, and artwork. Submit via online submission system.

M0005 365 Tomorrows

Magazine
United States

submissions@365tomorrows.com

https://365tomorrows.com

Types: Fiction
Formats: Short Fiction
Subjects: Science Fiction
Markets: Adult

Send: Full text

Website publishing daily flash fiction up to 600 words. Accepts all kinds of science fiction. Submit via form on website.

M0006 aaduna

Magazine
144 Genesee Street Suite 102-259, Auburn, New York 13021
United States

submissionsmanager@aaduna.org

http://www.aaduna.org

Types: Fiction; Nonfiction; Poetry
Subjects: Literary
Markets: Adult

Send: Full text
How to send: Email

Publishes fiction, poetry, and nonfiction. Submissions must be sent both by post and by email. See website for full guidelines.

M0007 AARP The Magazine

Magazine
c/o Editorial Submissions, 601 E St. NW, Washington, DC 20049
United States

AARPMagazine@aarp.org

https://www.aarp.org/magazine/

Types: Nonfiction
Formats: Articles; Essays
Subjects: Cookery; Finance; Health; Lifestyle; Travel
Markets: Adult

Send: Query
Don't send: Full text
How to send: Email

Magazine for those over 50. Rarely uses unsolicited ideas but will review those submitted in accordance with the guidelines on the website.

M0008 About Place Journal

Magazine
PO Box 24, Black Earth, WI 53515-0424
United States

blackearthinstitute@gmail.com

https://aboutplacejournal.org

Fiction > *Short Fiction*: Literary

Nonfiction
  Essays: General
  Short Nonfiction: Creative Nonfiction

Poetry > *Any Poetic Form*

Closed to approaches.

Publishes poetry, fiction, and essays / creative nonfiction. Accepts submissions during specific submission windows. See website for details and for themes.

M0009 Abramelin

Magazine
United States

nessaralindaran@aol.com

http://thegiantgilamonsters.com/abramelin

Types: Poetry
Subjects: Literary
Markets: Adult

Send: Full text
How to send: Email

Publishes modern, literary poetry. Send submissions by email, but no attachments. See website for full guidelines.

Editor: Vanessa Kittle

M0010 The Account
Magazine
United States

poetryprosethought@gmail.com

http://theaccountmagazine.com

Types: Fiction; Nonfiction; Poetry
Formats: Essays; Short Fiction
Subjects: Literary
Markets: Adult

Send: Full text

Accepts poetry, fiction, and creative nonfiction, between May 1 and September 1, annually, and between November 15 and March 1. Send 3-5 poems, essays up to 6,000 words, or fiction between 1,000 and 6,000 words, through online submission system. Each piece of work must be accompanied by an account between 150 and 500 words, giving voice to the artist's approach.

Editors: Brianna Noll, Poetry Editor; Jennifer Hawe, Nonfiction Editor; M. Milks, Fiction Editor; Tyler Mills, Editor-in-Chief; Christina Stoddard, Managing Editor/ Publicist

M0011 Accountancy Age
Magazine
United Kingdom

michael.mccaw@contentive.com

https://www.accountancyage.com

PROFESSIONAL > **Nonfiction** > *Articles*
Accounting; Business; Finance

Weekly magazine publishing articles on accountancy, business, and the financial world.

Editors: Michael McCaw; Beth McLoughlin

M0012 ACR Journal
Magazine
United Kingdom

Magazine Publisher: Warners Group Publications

M0013 Acumen
Magazine
6 The Mount, Higher Furzeham, Brixham, South Devon, TQ5 8QY
United Kingdom
Tel: +44 (0) 1803 851098

patriciaoxley6@gmail.com

http://www.acumen-poetry.co.uk

Types: Nonfiction; Poetry
Formats: Articles
Subjects: Literary; Literary Criticism
Markets: Adult

Send: Full text
How to send: Email

Magazine publishing poetry, articles, and features connected to poetry. Send submissions with SAE and author details on each page, or submit by email as Word attachment. See website for full submission guidelines.

Editor: Patricia Oxley

M0014 Ad Astra
Magazine
United States

adastra@nss.org

https://space.nss.org/ad-astra-the-magazine-of-the-national-space-society/

Nonfiction
Articles: Space
News: Space

Send: Query; Author bio; Writing sample; Full text
How to send: Email

Non-technical magazine, reporting on a broad range of space-related topics, including domestic and international space policy and programs, transportation, commercialisation, planetary science, extraterrestrial resources, colonisation, education, and space advocacy. No science fiction or UFO stories. Accepts unsolicited mss, but prefers queries from writers seeking assignments, including details of author expertise, credits, and writing samples.

Editor: Frank Sietzen Jr

M0015 The Adroit Journal
Magazine
United States

editors@theadroitjournal.org

http://www.theadroitjournal.org

Types: Fiction; Poetry
Formats: Short Fiction
Subjects: Literary
Markets: Adult

Closed to approaches.

Submit up to three pieces of prose up to 3,000 words each, or up to six poems of any length, during open submission periods. Currently closed to submissions until October 1, 2018.

M0016 After Happy Hour Review
Magazine
4750 Centre Avenue, Apt 60, Pittsburgh, PA 15213
United States

hourafterhappyhour@gmail.com

https://afterhappyhourreview.com/

Types: Fiction; Nonfiction; Poetry
Subjects: Commercial; Contemporary; Experimental; Literary; Traditional
Markets: Adult

Send: Full text
How not to send: Email

An online journal. We gravitate towards work that is quirky, accessible, and unconventional. An ideal piece might cover a subject few people write about or cover familiar subjects from an unexpected angle.

Editor: Mike Good, Jason Peck

M0017 Agenda
Magazine
Harts Cottage, Stonehurst Lane, Five Ashes, Mayfield, East Sussex, TN20 6LL
United Kingdom
Tel: +44 (0) 1825 831994

submissions@agendapoetry.co.uk

http://www.agendapoetry.co.uk

Types: Poetry
Formats: Essays; Reviews
Subjects: Literary; Literary Criticism
Markets: Adult

Send: Full text
How to send: Email

Publishes poems, critical essays, and reviews. Send up to five poems or up to two essays / reviews with email address, age, and short bio. No previously published material. Submit by email only, with each piece in a separate Word attachment. Accepts work only during specific submission windows – see website for current status.

Editor: Patricia McCarthy

M0018 Agony Opera
Online Magazine
188 A/23 Maniktala Main Road, Parvati Residency, flat-304, Opposite Kankurgachhi post office
India
Tel: +919831778983

hiyamukherjeephysics@gmail.com

https://www.agonyopera.com

Fiction in Translation > *Short Fiction*
Contemporary; Culture; Erotic; Experimental; Fantasy; Literary; New Age; Philosophy; Politics; Social Commentary; Speculative; Surreal

Fiction > *Short Fiction*
Contemporary; Culture; Erotic; Experimental; Fantasy; Literary; New Age;

Philosophy; Politics; Social Commentary; Speculative; Surreal

Poetry in Translation > *Any Poetic Form*
Experimental; Literary; Surreal

Poetry > *Any Poetic Form*
Experimental; Literary; Surreal

How to send: Email

We like things edgy, experimental (be it in language or form), surreal, magic-real, speculative, avant-garde. In short anything out of the box.

We have a soft spot for literature which makes a staunch stand on politics. And by politics, we mean the politics regarding the rights of the 99%, not the other way round. Though, we must admit socialist realism doesn't excite us that much.

M0019 Agricultural History
Magazine
Kennesaw State University, Dept. of History and Philosophy, 402 Bartow Ave., Kennesaw, GA 30144
United States

aghistory@kennesaw.edu

http://www.aghistorysociety.org/journal/

Types: Nonfiction
Formats: Articles
Subjects: History; Nature
Markets: Academic

Send: Full text

Publishes articles on all aspects of the history of agriculture and rural life with no geographical or temporal limits. Submit via online submission system. See website for full guidelines.

Editor: Albert Way

M0020 Air & Space Magazine
Magazine
Smithsonian Institution, PO Box 37012, MRC 513, Washington, DC 20013-7012
United States
Tel: +1 (202) 633-6070
Fax: +1 (202) 633-6085

editors@si.edu

https://www.airspacemag.com
https://www.facebook.com/AirSpaceMag
https://twitter.com/airspacemag
http://instagram.com/airspacemag

Magazine Publisher / Book Publisher: Smithsonian Institution (**P0821**)

Nonfiction > *Articles*
Aviation; Military Aviation; Space

Send: Query
How to send: Email; Online submission system

General interest magazine about flight. Submit proposal by email or through online submission system.

Editor: George Larson

M0021 AIR International
Magazine
PO BOX 100, Stamford, PE9 1XQ
United Kingdom
Tel: +44 (0) 1780 755131
Fax: +44 (0) 1780 751323

airint@keypublishing.com

http://www.airinternational.com

Types: Nonfiction
Formats: Articles; News
Subjects: Design; Technology; Warfare
Markets: Adult

Send: Full text

Aviation magazine covering military and civilian aircraft. Happy to receive contributions.

Editor: Mark Ayton

M0022 Aliterate
Magazine
United States

editor@aliterate.org

https://www.aliterate.org

Types: Fiction
Formats: Short Fiction
Subjects: Contemporary; Fantasy; Horror; Literary; Romance; Science Fiction; Thrillers; Westerns
Markets: Adult

Closed to approaches.

Closed to submissions, but plans to re-open before 2019. Check website for current status. Biannual print journal dedicated to "literary genre fiction". Accepts stories between 2,500 and 8,000 words. No poetry, erotica, inspirational fiction, polemics, nonfiction, gore, fanfic, or young adult fiction. Accepts submissions by email only.

Editor: R.S. Mason

M0023 Amazing! Magazine
Magazine
Amazing Publishing Limited, 4 Old Park Lane, Mayfair, London, W1K 1QW
United Kingdom
Tel: +44 (0) 20 3633 2531

hello@amazing.org.uk

https://amazing.org.uk

Types: Nonfiction
Markets: Children's

Send: Query
Don't send: Full text
How not to send: Email

Monthly printed magazine for children aged 6-12 that makes learning fun. Each issue covers maths, english, science, history, geography, and more. Inside are articles, facts, stories, debates, activities, puzzles, and jokes.

Editor: Yousuf Aslam

M0024 Ambit
Magazine
Staithe House, Main Road, Brancaster Staithe, Norfolk, PE31 8BP
United Kingdom
Tel: +44 (0) 7715 233221

contact@ambitmagazine.co.uk

http://ambitmagazine.co.uk

Types: Fiction; Poetry
Formats: Short Fiction
Subjects: Arts; Literary
Markets: Adult

Send: Full text

An international magazine. Potential contributors are advised to read a copy before submitting work. Send up to 5 poems, a story up to 5,000 words, or flash fiction up to 1,000 words. Submit via online portal, or by post if unable to use online portal. No submissions by email. Accepts submission only during specific submission windows – see website for details.

M0025 America's Civil War
Magazine
United States

acw@historynet.com

http://americascivilwarmag.com
https://www.historynet.com/magazines/mag-acw

Magazine Publisher: HistoryNet LLC

Nonfiction > *Articles:* American Civil War

Publishes material on the American Civil War, including features and articles for columns on the subjects of weapons, units, eye-witness accounts, and profiles of figures involved.

M0026 America's Pharmacist
Magazine
National Community Pharmacists Association, 100 Daingerfield Road, Alexandria, VA 22314
United States
Tel: +1 (703) 683-8200
Fax: +1 (703) 683-3619

http://www.ncpanet.org/newsroom/america's-pharmacist

Types: Nonfiction
Formats: Articles; News
Subjects: Business; Health
Markets: Professional

Magazine aimed at independent community pharmacists, publishing articles on business, management, and the latest legal and regulatory information.

M0027 American Book Review

Magazine
School of Arts & Sciences, University of Houston-Victoria, 3007 N. Ben Wilson, Victoria, TX 77901
United States
Tel: +1 (361) 570-4848

americanbookreview@uhv.edu

http://americanbookreview.org

Nonfiction > *Reviews*
   Cultural Criticism; Fiction as a Subject; Literary Criticism; Poetry as a Subject

Closed to approaches.

Specializes in reviews of frequently neglected works of fiction, poetry, and literary and cultural criticism from small, regional, university, ethnic, avant-garde, and women's presses. In nonfiction, reviews important books of criticism, biographies, and cultural studies. No reviews of "how-to" or "self-help" books. Would consider a review of innovative children's literature, but not usually part of the preferred content. Prefers books that have been published in the past six months, but will review books that have been published in the past year. No unsolicited reviews.

Editor: Lisa Savage

M0028 American Heritage

Online Magazine
United States

https://www.americanheritage.com
https://www.facebook.com/ameriheritage/
https://twitter.com/AmeriHeritage

Nonfiction > *Articles*
   American History; Culture; Food; Travel; United States

Magazine of American history, travel, food and culture. Originally a print magazine, now an online magazine as of 2017.

Editor: Richard Snow

M0029 American History

Magazine
1919 Gallows Road, Suite 400, Vienna, VA 22182
United States

americanhistory@historynet.com

http://www.historynet.com

Magazine Publisher: HistoryNet LLC

Types: Nonfiction
Formats: Articles
Subjects: History
Markets: Adult

Send: Full text
How to send: Email

Magazine of American history for a general readership. Send stories or ideas by post or by email. See website for full guidelines.

M0030 The American Poetry Journal (APJ)

Magazine
United States

apjpoetry@gmail.com

https://www.apjpoetry.org

Types: Poetry
Markets: Adult

Send: Full text

Publishes three issues per year in print and online editions, an annual anthology, and a chapbook series. Publishes poetry from diverse backgrounds and orientations, from new and established voices. We publish work that is committed, distinct and moving.

Editor: Jessica Fischoff

M0031 The American Poetry Review

Magazine
1906 Rittenhouse Square, 3rd Floor, Philadelphia, PA 19103
United States

escanlon@aprweb.org

https://aprweb.org

Types: Nonfiction; Poetry
Formats: Essays; Interviews; Reviews
Subjects: Contemporary; Literary; Literature
Markets: Adult

Send: Full text

Publishes poetry and literary prose. No previously published material. Send up to five poems or a piece of prose via online submission system ($3 charge) or by post with SASE. Accepts simultaneous submissions if notice of acceptance elsewhere is given. Six month response time.

Editor: Elizabeth Scanlon

M0032 American Quarter Horse Journal

Magazine
American Quarter Horse Association, 1600 Quarter Horse Drive, Amarillo, TX 79104
United States
Tel: +1 (806) 376-4811

https://www.aqha.com

Types: Nonfiction
Formats: Articles
Subjects: Business; How To; Lifestyle; Nature
Markets: Adult

Send: Query
Don't send: Full text

Magazine covering horse ownership, horse breeding, and Western lifestyle. Send query with published clips.

M0033 American Snowmobiler

Magazine
United States

editor@amsnow.com

http://www.amsnow.com

Types: Nonfiction
Formats: Articles
Subjects: Hobbies; How To; Leisure; Technology; Travel
Markets: Adult

Send: Full text
How to send: Email

Magazine publishing material relating to snowmobiles, their use and modification, etc. Send query or complete ms by email. See website for full guidelines.

M0034 Amethyst Review

Magazine
United Kingdom

Sarah.Poet@gmail.com

https://amethystmagazine.org

Types: Fiction; Nonfiction; Poetry
Formats: Short Fiction
Subjects: Religion
Markets: Adult

Send: Full text
How to send: Email

Publishes work that engages in some way with spirituality or the sacred. Submit up to five poems (of any length) and / or prose pieces of up to 2,000 words. Simultaneous submissions if notification of acceptance elsewhere is provided. No previously published work. Send submissions by email with author bio of around 50 words. See website for full guidelines.

Editor: Sarah Law

M0035 Anaverde Magazine

Magazine
38713 Tierra Subida Avenue #128, Palmdale, CA 93551
United States
Tel: +1 (661) 200-9156

hello@anaverde-magazine.com

http://www.anaverde-magazine.com
http://www.facebook.com/anaverdemagazine
http://www.twitter.com/anaverdemagazine
https://www.instagram.com/anaverdemagazine

Fiction > *Short Fiction*

Nonfiction
   Articles: Arts; Beauty; Crafts; Culture; Design; Entertainment; Fashion; Finance; Gardening; Health; Hobbies; Leisure;

Lifestyle; Nature; Spirituality; Women's Interests
Interviews: General

Send: Full text
How to send: Email

First issue in June 2020. The publication is mailed directly to the residents in the Anaverde community, which is located in the Antelope Valley.

Editors: Malena Jackson; Samantha Jennings

M0036 The Antigonish Review

Magazine
PO Box 5000, Antigonish, Nova Scotia, B2G 2W5
Canada
Tel: +1 (902) 867-3962
Fax: +1 (902) 867-5563

tar@stfx.ca

https://antigonishreview.com
https://twitter.com/antigonishrevie
https://www.facebook.com/The-Antigonish-Review-332083480162513/
https://www.linkedin.com/in/the-antigonish-review-7602052a

Fiction in Translation > *Short Fiction*: Literary

Fiction > *Short Fiction*: Literary

Nonfiction > *Essays*
  Creative Nonfiction; Culture; History; Memoir; Sport; Travel

Poetry in Translation > *Any Poetic Form*

Poetry > *Any Poetic Form*

Send: Full text
How to send: Submittable
How not to send: Post; Email

Costs: A fee is charged upon submission. $5 for prose; $2 for poetry.

Submit via online portal only. Submit no more than 6-8 poems (preferably 3-4) and submit no more till a response is received. Considers poetry on any subject written from any point of view and in any form. For fiction, send only one story at a time. Also publishes poetry and prose translated into English from other languages (be sure to indicate source language). Also considers critical articles and essays that are fresh, vigorous, and free from jargon. Welcomes creative nonfiction. No email submissions, postal submissions, or simultaneous submissions.

M0037 The Antioch Review

Magazine
PO Box 148, Yellow Springs, OH 45387
United States
Tel: +1 (937) 769-1365

cdunlevy@antiochcollege.edu

http://review.antiochcollege.org

Fiction > *Short Fiction*

Nonfiction
  Essays: General
  Reviews: Literature

Poetry > *Any Poetic Form*

Send: Full text; Self-Addressed Stamped Envelope (SASE)
How to send: Post
How not to send: Online

Send MS with SASE for return. Strongly encourages potential contributors to buy a sample copy and peruse the magazine before submitting. Considers fiction from September 1 to May 31 only, and accepts poetry from September 1 to April 30 only. Do not mix poetry and prose submissions in the same envelope. No email submissions or unsolicited book reviews.

Editor: Robert S. Fogarty

M0038 AntiqueWeek

Magazine
PO Box 90, 27 North Jefferson Street, Knightstown, IN 46148-0090
United States
Tel: +1 (765) 345-5133

cswaim@antiqueweek.com

http://www.antiqueweek.com

Types: Nonfiction
Formats: Articles
Subjects: Antiques
Markets: Adult; Professional

Send: Query
Don't send: Full text

Publishes articles on antiques for collectors, dealers, and auctioneers.

Editor: Connie Swaim

M0039 APICS Magazine

Magazine
8430 West Bryn Mawr Avenue, Suite 1000, Chicago, IL 60631
United States

editorial@apics.org

http://www.apics.org

Types: Nonfiction
Formats: Articles
Subjects: Business
Markets: Professional

Send: Full text

Publishes articles on supply chain management.

M0040 Architectural Record

Magazine
350 5th Ave, Suite 6000, New York, NY 10118
United States

Tel: +1 (646) 849-7100
Fax: +1 (646) 849-7148

mcguiganc@bnpmedia.com

https://www.architecturalrecord.com

Types: Nonfiction
Formats: Articles
Subjects: Architecture; Design
Markets: Professional

Send: Query
Don't send: Full text

Magazine for architects and designers.

M0041 Arena Fantasy

Magazine
Arena Fantasy Magazine, 12 Edward Stone Rise, Chipping Norton, Oxfordshire, OX7 5EP
United Kingdom
Tel: +44 (0) 7528 924361

arenafantasymagazine@gmail.com

https://arenafantasymagazine.carrd.co

Types: Fiction; Nonfiction
Formats: Articles
Subjects: Commercial; Fantasy; Literary; Traditional
Markets: Adult; Young Adult

Send: Full text
How to send: Email

Fantasy ezine that publishes every quarter. We specialise in fantasy stories as well as articles that help authors old and new. There are also competitions and a myriad of tools that will help you grow as an author. Submissions – Prose and Artwork Query via email initially. Your query should contain your Name, Pseudonym email address and contact details. Please give us a brief overview of your piece and a brief bio of anything you have published before if we like your work we will let you know and invite you to submit your piece.

Editor: Andy Hesford

M0042 Areopagus Magazine

Magazine
United Kingdom

editor@areopagus.org.uk

https://www.areopagus.org.uk

Fiction > *Short Fiction*
  Christianity; Evangelism

Nonfiction > *Articles*
  Christianity; Evangelism

Poetry > *Any Poetic Form*
  Christianity; Evangelism

Send: Full text
How to send: Email; Domestic Post

Costs: A subscription is required in order to submit. £5 for electronic subscription / £15 for print.

A Christian-based arena for creative writers. A forum for debate on contemporary issues relating to Christianity and wider issues. A chance for new writers to have their work published for the first time. We can only consider MSS which are submitted by subscribers to the magazine. Subscribers may submit by email, or by post if within the UK.

Editor: Julian Barritt

M0043 Arizona Wildlife Views

Magazine
Arizona Game and Fish Department, 5000 W. Carefree Highway, Phoenix, AZ 85086-5000
United States
Tel: +1 (623) 236-7216

hrayment@azgfd.gov

https://www.azgfd.com/media/magazine/

Types: Nonfiction
Formats: Articles
Subjects: How To; Leisure; Nature
Markets: Adult

Publishes articles on the wildlife and outdoors or Arizona, including general interest, how-to, photo features, popularized technical material on Arizona wildlife and wildlife management, habitat issues, outdoor recreation (involving wildlife, boating, fishing, hunting, bird watching, animal observation, off-highway vehicle use, etc.), and historical articles about wildlife and wildlife management. No "me and Joe" articles, anthropomorphism of wildlife or opinionated pieces not based on confirmable facts.

Editor: Heidi Rayment

M0044 Arkansas Review

Magazine
Department of English and Philosophy, PO Box 1890, State University, AR 72467
United States
Tel: +1 (870) 972-3043
Fax: +1 (870) 972-3045

arkansasreview@astate.edu

http://arkreview.org

Types: Fiction; Nonfiction; Poetry
Formats: Articles; Essays; Short Fiction
Subjects: Anthropology; Arts; Culture; History; Literature; Music; Politics; Sociology
Markets: Academic; Adult

Send: Full text
How to send: Email

Publishes articles in various disciplines focusing on the seven-state Mississippi River Delta, aimed at a general academic audience. Also publishes creative work including poetry, essays, fiction, and artwork that evoke or respond to the culture or nature of the delta. Academic articles should be submitted by post or by email. Creative material should be

submitted through online system. Allow 3-12 months for response.

Editor: Marcus Tribbett

M0045 The Armourer

Magazine
United Kingdom

Magazine Publisher: Warners Group Publications

M0046 Art + Framing Today

Magazine
2 Wye House, 6 Enterprise Way, London, SW18 1FZ
United Kingdom
Tel: +44 (0) 20 7381 6616

Lynn@fineart.co.uk

https://www.fineart.co.uk/art_and_framing_today.aspx

Types: Nonfiction
Formats: Articles; Interviews
Subjects: Arts; Business
Markets: Professional

Trade journal for the art, framing and printing industries.

Editor: Lynn Jones

M0047 Art Quarterly

Magazine
Art Fund, 2 Granary Square, King's Cross, London, N1C 4BH
United Kingdom
Tel: +44 (0) 20 7225 4856

artquarterly@artfund.org

https://www.artfund.org/about-us/art-quarterly

Types: Nonfiction
Formats: Articles
Subjects: Arts
Markets: Adult

Arts magazine publishing features on artists, galleries and museums.

M0048 ARTEMISpoetry

Magazine
3 Springfield Close, East Preston, West Sussex, BN16 2SZ
United Kingdom

editor@poetrypf.co.uk

http://www.secondlightlive.co.uk/artemis.shtml

Types: Poetry
Subjects: Literary
Markets: Adult

Send: Full text
How to send: Email

For poems by women. Submit up to four poems, up to 200 lines total, by post only. Poems must be unpublished and not out for

submission elsewhere. See website for full guidelines.

Editors: Kathy Miles; Lyn Moir; Dilys Wood

M0049 Arthritis Today

Magazine
1355 Peachtree St NE, 6th Floor, Atlanta, GA 30309
United States
Tel: +1 (404) 872-7100

https://www.arthritis.org

Types: Nonfiction
Formats: Articles; News
Subjects: Health; Medicine
Markets: Adult

Send: Query
Don't send: Full text
How to send: Email

Consumer health magazine aimed at sufferers of arthritis.

M0050 Artists & Illustrators

Magazine
The Chelsea Magazine Company, Jubilee House, 2 Jubilee Place, London, SW3 3TQ
United Kingdom

info@artistsandillustrators.co.uk

https://www.artistsandillustrators.co.uk

Types: Nonfiction
Formats: Articles
Subjects: Arts; How To
Markets: Adult; Professional

Publishes articles for both amateur and professional artists.

M0051 Arts & Letters

Magazine
United Kingdom
Tel: +1 (478) 445-1289

https://artsandletters.gcsu.edu
https://artsandletters.submittable.com/submit
https://www.facebook.com/artslettersgc
https://twitter.com/ArtsLettersGC
https://artsandlettersjournal.tumblr.com/

Fiction > *Short Fiction*: Literary

Nonfiction > *Short Nonfiction*: Creative Nonfiction

Poetry > *Any Poetic Form*

Send: Full text
How to send: Submittable

Costs: A fee is charged upon submission. $3 submission fee.

Send between four and six poems, or up to 25 pages (typed, double-spaced) of fiction or creative nonfiction. Accepts submissions between August 1 and January 31.

Editor: Martin Lammon

M0052 Ask

Magazine
United States

Magazine Publisher: Cricket Media, Inc.

M0053 Assaracus

Magazine
United States

info@siblingrivalrypress.com

https://siblingrivalrypress.com/assaracus/

Types: Poetry
Subjects: Literary
Markets: Adult

Journal of gay poetry. While contributors should self-identify as gay, poems need not have a gay theme. See website for calls for submissions.

M0054 Athletic Business

Magazine
22 E. Mifflin St., Suite 910, Madison, WI 53703
United States

editors@athleticbusiness.com

https://www.athleticbusiness.com

Types: Nonfiction
Formats: Articles
Subjects: Health; Leisure; Sport
Markets: Professional

Magazine for Athletic, Fitness and Recreation Professionals.

M0055 Atlanta Review

Magazine
Suite 333, 686 Cherry St. NW, Atlanta, GA 30332-0161
United States

atlantareview@gatech.edu

http://atlantareview.com
https://atlantareview.submittable.com/submit
https://twitter.com/ATLReview
https://www.facebook.com/atlantareview
https://www.instagram.com/atlantareviewpojo/

Poetry > *Any Poetic Form*

Send: Full text; Self-Addressed Stamped Envelope (SASE)
How to send: Submittable; Post

Costs: A fee is charged for online submissions. $3.

Accepts submissions of poetry between January 1 and June 1, and between September 15 and December 1. Submit online ($3 submission fee) or by post with SASE.

M0056 The Atlantic

Magazine
United States

politics@theatlantic.com
culture@theatlantic.com
science@theatlantic.com
family@theatlantic.com
education@theatlantic.com
global@theatlantic.com
ideas@theatlantic.com
fiction@theatlantic.com
poetry@theatlantic.com

https://www.theatlantic.com
https://support.theatlantic.com/hc/en-us/articles/360011374734-Submit-a-piece-for-editorial-consideration-at-The-Atlantic
https://www.facebook.com/TheAtlantic
https://www.instagram.com/theatlantic
https://www.youtube.com/user/TheAtlantic
https://twitter.com/TheAtlantic
https://www.linkedin.com/company/the-atlantic
https://flipboard.com/@theatlantic

Fiction > *Short Fiction*

Nonfiction > *Articles*
   Business; Culture; Education; Family; Health; International; Literature; Politics; Science; Technology

Poetry > *Any Poetic Form*

Send: Pitch; Full text
How to send: Word file email attachment; PDF file email attachment; In the body of an email

Always interested in great nonfiction, fiction, and poetry. A general familiarity with what we have published in the past is the best guide to what we're looking for. All manuscripts should be submitted as a Word document or PDF. Succinct pitches may be submitted in the body of an email.

Editor: Cullen Murphy

M0057 Auroras & Blossoms Creative Arts Journal

Online Magazine

https://abpoetryjournal.com

Fiction > *Short Fiction*

Nonfiction > *Essays*

Does not want:

> **Fiction** > *Short Fiction*
> Erotic; Politics
>
> **Nonfiction** > *Essays*
> Erotic; Politics

Send: Full text
How to send: Online submission system

Costs: A fee is charged upon submission. Cost varies depending on length.

Publishes short stories, flash fiction, essays, and six-word stories that are positive and uplifting in nature. Material must be suitable for all age groups.

M0058 Auroras & Blossoms Poetry Journal

Online Magazine
United Kingdom

info@abpoetryjournal.com

https://www.abpoetryjournal.com

ADULT > *Poetry* > *Any Poetic Form*

YOUNG ADULT > *Poetry* > *Any Poetic Form*

How to send: Email

Costs: A fee is charged upon submission. Free to submit within certain limits. Charges for submitting more or longer pieces.

Electronic poetry journal co-founded by two authors. They are family friendly, publishing "positive poetry/content. Positive as in stimulating, optimistic, confident, uplifting, inspirational." They accept work from adult writers/poets and teen poets (13-16).

We are a family-friendly magazine, so we expect clean language. No dirty words at all. We also don't want anything related to erotica or politics.

Apart from that, we are open to everything, as long as the message is good and uplifting.

When poets send us their pieces, we ask them to tell us why they think they would make a good fit for the journal. We want to ensure that they understand that the message is just as important as the language itself. There must be an energy behind the pieces that really make us think hard and ultimately inspires the reader, not just the poet themselves.

Editors / Poets: David Ellis; Cendrine Marrouat

M0059 Auto Express

Magazine
31-32 Alfred Place, London, WC1E 7DP
United Kingdom
Tel: +44 (0) 20 3890 3890

steve_fowler@dennis.co.uk

http://www.autoexpress.co.uk

Types: Nonfiction
Formats: Articles; News; Reviews
Subjects: How To; Men's Interests; Technology; Travel
Markets: Adult

Publishes motoring news, features, test drives, etc. Welcomes news items and fillers up to 100 words and leads up to 300 words, but no submissions of complete features. Send ideas for features in first instance.

Editor: Steve Fowler

M0060 Aviation History

Magazine
1919 Gallows Road, Ste 400, Vienna, VA

22182
United States

aviationhistory@historynet.com

http://www.historynet.com/aviation-history

Magazine Publisher: HistoryNet LLC

Types: Nonfiction
Formats: Articles
Subjects: History; Travel; Warfare
Markets: Adult

Publishes articles on the history of military and civil aviation.

M0061 The Awakenings Review

Magazine
The Awakenings Project, PO Box 177, Wheaton, IL 60187
United States

ar@awakeningsproject.org

http://awakeningsproject.org

Types: Fiction; Nonfiction; Poetry
Formats: Essays; Short Fiction
Subjects: Literary
Markets: Adult

Send: Full text
How not to send: Email

Publishes poetry, short stories, and essays by people who have had a personal experience with mental illness.

M0062 Awen

Magazine
Atlantean Publishing, 4 Pierrot Steps, 71 Kursaal Way, Southend-on-Sea, Essex, SS1 2UY
United Kingdom

atlanteanpublishing@hotmail.com

http://atlanteanpublishing.wikia.com/wiki/Awen

Book Publisher / Magazine Publisher:
Atlantean Publishing (**P0056**)

Fiction > *Short Fiction*

Poetry > *Any Poetic Form*

How to send: Email; Post

Now normally eight A4 sides in length, it contains poetry and short prose fiction and has appeared four times a year since 2013. Submit by post or by email.

Editor: David-John Tyrer

M0063 Backcountry Magazine

Magazine
60 Main Street, PO Box 190, Jeffersonville, VT 05464
United States
Tel: +1 (802) 644-6606

lucy@backcountrymagazine.com

https://backcountrymagazine.com

Types: Nonfiction
Formats: Articles
Subjects: Adventure; Hobbies; Leisure; Sport
Markets: Adult

Send: Query
Don't send: Full text

Magazine of skiing and snowboarding. Send query by email.

Editor: Lucy Higgins

M0064 Bacopa Literary Review

Magazine
United States

https://writersalliance.org/bacopa-literary-review/

Fiction > *Short Fiction*: Literary

Nonfiction > *Short Nonfiction*: Creative Nonfiction

Poetry > *Any Poetic Form*

Closed to approaches.

Annual print journal publishing short stories, creative nonfiction, poetry, and prose poetry. Accepts submissions only through annual contest that runs from March 18 to May 17 annually.

M0065 Bad Nudes

Magazine
Canada

submit.badnudes@gmail.com

http://www.badnudes.com

Types: Fiction; Poetry
Formats: Short Fiction
Subjects: Experimental; Literary
Markets: Adult

Send: Full text
How to send: Email

Strives to pair bold, experimental poetry and fiction with innovative design to create a magazine that is both relevant and thought-provoking. Submit one story up to 3,000 words, or up to five poems up to ten pages total.

M0066 Bad Pony

Online Magazine
United States

badponymag@gmail.com

https://www.badponymag.com

Fiction > *Short Fiction*: Literary

Nonfiction > *Short Nonfiction*: Literary

Poetry > *Any Poetic Form*

Closed to approaches.

Online magazine publishing poetry, fiction, and nonfiction that "speak to our bad selves".

Send submissions by email. See website for full guidelines.

M0067 The Baffler

Magazine
19 West 21st Street #1001, New York, NY 10010
United States
Tel: +1 (212) 390-1569

https://thebaffler.com

Types: Fiction; Nonfiction; Poetry
Formats: Articles; Essays; Short Fiction
Subjects: Comedy / Humour; Culture; Politics; Satire
Markets: Adult

Send: Query
Don't send: Full text

Describes itself as "America's leading voice of interesting and unexpected left-wing political criticism, cultural analysis, short stories, poems and art". Submit pitch using online form on website.

Editor: Jonathon Sturgeon

M0068 The Bangalore Review

Magazine
India

submissions@bangalorereview.com

http://bangalorereview.com

Types: Fiction; Nonfiction; Poetry; Translations
Formats: Essays; Reviews; Short Fiction
Subjects: Arts; Culture; Literary; Literature; Philosophy
Markets: Adult

Send: Full text
How to send: Email

Online literary journal publishing literary fiction and nonfiction, reviews, poetry, art and photographic essays. See website for submission guidelines.

M0069 Banipal

Magazine
1 Gough Square, London, EC4A 3DE
United Kingdom

editor@banipal.co.uk

http://www.banipal.co.uk

Types: Fiction; Poetry; Translations
Formats: Articles; Reviews; Short Fiction
Markets: Adult

Send: Query
Don't send: Full text
How to send: Email

Contemporary Arab authors in English translations. Publishes new and established writers, and diverse material including translations, poetry, short stories, novel excerpts, profiles, interviews, appreciations, book reviews, reports of literary festivals, conferences, and prizes. Welcomes submissions by post, but queries only by email. Unsolicited email submissions with attachments will be automatically deleted. Response in 3-6 months.

Editor: Margaret Obank

M0070 Bare Fiction Magazine

Magazine
177 Copthorne Road, Shrewsbury, Shropshire, SY3 8NA
United Kingdom

info@barefiction.co.uk

https://www.barefictionmagazine.co.uk

Types: Fiction; Nonfiction; Poetry; Scripts
Formats: Essays; Interviews; Reviews; Short Fiction; Theatre Scripts
Subjects: Drama; Literary; Literature
Markets: Adult

Closed to approaches.

Closed to submissions as at March 2019. Check website for current status. Publishes poetry, fiction and plays, literary review, interviews and commentary. Does not accept submissions at all times – check website for current status and sign up to newsletter to be notified when submissions next open.

M0071 Barking Sycamores

Magazine
United States

barkingsycamores@gmail.com

https://barkingsycamores.wordpress.com

Types: Fiction; Nonfiction; Poetry
Formats: Reviews; Short Fiction
Subjects: Literary
Markets: Adult

Send: Full text

A literary journal entirely edited and operated by transgender queer neurodivergent people of colour. Publishes poetry, artwork, short fiction, creative nonfiction, and hybrid genre work by emerging and established neurodivergent writers. Also book reviews. Submit up to five poems; up to five short stories up to 1,000 words each; creative nonfiction up to 8,500 words; or book reviews up to 1,000 words, via online submission system.

Editors: V.E. Maday; N.I. Nicholson

M0072 Barren Magazine

Magazine
United States

info@barrenmagazine.com

https://barrenmagazine.com

Types: Fiction; Nonfiction; Poetry
Formats: Short Fiction

Subjects: Literary; Photography
Markets: Adult

Send: Full text
How to send: Email

An Alt.Lit Introspective. A literary publication that features fiction, poetry, creative nonfiction, and photography for hard truths, long stares, and gritty lenses. We revel in the shadow-spaces that make up the human condition, and aim to find antitheses to that which defines us: light in darkness; beauty in ugliness; peace in disarray. We invite you to explore it with us.

Editor: Jason D. Ramsey

M0073 Bartender

Magazine
PO Box 157, Spring Lake, NJ 07762
United States
Tel: +1 (732) 449-4499

barmag2@gmail.com

https://bartender.com

Types: Nonfiction
Formats: Articles; News
Subjects: Business; Leisure
Markets: Professional

Magazine for establishments which mix drinks on site.

Editor: Jackie Foley

M0074 BBC Countryfile Magazine

Magazine
Eagle House, Colston Avenue, Bristol, BS1 4ST
United Kingdom
Tel: +44 (0) 1173 147399

editor@countryfile.com

http://www.countryfile.com

Types: Nonfiction
Formats: Articles
Subjects: Nature
Markets: Adult

Send: Query
Don't send: Full text

Magazine on British countryside and rural life. Send queries with ideas by email. No unsolicited mss.

Editor: Fergus Collins

M0075 BBC Focus

Magazine
Immediate Media, 9th floor, Tower House, Fairfax Street, Bristol, BS1 3BN
United Kingdom
Tel: +44 (0) 1173 008755

editorialenquiries@sciencefocus.com

https://www.sciencefocus.com

Types: Nonfiction
Formats: Articles; News
Subjects: Science; Technology
Markets: Adult

Send: Query
Don't send: Full text
How to send: Email

Publishes news and articles on science and technology. Accepts queries from previously published science writers only.

M0076 Beano

Magazine
United Kingdom

Newspaper Publisher / Magazine Publisher: DC Thomson Media

M0077 Beat Scene

Magazine
United Kingdom

kevbeatscene@gmail.com

https://www.beatscene.net

Nonfiction > *Articles*: Beat Generation

A magazine about the Beat Generation, Jack Kerouac, William Burroughs, Allen Ginsberg, Lawrence Ferlinghetti, Gary Snyder, Michael McClure, Philip Whalen, Anne Waldman, Joanne Kyger, Charles Bukowski and others.

Editor: Kevin Ring

M0078 BedTimes

Magazine
501 Wythe Street, Alexandria, VA 22314
United States
Tel: +1 (703) 683-8371
Fax: +1 (703) 683-4503

mbest@sleepproducts.org

https://bedtimesmagazine.com

Types: Nonfiction
Formats: Articles; News
Subjects: Business
Markets: Professional

Send: Query
Don't send: Full text
How to send: Email

Publishes news, trends and issues of interest to mattress manufacturers and their suppliers, as well as more general business stories. Send queries, CV, and writing samples by email.

Editor: Mary Best

M0079 Bella

Magazine
Academic House, 24-28 Oval Road, London, NW1 7DT
United Kingdom

Bella.Hotline@bauermedia.co.uk

https://www.bellamagazine.co.uk
https://twitter.com/#!/bellamagazineUK
http://facebook.com/bellamagazineUK
https://www.instagram.com/bellamagazineuk/

Magazine Publisher: H Bauer Publishing

Nonfiction > *Articles*
   Celebrity; Diet; Fashion; Real Life Stories; Travel

Send: Query
How to send: Email

Human interest magazine for women, publishing articles on celebs, diet, style, travel, and real-life stories. Send query by email.

Editor: Jayne Marsden

M0080 Bellingham Review
Magazine
MS-9053, Western Washington University, Bellingham, WA 98225
United States
Tel: +1 (360) 650-4863

bellingham.review@wwu.edu

http://bhreview.org

Types: Fiction; Nonfiction; Poetry
Formats: Essays; Short Fiction
Subjects: Literary
Markets: Adult

Send submissions of prose up to 6,000 words, or up to three poems, via online submission system only. Submit material between September 15 and December 1 only. Simultaneous submissions accepted provided immediate notification is given of acceptance elsewhere.

Editor: Bailey Cunningham

M0081 Belmont Story Review
Magazine
United States

belmontstoryreview@gmail.com

https://belmontstoryreview.wixsite.com/website
https://belmontstoryreview.submittable.com/submit

Fiction > *Short Fiction*

Nonfiction > *Short Nonfiction*: Creative Nonfiction

Poetry > *Any Poetic Form*

Send: Full text
How to send: Submittable

Established in 2016, the magazine aims to surprise and delight readers through an eclectic mix of storytelling which includes fiction, personal essay, poetry, songwriting, drama, graphic narrative, and photography; as well as creative reportage, including coverage of music, film, creativity and collaboration, and the intersection of faith and culture.

We seek to publish new and established writers passionate about their craft, fearlessly encountering difficult ideas, seeking to explore human experience in all its broken blessedness.

M0082 Best
Magazine
United Kingdom

best@hearst.co.uk

https://www.hearst.co.uk/brands/best
https://www.facebook.com/bestmagazine/
https://twitter.com/BestMagOfficial

Magazine Publisher: Hearst Magazines UK

Nonfiction > *Articles*
   Beauty; Celebrity; Diet; Fashion; Finance; Real Life Stories; Recipes; TV

Jam packed with amazing real-life stories, showbiz news, diet, recipes, fashion, beauty advice and so much more.

Editors: for fiction Pat Richardson.; Louise Court. For features contact Helen Garston or Charlotte Seligman

M0083 Better Than Starbucks
Magazine
146 Lake Constance, West Palm Beach, FL 33411
United States
Tel: +1 (561) 719-8627

betterthanstarbucks2@gmail.com

https://www.betterthanstarbucks.org

ADULT

Fiction > *Short Fiction*

Nonfiction > *Short Nonfiction*
   Creative Nonfiction; Memoir; Personal Essays

Poetry in Translation > *Any Poetic Form*

Poetry
   Any Poetic Form: Africa; Comedy / Humour; International
   Experimental Poetry: General
   Formal Poetry: General
   Free Verse: General
   Haiku: General

CHILDREN'S > **Poetry** > *Any Poetic Form*

Send: Full text; Author bio
How to send: Email

Publishes African Poetry, International Poetry, Prose Poetry, Forms as well as Formal Poetry, Poetry Translations, Experimental Poetry and poetry for children. Encourages sentiment in poetry. Also publishes Fiction, Flash Fiction, Micro Fiction and Creative Nonfiction. Submitted opinion pieces will be considered.

Editor: Vera Ignatowitsch

M0084 Big Fiction
Online Magazine
Seattle University, English Dept, c/o Juan Carlos Reyes, P.O. Box 222000, Seattle, WA 98122-1090
United States

editors@bigfiction.com

https://www.bigfictionmagazine.org

Fiction > *Novelette*

Nonfiction
   Essays: General
   Reviews: Fiction as a Subject
   Short Nonfiction: Creative Nonfiction

Send: Full text
How to send: Submittable

Costs: A fee is charged upon submission. $5 for novelettes; $3 for essays.

Literary magazine devoted to longer short fiction, between 7,500 and 20,000 words.

M0085 The Big Ugly Review
Online Magazine
2703 Seventh Street, Box 345, Berkeley, CA 94710
United States

elizabethstix@gmail.com

http://www.biguglyreview.com

Types: Fiction; Nonfiction; Poetry
Formats: Essays
Subjects: Commercial; Experimental; Literary
Markets: Adult

Send full MS as Word or Word-compatible attachment by email. Publishes poetry, fiction, flash fiction, creative nonfiction and personal essays in themed issues online. All material submitted must be related to theme for upcoming issue, which is available on website along with individual email addresses for different editors.

Editor: Elizabeth Bernstein

M0086 BIGnews
Magazine
United States

http://www.mainchance.org

Fiction > *Short Fiction*

Nonfiction
   Articles: Arts; Literature
   Essays: Arts; Literature
   Interviews: Arts; Literature

Publishes features, interviews, personal essays, short stories, and serialised novels from the outsider's perspective. Interested in presenting the art and literature of the outsider, rather than simply drumming up sympathy for the homeless.

Editor: Ron Grunberg

M0087 Bikers Club
Online Magazine
7B Tejal Bhuvan, N.P.Thakkar Road, Vile
Parle, Mumbai 400057
India
Tel: +91 9820189969

rm@bikersclub.in

https://www.bikersclub.in
https://www.facebook.com/bikersclubapp/
https://www.instagram.com/bikersclubapp/
https://twitter.com/Bikersclubapp

Nonfiction
  Articles: Biker Lifestyle; Motorbikes;
  Motorcycling; Motorsports; Travel
  Interviews: Motorbikes; Motorcycling;
  Motorsports
  Reviews: Motorbikes

Send: Full text
How to send: Email

Monthly digitally issued magazine dedicated to
the bikers and the traveller worldwide. It
includes interview, reviews of bikes and
destinations, lifestyles, shout out, current
affairs and travel stories.

Editor: Rahul Mehta

M0088 Birdwatch
Magazine
Warners Group Publications, The Maltings,
West Street, Bourne, Lincolnshire, PE10 9PH
United Kingdom
Tel: +44 (0) 20 8881 0550

http://www.birdwatch.co.uk

Magazine Publisher: Warners Group
Publications

Types: Nonfiction
Formats: Articles; News
Subjects: Nature
Markets: Adult

Magazine of birds and birdwatching,
publishing articles, news, and features.

Editor: Dominic Mitchell

M0089 The Bitter Oleander
Magazine
4983 Tall Oaks Drive, Fayetteville, NY 13066-
9776
United States

info@bitteroleander.com

https://www.bitteroleander.com

Book Publisher / Magazine Publisher: The
Bitter Oleander Press (**P0097**)

Fiction > *Short Fiction*: Literary

Poetry > *Any Poetic Form*

Send: Full text
How to send: Submittable; Post

Send fiction up to 2,500 words, or up to eight
poems, through online submission system or
by post with SASE.

Editor: Paul B. Roth

M0090 BizTimes Milwaukee
Magazine
126 N. Jefferson St., Suite 403, Milwaukee,
WI 53202
United States
Tel: +1 (414) 336-7120
Fax: +1 (414) 277-8191

https://www.biztimes.com

Types: Nonfiction
Formats: Articles; News
Subjects: Business
Markets: Professional

Publishes news and analysis for business
leaders in southeastern Wisconsin.

M0091 Black Beauty & Hair
Magazine
United Kingdom

info@blackbeautyandhair.com

http://www.blackbeautyandhair.com
https://www.facebook.com/
BlackBeautyandHair
https://twitter.com/BlackBeautyMag
https://www.youtube.com/user/
blackbeautymag
http://instagram.com/BlackBeautyMag
https://www.pinterest.com/blackbeautyhair/

Nonfiction > *Articles*
  Beauty; Fashion; Hairstyles; Weddings

Publishes articles and features on black hair,
beauty, fashion, and lifestyle. Also publishes
bridal features.

Editor: Irene Shelley

M0092 Black Static
Magazine
TTA Press, 5 Martins Lane, Witcham, Ely,
Cambs, CB6 2LB
United Kingdom

http://ttapress.com

Types: Fiction
Formats: Short Fiction
Subjects: Fantasy; Horror
Markets: Adult

Send: Full text

Publishes short stories of horror and dark
fantasy. See website for full guidelines and
online submission system.

Editor: Andy Cox

M0093 Blithe Spirit
Magazine
United Kingdom

ed.blithespirit@gmail.com

http://britishhaikusociety.org.uk

Poetry > *Haiku*

Send: Full text
How to send: Email

Only accepts submissions from members,
however members do not enjoy an automatic
right to publication – quality is key. Non-
members may appear as featured writers. All
work must be original. Submissions should be
sent by email with a covering note.

Editor: Caroline Skanne

M0094 Blue Collar Review
Magazine
PO 11417, Norfolk, VA 23517
United States

red-ink@earthlink.net

http://www.partisanpress.org

Types: Fiction; Poetry
Formats: Essays; Reviews; Short Fiction
Subjects: Literary
Markets: Adult

Send: Full text
How not to send: Email

Magazine that aims to "expand and promote a
progressive working class vision of culture that
inspires us and that moves us forward as a
class". Submit up to five poems or short
stories, essays, or reviews up to 1,000 words
by post with SASE for response.

M0095 Body
Magazine
United States

https://bodyliterature.com

Types: Fiction; Nonfiction; Poetry;
Translations
Formats: Essays; Interviews; Short Fiction
Subjects: Literary; Literary Criticism
Markets: Adult

Send: Full text

Online journal publishing poetry, fiction, and
nonfiction (including personal essays, criticism
and art interviews). Submit up to five poems or
prose up to 10 pages through online
submission system. Accepts simultaneous
submissions.

M0096 BoxOffice Magazine
Magazine
63 Copps Hill Road, Ridgefield, CT 06877
United States
Tel: +1 (203) 438-8389

ken@boxoffice.com

https://pro.boxoffice.com

Types: Nonfiction
Formats: Articles; Film Scripts; News

Subjects: Business; Entertainment; Media
Markets: Professional

Magazine for professionals in the film industry.

Editor: Kenneth James Bacon

M0097 Boys' Life
Magazine
1325 West Walnut Hill Lane, PO Box 152079, Irving, TX 75015-2079
United States
Tel: +1 (866) 584-6589

https://boyslife.org
https://facebook.com/boyslife
https://twitter.com/boyslife
https://instagram.com/boyslifemagazine#
https://www.youtube.com/user/
BoysLifeMagazine
https://www.pinterest.com/boyslife/

CHILDREN'S > **Nonfiction** > *Articles*
Comedy / Humour; Games; Hobbies; Leisure; Outdoor Activities

Magazine aimed at boys aged between 6 and 18. Includes games, jokes, contests, giveaways, and articles on hobbies and outdoor activities.

M0098 Brain, Child
Magazine
PO Box 714, Lexington, VA 24450
United States
Tel: +1 (540) 463-4817

editor@brainchildmag.com

http://www.brainchildmag.com

Types: Fiction
Formats: Articles; Essays; News; Reviews; Short Fiction
Subjects: Comedy / Humour

Closed to approaches.

Magazine on modern motherhood. Send MSS with cover letter and SASE, or pasted into the body of an email with "Submission" in the subject heading. For features, news items, and debate essays query first with clips. Simultaneous submissions are accepted, provided immediate notification is given of acceptance elsewhere.

Core focus is on insightful personal essays, using illustrative anecdotes, a personal voice, and a down-to-earth tone. Humour is appreciated. Sentimentality isn't.

Also publishes more traditional features based on reporting rather than introspection. Also publishes short fiction, parody, and book reviews. See website for full details.

Editor: Jennifer Niesslein and Stephanie Wilkinson

M0099 Briar Cliff Review
Magazine
3303 Rebecca Street, Sioux City, IA 51104-

2100
United States

currans@briarcliff.edu

http://www.bcreview.org

Types: Fiction; Nonfiction; Poetry
Formats: Essays; Short Fiction
Subjects: Literary
Markets: Adult

Send: Full text

Publishes poetry, fiction, nonfiction and Siouxland essays. Submit online for $3 fee or by post with SASE. See website for full details.

Editor: Tricia Currans-Sheehan

M0100 Brick
Magazine
P.O. Box 609, STN P, Toronto, ON, M5S 2Y4
Canada

info@brickmag.com

https://brickmag.com/
https://twitter.com/brickMAG
https://facebook.com/brickmagazine
https://instagram.com/brickliterary

Nonfiction

Essays: Arts; City and Town Planning; Dance; Food; History; Literature; Music; Photography; Science; Sport; Travel; Writing
Interviews: Arts; Literature; Performing Arts
Reviews: Arts; Literature; Performing Arts
Short Nonfiction: Literary; Memoir

Send entire submission in first instance. Please read magazine before submitting. Accepts unsolicited nonfiction submissions on a variety of subjects between March 1 and April 30 and between September 1 and October 31 each year. No unsolicited fiction or poetry.

Editor: Vivien Leong

M0101 British Medical Journal (BMJ)
Magazine
BMA House, Tavistock Square, London, WC1H 9JP
United Kingdom
Tel: +44 (0) 20 7387 4410
Fax: +44 (0) 20 7383 6418

papersadmin@bmj.com

https://www.bmj.com

Types: Nonfiction
Formats: Articles; News
Subjects: Medicine
Markets: Professional

Leading medical journal for healthcare professionals. Papers can be submitted using online submission system available via website.

Editor: Fiona Godlee

M0102 British Railway Modelling
Magazine
United Kingdom

Magazine Publisher: Warners Group Publications

M0103 Brittle Star
Magazine
Diversity House, 72 Nottingham Road, Arnold, Nottingham, NG5 6LF
United Kingdom

brittlestar.subs@gmail.com

http://www.brittlestar.org.uk
http://www.twitter.com/brittlestarmag

Fiction > *Short Fiction:* Literary

Poetry > *Any Poetic Form*

Send: Full text; Self-Addressed Stamped Envelope (SASE)
How to send: Domestic Post; Email attachment

Publishes original and unpublished poetry and short stories. Send 1-4 poems or 1-2 stories of up to 2,000 words each. Include short bio of up to 40 words. No simultaneous submissions. Also reviews of first, full poetry collections and single-author short fiction collections.

M0104 The Broons
Magazine
United Kingdom

Newspaper Publisher / Magazine Publisher: DC Thomson Media

M0105 Bunbury Magazine
Magazine
United Kingdom

submissions@bunburymagazine.com

https://bunburymagazine.com

Types: Fiction; Nonfiction; Poetry
Formats: Articles; Reviews; Short Fiction
Subjects: Literary
Markets: Adult

Send: Full text
How to send: Email

Online literary magazine. Publishes anything from poetry to artwork, flash fiction to graphic story, life writing to photography, plus reviews and articles. Send submissions by email. See website for full guidelines, and for current issue theme.

M0106 The Burlington Magazine
Magazine
14-16 Duke's Road, London, WC1H 9SZ
United Kingdom
Tel: +44 (0) 20 7388 1228

mhall@burlington.org.uk

http://www.burlington.org.uk

Types: Nonfiction
Formats: Articles; Reviews
Subjects: Arts; History
Markets: Adult

Monthly magazine devoted to the fine and decorative arts. Publishes concise articles based on original research, presenting new works, art-historical discoveries and fresh interpretations.

Editor: Michael Hall

M0107 The Burnt Candle

Magazine
Hamilton House, Nottingham, NG5 1AE
United Kingdom

theburntcandle@compsncalls.com

https://www.compsncalls.com/burntcandle.html

Types: Fiction; Poetry
Formats: Short Fiction
Subjects: Commercial; Crime; Drama; Erotic; Fantasy; Literary; Literature; Mystery; Romance; Suspense; Thrillers
Markets: Adult

Send: Full text
How to send: Email

Magazine looking for original, well-written, powerful and emotional stories. Also open for poetry. New and up-and-coming writers are just as welcome as established writers.

Editor: Judith Darcey-Blake

M0108 Business London

Magazine
210 Dundas St., Suite 201, London, ON N6A 5J3
Canada

sajones@postmedia.com

https://lfpress.com/category/business-london/

Media Company: The London Free Press

PROFESSIONAL > **Nonfiction** > *Articles*: Business

Business magazine for southwestern Ontario.

Editor: Sarah Jones

M0109 Button

Magazine
PO Box 77, Westminster, MA 01473
United States

sally@moonsigns.net

http://www.moonsigns.net/Button-frame.htm

Fiction > *Short Fiction*

Poetry > *Any Poetic Form*

Send: Full text
How to send: Post; Email if overseas
How not to send: Email if not overseas

Send SASE for writers guidelines, and / or purchase a copy of the magazine for guidance on style. Magazine of poetry, fiction, and gracious living.

Editor: Sally Cragin

Fiction Editor: W.M. Davies

M0110 Cabildo Quarterly

Magazine
United States

cabildoquarterly@gmail.com

https://cabildoquarterly.tumblr.com

Types: Fiction; Poetry
Formats: Short Fiction
Subjects: Literary
Markets: Adult

Send: Full text
How to send: Email

Punk-influenced broadsheet journal based in Cape Cod and Bangor ME. Publishes material both in print and online. Send one or two unpublished stories or up to five unpublished poems, by email. See website for full guidelines and separate email address for poetry submissions.

M0111 Cadaverous Magazine

Magazine
United States

cadaverousmagazine@gmail.com

https://cadaverousmagazine.wixsite.com/litmag

Types: Fiction; Poetry
Subjects: Horror; Literary
Markets: Academic; Adult; Young Adult

Send: Full text
How to send: Email

A not-for-profit online supernatural horror (global) literary magazine. We feature: poetry, prose, fiction, flash fiction, art and photography. We accept submissions from writers and artists of all ages from all across the globe. They must be at least 13 years old.

Editor: Alexa Findlay

M0112 Caesura

Magazine
Poetry Center San José, 1650 Senter Road, San Jose, CA 95112-2599
United States

caesura@pcsj.org

http://www.pcsj.org/caesura.html

Types: Fiction; Nonfiction; Poetry
Formats: Interviews; Reviews; Short Fiction
Subjects: Literary; Literary Criticism
Markets: Adult

Literary journal publishing poems, short fiction, nonfiction, critical work, book reviews, and interviews.

M0113 The Cafe Irreal

Magazine
United States

editors@cafeirreal.com

http://cafeirreal.alicewhittenburg.com

Types: Fiction
Formats: Short Fiction
Subjects: Literary
Markets: Adult

Send: Full text
How to send: Email

Quarterly webzine publishing fantastic fiction resembling the work of writers such as Franz Kafka and Jorge Luis Borges. Send stories up to 2,000 in the body of an email. No simultaneous submissions.

M0114 Cake Craft

Magazine
United Kingdom

Magazine Publisher: Warners Group Publications

M0115 Cake Craft Guides

Magazine
United Kingdom

Magazine Publisher: Warners Group Publications

M0116 California Quarterly

Magazine
PO Box 7126, Orange, CA 92863
United States

apc@californiastatepoetrysociety.org

https://www.californiastatepoetrysociety.org

Types: Poetry; Translations
Subjects: Literary
Markets: Adult

Send: Full text

We are open to poets anywhere, any style or theme The only criterion is quality. Prefer poems of one page (40 lines) but two pages (80 lines) maximum. Submit no more than 6 poems. Include SASE or email address for response.

M0117 Campervan

Magazine
United Kingdom

Magazine Publisher: Warners Group Publications

M0118 Camping Magazine

Magazine
United Kingdom

Magazine Publisher: Warners Group
Publications

M0119 Canadian Yachting
Magazine
538 Elizabeth Street, Midland, Ontario, L4R
2A3
Canada

elissacampbell@kerrwil.com

http://www.kerrwil.com

Types: Nonfiction
Formats: Articles; News
Subjects: Technology; Travel
Markets: Adult

Describes itself as the premier boating
magazine in Canada.

M0120 Candis
Magazine
Newhall Publications Ltd, Newhall Lane,
Hoylake, Wirral, CH47 4BQ
United Kingdom
Tel: +44 (0) 1516 323232

info@newhallpublishing.com

https://www.candis.co.uk

Types: Nonfiction
Formats: Articles
Subjects: Cookery; Health; Lifestyle; Travel
Markets: Adult

Publishes features on food, health, travel, and
charity.

M0121 Caravan
Magazine
United Kingdom

Magazine Publisher: Warners Group
Publications

M0122 The Caribbean Writer
Magazine
University of the Virgin Islands, RR 1, Box
10,000, Kingshill, St Croix USVI 00850
United States
Tel: +1 (340) 692-4152
Fax: +1 (340) 692-4122

submit@TheCaribbeanWriter.com

http://TheCaribbeanWriter.com

Types: Fiction; Nonfiction; Poetry; Scripts;
Translations
Formats: Essays; Interviews; Reviews; Short
Fiction
Subjects: Drama; Literary
Markets: Adult

Send: Full text
How to send: Email

An international magazine with a regional
focus. Explores the diverse and multi-ethnic
culture in poetry, short fiction, personal essays,
creative nonfiction, and short plays.

Editor: Alscess Lewis-Brown

M0123 Cat World
Magazine
PO Box 2258, Pulborough, West Sussex,
RH20 9BA
United Kingdom
Tel: +44 (0) 1903 884988

support@ashdown.co.uk

http://www.catworld.co.uk

Types: Nonfiction
Formats: Articles; News
Subjects: Comedy / Humour; Nature
Markets: Adult

Publishes articles about cats and cat ownership.

M0124 Charleston Magazine
Magazine
PO Box 1794, Mount Pleasant, SC 29465-1794
United States
Tel: +1 (888) 242-7624

dshankland@charlestonmag.com

http://charlestonmag.com

Types: Nonfiction
Formats: Articles; News
Subjects: Arts; Culture; Current Affairs;
Gardening; Leisure; Lifestyle; Travel
Markets: Adult

Magazine covering the city of Charleston and
surrounding areas.

Editor: Darcy Shankland

M0125 Charleston Style and Design Magazine
Magazine
United States

publisher7@bellsouth.net

https://www.charlestonstyleanddesign.com
https://www.facebook.com/Charleston-Style-
Design-Magazine-108903839161607/
https://www.instagram.com/
chasstyleanddesign/
https://twitter.com/CharlestonSDMa1
https://www.pinterest.com/charlestonsdmag/

Types: Nonfiction
Formats: Articles
Subjects: Antiques; Architecture; Arts; Beauty;
Design; Fashion; Health; Lifestyle; Travel
Markets: Adult

Design and lifestyle magazine for the
Lowcountry, covering architects, designers and
builders, home projects, lifestyle trends,
restaurants, wines, fashions, art galleries, and
travel destinations.

Editor: Mary Love

M0126 Chat
Magazine
TI Media, 161 Marsh Wall, London, London,

E14 9AP
United Kingdom
Tel: +44 (0) 20 3148 5000

chat_magazine@ti-media.com

https://www.ti-media.com

Types: Nonfiction
Formats: Articles
Subjects: Comedy / Humour; Lifestyle;
Women's Interests
Markets: Adult

Send: Full text

General interest women's magazine. Approach
in writing with ideas only after becoming
familiar with the magazine and the kind of
material it publishes. No fiction.

M0127 CHEST
Magazine
2595 Patriot Boulevard, Glenview, IL 60026
United States
Tel: +1 (224) 521-9800
Fax: +1 (224) 521-9801

poetrychest@aol.com

https://journal.chestnet.org

Types: Nonfiction; Poetry
Formats: Articles; News
Subjects: Medicine
Markets: Professional

Send: Full text
How to send: Email

Medical journal for chest physicians. Also
publishes poetry up to 350 words relating to
the concerns of healthcare providers. Send
submissions by email. See website for full
details.

M0128 Cholla Needles
Magazine
United States

editor@chollaneedles.com

https://www.chollaneedles.com

Poetry > *Any Poetic Form*: Literary

Send: Full text
How to send: Email

We look for poetry that reaches readers, with a
special emphasis on poetry that readers desire
to return to. Each issue contains 10 distinctly
different poets, and we are very happy to
introduce new writers to our audience in each
issue. We have no restriction as to writing style
or format, but do expect that the work
submitted is ready for an audience. Payment in
US is by contributor's copy, and outside the
US is by pdf copy.

M0129 The Christian Science Monitor
Magazine
210 Massachusetts Avenue, Boston, MA

02115
United States
Tel: +1 (617) 450-2300

https://www.csmonitor.com

Types: Nonfiction
Formats: Articles; Essays; News
Subjects: Culture; Current Affairs; Finance; Literature; Nature; Religion; Science
Markets: Adult

Send: Full text

Accepts new writers' work on spec only. Approach via contact forms on website.

Editor: Mark Sappenfield

M0130 Christianity & Literature
Magazine
Department of English, Azusa Pacific University, 901 E. Alosta Avenue, Azusa, CA 91702-7000
United States

cal@apu.edu

https://www.christianityandliterature.com/journal

Types: Nonfiction; Poetry
Formats: Articles; Essays; Reviews
Subjects: Literature; Religion
Markets: Academic; Adult

Send: Full text

Journal devoted to the scholarly exploration of how literature engages Christian thought, experience, and practice. Submit articles and essays via online submission system. Send poems by post only. Book reviews by invitation only. See website for full details.

Editor: Mark Eaton

M0131 Church Music Quarterly
Magazine
RSCM, 19 The Close, Salisbury, Wiltshire, SP1 2EB
United Kingdom
Tel: +44 (0) 1722 424848

cmq@rscm.com

https://www.rscm.org.uk/our-resources/magazines/church-music-quarterly/

Nonfiction > *Articles:* Church Music

Send: Full text
How to send: Email; Post

Publishes reports, press releases and letters on or related to church music.

Editor: Esther Jones

M0132 The Cincinnati Review
Magazine
PO Box 210069, Cincinnati, Ohio 45221-0069
United States

editors@cincinnatireview.com

https://www.cincinnatireview.com/
https://facebook.com/CincinnatiReview
https://twitter.com/CincinnReview
https://www.youtube.com/channel/UCbDPomwAnBAddHtuKKh4HqA

Fiction > *Short Fiction:* Literary

Nonfiction > *Short Nonfiction*
Creative Nonfiction; Literary

Poetry in Translation > *Any Poetic Form*

Poetry > *Any Poetic Form*

How to send: Online submission system

Submit up to ten pages of poetry, up to forty pages of double-spaced fiction, or up to twenty pages of double-spaced literary nonfiction between September 1 and January 1. Accepts micro submissions year-round, except when accepting contest submissions.

Editors: Michael Griffith; Kristen Iversen; Rebecca Lindenberg

Fiction Editor: Brock Clarke

Managing Editor: Nicola Mason

Poetry Editor: Jim Cummins

M0133 Cirque
Magazine
United States

cirquejournal@gmail.com

https://cirquejournal.com

Fiction > *Short Fiction:* North Pacific Rim

Nonfiction
Reviews: North Pacific Rim
Short Nonfiction: North Pacific Rim

Poetry > *Any Poetic Form:* North Pacific Rim

Scripts > *Theatre Scripts:* North Pacific Rim

Send: Full text
How to send: Submittable

Publishes short stories, poems, creative nonfiction, translations, and plays by writers born in, or resident for at least five years in, the North Pacific Rim (Alaska, Washington, Oregon, Idaho, Montana, Hawaii, Yukon Territory, Alberta, and British Columbia). Submit via online submission system.

Editor: Sandra Kleven

M0134 Civil War Times
Magazine
United States

Magazine Publisher: HistoryNet LLC

M0135 Classic & Sports Car
Magazine
United Kingdom

https://www.classicandsportscar.com
https://www.facebook.com/candscmagazine

https://twitter.com/candscmagazine?lang=en
https://www.youtube.com/user/candscmagazine
https://www.instagram.com/classicandsportscar

Magazine Publisher: Haymarket Media Group

Nonfiction > *Articles*
Classic Cars; Sports Cars

Describes itself as "the world's best-selling classic car magazine, and the undisputed authority for anyone buying, owning, selling, maintaining or even just dreaming about classic cars".

Editor: James Elliott

Editor-in-Chief: Alastair Clements

M0136 Classical Singer
Magazine
PO Box 1710, Draper, UT 84020
United States

support@csmusic.net

https://csmusic.net

Types: Nonfiction
Formats: Articles; News
Subjects: Music
Markets: Professional

Magazine for professional classical singers.

M0137 Click
Magazine
United States

Magazine Publisher: Cricket Media, Inc.

M0138 Clubhouse Magazine
Magazine
Focus on the Family, 8605 Explorer Drive, Colorado Springs, CO 80920
United States
Tel: +1 (800) 232-6459

https://www.clubhousemagazine.com

Types: Fiction; Nonfiction
Formats: Essays; Interviews; Short Fiction
Subjects: Comedy / Humour; Fantasy; History; Religion; Science Fiction
Markets: Children's

Send: Full text

Magazine for boys and girls aged 8-12 providing wholesome, educational material with Scriptural or moral insight. Avoid bible stories, poems, and strictly informational pieces. See website for full guidelines.

Assistant Editor: Rachel Pfeiffer

M0139 Coin Collector
Magazine
United Kingdom

Magazine Publisher: Warners Group Publications

M0140 Coin News

Magazine
No 40, Southernhay East, Exeter, Devon, EX1
1PE
United Kingdom
Tel: +44 (0) 1404 46972

info@tokenpublishing.com

https://www.tokenpublishing.com

Types: Nonfiction
Formats: Articles; News
Subjects: Hobbies
Markets: Adult

Magazine covering coin collecting.

M0141 Collectors Magazine

Magazine
United Kingdom

Magazine Publisher: Warners Group
Publications

M0142 The Common Tongue Magazine

Online Magazine
United States

kade@commontonguezine.com

https://www.commontonguezine.com
https://twitter.com/commontonguemag
https://www.facebook.com/
commontonguezine/

Fiction > *Short Fiction*: Dark Fantasy

Nonfiction > *Articles*
   Fantasy; Writing

Poetry > *Any Poetic Form*: Dark Fantasy

Send: Full text
How to send: Online submission system

Writer's submissions must adhere to our
guidelines to be considered for publication in
our magazine. While we allow our writers a
vast amount of room for creativity and writer's
interpretation, we want to be sure that they
support us in our quest for retaining that dark,
dangerous tone that invokes our brand image.

We currently pay 0.03-0.06 cents USD per
word for successful submissions.

We invite all writers, regardless of level, to
submit their short story submissions. We
appreciate everyone's interest in the magazine
and seek to honor that interest. While we are
proud of being a leader in fantasy publications,
we are also foremost writers and artists, and so
we have extreme pride in supporting our
contributors and those that make this all
possible.

If you are interested in submitting short stories
to be published in our quarterly magazine,
please review the writer guidelines to be
considered on our website.

M0143 Condé Nast Traveller

Magazine
United Kingdom

https://www.cntraveller.com
https://www.facebook.com/CNTraveller/
https://twitter.com/cntraveller
https://www.instagram.com/condenasttraveller/
https://www.youtube.com/user/
condenasttraveller
https://www.pinterest.co.uk/cntraveller/

Magazine Publisher: Condé Nast Britain

Nonfiction > *Articles*: Travel

A luxury travel magazine aimed at the
upmarket, independent traveller.

Editor: Abigail Chisman

M0144 Conjunctions

Magazine
21 East 10th St., #3E, New York, NY 10003
United States

conjunctions@bard.edu

http://www.conjunctions.com
http://www.facebook.com/pages/Conjunctions/
133404885505
https://www.instagram.com/_conjunctions/
https://twitter.com/_conjunctions

Fiction > *Short Fiction*: Literary

Nonfiction > *Short Nonfiction*: Creative
Nonfiction

Poetry > *Any Poetic Form*

Closed to approaches.

Publishes short and long form fiction, poetry,
and creative nonfiction. No academic essays or
book reviews. Do not query or send samples –
submit complete ms through by post with
SASE. See website for full guidelines.

Editor: Bradford Morrow

M0145 Construction Equipment Guide

Magazine
470 Maryland Drive, Fort Washington, PA
19034
United States
Tel: +1 (800) 523-2200

cmongeau@cegltd.com

https://www.constructionequipmentguide.com

Types: Nonfiction
Formats: News
Subjects: Business; Technology
Markets: Professional

Covers the United States with four regional
newspapers offering construction industry
news and information, and new and used
construction equipment for sale.

Editors: Christine Allen; Craig Mongeau

M0146 Coping with Cancer Magazine

Magazine
PO Box 682268, Franklin, TN 37068-2268
United States
Tel: +1 (615) 790-2400

info@copingmag.com

https://www.copingmag.com

Types: Nonfiction; Poetry
Formats: Articles
Subjects: Health; Medicine
Markets: Adult

Send: Full text
How to send: Email

Publishes articles, poems, reflections, and
professional advice relating to cancer. See
website for full submission guidelines.

M0147 Copper Nickel

Magazine
United States

wayne.miller@ucdenver.edu

http://copper-nickel.org

Types: Fiction; Nonfiction; Poetry;
Translations
Formats: Essays; Short Fiction
Subjects: Literary
Markets: Adult

Send: Full text

Submit four to six poems, or one story or one
essay at a time. Wait at least six months
between submissions. Submit via online
submission system.

Fiction Editor: Teague Bohlen

Fiction Editor / Nonfiction Editor: Joanna
Luloff

Managing Editor: Wayne Miller

Poetry Editors: Brian Barker; Nicky Beer

M0148 The Corridor of Uncertainty

Magazine
United Kingdom

clarky@corridorofuncertainty.com

https://www.corridorofuncertainty.com
https://twitter.com/clarkyfanzine

Types: Nonfiction
Formats: Articles
Subjects: Sport
Markets: Adult

How to send: Email

A Yorkshire cricket fansite which encourages
discussion on Yorkshire cricket and cricket in
general.

Editor: James Buttler

M0149 Cosmopolitan

Magazine
House of Hearst, 30 Panton Street, London,
SW1Y 4AJ
United Kingdom
Tel: +44 (0) 1858 438423

cosmopolitan-UK@hearst.co.uk

https://www.cosmopolitan.com/uk
https://facebook.com/cosmopolitanuk
https://twitter.com/CosmopolitanUK
https://www.pinterest.com/cosmopolitanuk/
https://instagram.com/cosmopolitanuk
https://www.youtube.com/user/cosmopolitanuk

Magazine Publisher: Hearst Magazines UK

Nonfiction > *Articles*
Beauty; Current Affairs; Entertainment;
Fashion; Health; Politics; Relationships; Sex

Magazine aimed at modern-minded women in
their mid-twenties, including a range of
articles, particularly on careers, relationships,
and news.

Editor: Sam Baker

Features Editor: Catherine Gray

M0150 Country Life

Magazine
Pinehurst 2, Pinehurst Road, Farnborough
Business Park, Farnborough, Hants, GU14
7BF
United Kingdom
Tel: +44 (0) 1252 555062

mark.hedges@ti-media.com

https://www.countrylife.co.uk

Types: Nonfiction
Formats: Articles; News
Subjects: Architecture; Arts; Current Affairs;
Lifestyle; Nature; Sport
Markets: Adult

Magazine covering all aspects of country
living. Looks for strong, well informed
material rather than material by amateur
enthusiasts.

Editor: Mark Hedges

M0151 Country Living

Magazine
House of Hearst, 30 Panton Street, London,
SW1Y 4AJ
United Kingdom

https://www.countryliving.com
https://www.facebook.com/countrylivinguk
https://twitter.com/countrylivinguk
https://www.pinterest.com/UKcountryliving/
https://www.instagram.com/countrylivinguk/

Magazine Publisher: Hearst Magazines UK

Nonfiction > *Articles*
Country Lifestyle; Countryside; Crafts;
Houses; Nature; Recipes; Travel; Wellbeing

Magazine for people who love the country,
whether they live in it or not. Includes articles
on the countryside, wildlife, conservation,
gardens, houses, rural life, etc.

Editor: Susy Smith

M0152 Country Smallholding

Magazine
Archant SW, Unit 3, Old Station Road,
Barnstaple, EX32 8PB
United Kingdom
Tel: +44 (0) 1271 341652

editorial.csh@archant.co.uk

https://www.countrysmallholding.com/
https://www.facebook.com/
countrysmallholding
https://twitter.com/ctysmallholding

Nonfiction > *Articles*
Country Lifestyle; Countryside; Gardening;
Self-Sufficiency; Smallholdings

Magazine for smallholders, small farmers and
landowners, and those interested in both rural
and urban self-sufficiency.

Editor: Diane Cowgill

M0153 Cowboys & Indians

Magazine
Three Forest Plaza, 12221 Merit Drive, Suite
1610, Dallas, Texas 75251
United States
Tel: +1 (386) 246-0179

queries@cowboysindians.com

https://www.cowboysindians.com
https://www.facebook.com/cowboysindians/
http://pinterest.com/cowboysindians/
http://www.twitter.com/CI_Magazine
http://instagram.com/
cowboysindiansmagazine#

Nonfiction > *Articles*
American West; Arts; Culture;
Entertainment; Fashion; Food and Drink;
Houses; Ranch Lifestyle; Ranches; Travel

Magazine focusing on the past and present of
the American West, including both historical
and lifestyle material.

M0154 Crab Orchard Review

Magazine
Southern Illinois University, Department of
English, 1000 Faner Drive, Mail Code 4503,
Southern Illinois University Carbondale,
Carbondale, IL 62901
United States
Tel: +1 (618) 453-6833
Fax: +1 (618) 453-8224

https://craborchardreview.siu.edu

Fiction > *Short Fiction*

Nonfiction > *Essays*

Poetry > *Any Poetic Form*

Closed to approaches.

Closed to submissions for the foreseeable
future following the death of the editor in
December 2019. Check website for current
status.

Editors: Allison Joseph; Jon Tribble

Prose Editor: Carolyn Alessio

M0155 Crannog Magazine

Magazine
Ireland

submissions@crannogmagazine.com

http://www.crannogmagazine.com

Fiction > *Short Fiction*: Literary

Poetry > *Any Poetic Form*

Send: Full text

A literary magazine publishing fiction and
poetry only. No reviews or nonfiction.
Published twice yearly in March and
September. Accepts submissions in June and
November. Authors who have been previously
published in the magazine are recommended to
purchase a copy of the current issue (or take
out a subscription); for authors who have not
been previously published in the magazine this
is a requirement. Send up to one story or up to
three poems by email only. No postal
submissions.

Editor: Sandra Bunting, Tony O'Dwyer, Ger
Burke, Jarlath Fahy

M0156 Crazyhorse

Magazine
Department of English, College of Charleston,
66 George Street, Charleston, SC 29424
United States
Tel: +1 (843) 953-4470

crazyhorse@cofc.edu

https://crazyhorse.cofc.edu
https://www.facebook.com/
CrazyhorseLiteraryJournal
https://twitter.com/crazyhorselitjo

Fiction > *Short Fiction*

Nonfiction > *Short Nonfiction*: Creative
Nonfiction

Poetry > *Any Poetic Form*

Send: Full text
How to send: Submittable

Costs: A fee is charged upon submission.
$3.00.

Send between 2,500 and 8,500 words of prose
or 3-5 poems via online submission system.
Accepts submissions between September 1 and
May 31 (except for January).

Editor: Garrett Doherty

M0157 Creative Knitting

Magazine
United States

https://www.creativeknittingmagazine.com

Types: Nonfiction
Subjects: Crafts; Design; Hobbies
Markets: Adult

Knitting magazine, featuring clear instructions for classic and current trends in knitting design.

M0158 Crimewave

Magazine
United Kingdom

http://www.ttapress.com/crimewave/

Magazine Publisher / Book Publisher: TTA Press (**P0878**)

Fiction > *Short Fiction*
  Crime; Mystery

Send: Full text
How to send: Submittable

Publishes crime and mystery short stories. See website for complete guidelines.

Editor: Andy Cox

M0159 Critical Quarterly

Magazine
Newbury, Crediton, Devon, EX17 5HA
United Kingdom

CQpoetry@gmail.com

http://onlinelibrary.wiley.com/journal/10.1111/(ISSN)1467-8705

Types: Fiction; Nonfiction; Poetry
Formats: Essays; Short Fiction
Subjects: Culture; Literary; Literary Criticism
Markets: Adult

Send: Full text
How to send: Email

Publishes literary criticism, cultural studies, poetry and fiction. Send submissions by email. See website for separate email address for submissions of criticism.

Editors: Clare Bucknell; Colin MacCabe

M0160 CrossStitcher

Magazine
United Kingdom

Magazine Publisher: Warners Group Publications

M0161 Cruising World

Magazine
55 Hammarlund Way, Middletown, RI 02842
United States
Tel: +1 (401) 845-5100
Fax: +1 (401) 845-5180

editor@cruisingworld.com

https://www.cruisingworld.com
https://www.facebook.com/cruisingworld/
https://twitter.com/cruisingworld/
https://www.instagram.com/cruisingworldmag/
https://www.youtube.com/c/cruisingworld

Nonfiction > *Articles*
  Boats; Sailing

Send: Full text
How to send: Email

Magazine for owners of sailboats between 20 and 50 feet in length. Authors should familiarise themselves with the magazine before approaching.

M0162 Crystal Magazine

Magazine
3 Bowness Avenue, Prenton, Birkenhead, CH43 0SD
United Kingdom
Tel: +44 (0) 1516 089736

christinecrystal@hotmail.com

http://www.christinecrystal.blogspot.com

Fiction > *Short Fiction*
  Adventure; Comedy / Humour; Fantasy; Horror; Mystery; Romance; Science Fiction; Suspense; Thrillers; Westerns

Nonfiction > *Articles*
  Comedy / Humour; Hobbies; Literature; Nature; Travel

Poetry > *Any Poetic Form*

Send: Full text
How to send: Email

CRYSTAL MAGAZINE: A4, 40-page, spiral-bound bi-monthly

FOR: subscribers only

CONTENTS: poems, stories (true and fiction) and articles

COLOUR IMAGES: carefully selected to enhance work

WORDSMITHING: a very popular regular feature written just for the Magazine

LETTERS: usually pages

NEWS: an opportunity to share writing achievements

EXTRA: occasionally free booklets, bumper issues, gifts

COMPETITIONS: open to everyone

Editor: Christine Carr

M0163 Cumbria

Magazine
Country Publications Limited, The Gatehouse, Skipton Castle, Skipton, BD23 1AL
United Kingdom
Tel: +44 (0) 1756 701381
Fax: +44 (0) 1756 701326

johnm@dalesman.co.uk

http://www.cumbriamagazine.co.uk

Types: Nonfiction
Formats: Articles
Subjects: Nature; Travel
Markets: Adult

Regional magazine focusing on the nature of and walks in the Lake District.

Editor: John Manning

M0164 Curve

Magazine
United States

editor@curvemag.com

http://www.curvemag.com

Types: Nonfiction
Formats: Articles; Film Scripts; News; TV Scripts
Subjects: Culture; Entertainment; Lifestyle; Literature
Markets: Adult

Magazine of lesbian culture, entertainment, and lifestyle.

Editor: Merryn Johns

M0165 Cyphers

Magazine
3 Selskar Terrace, Ranelagh, Dublin 6
Ireland

letters@cyphers.ie

http://www.cyphers.ie

Types: Fiction; Poetry; Translations
Formats: Short Fiction
Subjects: Literary
Markets: Adult

Send: Full text
How not to send: Email

Publishes poetry and fiction in English and Irish, from Ireland and around the world. Translations are welcome. No unsolicited critical articles. Submissions by post only. Attachments sent by email will be deleted. See website for full guidelines.

M0166 Daily Science Fiction

Magazine
United States

https://dailysciencefiction.com

Types: Fiction
Formats: Short Fiction
Subjects: Fantasy; Science Fiction
Markets: Adult

Send: Full text

Publishes speculative fiction stories from 100 to 1,500 words, including science fiction, fantasy, slipstream, etc. Send submissions through online submissions system

M0167 DairyBusiness

Magazine
1350C W Southport Road Suite 297,
Indianapolis, IN 46217
United States
Tel: +1 (317) 721-4694

WebContact@DairyBusiness.com

https://www.dairybusiness.com

Types: Nonfiction
Formats: Articles; Interviews
Subjects: Business; Nature
Markets: Professional

Magazine covering the large-herd commercial dairy industry.

M0168 Dalesman

Magazine
The Gatehouse, Skipton Castle, Skipton, North Yorkshire, BD23 1AL
United Kingdom
Tel: +44 (0) 1756 701033

jon@dalesman.co.uk

http://www.dalesman.co.uk

Book Publisher / Magazine Publisher:
Dalesman Publishing Co. Ltd (**P0209**)

Nonfiction > *Articles:* Yorkshire

Magazine publishing material of Yorkshire interest.

Editor: Paul Jackson

M0169 The Dalhousie Review

Magazine
Dalhousie University, Halifax, Nova Scotia, B3H 4R2
Canada

dalhousie.review@dal.ca

https://ojs.library.dal.ca/dalhousiereview

Types: Fiction; Nonfiction; Poetry
Formats: Essays; Reviews; Short Fiction
Subjects: Literary
Markets: Adult

Send: Full text
How to send: Email

Publishes fiction, poetry, essays, and book reviews. Submit up to five poems at a time. Query before submitting reviews. See website for full submission guidelines.

M0170 Dame

Magazine
United States

editorial@damemagazine.com

https://www.damemagazine.com

Types: Nonfiction
Formats: Articles; Essays; News
Subjects: Arts; Business; Culture; Finance; Health; Nature; Politics; Science; Technology; Women's Interests
Markets: Adult

Magazine of news and opinion from a female perspective.

Editor: Kera Bolonik

M0171 Dancing Times

Magazine
United Kingdom
Tel: +44 (0) 20 7250 3006

https://www.facebook.com/1dancingtimes/
https://twitter.com/dancingtimes

Nonfiction
Articles: Dance
News: Dance
Reviews: Dance

Monthly magazine of dance, publishing features, news, and review.

M0172 DargonZine

Magazine
United States

editor@dargonzine.org

http://dargonzine.org

Types: Fiction
Formats: Short Fiction
Subjects: Fantasy
Markets: Adult

Send: Full text

Electronic magazine publishing fantasy fiction based in a shared world, where authors write in a common milieu, sharing settings, mythos, and characters. To submit, writers need to join (free until a year after first publication) and work with a mentor to produce a piece of work that will fit the shared world.

M0173 The Dark Horse

Magazine
3A Blantyre Mill Road, Bothwell, South Lanarkshire, G71 8DD
United Kingdom

http://thedarkhorsemagazine.com

Types: Poetry
Subjects: Literary
Markets: Adult

Send: Full text

International literary magazine committed to British, Irish and American poetry. Send submissions by post only, to UK or US editorial addresses. No simultaneous submissions. See website for full guidelines.

Editor: Gerry Cambridge

M0174 Dark Tales

Magazine
7 Offley Street, Worcester, WR3 8BH
United Kingdom

stories@darktales.co.uk

http://www.darktales.co.uk

Fiction > *Short Fiction*
Horror; Speculative

Send: Full text
How to send: Email; Post

Costs: A fee is charged upon submission; Offers services that writers have to pay for.

Created as an outlet primarily for unpublished writers of sci-fi, dark fantasy and horror short stories. Published stories are the winners and shortlisted entries from the monthly competition (£4 entry fee). Also offers optional critiques.

Editor: Sean Jeffery

M0175 Darts World

Magazine
United Kingdom

info@dartsworld.com

https://www.dartsworld.com
https://www.facebook.com/dartsworldmagazine
https://twitter.com/darts_world

Nonfiction
Articles: Darts
News: Darts

Publishes articles and news on the subject of darts only.

Editor: Tony Wood

M0176 The Dawntreader

Magazine
24 Forest Houses, Halwill, Beaworthy, Devon, EX21 5UU
United Kingdom

dawnidp@gmail.com

https://www.indigodreams.co.uk/the-dawntreader

Types: Fiction; Nonfiction; Poetry
Formats: Articles; Short Fiction
Subjects: Literary; Nature; Spirituality
Markets: Adult

Send: Full text

A quarterly publication specialising in myth, legend; in the landscape, nature; spirituality and love; the mystic, the environment. Welcomes poetry up to 40 lines, and prose, articles, and local legends up to 1,000 words.

Editor: Ronnie Goodyer

M0177 Decision

Magazine
United States

https://decisionmagazine.com
https://www.facebook.com/Decisionmagazine/
https://twitter.com/DecisionNews

Nonfiction
 Articles: Christianity; Evangelism; Politics
 News: Christianity; Evangelism; Politics

Magazine publishing news and articles of relevance to Christians and evangelism.

Editor: Bob Paulson

M0178 Deracine

Magazine
United States

deracinemagazine@gmail.com

http://deracinemagazine.wordpress.com

Types: Fiction; Poetry
Subjects: Contemporary; Experimental; Gothic; Literary; Literature
Markets: Adult; Professional; Young Adult

Send: Full text
How to send: Email

A literary magazine featuring dark, psychological fiction, poetry, and art. Started in 2017, we are a nonprofit publication. Our goal is to share literature that raises awareness of and expresses psychological issues and feelings of displacement through the literary gothic. We're open to a variety of styles, including writing that is minimalistic or that has elements of fantasy or horror, so long as it fits within our theme.

Editor: Victoria Elghasen and Michelle Baleka

M0179 Descant

Magazine
c/o TCU Department of English, Box 297270, 2850 S. University Dr., Fort Worth, TX 76129
United States

descant@tcu.edu

https://descant.tcu.edu

Types: Fiction; Poetry
Formats: Short Fiction
Subjects: Literary
Markets: Adult

Send: Full text

Submit one story up to 5,000 words, or up to five poems via online submission system, or by post with SASE. Closed to submissions in April, May, June, July, and August. See website for full guidelines.

M0180 Diecast Collection

Magazine
United Kingdom

Magazine Publisher: Warners Group Publications

M0181 Digital Engineering

Magazine
111 Speen Street, Ste 200, Framingham MA 01701

United States
Tel: +1 (508) 663-1500

de-editors@digitaleng.news

http://www.digitaleng.news

Types: Nonfiction
Formats: Articles; News
Subjects: Design; Technology
Markets: Professional

Magazine covering the use of computers and other digital technology for design / engineering.

M0182 Diver Magazine

Magazine
Suite B, 74 Oldfield Road, Hampton, Middlesex, TW12 2HR
United Kingdom
Tel: +44 (0) 20 8941 8152

nigel@divermag.co.uk

https://divernet.com/contact/

Formats: Articles; News
Subjects: Hobbies; Sport; Technology; Travel
Markets: Adult

Magazine covering every aspect of recreational scuba diving, especially in the realms of gear testing and surveys, diving holiday destinations, and advances in technology and techniques.

M0183 Dogs Monthly

Magazine
The Old Print House, 62 The High Street, Chobham, Surrey, GU24 8AA
United Kingdom
Tel: +44 (0) 1276 858880

https://dogsmonthly.co.uk
https://www.facebook.com/DogsMonthly
https://www.instagram.com/dogsmonthlymagazine/
https://twitter.com/dogsmonthly

Nonfiction > *Articles*: Dogs

Send: Query
How to send: Online contact form; Phone; Post

Magazine for dog enthusiasts publishing articles on breeds, topical news, and features. Contact through form on website, or by phone or post in first instance.

Editor: Caroline Davis

M0184 Dolls House and Miniature Scene

Magazine
United Kingdom

Magazine Publisher: Warners Group Publications

M0185 Dorset Life

Magazine
7, The Leanne, Sandford Lane, Wareham,

Dorset, BH20 4DY
United Kingdom
Tel: +44 (0) 1929 551264

editor@dorsetlife.co.uk

https://www.dorsetlife.co.uk

Types: Nonfiction
Formats: Articles
Markets: Adult

County magazine for Dorset.

Editor: Joël Lacey

M0186 Downstate Story

Magazine
1825 Maple Ridge, Peoria, IL 61614
United States
Tel: +1 (309) 688-1409

ehopkins7@prodigy.net

https://www.downstatestory.com

Types: Fiction
Formats: Short Fiction
Subjects: Literary
Markets: Adult

A regional magazine featuring mostly writers from Illinois and the Midwest. As of 2012, online only.

Editor: Elaine Hopkins

M0187 The Drake Magazine

Magazine
PO Box 11546, Denver, CO 80211
United States
Tel: +1 (303) 917-9006

info@drakemag.com

https://drakemag.com/
https://www.instagram.com/thedrakemagazine/
https://twitter.com/Drakemagazine
https://www.facebook.com/TheDrakeMagazine/
http://feeds.feedburner.com/Drakemag

Nonfiction > *Articles*: Fishing

Send: Query
Don't send: Full text
How to send: Post; Email

Fishing magazine publishing educational and entertaining fishing stories. Does not publish how-to and where-to stories, but rather pieces which tell stories in a literary way. See website for details.

Editor: Tom Bie

M0188 Dream Catcher

Magazine
109 Wensley Drive, Leeds, LS7 2LU
United Kingdom
Tel: +44 (0) 1904 733767

dreamcatchersubmissions@gmail.com

http://www.dreamcatchermagazine.co.uk

Types: Fiction; Nonfiction; Poetry; Translations
Formats: Interviews; Reviews; Short Fiction
Subjects: Literary
Markets: Adult

Send: Full text
How to send: Post

Send submissions by post, following guidelines on website. No electronic submissions.

Editor: Wendy Pratt

M0189 The Dublin Review
Magazine
PO Box 7948, Dublin 1
Ireland

enquiry@thedublinreview.com

https://thedublinreview.com

Types: Fiction; Nonfiction
Formats: Essays; Short Fiction
Subjects: Literary; Literary Criticism
Markets: Adult

Send: Full text

Publishes essays, criticism, reportage, and fiction for a general, intelligent readership. No poetry. Accepts submissions by post with email address for response, but prefers submissions by via form on website. Physical material is not returned, so do not include return postage. No response without email address.

M0190 E/The Environmental Magazine
Online Magazine
United States

http://www.emagazine.com
https://www.facebook.com/askearthtalk/
https://twitter.com/EEnviroMag

Nonfiction
 Articles: Environment; Nature; Sustainable Living
 News: Environment

Send: Query
How to send: Online contact form

Former print magazine (now online only) focusing on environmental issues, dispensing news and information and advising people on how they can make a difference. Potential contributors should query in the first instance via contact form on website.

Editor: Jim Motavalli

M0191 EAP: The Magazine
Magazine
United States

tod@exterminatingangel.com

http://exterminatingangel.com/eap-the-magazine/

Types: Fiction; Poetry
Formats: Short Fiction
Subjects: Literary
Markets: Adult

Online publication established in 2012. See website for latest issue and next deadline for submissions.

Editor: Tod Davies

M0192 Early American Life
Magazine
Firelands Media Group LLC, 16759 West Park Circle Drive, Chagrin Falls, Ohio 44023
United States
Tel: +1 (440) 543-8566

queries@firelandsmedia.com

https://www.ealonline.com

Types: Nonfiction
Formats: Articles
Subjects: Antiques; Architecture; Crafts; History
Markets: Adult

Send: Full text
How to send: Email

Magazine aimed at people with an interest in the style of the period 1600-1840 in America, and its use in their modern homes and lives. Covers architecture, antiques, etc. Will consider unsolicited mss but prefers initial queries by email.

M0193 Economica
Magazine
United Kingdom

economica@lse.ac.uk

https://onlinelibrary.wiley.com/journal/14680335

Types: Nonfiction
Formats: Articles
Subjects: Business; Finance
Markets: Academic

Send: Full text
How to send: Email

Academic journal or economics. See website for submission guidelines.

Editors: Nava Ashraf; Oriana Bandiera; Tim Besley; Francesco Caselli; Maitreesh Ghatak; Stephen Machin; Ian Martin; Gianmarco Ottaviano

M0194 The Economist
Magazine
The Adelphi, 1-11 John Adam Street, London, WC2N 6HT
United Kingdom
Tel: +44 (0) 20 7830 7000

https://www.economist.com
https://www.facebook.com/theeconomist
https://www.instagram.com/theeconomist

https://www.twitter.com/theeconomist
https://www.linkedin.com/company/the-economist
https://www.youtube.com/user/economistmagazine

Nonfiction
 Articles: Business; Current Affairs; Finance; Politics
 News: Business; Current Affairs; Finance; Politics

Magazine covering economics, business, finance, politics, and current affairs.

M0195 Ecotone
Magazine
Department of Creative Writing, University of North Carolina Wilmington, 601 South College Road, Wilmington, NC 28403-5938
United States

info@ecotonejournal.com

https://ecotonemagazine.org

Types: Fiction; Nonfiction; Poetry
Subjects: Literary
Markets: Adult

Send: Full text

Publishes work from a wide range of voices. Particularly interested in hearing from writers historically underrepresented in literary publishing and in place-based contexts: people of colour, Indigenous people, people with disabilities, gender-nonconforming people, LGBTQIA+, women, and others. Check website for specific reading periods and submit prose up to 30 double-spaced pages or 3-5 poems by post with SAE or using online system ($3 charge). No hard copy submissions from outside the US.

Editor: David Gessner

M0196 Edinburgh Review
Magazine
United Kingdom

https://edinburgh-review.com
https://www.facebook.com/Edinburgh-Review-202034306209/
https://twitter.com/EdinburghReview

Fiction > *Short Fiction*: Literary

Nonfiction > *Essays*
 Arts; Culture; Literary Criticism; Literature; Philosophy; Politics

Poetry > *Any Poetic Form*

Closed to approaches.

Publishes Scottish and international fiction and accessible essays on the relationship of philosophy to the visual and literary arts.

Editor: Brian McCabe

M0197 Edison Literary Review

Magazine
13 Waverly Drive East, Edison, NJ 08817
United States

http://edisonliteraryreview.org

Types: Poetry
Subjects: Literary
Markets: Adult

Submit 3-5 poems. Poems under 40 lines stand a better chance of acceptance. Will accept submissions by post with SASE, but prefers submissions via form on website.

M0198 The Ekphrastic Review

Online Magazine
Canada

theekphrasticreview@gmail.com

https://www.ekphrastic.net

Fiction > *Short Fiction*

Nonfiction
Articles: Arts
Interviews: Literature
Reviews: Literature
Short Nonfiction: General

Poetry in Translation > *Any Poetic Form:* Arts

Poetry > *Any Poetic Form:* Arts

Send: Full text
How to send: Email

Publishes poetry that responds to, explores, or is inspired by a piece of art, and fiction and nonfiction of any kind, including book interviews or profiles, and articles about ekphrastic writing. Accepts submissions during specific windows only (see website for details).

Editor: Lorette C. Luzajic

M0199 El Portal

Magazine
United States

el.portal@enmu.edu

https://elportaljournal.com

Types: Fiction; Nonfiction; Poetry
Formats: Essays; Short Fiction
Subjects: Literary
Markets: Adult

Send: Full text
How to send: Email

Accepts submissions of flash fiction up to 500 words, short stories and creative nonfiction up to 4,000 words, or up to five poems, by email. See website for full guidelines.

Editor: Jennifer Baros

M0200 Electronic Musician

Magazine
NewBay Media, LLC, 28 East 28th Street,
12th floor, New York, NY 10016
United States

gino@ginorobair.com

https://www.emusician.com

Types: Nonfiction
Formats: Articles; News; Reviews
Subjects: Business; Music; Technology
Markets: Adult

Magazine covering all aspects of music production: performance, recording, and technology. Includes product news and reviews on the latest equipment and services, tips and techniques, gear reviews, and insights from top artists.

Editor: Gino Robair

M0201 The Elks Magazine

Magazine
425 West Diversey Parkway, Chicago, IL 60614
United States

magnews@elks.org

https://www.elks.org/elksmag/

Nonfiction > *Articles*
Americana; Finance; Health; History; Leisure; Nature; Retirement; Science; Sport; Technology

Send: Full text; Self-Addressed Stamped Envelope (SASE)
How to send: Post; Email

Publishes features of general interest. Seeks articles that are fresh, thought provoking, well researched, and well documented. Typical readership consists of individuals over 40, with some college, an above-average income, from towns of half a million or less. Send submissions by email or by post with SASE. No religious, political, or first-person articles, or poetry.

Editor: Anna L. Idol

M0202 Elle

Magazine
30 Panton Street, Leicester Square, London, SW1Y 4AJ
United Kingdom
Tel: +44 (0) 1858 438796

ellefeatures@elleuk.com

https://www.elle.com/uk/
https://www.facebook.com/ELLEuk
https://twitter.com/ELLEUK
https://www.pinterest.com/ellemag/
https://www.instagram.com/elleuk/
https://www.youtube.com/user/ELLEUKTV

Magazine Publisher: Hearst Magazines UK

Nonfiction
Articles: Beauty; Culture; Fashion; Horoscopes; Lifestyle
News: Celebrity

Send: Query; Author bio
How to send: Email

For features, send query with CV by email.

Editor: Lorraine Candy

Features Editor: Anna Pursglove

M0203 Empire

Magazine
United Kingdom

https://www.empireonline.com
http://facebook.com/empiremagazine
http://twitter.com/empiremagazine

Magazine Publisher: H Bauer Publishing

Nonfiction
Articles: Cinemas / Movie Theaters; Film Industry; Films; Technology
News: Cinemas / Movie Theaters; Film Industry; Films; Technology
Reviews: Films; Technology

Magazine of films and film-makers, as well as some attention to supporting technologies. Publishes behind-the-scenes articles, news, and reviews.

Editor: Colin Kennedy

M0204 Emrys Journal

Magazine
The Emrys Foundation, 201 West Stone Avenue, Suite D, Greenville, SC 29609
United States
Tel: +1 (864) 202-4906

info@emrys.org

http://www.emrys.org

Types: Fiction; Nonfiction; Poetry
Formats: Short Fiction
Subjects: Literary
Markets: Adult

Send: Full text

Literary journal publishing fiction, poetry, and creative nonfiction. Submit up to three poems or prose up to 5,000 words between August 1 and November 1 annually, via online submission system. No postal submissions. $250 awarded to one piece selected from each category.

Editor: Katherine Burgess

M0205 Enchanted Living

Magazine
United States

submissions@faeriemag.com

https://enchantedlivingmag.com

Types: Fiction; Nonfiction; Poetry
Formats: Articles
Subjects: Arts; Beauty; Crafts; Design; Fantasy; Fashion; Nature; Travel
Markets: Adult

Send: Full text
How to send: Email

A quarterly print magazine that celebrates all things enchanted. Publishes photography, recipes, original fiction and poetry, travel pieces, artist profiles, home decor, otherworldly beauty tips, craft tutorials, and more. Send submissions by email. See website for specific email address for poetry.

M0206 **The Engravers Journal**
Magazine
P.O. Box 318, Brighton, MI 48116-0318
United States
Tel: +1 (810) 229-5725
Fax: +1 (810) 229-8320

editor@engraversjournal.com

http://www.engraversjournal.com

Types: Nonfiction
Formats: Articles
Subjects: Business; How To; Technology
Markets: Professional

Magazine offering practical advice and trade-oriented articles for the recognition and personalisation industry.

M0207 **Entrepreneur**
Magazine
18061 Fitch, Irvine CA, 92614
United States

https://www.entrepreneur.com/
https://www.facebook.com/EntMagazine
https://twitter.com/entrepreneur
https://www.linkedin.com/company/
entrepreneur-media
https://www.pinterest.com/entrepreneurmedia
https://www.instagram.com/entrepreneur/
https://www.youtube.com/user/
EntrepreneurOnline

Nonfiction > *Articles*
Business; Entrepreneurship; Finance; How To

Magazine for people who have started and are running their own business, providing news o current trends, practical how-to articles, features on combining work and life, etc. Runs features and several regular columns, as well as an inner magazine on start-ups.

Editor: Karen Axelton

M0208 **EQy Magazine (Scottish Equestrian Year)**
Magazine
Wyvex Media, Fettes Park, 496 Ferry Road, Edinburgh, EH5 2DL
United Kingdom
Tel: +44 (0) 1315 511000

heddy@eqymagazine.co.uk

https://www.eqymagazine.co.uk

Types: Nonfiction
Subjects: Nature
Markets: Adult

Luxury magazine published once a year, covering Scottish equestrianism.

M0209 **Erotic Review**
Magazine
United Kingdom

editorial@ermagazine.org

http://eroticreviewmagazine.com

Types: Fiction; Nonfiction
Formats: Articles; Reviews; Short Fiction
Subjects: Erotic; Lifestyle
Markets: Adult

Send: Full text
How to send: Email

Literary lifestyle publication about sex and sexuality aimed at sophisticated, intelligent and mature readers. Print version has been retired and is now online only. Publishes features, articles, short stories, and reviews. See website for full submission guidelines.

Editor / Literary Agent: Jamie Maclean
(L0903)

M0210 **Essence**
Magazine
241 37th Street, 4th floor, Brooklyn, NY 11232
United States

toletters@essence.com

http://www.essence.com

Types: Nonfiction
Formats: Articles
Subjects: Beauty; Culture; Entertainment; Fashion; Health; Lifestyle; Politics
Markets: Adult

Magazine of black culture.

M0211 **Event**
Magazine
PO Box 2503, New Westminster, BC, V3L 5B2
Canada
Tel: +1 (604) 527-5293

event@douglascollege.ca

http://event.douglas.bc.ca

Types: Fiction; Nonfiction; Poetry
Formats: Reviews
Subjects: Literary
Markets: Adult

Closed to approaches.

Closed to submissions as at October 2019. Check website for current status. Send one story or up to eight poems via online submission system only. Occasional

unsolicited reviews published – query before submitting.

M0212 **Fabula Argentea**
Magazine
United States

fabargmagazine@gmail.com

https://www.fabulaargentea.com

Types: Fiction
Formats: Short Fiction
Markets: Adult

Send: Full text

Online magazine publishing fiction up to 8,000 words. Submit via online submission system.

M0213 **Faces**
Magazine
1751 Pinnacle Drive, Suite 600, McLean, VA 22102
United States

faces@cricketmedia.com

http://cricketmedia.com/Faces-travel-magazine-for-kids

Magazine Publisher: Cricket Media, Inc.

CHILDREN'S
Fiction > *Short Fiction:* Folklore, Myths, and Legends

Nonfiction
Articles: Culture; Lifestyle; Travel
Interviews: Culture; Lifestyle; Travel

Send: Query
Don't send: Full text
How to send: Email

Magazine for children aged 9-14 covering the ways in which people living in other countries and cultures live. All issues are themed so essential to check upcoming themes before querying. Send query with one-page outline of proposed article and detailed bibliography of materials. See website for full details.

Editor: Elizabeth Crooker Carpentiere

M0214 **Families First**
Magazine
Mothers' Union Publishing, Mary Sumner House, 24 Tufton Street, London, SW1P 3RB
United Kingdom
Tel: +44 (0) 20 7222 5533
Fax: +44 (0) 20 7227 9737

mu@mothersunion.org

https://www.mothersunion.org/FamiliesFirst

Types: Nonfiction
Formats: Articles
Subjects: Lifestyle; Religion
Markets: Adult

Publishes features on family life, social issues, marriage, Christian faith, etc. No fiction or poetry.

Editor: Catherine Butcher

M0215 Farm & Ranch Living

Magazine
1610 North 2nd Street, Suite 102, Milwaukee, WI 53212
United States

feedback@farmandranchliving.com

http://www.farmandranchliving.com

PROFESSIONAL > **Nonfiction** > *Articles*: Farming

Send: Full text
How to send: Online submission system

Reader-written magazine about farming and life on a ranch, publishing personal stories and photographs. Submit via online submission system.

M0216 Farming Magazine

Magazine
United States
Tel: +1 (330) 674-1892

editor@farmingmagazine.net

https://www.farmingmagazine.net

Types: Nonfiction
Formats: Articles
Subjects: Lifestyle; Nature
Markets: Adult; Professional

Send: Full text
How to send: Email

Magazine that celebrates the joys of farming well and living well on a small, ecologically-conscious scale.

M0217 Fashion x Film

Magazine
United States

info@fashionxfilm.com

https://fashionxfilm.com

Types: Nonfiction
Formats: Articles; Film Scripts
Subjects: Beauty; Culture; Fashion
Markets: Academic; Adult

Send: Full text
How to send: Email

Online publication dedicated to unravelling the hidden meaning of fashion in film, be it through a single work, a director's oeuvre, or some common theme. Aims for an academic, cerebral tone. Send queries or complete submissions by email. See website for full guidelines.

M0218 Faultline

Magazine
UCI Department of English, 435 Humanities Instructional Building, Irvine, CA 92697-2650
United States
Tel: +1 (949) 824-1573

faultline@uci.edu
ucifaultline@gmail.com

https://faultline.sites.uci.edu/
https://www.facebook.com/uci.faultline
https://twitter.com/faultline_journ

Fiction in Translation > *Short Fiction*

Fiction > *Short Fiction*

Nonfiction in Translation > *Short Nonfiction*: Creative Nonfiction

Nonfiction > *Short Nonfiction*: Creative Nonfiction

Poetry in Translation > *Any Poetic Form*

Poetry > *Any Poetic Form*

Send: Full text
How to send: Submittable

Send up to five poems or up to 20 pages of fiction or creative nonfiction, between October 15 and December 15 only.

Fiction Editor: Sara Joyce Robinson

Poetry Editor: Lisa P. Sutton

M0219 FellowScript

Magazine
c/o Box 463, Glendon, Alberta
Canada
Tel: +1 (780) 646-3068

fellowscripteditor2@gmail.com

https://inscribe.org/fellowscript/

Types: Nonfiction; Poetry
Formats: Articles; Reviews
Subjects: Hobbies; Religion
Markets: Adult

Magazine for Christian writers. Includes articles and book and market reviews of interest to writers, and also poetry. See website for full guidelines.

Editor: Nina Morey

M0220 Feminist Studies

Magazine
4137 Susquehannna Hall, 4200 Lehigh Road, University of Maryland, College Park, MD 20742
United States
Tel: +1 (301) 405-7415
Fax: +1 (301) 405-8395

info@feministstudies.org
submit@feministstudies.org
creative@feministstudies.org
art@feministstudies.org
review@feministstudies.org

http://www.feministstudies.org

ACADEMIC > **Nonfiction** > *Essays*
Cultural Criticism; Literary Criticism

ADULT
Fiction > *Short Fiction*: Feminism

Nonfiction > *Articles*

Arts; Culture; Feminism

Poetry > *Any Poetic Form*: Feminism

Send: Full text; Proposal; Writing sample; Author bio
How to send: Email

Feminist journal publishing research and criticism, creative writing, art, essays, and other forms of writing and visual expression. See website for submission guidelines and specific submission email addresses.

M0221 Fenland Poetry Journal

Magazine
PO Box 234, Wisbech, PE14 4EZ
United Kingdom

fenlandpoetryjournal@gmail.com

https://fenlandpoetryjournal.co.uk

Poetry > *Any Poetic Form*
Contemporary; Literary

Closed to approaches.

Contemporary poetry journal accepting submissions from anywhere in the world, though particularly encouraged from Fenland. No line limits. Send up to six poems by post only with SASE. No email submissions.

M0222 FHM

Online Magazine
United Kingdom

editor@fhm.com

http://www.fhm.com

Nonfiction
Articles: Cars; Entertainment; Fashion; Lifestyle; Sex; Sport
Interviews: General

Formerly the world's best-selling print male lifestyle magazine, now an online magazine.

Editor: Ross Brown

M0223 Fiction

Magazine
c/o Department of English, City College of New York, Convent Ave. at 138th Street, New York, NY 10031
United States

fictionmageditors@gmail.com

http://www.fictioninc.com
http://submissions.fictioninc.com/
http://instagram.com/fiction.magazine
https://twitter.com/fictionmag
https://www.facebook.com/fiction.mag/

Fiction > *Short Fiction*: Literary

Send: Full text
How to send: Online submission system; Post
How not to send: Email

Accepts short stories, novelettes, and novellas of any length (though staying under 5,000 words is encouraged). Submit by post or using online submission system between October 15 and April 15 only.

Editor: Mark J. Mirsky

M0224 The Fiddlehead

Magazine
Campus House, 11 Garland Court, University of New Brunswick, PO Box 4400, Fredericton NB, E3B 5A3
Canada
Tel: +1 (506) 453-3501

fiddlehd@unb.ca

https://thefiddlehead.ca
https://twitter.com/TheFiddlehd
http://www.facebook.com/pages/The-Fiddlehead-Atlantic-Canadas-International-Literary-Journal/174825212565312

Fiction
   Novel Excerpts; *Short Fiction*
Nonfiction > *Short Nonfiction*: Creative Nonfiction

Poetry > *Any Poetic Form*

Send: Query; Author bio; Full text; Self-Addressed Stamped Envelope (SASE)
How to send: Submittable; Post

Publishes poetry, fiction, and creative nonfiction in a variety of styles, including experimental genres. Also publishes excerpts from longer works, and reviews. Submit up to six poems, or a piece of fiction up to 6,000 words. All submissions must be original and unpublished. Prefers submissions through online submission system (Feb 15 to April 30 and Sep 15 to November 30 only), but will accept submissions by post. See website for full details.

M0225 Film Review

Online Magazine
United States

https://filmreviewonline.com
https://www.facebook.com/Film-Review-Online-139186982814321

Nonfiction
   Interviews: Celebrity; Entertainment; Films; TV
   News: Cinemas / Movie Theaters; Film Industry; Films; TV
   Reviews: Films; TV

Film and TV website publishing reviews, profiles, interviews, and news. Includes editors based in New York, Los Angeles, and London.

Editor: Neil Corry

M0226 Five Points

Magazine
Georgia State University, P.O. Box 3999, Atlanta, GA 30302-3999
United States

http://fivepoints.gsu.edu

Fiction in Translation
   Novel Excerpts: Literary
   Short Fiction: Literary

Fiction > *Short Fiction*: Literary

Nonfiction in Translation > *Essays*

Nonfiction > *Short Nonfiction*
   General, and in particular: Literary

Poetry in Translation > *Any Poetic Form*

Poetry > *Any Poetic Form*

Send: Full text
How to send: Submittable
How not to send: Post

Costs: A fee is charged upon submission.

Welcomes unsolicited submissions of fiction, poetry, flash fiction and nonfiction, and literary nonfiction. Submit through online submission system.

Editor: Megan Sexton

M0227 Five:2:One

Magazine
United States

http://five2onemagazine.com

Types: Fiction; Nonfiction; Poetry
Formats: Essays; Short Fiction
Subjects: Experimental; Literary
Markets: Adult

Send: Full text

Publishes fiction of 1,000 words or more; visual / experimental / written poetry of 120 words or more; and nonfiction / essays / manifestos of 1,000 words or more. Submit online through website.

M0228 Flaneur

Online Magazine
United Kingdom

editor@flaneur.me.uk

http://www.flaneur.me.uk

Nonfiction > *Articles*
   Arts; Films; Food and Drink; Literature; Music; Politics; Sport; TV; Theatre; Travel

Send: Full text
How to send: In the body of an email

Online magazine of arts, culture, politics, and sport.

Editor: J Powell

M0229 Flash: The International Short-Short Story Magazine

Magazine
Department of English, University of Chester, Parkgate Road, Chester, CH1 4BJ
United Kingdom

flash.magazine@chester.ac.uk

http://www.chester.ac.uk/flash.magazine

Types: Fiction
Formats: Short Fiction
Subjects: Literary
Markets: Adult

Send: Full text
How to send: Email

Publishes flash fiction up to 360 words, including the title. Send up to four pieces per issue. Attach submissions to a single email. See website for full submission guidelines.

Editors: Dr Peter Blair; Dr Ashley Chantler

M0230 Florida Monthly

Magazine
999 Douglas Avenue, Suite 3301, Altamonte Springs, FL 32714
United States
Tel: +1 (407) 816-9596
Fax: +1 (407) 816-9373

editorial@floridamagazine.com

https://www.floridamagazine.com

Types: Nonfiction
Formats: Articles; Interviews; News; Reviews
Subjects: Business; Finance; Health; History; Lifestyle; Sport; Travel
Markets: Adult

General interest magazine covering Florida. Send query with published clips.

M0231 Fly Fishing & Fly Tying Magazine

Magazine
Locus Centre, The Square, Aberfeldy, Perthshire, PH15 2DD
United Kingdom
Tel: +44 (0) 1887 829868
Fax: +44 (0) 1887 829856

MarkB.ffft@btinternet.com

http://flyfishing-and-flytying.co.uk

Types: Nonfiction
Formats: Articles; Reviews
Subjects: Nature; Sport
Markets: Adult

Magazine publishing articles and reviews relating to fly fishing and fly tying.

Editor: Mark Bowler

M0232 Focus

Magazine
United Kingdom

https://bsfa.co.uk/bsfa-publications/focus/

Professional Body: BSFA (British Science Fiction Association)

Nonfiction > *Articles*
   Creative Writing; Science Fiction

Poetry > *Any Poetic Form*: Science Fiction

Send: Query
How to send: Online contact form

Writing magazine, devoted to the craft and practice of writing genre fiction. Publishes articles on writing science fiction, and science fiction poetry. Make contact via contact form on website.

Editor: Dev Agarwal

M0233 Folio

Magazine
United States

folio.editors@gmail.com

https://www.american.edu/cas/literature/folio/
https://www.facebook.com/FolioLitJournal/
https://twitter.com/FolioLitJournal
https://www.linkedin.com/in/folio-literary-journal-a235a8b4
http://folio-lit-journal.tumblr.com/

Fiction > *Short Fiction*: Literary

Nonfiction > *Essays*: Creative Nonfiction

Poetry > *Any Poetic Form*

Send: Full text
How to send: Submittable

Accepts submissions of fiction, nonfiction, and poetry on specific themes during specific submission windows. See website for details.

M0234 Fortean Times: The Journal of Strange Phenomena

Magazine
Dennis Publishing, 31-32 Alfred Place, London, WC1E 7DP
United Kingdom

drsutton@forteantimes.com

http://subscribe.forteantimes.com

Types: Nonfiction
Formats: Articles; News; Reviews
Markets: Adult

Publishes accounts of strange phenomena, experiences, curiosities, mysteries, prodigies, and portents. No fiction or poetry.

Editor: David Sutton

M0235 The Fourth River

Magazine
United States

4thriver@gmail.com

https://www.thefourthriver.com
https://twitter.com/thefourthriver
https://www.instagram.com/thefourthriver/
https://www.facebook.com/TheFourthRiver

Fiction > *Short Fiction*: Literary

Nonfiction > *Short Nonfiction*: Creative Nonfiction

Poetry > *Any Poetic Form*

Closed to approaches.

Costs: A fee is charged upon submission. $3 submission fee.

Print and digital literary magazine publishing creative writing that explores the relationship between humans and their environments, whether natural or man-made. Submit 3-5 poems or prose up to 4,000 words between July 1 and September 1 for print, or December 1 and February 1 for online, via online submission system. No submissions by email.

M0236 The Frogmore Papers

Magazine
21 Mildmay Road, Lewes, East Sussex, BN7 1PJ
United Kingdom

frogmorepress@gmail.com

http://www.frogmorepress.co.uk

Fiction
 Novel Excerpts; *Short Fiction*
Poetry > *Any Poetic Form*

Send: Full text; Self-Addressed Stamped Envelope (SASE)
How to send: Domestic Post; Email if overseas

Poetry and prose by new and established authors. There is no house style but the extremes of tradition and experiment are equally unlikely to find favour.

Send between four and six poems, or up to two prose pieces.

Editor: Jeremy Page

M0237 Fugue

Magazine
United States

fugue@uidaho.edu

http://www.fuguejournal.com

Fiction > *Short Fiction*

Nonfiction > *Essays*

Poetry > *Any Poetic Form*

Send: Full text

Submit up to 5 poems, up to two short shorts, one story, or one essay per submission. Accepts submissions online only, between September 1 and May 1. Submission service charges $3 per submission.

Editors: Scott Dorsch; Ryan Downum; Emmy Newman; Steven Pfau; Clare Shearer; Keene Short

M0238 Funny Times

Magazine
PO Box 18530, Cleveland Heights, OH 44118
United States
Tel: +1 (888) 386-6984
Fax: +1 (216) 371-8696

info@funnytimes.com

https://funnytimes.com
https://www.facebook.com/TheFunnyTimes

Fiction
 Cartoons: Business; Comedy / Humour; Current Affairs; Food; Pets; Politics; Relationships; Religion; Technology
 Short Fiction: Business; Comedy / Humour; Current Affairs; Food; Pets; Politics; Relationships; Religion; Technology

Send: Full text; Self-Addressed Stamped Envelope (SASE)
How to send: Post

Send query with SASE and details of previous publishing history (where applicable). Publishes funny stories and cartoons only. No fax or email submissions.

Editor: Raymond Lesser, Susan Wolpert

M0239 The Furrow

Magazine
St Patrick's College, Maynooth, Co. Kildare
Ireland
Tel: 01-7083741
Fax: 01-7083908

editor.furrow@spcm.ie

https://thefurrow.ie

Formats: Articles
Subjects: Religion
Markets: Adult

A monthly journal for the contemporary Church, providing a forum for discussion of challenges facing the Church today and of the resources available to meet them.

Editor: Pádraig Corkery

M0240 The Future Fire

Online Magazine
United Kingdom

fiction@futurefire.net
nonfiction@futurefire.net

http://futurefire.net

Fiction > *Short Fiction*
 Environment; Feminism; LGBTQIA; Postcolonialism; Speculative

Nonfiction > *Reviews*
 Arts; Films; Magazines; Published Books

Poetry > *Any Poetic Form*
 Environment; Feminism; LGBTQIA; Postcolonialism; Speculative

Send: Full text
How to send: Email attachment

Magazine of social political and speculative cyber fiction. Publishes short stories generally up to 10,000 words, however may consider stories up to 17,500. Also publishes nonfiction reviews. Accepts email submissions for fiction; for reviews send query by email before submitting material. See website for full submission guidelines.

Editors: Djibril Alayad; Bruce Stenning

M0241 Gallows Hill

Magazine
United States

josh@gallowshillmagazine.com

https://gallowshillmagazine.com

Types: Fiction; Nonfiction; Poetry
Formats: Interviews; News; Reviews
Subjects: Horror
Markets: Adult

Send: Full text

Print and online horror magazine publishing fiction up to 12,000 words (online) or 6,000 words (print), dark poetry, and nonfiction, including creative nonfiction, stranger-than-fiction, real life horror, movie and book reviews, and horror community reviews. Submit through online submission system.

M0242 Garden & Gun

Magazine
701 E. Bay Street, #115, Charleston, SC 29403
United States

editorial@gardenandgun.com

https://gardenandgun.com

Types: Nonfiction
Formats: Articles
Subjects: Arts; Cookery; Culture; Gardening; Lifestyle; Music; Sport; Travel
Markets: Adult

Lifestyle magazine devoted to to the New South and the Caribbean.

M0243 Garden Rail

Magazine
United Kingdom

Magazine Publisher: Warners Group Publications

M0244 The Garden

Magazine
The Royal Horticultural Society, 80 Vincent Square, London, SW1P 2PE
United Kingdom
Tel: +44 (0) 20 3176 5800

thegarden@rhs.org.uk

https://www.rhs.org.uk/about-the-rhs/publications/the-garden

Magazine Publisher: The Royal Horticultural Society (RHS)

Nonfiction > *Articles*: Gardening

Gardening magazine publishing practical garden design ideas, plant profiles and outstanding gardens large and small. Also carries news of flower shows, special garden openings, books, etc.

Editor: Ian Hodgson

M0245 Geochemistry: Exploration, Environment, Analysis

Magazine
United Kingdom

Book Publisher / Magazine Publisher: The Geological Society Publishing House (**P0317**)

M0246 Gertrude

Online Magazine
United States

EditorGertrudePress@gmail.com

https://www.gertrudepress.org

Fiction > *Short Fiction*
General, and in particular: LGBTQIA

Nonfiction
Essays: Creative Nonfiction; LGBTQIA
Short Nonfiction: Creative Nonfiction; LGBTQIA; Memoir
Poetry > *Any Poetic Form*
General, and in particular: LGBTQIA

Send: Full text
How to send: Submittable

Costs: A fee is charged upon submission. £3 submission fee.

Online LGBTQA journal publishing fiction, poetry, and creative nonfiction. Subject matter need not be LGBTQA-specific, and writers from all backgrounds are welcomed. Submit fiction or creative nonfiction up to 3,000 words, or up to five poems (no line limit, but under 40 lines preferred), via online submission system. For book reviews and interviews, email editor with proposal. See website for full guidelines.

Editor: Tammy

M0247 Get Creative With...

Magazine
United Kingdom

Magazine Publisher: Warners Group Publications

M0248 Gibbons Stamp Monthly

Magazine
399 Strand, London, WC2R 0LX
United Kingdom
Tel: +44 (0) 1425 472363

http://www.gibbonsstampmonthly.com

Types: Nonfiction
Formats: Articles; News
Subjects: Hobbies
Markets: Adult

Magazine publishing features and news relating to stamps.

M0249 The Gin Kin

Online Magazine
United Kingdom

https://www.theginkin.com

Newspaper Publisher / Magazine Publisher: DC Thomson Media

M0250 Golf Monthly

Magazine
Pinehurst 2, Pinehurst Road, Farnborough Business Park, Farnborough, Hampshire, GU14 7BF
United Kingdom
Tel: +44 (0) 1252 555197

golfmonthly@timeinc.com

http://www.golf-monthly.co.uk

Types: Nonfiction
Formats: Articles
Subjects: Sport
Markets: Adult

Send: Query
Don't send: Full text

Golfing magazine. Publishes profiles on players, and general features and columns. Welcomes unsolicited MSS but approach in writing with ideas first. No instruction material from external contributors.

Editor: Michael Harris

M0251 Good Homes

Magazine
United Kingdom

https://www.goodhomesmagazine.com
https://www.facebook.com/GoodHomes
https://uk.pinterest.com/goodhomes/
https://twitter.com/GoodHomesMag
https://www.instagram.com/goodhomesmag/

Magazine Publisher: Media 10

Nonfiction > *Articles*
Decorating; Interior Design

Magazine of decorating and interior design.

Editor: Lisa Allen

M0252 Good Housekeeping

Magazine
72 Broadwick Street, London, W1F 9EP
United Kingdom
Tel: +44 (0) 20 7439 5000
Fax: +44 (0) 20 7437 6886

goodh.mail@hearst.co.uk

http://www.goodhousekeeping.co.uk

Types: Nonfiction
Formats: Articles
Subjects: Cookery; Health; Lifestyle; Women's Interests
Markets: Adult

Monthly glossy women's magazine publishing material on health, lifestyle, cookery, etc.

Editor: Lindsay Nicholson

M0253 The Good Ski Guide
Magazine
1 Esher Place Avenue, KT10 8PU
United Kingdom
Tel: +44 (0) 1372 469874

johnh@goodholidayideas.com

https://www.goodskiguide.com/
https://www.facebook.com/goodskiguide.
official
https://twitter.com/officialGSG
https://www.youtube.com/goodskiguideoffical

Nonfiction > *Articles*
Skiing; Travel

Magazine of skiing and ski resorts.

Editors: Nick Dalton; John Hill

M0254 Granta
Magazine
12 Addison Avenue, Holland Park, London,
W11 4QR
United Kingdom
Tel: +44 (0) 20 7605 1360
Fax: +44 (0) 20 7605 1361

editorial@granta.com

https://granta.com

Fiction > *Short Fiction*

Nonfiction > *Short Nonfiction*

Poetry > *Any Poetic Form*

Send: Full text
How to send: Submittable

Costs: A fee is charged upon submission. £3
for prose; £2 for poems.

Submit one story or essay, or up to four poems,
via online submission system. £3 charge for
prose submissions; £2 for poems. No specific
length limits for prose, but most pieces are
between 3,000 and 6,000 words. Unlikely to
read anything over 10,000 words.

Editor: Sigrid Rausing

M0255 Grazia
Magazine
Media House, Peterborough Business Park,
Lynch Wood, Peterborough, PE2 6EA
United Kingdom
Tel: +44 (0) 1858 438884

graziadaily@graziamagazine.co.uk

https://graziadaily.co.uk

Types: Nonfiction
Formats: Articles; News
Subjects: Beauty; Fashion; Lifestyle; Women's
Interests
Markets: Adult

Weekly glossy women's magazine published
for more than 50 years in Italy, now brought to

the UK market. Publishes articles and news
aimed at women aged between 25 and 45.

M0256 The Great Outdoors (TGO)
Magazine
Kelsey Media Ltd, Cudham Tithe Barn,
Berry's Hill, Cudham, Kent, TN16 3AG
United Kingdom
Tel: +44 (0) 1959 541444

carey.davies@kelsey.co.uk

https://www.tgomagazine.co.uk

Types: Nonfiction
Formats: Articles; News
Subjects: Hobbies; Leisure; Sport; Travel
Markets: Adult

Send: Query
Don't send: Full text

Magazine publishing features and news articles
on outdoor pursuits, including walking and
back-packing, etc. Query editor by email in
first instance.

Editor: Carey Davies

M0257 Grit
Magazine
1503 S.W. 42nd St., Topeka, KS 66609
United States
Tel: +1 (785) 274-4300
Fax: +1 (785) 274-4305

Letters@grit.com

https://www.grit.com
https://www.facebook.com/GritMagazine/
https://www.pinterest.com/gritmagazine
https://www.instagram.com/grit1882/
https://www.youtube.com/user/
MotherEarthNewsMag
https://twitter.com/GritMagazine

Nonfiction > *Articles*
Farming; Gardening; Rural Living; Urban
Farming

Send: Query
Don't send: Full text
How to send: Word file email attachment

Family magazine distributed across America,
with a positive approach to life, providing a
voice for rural lifestyle farmers. Potential
contributors must be knowledgeable on rural
life. Send query in first instance, preferably by
email (with the word "Query" in the subject
line).

Editor: K.C. Compton

Editorial Director: Oscar H. Will

M0258 GUD Magazine
Magazine
United States

mike@ktf-design.com

http://www.gudmagazine.com

Types: Fiction; Nonfiction; Poetry
Formats: Articles; Essays; Interviews; Short
Fiction
Subjects: Arts; Comedy / Humour; Fantasy;
History; Horror; Literary; Mystery; Romance;
Science Fiction; Suspense
Markets: Adult

Closed to approaches.

Note: Closed to submissions as at November
2016. See website for current status. What
you've been looking for in a magazine.
Published two times a year, we provoke with
words and art. We bring you stories that
engage. Essays and interviews that make you
think harder. Poetry that bares reality, more
subtly interprets what it means to be human.
We're aiming to make each issue roughly two
hundred pages of content, 450 words (or a
single poem or piece of art) per page.
Information for how to subscribe will be
available shortly. Subscribe and discover a new
magazine that looks good, feels good in the
hand, and delivers content that will make you
hungry for more.

Editor: Kaolin Fire, Mike Coombes, Sue
Miller, Sal Coraccio

M0259 Gulf Coast: A Journal of Literature and Fine Arts
Magazine
4800 Calhoun Road, Houston, TX 77204-3013
United States

gulfcoastme@gmail.com

http://www.gulfcoastmag.org

Types: Fiction; Nonfiction; Poetry
Formats: Essays; Interviews; Reviews
Subjects: Literary
Markets: Adult

Send: Full text

Submit up to five poems, or fiction or essays
up to 7,000 words, by post or via online
submission manager. For other material, send
query by email to address on website. $2.50
submission fee. Accepts material September 1
to March 1, annually.

Editor: Luisa Muradyan Tannahill

M0260 Gutter Magazine
Magazine
United Kingdom

contactguttermagazine@gmail.com

https://www.guttermag.co.uk/

Fiction > *Short Fiction*
International; Literary; Scotland

Nonfiction > *Essays*
Creative Nonfiction; International; Literary;
Scotland

Poetry > *Any Poetic Form*
International; Scotland

Scripts > *Theatre Scripts*
  International; Literary; Scotland

Closed to approaches.

Publishes poetry, short stories, and drama. Publishes work by writers born or living in Scotland alongside international writing. Send up to five poems up to 120 lines total, or prose up to 3,000 words. Submit through online submission system. See website for full guidelines.

Editors: Colin Begg; Kate MacLeary; Laura Waddell

M0261 **Haiku Journal**
Magazine
Prolific Press Inc., ICO HJ Editor, PO Box 5315, Johnstown, PA 15904
United States

Editor@HaikuJournal.org

https://haikujournal.org

Types: Poetry
Subjects: Literary
Markets: Adult

Send: Full text

Magazine publishing Haiku. Submit via online submission system available on website.

Editor: Glenn Lyvers

M0262 **Haikuniverse**
Magazine
United States

info@haikuniverse.com

http://www.haikuniverse.com

Types: Poetry
Subjects: Literary
Markets: Adult

Send: Full text

Daily online publication of haiku and micro-poems. Submit online using website submission form.

M0263 **Hair**
Magazine
United Kingdom

http://hairmagazine.co.uk

Magazine Publisher: Haversham Publications Ltd

Nonfiction > *Articles*: Hairstyles

Magazine on hair and beauty, publishing articles and features on trends in fashion and hair styling.

M0264 **Harper's Bazaar**
Magazine
The National Magazine Company Ltd, 72 Broadwick Street, London, W1F 9EP

United Kingdom
Tel: +44 (0) 20 7439 5000

Justine.picardie@hearst.co.uk

http://www.harpersbazaar.co.uk

Types: Nonfiction
Formats: Articles; Film Scripts; News; Theatre Scripts
Subjects: Arts; Beauty; Business; Fashion; Health; Lifestyle; Travel; Women's Interests
Markets: Adult

Send: Query
Don't send: Full text

Women's glossy magazine aimed at discerning, style-conscious, intelligent 30+ women who are cultured, well-travelled and independent.

Editor: Justine Picardie

M0265 **Harper's Magazine**
Magazine
666 Broadway, 11th Floor, New York, NY 10012
United States
Tel: +1 (212) 420-5720

harpers@harpers.org

https://harpers.org
https://twitter.com/Harpers
https://www.facebook.com/HarpersMagazine/
https://www.instagram.com/harpersmagazine/

Fiction > *Short Fiction*

Nonfiction
  Articles: Culture; Current Affairs; Environment; Journalism; Politics; Society
  Essays: Culture; Current Affairs; Environment; Politics; Society

Send: Query; Full text; Self-Addressed Stamped Envelope (SASE)
How to send: Post
How not to send: Email

Current affairs magazine publishing topical essays, and fiction. Considers unsolicited fiction MSS, however no unsolicited nonfiction (query in first instance). All queries and submissions must be sent by post.

Editor: Roger D. Hodge

M0266 **Harpur Palate**
Magazine
Binghamton University, English Department, P.O. Box 6000, Binghamton, NY 13902-6000
United States

harpur.palate@gmail.com

https://harpurpalate.binghamton.edu
https://twitter.com/harpurpalate
https://www.instagram.com/harpurpalate
https://www.facebook.com/harpurpalate
https://harpurpalate.submittable.com/submit

Fiction > *Short Fiction*

Nonfiction > *Short Nonfiction*: Creative Nonfiction

Poetry > *Any Poetic Form*

Send: Full text
How to send: Submittable

Submit up to five poems, up to 15 pages total; prose up to 5,500 words; or three pieces of short prose up to 1,000 words each. Submit through online submission system.

M0267 **Heat Pumps Today**
Magazine
United Kingdom

Magazine Publisher: Warners Group Publications

M0268 **The Helix**
Magazine
United States

helixmagazine@gmail.com

https://helixmagazine.org

Types: Fiction; Nonfiction; Poetry; Scripts
Formats: Essays; Short Fiction
Subjects: Drama; Literary
Markets: Adult

Send: Full text

Publishes fiction, creative nonfiction, poetry, plays, and art. Submit up to four pieces of prose up to 3,000 words each, or up to four poems.

Editor: Victoria-Lynn Bell

M0269 **Hello!**
Magazine
Wellington House, 69-71 Upper Ground, London, SE1 9PQ
United Kingdom
Tel: +44 (0) 20 7667 8721

holly.nesbitt-larking@hellomagazine.com

https://www.hellomagazine.com

Types: Nonfiction
Formats: Articles; Interviews; News
Subjects: Beauty; Culture; Fashion; Lifestyle; Women's Interests
Markets: Adult

Magazine of celebrity and lifestyle.

Editor: Holly Nesbitt-Larking

M0270 **Here Comes Everyone**
Magazine
United Kingdom

http://herecomeseveryone.me

Types: Fiction; Nonfiction; Poetry
Formats: Articles
Subjects: Literary
Markets: Adult

Send: Full text

Biannual literature and arts magazine publishing poetry, fiction, articles, and artwork. Each issue is themed. See website for upcoming themes and to submit.

Editors: Matthew Barton; Raef Boylan

M0271 Hi-Fi News
Magazine
United Kingdom

https://www.hifinews.com
https://www.facebook.com/pages/Hi-Fi-News-Record-Review/299204350193416
https://twitter.com/hifinewsmag

Magazine Publisher: AV Tech Media Ltd

Nonfiction
 News: Audio Technology
 Reviews: Audio Technology

Reviews audiophile-oriented sound-reproduction and recording equipment, and includes information on new products and developments in audio.

Editor: Paul Miller

M0272 History Scotland
Magazine
United Kingdom

Magazine Publisher: Warners Group Publications

M0273 History Today
Magazine
2nd Floor, 9 Staple Inn, London, WC1V 7QH
United Kingdom
Tel: +44 (0) 20 3219 7810

p.lay@historytoday.com

http://www.historytoday.com

Types: Nonfiction
Formats: Articles
Subjects: History
Markets: Adult

Historical magazine publishing short articles (600-1,000 words); mid-length articles (1,300-2,200 words) and feature articles (3,500 to 4,000 words). Send query by email with proposal and details of your career / academic background. See website for full guidelines.

M0274 Horse and Rider
Magazine
DJ Murphy Publishers Ltd, Olive Studio, Grange Road, Tilford, Farnham, Surrey, GU10 2DQ
United Kingdom
Tel: +44 (0) 1428 601020

editor@djmurphy.co.uk

https://www.horseandrideruk.com

Magazine Publisher: DJ Murphy Publishers Ltd

Nonfiction > *Articles*

Equestrian; Horses

Magazine on horses, including news, instructional features, etc. Aimed mainly at horse-owners.

Editor: Louise Kittle

M0275 Hotel Amerika
Magazine
C/O The Department of Creative Writing, Columbia College Chicago, 600 South Michigan Avenue, Chicago, IL 60605
United States
Tel: +1 (312) 369-8175

http://www.hotelamerika.net

Fiction > *Short Fiction*: Literary

Nonfiction > *Essays*

Poetry > *Any Poetic Form*

Send: Full text
How to send: Submittable

Costs: A fee is charged upon submission. $3.00.

Submissions will be considered between September 1 and April 1. Materials received after April 1 and before September 1 will not be considered.

Editor: David Lazar

M0276 House & Garden
Magazine
United Kingdom

houseandgarden@condenast.co.uk

http://www.houseandgarden.co.uk

Types: Nonfiction
Formats: Articles
Subjects: Architecture; Cookery; Design; Gardening; Lifestyle; Travel
Markets: Adult

Publishes articles on gardens, architecture, home decor, recipes, travel, and lifestyle.

Editor: Hatta Byng

M0277 Hoxie Gorge Review
Magazine
United States

editor@hoxiegorgereview.com

http://hoxiegorgereview.com

Types: Fiction; Nonfiction; Poetry
Subjects: Literary
Markets: Adult

Send: Full text

Online literary journal publishing poetry, fiction, and creative nonfiction. Submit via website through online submission system.

Editor: Heather Bartlett

M0278 Hunger Mountain
Magazine
36 College Street, Montpelier, VT 05602
United States
Tel: +1 (802) 828-8844

hungermtn@vcfa.edu

https://hungermtn.org

Fiction in Translation > *Short Fiction*: Literary

Fiction > *Short Fiction*: Literary

Nonfiction in Translation > *Short Nonfiction*: Creative Nonfiction

Nonfiction > *Short Nonfiction*: Creative Nonfiction

Poetry in Translation > *Any Poetic Form*

Poetry > *Any Poetic Form*

Closed to approaches.

Submit prose up to 8,000 words, or up to three flash pieces, or up to five poems, via online submission system. Accepts general submissions between May 1 and October 15, and contest submissions between November 1 and March 1.

Editor: Caroline Mercurio

M0279 Ibbetson Street
Magazine
25 School Street, Somerville, MA 02143
United States
Tel: +1 (617) 628-2313

tapestryofvoices@yahoo.com

http://ibbetsonpress.com

Types: Poetry
Subjects: Literary
Markets: Adult

Publishes poetry that is not too abstract. Looks for simplicity and economy of words. Send 3-5 poems with author bio in the body of an email with "Poetry Submission" in the subject line. No attachments.

Editors: Harris Gardner; Lawrence Kessenich; Emily Pineau

M0280 Ibsen Studies
Magazine
Norway

https://www.tandfonline.com/toc/sibs20/current

Types: Nonfiction
Formats: Articles; Essays
Subjects: Literature
Markets: Academic

Publishes scholarly articles on the life and works of Henrik Ibsen. See website for submission guidelines.

Editor: Ellen Rees

M0281 Idaho Review

Magazine
Boise State University, 1910 University Drive,
Boise, Idaho 83725
United States

mwieland@boisestate.edu

https://www.idahoreview.org
https://theidahoreview.submittable.com/submit
http://www.facebook.com/
10213528569031037
http://twitter.com/idahoreview
http://www.instagram.com/theidahoreview

Fiction > *Short Fiction*: Literary

Nonfiction
  Essays: General
  Short Nonfiction: Creative Nonfiction

Poetry > *Any Poetic Form*

Send: Full text; Self-Addressed Stamped
Envelope (SASE)
How to send: Submittable; Post

Costs: A fee is charged for online submissions.
$3 to submit online.

Annual literary journal publishing poetry and
fiction. No specific limit for fiction, but most
of the stories accepted are under 25 double-
spaced pages. For poetry, submit up to five
poems. Reading period runs from September to
March (see website for specific dates for this
year). Accepts submissions by post with
SASE, but prefers submissions through online
submission system ($3 fee).

M0282 Identity Theory

Magazine
United States

editor@identitytheory.com

http://www.identitytheory.com

Types: Fiction; Nonfiction; Poetry
Formats: Essays; Interviews; Short Fiction
Subjects: Literary
Markets: Adult

Send: Full text

Online literary magazine. Send fiction or
essays up to 4,000 words through Submittable
or through specific email address, or 3-5
unpublished poems in the body of an email.
See website for different email addresses for
different types of submissions.

Editor: Matt Borondy

M0283 Improve Your Coarse Fishing

Magazine
Media House, Peterborough Business Park,
Peterborough, PE2 6EA
United Kingdom
Tel: +44 (0) 1733 395102

ben.miles@bauermedia.co.uk

https://www.anglingtimes.co.uk/magazines/
improve-your-coarse-fishing/

Formats: Articles; News
Subjects: Leisure; Sport
Markets: Adult

Magazine on coarse fishing.

Editor: Ben Miles

M0284 The Independent Publishing Magazine

Magazine
United Kingdom

mickrooney@
theindependentpublishingmagazine.com

http://www.
theindependentpublishingmagazine.com

Types: Nonfiction
Formats: Articles; News
Subjects: Media
Markets: Adult

Magazine covering the self-publishing industry
specifically and the wider publishing industry
generally.

Editor: Mick Rooney

M0285 Indiana Review

Magazine
Indiana University, Indiana Review Journal,
Department of English, Lindley 215, 150 S
Woodlawn Ave, Bloomington, IN 47405-7104
United States

inreview@indiana.edu

https://indianareview.org
https://twitter.com/indianareview
https://www.facebook.com/IndianaReview

Fiction in Translation > *Short
Fiction*: Literary

Fiction > *Short Fiction*: Literary

Nonfiction in Translation > *Essays*

Nonfiction > *Essays*

Poetry in Translation > *Any Poetic Form*

Poetry > *Any Poetic Form*

Closed to approaches.

Costs: A fee is charged upon submission.

Send fiction or nonfiction up 6,000 words or 3-
6 poems per submission, during specific
submission windows only (see website for
details). No submissions by post or by email –
all submissions must be made through online
submission manager ($3 fee). See website for
full guidelines, and to submit.

Editor: Tessa Yang

Editor-in-Chief: Mariah Gese

M0286 Infinite Rust

Magazine
Texas Southern University, Department of
English – MLK 107, 3100 Cleburne Street,
Houston, TX 77004
United States

editor@infiniterust.com

http://www.infiniterust.com

Types: Fiction; Nonfiction; Poetry
Formats: Articles; Essays; Interviews; Short
Fiction
Subjects: Arts; Autobiography; Contemporary;
Culture; Current Affairs; Experimental;
History; Lifestyle; Literary; Literary Criticism;
Music; Philosophy; Photography; Politics;
Satire; Sociology; Spirituality; Travel;
Women's Interests
Markets: Academic; Adult; Professional

Send: Full text
How to send: Email

University-affiliated quarterly online literary
arts journal showcasing creative work. We
publish short fiction, poetry, creative
nonfiction, and essays, as well as art and
photography. The goal of our publication is to
assemble a variety of literary and artistic styles
as well as a broad range of voices,
perspectives, and life experiences. We accept
unsolicited submissions year-round, however
the submission deadline for our Spring 2019
issue is February 28, 2019. We are interested
in unexpected new perspectives, originality of
language, creative vision, and high-quality
content. Send us your best work, we are
excited to read it. Please include a brief author
bio of no more than 100 words. Limit
submissions to no more than 2,500 words of
prose, five poems, or five artworks or
photographic images. Works previously
published elsewhere cannot be submitted.
Simultaneous and multiple submissions are
fine. Please notify if work gets accepted for
publication elsewhere. Contributors retain all
rights to their work. We do not charge a
submission fee. Please visit our website to
view our current issue and to submit your
work.

Editors: Dr. Michael Sollars; Marjorie Ward

M0287 InfoWorld

Online Magazine
492 Old Connecticut Path, PO Box 9208,
Framingham, MA 01701
United States

https://www.infoworld.com
https://www.linkedin.com/company/164364
https://twitter.com/infoworld
https://www.facebook.com/InfoWorld

Magazine Publisher: IDG Communications,
Inc.

PROFESSIONAL > **Nonfiction** > *Articles*
  Computers; Technology

Closed to approaches.

The leading voice in emerging enterprise technology, is the go-to resource for developers, architects, and business leaders launching next-generation initiatives on scalable cloud platforms, where such future-focused tech as AI/machine learning, big data analytics, and NoSQL databases evolve continuously. Does not publish contributed articles.

Editor: Steve Fox, Editor in Chief

M0288 InJoy Magazine
Magazine
2302 Noblewood Road, Edgewater, MD 21037
United States
Tel: +1 (660) 281-4488

cjsmith@injoymagazine.com

http://www.injoymagazine.com

Types: Fiction; Poetry
Formats: Articles; Reviews; Short Fiction
Subjects: Arts; Beauty; Comedy / Humour; Culture; Entertainment; Fashion; Hobbies; How To; Romance; Spirituality; Women's Interests

Send: Full text
How to send: Email

Provides a collaborative platform for art, encouragement and enjoying life. Our target audience is Women in all walks of life seeking to connect with others, share stories and laugh.

Editor: Crystal Smith

M0289 Ink Sweat and Tears
Online Magazine
United Kingdom

inksweatandtearssubmissions@gmail.com

http://www.inksweatandtears.co.uk

Nonfiction > *Reviews*
Literature; Poetry as a Subject

Poetry
Any Poetic Form; Haibun; Haiga; Haiku; Prose Poetry

Closed to approaches.

UK-based webzine publishing poetry, prose, prose-poetry, word and image pieces, and poetry reviews. Send 4-6 pieces by email only. Accepts unsolicited reviews of poetry and short story collections. See website for full guidelines.

Editor: Helen Ivory

M0290 Inspiralist
Online Magazine
United Kingdom

Newspaper Publisher / Magazine Publisher: DC Thomson Media

M0291 Insurance Age
Magazine
Infopro Digital, 133 Houndsditch, London, EC3A 7BX
United Kingdom
Tel: +44 (0) 20 7316 9000
Fax: +44 (0) 20 7681 3401

sian.barton@infopro-digital.com

https://www.insuranceage.co.uk

Types: Nonfiction
Formats: Articles; News
Subjects: Business; Finance
Markets: Professional

Publishes news and features on the insurance industry.

Editor: Sian Barton

M0292 The Interpreter's House
Magazine
37A Spencer Street, Holywood, County Down, Northern Ireland, BT18 9DN
United Kingdom

interpretershousesubmissions@gmail.com

http://www.theinterpretershouse.com

Types: Fiction; Poetry
Formats: Short Fiction
Subjects: Literary
Markets: Adult

Send: Full text

Send up to five poems or up to two short stories by email in a single Word attachment, or by post with SAE. Accepts work in October, February, and June.

Editor: Georgi Gill

M0293 Interzone
Magazine
TTA Press, 5 Martins Lane, Witcham, Ely, Cambs, CB6 2LB
United Kingdom

http://ttapress.com

Types: Fiction
Formats: Short Fiction
Subjects: Fantasy; Science Fiction
Markets: Adult

Send: Full text

Publishes science fiction and fantasy short stories up to about 10,000 words. No simultaneous submissions, multiple submissions or reprints. See website for full guidelines and online submission system.

Editor: Andy Cox

M0294 Investors Chronicle
Magazine
United Kingdom

john.hughman@ft.com

https://www.investorschronicle.co.uk

Types: Nonfiction
Formats: Articles; News
Subjects: Business; Finance
Markets: Professional

Magazine for investors.

Editor: John Hughman

M0295 The Iowa Review
Magazine
The University of Iowa, 308 English-Philosophy Building, Iowa City, IA 52242
United States
Tel: +1 (319) 335-0462
Fax: +1 (319) 335-2535

iowa-review@uiowa.edu

http://www.iowareview.org

Types: Fiction; Poetry; Translations
Formats: Essays; Reviews; Short Fiction
Subjects: Literary
Markets: Adult

Send: Full text

Publishes poetry, fiction, and nonfiction. Submit in September, October, and November only, via online submission system ($4 charge for non-subscribers) or by post with SASE. Accepts prose up to 25 pages and poetry up to 8 pages (query by email if your poem is longer). Do not mix genres in a single envelope. Work must be unpublished. Simultaneous submissions accepted if immediate notification of acceptance elsewhere is given.

Editor: Lynne Nugent

M0296 Ireland's Own
Magazine
Channing House, Rowe Street, Wexford
Ireland

info@irelandsown.ie

https://irelandsown.ie

Types: Fiction; Nonfiction
Formats: Articles; Short Fiction
Subjects: Literary; Traditional
Markets: Adult; Children's; Young Adult

Magazine publishing stories and articles of Irish interest for the whole family, plus puzzles and games.

Editor: Sean Nolan

M0297 Irish Journal of Medical Science
Magazine
RAMI Office, Setanta House, 2nd Floor, Setanta Place, Dublin 2
Ireland
Tel: +353 1 633 4820

helenmoore@rcpi.ie

http://www.springer.com/medicine/internal/journal/11845

Types: Nonfiction
Formats: Articles; News
Subjects: Medicine
Markets: Academic; Professional

Quarterly medical science journal providing a forum for the exchange of scientific information, and promoting academic discussion.

Editors: Helen Moore; William P. Tormey

M0298 Irish Medical Times
Magazine
Ireland
Tel: +353 (0) 1 817

editor@imt.ie

https://www.imt.ie

Types: Nonfiction
Formats: Articles; News
Subjects: Medicine
Markets: Professional

Newspaper for medical professionals.

Editor: Lloyd Mudiwa

M0299 Irish Pages
Magazine
129 Ormeau Road, Belfast, BT7 1SH
United Kingdom
Tel: +44 (0) 2890 434800

editor@irishpages.org

https://irishpages.org

Types: Fiction; Nonfiction; Poetry; Translations
Formats: Essays; Reviews; Short Fiction
Subjects: Autobiography; History; Literary; Nature; Science
Markets: Adult

Send: Full text
How not to send: Email

Non-partisan and non-sectarian literary journal publishing writing from the island of Ireland and elsewhere in equal measure. Publishes work in English, and in the Irish Language or Ulster Scots with English translations or glosses. Accepts submissions throughout the year by post only with stamps, coupons or cash for return postage (no self-addressed envelope is needed). See website for more details.

M0300 Iron Cross
Magazine
United Kingdom

Magazine Publisher: Warners Group Publications

M0301 Island
Magazine
PO Box 4703, Hobart TAS 7000

Australia
Tel: +61 (0) 3 6234 1462

admin@islandmag.com

https://islandmag.com

Types: Fiction; Poetry
Formats: Articles; Essays; Short Fiction
Markets: Adult

Welcomes submissions of nonfiction, fiction and poetry from Australia, New Zealand and the Pacific, as well as from Australians living abroad. See website for details and to submit using online submission system.

M0302 J Journal
Magazine
Department of English, John Jay College of Criminal Justice, 524 West 59th Street, 7th Floor, New York, NY 10019
United States

submissionsjjournal@gmail.com

http://jjournal2.jjay.cuny.edu/jjournal/

Types: Fiction; Nonfiction; Poetry
Formats: Essays; Short Fiction
Subjects: Crime; Legal; Literary
Markets: Adult

Send: Full text
How to send: Email

Publishes fiction, creative nonfiction (1st person narrative, personal essay, memoir) and poetry that examines questions of justice, either obliquely or directly addressing crime and the criminal justice system. Unlikely to publish genre fiction. Send up to three poems or prose up to 6,000 words.

M0303 J.J. Outre Review
Magazine
United States

thejjoutrereview@gmail.com

https://darkpassagespublishing.com

Types: Fiction
Formats: Short Fiction
Subjects: Adventure; Crime; Experimental; Fantasy; Horror; Literary; Mystery; Science Fiction; Suspense; Thrillers
Markets: Adult

Send: Full text

Semi-annual online journal with an annual print issue. Publishes genre fiction with strong literary elements. Welcomes the bizarre and experimental. Not interested in zombies, vampires, werewolves, fairies, shapeshifters or fan-fic. Submit up to three stories at a time via online submission system.

M0304 Jaggery
Magazine
United States

editor@jaggerylit.com

http://jaggerylit.com

Types: Fiction; Nonfiction; Poetry
Formats: Essays; Interviews; Reviews; Short Fiction
Markets: Adult

Send: Full text

Publishes fiction, poetry, essays, interviews and reviews from or about South Asia and its diasporas. Submit online via online submission system.

Editor: Anu Mahadev

M0305 Jewish Chronicle
Magazine
United Kingdom

editorial@thejc.com

https://www.thejc.com
https://www.instagram.com/thejewishchronicle/
https://twitter.com/jewishchron
https://www.facebook.com/pages/The-Jewish-Chronicle/99875692725
https://www.pinterest.co.uk/thejewishchroni/

Nonfiction
 Articles: Jewish Culture; Judaism; Lifestyle
 News: Jewish Culture; Judaism; Sport

Weekly paper publishing material of Jewish interest. No fiction.

M0306 Josephine Quarterly
Magazine
United States

https://www.josephinequarterly.com

Types: Poetry
Subjects: Literary
Markets: Adult

Online poetry journal. Submit up to five poems of any length via online submission system.

M0307 Journal of Apicultural Research
Magazine
United Kingdom

https://www.tandfonline.com/toc/tjar20/current

ACADEMIC > **Nonfiction** > *Articles:* Apiculture (Beekeeping)

Send: Full text
How to send: Online submission system

Publishes research articles, theoretical papers, notes, comments and authoritative reviews on scientific aspects of the biology, ecology, natural history and culture of all types of bee.

M0308 Journal of the Geological Society
Magazine
United Kingdom

Book Publisher / Magazine Publisher: The Geological Society Publishing House (**P0317**)

M0309 Juniper

Magazine
United Kingdom

Newspaper Publisher / Magazine Publisher: DC Thomson Media

M0310 Kaimana: Literary Arts Hawai'i

Magazine
United States

reimersa001@hawaii.rr.com

http://www.hawaii.edu/hlac/kaimana.htm

Types: Fiction; Poetry
Formats: Short Fiction
Subjects: Literary
Markets: Adult

Send: Full text
How not to send: Email

Publishes poetry and fiction, with a particular (but not exclusive) interest in work which makes reference to the Pacific / Asia / Polynesia / Hawai'i. Send complete ms with SASE. No submissions by email.

M0311 Kairos

Magazine
United States

submissions.kairos@gmail.com

http://kairoslit.com

Types: Fiction; Nonfiction; Poetry
Formats: Articles; Short Fiction
Subjects: Literary
Markets: Adult

Send: Full text
How to send: Email

Publishes poetry, fiction, creative nonfiction, and opinion / editorial pieces. Submit up to five poems or prose up to 10,000 words.

M0312 Kaleidoscope

Magazine
701 South Main Street, Akron, OH 44311-1019
United States
Tel: +1 (330) 762-9755

kaleidoscope@udsakron.org

http://www.udsakron.org/kaleidoscope.aspx

Types: Fiction; Poetry
Formats: Articles; Reviews; Short Fiction
Subjects: Arts; Autobiography; Culture; Health; Literary; Sociology
Markets: Adult

Send: Full text
How to send: Email

Publishes material examining experiences of disability through literature and the fine arts. Seeking material that challenges and overcomes stereotypical, patronising, and sentimental attitudes about disability. Writers with and without disabilities are welcome to submit their work. Writers should avoid using offensive language and always put the person before the disability. All MSS should be submitted by email or through the website. Poetry submissions should consist of up to five poems and use strong imagery and evocative language. Short stories should demonstrate effective technique, thought-provoking subject matter, and a mature grasp of the art of story-telling.

Editor: Gail Willmott

M0313 The Kenyon Review

Magazine
Finn House, 102 W. Wiggin Street, Kenyon College, Gambier, OH 43022-9623
United States
Tel: +1 (740) 427-5208
Fax: +1 (740) 427-5417

kenyonreview@kenyon.edu

https://kenyonreview.org

Types: Fiction; Nonfiction; Poetry; Scripts; Translations
Formats: Essays; Reviews; Short Fiction
Subjects: Arts; Literary
Markets: Adult

Submit through online submission system. Send short fiction up to 7,500 words, poetry up to six poems, or plays or excerpts up to 30 pages, with SASE. Translations are also accepted, but author is responsible for permissions. No unsolicited interviews or submissions by email or post.

Editor: David H. Lynn

Managing Editor: Abigail Wadsworth Serfass

M0314 La Presa

Magazine
United States

leegould@embajadoraspress.com

https://embajadoraspress.com/index.php/la-presa/

Types: Fiction; Nonfiction; Poetry
Formats: Essays; Short Fiction
Subjects: Autobiography; Literary
Markets: Adult

Send: Full text
How to send: Email

Publishes poetry and prose, in English and Spanish, by writers from Canada, the US, and Mexico. Publishes poems and poem sequences, creative nonfiction, fiction, memoir, flash fiction, essays and vignettes. Also eager to publish longer work. Send submissions by email.

M0315 LabLit.com

Magazine
United States

editorial@lablit.com

http://www.lablit.com

Types: Fiction; Nonfiction; Poetry
Formats: Essays; Interviews; Short Fiction
Subjects: Comedy / Humour; Science
Markets: Adult

Send: Full text
How to send: Email

Magazine for scientists and non-scientists, publishing profiles, interviews, essays, humour, cartoons, reviews, poetry, and fiction related to science (but no science fiction). Send submissions by email.

Editor: Dr Jennifer Rohn

M0316 Lake Relo

Magazine
2820 Bagnell Dam Boulevard, #1B, Lake Ozark, MO 65049
United States
Tel: +1 (573) 365-2323
Fax: +1 (573) 365-2351

SPublishingCO@msn.com

http://www.
relocatingtothelakeoftheozarks.com

Types: Nonfiction
Formats: Articles
Subjects: Entertainment; Lifestyle; Travel
Markets: Adult

Magazine for people relocating to the Lake Ozark area.

M0317 Land Rover Monthly

Magazine
United Kingdom

Magazine Publisher: Warners Group Publications

M0318 Landfall

Magazine
Otago University Press, PO Box 56, Dunedin 9054
New Zealand
Tel: +64 (0) 3 479 4155

landfall.press@otago.ac.nz

http://www.otago.ac.nz/press/landfall

Types: Fiction; Nonfiction; Poetry
Formats: Essays
Subjects: Arts; Biography; Literary; Literary Criticism
Markets: Adult

Send: Full text
How to send: Email

Open to work by New Zealand and Pacific writers or by writers whose work has a connection to the region in subject matter or location. Work from Australian writers is occasionally included as a special feature. Send up to five poems or up to two pieces of prose per issue. Preferred length is 3,000 words, but longer pieces will be considered.

M0319 Leisure Painter

Magazine
The Artists' Publishing Company Ltd., Caxton House, 63-65 High Street, Tenterden, Kent TN30 6BD
United Kingdom
Tel: +44 (0) 1580 763315

http://www.painters-online.co.uk

Magazine Publisher: Warners Group Publications

Types: Nonfiction
Formats: Articles
Subjects: Arts; Hobbies; How To
Markets: Adult

Magazine offering artistic inspiration, guidance, tuition and encouragement for beginners and amateur artists. Includes features and step-by-step painting and drawing demonstrations.

Editor: Ingrid Lyon

M0320 LGC (Local Government Chronicle)

Magazine
EMAP Publishing Limited, Telephone House, 69 – 77 Paul Street, London, EC2A 4NQ
United Kingdom
Tel: +44 (0) 20 3953 2774

lgcnews@emap.com

https://www.lgcplus.com

Types: Nonfiction
Formats: Articles; News
Subjects: Business; Politics; Sociology
Markets: Professional

Magazine aimed at managers in local government.

Editor: Nick Golding

M0321 Life and Work

Magazine
121 George Street, Edinburgh, EH2 4YN
United Kingdom
Tel: +44 (0) 1312 255722

magazine@lifeandwork.org

https://www.lifeandwork.org

Types: Nonfiction
Formats: Articles; News
Subjects: Religion
Markets: Adult

Magazine of the Church of Scotland.

M0322 Light & Life

Magazine
United States

https://lightandlifemagazine.com
https://twitter.com/lightandlifemag
https://www.facebook.com/lightandlifemagazine
https://www.youtube.com/channel/UCr8nd1V-UnRFTBeCTSPB68A
https://vimeo.com/llcomm
https://www.linkedin.com/company/559925
https://www.flickr.com/photos/llcomm/

Nonfiction > *Articles*: Methodism

Send: Full text
How to send: Email

Bimonthly magazine that exists to promote thoughtful Christian discipleship from a Wesleyan-Arminian perspective. Submit to the Executive Editor by email.

Editor: Doug Newton

Executive Editor: Jeff Finley

M0323 Lighthouse

Magazine
United Kingdom

submissions@lighthouse.gatehousepress.com

http://www.gatehousepress.com/lighthouse/

Types: Fiction; Poetry
Formats: Short Fiction
Subjects: Contemporary; Literary
Markets: Adult

Send: Full text
How to send: Email

Magazine of contemporary fiction and poetry, aimed at a UK audience. Submit up to four poems, one piece of fiction or up to two flash fictions by email as attachments. No previously published material or simultaneous submissions. See website for full guidelines.

M0324 The Linguist

Magazine
Chartered Institute of Linguists (CIOL), 7th Floor, 167 Fleet Street, London, EC4A 2EA
United Kingdom
Tel: +44 (0) 20 7940 3100

https://www.ciol.org.uk/the-linguist

Types: Nonfiction
Formats: Articles; News
Subjects: Science
Markets: Professional

Magazine for language professionals.

M0325 Literary Mama

Online Magazine
United States

LMinfo@literarymama.com
LMreviews@literarymama.com
LMnonfiction@literarymama.com
LMfiction@literarymama.com
LMpoetry@literarymama.com

https://literarymama.com
http://www.facebook.com/litmama
http://twitter.com/literarymama
https://www.instagram.com/literary_mama/

Fiction > *Short Fiction*: Motherhood

Nonfiction
Reviews: Motherhood; Published Books
Short Nonfiction: Creative Nonfiction; Motherhood
Poetry > *Any Poetic Form*: Motherhood

Send: Full text; Query
How to send: In the body of an email

Online magazine publishing fiction, poetry, creative nonfiction, and book reviews focusing on mother writers, and the complexities and many faces of motherhood. Accepts submissions in the text of emails only – no snail mail submissions. See website for full submission guidelines.

Editor: Amy Hudock

M0326 Litro Magazine

Magazine
90 York Way, London, N1 9AG
United Kingdom

info@litro.co.uk
editor@litro.co.uk

https://www.litro.co.uk
https://www.facebook.com/Litromedia/
https://open.spotify.com/show/78fpfD5ejecJXXdsVHGJqb
https://www.instagram.com/litromedia/
https://twitter.com/litromagazine

Fiction > *Short Fiction*

Nonfiction > *Short Nonfiction*
Literary Journalism; Memoir; Travel

Accepts short fiction, flash/micro fiction, nonfiction (memoir, literary journalism, travel narratives, etc), and original artwork (photographs, illustrations, paintings, etc) based on the designated monthly theme. Works translated into English are also welcome. See website for upcoming themes.

M0327 Little Rose Magazine

Magazine
460 N 50 E, Apt 460, Orem, UT 84057
United States

littlerosemagazine@gmail.com

https://littlerosemagazine.weebly.com/

Types: Fiction; Nonfiction; Poetry
Formats: Articles; Essays; Interviews; Short Fiction
Subjects: Arts; Autobiography; Contemporary; Culture; Current Affairs; Entertainment; Experimental; Lifestyle; Literary; Literature; Photography; Politics; Psychology; Religion; Self Help; Sociology; Technology; Traditional

Markets: Academic; Adult; Professional; Young Adult

Send: Full text
How to send: Email

A Utah-based online magazine of literature and art, aiming to confront issues of identity, such as gender, race, class, religion, intersectionality, internet identity, and culture. We want to give artists and authors a space to reveal everything about the human experience – the good, bad, ugly, and everything in between.

Editor: Kendra Nuttall

M0328 Living

Magazine
United Kingdom

Newspaper Publisher / Magazine Publisher: DC Thomson Media

M0329 Loaded

Online Magazine
United Kingdom

https://loaded.co.uk
https://www.facebook.com/LoadedMagazine
https://twitter.com/loadedonline
https://www.pinterest.com/loadedonline/

Nonfiction
   Articles: Entertainment; Lifestyle; Sport; Women
   News: General

Online men's lifestyle magazine. Originally a print publication, now online only.

Editors: Scott Manson; Andrew Woods

M0330 The London Magazine

Magazine
Flat 5, 11 Queen's Gate, London, SW7 5EL
United Kingdom
Tel: +44 (0) 20 7584 5977

info@thelondonmagazine.org

http://thelondonmagazine.org

Types: Fiction; Nonfiction; Poetry
Formats: Articles; Essays; Reviews; Short Fiction
Subjects: Arts; Autobiography; Literary; Literary Criticism
Markets: Adult

Send: Full text

Send submissions through online submission system or by email. Does not normally publish science fiction or fantasy writing, or erotica. Will consider postal submissions, but prefers submissions electronically. See website for full guidelines and to access online submission system.

M0331 London Review of Books

Magazine
28 Little Russell Street, London, WC1A 2HN
United Kingdom
Tel: +44 (0) 20 7209 1101
Fax: +44 (0) 20 7209 1151

edit@lrb.co.uk

https://www.lrb.co.uk

Types: Nonfiction; Poetry
Formats: Articles; Essays; Film Scripts; Reviews
Subjects: Arts; Culture; Literary; Literature; Politics; Science
Markets: Adult

Publishes poems, reviews, reportage, memoir, articles, and blogposts. Send submissions by email or by post (with SAE).

M0332 Long Life Magazine

Magazine
Cryonics Institute, 24355 Sorrentino Court, Clinton Township, MI 48035
United States
Tel: +1 (586) 791-5961

info@cryonics.org

http://www.cryonics.org/resources/long-life-magazine

Types: Fiction; Nonfiction; Poetry
Formats: Articles; Essays; Short Fiction
Subjects: Science; Technology
Markets: Adult

Send: Full text

Magazine on the subject of cryonics, publishing articles and essays covering the various aspects and challenges of being frozen and then re-animated. Welcomes poetry and occasionally accepts fiction, provided cryonics are central. No horror or stories portraying a dismal future.

M0333 Long Poem Magazine

Magazine
20 Spencer Rise, London, NW5 1AP
United Kingdom

longpoemmagazine@gmail.com

http://longpoemmagazine.org.uk

Types: Nonfiction; Poetry
Formats: Essays; Reviews
Subjects: Literary; Literature
Markets: Adult

Closed to approaches.

Magazine dedicated to publishing long poems and sequences. Publishes unpublished poems of at least 75 lines (but no book length poems). Also publishes essays on aspects of the long poem and reviews of books featuring long poems or sequences. Send submissions by email as Word file attachments. Does not

accept poems submitted in the body of emails. See website for full guidelines and submission months. Poems submitted outside submission months will be discarded.

M0334 Louisiana Literature

Magazine
United States

lalit@selu.edu

http://www.louisianaliterature.org
https://twitter.com/LaLiterature
https://louisianaliterature.submittable.com/submit

Fiction > *Short Fiction*: Literary

Nonfiction > *Essays*: Creative Nonfiction

Poetry > *Any Poetic Form*

Send: Full text
How to send: Submittable

Literary journal publishing fiction, poetry, and creative nonfiction. Submit via online system available at the website.

Editor: Dr Jack Bedell

M0335 The Lyric

Magazine
PO Box 110, Jericho, VT 05465
United States

themuse@thelyricmagazine.com

https://thelyricmagazine.com

Types: Poetry
Subjects: Literary; Traditional
Markets: Adult

Send: Full text
How to send: Email

Publishes rhymed verse in traditional forms, with an occasional piece of blank or free verse. Poems must be original, unpublished, and not under consideration elsewhere. Send submissions by post with SASE if return required (not necessary if email response is sufficient). No submissions by email unless from outside the US.

Editor: Jean Mellichamp Milliken

M0336 The MacGuffin

Magazine
Schoolcraft College, 18600 Haggerty Road, Livonia, MI 48152
United States
Tel: +1 (734) 462-5327

macguffin@schoolcraft.edu

https://schoolcraft.edu/macguffin

Types: Fiction; Nonfiction; Poetry
Formats: Short Fiction
Subjects: Experimental; Literary; Traditional
Markets: Adult

Send: Full text
How to send: Email

Publishes fiction, creative nonfiction, and poetry. Send complete MS by post with return postage, or by email as a Word document attachment. Submissions in the body of the email will not be accepted. Submit up to five poems or up to two stories.

M0337 Machine Knitting Monthly

Magazine
PO Box 1479, Maidenhead, Berkshire, SL6 8YX
United Kingdom
Tel: +44 (0) 1628 783080

mail@machineknittingmonthly.net

https://machineknittingmonthly.net

Nonfiction > *Articles*: Knitting

Editor: Anne Smith

M0338 MacroMicroCosm

Magazine
Canada

literary@vraeydamedia.ca

https://www.vraeydamedia.ca/macromicrocosm

Types: Fiction; Nonfiction; Poetry
Formats: Interviews; Reviews
Subjects: Fantasy; Literary; Literary Criticism; Philosophy; Science; Science Fiction
Markets: Adult

Send: Full text
How to send: Email

A quarterly digital literary and art journal dedicated to speculative fiction, art and literary criticism. Send submissions by email.

M0339 Mad

Magazine
United States

Customer_Service@Mad-Magazine.us

https://www.madmagazine.com

Formats: Articles
Subjects: Comedy / Humour; Current Affairs; Politics; Satire; Sport
Markets: Adult; Young Adult

Send: Query
Don't send: Full text

Humour magazine welcoming pitches of up to three article ideas via the form on the website.

M0340 Magma

Magazine
23 Pine Walk, Carshalton, SM5 4ES
United Kingdom

info@magmapoetry.com

https://magmapoetry.com

Types: Nonfiction; Poetry
Formats: Reviews
Subjects: Literary; Literature
Markets: Adult

Send: Full text

Prefers submissions through online submission system. Postal submissions accepted from the UK only, and must include SAE. No submissions by email. Accepts poems and artwork. Poems are considered for one issue only – they are not held over from one issue to the next. Seeks poems that give a direct sense of what it is to live today – honest about feelings, alert about world, sometimes funny, always well crafted. Also publishes reviews of books and pamphlets of poetry. See website for details.

Editor: Laurie Smith

M0341 Making Cards

Magazine
United Kingdom

Magazine Publisher: Warners Group Publications

M0342 Management Today

Magazine
Bridge House, 69 London Road, Twickenham, TW1 3SP
United Kingdom
Tel: +44 (0) 20 8267 4967

adam.gale@haymarket.com

https://www.managementtoday.co.uk

Types: Nonfiction
Formats: Articles
Subjects: Business
Markets: Professional

Send: Query
Don't send: Full text
How to send: Email

Publishes features and articles on general business and management topics. Send query with brief synopsis by email only.

Editor: Adam Gale

M0343 Manoa

Magazine
University of Hawai'i at Mānoa, Department of English, 1733 Donaghho Road, Honolulu, HI 96822
United States
Tel: +1 (808) 956-3070
Fax: +1 (808) 956-3083

mjournal-l@lists.hawaii.edu

https://manoa.hawaii.edu/manoajournal/

ACADEMIC > **Nonfiction** > *Essays*
Asia; Culture; Literature; Pacific

ADULT
Fiction in Translation > *Short Fiction*
Asia; Pacific

Fiction > *Short Fiction*
Asia; Pacific

Poetry in Translation > *Any Poetic Form*
Asia; Pacific

Poetry > *Any Poetic Form*
Asia; Pacific

Closed to approaches.

A Pacific journal, however material does not need to be related to the Pacific, or by authors from the region.

Editor: Frank Stewart

M0344 marie claire

Magazine
300 West 57th Street, New York, NY 10019
United States

https://www.marieclaire.com
https://www.facebook.com/MarieClaire
https://twitter.com/marieclaire
https://www.pinterest.com/MarieClaire
https://instagram.com/marieclairemag
https://www.youtube.com/c/MarieClaire

Nonfiction > *Articles*
Beauty; Career Development; Celebrity; Culture; Fashion; Finance; Fitness; Food and Drink; Health; Horoscopes; Politics; Relationships; Sex; Travel; Women's Interests

Lifestyle magazine aimed at the younger working woman.

M0345 Maritime Journal

Magazine
Spinnaker House, Waterside Gardens, Fareham, Hampshire, PO16 8SD
United Kingdom
Tel: +44 (0) 1329 825335
Fax: +44 (0) 1329 550192

editor@maritimejournal.com

http://www.maritimejournal.com

Types: Nonfiction
Formats: Articles; News
Subjects: Business; Travel
Markets: Professional

Magazine providing insight for the European commercial marine business.

M0346 Marlin

Magazine
World Publications, 460 North Orlando Ave, Suite 200, Winter Park, FL 32789
United States

editor@marlinmag.com

https://www.marlinmag.com
https://www.facebook.com/marlinmag/
https://twitter.com/MarlinMagazine/
http://instagram.com/marlinmag/
http://www.youtube.com/MarlinMagazine/

Nonfiction > *Articles*
Boats; How To; Offshore Gamefishing;
Travel

Publishes articles, features, and news items
relating to offshore fishing, destinations,
personalities, fishery regulations, the boating
industry and related topics, including how-to
and technical information.

Editor: Dave Ferrel

M0347 The Massachusetts Review

Magazine
Photo Lab 309, University of Massachusetts,
Amherst, MA 01003
United States
Tel: +1 (413) 545-2689
Fax: +1 (413) 577-0740

massrev@external.umass.edu

http://www.massreview.org
https://www.facebook.com/pages/The-
Massachusetts-Review/40580092594
https://twitter.com/MassReview
http://instagram.com/themassachusettsreview?
ref=badge
http://themassreview.tumblr.com/

Fiction in Translation > *Short
Fiction*: Literary

Fiction > *Short Fiction*: Literary

Nonfiction in Translation > *Essays*
Arts; Current Affairs; Drama; Literature;
Music; Philosophy; Science

Nonfiction
Articles: Arts; Current Affairs; Drama;
Literature; Music; Philosophy; Science
Essays: Arts; Current Affairs; Drama;
Literature; Music; Philosophy; Science
Poetry in Translation > *Any Poetic Form*

Poetry > *Any Poetic Form*

Send: Full text; Self-Addressed Stamped
Envelope (SASE)
How to send: Post; Online submission system;
Email

Costs: A fee is charged for online submissions.
$3.

Send one story of up to 25–30 pages or up to
six poems of any length (though rarely
publishes poems of more than 100 lines).
White people may not submit between May 1
and September 30. Others may submit year-
round, and may use email if the online
submission system is closed. White people are
not permitted to submit by email. Articles and
essays of breadth and depth are considered, as
well as discussions of leading writers; of art,
music, and drama; analyses of trends in
literature, science, philosophy, and public
affairs. No plays, reviews of single books, or
submissions by fax or email.

Editor: David Lenson

M0348 Maxim

Magazine
United States

Editor@maxim.com

https://www.maxim.com
https://www.facebook.com/maximmagazine
https://twitter.com/MaximMag
https://www.youtube.com/user/
videosbyMaxim
https://www.instagram.com/maximmag
https://pinterest.com/maximmag

Nonfiction > *Articles*
Cars; Entertainment; Fashion; Food and
Drink; Luxury Lifestyle; Sport; Technology;
Travel; Women

Glossy magazine for men publishing articles
and features on entertainment, fashion, sex,
sport, travel, motoring, and tech. No poetry or
fiction.

Editor: Tom Loxley

M0349 Medal News

Magazine
No 40, Southernhay East, Exeter, Devon, EX1
1PE
United Kingdom
Tel: +44 (0) 1404 46972

info@tokenpublishing.com

http://www.tokenpublishing.com

Types: Nonfiction
Formats: Articles; News
Subjects: History; Warfare
Markets: Adult

Send: Full text

Magazine covering medals and the history
surrounding them. Welcomes unsolicited MSS,
but prior approach by phone or in writing
preferred.

M0350 Men's Health

Magazine
Hearst UK, 30 Panton Street, Leicester Square,
London, SW1Y 4AJ
United Kingdom

https://www.menshealth.com/uk

Types: Nonfiction
Formats: Articles
Subjects: Health; Lifestyle; Medicine; Men's
Interests
Markets: Adult

Publishes articles related to the health of men,
including such topics as fitness, stress, sex,
nutrition, and health in general.

M0351 Metropolis Magazine

Magazine
101 Park Ave, 4th Floor, New York, NY
10178
United States
Tel: +1 (212) 934-2800

info@metropolismag.com

https://www.metropolismag.com/
https://www.facebook.com/MetropolisMag
https://twitter.com/MetropolisMag
https://www.linkedin.com/company/
metropolis-magazine
https://www.instagram.com/metropolismag/

Magazine Publisher: Sandow

Nonfiction > *Articles*
Architecture; Arts; City and Town Planning;
Culture; Design; Interior Design; Sustainable
Living; Technology

Magazine examining contemporary life
through design: architecture, interior design,
product design, graphic design, crafts,
planning, and preservation.

M0352 MHQ

Magazine
United States

Magazine Publisher: HistoryNet LLC

M0353 Midway Journal

Magazine
United States

editors@midwayjournal.com

http://midwayjournal.com

Types: Fiction; Nonfiction; Poetry
Subjects: Literary
Markets: Adult

Send: Full text

Accepts submissions of fiction, poetry, and
creative nonfiction via online submission
system between January 1 and May 1 each
year. Seeks aesthetically ambitious work that
invokes the colliding and converging energies
of the fairgrounds. See website for full
guidelines.

Fiction Editor: Ralph Pennel

Nonfiction Editor: Allie Mariano

Poetry Editor: Paige Riehl

M0354 Military History

Magazine
1919 Gallows Road, Ste 400, Vienna, VA
22182
United States

militaryhistory@historynet.com

https://www.historynet.com/magazines/mag-
mh

Magazine Publisher: HistoryNet LLC

Nonfiction > *Articles*: Military History

Send: Query
Don't send: Full text
How to send: Email

Magazine of military history. No unsolicited
MSS. Send one-page query with details of any

previous writing experience. Potential contributors advised to familiarise themselves with the magazine before approaching.

Editor: Michael Robbins

M0355 Miniature Wargames
Magazine
United Kingdom

Magazine Publisher: Warners Group Publications

M0356 Modern Literature
Magazine
Chennai
India

editor@modernliterature.org

https://www.modernliterature.org/

Types: Fiction; Nonfiction; Poetry
Formats: Interviews; Reviews
Subjects: Experimental; Literary; Literature
Markets: Academic; Adult

Send: Full text
How to send: Email

An international, online literary magazine, focusing on the latest trends in literature. Fiction, nonfiction, poetry, interviews and many more interesting articles can be found. New articles are welcome.

Editor: Rajesh Subramanian

M0357 Modern Poetry in Translation
Magazine
United Kingdom

http://modernpoetryintranslation.com
https://twitter.com/MPTmagazine
https://www.instagram.com/modernpoetryintranslation/

Poetry in Translation > *Any Poetic Form*

Send: Full text
How to send: Submittable

Respected poetry series originally founded by prominent poets in the sixties. New Series continues their editorial policy: translation of good poets by translators who are often themselves poets, fluent in the foreign language, and sometimes working with the original poet. Publishes translations into English only. No original English language poetry. Send submissions via online submission system.

M0358 Moneywise
Magazine
First Floor, Standon House, 21 Mansell Street, London, E1 8AA
United Kingdom

editorial@moneywise.co.uk

http://www.moneywise.co.uk

Types: Nonfiction
Formats: Articles; News
Subjects: Business; Finance
Markets: Adult

Helps people learn how to make the most of their money, helping them to identify the right investment products, and avoid the unnecessary costs associated with some financial products.

M0359 Monomyth
Magazine
Atlantean Publishing, 4 Pierrot Steps, 71 Kursaal Way, Southend-on-Sea, Essex, SS1 2UY
United Kingdom

atlanteanpublishing@hotmail.com

https://atlanteanpublishing.fandom.com/wiki/Monomyth

Fiction > *Short Fiction*

Poetry > *Any Poetic Form*

Send: Full text; Self-Addressed Stamped Envelope (SASE)
How to send: Email; Post

Features mostly short fiction, covering a wide variety of genres but often quirky, offbeat or fantastical. Send submissions by email or by post with SAE / email address for response. See website for full guidelines.

Editor: David-John Tyrer

M0360 The Moth
Magazine
Ardan Grange, Milltown, Belturbet, Co. Cavan
Ireland
Tel: 353 (0) 87 2657251

submissions@themothmagazine.com

https://www.themothmagazine.com

Fiction > *Short Fiction*: Literary

Poetry > *Any Poetic Form*

Send: Full text
How to send: Email; Post

Submit up to six poems or up to two short stories by post or by email. Accepts fiction submissions between September and April only. Poetry submissions are open all year. See website for full submission guidelines.

Editor: Rebecca O'Connor

M0361 Motor Boat & Yachting
Magazine
United Kingdom

mby@futurenet.com

https://www.mby.com
https://www.youtube.com/user/ybwtv
https://www.facebook.com/motorboatandyachting
https://twitter.com/mbymagazine

https://www.instagram.com/motorboat_and_yachting/

Magazine Publisher: Future

Nonfiction > *Articles*
Motor Boats; Yachts

Magazine publishing news and features related to motor boats and motor cruising.

Editor: Hugo Andreae

M0362 Motorcaravan Motorhome Monthly (MMM)
Magazine
Warners Group Publications, The Maltings, West Street, Bourne, LINCS, PE10 9PH
United Kingdom

https://www.outandaboutlive.co.uk/motorhomes

Magazine Publisher: Warners Group Publications

Nonfiction > *Articles*
Motorhomes; Travel

Publishes articles on motorhome travel.

Editor: Mike & Jane Jago
Managing Editor: Daniel Atwood

M0363 Motorcycle News (MCN)
Magazine
Media House, Lynch Wood, Peterborough, PE2 6EA
United Kingdom
Tel: +44 (0) 1858 438884

andy.calton@motorcyclenews.com

https://www.motorcyclenews.com

Types: Nonfiction
Formats: Articles
Subjects: Leisure; Technology; Travel
Markets: Adult

Magazine for motorbike enthusiasts.

Editor: Andy Calton

M0364 The Motorship
Magazine
Mercator Media Ltd, Spinnaker House, Waterside Gardens, Fareham, Hampshire, PO16 8SD
United Kingdom
Tel: +44 (0) 1329 825335
Fax: +44 (0) 1329 550192

editor@motorship.com

http://www.motorship.com

Types: Nonfiction
Formats: Articles; News
Subjects: Business; Technology; Travel
Markets: Professional

Magazine aimed at marine technology professionals.

M0365 Mountain Living

Magazine
United States

https://www.mountainliving.com
https://www.facebook.com/mountainlivingmag
https://www.instagram.com/
mountainlivingmag/
https://www.pinterest.com/mtnlivingmag/

Nonfiction > *Articles*
  Architecture; Interior Design; Luxury
  Lifestyle; Mountain Lifestyle

Send: Query
How to send: Email

Magazine featuring mountain residences, from
luxurious high-country retreats to charming
guest cabins, with styles that range from
traditional to contemporary. Submit via email
and include a brief description of the home
with size, location and any distinctive details.

Editor: Irene Rawlings, Editor in Chief

Editor-in-Chief: Darla Worden

M0366 Moving Worlds: A Journal of Transcultural Writings

Magazine
School of English, University of Leeds, Leeds,
LS2 9JT
United Kingdom
Tel: +44 (0) 1133 434792
Fax: +44 (0) 1133 434774

mworlds@leeds.ac.uk

http://www.movingworlds.net

Types: Fiction; Poetry; Translations
Formats: Articles; Essays
Subjects: Culture; Experimental; Literary;
Literary Criticism
Markets: Academic; Adult

Biannual international magazine for creative
work as well as criticism, literary as well as
visual texts, writing in scholarly as well as
more personal modes, in English and
translations into English. It is open to
experimentation, and represents work of
different kinds and from different cultural
traditions. Its central concern is the
transcultural.

Editors: Shirley Chew; Stuart Murray

M0367 Mslexia

Magazine
PO Box 656, Newcastle upon Tyne, NE99 1PZ
United Kingdom

postbag@mslexia.co.uk

https://mslexia.co.uk

Fiction > *Short Fiction*

Nonfiction > *Articles*

Poetry > *Any Poetic Form*

Send: Full text
How to send: Online submission system

By women, for women who write, who want to
write, who teach creative writing or who have
an interest in women's literature and creativity.
It is a mixture of original work, features, news,
views, advice and listings. The UK's only
magazine devoted to women writers and their
writing.

See website for themes of upcoming issues /
competitions.

Publishes features, columns, reviews, flash
fiction, and literature listings. Some themes are
open to subscribers only. Submit via online
submission system on website.

M0368 Muse

Magazine
United States

Magazine Publisher: Cricket Media, Inc.

M0369 My Weekly

Magazine
D C Thomson & Co Ltd, My Weekly, 2 Albert
Square, Dundee, DD1 1DD
United Kingdom
Tel: +44 (0) 1382 223131
Fax: +44 (0) 1382 452491

sjohnstone@dctmedia.co.uk

https://www.myweekly.co.uk/

Newspaper Publisher / Magazine Publisher:
DC Thomson Media

Types: Fiction; Nonfiction
Formats: Articles
Subjects: Beauty; Cookery; Crafts; Fashion;
Finance; Gardening; Health; Lifestyle; Travel;
Women's Interests
Markets: Adult

Weekly women's magazine aged at the over-
50s, publishing a mix of lifestyle features, true
life stories, and fiction.

Editor: S. Johnstone

M0370 Mystery Weekly Magazine

Magazine
United States

https://www.mysteryweekly.com

Fiction > *Short Fiction*: Mystery

Send: Full text
How to send: Online submission system

Submit mysteries between 2,500 and 7,500
words through online submission system
available on website.

M0371 Nailpolish Stories

Magazine
United States

ncmonaghan@gmail.com

https://nailpolishstories.wordpress.com

Types: Fiction
Markets: Adult

Send: Full text
How to send: Email

Online literary journal publishing stories
exactly 25 words long. All stories must use a
nail polish colour as the title. Submit by email.

Editor: Nicole Monaghan

M0372 Nanoism

Magazine
United States

editor@nanoism.net

http://nanoism.net

Types: Fiction
Formats: Short Fiction
Subjects: Literary
Markets: Adult

Send: Full text
How to send: Email

Twitterzine publishing short stories up to 140
characters. Also accepts serials of up to 3-7
parts, though each must be able to stand on its
own. Submit no more than once per week, by
email.

M0373 Narrow Gauge World

Magazine
United Kingdom

Magazine Publisher: Warners Group
Publications

M0374 Nashville Review

Magazine
United States

thenashvillereview@gmail.com

https://as.vanderbilt.edu/nashvillereview

Types: Fiction; Nonfiction; Poetry;
Translations
Formats: Essays; Short Fiction
Subjects: Literary
Markets: Adult

Send: Full text

Submit short stories and novel excerpts up to
8,000 words, or three flash fiction pieces
(1,000 words each), 1-3 poems (up to ten pages
total), or creative nonfiction including memoir
excerpts, essays, imaginative meditations, up
to 8,000 words, via online submission system
during the three annual reading periods:
January, May, and September.

M0375 Nature

Magazine
The Macmillan Building, 4-6 Crinan Street,
London, N1 9XW

United Kingdom
Tel: +44 (0) 20 7833 4000
Fax: +44 (0) 20 7843 4596

nature@nature.com

http://www.nature.com

Types: Nonfiction
Formats: Articles; News
Subjects: Science
Markets: Academic; Adult; Professional

Journal covering all aspects of science. Scope for freelance writers with specialist knowledge.

Editor: Philip Campbell

M0376 NB Magazine
Magazine
172 Winsley Road, Bradford-on-Avon,
Wiltshire, BA15 1NY
United Kingdom
Tel: +44 (0) 1225 302266

info@nbmagazine.co.uk

https://nbmagazine.co.uk

Nonfiction > *Articles*: Book Publishing

Magazine and online platform for book lovers, book clubs and all round bibliophiles. Publishes articles and features on books and the book trade, as well as extracts from books.

M0377 Neon
Magazine
United Kingdom

subs@neonmagazine.co.uk

https://www.neonmagazine.co.uk

Fiction > *Short Fiction*
Dark; Literary; Speculative; Surreal

Poetry
Any Poetic Form: Dark; Literary; Surreal
Graphic Poems: Dark; Literary; Surreal

Send: Full text
How to send: Email

Quarterly online magazine publishing stylised poetry and prose, particularly the new, experimental, and strange. Welcomes genre fiction. Dark material preferred over humour; free verse preferred over rhyme. Send work pasted into the body of an email with a biographical note and the word "Submission" in the subject line.

Editor: Krishan Coupland

M0378 New England Review
Magazine
Middlebury College, Middlebury, VT 05753
United States
Tel: +1 (802) 443-5075

nereview@middlebury.edu

https://www.nereview.com
https://newenglandreview.submittable.com/
submit

https://www.facebook.com/
NewEnglandReviewMiddlebury/
https://twitter.com/nerweb

Fiction
Novel Excerpts; *Novellas*; *Short Fiction*
Nonfiction in Translation > *Essays*

Nonfiction
Essays: Personal Essays
Short Nonfiction: Arts; Cultural Criticism; Environment; Films; Literary Criticism; Travel
Poetry > *Any Poetic Form*

Scripts > *Theatre Scripts*: Drama

How to send: Submittable

Welcomes submissions in fiction, poetry, nonfiction, drama, and translation. Different submission windows for different categories of work. See website for details.

Editor: Stephen Donadio

M0379 New Orleans Review
Online Magazine
United States

noreview@loyno.edu

https://www.neworleansreview.org
https://www.facebook.com/neworleans.review/
https://twitter.com/NOReview

Fiction > *Short Fiction*: Literary

Nonfiction
Reviews: Literature
Short Nonfiction: General

Poetry > *Any Poetic Form*

Send: Full text
How to send: Submittable

Costs: A fee is charged upon submission. $3 per submission.

A journal of contemporary literature and culture. Send one story or piece of nonfiction up to 5,000 words, or up to five poems via online submission system.

Editor: Christopher Chambers

M0380 New Scientist
Magazine
110 High Holborn, London, WC1V 6EU
United Kingdom

richard.webb@newscientist.com

http://www.newscientist.com

Types: Nonfiction
Formats: Articles; News; Reviews
Subjects: Science; Technology
Markets: Adult; Professional

Weekly science magazine. No unsolicited MSS but accepts pitches by email. See website for more details and specific contact details and focus areas for the different editors. Reviews are commissioned.

Editor: Richard Webb

M0381 The New Shetlander
Magazine
United Kingdom

vas@shetland.org

https://www.shetland-communities.org.uk/
subsites/vas/the-new-shetlander.htm

Fiction > *Short Fiction*
Literary; Shetland

Nonfiction > *Articles*
Arts; Culture; History; Literature; Politics; Shetland

Poetry > *Any Poetic Form*: Shetland

Send: Full text
How to send: Email

Publishes short stories, poetry, and historical articles with a Shetland interest. Contributions and enquiries may be sent by email.

Editors: Laureen Johnson; Brian Smith

M0382 New Welsh Reader
Magazine
United Kingdom

editor@newwelshreview.com

https://newwelshreview.com/new-welsh-reader

Fiction > *Short Fiction*: Literary

Nonfiction
Essays: General
Short Nonfiction: Creative Nonfiction

Poetry > *Any Poetic Form*

Send: Full text
How to send: Online submission system

Focus is on Welsh writing in English, but has an outlook which is deliberately diverse, encompassing broader UK and international contexts. For feature articles, send 300-word query by email. Submit through online submission system only. Postal submissions will be returned unopened. Full details available on website.

Editor: Gwen Davies

M0383 Nine Muses Poetry
Magazine
United Kingdom

ninemusespoetry@talktalk.net

https://ninemusespoetry.com

Types: Poetry
Subjects: Literary
Markets: Adult

Send: Full text

A webzine featuring all forms of poetry by new, emerging and established poets, showcasing the best of contemporary poetry.

Editor: Annest Gwilym

M0384 No.1
Magazine
United Kingdom

Newspaper Publisher / Magazine Publisher:
DC Thomson Media

M0385 The North
Magazine
The Poetry Business, Campo House, 54
Campo Lane, Sheffield, S1 2EG
United Kingdom
Tel: +44 (0) 1144 384074

office@poetrybusiness.co.uk

https://poetrybusiness.co.uk

Poetry > *Any Poetic Form*: Contemporary

Closed to approaches.

Send up to 6 poems with SASE / return
postage. We publish the best of contemporary
poetry. No "genre" or derivative poetry.
Submitters should be aware of, should
preferably have read, the magazine before
submitting. See our website for notes on
submitting poems. No submissions by email.
Overseas submissions may be made through
online submission system.

Editors: Ann Sansom; Peter Sansom

M0386 Nursery World
Magazine
MA Education, St Jude's Church, Dulwich
Road, London, SE24 0PB
United Kingdom
Tel: +44 (0) 20 7501 6693

liz.roberts@markallengroup.com

https://www.nurseryworld.co.uk

Types: Nonfiction
Formats: Articles; News
Markets: Professional

Magazine aimed at professionals dealing with
the care of children in nurseries, primary
schools, childcare, etc.; nannies and foster
parents; and those involved with caring for
expectant mothers, babies, and young children.

Editor: Liz Roberts

M0387 Nursing Times
Magazine
EMAP Publishing Company, 7th Floor,
Vantage London, Great West Road, Brentford,
TW8 9AG
United Kingdom
Tel: +44 (0) 20 3953 2707
Fax: +44 (0) 20 7874 0505

jenni.middleton@emap.com

http://www.nursingtimes.net

Types: Nonfiction
Formats: Articles
Subjects: Contemporary; Health; Medicine
Markets: Professional

Magazine aimed at nurses, covering all aspects
of health care and nursing.

Editor: Jenni Middleton

M0388 OBRA / Aftifact
Magazine
United States

editors@obraartifact.com

https://obraartifact.com

Types: Fiction; Nonfiction; Poetry;
Translations
Formats: Essays
Subjects: Experimental; Literary
Markets: Adult

Closed to approaches.

Closed to submissions as at September 2019.
Check website for current status. Publishes
fiction, creative nonfiction, essays, and poetry,
for print and online publication. Submit via
online submission system.

Editor: Carley Fockler

M0389 Obsidian: Literature in
the African Diaspora
Magazine
Illinois State University, Williams Hall Annex,
Normal, IL 61790
United States

https://obsidianlit.org

Fiction > *Short Fiction*: African Diaspora

Poetry > *Any Poetic Form*: African Diaspora

Scripts > *Theatre Scripts*: African Diaspora

Send: Full text
How to send: Submittable

Publishes scripts, fiction, and poetry focused
on Africa and her Diaspora. Reading period
runs from September 15 to January 15. See
website for submission guidelines and to
submit via online submission system.

M0390 The Official Jacqueline
Wilson Mag
Magazine
United Kingdom

Newspaper Publisher / Magazine Publisher:
DC Thomson Media

M0391 OK! Magazine
Magazine
The Northern & Shell Building, 10 Lower
Thames Street, London, EC3R 6EN
United Kingdom
Tel: +44 (0) 20 8612 7000

charlotte.seligman@reachplc.com

https://www.ok.co.uk

Types: Nonfiction
Formats: Articles; Interviews

Subjects: Women's Interests
Markets: Adult

Send: Query
Don't send: Full text

Celebrity magazine, welcoming ideas for
features and interviews/pictures of celebrities.

Editor: Charlotte Seligman

M0392 Old Glory
Magazine
United Kingdom
Tel: +44 (0) 7943 02158

colin.tyson@kelseymedia.co.uk

https://www.oldglory.co.uk
https://www.facebook.com/OldGloryMag/

Magazine Publisher: Kelsey Media

Nonfiction > *Articles*
History; Steam Engines; Steam Power

Publishes articles, features, and news covering
industrial and transport heritage in the United
Kingdom and overseas, particularly vintage
vehicles and the preservation and restoration of
steam engines.

Editor: Colin Tyson

M0393 Old Red Kimono
Magazine
Georgia Highlands College, 3175 Cedartown
Hwy SE, Rome, GA 30161
United States

napplega@highlands.edu

https://www2.highlands.edu/site/ork

Types: Fiction; Poetry
Formats: Short Fiction
Subjects: Literary
Markets: Adult

Send: Full text
How to send: Email

Annual student-edited literary magazine. Send
3-5 poems or short stories up to 1,500 words
by post or by email. Submissions from
contributors outside the university are
considered between October and February each
year.

Editor: Steven Godfrey

M0394 Oor Wullie
Magazine
United Kingdom

Newspaper Publisher / Magazine Publisher:
DC Thomson Media

M0395 Orbis International
Literary Journal
Magazine
17 Greenhow Avenue, West Kirby, Wirral,
CH48 5EL
United Kingdom

carolebaldock@hotmail.com

http://www.orbisjournal.com

Types: Fiction; Nonfiction; Poetry
Formats: Articles; Essays; News; Reviews;
Short Fiction
Subjects: Arts; Comedy / Humour; Literary;
Women's Interests
Markets: Adult

Send: Full text

One of the longest running UK magazines;
established 1969 And one of the most highly
regarded; Peter Finch, Chief Executive of the
Welsh Academi includes this magazine in his
Top 10 publications (The Poetry Business).
Around one third of the poems in each issue
are from Overseas (and around one fifth of
subscribers):read, enjoy, inwardly digest; and
improve your chances of being published
abroad. One of the few magazines which is
also a useful resource. Includes news items,
competition listings and magazine reviews.
One of the few magazines to provide
contributors with proofs and editorial critique.
Readers' Award: £50 for the piece receiving
the most votes, plus £50 between four runners-
up. Submissions by post only, unless overseas.

Editor: Carole Baldock

M0396 The Orchid Review

Magazine
United Kingdom

Magazine Publisher: The Royal Horticultural
Society (RHS)

M0397 Our Dogs

Magazine
Northwood House, Greenwood Business
Centre, Regent Road, Salford, M5 4QH
United Kingdom
Tel: +44 (0) 1617 094571
Fax: +44 (0) 844 504 9013

alismith@ourdogs.co.uk

http://www.ourdogs.co.uk

Types: Nonfiction
Formats: Articles; News
Subjects: Hobbies; How To
Markets: Adult; Professional

Magazine on the showing and breeding of
pedigree dogs.

Editor: Alison Smith

M0398 Overtime

Magazine
PO Box 250382, Plano, TX 75025-0382
United States

overtime@workerswritejournal.com

http://www.workerswritejournal.com/overtime.
htm

Types: Fiction
Formats: Short Fiction
Subjects: Literary
Markets: Adult

Send: Query
Don't send: Full text
How to send: Email

A series of one-story chapbooks, publishing
stories between 5,000 and 10,000 words, where
work is a central theme.

Editor: David LaBounty

M0399 Oxford Poetry

Magazine
c/o Partus Press, Suite 270, 266 Banbury Road,
Oxford, OX2 7DL
United Kingdom

editors@oxfordpoetry.co.uk

http://www.oxfordpoetry.co.uk

Book Publisher / Magazine Publisher: Partus
Press

Nonfiction
  Articles: Literature
  Essays: Literature
  Interviews: Literature
  Reviews: Literature

Poetry in Translation > *Any Poetic Form*

Poetry > *Any Poetic Form*

How to send: Submittable

Publishes poems, interviews, reviews, and
essays. Accepts unpublished poems on any
theme and of any length during specific
biannual submission windows, which are
announced on the website. Send up to four
poems by email. See website for full details.

M0400 Pacifica Literary Review

Magazine
Seattle, WA
United States

pacificalitreview@gmail.com

http://www.pacificareview.com

Types: Fiction; Nonfiction; Poetry
Subjects: Literary
Markets: Adult

Send: Full text

Accepts poetry, fiction, and creative
nonfiction. Prose should be under 5,000 words.
Flash fiction up to 1,000 words. Will consider
novel excerpts, but must work as stand alone
entities. For poetry and flash fiction submit a
maximum of three pieces at a time. Send
submissions through online submission system.
See website for full guidelines.

Editor: Matt Muth

M0401 pacificREVIEW

Magazine
Dept. of English and Comparative Literature,
San Diego State University, 5500 Campanile
Dr., San Diego, CA 92182-6020
United States

pacrevjournal@gmail.com

https://pacificreview.sdsu.edu

Types: Fiction; Nonfiction; Poetry
Formats: Essays; Short Fiction
Markets: Adult

Closed to approaches.

Closed as at September 2019. Check website
for current status. Publishes poems, fiction
(short stories, flash fiction and excerpts that
stand alone), memoir, creative non-fiction,
essays, comics, visual art, photography,
documented performance and hybrid.

M0402 Packingtown Review

Magazine
United States

packingtownreview@gmail.com

http://www.packingtownreview.com

Types: Fiction; Nonfiction; Poetry; Scripts;
Translations
Subjects: Drama; Literary; Literary Criticism
Markets: Adult

Send: Full text
How to send: Email

Submit 3-5 poems, fiction, criticism, or
creative nonfiction up to 4,000 words, drama
up to 15 pages, or translations, with 60-word
bio in the third person. Send as attachment by
email. See website for full guidelines.

M0403 The Paddock Review

Magazine
United States

https://paddockreview.com

Types: Poetry
Subjects: Literary
Markets: Adult

Send: Full text

Submit 1-3 poems through online submission
system. Accepts previously published poems
and simultaneous submissions. Include short
bio.

M0404 Pain

Magazine
United Kingdom

pain@partuspress.com

https://www.painpoetry.co.uk
https://partus.submittable.com/submit

Book Publisher / Magazine Publisher: Partus
Press

Nonfiction
  Articles: Literature
  Essays: Creative Nonfiction

Poetry > *Any Poetic Form*

Closed to approaches.

Costs: A fee is charged upon submission. £3.00 fee per submission.

Publishes unpublished poems as well as short essays and articles with a literary focus.

M0405 Parchment Craft
Magazine
United Kingdom

Magazine Publisher: Warners Group Publications

M0406 The Paris Review
Magazine
544 West 27th Street, New York, NY 10001
United States
Tel: +1 (212) 343-1333

queries@theparisreview.org

https://www.theparisreview.org
https://www.facebook.com/parisreview
https://twitter.com/parisreview
http://theparisreview.tumblr.com/

Fiction > *Short Fiction*: Literary

Nonfiction
  Interviews; *Short Nonfiction*
Poetry > *Any Poetic Form*

Closed to approaches.

Send submissions through online submission system only. Postal submissions are suspended at this time. All submissions must be in English and previously unpublished, though translations are acceptable if accompanied by copy of the original text. Simultaneous submissions accepted as long as immediate notification is given of acceptance elsewhere.

Executive Editor: Brigid Hughes

M0407 Park & Holiday Home Inspiration
Magazine
United Kingdom

Magazine Publisher: Warners Group Publications

M0408 Park Home and Holiday Caravan
Magazine
Kelsey Publishing, Cudham Tithe Barn, Berry's Hill, Cudham, Kent, TN16 3AG
United Kingdom
Tel: +44 (0) 1959 541444

phhc.ed@kelsey.co.uk

https://www.parkhomemagazine.co.uk

Types: Nonfiction
Formats: Articles; News
Subjects: Hobbies; How To; Lifestyle; Travel
Markets: Adult

Magazine for those owning holiday caravans or living in residential park homes.

Editor: Alex Melvin

M0409 Peace and Freedom
Magazine
United Kingdom

p_rance@yahoo.co.uk

http://pandf.booksmusicfilmstv.com/

Fiction > *Short Fiction*
  Environment; Social Issues

Nonfiction
  Articles: Environment; Social Issues
  Essays: Environment; Social Issues
Poetry > *Any Poetic Form*
  Environment; Social Issues

Magazine publishing poetry, fiction, and articles, with an emphasis on social, humanitarian and environmental issues. Also publishes interviews of animal welfare/environmental/human rights campaigners, writers, poets, artists, film, music and TV personalities, up to 1,000 words. Reviews of books / records / events etc. up to 50 words also considered. Email submissions accepted for reviews, short stories, and interviews ONLY.

Editor: Paul Rance

M0410 People's Friend Pocket Novels
Magazine
DC Thomson & Co. Ltd, 2 Albert Square, Dundee, DD1 9QJ
United Kingdom
Tel: +44 (0) 1382 223131

tsteel@dcthomson.co.uk

http://www.thepeoplesfriend.co.uk

Types: Fiction
Subjects: Romance
Markets: Adult

Send: Query
Don't send: Full text
How to send: Email

Publishes romance and family fiction between 40,000 and 42,000 words, aimed at adults aged over 30. Send query by post or by email (preferred) with synopsis and first two chapters in first instance. See website for more information.

Editor: Tracey Steel

M0411 The People's Friend
Magazine
DC Thomson & Co. Ltd., 2 Albert Square,

Dundee, DD1 9QJ
United Kingdom
Tel: +44 (0) 1382 223131

peoplesfriend@dcthomson.co.uk

http://www.thepeoplesfriend.co.uk

Newspaper Publisher / Magazine Publisher: DC Thomson Media

Types: Fiction; Nonfiction; Poetry
Formats: Articles; Short Fiction
Subjects: Adventure; Cookery; Crafts; Crime; Hobbies; Mystery; Nature; Romance; Thrillers; Traditional; Travel; Women's Interests
Markets: Adult

Publishes complete short stories (1,200-3,000 words (4,000 for specials)) and serials, focusing on character development rather than complex plots, plus 10,000-word crime thrillers. Also considers nonfiction from nature to nostalgia and from holidays to hobbies, and poetry. Guidelines available on website.

M0412 Period Living
Magazine
Future Publishing Limited, Quay House, The Ambury, Bath, BA1 1UA
United Kingdom

realhomes@futurenet.com

https://www.realhomes.com/period-living

Types: Nonfiction
Formats: Articles
Subjects: Crafts; Design; Gardening
Markets: Adult

Magazine on renovating and decorating period homes, or in a period style.

M0413 Petroleum Geoscience
Magazine
United Kingdom

Book Publisher / Magazine Publisher: The Geological Society Publishing House (**P0317**)

M0414 Phase 2 Magazine
Magazine
United States

submissions@darkfuturesfiction.net

http://www.darkfuturesfiction.net

Types: Fiction; Nonfiction; Poetry
Formats: Reviews
Subjects: Science Fiction
Markets: Adult

Send: Full text
How to send: Email

Science fiction magazine publishing fiction up to 1,500 words; reviews up to 800 words; and poetry up to 19 lines. See website for full guidelines.

M0415 The Photographer

Magazine
The British Institute of Professional Photography, The Artistry House, 16 Winckley Square, Preston, PR1 3JJ
United Kingdom
Tel: +44 (0) 1772 367968

editor@bipp.com

http://www.bipp.com

Types: Nonfiction
Formats: Articles; News; Reviews
Subjects: Photography
Markets: Professional

Photography magazine for professional photographers.

M0416 Pianist

Magazine
United Kingdom

Magazine Publisher: Warners Group Publications

M0417 Picture Postcard Monthly

Magazine
6 Carmarthen Avenue, Drayton, Portsmouth, Hampshire, PO6 2AQ
United Kingdom
Tel: +44 (0) 2392 423527

info@picturepostcardmagazine.co.uk

http://www.picturepostcardmagazine.co.uk

Types: Nonfiction
Formats: Articles; News; Reference
Subjects: Arts; Hobbies; Photography
Markets: Adult

Magazine for postcard collectors, publishing news, views, stories and feature articles.

Editor: Mark Wingham

M0418 Pilot

Magazine
Evolution House, 2-6 Easthampstead Road, Wokingham, RG40 2EG
United Kingdom

philip.whiteman@archant.co.uk

https://www.pilotweb.aero

Magazine Publisher: Archant

ADULT > *Nonfiction* > *Articles*
Air Travel; Piloting

PROFESSIONAL > *Nonfiction* > *Articles*
Air Travel; Piloting

Send: Full text
How to send: Email

Aimed at private, commercial and would-be flyers, including enthusiasts.

Editor: Nick Bloom

M0419 Pirene's Fountain

Magazine
United States

pirenesfountain@gmail.com

http://pirenesfountain.com

Types: Poetry
Subjects: Literary
Markets: Adult

Send: Full text
How to send: Email

Send between three and eight previously unpublished poems in the body of an email with a brief bio, between May 1 and August 1 annually.

M0420 Planet

Magazine
PO Box 44, Aberystwyth, Ceredigion, SY23 3ZZ
United Kingdom
Tel: +44 (0) 1970 611255

submissions@planetmagazine.org.uk

http://www.planetmagazine.org.uk

Types: Fiction; Nonfiction; Poetry
Formats: Articles; Reviews; Short Fiction; Theatre Scripts
Subjects: Arts; Current Affairs; Literary; Literature; Music; Politics
Markets: Adult

Send: Full text
How to send: Email

Publishes mostly commissioned material, but will accept ideas for articles and reviews, and unsolicited submissions of fiction and poetry. Submit one piece of short fiction between 1,500 and 2,500 words, or 4-6 poems at a time. A range of styles and themes are accepted, but postal submissions will not be considered unless adequate return postage is provided. If you have an idea for a relevant article send a query with brief synopsis.

Editor: Emily Trahair

M0421 The Plant Review

Magazine
United Kingdom

Magazine Publisher: The Royal Horticultural Society (RHS)

M0422 Platinum Magazine

Magazine
United Kingdom

Newspaper Publisher / Magazine Publisher: DC Thomson Media

M0423 PN Review

Magazine
4th Floor, Alliance House, 30 Cross Street, Manchester, M2 7AQ
United Kingdom
Tel: +44 (0) 161 834 8730
Fax: +44 (0) 161 832 0084

PNRsubmissions@carcanet.co.uk

http://www.pnreview.co.uk

Types: Poetry; Translations
Formats: Articles; Interviews; News; Reviews
Markets: Adult

Send: Query
Don't send: Full text

Send query with synopsis and sample pages, after having familiarised yourself with the magazine. Accepts prose up to 15 double-spaced pages or 4 poems / 5 pages of poetry. Bimonthly magazine of poetry and poetry criticism. Includes editorial, letters, news, articles, interviews, features, poems, translations, and a substantial book review section. No short stories, children's prose / poetry, or non-poetry related work (academic, biography etc.). Accepts electronic submissions from individual subscribers only – otherwise only hard copy submissions are considered.

Editor: Michael Schmidt

M0424 Poetica Magazine

Magazine
5215 Colley Avenue #138, Norfolk, VA 23508
United States

poeticapublishing@aol.com

http://www.poeticamagazine.com

Types: Poetry
Subjects: Contemporary; Literary
Markets: Adult

Publishes contemporary Jewish poetry. Submit via online submission manager.

Editor: Michal Mahgerefteh

M0425 Poetry Ireland Review

Magazine
11 Parnell Square East, Dublin 1, D01 ND60
Ireland
Tel: +353 (0)1 6789815
Fax: +353 (0)1 6789782

pir@poetryireland.ie
info@poetryireland.ie

https://www.poetryireland.ie

Nonfiction
 Articles: Poetry as a Subject
 Reviews: Poetry as a Subject

Poetry > *Any Poetic Form*

Send: Full text; Proposal
How to send: Post; Submittable

Send up to six poems through online submission system, or by post. Poetry is accepted from around the world, but must be previously unpublished. No sexism or racism.

Articles and reviews are generally commissioned, however proposals are welcome. No unsolicited reviews or articles.

Editor: Colette Bryce

M0426 Poetry London

Magazine
Goldsmiths, University of London, New Cross, London, SE14 6NW
United Kingdom
Tel: +44 (0) 20 8228 5707

admin@poetrylondon.co.uk

http://www.poetrylondon.co.uk

Types: Nonfiction; Poetry; Translations
Formats: Articles; Reviews
Subjects: Contemporary; Literary
Markets: Adult

Send: Full text
How not to send: Email

Send up to six poems with SASE or adequate return postage. Considers poems by both new and established poets. Also publishes book reviews. No submissions by email.

Editors: Martha Kapos; Ahren Warner

M0427 The Poetry Review

Magazine
The Poetry Society, 22 Betterton Street, London, WC2H 9BX
United Kingdom
Tel: +44 (0) 20 7420 9880
Fax: +44 (0) 20 7240 4818

poetryreview@poetrysociety.org.uk

https://poetrysociety.org.uk/

Nonfiction
  Essays: Poetry as a Subject
  Reviews: Poetry as a Subject

Poetry in Translation > *Any Poetic Form*

Poetry > *Any Poetic Form*

Send: Full text
How to send: Submittable

Describes itself as "one of the liveliest and most influential literary magazines in the world", and has been associated with the rise of the New Generation of British poets – Carol Ann Duffy, Simon Armitage, Glyn Maxwell, Don Paterson... though its scope extends beyond the UK, with special issues focusing on poetries from around the world. Send up to 6 unpublished poems, or literary translations of poems, through online submission system.

M0428 Poetry Wales

Magazine
Suite 6, 4 Derwen Road, Bridgend, CF31 1LH
United Kingdom
Tel: +44 (0) 1656 663018

editor@poetrywales.co.uk

https://poetrywales.co.uk
http://twitter.com/poetrywales
http://facebook.com/poetrywales
http://instagram.com/poetrywales

Nonfiction
  Articles: Poetry as a Subject
  Reviews: Poetry as a Subject; Published Books
Poetry > *Any Poetic Form*

Send: Full text
How to send: Submittable; Post; Word file email attachment
How not to send: PDF file email attachment

Publishes poetry, features, and reviews from Wales and beyond. Submit via online submission system. Also runs competitions.

Editor: Nia Davies

M0429 The Political Quarterly

Magazine
United Kingdom

submissions@politicalquarterly.org.uk

http://www.politicalquarterly.org.uk

Types: Nonfiction
Formats: Articles
Subjects: Politics
Markets: Adult

Send: Full text
How to send: Email

Magazine covering national and international politics. Accepts unsolicited articles.

M0430 The Pool

Magazine
United Kingdom

hello@thepoolltd.com

https://www.the-pool.com

Types: Nonfiction
Formats: Articles; News
Subjects: Arts; Beauty; Culture; Fashion; Health; Lifestyle; Women's Interests
Markets: Adult

Send: Query
Don't send: Full text
How to send: Email

Online platform for news and comment aimed at women. Send proposals by email.

M0431 Popshot Quarterly

Magazine
United Kingdom

submit@popshotpopshot.com

https://www.popshotpopshot.com

Fiction > *Short Fiction*: Literary

Poetry > *Any Poetic Form*

Send: Full text
How to send: Email

Publishes flash fiction, short stories, and poetry on the theme of the current issue (see website). Submit by email.

M0432 Prac Crit

Magazine
United Kingdom

editors@praccrit.com

http://www.praccrit.com

Types: Nonfiction
Formats: Essays; Interviews
Subjects: Contemporary; Literary; Literary Criticism
Markets: Adult

Send: Query
Don't send: Full text
How to send: Email

Publishes close analysis of poems; essays; interviews; and reflections from poets. Most articles are commissioned, but will accept proposals for essays or interviews. No direct submissions of poetry.

M0433 Practical Boat Owner Magazine

Magazine
2 Pinehurst, Pinehurst Road, Farnborough Business Park, Farnborough, Hants, GU14 7BF
United Kingdom
Tel: +44 (0) 1252 555213

pbo@futurenet.com

https://www.pbo.co.uk

Magazine Publisher: Future

Nonfiction > *Articles*: Boats

Cruising boats magazine covering both power and sail. Publishes technical articles on maintenance, restoration, modifications, etc.

M0434 Practical Caravan

Magazine
Future Publishing Limited, Quay House, The Ambury, Bath, BA1 1UA
United Kingdom

https://www.practicalcaravan.com

Types: Nonfiction
Formats: Articles; Reviews
Subjects: Leisure; Travel
Markets: Adult

Publishes material relating to caravanning and touring caravans, including features, reviews, travel pieces, etc. No static van or motorcaravan stories. Features must be accompanied by photos.

M0435 Practical Fishkeeping

Magazine
The Maltings, West Street, Bourne, Lincolnshire, PE10 9PH

United Kingdom
Tel: +44 (0) 1778 391194

editorial@practicalfishkeeping.co.uk

https://www.practicalfishkeeping.co.uk
https://www.facebook.com/PFKmag/
https://www.twitter.com/PFKmagazine
https://www.instagram.com/pfkmag/
https://www.youtube.com/channel/UC--fz-
Y9Zn6cZ-XKcIBjeGw

Magazine Publisher: Warners Group
Publications

Nonfiction > *Articles*: Pet Fish

Publishes practical articles on all aspects of
keeping fish.

Editor: Karen Youngs

M0436 The Practising Midwife
Magazine
Saturn House, Mercury Rise, Altham Industrial
Park, Altham, Lancashire, BB5 5BY
United Kingdom

info@all4maternity.com

https://www.all4maternity.com
https://twitter.com/all4maternity
https://www.facebook.com/all4maternity/

PROFESSIONAL > **Nonfiction**
  Articles: Midwifery
  News: Midwifery

How to send: Online submission system

Publishes accessible, authoritative and readable
information for midwives, students and other
professionals in the maternity services.

Editors: Claire Feeley; Laura Yeates

M0437 The Practitioner
Magazine
United Kingdom

editor@thepractitioner.co.uk

https://www.thepractitioner.co.uk

PROFESSIONAL > **Nonfiction**
  Articles: Health; Medicine
  News: Health; Medicine

Send: Query; Full text
How to send: Email

Monthly magazine for General Practitioners,
covering latest clinical issues. Considers ideas
for articles and submissions of case reports.

Editor: Corinne Short

M0438 Press Gazette
Magazine
40 Hatton Garden, London, EC1N 8EV
United Kingdom
Tel: +44 (0) 20 7936 6433

pged@pressgazette.co.uk

http://www.pressgazette.co.uk

Types: Nonfiction
Formats: Articles; News
Subjects: Current Affairs; Media
Markets: Professional

Send: Query
Don't send: Full text
How to send: Email

Publishes news, features, and analysis related
to all areas of journalism: print, broadcasting,
online; national, regional, magazines, etc. Pitch
stories by phone or by email.

Editor: Freddy Mayhew

M0439 Pride
Magazine
1 Garrat Lane, London, SW18 4AQ
United Kingdom
Tel: +44 (0) 20 8871 4443

editor@pridemagazine.com

http://pridemagazine.com
http://www.facebook.com/PrideMagazine
http://www.instagram.com/pridemaguk

Nonfiction
  Articles: Beauty; Career Development;
  Entertainment; Fashion; Hairstyles; Health;
  Lifestyle
  News: Ethnic Groups; Social Issues

Magazine aimed at black women. Publishes
news, and articles and features on
entertainment, hair, beauty, and fashion.

Editor: CJ Cushnie

M0440 Proceedings of the Yorkshire Geological Society
Magazine
United Kingdom

Book Publisher / Magazine Publisher: The
Geological Society Publishing House (**P0317**)

M0441 The Progressive Populist
Magazine
PO Box 819, Manchaca, Texas 78652
United States
Tel: +1 (512) 828-7245

populist@usa.net

http://www.populist.com

Types: Nonfiction
Formats: Articles; Essays; News
Subjects: Business; Finance; Lifestyle; Politics
Markets: Adult

Send: Query
Don't send: Full text
How to send: Email

Fortnightly newspaper reporting on issues of
interest to workers, small-business owners and
family farmers and ranchers.

Editor: Jim Cullen

M0442 Prole
Magazine
United Kingdom

submissionspoetry@prolebooks.co.uk
submissionsprose@prolebooks.co.uk

https://prolebooks.co.uk
https://facebook.com/Prole-236155444300
https://twitter.com/Prolebooks

Fiction > *Short Fiction*: Literary

Nonfiction > *Short Nonfiction*: Creative
Nonfiction

Poetry > *Any Poetic Form*

Send: Full text
How to send: In the body of an email

Publishes accessible literature of high quality,
including poetry, short fiction, and creative
nonfiction. Seeks to appeal to a wide audience
and avoid literary elitism (obscure references
and highly stylised structures and forms are
unlikely to find favour). No previously
published material or simultaneous
submissions. Submit one piece of prose or up
to five poems (or three longer poems) in the
body of an email, with your name, contact
details, word count and third person author bio
up to 100 words. See website for appropriate
email addresses for prose and poetry
submissions, and full submission guidelines.
No attachments.

M0443 Prospect
Magazine
United Kingdom

editorial@prospect-magazine.co.uk

https://prospectmagazine.co.uk

Types: Nonfiction
Formats: Articles; Essays; Reviews
Subjects: Arts; Culture; Current Affairs;
Literature; Politics
Markets: Adult

Intelligent magazine of current affairs and
cultural debate. No news features. Almost all
articles are commissioned from regular writers,
but will consider unsolicited nonfiction
submissions if suitable for the magazine, but
no unsolicited fiction submissions. Does not
publish any poetry. No postal submissions or
telephone pitches. Submit by email only.

Editor: Tom Clark

M0444 Psychic News
Magazine
Unit 2, Griggs Business Centre, West Street,
Coggeshall, Essex, CO6 1NT
United Kingdom
Tel: +44 (0) 1376 563091

pneditorials@gmail.com

https://www.psychicnews.org.uk
https://www.facebook.com/psychicnews/
https://twitter.com/psychicnewsmag

Nonfiction > *Articles*: Spirituality

Magazine of the paranormal, covering ghosts, spiritual healing, psychic research, etc.

Editor: Tony Ortzen

M0445 Publishers Weekly
Magazine
United States

jmilliot@publishersweekly.com

https://www.publishersweekly.com

Types: Nonfiction
Formats: Articles; News; Reviews
Subjects: Business; Literature
Markets: Professional

Weekly news magazine aimed at publishers, booksellers, librarians, literary agents, authors and the media, providing news and feature articles relating to the book industry, but best known for its pre-publication book reviews.

Editor: Jim Milliot

M0446 Pulse
Magazine
Cogora Limited, 140 London Wall, London, EC2Y 5DN
United Kingdom
Tel: +44 (0) 20 7214 0567

jaimiekaffash@cogora.com

http://www.pulsetoday.co.uk

Types: Nonfiction
Formats: Articles
Subjects: Medicine
Markets: Professional

Magazine aimed at GPs.

Editor: Jaimie Kaffash

M0447 Pushing Out the Boat
Magazine
United Kingdom

info@pushingouttheboat.co.uk

https://www.pushingouttheboat.co.uk

Fiction > *Short Fiction*: Literary

Poetry > *Any Poetic Form*

Scripts > *Theatre Scripts*

Closed to approaches.

Magazine of prose, poetry and visual arts, based in North-East Scotland. Welcomes work in English, Doric or Scots. Submit via online submission system during open reading periods. See website for details.

M0448 Qu
Magazine
United States

qulitmag@queens.edu

http://www.qulitmag.com

Fiction > *Short Fiction*: Literary

Nonfiction > *Essays*

Poetry > *Any Poetic Form*

Scripts
    Film Scripts; *TV Scripts*; *Theatre Scripts*

Closed to approaches.

Submit prose or poems via online submission system. $2 fee. Does not accept international submissions.

M0449 Quail Bell
Magazine
United States

submissions@quailbellmagazine.com

http://www.quailbellmagazine.com

Types: Fiction; Nonfiction; Poetry
Formats: Articles; Short Fiction
Subjects: Literary; Women's Interests
Markets: Adult

Send: Full text
How to send: Email

Feminist magazine. Send submissions by email. See website for full guidelines.

M0450 Qualified Remodeler
Magazine
United States
Tel: +1 (847) 920-5996

Patrick@SOLAbrands.com

http://www.qualifiedremodeler.com

Types: Nonfiction
Formats: Articles; News
Subjects: Business; Design; How To; Technology
Markets: Professional

Send: Query
Don't send: Full text

Magazine aimed at residential remodelling contractors. Particularly interested in business management issues. Send query with published clips.

Editor: Patrick O'Toole

M0451 Quarter After Eight
Magazine
United States

editor@quarteraftereight.org

http://www.quarteraftereight.org

Types: Fiction; Nonfiction; Poetry; Scripts; Translations
Formats: Interviews; Reviews

Subjects: Drama; Experimental
Markets: Adult

Send: Full text

Publishes fiction, poetry, and nonfiction. Submit one story or essay or up to three flash prose pieces or four poems via online submission system. Accepts online submissions between October 15 and April 15 only.

M0452 Quarterly Journal of Engineering Geology and Hydrogeology
Magazine
United Kingdom

Book Publisher / Magazine Publisher: The Geological Society Publishing House (**P0317**)

M0453 R.kv.r.y. Quarterly Literary Journal
Magazine
United States

r.kv.r.y.editor@gmail.com

http://rkvryquarterly.com

Types: Fiction; Nonfiction; Poetry
Formats: Essays; Short Fiction
Subjects: Literary
Markets: Adult

Closed to approaches.

Closed to submissions as at November 2019. Check website for current status. Literary journal publishing works relating to acts, processes, or instances of recovery. Submit up to 3,000 words for prose, up to 1,000 words for flash fiction, or up to three poems, via online submission system. £3 submission charge. Closed to submissions during the summer months.

M0454 Rabid Oak
Magazine
United States

rabidoak@gmail.com

https://rabidoak.com

Types: Fiction; Nonfiction; Poetry
Subjects: Literary
Markets: Adult

Closed to approaches.

Online literary journal. Send up to five poems or two pieces of fiction or nonfiction (up to 1,000 words) in a Word document attachment.

M0455 Race & Class
Magazine
United Kingdom

raceandclass@irr.org.uk

https://journals.sagepub.com/home/rac

Types: Nonfiction
Formats: Articles; Essays
Subjects: Sociology
Markets: Academic

Refereed, ISI-ranked journal on racism and imperialism in the world today.

Editors: Jenny Bourne; Hazel Waters

M0456 Racing Post

Magazine
Floor 7, Vivo Building, South Bank Central, 30 Stamford Street, London, SE1 9LS
United Kingdom

help@racingpost.com

https://www.racingpost.com

Nonfiction
   Articles: Horse Racing
   News: Horse Racing

Daily paper of horse racing, plus some general sport.

M0457 Radar Poetry

Magazine
United States

radarpoetry@gmail.com

https://www.radarpoetry.com

Poetry > *Any Poetic Form*

Send: Full text
How to send: Submittable

Electronic journal, published quarterly. Submit 3-5 original, previously unpublished poems through online submission system. Accepts submissions November 1 to January 1, and March 1 to May 1 annually.

Editors: Rachel Marie Patterson; Dara-Lyn Shrager

M0458 Radio User

Magazine
United Kingdom

https://www.radioenthusiast.co.uk/
https://www.facebook.com/radioenthusiasts/
https://twitter.com/renthusiasts

Magazine Publisher: Warners Group
Publications

Nonfiction > *Articles:* Radio Technology

Magazine relating to receiving and listening to radio signals, aimed at radio enthusiasts.

Editors: Elaine Richards; Georg Wiessala

M0459 The Railway Magazine

Magazine
Mortons Media Group Ltd, Morton Way, Horncastle, Lincolnshire, LN9 6JR
United Kingdom
Tel: +44 (0) 1507 529589

cmilner@mortons.co.uk

https://www.railwaymagazine.co.uk

Types: Nonfiction
Formats: Articles; News
Subjects: History; Technology; Travel
Markets: Adult

Magazine for the railway community, covering all aspects from steam through to modern rail developments.

Editor: Chris Milner

M0460 Ramsay's

Magazine
United Kingdom

Magazine Publisher: Warners Group
Publications

M0461 Reach

Magazine
IDP, 24 Forest Houses, Halwill, Beaworthy, Devon, EX21 5UU
United Kingdom

publishing@indigodreams.co.uk

http://www.indigodreams.co.uk/reach-poetry/4563791643

Poetry > *Any Poetic Form:* Literary

Send: Full text
How to send: Email

Accepting submissions from subscribers only until 2021.

Publishes quality poetry from both experienced and new poets. Formal or free verse, haiku... everything is considered. Subscribers can comment on and vote for poetry from the previous issue, the winner receiving £50, plus regular in-house anthologies and competitions. Receives no external funding and depends entirely on subscriptions. Submit up to two poems by email. No simultaneous submissions.

Editor: Ronnie Goodyer

M0462 The Reader

Magazine
The Mansion House, Calderstones Park, Liverpool, L18 3JB
United Kingdom
Tel: + 44 (0) 1517 292200

magazine@thereader.org.uk

https://www.thereader.org.uk
https://www.thereader.org.uk/what-we-do/the-reader-magazine/
https://twitter.com/thereaderorg
https://www.facebook.com/thereaderorg
https://www.instagram.com/thereaderorg/

Nonfiction > *Articles:* Literature

Magazine of charity promoting shared reading through reading aloud groups. No longer publishes original fiction and poetry.

M0463 Reason

Magazine
5737 Mesmer Avenue, Los Angeles, CA 90230
United States
Tel: +1 (310) 391-2245
Fax: +1 (310) 390-8986

submissions@reason.com

http://reason.com

Types: Nonfiction
Formats: Articles; Essays; News; Reviews
Subjects: Culture; Current Affairs; Finance; Politics; Science
Markets: Adult

Send: Full text
How to send: Email

Publishes articles and essays on politics, economics, culture, and science, from a broad-minded libertarian perspective. Accepts unsolicited MSS but prefers queries in writing either by post with SASE or by email.

Editor: Brian Doherty, Associate Editor

M0464 Red Magazine

Magazine
30 Panton Street, Leicester Square, London, SW1Y 4AJ
United Kingdom

https://www.redonline.co.uk

Types: Nonfiction
Formats: Articles; News; Reviews
Subjects: Beauty; Cookery; Design; Fashion; Lifestyle; Travel; Women's Interests
Markets: Adult

Send: Query
Don't send: Full text

Magazine aimed at women in their thirties. Usually uses regular contributors, but will consider queries for ideas.

M0465 Relevant

Magazine
United States

submissions@relevantmediagroup.com

https://relevantmagazine.com

Types: Nonfiction
Formats: Articles
Subjects: Culture; Lifestyle; Religion
Markets: Adult

Send: Full text
How to send: Email

Christian lifestyle magazine aimed at adults in their 20s and 30s, covering faith, culture, and "intentional living".

M0466 Report

Magazine
Association of Teachers and Lecturers, 7 Northumberland Street, London, WC2N 5RD

United Kingdom
Tel: +44 (0) 20 7930 6441
Fax: +44 (0) 20 7930 1359

http://www.atl.org.uk

Types: Nonfiction
Formats: Articles
Markets: Professional

Magazine for teachers and lecturers publishing articles of practical interest to the target audience.

M0467 Reptiles

Magazine
United States

reptiles@chewy.com

http://www.reptilesmagazine.com

Types: Nonfiction
Formats: Articles
Subjects: Hobbies; Nature
Markets: Adult

Send: Query
Don't send: Full text
How to send: Email

Magazine publishing material relating to reptiles and amphibians. Send query by email.

M0468 Resurgence & Ecologist

Magazine
The Resurgence Centre, Fore Street, Hartland, Bideford, Devon, EX39 6AB
United Kingdom

brendan@theecologist.org

https://theecologist.org

Nonfiction
 Articles: Environment
 News: Environment

Aims to foster a greater connection to nature in order to enhance personal wellbeing, support resilient communities and inform social change towards regenerative societies that enrich rather than deplete our natural environment.

Editor: Zac Goldsmith

M0469 The Rialto

Magazine
PO Box 309, Aylsham, Norwich, NR11 6LN
United Kingdom

info@therialto.co.uk

https://www.therialto.co.uk

Types: Nonfiction; Poetry
Formats: Articles; Reviews
Subjects: Literary
Markets: Adult

Send: Full text

Send up to six poems with SASE or adequate return postage, or submit through online

submission system. No submissions by email. Reviews and articles commissioned.

Editor: Michael Mackmin

M0470 Right Start Online

Online Magazine
United Kingdom

info@rightstartonline.co.uk

https://www.rightstartonline.co.uk

Nonfiction > *Articles:* Parenting

Magazine covering pre-school children's health, lifestyle, development, education, etc. Contact the editor by email to discuss editorial opportunities.

Editor: Lynette Lowthian

M0471 Ripcord.

Magazine
United States

ndowney@ripcordmagazine.org

https://www.ripcordmagazine.org

Types: Fiction; Poetry
Formats: Essays; Short Fiction
Subjects: Experimental; Literary
Markets: Adult

Send: Full text
How to send: Email

An online multimedia literary magazine where we celebrate stories in all their forms, no matter how bizarre or unconventional those forms may be. We want to create a platform that embraces diverse, exciting, and inventive narratives. Whether it's a poem, a short story, a photo set, a performance piece, or something even weirder, if it's quality and has a narrative we can sink our teeth into, it's for us. We help tell the stories that would otherwise be lost, and yours could be next. Send us something that helps us see the world in a new way.

Editor: Noelle Downey

M0472 Riptide

Magazine
The Department of English, The University of Exeter, Queen's Building, Queen's Drive, Exeter, EX4 6QH
United Kingdom

editors@riptidejournal.co.uk

http://www.riptidejournal.co.uk
http://twitter.com/#!/RiptideJournal
http://www.facebook.com/pages/Riptide-Journal/161555683865263

Fiction > *Short Fiction:* Literary

Poetry > *Any Poetic Form*

Closed to approaches.

Bi-annual anthology of new short fiction and poetry by both established and emerging writers. Send one unpublished original story up

to 5,000 words or up to five poems up to 40 lines each, by post or as a Word file email attachment.

M0473 Rising Innovator

Online Magazine
United States

editorial@risinginnovator.com

https://www.risinginnovator.com
https://docs.google.com/document/d/1_YIzJeFywByFcqOfNEod86dNiAR1MnTQbtSUXERqDn4/edit
https://facebook.com/risinginnovator/
https://www.linkedin.com/company/rising-innovator
https://www.instagram.com/risinginnovator/
https://twitter.com/risinginnovate
https://pinterest.com/risinginnovator

ADULT > **Nonfiction** > *Articles*
 Business; Entrepreneurship

CHILDREN'S > **Nonfiction** > *Articles*
 Business; Entrepreneurship

PROFESSIONAL > **Nonfiction** > *Articles*
 Business; Education; Entrepreneurship

Send: Pitch
How to send: Email; Online contact form

A web-only publication to support entrepreneurship in children. We have three basic targets: children aged 8 to 18, their parents, and any school staff that teach entrepreneurship. We offer news, profiles, guides, advice, and any articles of interest to our audience. We also offer a few free online tools as well, such as a quiz that helps children select a business idea.

Because of our different targets, sometimes we solicit the same content to be written for two different audiences. We keep content differentiated on our website. If you have further questions then please refer to the guidelines above or email us.

M0474 River Heron Review

Magazine
PO Box 543, New Hope, PA 18953
United States

riverheronreview@gmail.com

http://www.riverheronreview.com

Types: Poetry
Subjects: Contemporary; Experimental; Literary; Satire; Traditional
Markets: Adult

Send: Full text
How to send: Email

Established to support the arts through the sharing of poetry in our online journal, at readings, workshops and by making public the transformative power of poetic expression. We hope to contribute to the expansion of a community of poets, to establish a creative outlet that does not discriminate by age, race, or sexual orientation in order to offer voice to all and to represent poetry in its many forms, styles, perspectives, and intentions.

Editor: Robbin Farr, Judith Lagana

M0475 River Hills Traveler

Magazine
212 E Main Street, Neosho, MO 64850
United States
Tel: +1 (417) 451-3798
Fax: +1 (417) 451-3798

jimmy@riverhillstraveler.com

http://www.riverhillstraveler.com

Types: Nonfiction
Formats: Articles
Subjects: Hobbies; Nature; Sport
Markets: Adult

Send: Query
Don't send: Full text
How to send: Email

Magazine covering outdoor sports and nature in the southeast quarter of Missouri, the east and central Ozarks. Send query by email with writing samples.

Editor: Jimmy Sexton

M0476 The Road Not Taken: The Journal of Formal Poetry

Magazine
United States

TheRoadNotTakenJournal@gmail.com

http://www.journalformalpoetry.com

Types: Poetry
Subjects: Literary
Markets: Adult

Send: Full text
How to send: Email

Publishes metrical poetry in modern English. See website for previous issues and full guidelines. Submit 3-5 poems by email during specific reading periods (August 15 – October 15; January 15 – March 15; and April 1 – June 15).

Editors: Kathryn Jacobs; Rachel Jacobs

M0477 Romantic Homes

Magazine
17890 Sky Park Circle, Suite 250, Irvine, CA 92614
United States

mdombrowski@engagedmediainc.com

https://www.romantichomes.com

Types: Nonfiction
Formats: Articles
Subjects: Design; How To
Markets: Adult

Publishes elegant inspiration for everyday life, including decorating ideas and entertaining advice.

Editor: Margie Monin Dombrowski

M0478 Rugby World

Magazine
2nd Floor, Pinehurst 2, Pinehurst Road, Farnborough Business Park, Farnborough, Hampshire, GU14 7BF
United Kingdom
Tel: +44 (0) 01252 555272

sarah.mockford@futurenet.com

https://www.rugbyworld.com
https://www.facebook.com/rugbyworldmagazine
https://www.youtube.com/user/rugbyworld08
https://twitter.com/rugbyworldmag

Nonfiction
 Articles: Rugby
 News: Rugby

Send: Query; Author bio; Synopsis

Magazine publishing news and articles related to rugby. Send idea with coverline, headline, and 50-word synopsis, along with brief resume of your experience.

Editor: Sarah Mockford

M0479 Running

Magazine
Kelsey Media, Cudham Tithe Barn, Berry's Hill, Cudham, Kent, TN16 3AG
United Kingdom

rf.ed@kelsey.co.uk

https://www.runnersradar.com

Types: Nonfiction
Formats: Articles
Subjects: Health; Hobbies; Leisure; Sport
Markets: Adult

Magazine for runners, including advice on health, fitness, and injury.

M0480 Rural Builder

Magazine
Shield Wall Media LLC, PO Box 255, Iola, WI 54945
United States

karen@shieldwallmedia.com

http://www.ruralbuilder.com

Types: Nonfiction
Formats: Articles; News
Subjects: Architecture; Business; Design; How To
Markets: Professional

Magazine for builders and suppliers of primarily low-rise agricultural and small retail and municipal structures in cities with populations under 250,000.

M0481 S/tick

Magazine
Canada

editor@dontdiepress.org

https://www.dontdiepress.org/stickmag/

Types: Fiction; Poetry
Formats: Short Fiction
Subjects: Literary; Women's Interests
Markets: Adult

Send: Full text
How to send: Email

Online magazine publishing feminist prose and poetry. Send up to five poems or up to 2,000 words of prose by email. See website for full guidelines.

Editor: Sarah-Jean Krahn

M0482 Sable

Online Magazine
SAKS Publications, PO Box 33504, London, E9 7YE
United Kingdom

editorial@sablelitmag.org
micro@sablelitmag.org

http://www.sablelitmag.org
https://www.facebook.com/SABLELitmag.org
https://twitter.com/SABLELitMag

Fiction > *Short Fiction*

Nonfiction > *Reviews*

Send: Full text
How to send: Email

A showcase of new creative work by writers of colour. Publishes reviews and flash fiction up to 600 words.

M0483 Sacramento Magazine

Magazine
5750 New King Drive, Suite 100, Troy, MI 48098
United States
Tel: +1 (866) 660-6247

darlena@sacmag.com

http://www.sacmag.com

Types: Nonfiction
Formats: Articles
Subjects: Arts; Culture; Health; Lifestyle; Travel
Markets: Adult

Magazine covering culture, events, and entertainment in and around Sacramento.

Editor: Darlena Belushin McKay

M0484 Saddlebag Dispatches

Magazine
United States

submissions@saddlebagdispatches.com

https://saddlebagdispatches.com

Types: Fiction; Nonfiction; Poetry
Formats: Articles; Short Fiction
Subjects: Westerns
Markets: Adult

Send: Full text
How to send: Email

Publishes fiction, nonfiction, and poetry about the American West. Looks for themes of open country, unforgiving nature, struggles to survive and settle the land, freedom from authority, cooperation with fellow adventurers, and other experiences that human beings encounter on the frontier. Send submissions by email. See website for full guidelines.

M0485 Saga Magazine

Magazine
Saga Publishing Ltd, The Saga Building, Enbrook Park, Folkestone, Kent, CT20 3SE
United Kingdom
Tel: +44 (0) 1303 771111

https://www.saga.co.uk/magazine

Types: Nonfiction
Formats: Articles; Interviews
Subjects: Lifestyle
Markets: Adult

Send: Query
Don't send: Full text

Magazine for older people.

M0486 SAIL Magazine

Magazine
23a Glendale Street, Salem, MA 01970
United States
Tel: +1 (860) 767-3200
Fax: +1 (860) 767-1048

sailmail@sailmagazine.com

https://www.sailmagazine.com

Types: Nonfiction
Formats: Articles
Subjects: Leisure; Sport; Travel
Markets: Adult

Sailing magazine covering boats, DIY, cruising, racing, equipment, etc.

Editor: Adam Cort

M0487 San Diego Home / Garden Lifestyles

Magazine
4577 Viewridge Avenue, San Diego, CA 92123
United States
Tel: +1 (858) 571-0529

ditler@sdhg.net

https://www.sandiegohomegarden.com

Types: Nonfiction
Formats: Articles
Subjects: Arts; Culture; Design; Gardening;

Lifestyle
Markets: Adult

Lifestyle magazine for residents of San Diego city and county.

Editor: Eva Ditler

M0488 Sarasvati

Magazine
24 Forest Houses, Halwill, Beaworthy, Devon, EX21 5UU
United Kingdom

dawnidp@gmail.com

http://www.indigodreams.co.uk/sarasvati/

Types: Fiction; Poetry
Formats: Short Fiction
Markets: Adult

Showcases poetry and prose. Each contributor will have three to four A5 pages available to their work. Submit up to five poems, or prose up to 1,000 words.

Editor: Dawn Bauling

M0489 Saveur

Magazine
PO Box 6364, Harlan, IA 51593
United States
Tel: +1 (515) 237-3697

edit@saveur.com

https://www.saveur.com

Types: Nonfiction
Formats: Articles
Subjects: Cookery; Culture; Travel
Markets: Adult

Send: Query
Don't send: Full text

Welcomes pitches from writers who want to tell amazing stories about food and travel. Queries should include a brief summary of the proposed article and proposed timescale, along with any links to past work. Response only if interested.

M0490 Scale Auto

Magazine
Kalmbach Publishing Co., 21027 Crossroads Circle, Waukesha, WI 53187-1612
United States

msavage@kalmbach.com

http://www.scaleautomag.com

Types: Nonfiction
Formats: Articles; Reviews
Subjects: Hobbies; How To
Markets: Adult

Send: Full text

Magazine for model car enthusiasts. See website for full submission guidelines.

Editor: Mark Savage

M0491 Scientific American

Magazine
1 New York Plaza, Suite 4500, New York, NY 10004
United States

editors@sciam.com

https://www.scientificamerican.com

Types: Nonfiction
Formats: Articles
Subjects: Health; Psychology; Science; Technology
Markets: Adult

Send: Query
Don't send: Full text
How to send: Email

Welcomes ideas for articles on recent scientific discoveries, technical innovations and overviews of ongoing research. Send proposals by email or by post. See website for full details.

M0492 Scintilla

Magazine
United Kingdom

subscriptions@vaughanassociation.org

http://www.vaughanassociation.org

Types: Fiction; Nonfiction; Poetry
Formats: Articles; Essays
Subjects: Drama; Health; Literary; Nature; Science; Spirituality
Markets: Adult

Send: Full text

An international, peer-reviewed journal of literary criticism, prose, and new poetry in the metaphysical tradition. Submit using online submission form.

Editors: Erik Ankerberg; Damian Walford Davies; Dr. Kevin Mills; Joseph Sterrett

M0493 The Scots Magazine

Magazine
D.C. Thomson & Co. Ltd, 1 Albert Square, Dundee, DD1 1DD
United Kingdom
Tel: +44 (0) 1382 223131

mail@scotsmagazine.com

http://www.scotsmagazine.com

Newspaper Publisher / Magazine Publisher: DC Thomson Media

Types: Nonfiction
Formats: Articles; Reviews
Subjects: History; Leisure; Lifestyle; Literature; Music; Nature
Markets: Adult

Send: Query
Don't send: Full text
How to send: Email

Scottish interest magazine publishing material covering history, folklore, wildlife, outdoor pursuits, Scottish personalities, etc. Send initial query by post or by email.

Editor: John Methven

M0494 Scottish Caravans & Motorhomes

Magazine
United Kingdom

Newspaper Publisher / Magazine Publisher: DC Thomson Media

M0495 Scottish Field

Magazine
Fettes Park, 496 Ferry Road, Edinburgh, EH5 2DL
United Kingdom
Tel: +44 (0) 1315 511000
Fax: +44 (0) 1315 517901

editor@scottishfield.co.uk

https://www.scottishfield.co.uk
https://www.facebook.com/scottishfield
http://www.twitter.com/scottishfield

Nonfiction > *Articles*
Beauty; Culture; Fashion; Food and Drink; Gardening; Interior Design; Lifestyle; Outdoor Activities; Scotland; Travel

Lifestyle magazine publishing articles and features of general Scottish interest.

Editors: Richard Bath; Claire Grant

M0496 Scottish Journal of Geology

Magazine
United Kingdom

Book Publisher / Magazine Publisher: The Geological Society Publishing House (**P0317**)

M0497 Scottish Wedding

Magazine
United Kingdom

Newspaper Publisher / Magazine Publisher: DC Thomson Media

M0498 Screem

Magazine
41 Mayer Street, Wilkes Barre, PA 18702
United States

Screemagazine@msn.com

http://screemag.com

Types: Nonfiction
Formats: Articles; News
Subjects: Horror
Markets: Adult

Send: Query
Don't send: Full text

Magazine publishing articles relating to Horror. Query in first instance.

M0499 Screen International

Magazine
Zetland House, 5-25 Scrutton Street, London, EC2A 4HJ
United Kingdom
Tel: +44 (0) 20 8102 0900

info@mbi.london

https://www.screendaily.com
https://www.facebook.com/ScreenDaily/
https://twitter.com/screendaily
https://www.linkedin.com/company-beta/2298039/
https://www.youtube.com/channel/UCKV7nCATTd4LFbD93ScBUoA
https://www.instagram.com/screendaily/?hl=en

Magazine Publisher: Media Business Insights (MBI)

PROFESSIONAL > **Nonfiction** > *Articles*
Cinemas / Movie Theaters; Film Industry; Films; TV

International trade paper for the film and television industries.

Editors: Leo Barraclough; Matt Mueller

M0500 Scribble

Magazine
14 The Park, Stow on the Wold, Cheltenham, Glos., GL54 1DX
United Kingdom
Tel: +44 (0) 1451 831053

enquiries@parkpublications.co.uk

http://www.parkpublications.co.uk/scribble.html

Magazine Publisher: Park Publications

Fiction > *Short Fiction*

Send: Full text
How to send: Email; Post

Costs: A fee is charged upon submission. £3. Free for subscribers.

Accepts short stories on any subject from new and experienced writers. Each quarter prizes of £75, £25, and £15 will be awarded for the best three stories in the edition. These competitions are free to annual subscribers, who also have the option to submit by email. See website for further details.

Editor: David Howarth

M0501 Seen and Heard

Magazine
United Kingdom

nagalro@nagalro.com

http://www.nagalro.com/seen-and-heard-journal/seen-and-heard.aspx

Types: Nonfiction
Formats: Articles; News
Subjects: Legal
Markets: Academic; Professional

Association magazine for children's guardians, family court advisers and independent social workers who work with children and parents in family court proceedings. Provided free to members. See website for submission guidelines.

Editor: Rodney Noon

M0502 Sentinel Literary Quarterly

Magazine
120 Warland Road, London, SE18 2ET
United Kingdom
Tel: +44 (0) 7812 755751

editor@sentinelquarterly.com

https://sentinelquarterly.com
http://www.facebook.com/pages/Sentinel-Literary-Quarterly/99050249348
http://twitter.com/sentinelpoetry

Fiction
Novel Excerpts; Short Fiction
Nonfiction
Essays; Interviews; Reviews
Poetry > *Any Poetic Form*

Scripts > *Theatre Scripts*

Send: Full text
How to send: Email

Magazine publishing poetry on any subject, short stories and excerpts from novels on any theme, academic essays, reviews, and interviews. Submit by email only; send 6 poems up to 60 lines each, or one long poem up to 200 lines with two shorter poems, or one piece of prose. Turnaround in 6 weeks. No simultaneous submissions.

M0503 Sewing World

Magazine
United Kingdom

sw@mytimemedia.com

https://www.sewingworldmagazine.com

Types: Nonfiction
Formats: Articles; Interviews; News
Subjects: Crafts; Hobbies
Markets: Adult

Send: Full text
How to send: Email

Sewing magazine, publishing inspirational projects, sewing techniques, interviews and features as well as all the latest news, products and fabrics. Submit projects and articles by email.

M0504 Ships Monthly Magazine

Magazine
Kelsey Publishing Group, Cudham Tithe Barn,
Berrys Hill, Cudham, Kent, TN16 3AG
United Kingdom
Tel: +44 (0) 1959 541444

ships.monthly@btinternet.com

https://shipsmonthly.com

Types: Nonfiction
Formats: Articles; News
Subjects: Design; History; Technology; Travel
Markets: Adult; Professional

Send: Query
Don't send: Full text
How to send: Email

Magazine aimed at ship enthusiasts and
maritime professionals. Publishes news and
illustrated articles related to all kinds of ships,
including reports on the ferry, cruise, new
building and cargo ship scene as well as navies
across the world.

Editor: Nicholas Leach

M0505 Shooter Literary Magazine

Magazine
United Kingdom

submissions.shooterlitmag@gmail.com

https://shooterlitmag.com

Types: Fiction; Nonfiction; Poetry
Formats: Essays
Subjects: Literary
Markets: Adult

Send: Full text

Publishes literary fiction, poetry, creative
nonfiction and narrative journalism relating to
specific themes for each issue. Send one piece
of prose between 2,000 and 7,500 words or up
to three poems per issue, by email. See website
for current theme and full submission
guidelines.

M0506 Shout

Magazine
United Kingdom

Newspaper Publisher / Magazine Publisher:
DC Thomson Media

M0507 Sinister Wisdom

Magazine
2333 McIntosh Road, Dover, FL 33527
United States
Tel: +1 (813) 502-5549

julie@sinisterwisdom.org

http://www.sinisterwisdom.org

Types: Fiction; Nonfiction; Poetry
Formats: Essays; Short Fiction

Subjects: Arts; Culture; Women's Interests
Markets: Adult

Send: Full text

Multicultural lesbian literary and art journal.
Material may be in any style or form, or
combination of forms. Submit five poems, two
short stories or essays, OR one longer piece of
up to 5,000 words, via online submission
system.

Editor: Julie R. Enszer

M0508 SisterShip Magazine

Magazine
59 Bellemount Lane
Australia

editor@sistershipmagazine.com

https://www.sistershipmagazine.com

Types: Nonfiction
Formats: Articles; Essays; Interviews; News;
Reference; Reviews
Subjects: Adventure; Arts; Autobiography;
Business; Comedy / Humour; Commercial;
Contemporary; Cookery; Crafts; Culture;
Current Affairs; Drama; Entertainment;
Health; History; Hobbies; How To; Legal;
Leisure; Lifestyle; Literary; Literature; Nature;
Photography; Satire; Science; Self Help; Sport;
Travel; Women's Interests
Markets: Adult

Send: Full text
How to send: Email

First launched thirty years ago, this magazine
has been taken out of drydock, refitted, and is
now ready to set sail! Our team have been busy
in the "shipyard" for over twelve months, but
now it's time to share our work and ideas with
you. Just like going to sea, it's all about taking
the plunge and casting off, if you wait until
everything is perfect you'll never leave the
marina! We are about to untie the lines. We are
an international magazine; written by women
for women on the water. We are THE first
boating magazine for women, our ethos is:
Belong: Share passions with like-minded
people; Encourage: Support women, assist,
advise, share, trust; Inspire: Creating ideas,
thoughts, hopes, dreams; Inform: Promote
safety, topical, newsy, fresh, detail; and
Entertain: Be exciting, new, fun, rich, safe,
honest, reliable. We'd love you to join us on
our journey.

Editor: Jackie Parry and Shelley Wright

M0509 Ski+board

Magazine
United Kingdom
Tel: +44 (0) 20 8410 2010

harriet.johnston@skiclub.co.uk

https://www.skiclub.co.uk

Types: Nonfiction
Formats: Articles; News; Reviews

Subjects: Sport; Travel
Markets: Adult

Send: Query
Don't send: Full text

Magazine publishing articles, reviews, features
and news relating to skiing and snowboarding.

Deputy Editor: Harriet Johnston

M0510 Skier & Snowboarder Magazine

Magazine
The Lodge, West Heath, Ashgrove Road,
Sevenoaks, Kent, TN13 1ST
United Kingdom
Tel: +44 (0) 07768 670158

https://www.skierandsnowboarder.com

Types: Nonfiction
Formats: Articles
Subjects: Sport
Markets: Adult

Magazine publishing features on skiing.
Contact via form on website.

M0511 Slime Factory

Magazine
United Kingdom

Newspaper Publisher / Magazine Publisher:
DC Thomson Media

M0512 Smart Retailer

Magazine
PO Box 5000, N7528 Aanstad Road, Iola, WI
54945-5000
United States
Tel: +1 (715) 445-5000
Fax: +1 (715) 445-4053

danb@jonespublishing.com

http://smart-retailer.com

Types: Nonfiction
Formats: Articles; Interviews; News
Subjects: Business; Finance; How To; Legal
Markets: Professional

Send: Full text
How to send: Email

Trade magazine for independent gift retailers.
Send complete ms by email with CV and
published clips.

Editor: Dan Brownell

M0513 Smithsonian Magazine

Magazine
Capital Gallery, Suite 6001, MRC 513, PO
Box 37012, Washington, DC 20013
United States
Tel: +1 (202) 275-2000

smithsonianmagazine@si.edu

http://www.smithsonianmag.com

Magazine Publisher / Book Publisher: Smithsonian Institution (**P0821**)

Types: Nonfiction
Formats: Articles
Subjects: Anthropology; Archaeology; Arts; Culture; History; Lifestyle; Nature; Science; Technology
Markets: Adult

Send: Query
Don't send: Full text

Publishes articles on archaeology, arts, different lifestyles, cultures and peoples, nature, science and technology. Submit proposal through online form on website.

M0514 Smoke

Magazine
1-27 Bridport Street, Liverpool, L3 5QF
United Kingdom
Tel: +44 (0) 7710 644325

windowsproject@btinternet.com

https://smokemagazine.wordpress.com

Writing Group: The Windows Project

Poetry > *Any Poetic Form*

Send: Full text; Self-Addressed Stamped Envelope (SASE)
How to send: Post

New writing, poetry and graphics by some of the best established names alongside new work from Merseyside, from all over the country and the world.

M0515 SnoWest

Magazine
360 B Street, Idaho Falls, ID 83402
United States
Tel: +1 (208) 524-7000
Fax: +1 (208) 522-5241

https://www.snowest.com

Types: Nonfiction
Formats: Articles
Subjects: Leisure; Sport
Markets: Adult

Send: Query
Don't send: Full text

Snowmobiling magazine. Send query with published clips.

M0516 Somerset Home

Magazine
22992 Mill Creek Drive, Laguna Hills, CA 92653
United States

somersethome@stampington.com

https://stampington.com/somerset-home

Types: Nonfiction
Formats: Articles

Subjects: Design
Markets: Adult

Send: Query
Don't send: Full text

Home decor magazine.

M0517 Songwriting & Composing Magazine

Magazine
Westland House, 2 Penlee Close, Praa Sands, Penzance, Cornwall, TR20 9SR
United Kingdom
Tel: +44 (0) 1736 761112

gisc@btconnect.com

http://songwriters-guild.co.uk/magazine.htm

Types: Nonfiction
Formats: Articles
Subjects: Business; Music
Markets: Professional

Magazine free for guild members, publishing articles of interest to professional composers and songwriters.

M0518 South

Magazine
PO Box 9338, Wimborne, BH21 9JA
United Kingdom

south@southpoetry.org

http://www.southpoetry.org

Types: Poetry
Markets: Adult

Send: Full text
How not to send: Email

Submit up to three poems by post (two copies of each), along with submission form available on website. No previously published poems (including poems that have appeared on the internet). Submissions are not returned. See website for full details. No translations or submissions by email.

Editors: Peter Keeble; Anne Peterson; Chrissie Williams

M0519 Southern Humanities Review

Magazine
9088 Haley Center, Auburn University, Auburn, AL 36849
United States
Tel: +1 (334) 844-9088

shr@auburn.edu

http://www.southernhumanitiesreview.com
https://www.facebook.com/southernhumanitiesreview
https://twitter.com/SouthernHReview
https://www.instagram.com/southernhumanitiesreview/
https://www.youtube.com/channel/UCnywOlZbBtEX7OFYMUMSQsg

Fiction > *Short Fiction*

Nonfiction > *Essays*
Creative Nonfiction; Literary Journalism; Literary; Lyric Essays; Memoir; Personal Essays; Travel

Poetry > *Any Poetic Form*

Send: Full text
How to send: Submittable
How not to send: Post; Email

Submissions for all fiction and nonfiction are open from August 24 until November 1 in the fall and from January 15 until March 14 in the spring. Poetry submissions are open from August 24 until September 7 in the fall and from January 15 until March 14 in the spring. Submissions for online fiction features are open year-round.

Editors: Anton DiSclafani; Virginia M. Kouidis; Dan Latimer; Rose McLarney

M0520 Southern Theatre

Magazine
3309 Northampton Drive, Greensboro, NC 27408-5224
United States
Tel: +1 (336) 292-6041
Fax: +1 (336) 294-3292

deanna@setc.org

https://www.setc.org/publications-resources/southern-theatre/

Types: Nonfiction
Formats: Articles; Theatre Scripts
Markets: Adult

Send: Full text
How to send: Email

Theatre magazine focusing on the 10 Southeastern states of the US. Submit by post or email.

Editor: Deanna Thompson

M0521 The Sow's Ear

Magazine
United States

sowsearsubmit@gmail.com

http://www.sowsearpoetry.org
https://www.facebook.com/SowsEarPoetryReview?ref=hl
https://twitter.com/SowsEarPR

Poetry > *Any Poetic Form*

Send: Full text
How to send: Post; Email

Submissions of fine poetry in any style and length. Wants work that is carefully crafted, keenly felt, and freshly perceived. Like poems with voice, specificity, delight in language, and a meaning that unfolds.

Art Editor: Kristin Zimet

Editor: Janet Harrison

M0522 Speciality Food

Magazine
Aceville Publications Ltd., 21-23 Phoenix
Court, Hawkins Road, Colchester, Essex, CO2
8JY
United Kingdom
Tel: +44 (0) 1206 505981

holly.shackleton@aceville.co.uk

https://www.specialityfoodmagazine.com

Types: Nonfiction
Formats: Articles; News
Subjects: Business; Cookery
Markets: Professional

Trade magazine for the food and drink
industry.

Editor: Holly Shackleton

M0523 Specialty Fabrics Review

Magazine
1801 County Road B W, Roseville, MN
55113-4061
United States
Tel: +1 (651) 222-2508

generalinfo@ifai.com

https://specialtyfabricsreview.com

Types: Nonfiction
Formats: Articles
Subjects: Business; Design
Markets: Professional

Magazine covering the industrial textiles
industry.

M0524 The Spectator

Magazine
The Spectator (1828) Ltd, 22 Old Queen
Street, London, SW1H 9HP
United Kingdom
Tel: +44 (0) 20 7961 0200

editor@spectator.co.uk

http://www.spectator.co.uk

Formats: Articles
Subjects: Arts; Current Affairs; Literature;
Politics
Markets: Adult

Magazine of politics, literature, and arts.

Editor: Fraser Nelson

M0525 Spirituality & Health

Magazine
United States
Tel: +1 (844) 375-3755

editors@spiritualityhealth.com

https://spiritualityhealth.com

Types: Nonfiction
Formats: Articles; Interviews; Reviews
Subjects: Health; Lifestyle; Spirituality
Markets: Adult

Send: Full text
How to send: Email

Magazine that aims to help people improve
their lives both physically and spiritually. Send
submissions by email. No attachments.
Response not guaranteed. See website for full
guidelines.

M0526 Spitball

Magazine
536 Lassing Way, Walton, KY 41094
United States

spitball5@hotmail.com

http://www.spitballmag.com

Types: Fiction; Poetry
Formats: Reviews; Short Fiction
Subjects: Literary; Sport
Markets: Adult

Send: Full text
How not to send: Email

Literary baseball magazine, publishing poems,
fiction, prose, art, and book reviews relating to
baseball. Potential contributors must publish a
sample copy ($6) before submitting. See
website for full guidelines.

M0527 Sports Afield

Magazine
P.O. Box 271305, Fort Collins, CO 80527
United States

editorinchief@sportsafield.com

http://sportsafield.com

Types: Nonfiction
Formats: Articles
Subjects: Adventure; Nature; Sport
Markets: Adult

Send: Full text
How to send: Email

Hunting adventure magazine. Publishes articles
on high-end hunting and shooting, and
coverage of guns, optics, clothing, and other
equipment. Send complete ms by email only.
See website for full guidelines.

M0528 Stamp Collector

Magazine
United Kingdom

Magazine Publisher: Warners Group
Publications

M0529 Stanford Magazine

Magazine
United States

stanford.magazine@stanford.edu

https://stanfordmag.org

Types: Nonfiction
Formats: Articles; Essays
Markets: Academic; Adult

University alumni magazine.

M0530 Stitch

Magazine
United Kingdom

Magazine Publisher: Warners Group
Publications

M0531 StoryNews

Magazine
United States

jess@storynews.net

https://www.storynews.net

Types: Nonfiction
Formats: Essays
Subjects: Arts; Culture; Current Affairs;
Literature; Media; Politics
Markets: Adult

Send: Full text
How not to send: Email

An online literary journal committed to
showcasing the human stories behind
headlines. We're seeking nonfiction writing as
well as visual, audio, and multimedia art that
tells a true story in response to news articles,
capturing something unique, special, and
personal about the way you see the world. Our
mission isn't to convert folks to new political
ideologies, but to give people of all
backgrounds insights into each other's
worldviews for the sake of understanding and
more open dialogues, both personally and
globally. All stories are welcome – so long as
they are honest, thoughtful, vulnerable, and
free of hate speech or bigotry. Our full
submission guidelines are accessible on our
website.

Editor: Jess Millman

M0532 Strategic Finance

Magazine
United States

aschulman@imanet.org

https://sfmagazine.com

Types: Nonfiction
Formats: Articles
Subjects: Finance
Markets: Professional

Send: Full text

Publishes articles that help financial
professionals perform their jobs more
effectively, advance their careers, grow
personally and professionally, and make their
organisations more profitable.

M0533 Studio One

Magazine
Murray Hall 170, College of St. Benedict, 37
South College Avenue, St Joseph, MN 56374
United States

studio1@csbsju.edu

https://digitalcommons.csbsju.edu/studio_one/

Types: Fiction; Nonfiction; Poetry
Formats: Essays; Short Fiction
Subjects: Literary
Markets: Adult

Send: Full text
How to send: Email

Literary and visual arts magazine published each spring. Founded in 1976 as a print publication. Online only since 2012. Prefers email submissions, but will accept submissions by post. See website for full guidelines.

M0534 Stylist

Magazine
26-34 Emerald Street, London, WC1N 3QA
United Kingdom
Tel: +44 (0) 20 7611 9700

reception@stylist.co.uk

https://www.thestylistgroup.com

Types: Nonfiction
Formats: Articles; News
Subjects: Beauty; Entertainment; Fashion; Lifestyle; Women's Interests
Markets: Adult

Magazine of feminism, fashion, beauty, lifestyle trends, and news.

M0535 Subtropics

Magazine
PO Box 112075, 4008 Turlington Hall, University of Florida, Gainesville, FL 32611-2075
United States

subtropics@english.ufl.edu

http://subtropics.english.ufl.edu
http://www.facebook.com/subtropicsmag/
https://twitter.com/subtropicsmag/

Fiction > *Short Fiction*: Literary

Nonfiction > *Essays*

Poetry > *Any Poetic Form*

Send: Full text
How to send: Submittable

Costs: A fee is charged upon submission. $3.00 for each submission.

Publishes literary fiction, essays, and poetry, of any length. Submit via online submission system during open windows. $3 charge per submission.

Editor: David Leavitt

Managing Editor: Mark Mitchell

Poetry Editors: Ange Mlinko; Sidney Wade

M0536 Successful Meetings

Magazine
100 Lighting Way, Secaucus, NJ 07094-3626

United States
Tel: +1 (201) 902-1978

ledelstein@ntmllc.com

http://www.successfulmeetings.com

Formats: Articles
Subjects: Business
Markets: Professional

Magazine for multi-tasking meeting planners.

Editor: Loren Edelstein

M0537 Sunshine Artist

Magazine
N7528 Aanstad Road, PO Box 5000, Iola, WI 54945
United States
Tel: +1 (800) 597-2573

editor@sunshineartist.com

http://www.sunshineartist.com

Types: Nonfiction
Formats: Reviews
Subjects: Arts; Crafts
Markets: Professional

Send: Full text

Publishes reviews of fine art fairs, festivals, events, and small craft shows around the country, for professionals making a living through art shows.

Editor: Joyce Greenholdt

Managing Editor: Melissa Jones

M0538 Surface

Magazine
One World Trade Center 32nd Floor, New York, NY 10007
United States
Tel: +1 (212) 229-1500

editorial@surfacemag.com

https://www.surfacemag.com

Formats: Articles
Subjects: Architecture; Arts; Contemporary; Culture; Design
Markets: Adult

American magazine of global contemporary design. Covers architecture, art, design, fashion, and travel, with a focus on how these fields shape and are shaped by contemporary culture.

M0539 Sweet Princess Magic

Magazine
United Kingdom

Newspaper Publisher / Magazine Publisher: DC Thomson Media

M0540 Swimming Times Magazine

Magazine
Sport Park, 3 Oakwood Drive, Loughborough, Leicestershire, LE11 3QF
United Kingdom
Tel: +44 (0) 1509 632230
Fax: +44 (0) 1509 618701

swimmingtimes@swimming.org

http://www.swimming.org/swimengland/subscribe-to-swimming-times-magazine/

Types: Nonfiction
Formats: Articles; Interviews
Subjects: Sport
Markets: Adult

Magazine featuring coaching tips, teaching articles and club stories plus interviews and features from across the swimming community.

Editor: P. Hassall

M0541 Tabletop Gaming

Magazine
United Kingdom

Magazine Publisher: Warners Group Publications

M0542 Tagvverk

Magazine
United States

tagvverk@gmail.com

http://tagvverk.info

Types: Fiction; Nonfiction; Poetry
Formats: Essays; Reviews
Subjects: Literary; Literary Criticism
Markets: Adult

Closed to approaches.

Online magazine publishing poetry, fiction, essays, reviews, criticisms, visual poems and multimedia projects. Send submissions by email.

Editors: Miriam Karraker; Barrett White

M0543 Tahoma Literary Review

Magazine
United States

poetry@tahomaliteraryreview.com
fiction@tahomaliteraryreview.com
nonfiction@tahomaliteraryreview.com

https://tahomaliteraryreview.com

Fiction > *Short Fiction*
Experimental; Literary

Nonfiction
Essays: General, and in particular: Experimental; Lyric Essays
Short Nonfiction: Narrative Nonfiction

Poetry
Formal Poetry; Free Verse; Long Form Poetry

Send: Full text
How to send: Submittable

Costs: A fee is charged upon submission. $4 for poetry and flash prose; $5 for longer prose. Submissions are free for anyone who self-identifies as a historically marginalised writer.

Publishes poetry, fiction, and nonfiction. Charges $4 submission fee for short works; $5 submission fee for long works. Submit online through online submission system.

M0544 Takahe
Magazine
PO Box 13 335, Christchurch 8141
New Zealand

secretary@takahe.org.nz

https://www.takahe.org.nz
https://twitter.com/takahemagazine

Fiction > *Short Fiction*: Literary

Nonfiction
Essays: Cultural Criticism; New Zealand; South Pacific
Reviews: Published Books

Poetry > *Any Poetic Form*

Send: Full text; Author bio
How to send: Email attachment; Domestic Post

Submit up to four poems, or short stories up to 3,000 words, by email (preferred) or hard copy by post (New Zealand submissions only). See website for full details.

Art Editor / Essays Editor: Andrew Paul Wood

Fiction Editor: Zoë Meager

Poetry Editors: Jeni Curtis; Gail Ingram

Reviews Editor: Michelle Elvy

M0545 Take a Break
Magazine
United Kingdom

feedback@takeabreak.co.uk

https://takeabreak.co.uk
http://www.facebook.com/takeabreakmag
http://instagram.com/takeabreak.mag
https://twitter.com/takeabreakmag
https://www.youtube.com/channel/
UCWNCQhPiJ5WXsMi0Fnpmuag

Magazine Publisher: H Bauer Publishing

Nonfiction > *Articles*
Beauty; Cookery; Fashion; Health; Pets; Real Life Stories; Travel

Weekly magazine publishing compelling true-life stories, the latest health, fashion and beauty tips, plus cookery and travel.

Editor: John Dale

M0546 Take a Break's Take a Puzzle
Magazine
Academic House, 24-28 Oval Road, London, NW1 7DT
United Kingdom

puzzlesfeedback@bauer.co.uk

https://www.puzzlemagazines.co.uk/puzzle-magazines/take-a-puzzle

Types: Nonfiction
Subjects: Hobbies
Markets: Adult

Magazine of puzzles. Welcomes ideas.

M0547 Tampa Review
Magazine
University of Tampa Press, The University of Tampa, 401 West Kennedy Blvd., Tampa, FL 33606-1490, Box 19F
United States
Tel: (813) 253-6266
Fax: (813) 253-6266

utpress@ut.edu

https://tampareview.ut.edu

Types: Fiction; Nonfiction; Poetry; Translations
Formats: Essays; Interviews; Short Fiction
Subjects: Commercial; Culture; Experimental; Fantasy; History; Literary
Markets: Adult

Closed to approaches.

Submit 3-6 poems or one piece of prose up to 5,000 words with SASE between September and December only. Submissions received prior to August are returned unread. No submisisons by email or simultaneous submissions.

Editor: Richard Mathews

Fiction Editor: Lisa Birnbaum and Kathleen Ochshorn

Nonfiction Editor: Elizabeth Winston

Poetry Editor: Donald Morrill and Martha Serpas

M0548 Tate Etc.
Magazine
Tate, Millbank, London, SW1P 4RG
United Kingdom
Tel: +44 (0) 20 7887 8606

https://www.tate.org.uk/tate-etc

Types: Nonfiction
Formats: Articles
Subjects: Arts; Contemporary; History
Markets: Adult

Magazine of the visual arts, aiming to blend the historic with the contemporary.

Assistant Editor: Enrico Tassi

Editor: Aaron Juneau, Assistant Editor

M0549 TD Magazine
Magazine
United States
Tel: +1 (703) 299-8723

submissions@td.org

https://www.td.org/td-magazine

Types: Nonfiction
Formats: Articles
Subjects: Business
Markets: Professional

Send: Query
Don't send: Full text
How to send: Email

Magazine for talent development professionals. No unsolicited mss. Send query with outline up to 100 words.

M0550 Tears in the Fence
Magazine
Portman Lodge, Durweston, Blandford Forum, Dorset, DT11 0QA
United Kingdom
Tel: +44 (0) 7824 618708

tearsinthefence@gmail.com

http://tearsinthefence.com

Types: Fiction; Nonfiction; Poetry; Translations
Formats: Essays; Interviews; Reviews; Short Fiction
Subjects: Literary
Markets: Adult

Send: Full text
How to send: Email

International literary magazine publishing poetry, fiction, prose poems, essays, translations, interviews and reviews. Publishes fiction as short as 100 words or as long as 3,500. Maximum 6 poems per poet per issue. No simultaneous submissions or previously published material. Send submissions by post or by email as an attachment and in the body of the email.

Editor: David Caddy

M0551 Teen Breathe
Magazine
GMC Publications Ltd, 86 High Street, Lewes, BN7 1XU
United Kingdom
Tel: +44 (0) 1273 477374

hello@breathemagazine.co.uk

https://www.teenbreathe.co.uk

Types: Nonfiction
Formats: Articles
Subjects: Health; Lifestyle
Markets: Young Adult

Send: Full text

Magazine for young people who want to find time for themselves. Focuses on Wellbeing, Mindfulness, Creativity and Escaping. Experienced writers should send ideas with examples of previous work. New writers should submit complete articles. Submit using forms on website.

M0552 The Temz Review

Online Magazine
London, ON
Canada

thetemzreview@gmail.com

https://www.thetemzreview.com

Fiction > *Short Fiction*: Literary

Nonfiction > *Reviews*: Literature

Poetry > *Any Poetic Form*

Send: Full text
How to send: Moksha

Quarterly online magazine. Submit one piece of fiction or creative nonfiction (or more than one if under 1,000 words) or 1-8 poems via online submission system. For reviews, send query by email.

M0553 Texas Monthly

Magazine
PO Box 1569, Austin, TX 78767-1569
United States
Tel: +1 (512) 320-6900
Fax: +1 (512) 476-9007

news@texasmonthly.com

https://www.texasmonthly.com

Formats: Articles; Film Scripts; News; TV Scripts
Subjects: Culture; Lifestyle; Music; Politics; Travel
Markets: Adult

Monthly magazine covering Texas.

M0554 That's Life!

Magazine
FREEPOST LON12043, H Bauer Publishing, London, NW1 1YU
United Kingdom

stories@thatslife.co.uk

http://www.thatslife.co.uk

Types: Nonfiction
Formats: Articles; News
Subjects: Lifestyle
Markets: Adult

Publishes nonfiction true life stories. See website for details.

M0555 Thick With Conviction

Magazine
United States

twczine@gmail.com

http://twczine.blogspot.com

Types: Poetry
Subjects: Literary
Markets: Adult

Send: Full text
How to send: Email

Online magazine publishing poems that are unique or thought provoking. No religious poems, nature poems, greeting card styled poems or teenage angst. Send submissions in the body of an email with bio up to 75 words and author photo.

Editor: Arielle LaBrea

M0556 This Is

Magazine
United Kingdom

Newspaper Publisher / Magazine Publisher:
DC Thomson Media

M0557 This Is Bill Gorton

Magazine
Hacienda Publishing, 300 State Street, PO Box 92951, Southlake, TX 76092
United States
Tel: +1 (936) 468-5759

thisisbillgorton@gmail.com

http://thisisbillgorton.org

Types: Fiction; Nonfiction
Formats: Short Fiction
Subjects: Literary
Markets: Adult

Send: Full text

Accepts fiction and nonfiction of any length. Submit via online submission system.

Editors: Andrew Brininstool; Joshua Hines

M0558 This Is Little Baby Bum

Magazine
United Kingdom

Newspaper Publisher / Magazine Publisher:
DC Thomson Media

M0559 The Threepenny Review

Magazine
PO Box 9131, Berkeley, CA 94709
United States
Tel: +1 (510) 849-4545

wlesser@threepennyreview.com

http://www.threepennyreview.com

Fiction > *Short Fiction*: Literary

Nonfiction > *Articles*
   Arts; Culture; Literature

Poetry > *Any Poetic Form*

Closed to approaches.

National literary magazine with coverage of the visual and performing arts. Send complete MS by post with SASE or by email as a single Word file attachment. No previously published material, simultaneous submissions, or submissions from September to December. Prospective contributors are advised to read the magazine before submitting.

Editor: Wendy Lesser

M0560 The Times Literary Supplement (TLS)

Magazine
1 London Bridge Street, London, SE1 9GF
United Kingdom
Tel: +44 (0) 20 7782 5000

letters@the-tls.co.uk

https://www.the-tls.co.uk

Types: Nonfiction; Poetry
Formats: Articles; Film Scripts; News; Reviews; Theatre Scripts
Subjects: Arts; History; Literature; Philosophy; Science
Markets: Adult

Send: Query
Don't send: Full text

Publishes coverage of the latest and most important publications, as well as current theatre, opera, exhibitions and film. Also publishes letters to the editor and poetry. Send books for review by post. For poetry, submit up to six poems with SASE. Letters to the Editor may be sent by post or by email to the address provided on the website.

Editor: Stig Abell

M0561 Tin House Magazine

Magazine
United States

alana@tinhouse.com

http://www.tinhouse.com

Types: Fiction; Nonfiction; Poetry
Formats: Essays; Short Fiction
Subjects: Literary
Markets: Adult

Closed to approaches.

Publishes unpublished fiction, nonfiction, and poetry through daily blog. Submit via online submission system.

Editor: Alana Csaposs

M0562 Tocher

Magazine
School of Scottish Studies Archives, University of Edinburgh, 29 George Square, Edinburgh, EH8 9LD
United Kingdom

scottish.studies.arhives@ed.ac.uk

https://www.ed.ac.uk/literatures-languages-cultures/celtic-scottish-studies/research/publications/in-house/tocher

ACADEMIC > **Nonfiction** > *Articles*
Culture; Folklore, Myths, and Legends; Music; Scotland

ADULT
Fiction in Translation > *Short Fiction*: Scotland

Fiction > *Short Fiction*: Scotland

The journal contains traditional Scottish songs, stories, music, customs, beliefs, local history, rhymes and riddles transcribed from tapes held in the sound archive.

M0563 Total Film
Magazine
Future Publishing Limited, Quay House, The Ambury, Bath, BA1 1UA
United Kingdom
Tel: +44 (0) 1225 442244

jane.crowther@futurenet.com

https://www.futureplc.com/brand/total-film/

Types: Nonfiction
Formats: Articles; Film Scripts; Interviews; Reviews
Subjects: Comedy / Humour
Markets: Adult

"A cheeky, irreverent but always passionate and authoritative look at every part of the film world".

M0564 Toy Collectors Price Guide
Magazine
United Kingdom

Magazine Publisher: Warners Group Publications

M0565 Traction
Magazine
United Kingdom

Magazine Publisher: Warners Group Publications

M0566 Trout & Salmon
Magazine
Media House, Peterborough Business Park, Peterborough, PE2 6EA
United Kingdom
Tel: +44 (0) 1733 468000

troutandsalmon@bauermedia.co.uk

https://www.troutandsalmon.com

Types: Nonfiction
Formats: Articles
Subjects: Hobbies; Leisure; Sport
Markets: Adult

Magazine publishing articles on the fishing of salmon and trout.

Editor: Andrew Flitcroft

M0567 Trucking
Magazine
Kelsey Media Ltd, Cudham Tithe Barn, Berry's Hill, Cudham, Kent TN16 3AG
United Kingdom
Tel: +44 (0) 1959 541444

trucking.ed@kelsey.co.uk

https://truckingmag.co.uk

Types: Nonfiction
Formats: Articles; News
Subjects: Business; Travel
Markets: Professional

Magazine for owners, drivers, and operators of road haulage vehicles.

M0568 TV Times
Magazine
United Kingdom

colin.tough@futurenet.com

https://www.futureplc.com/brand/tv-times/

Magazine Publisher: Future

Nonfiction > *Articles*
Entertainment; TV

Magazine publishing television news, listings, and articles.

M0569 The 2River View
Magazine
University City, MO 63130
United States

Be1ong@2river.org

http://www.2river.org

Types: Poetry
Subjects: Literary
Markets: Adult

Send: Full text

Considers unpublished poems only. Submit via online submission system. See website for more details.

Editor: Richard Long

M0570 UCity Review
Magazine
United States

editors@ucityreview.com

http://www.ucityreview.com

Types: Poetry
Subjects: Literary
Markets: Adult

Send: Full text
How to send: Email

Online magazine accepting submissions of poetry year-round. Submit up to six poems in .doc or .docx format, by email.

M0571 Ulster Tatler
Magazine
39 Boucher Road, Belfast, BT12 6UT
United Kingdom
Tel: +44 (0) 28 9066 3311

edit@ulstertatler.com
info@ulstertatler.com

https://www.ulstertatler.com
https://www.facebook.com/ulstertatlermag/
https://twitter.com/ulstertatlermag
https://www.youtube.com/channel/UCHH_sMGsPuy8i0VUj5L0_kA
https://www.instagram.com/ulstertatler/

Nonfiction > *Articles*
Fashion; High Society; Lifestyle

Lifestyle and society magazine based in Northern Ireland, covering Northern Ireland social events and local fashions.

Editor: Chris Sherry

Features Editor: James Sherry

Fiction Editor: Richard Sherry

M0572 Umbrella Factory
Magazine
United States

https://umbrellafactorymagazine.com

Types: Fiction; Nonfiction; Poetry
Formats: Short Fiction
Subjects: Literary
Markets: Adult

Send: Full text

Submit fiction between 1,000 and 5,000 words, three poems, or a piece of nonfiction. Submit through online submission system. See website for full guidelines.

Editors: Anthony ILacqua; Sharyce Winters

M0573 Understorey Magazine
Magazine
Alexa McDonough Institute for Women, Gender and Social Justice, Mount Saint Vincent University, 166 Bedford Highway, Halifax, NS, B3M 2J6
Canada

editor@understoreymagazine.ca

https://understoreymagazine.ca

Fiction > *Short Fiction*
Feminism; Women's Issues; Women

Nonfiction > *Short Nonfiction*
Creative Nonfiction; Feminism; Women's Issues; Women

Poetry > *Any Poetic Form*
Feminism; Women's Issues; Women

How to send: Email

Publishes fiction, poetry, and creative nonfiction by Canadian women. Send prose up to 1,500 words or up to five poems by email. See website for full guidelines.

M0574 Unfit Magazine

Magazine
Eugene, OR 97401
United States

contact@unfitmag.com

http://unfitmag.com

Magazine Publisher: Longshot Press

Fiction > *Short Fiction*
Adventure; Alien Invasion; Alternative History; Cyberpunk; Genetics; Military; Post-Apocalyptic; Science Fiction; Space Opera; Time Travel

Send: Full text
How to send: Online submission system

This magazine is about fiction that isn't fit for "them". What do I mean by "them"? Who in particular are "they"? They are the government. They are your parents. They are your teachers. They are everywhere.

Editor: Daniel Scott White

M0575 Unicorn Universe

Magazine
United Kingdom

Newspaper Publisher / Magazine Publisher: DC Thomson Media

M0576 Unreal Magazine

Magazine
United States

contact@unrealmag.com

https://unrealmag.com

Magazine Publisher: Longshot Press

Fiction > *Short Fiction*
Adventure; Alternative History; Comedy / Humour; Experimental; Fairy Tales; Fantasy; Folklore, Myths, and Legends; Gaslamp Fantasy; High / Epic Fantasy; Historical Fiction; Magical Realism; Military; Superhero Fantasy; Sword and Sorcery

Nonfiction > *Articles*
Fantasy; Magical Realism

Send: Full text
How to send: Online submission system

We want stories that are well written, intelligent, and enjoyable to read. We are looking for stories with metaphors and emotional ambience and imaginative descriptive writing.

M0577 US Equestrian Magazine

Magazine
United States Equestrian Federation (USEF), 4047 Iron Works Parkway, Lexington, KY

40511
United States
Tel: +1 (859) 258-2472
Fax: +1 (859) 231-6662

goakford@usef.org

http://www.usef.org
https://www.usef.org/media/equestrian-magazine

Nonfiction > *Articles*
Equestrian; Horses

Send: Query
How to send: Email

Magazine publishing articles, features, and interviews about horses and people related to them.

Editors: Glenye Oakford; Brian Sosby

M0578 Vagabond City

Magazine
United States

vagabondcityliterary@gmail.com

https://vagabondcitylit.com

Types: Nonfiction; Poetry; Translations
Formats: Essays; Interviews; Reviews
Subjects: Literary
Markets: Adult

Send: Full text
How to send: Email

Electronic magazine featuring poetry, poetry in translation, art, creative nonfiction, essays, interviews, and reviews by marginalised creators. Submit up to five pieces at a time in the body of an email or as a Word file attachment. See website for full guidelines.

M0579 Vallum

Magazine
5038 Sherbrooke West, PO Box 23077 CP Vendome Station, Montreal, Quebec, H4A 1T0 Canada
Tel: +1 (514) 937-8946

editors@vallummag.com

http://www.vallummag.com

Types: Nonfiction; Poetry
Formats: Essays; Interviews; Reviews
Subjects: Contemporary
Markets: Adult

How to send: Submittable

Send 4-7 poems, essays of 4-6 pages, interviews of 3-5 pages, reviews of 1-3 pages, through online submission system only. No fiction, plays, movie scripts, memoir, or creative nonfiction. Check website for submission windows and themes.

M0580 Vegetarian Living

Magazine
Select Publisher Services, PO Box 6337,

Bournemouth, BH1 9EH
United Kingdom
Tel: +44 (0) 1202 586848

editorial@vegmag.co.uk

http://www.vegetarianliving.co.uk

Types: Nonfiction
Formats: Articles
Subjects: Cookery; Health
Markets: Adult

Magazine for those interested in vegetarian and vegan cooking.

M0581 Veggie

Magazine
United Kingdom

https://www.vegetarianrecipesmag.com

Nonfiction > *Articles*
Health; Vegetarian Cooking; Vegetarian Food; Vegetarianism

Magazine of vegetarian food, wellness, and lifestyle.

Editors: Sian Bunney; Rachael Perrett

M0582 Verbicide

Magazine
United States

info@scissorpress.com

https://www.verbicidemagazine.com

Types: Fiction; Nonfiction
Formats: Articles; Interviews; Reviews; Short Fiction
Subjects: Entertainment; Music
Markets: Adult

Send: Full text
How to send: Email

Entertainment periodical, online-only since 2009. Accepts short stories between 500 and 3,000 words. For features or music reviews contact by email in advance. See website for specific email addresses and full submission guidelines.

M0583 Vietnam

Magazine
United States

Magazine Publisher: HistoryNet LLC

M0584 Viz

Magazine
Dennis Publishing Ltd, 31-32 Alfred Place, London, WC1E 7DP
United Kingdom

viz@viz.co.uk

http://www.viz.co.uk

Types: Fiction
Formats: Articles
Subjects: Comedy / Humour
Markets: Adult

Magazine of adult humour, including cartoons, spoof articles, etc.

M0585 Waccamaw

Magazine
United States

http://waccamawjournal.com

Types: Fiction; Nonfiction; Poetry
Formats: Essays
Subjects: Literary
Markets: Adult

Send: Full text

Online literary journal publishing poems, stories, and essays. Submit prose up to 6,000 words or 3-5 poems between January 15 and February 15 or August 1 and August 31 annually. Submit via online submission system only.

M0586 The Wallace Stevens Journal

Magazine
University of Antwerp, Prinsstraat 13, 2000 Antwerp
Belgium

bart.eeckhout@uantwerp.be

https://www.press.jhu.edu/journals/wallace-stevens-journal

Types: Nonfiction; Poetry
Formats: Articles; Essays
Subjects: Literary; Literary Criticism
Markets: Academic; Adult

Send: Full text
How to send: Email

Publishes articles and essays on all aspects of Wallace Stevens' poetry and life. Also accepts poetry inspired by the poet. See website for full submission guidelines.

Editor: Bart Eeckhout

M0587 Walloon Writers Review

Magazine
United States

https://walloonwriters.com

Types: Fiction; Nonfiction; Poetry
Formats: Essays
Subjects: Literary
Markets: Adult

Publishes stories, poetry, and creative writing inspired by or about Northern Michigan and the Upper Peninsula.

M0588 Wasafiri

Magazine
c/o School of English and Drama, Queen Mary, University of London, Mile End Road, London, E1 4NS
United Kingdom
Tel: +44 (0) 20 7882 2686

wasafiri@qmul.ac.uk

http://www.wasafiri.org

Types: Fiction; Nonfiction; Poetry
Formats: Articles; Essays; Interviews; Reviews; Short Fiction
Subjects: Culture; Literary; Literary Criticism
Markets: Academic; Adult

Closed to approaches.

The indispensable journal of contemporary African, Asian Black British, Caribbean and transnational literatures.

In over fifteen years of publishing, this magazine has changed the face of contemporary writing in Britain. As a literary magazine primarily concerned with new and postcolonial writers, it continues to stress the diversity and range of black and diasporic writers world-wide. It remains committed to its original aims: to create a definitive forum for the voices of new writers and to open up lively spaces for serious critical discussion not available elsewhere. It is Britain's only international magazine for Black British, African, Asian and Caribbean literatures. Get the whole picture, get the magazine at the core of contemporary international literature today.

Submit via online submissions portal only (see website).

Editor: Malachi McIntosh

M0589 Westview

Magazine
Southwestern Oklahoma State University, 100 Campus Drive, Weatherford, OK 73096
United States

westview@swosu.edu

https://dc.swosu.edu/westview/

Types: Fiction; Nonfiction; Poetry
Formats: Short Fiction
Markets: Adult

Send: Full text
How to send: Email

Publishes unpublished short fiction, poetry, prose poems, creative nonfiction, and artwork. Accepts submissions year-round and supports emerging writers and artists. Electronic submissions only.

Editor: Amanda Smith

M0590 What Motorhome

Magazine
United Kingdom

Magazine Publisher: Warners Group Publications

M0591 What's on TV

Magazine
Time Inc. (UK) Ltd, 161 Marsh Wall, London,

E14 9AP
United Kingdom

michelle.briant@timeinc.com

https://www.whatsontv.co.uk

Types: Nonfiction
Formats: Articles; TV Scripts
Subjects: Entertainment; Media
Markets: Adult

Magazine publishing articles on TV programmes, soaps, celebrities, etc.

M0592 The White Review

Magazine
A.104 Fuel Tank, 8-12 Creekside, London, SE8 3DX
United Kingdom

submissions@thewhitereview.org

http://www.thewhitereview.org

Types: Fiction; Nonfiction; Poetry
Formats: Essays; Reviews; Short Fiction
Subjects: Arts; Culture; Literary; Literature
Markets: Adult

Send: Full text
How to send: Email

Print and online arts and literature magazine. Publishes cultural analysis, reviews, and new fiction and poetry. Accepts nonfiction year-round but only accepts poetry and fiction in specific submission windows. Prose submissions should be a minimum of 1,500 words. See website for guidelines and submit by email.

M0593 WI Life

Magazine
104 New Kings Road, London, SW6 4LY
United Kingdom
Tel: +44 (0) 20 7731 5777 ext 217

wilife@nfwi.org.uk

https://www.thewi.org.uk/wie-and-wi-life

Types: Nonfiction
Formats: Articles
Subjects: Cookery; Crafts; Gardening; Nature; Women's Interests
Markets: Adult

Magazine for Women's Institute membership. Welcomes contributions from WI members.

M0594 Woman & Home

Magazine
161 Marsh Wall, London, E14 9AP
United Kingdom
Tel: +44 (0) 20 3148 5000

https://www.womanandhome.com

Magazine Publisher: Future

Nonfiction > *Articles*
  Beauty; Fashion; Food; Health; Lifestyle; Travel; Wellbeing; Women's Interests

Our mission is to keep 40+ women informed on the subjects that matter to them, so they can live smarter, healthier and happier lives. We publish celebrity news for grown-ups, as well as informative, no-nonsense health and wellbeing features about subjects like the menopause. We speak to internationally renown experts to give up-to-date advice on dieting and weight-loss plans. We aim to delight you with delicious – and healthy – recipes. And to inspire your next holiday destinations with travel recommendations both near and far. We filter through the latest fashion and beauty noise to offer you advice on the trends you'll want to try, because they're flattering as well as stylish.

Editor: Catherine Westwood

M0595 Woman's Weekly

Magazine
Time Inc (UK), 161 Marsh Wall, London, E14 9AP
United Kingdom

womansweeklypostbag@timeinc.com

http://www.womansweekly.com

Types: Fiction; Nonfiction
Formats: Articles; News; Short Fiction
Subjects: Beauty; Contemporary; Cookery; Crafts; Fashion; Gardening; Health; Travel; Women's Interests
Markets: Adult

Send: Query
Don't send: Full text
How not to send: Email

Publishes features of interest to women over forty, plus fiction between 1,000 and 2,000 words and serials in four or five parts of 3,400 words each. Only uses experienced journalists for nonfiction. No submissions by email. Submit by post with SAE.

Editor: Diane Kenwood

Features Editor: Sue Pilkington

Fiction Editor: Gaynor Davies

M0596 Woman's Weekly Fiction Special

Magazine
Time Inc (UK), 161 Marsh Wall, London, E14 9AP
United Kingdom

womansweeklypostbag@timeinc.com

https://www.womansweekly.com

Types: Fiction
Formats: Short Fiction
Subjects: Women's Interests
Markets: Adult

Publishes short stories for women between 1,000 and 8,000 words. Send stories by post with SAE – no correspondence by email.

Editor: Gaynor Davies

M0597 Women Together

Magazine
SWI, 42 Heriot Row, Edinburgh, EH3 6ES
United Kingdom

magazine@theswi.org.uk

https://www.theswi.org.uk

Types: Nonfiction
Formats: Articles
Subjects: Cookery; Crafts; Health; Hobbies; Lifestyle; Literature; Travel; Women's Interests
Markets: Adult

Send: Full text
How to send: Email

Looking for features on a wide range of subjects including crafts, food and drink, women's issues, travel, health, lifestyle and general interest. Send articles / features between 600 and 1,200 words by post or by email.

M0598 The World of Interiors

Magazine
Vogue House, Hanover Square, London, W1S 1JU
United Kingdom
Tel: +44 (0) 20 7499 9080

augusta.pownall@condenast.co.uk

http://www.worldofinteriors.co.uk

Types: Nonfiction
Formats: Articles
Subjects: Design
Markets: Adult

Send: Query
Don't send: Full text

Magazine publishing material related to interiors. All material commissioned. Send query with photos and article synopsis / ideas.

M0599 Xavier Review

Magazine
United States

radamo@xula.edu

http://www.xavierreview.com

Types: Fiction; Nonfiction; Poetry
Formats: Essays; Interviews; Reviews; Short Fiction
Subjects: Literary; Literary Criticism; Religion
Markets: Adult

Send: Full text
How to send: Email

Publishes poetry, fiction, essays, reviews, and interviews. Prefers email submissions with attachments to postal submissions. Send 3-6 poems, or one piece of prose.

Editor: Ralph Adamo

M0600 Yachting World

Magazine
United Kingdom

yachting.world@timeinc.com

https://www.yachtingworld.com

Types: Nonfiction
Formats: Articles; News
Subjects: Leisure; Sport
Markets: Adult

Publishes news and features relating to yacht racing, yachting events, and cruising.

Editor: Elaine Bunting

M0601 The Yale Review

Magazine
United States

theyalereview@gmail.com

https://yalereview.yale.edu
https://www.facebook.com/YaleReview/
https://www.instagram.com/yalereview/
https://twitter.com/YaleReview

Fiction > *Short Fiction*: Literary

Nonfiction > *Essays*
    Arts; Cultural Criticism; Films; History; Literary Criticism; Memoir; Music; Politics; TV

Poetry > *Any Poetic Form*

Send: Full text
How to send: Submittable

Open for submissions of poetry, nonfiction, and fiction from October 5 to November 3, 2020.

Editor: Meghan O'Rourke

M0602 The Yalobusha Review

Magazine
United States

yreditors@gmail.com

https://yr.olemiss.edu

Types: Fiction; Poetry
Formats: Short Fiction
Subjects: Literary; Literature
Markets: Adult

Send: Full text

Submit 3-5 poems, one short story up to 5,000 words, or up to three shorter stories up to 1,000 words each. Accepts a certain number of free entries per month. Once the limit has been reached writers can wait till the next month, or make payment to submit.

Editors: Helene Achanzar; Lara Avery; Linda Masi; Nicholas Sabo

Fiction Editor: Victoria Hulbert

Poetry Editor: Mason Wray

Senior Editors: Sarah Heying; Andy Sia

M0603 Yellow Mama Webzine

Magazine
United States

crosmus@hotmail.com

http://blackpetalsks.tripod.com/yellowmama

Types: Fiction
Subjects: Horror; Literary
Markets: Adult

Send: Full text
How to send: Email

Webzine publishing fiction and poetry. Seeks cutting edge, hardboiled, horror, literary, noir, psychological / horror. No fanfiction, romance, swords & sorcery, fantasy, or erotica. Send submissions by email. See website for full guidelines.

M0604 Yemassee

Magazine
Department of English, University of South Carolina, Columbia, SC 29208
United States

editor@yemasseejournal.org

http://yemasseejournal.org

Types: Fiction; Nonfiction; Poetry
Formats: Essays; Reviews; Short Fiction
Subjects: Literary
Markets: Adult

Publishes poetry, fiction, and nonfiction. Submit 3-5 poems or pieces of flash fiction up to 1,000 words, or a longer short story up to 8,000 words (1,000 words to 5,000 words preferred), via online submission system. See website for full guidelines. $3 submission fee. $6 for expedited submissions.

Editors: Cody Hosek; Dylan Nutter; Victoria Romero

M0605 Your Best Ever Christmas

Magazine
United Kingdom

Newspaper Publisher / Magazine Publisher:
DC Thomson Media

M0606 Your Cat

Magazine
Warners Group Publications Plc, The Maltings,
West Street, Bourne, Lincolnshire, PE10 9PH
United Kingdom
Tel: +44 (0) 1778 395070

editorial@yourcat.co.uk

https://www.yourcat.co.uk

Magazine Publisher: Warners Group Publications

Types: Fiction; Nonfiction
Formats: Articles; Short Fiction
Subjects: How To
Markets: Adult

Practical magazine covering the care of cats and kittens.

Editor: Chloë Hukin

M0607 Your Dog

Magazine
The Maltings, West Street, Bourne,
Lincolnshire, PE10 9PH
United Kingdom
Tel: +44 (0) 1778 395070

editorial@yourdog.co.uk

https://www.yourdog.co.uk

Magazine Publisher: Warners Group Publications

Nonfiction
   Articles: Dogs
   News: Dogs

Publishes news and articles aimed at dog owners, offering practical advice and some personal experience pieces.

Editor: Sarah Wright

M0608 Zetetic: A Record of Unusual Inquiry

Magazine
United States

http://zeteticrecord.org

Types: Fiction; Nonfiction; Poetry
Formats: Short Fiction
Subjects: Literary
Markets: Adult

Online magazine publishing fiction, nonfiction, and poetry. Accepts prose between 100 and 2,500 words, or up to three poems between three and 100 lines.

M0609 Zoetrope: All-Story

Magazine
916 Kearny Street, San Francisco, CA 94133
United States
Tel: +1 (415) 788-7500

info@all-story.com

http://www.all-story.com

Types: Fiction; Scripts
Formats: Short Fiction
Subjects: Literary
Markets: Adult

Closed to approaches.

Closed to submissions from June 1, 2018, to May 31, 2019. Send short stories or one act-plays up to 7,000 words only, with SASE. No excerpts from larger works, screenplays, treatments, poetry, multiple submissions (no more than one story or play at a time), or submissions by email. No submissions between June 1 and August 31.

M0610 Zone 3

Magazine
APSU Box 4565, Clarksville, TN 37044
United States
Tel: +1 (931) 221-7031

https://www.zone3press.com

Book Publisher / Magazine Publisher: Zone 3 Press

Fiction > *Short Fiction*
   Contemporary; Literary

Nonfiction > *Short Nonfiction*
   Contemporary; Creative Nonfiction; Literary

Poetry > *Any Poetic Form*

Send: Full text
How to send: Submittable
How not to send: Email

Costs: A fee is charged upon submission. $3 for white people; free for everyone else.

Publishes fiction, poetry, and creative nonfiction. Accepts submissions through online submission system between August 1 and April 1 annually. $3 submission fee per submission for white people.

Editor: Susan Wallace

Book Publishers

For the most up-to-date listings of these and hundreds of other book publishers, visit https://www.firstwriter.com/publishers

To claim your free access to the site, please see the back of this book.

P0001 **42 Miles Press**
Book Publisher
English Department, Indiana University South Bend, 1700 Mishawaka Avenue, P.O. Box 7111, South Bend, IN 46634-7111
United States

42milespress@gmail.com

https://42milespress.com

Types: Poetry
Subjects: Literary
Markets: Adult

Closed to approaches.

Publishes books and chapbooks of poetry. Currently only accepts submissions via its annual poetry competition, which runs from December 1 to March 15 and costs $25 to enter.

Editor: David Dodd Lee

P0002 **4RV Biblical Based**
Publishing Imprint
United States

Book Publisher: 4RV Publishing (**P0006**)

Fiction > *Novels*: Christianity

Nonfiction > *Nonfiction Books*: Christianity

Publishes fiction and nonfiction based on the Bible, including Christian works.

P0003 **4RV Children's Corner**
Publishing Imprint
United States

Book Publisher: 4RV Publishing (**P0006**)

CHILDREN'S > **Fiction**
Chapter Books; *Early Readers*; *Picture Books*

Closed to approaches.

Publishes books for any aged reader below 5th grade.

P0004 **4RV Fiction**
Publishing Imprint
United States

Book Publisher: 4RV Publishing (**P0006**)

ADULT > **Fiction** > *Novels*

General, and in particular: Fantasy; Romance; Science Fiction

NEW ADULT > **Fiction** > *Novels*

Does not want:

Fiction > *Novels*: Erotic

Publishes novels for adults or young people with high reading abilities.

P0005 **4RV Nonfiction**
Publishing Imprint
United States

Book Publisher: 4RV Publishing (**P0006**)

Nonfiction > *Nonfiction Books*

Publishes nonfiction works above Young Adult.

P0006 **4RV Publishing**
Book Publisher
35427 State Highway 58, Hydro, OK 73048
United States
Tel: +1 (405) 820-9640

President@4rvpublishingllc.com
vp_operations@4rvpublishingllc.com
art_director@4rvpublishingllc.com

https://www.4rvpublishing.com
https://www.facebook.com/4RV-Publishing-LLC-20479523692/
https://twitter.com/4RV
https://www.youtube.com/user/4RVPublishingLLC

ADULT
  Fiction > *Novels*
   General, and in particular: Christianity; Fantasy; Romance; Science Fiction

  Nonfiction > *Nonfiction Books*

CHILDREN'S > **Fiction**
  Chapter Books; *Early Readers*; *Middle Grade*; *Picture Books*
TEEN > **Fiction** > *Novels*

YOUNG ADULT > **Fiction** > *Novels*

Does not want:

Fiction > *Novels*: Erotic

Send: Query; Synopsis; Writing sample
How to send: Email attachment

Accepts most genres of fiction and nonfiction books for all ages, including nonfiction, mystery, romance, mainstream, western, Christian, and science-fiction, as well as children's books, middle grade and young adult novels. No poetry or graphic sex or violence. Language should not be overly profane or vulgar. Accepts submissions by email from the US, UK, and Australia. Not accepting children's books as at September 2020. See website for current status and full guidelines.

Publishing Imprints: 4RV Biblical Based (**P0002**); 4RV Children's Corner (**P0003**); 4RV Fiction (**P0004**); 4RV Nonfiction (**P0005**); 4RV Tweens & Teens (**P0007**); 4RV Young Adult (**P0008**)

P0007 **4RV Tweens & Teens**
Publishing Imprint
United States

Book Publisher: 4RV Publishing (**P0006**)

CHILDREN'S > **Fiction** > *Middle Grade*

TEEN > **Fiction** > *Novels*

Publishes books for teens and tweens grades 5-8.

P0008 **4RV Young Adult**
Publishing Imprint
United States

Book Publisher: 4RV Publishing (**P0006**)

YOUNG ADULT > **Fiction** > *Novels*

Publishes books for young adults aged 14-18.

P0009 **4th Estate**
Publishing Imprint
The News Building, 1 London Bridge Street, London, SE1 9GF
United Kingdom
Tel: +44 (0) 20 8741 7070

4thestate.marketing@harpercollins.co.uk

http://www.4thestate.co.uk

Book Publisher: HarperCollins UK (**P0382**)

Types: Fiction; Nonfiction
Formats: Reference
Subjects: Biography; Comedy / Humour;
Current Affairs; Literary; Science; Travel
Markets: Adult

Closed to approaches.

Strong reputation for Literary and nonfiction.
No unsolicited mss.

P0010 6th
Publishing Imprint

Publishing Imprint: O-Books

P0011 6th Books
Publishing Imprint

Book Publisher: John Hunt Publishing Ltd

P0012 7.13 Books
Book Publisher
United States

leland@713books.com

https://713books.com

Types: Fiction
Formats: Short Fiction
Subjects: Comedy / Humour; Literary
Markets: Adult

Publishes novels and short story collections
between 45,000 and 100,000 words. Only
accepts work from writers who have not yet
published a book of literary fiction.
Particularly looking for female and LGBTQ
voices. Submit via online submission system.
$7.13 fee per submission.

Editors: Leland Cheuk; Hasanthika Sirisena

P0013 A-R Editions
Book Publisher
1600 Aspen Cmns, Suite 100, Middleton WI
53562
United States
Tel: +1 (608) 836-9000

info@areditions.com

https://www.areditions.com
https://www.facebook.com/areditions

Nonfiction > *Nonfiction Books*: Music

Send: Query; Proposal
How to send: Email; File sharing service

Publisher of modern critical editions of music
based on current musicological research, aimed
at scholars and performers. See website for
submission guidelines.

Managing Editor: Paul L. Ranzini

Publishing Imprint: Greenway Music Press
(P0340)

P0014 a...p press
Book Publisher
United States

afterthepause@gmail.com

https://afterthepause.com/a-p-press/

Types: Fiction; Poetry
Formats: Short Fiction
Subjects: Experimental
Markets: Adult

Send: Full text

Publishes poetry, flash fiction, visual poetry,
experimental poetry, and any combination
thereof. Manuscripts must be at least 50 pages.
Send submissions by email.

P0015 Abacus
Publishing Imprint

Publishing Imprint: Little, Brown Book Group
(P0532)

P0016 ABC-CLIO
Book Publisher
PO Box 1911, Santa Barbara, CA 93116-1911
United States
Tel: +1 (800) 368-6868
Fax: +1 (805) 968-1911

CustomerService@abc-clio.com

https://www.abc-clio.com/
https://www.facebook.com/ABCCLIO
https://twitter.com/ABC_CLIO
https://www.youtube.com/user/ABCCLIOLive
https://www.linkedin.com/company/abc-clio/

ACADEMIC > **Nonfiction** > *Reference*
General, and in particular: History;
Sociology

Publishes academic reference works and
periodicals primarily on topics such as history
and social sciences for educational and public
library settings.

Publishing Imprints: ABC-CLIO / Greenwood
(P0017); Libraries Unlimited (*P0521*); Praeger
(*P0717*)

P0017 ABC-CLIO / Greenwood
Publishing Imprint
Acquisitions Department, ABC-
CLIO/Greenwood, ABC-CLIO, PO Box 1911,
Santa Barbara, CA 93116-1911
United States
Tel: +1 (800) 368-6868

acquisition_inquiries@abc-clio.com

http://www.abc-clio.com

Book Publisher: ABC-CLIO **(P0016)**

Types: Nonfiction
Formats: Reference
Subjects: Arts; Biography; Business; Crime;
Culture; Current Affairs; Finance; Health;
History; Legal; Nature; Politics; Psychology;
Religion; Science; Sociology; Technology;
Warfare; Women's Interests
Markets: Academic; Adult

Send: Query
Don't send: Full text

Publisher of general nonfiction and reference
covering history, humanities, and general
interest topics across the secondary and higher
education curriculum. No fiction, poetry, or
drama. Welcomes proposals in appropriate
areas. See website for specific imprint / editor
contact details.

P0018 Abdo Publishing Co
Book Publisher
1920 Lookout Drive, North Mankato MN
56003
United States
Tel: +1 (800) 800-1312
Fax: +1 (800) 862-3480

fiction@abdobooks.com

http://abdopublishing.com

Types: Fiction; Nonfiction
Subjects: Anthropology; Arts; Biography;
Cookery; Crafts; Culture; Current Affairs;
Design; Entertainment; History; Hobbies;
Medicine; Politics; Religion; Science;
Sociology; Sport; Technology; Travel; Warfare
Markets: Children's

Send: Query
Don't send: Full text

Publishes nonfiction, educational material for
children up to the 12th grade, plus fiction
series for children. Not accepting nonfiction
submissions as at May 2017 (see website for
current situation). Writers with a concept for a
fiction series should send samples of
manuscripts by email.

Editor: Paul Abdo

P0019 Absolute Classics
Publishing Imprint

Book Publisher: Oberon Books **(P0628)**

P0020 Abuzz Press
Book Publisher
United States

https://www.abuzzpress.com

Types: Fiction; Nonfiction
Subjects: Erotic; How To; New Age; Romance
Markets: Adult

Publishes nonfiction, adult colouring books,
how-to, new age, erotica (including erotic
nonfiction and erotic romance), and
exceptional fiction. No poetry, short story
collections, books with colour interiors, or
illegal material. Send submissions via form on
website.

P0021 Acair Ltd
Book Publisher
An Tosgan, 54 Seaforth Road, Stornoway, Isle
of Lewis, HS1 2SD

United Kingdom
Tel: +44 (0) 1851 703020

info@acairbooks.com

https://www.acairbooks.com
https://www.facebook.com/acairbooks
https://twitter.com/AcairBooks
https://www.pinterest.co.uk/acairbooks/

ADULT
Fiction in Translation > *Novels*: Gaelic

Nonfiction in Translation > *Nonfiction Books*: Gaelic

Nonfiction > *Nonfiction Books*

Poetry in Translation > *Any Poetic Form*: Gaelic

CHILDREN'S > **Fiction in Translation**
Novels: Gaelic
Picture Books: Gaelic

Publishes a wide range of Gaelic, English and Bilingual books, including children's fiction. 75% of children's books published are exclusively Gaelic.

P0022 Addison Wesley
Publishing Imprint
United States

Book Publisher: Pearson (**P0670**)

ACADEMIC > **Nonfiction** > *Nonfiction Books*
Computer Science; Finance; Mathematics; Statistics

Publishes academic textbooks, learning programs, and multimedia in the areas of computer science, economics, finance, mathematics and statistics.

P0023 Adonis and Abbey Publishing
Book Publisher
Adonis & Abbey Publishers Ltd, P.O. Box 43418, London, SE11 4XZ, United Kingdom
United Kingdom
Tel: +44 (0) 20 7793 8893

editor@adonis-abbey.com

http://www.adonisandabbey.com

Types: Nonfiction
Formats: Reference
Subjects: Anthropology; Culture; Current Affairs; History; Lifestyle; Literary; Traditional
Markets: Academic; Adult

Send: Full text

This press is actively seeking personal material from an experiential point of view while employing a vocabulary that will educate the reader with a real sense of presence. They are also seeking highly academic books on current events and history. Manuscripts with an African or African American veiw point are also saught. Query first.

P0024 AFK
Publishing Imprint

Book Publisher: Scholastic (**P0790**)

P0025 Agora Books
Book Publisher
55 New Oxford Street, London, WC1A 1BS
United Kingdom
Tel: +44 (0) 20 7344 1000

submissions@agorabooks.co

https://www.agorabooks.co

Literary Agency: Peters Fraser + Dunlop (**L1091**)

Types: Fiction
Subjects: Crime; History; Mystery; Suspense; Women's Interests
Markets: Adult

Send: Query
Don't send: Full text

Send synopsis and first three chapters (or 50 pages) as Word document attachments by email. See website for full guidelines.

P0026 Albert Whitman & Company
Book Publisher
250 South Northwest Highway, Suite 320, Park Ridge, Illinois 60068
United States
Tel: +1 (800) 255-7675
Fax: +1 (847) 581-0039

submissions@albertwhitman.com

http://www.albertwhitman.com

Types: Fiction; Nonfiction
Markets: Children's; Young Adult

Publishes picture books, middle-grade fiction, and young adult novels. Will consider fiction and nonfiction manuscripts for picture books for children ages 1 to 8, up to 1,000 words; middle-grade novels up to 35,000 words for children up to the age of 12; and young adult novels up to 70,000 words for ages 12-18. See website for full submission guidelines.

Editor-in-Chief: Kathleen Tucker

P0027 Alfred A. Knopf
Publishing Imprint
United States

Book Publisher: Knopf Doubleday Publishing Group (**P0498**)

P0028 Allison & Busby Ltd
Book Publisher
11 Wardour Mews, London, W1F 8AN
United Kingdom
Tel: +44 (0) 20 3950 7834

susie@allisonandbusby.com

http://www.allisonandbusby.com

Types: Fiction
Formats: Short Fiction
Subjects: Autobiography; Contemporary; Cookery; Crime; Culture; Fantasy; History; Literary; Mystery; Romance; Science Fiction; Self Help; Thrillers; Travel; Warfare; Women's Interests
Markets: Adult; Young Adult

How to send: Through a literary agent

Accepts approaches via a literary agent only. No unsolicited MSS or queries from authors.

Publishing Director: Susie Dunlop

P0029 Allworth Press
Book Publisher
307 West 36th Street, 11th Floor, New York, NY 10018
United States
Tel: +1 (212) 643-6816
Fax: +1 (212) 643-6819

allworthsubmissions@skyhorsepublishing.com

https://www.skyhorsepublishing.com/allworth-press/

Book Publisher: Skyhorse Publishing, Inc. (**P0817**)

Types: Nonfiction
Formats: Theatre Scripts
Subjects: Arts; Business; Crafts; Design; Photography
Markets: Adult

Send: Query
Don't send: Full text

Send query with 1-2 page synopsis, annotated chapter outline, market analysis, one or two sample chapters, and author CV. See website for full guidelines.

P0030 Allyn & Bacon
Publishing Imprint

Book Publisher: Pearson (**P0670**)

P0031 Alma Books Ltd
Book Publisher
Thornton House, Thornton Road, Wimbledon, London, SW19 4NG
United Kingdom

info@almabooks.com

https://www.almabooks.com
https://www.facebook.com/AlmaPublishing/
https://twitter.com/almabooks
https://www.pinterest.co.uk/almabooks/
https://www.instagram.com/almapublishing/

Fiction in Translation > *Novels*

Fiction > *Novels*

Nonfiction in Translation > *Nonfiction Books*

Nonfiction > *Nonfiction Books*

Send: Query
How to send: Email

Closed to submissions of contemporary fiction. Accepts proposals for translations of classic literature, and welcomes proposals and ideas for the Classics list.

Publishing Imprints: Alma Classics; Calder Publications Ltd (**P0140**)

P0032 Amber Books Ltd
Book Publisher
United House, North Road, London, N7 9DP
United Kingdom
Tel: +44 (0) 20 7520 7600

editorial@amberbooks.co.uk

https://www.amberbooks.co.uk

Types: Nonfiction
Formats: Reference
Subjects: History; Warfare
Markets: Adult

Send: Query
Don't send: Full text

Publishes illustrated nonfiction in a wide range of subject areas, particularly military. No fiction, biography or poetry. Send query with synopsis, contents lists, author CV, and one or two sample chapters by post or by email. Do not send SASE or IRCs or cash. Response not guaranteed.

P0033 American Catholic Press
Book Publisher
16565 S. State Street, South Holland, Illinois 60473
United States
Tel: +1 (708) 331-5485
Fax: +1 (708) 331-5484

acp@acpress.org

http://www.americancatholicpress.org

Nonfiction > *Nonfiction Books*
  Christianity; Church Music

Publishes books on the Roman Catholic liturgy, including new music for use in church services. No religious poetry.

Editorial Director: Rev. Michael Gilligan PhD

P0034 American Psychiatric Association Publishing
Book Publisher
800 Maine Avenue, S.W. Suite 900, Washington, DC 20024
United States
Tel: +1 (800) 368-5777
Fax: +1 (202) 403-3094

appi@psych.org

https://www.appi.org

Types: Nonfiction
Subjects: Health; Psychology; Science
Markets: Academic; Adult; Professional

Publishes books, journals, and multimedia on psychiatry, mental health, and behavioural science, aimed at psychiatrists, other mental health professionals, psychiatric residents, medical students, and the general public.

Editor: Laura Roberts

P0035 Amistad
Publishing Imprint

Book Publisher: HarperCollins (**P0378**)

P0036 Anchor Books
Publishing Imprint
United States

Book Publisher: Knopf Doubleday Publishing Group (**P0498**)

P0037 Anchorage Press, Inc.
Publishing Imprint

Book Publisher: Cressrelles Publishing Co. Ltd (**P0197**)

P0038 Andersen Press Ltd
Book Publisher
20 Vauxhall Bridge Road, London, SW1V 2SA
United Kingdom

anderseneditorial@penguinrandomhouse.co.uk

https://www.andersenpress.co.uk
https://twitter.com/andersenpresshttps://twitter.com/andersenpress
https://www.facebook.com/andersenpress

CHILDREN'S > **Fiction** > *Picture Books*

How to send: Through a literary agent

Publishes rhyming stories, but no poetry, adult fiction, fiction for older children, nonfiction, or short story collections. Accepts submissions through literary agents only.

P0039 Angry Robot
Book Publisher
Unit 11, Shepperton House, 89 Shepperton Road, London, N1 3DF
United Kingdom
Tel: +44 (0) 20 3813 6940

incoming@angryrobotbooks.com

https://www.angryrobotbooks.com

Book Publisher: Watkins Media (**P0949**)

Types: Fiction
Subjects: Fantasy; Science Fiction
Markets: Adult

How to send: Through a literary agent

Publisher of science fiction and fantasy. Accepts submissions through literary agents only, apart from a specific open door period held each year. See the company's social media for updates.

P0040 Anness Publishing Ltd
Book Publisher
Algores Way, Wisbech, Cambridgeshire, PE13 2TQ
United Kingdom

info@anness.com

http://www.aquamarinebooks.com

Types: Nonfiction; Poetry
Formats: Reference
Subjects: Arts; Cookery; Crafts; Design; Gardening; Health; History; Leisure; Lifestyle; Music; Nature; New Age; Photography; Religion; Science; Sport; Travel; Warfare
Markets: Adult; Children's

Describes itself as one of the largest independent book publishers in the UK.

Publishing Imprints: Armadillo (*P0052*); Lorenz Books (*P0538*); Peony Press (*P0690*); Southwater. (*P0826*)

P0041 Anthony Bourdain Books
Publishing Imprint

Book Publisher: HarperCollins (**P0378**)

P0042 Anvil Press Publishers
Book Publisher
P.O. Box 3008, MPO, Vancouver, B.C., V6B 3X5
Canada
Tel: +1 (604) 876-8710

info@anvilpress.com

https://www.anvilpress.com
https://www.facebook.com/Anvil-Press-115437275199047/
https://www.twitter.com/anvilpress
https://www.instagram.com/anvilpress_publishers/

Fiction > *Novels*

Nonfiction > *Nonfiction Books*
  Arts; Photography

Poetry > *Poetry Collections*

Scripts > *Theatre Scripts*: Drama

Closed to approaches.

Publisher designed to discover and nurture Canadian literary talent. Considers work from Canadian authors with SASE only. For prose, send query with synopsis and 20-30 pages; for poetry send 8-12 poems; and for drama send entire MS, unless excessively long. No submissions by email.

Editor: Brian Kaufman

P0043 Aphrodisia
Publishing Imprint

Book Publisher: Kensington Publishing Corp. (**P0488**)

P0044 Applause

Publishing Imprint
United States

Book Publisher: The Globe Pequot Press
(**P0324**)

P0045 Appletree Press Ltd

Book Publisher
Roycroft House, 164 Malone Road, Belfast,
BT9 5LL
United Kingdom
Tel: +44 (0) 28 90 243074
Fax: +44 (0) 28 90 246756

editorial@appletree.ie

http://www.appletree.ie

Types: Nonfiction
Markets: Adult

Send: Query
Don't send: Full text

Send query with synopsis, descriptive chapter
list, and two or three chapters by email.
Publishes small-format gift books and general
nonfiction books of Irish and Scottish interest.
No unsolicited MSS.

P0046 April Gloaming

Book Publisher
United States

inquiries.aprilgloaming@gmail.com

http://www.aprilgloaming.com

Types: Fiction; Nonfiction; Poetry
Subjects: Literary
Markets: Adult

Send: Query
Don't send: Full text

Nashville-based independent press that aims to
capture and better understand the Southern
soul, Southern writing, and the Southern holler.
Send submissions of poetry, fiction, creative
nonfiction, or graphic novels to the specific
email addresses given on the website.

P0047 Arabelle Publishing

Book Publisher
United States
Tel: +1 (804) 298-5082

http://www.arabellepublishing.com

Types: Nonfiction
Subjects: Autobiography; Business; Cookery;
Health; How To; Lifestyle; Religion; Women's
Interests
Markets: Adult; Children's; Professional

We are dedicated to glorifying God by
celebrating life through stories that reveal His
grace and love. We publish high-quality,
nonfiction books that inspire, impact, and
instruct. We bring communities and cultures
together by celebrating the regional history,
and the beauty found in the lives of ordinary

people who impact the communities in which
they live. As at November 2019, we are
accepting query submissions for the 2020
publication. Although we will consider all
great books, we are specifically accepting
queries for Health and Wellness books that are
biblically based, Christian Living, and Bible
Studies and Devotionals.

P0048 Arc Music

Publishing Imprint

Book Publisher: Arc Publications (**P0049**)

P0049 Arc Publications

Book Publisher
Nanholme Mill, Shaw Wood Road,
Todmorden, Lancs, OL14 6DA
United Kingdom
Tel: +44 (0) 1706 812338

info@arcpublications.co.uk

https://www.arcpublications.co.uk

Types: Poetry; Translations
Subjects: Contemporary; Music
Markets: Adult

Send: Full text

Send 16-24 poems by email as a Word / PDF
attachment, maximum one poem per page,
during December only. Submissions from
outside the UK and Ireland should be sent to
specific address for international submissions,
available on website. Cover letter should
include short bio and details of the
contemporary poets you read. See website for
full guidelines.

Publishing Imprint: Arc Music (*P0048*)

P0050 Arcadia Books

Book Publisher
Great West House, Great West Road,
Brentford, TW8 9DF
United Kingdom
Tel: +44 (0) 20 8960 4967

info@arcadiabooks.co.uk

http://arcadiabooks.co.uk

Types: Fiction; Translations
Subjects: Crime; Literary
Markets: Adult

Publisher of translated fiction, literary fiction
and crime.

P0051 Arcana

Publishing Imprint

Book Publisher: Aurelia Leo (**P0061**)

P0052 Armadillo

Publishing Imprint

Book Publisher: Anness Publishing Ltd
(**P0040**)

P0053 Arsenal Pulp Press

Book Publisher
202-211 East Georgia Street, Vancouver, BC,
V6A 1Z6
Canada
Tel: +1 (604) 687-4233
Fax: +1 (604) 687-4283

info@arsenalpulp.com

https://arsenalpulp.com

ADULT
  Fiction > *Novels*
    LGBTQIA; Literary

  Nonfiction > *Nonfiction Books*
    British Columbia; Culture; LGBTQIA;
    Literary; Politics; Regional; Sociology;
    Youth Culture

CHILDREN'S
  Fiction > *Novels*
    Diversity; LGBTQIA

  Nonfiction > *Nonfiction Books*
    Diversity; LGBTQIA

YOUNG ADULT
  Fiction > *Novels*: LGBTQIA

  Nonfiction > *Nonfiction Books*: LGBTQIA

Send: Synopsis; Outline; Writing sample;
Market info; Self-Addressed Stamped
Envelope (SASE)
How to send: Post
How not to send: Fax; Email; Phone

Publishes Cultural studies,
Political/sociological studies, Regional studies
and guides, in particular for British Columbia,
Cookbooks, Gay and lesbian fiction and
nonfiction (including young adult and
children's), Visual art, Multicultural fiction
and nonfiction, Literary fiction and nonfiction
(no genre fiction, such as mysteries, thriller, or
romance), Youth culture, Health, and books for
children (especially those that emphasise
diversity). Send query with synopsis, chapter
by chapter outline for nonfiction, writing
credentials, 50-page excerpt, and marketing
analysis. Include self-addressed envelope and
appropriate return postage (either Canadian
postage or IRCs), or email address for
response. See website for full details. No
submissions by fax or email, or queries by
phone.

P0054 Ascend Books, LLC

Book Publisher
7221 West 79th Street, Suite 206, Overland
Park, KS 66204
United States
Tel: +1 (913) 948-5500

bsnodgrass@ascendbooks.com

http://ascendbooks.com

Types: Nonfiction
Subjects: Entertainment; Sport
Markets: Adult; Children's

Send: Query
Don't send: Full text

Highly specialised publishing company with a burgeoning presence in sports, entertainment and commemoration events. Send query by post with SASE if return of material required. See website for full guidelines.

Editor: Bob Snodgrass

P0055 Ashley Drake Publishing Ltd

Book Publisher
PO Box 733, Cardiff, CF14 7ZY
United Kingdom

post@ashleydrake.com

http://www.ashleydrake.com

ACADEMIC > **Nonfiction** > *Nonfiction Books*
  Education; History; Medieval Literature; Politics; Scandinavia

ADULT > **Nonfiction**
  Nonfiction Books: Leisure; Sport
  Reference: Popular

Send: Proposal

Publishes English and Welsh language trade and academic books. Welcomes proposals. Forms for proposals can be found on the website.

Publishing Imprints: Gwasg Addysgol Cymru; Morgan Publishing; Scandinavian Academic Press; St David's Press; Welsh Academic Press (**P0960**); YDdraig Fach

P0056 Atlantean Publishing

Book Publisher; Magazine Publisher
United Kingdom

https://atlanteanpublishing.fandom.com/wiki/Atlantean_Publishing

Fiction > *Short Fiction*

Poetry > *Any Poetic Form*

Non-profit-making small press. Produces several serial publications and numerous one-off releases, specialising in poetry and short fiction, both 'general' and 'genre'.

Editor: David-John Tyrer

Magazine: Awen (**M0062**)

P0057 Atlantic Books

Book Publisher
Ormond House, 26-27 Boswell Street, London, WC1N 3JZ
United Kingdom
Tel: +44 (0) 20 7269 1610
Fax: +44 (0) 20 7430 0916

enquiries@atlantic-books.co.uk

https://atlantic-books.co.uk

Types: Fiction; Nonfiction
Subjects: Autobiography; Current Affairs; History; Literary; Politics
Markets: Adult

Send: Query
Don't send: Full text

Open to submissions of complete novels, extensive partials, or short stories, within the literary genre. Send submissions with a one line pitch and a one paragraph pitch, outlining the submission.

P0058 Atom

Publishing Imprint

Publishing Imprint: Little, Brown Book Group (**P0532**)

P0059 Atrium

Publishing Imprint

Book Publisher: Cork University Press (**P0187**)

P0060 Attic Press

Publishing Imprint

Book Publisher: Cork University Press (**P0187**)

P0061 Aurelia Leo

Book Publisher
4212 Algonquin Parkway, Louisville, KY 40211-2402
United States

subs@aurelialeo.com

https://aurelialeo.com

Fiction > *Short Fiction*
  Erotic Romance; Fantasy; LGBTQIA; Science Fiction

Closed to approaches.

Currently looking for lesbian, gay, bisexual, and transgender erotic romance with elements of sci-fi and fantasy for a themed anthology. 1,000 to 17,500 words.

Editor: Zelda Knight

Publishing Imprint: Arcana (*P0051*)

P0062 Aurora Metro Press

Book Publisher
67 Grove Avenue, Twickenham, TW1 4HX
United Kingdom
Tel: +44 (0) 20 3261 0000

submissions@aurorametro.com

https://aurorametro.com

Types: Fiction; Nonfiction; Scripts
Formats: Film Scripts; Theatre Scripts
Subjects: Biography; Comedy / Humour; Cookery; Culture; Drama; History
Markets: Adult; Young Adult

Send: Query
Don't send: Full text

Publishes fiction, plays/theatre texts, and both general and specialist nonfiction books across theatre, film, music, literature, and popular culture. Send synopsis and complete ms by email only. For play submissions, if a production is scheduled then the full script must be sent at least 6 weeks before opening night.

P0063 The Authority Guides

Book Publisher
SRA Books, Unit 3, Spike Island, 133 Cumberland Road, Bristol, BS1 6UX
United Kingdom
Tel: +44 (0) 1789 761345

http://authorityguides.co.uk

Types: Nonfiction
Subjects: Business
Markets: Professional

Publishes pocket-sized business books for entrepreneurs and business professionals.

P0064 Avalon Travel

Publishing Imprint
United States

Book Publisher: Perseus Books (**P0693**)

P0065 Avery

Publishing Imprint

Book Publisher: Penguin Publishing Group (**P0682**)

P0066 Avon

Publishing Imprint
United Kingdom

Book Publisher: HarperCollins UK (**P0382**)

P0067 Avon Books

Publishing Imprint
United States

https://www.harpercollins.com
https://www.harpercollins.com/pages/avonromance
https://twitter.com/avonbooks
https://www.instagram.com/avonbooks/
https://www.facebook.com/avonromance

Book Publisher: HarperCollins (**P0378**)

Fiction > *Novels*
  Contemporary Romance; Historical Romance; Romance; Supernatural / Paranormal Romance

Closed to approaches.

Publishing award-winning romance since 1941. Recognized for having pioneered the historical romance category and continues to publish in wide variety of other genres, including paranormal, urban fantasy, contemporary and regency.

P0068 Award Publications Limited
Book Publisher
The Old Riding School, The Welbeck Estate, Worksop, Nottinghamshire, S80 3LR
United Kingdom
Tel: +44 (0) 1909 478170

info@awardpublications.co.uk

http://www.awardpublications.co.uk

Types: Fiction; Nonfiction
Formats: Reference
Markets: Children's

Publishes children's fiction, nonfiction, and reference.

P0069 Axis Mundi
Publishing Imprint

Publishing Imprint: O-Books

P0070 Axis Mundi Books
Publishing Imprint

Book Publisher: John Hunt Publishing Ltd

P0071 AYNI BOOKS
Publishing Imprint

Book Publisher: John Hunt Publishing Ltd

P0072 Backbeat
Publishing Imprint
United States

Book Publisher: The Globe Pequot Press **(P0324)**

P0073 Bad Press Ink
Book Publisher
United Kingdom

enquiries@badpress.ink

https://badpress.ink

Types: Fiction
Markets: Adult

Publishes alternative books and niche lifestyle fiction. Complete online submission process on website.

Editors: Pat Blayney; Iain Parke

P0074 Baker Publishing Group
Book Publisher
6030 East Fulton Road, Ada, MI 49301
United States
Tel: +1 (616) 676-9185
Fax: +1 (616) 676-9573

http://bakerpublishinggroup.com

Fiction > *Novels*: Christianity

Nonfiction > *Nonfiction Books*: Christianity

Publishes high-quality writings that represent historic Christianity and serve the diverse interests and concerns of evangelical readers.

Book Publishers: Baker Academic; Baker Books; Brazos Press; Chosen Books; Fleming H. Revell

P0075 Balkan Press
Book Publisher
United States

wbernhardt@conclave.com

https://www.williambernhardt.com/balkan-press-submission-guidelines

Types: Fiction; Nonfiction; Poetry
Subjects: Literary
Markets: Adult

Send: Full text

Seeks poetry, fiction, and creative nonfiction of exceptional literary merit. Submit through online submission system. $10 submission fee.

P0076 Balzer + Bray
Publishing Imprint

Book Publisher: HarperCollins **(P0378)**

P0077 Bantam
Publishing Imprint
United States

http://www.randomhousebooks.com/imprints/

Book Publisher: Random House

Fiction > *Novels*

Nonfiction > *Nonfiction Books*

How to send: Through a literary agent

Publishes original works of fiction and nonfiction in all formats.

Magazine: island

P0078 Bantam Books
Publishing Imprint

Book Publisher: Transworld Publishers **(P0875)**

P0079 Bantam Press
Publishing Imprint

Book Publisher: Transworld Publishers **(P0875)**

P0080 Baobab Press
Book Publisher
121 California Avenue, Reno, NV 89503
United States
Tel: +1 (775) 786-1188

info@baobab.com

http://baobabpress.com

Types: Fiction; Nonfiction; Poetry
Formats: Short Fiction
Markets: Adult; Children's

Taking a break from short story submissions as at April 2019. Aims to re-
open later in 2019. Check website for current status.** Constantly strives to discover, cultivate, and nurture authors working in all genres. Publishes Creative Nonfiction, Short-Story, Novel, and Comic/Visual Narrative manuscripts (Comic/Visual Narrative manuscripts will not be considered without artwork). Also publishes children's picture and board books (send text with or without artwork). Submit via online submission system.

P0081 Barrington Stoke
Book Publisher
18 Walker Street, Edinburgh, EH3 7LP
United Kingdom
Tel: +44 (0) 131 225 4113

info@barringtonstoke.co.uk

https://www.barringtonstoke.co.uk

Types: Fiction; Nonfiction
Formats: Reference
Markets: Children's; Professional

Closed to approaches.

Commissions books via literary agents only. No unsolicited material. Publishes books for "reluctant, dyslexic, disenchanted and under-confident" readers and their teachers.

P0082 BatCat Press
Book Publisher
c/o Lincoln Park Performing Arts Charter School, One Lincoln Park, Midland, PA 15059
United States

batcatpress@gmail.com

https://batcatpress.com

Types: Fiction; Nonfiction; Poetry
Formats: Short Fiction
Subjects: Literary
Markets: Adult

Closed to approaches.

Publishes literary fiction, poetry, and creative nonfiction. Submit via online submission system.

P0083 Batsford
Publishing Imprint

Book Publisher: Pavilion Books Group Limited **(P0666)**

P0084 BBC Active
Publishing Imprint

Book Publisher: Pearson **(P0670)**

P0085 BBC Books
Publishing Imprint
United Kingdom

https://www.penguin.co.uk/company/publishers/ebury/bbc-books.html

Book Publisher: Ebury **(P0243)**

Nonfiction > *Nonfiction Books*
General, and in particular: Entertainment; Food and Drink; Nature; Popular Culture; TV

Specialises in TV and radio tie-ins, as well as food and drink, nature, and history, etc.

Editor: Stuart Biles

P0086 BCS (British Computer Society)
Book Publisher
United Kingdom
Tel: +44 (0) 1793 417417

publishing@bcs.uk

https://www.bcs.org/

PROFESSIONAL > **Nonfiction** > *Nonfiction Books*
Business; Cyber Security; Data and Information Systems; Finance; Leadership; Legal; Management; Procurement; Project Management; Service Management; Software Development

Publishes books for business and technology professionals.

Editor: Matthew Flynn

P0087 Be About It Press
Book Publisher
United States

zinebeaboutit@gmail.com

http://beaboutitpress.tumblr.com

Types: Fiction; Poetry
Formats: Short Fiction
Subjects: Literary
Markets: Adult

Publishes zines, ebooks, chapbooks, and other short form creative literature online and in print. Print chapbooks by solicitation only. Ebooks by solicitation or during an announced contest. See website for full details.

P0088 Beacon Publishing Group
Book Publisher
New York, NY
United States
Tel: +1 (800) 817-8480

submissions@beaconpublishinggroup.com

https://www.beaconpublishinggroup.com

Types: Fiction; Nonfiction
Markets: Adult

Send: Full text

A traditional publisher that specialises in fiction and nonfiction work.

Publishing Imprints: Fox Book Press (*P0300*); University Press (*P0919*)

P0089 becker&mayer! books
Publishing Imprint
11120 NE 33rd Place Suite 101, Bellevue, WA 98004
United States
Tel: +1 (425) 827-7120
Fax: +1 (425) 828-9659

mike.oprins@quarto.com

https://www.quartoknows.com/brand/2113/becker-mayer/

Book Publisher: The Quarto Group, Inc. (**P0739**)

Types: Nonfiction
Markets: Adult; Children's

Publishes illustrated nonfiction for adults and children.

Editor: Mike Oprins

P0090 becker&mayer! kids
Publishing Imprint

Book Publisher: The Quarto Group, Inc. (**P0739**)

P0091 Bello
Publishing Imprint

Book Publisher: Pan Macmillan (**P0659**)

P0092 Berkley
Publishing Imprint

Book Publisher: Penguin Publishing Group (**P0682**)

P0093 Bernard Babani (publishing) Ltd
Book Publisher
The Grampians, Shepherds Bush Road, London, W6 7NF
United Kingdom

enquiries@babanibooks.com

http://www.babanibooks.com

Types: Nonfiction
Subjects: Technology
Markets: Adult

Send: Query
Don't send: Full text

Publishes books on robotics, computing, and electronics. Always interested in hearing from potential authors. Send query by email with synopsis and details of your qualifications for writing on the topic.

P0094 Bess Press
Book Publisher
3565 Harding Avenue, Honolulu, HI 96816
United States
Tel: +1 (808) 734-7159
Fax: +1 (808) 732-3627

submission@besspress.com

https://www.besspress.com

Types: Nonfiction
Subjects: Culture; Lifestyle; Travel
Markets: Adult; Children's

Send: Query
Don't send: Full text

Publishes books about Hawai'i and the Pacific. All submissions should be sent by email. See website for full guidelines.

P0095 Birlinn Ltd
Book Publisher
West Newington House, 10 Newington Road, Edinburgh, EH9 1QS
United Kingdom
Tel: +44 (0) 131 668 4371
Fax: +44 (0) 131 668 4466

info@birlinn.co.uk

http://www.birlinn.co.uk

Types: Fiction; Nonfiction; Poetry
Formats: Reference
Subjects: Adventure; Architecture; Arts; Autobiography; Comedy / Humour; Culture; Current Affairs; Finance; History; Legal; Medicine; Nature; Politics; Sociology; Sport; Travel; Warfare
Markets: Adult; Children's

Send: Query
Don't send: Full text

Focuses on Scottish material: local, military, and Highland history; humour, adventure; reference, guidebooks, and folklore. Not currently accepting romantic fiction, science fiction, or short stories. Send query by post with SAE, synopsis, three sample chapters, and explanation of why you have chosen this publisher. No submissions by fax, email, or on disk. See website for full details.

P0096 Bitter Lemon Press
Book Publisher
47 Wilmington Square, London, WC1X 0ET
United Kingdom
Tel: +44 (0) 20 7278 3738

books@bitterlemonpress.com

http://www.bitterlemonpress.com

Types: Fiction
Subjects: Crime; Literary; Thrillers
Markets: Adult

How to send: Through a literary agent

Accepts submissions in the literary crime and thriller genres. Submissions may be sent by email and must come through a literary agent.

P0097 The Bitter Oleander Press
Book Publisher; Magazine Publisher
4983 Tall Oaks Drive, Fayetteville, NY 13066-9776
United States

info@bitteroleander.com

https://www.bitteroleander.com

Poetry > *Any Poetic Form*

Closed to approaches.

Publishes poetry collections and a journal of poetry and short fiction.

Magazine: The Bitter Oleander (**M0089**)

P0098 Black & White Publishing Ltd

Book Publisher
Nautical House, 104 Commercial Street, Edinburgh, EH6 6NF
United Kingdom
Tel: +44 (0) 1316 254500
Fax: +44 (0) 1316 254501

submissions@blackandwhitepublishing.com
mail@blackandwhitepublishing.com

https://blackandwhitepublishing.com
https://twitter.com/bwpublishing
https://www.facebook.com/
blackandwhitepublishing/
https://www.instagram.com/bwpublishing/
https://www.youtube.com/user/
blackandwhitePub

Fiction > *Novels*

Nonfiction > *Nonfiction Books*
Celebrity Memoir; Comedy / Humour; Food and Drink; Ireland; Lifestyle; Nature; Scotland; Sport

Send: Query; Proposal
How to send: Email; Through a literary agent

Publisher of general fiction and nonfiction. See website for an idea of the kind of books normally published. Accepts fiction submissions during specific submission windows only, or through a literary agent year-round. Check website for details and to submit via online submission system. No poetry, short stories, or work in languages other than English.

Editors: Campbell Brown; Alison McBride

Publishing Imprints: Ink Road (*P0449*); Itchy Coo (*P0457*)

P0099 Black Coffey Publishing

Book Publisher
23 Cromwell rd, Warley, Brentwood, Essex, CM14 5DT
United Kingdom

Paul@blackcoffeypublishing.com

http://www.blackcoffeypublishing.com

Types: Fiction
Formats: Short Fiction
Subjects: Adventure; Comedy / Humour; Commercial; Contemporary; Crime; Drama; Fantasy; Mystery; Satire; Science Fiction; Suspense; Thrillers; Westerns
Markets: Adult; Young Adult

Closed to approaches.

Not accepting submissions as at January 2019. Check website for current status. Specialist digital publisher actively looking for short stories in our 2012 release schedule. We scheduled to publish humorous short story collections on: + 'Office life' + 'Growing up in the 1970s' + 'Leaving home for the first time' Submisions can be made via our website.

Editor: Paul Coffey

P0100 Black Dog & Leventhal

Publishing Imprint
United States

Book Publisher: Perseus Books (**P0693**)

P0101 Black Heron Press

Book Publisher
PO Box 614, Anacortes, WA 98221
United States

https://blackheronpress.com

Fiction > *Novels*: Literary

Send: Query; Writing sample; Self-Addressed Stamped Envelope (SASE)
How to send: Post

Publisher of literary fiction. No submissions or queries by email. Send query with first 30-40 pages by post with SASE.

Publisher: Jerry Gold

P0102 Black Lizard

Publishing Imprint
United States

Book Publisher: Knopf Doubleday Publishing Group (**P0498**)

P0103 Black Swan

Publishing Imprint

Book Publisher: Transworld Publishers (**P0875**)

P0104 Blackfriars

Publishing Imprint

Publishing Imprint: Little, Brown Book Group (**P0532**)

P0105 Blink Publishing

Book Publisher
2.08 The Plaza, 535 Kings Road, London, SW10 0SZ
United Kingdom
Tel: +44 (0) 20 3770 8888

info@blinkpublishing.co.uk

http://www.blinkpublishing.co.uk

Types: Nonfiction
Subjects: Autobiography; Comedy / Humour; Cookery; Crime; Culture; History; Lifestyle;

Music; Sport; Travel; Warfare
Markets: Adult

Send: Query
Don't send: Full text

Publishes illustrated and non-illustrated adult nonfiction. No fiction. Send queries by email with one-page synopsis and first three chapters.

P0106 Bloodaxe Books Ltd

Book Publisher
Eastburn, South Park, Hexham, Northumberland, NE46 1BS
United Kingdom
Tel: +44 (0) 01434 611581

editor@bloodaxebooks.com

https://www.bloodaxebooks.com

Types: Poetry
Markets: Adult

Send: Query
Don't send: Full text

Submit poetry only if you have a track record of publication in magazines. If so, send sample of up to a dozen poems with SAE, or email address for response if outside the UK. No submissions by email or on disk. Poems from the UK sent without return postage will be recycled unread; submissions by email will be deleted unread. No longer accepting poets who have already published a full-length collection with another publisher. See website for full details.

Editorial Director: Neil Astley

P0107 Bloomberg BNA Books

Book Publisher
PO Box 7814, Edison, NJ 08818-7814
United States
Tel: +1 (800) 960-1220

https://www.bna.com

Formats: Reference
Subjects: Legal
Markets: Professional

Send: Query
Don't send: Full text

Publishes reference books written by and for lawyers. Send query with outline or table of contents, CV, market info, and estimated word count.

P0108 Bloomsbury Publishing Plc

Book Publisher
50 Bedford Square, London, WC1B 3DP
United Kingdom
Tel: +44 (0) 20 7631 5600
Fax: +44 (0) 20 7631 5800

contact@bloomsbury.com

https://www.bloomsbury.com

Types: Fiction; Nonfiction
Formats: Reference
Subjects: Arts; Business; Health; History;
Hobbies; Music; Nature; Science; Sport
Markets: Academic; Adult; Children's;
Professional

No longer accepting submissions of fiction, or
nonfiction other than in the following areas:
Academic; Education, Music, Military History,
Natural History, Nautical and Outdoors; Health
and Wellness; Business; Sport; Wildlife;
History; and Science. See website for full
submission guidelines.

Book Publishers: A & C Black Publishers
Limited; Bloomsbury Spark; Walker &
Company

Publishing Imprint: Absolute Press

P0109 Blue Guides Limited
Book Publisher
Winchester House, Dean Gate Avenue,
Taunton, Somerset, TA1 2UH
United Kingdom

editorial@blueguides.com

http://blueguides.com

Types: Nonfiction
Subjects: Culture; Travel
Markets: Adult

Publishes travel guides. Always on the lookout
for new authors. Contact by email in first
instance, giving an indication of your areas of
interest.

P0110 Blue Lamp Books
Publishing Imprint
United Kingdom

https://mangobooks.co.uk/pages/about-mango-
books

Book Publisher: Mango Books (**P0562**)

Nonfiction > *Nonfiction Books*: Police History

Publishes nonfiction books on police history.

P0111 Blue Rider Press
Publishing Imprint
United States

Book Publisher: Penguin Publishing Group
(**P0682**)

P0112 Bluebird
Publishing Imprint

Book Publisher: Pan Macmillan (**P0659**)

P0113 Bluemoose Books Ltd
Book Publisher
25 Sackville Street, Hebden Bridge, HX7 7DJ
United Kingdom

kevin@bluemoosebooks.com

http://www.bluemoosebooks.com

Types: Fiction
Markets: Adult

Send: Query
Don't send: Full text

Send query with synopsis and first three
chapters by email. No unsolicited MSS,
children's books, or young adult.

Editors: Hetha Duffy; Kevin Duffy

P0114 BMM
Publishing Imprint

Book Publisher: SportsBooks Limited (**P0830**)

P0115 Bodleian Library Publishing
Book Publisher
Broad Street, Oxford, OX1 3BG
United Kingdom
Tel: +44 (0) 1865 283850

publishing@bodleian.ox.ac.uk

https://www.bodleianshop.co.uk/
bodleianlibrarypublishing

Types: Nonfiction
Subjects: Arts; History; Literature
Markets: Academic; Adult

Send: Query
Don't send: Full text

Publishes books relating to the library
collections only.

P0116 The Bodley Head
Publishing Imprint
United Kingdom

Book Publisher: Vintage (**P0934**)

P0117 Bonneville Books
Publishing Imprint

Book Publisher: Cedar Fort (**P0155**)

P0118 Bonnier Books (UK)
Book Publisher
1.07-1.09, The Plaza, 535 Kings Road,
London, SW10 0SZ
United Kingdom
Tel: +44 (0) 20 3770 8888

hello@bonnierbooks.co.uk

https://www.bonnierbooks.co.uk

Types: Fiction; Nonfiction
Markets: Adult; Children's

How to send: Through a literary agent

Publishes adult fiction and nonfiction, and
children's books. Accepts approaches through
a literary agent only.

Book Publishers: Autumn Publishing Ltd; Hot
Key Books (**P0419**); The Templar Company
Limited (**P0854**)

P0119 Book House
Publishing Imprint

Book Publisher: The Salariya Book Company
(**P0778**)

P0120 Book Sales
Publishing Imprint

Book Publisher: The Quarto Group, Inc.
(**P0739**)

P0121 Bookouture
Book Publisher
United Kingdom

http://www.bookouture.com

https://twitter.com/bookouture

Fiction > *Novels*
Book Club Fiction; Chick Lit; Commercial;
Contemporary Romance; Cozy Mysteries;
Crime; Domestic Suspense; Historical
Fiction; Multicultural; Police Procedural;
Psychological Thrillers; Romantic Comedy;
Thrillers; Women's Fiction

Nonfiction > *Nonfiction Books*

Send: Full text
How to send: Online submission system

Publishes commercial fiction and some text-
lead nonfiction.

For most authors outside the bestseller lists,
traditional publishers simply aren't adding
enough value to justify low royalty rates. And
because authors aren't all experts in editing,
design, or marketing, self-publishing doesn't
get the most out of their books or time. Digital
publishing offers incredible opportunities to
connect with readers all over the world – but
finding the help you need to make the most of
them can be tricky.

That's why we bring both big publisher
experience and small team creativity. We
genuinely understand and invest in brands –
developing long-term strategies, marketing
plans and websites for each of our authors.

And we work with the most brilliant editorial,
design and marketing professionals in the
business to make sure that everything we do is
perfectly tailored to you and ridiculously good.

Combine all of that with an incredible 45%
royalty rate we think we're simply the perfect
combination of high returns and inspirational
publishing.

P0122 The Borough Press
Publishing Imprint
United Kingdom

Book Publisher: HarperCollins UK (**P0382**)

P0123 Brava
Publishing Imprint

Book Publisher: Kensington Publishing Corp. (**P0488**)

P0124 Brick Books
Book Publisher
PO Box 404, Toronto Station C, Toronto, ON M6J 3P5
Canada
Tel: +1 (519) 657-8579

prodbrick@gmail.com

http://www.brickbooks.ca

Types: Poetry
Markets: Adult

Send: Full text

Publishes poetry by Canadian citizens or landed immigrants only. Considers submissions between January 1 and April 30 only. Prospective authors are advised to familiarise themselves with other books from the publisher before sending a complete ms by post. No multiple submissions. Response in 3-4 months.

Editors: Cara-Lyn Morgan; Nick Thran

P0125 Bright Press
Publishing Imprint

Book Publisher: The Quarto Group, Inc. (**P0739**)

P0126 Bristol University Press
Book Publisher
1-9 Old Park Hill, Bristol, BS2 8BB
United Kingdom
Tel: +44 (0) 1179 545940

bup-info@bristol.ac.uk

http://bristoluniversitypress.co.uk

Types: Nonfiction
Subjects: Business; Current Affairs; Finance; Legal; Nature; Politics; Sociology
Markets: Academic

Send: Query
Don't send: Full text

Publishes scholarship and education in the social sciences. Send query with proposal by email.

Publishing Imprint: Policy Press (*P0710*)

P0127 The British Academy
Book Publisher
10–11 Carlton House Terrace, London, SW1Y 5AH
United Kingdom
Tel: +44 (0) 20 7969 5200

pubs@thebritishacademy.ac.uk

https://www.thebritishacademy.ac.uk
https://www.thebritishacademy.ac.uk/publishing/

ACADEMIC > **Nonfiction** > *Nonfiction Books*
Archaeology; Culture; History; Philosophy; Society

Registered charity publishing not for profit. Publishes humanities and social sciences, particularly history, philosophy, and archaeology.

P0128 The British Museum Press
Book Publisher
British Museum, Great Russell Street, London, WC1B 3DG
United Kingdom
Tel: +44 (0) 20 7323 8528

publicity@britishmuseum.org

https://www.britishmuseum.org/about_us/services/the_british_museum_press.aspx

Types: Nonfiction
Subjects: Archaeology; Arts; Culture; History
Markets: Academic; Adult; Children's

Publishes books inspired by the collections of the British Museum, covering fine and decorative arts, history, archaeology and world cultures.

P0129 Broadside Books
Publishing Imprint

Book Publisher: HarperCollins (**P0378**)

P0130 Broadview Press
Book Publisher
PO Box 1243, Peterborough, ON, K9J 7H5
Canada
Tel: +1 (705) 743-8990
Fax: +1 (705) 743-8353

customerservice@broadviewpress.com

http://www.broadviewpress.com

Types: Nonfiction
Subjects: Literature; Philosophy
Markets: Academic

Send: Query
Don't send: Full text

Publishes academic books on English and philosophy, aimed at undergraduates. Before sending a proposal send an email query to the appropriate editor (see website).

P0131 Bromley House Editions
Publishing Imprint

Book Publisher: Five Leaves Publications (**P0289**)

P0132 Brookside
Publishing Imprint

Book Publisher: New Island (**P0613**)

P0133 Brow Books
Book Publisher
Australia

info@browbooks.com

http://www.browbooks.com

Types: Fiction; Nonfiction; Translations
Formats: Short Fiction
Subjects: Literary
Markets: Adult

Send: Full text

Publishes literary fiction and nonfiction, including translations. Accepts submissions from anyone who identifies as Australian, particularly those who "identify as queer and/or trans and/or intersex and/or are of any colour, religion, or gender, and/or have a disability" [sic]. Submit via online submission system.

P0134 Burgess Lea Press
Publishing Imprint

Book Publisher: The Quarto Group, Inc. (**P0739**)

P0135 Burning Chair
Book Publisher
United Kingdom

info@burningchairpublishing.com

https://burningchairpublishing.com

Types: Fiction
Subjects: Adventure; Crime; Fantasy; History; Horror; Mystery; Science Fiction; Suspense; Thrillers
Markets: Adult; Young Adult

Closed to approaches.

Closed to submissions as at June 2020.

P0136 Business Books
Publishing Imprint

Book Publisher: John Hunt Publishing Ltd

P0137 Buster Books
Publishing Imprint

Book Publisher: Michael O'Mara Books Ltd (**P0586**)

P0138 C&T Publishing
Book Publisher
1651 Challenge Drive, Concord, CA 94520-5206
United States

support@ctpub.com

https://www.ctpub.com

Nonfiction > *Nonfiction Books*
Embroidery; Quilting; Sewing

Publishes books on sewing and related crafts.

Publishing Imprints: Crosley-Griffith (*P0201*); FunStitch Studio (*P0306*); Kansas City Star Quilts; Stash Books (*P0839*)

P0139 Caitlin Press Inc.
Book Publisher
8100 Alderwood Road, Halfmoon Bay, BC, V0N 1Y1
Canada
Tel: +1 (604) 885-9194

vici@caitlin-press.com

http://caitlin-press.com

Types: Fiction; Nonfiction; Poetry
Formats: Short Fiction
Subjects: Adventure; Arts; Autobiography; Comedy / Humour; Cookery; History; Nature; Photography; Politics; Sport; Travel; Women's Interests
Markets: Adult; Children's

Send: Query
Don't send: Full text

Publishes books on topics concerning or by writers from the British Columbia Interior and stories about and by British Columbia women. No submissions by fax or by email. See website for full guidelines.

Editors: Sarah Corsie; Vici Johnstone; Holly Vestad

P0140 Calder Publications Ltd
Publishing Imprint
3 Castle Yard, Richmond TW10 6TF
United Kingdom
Tel: +44 (0) 20 8940 6917

info@almabooks.com

https://almabooks.com/product-category/calder-collection/?imprint=4

Book Publisher: Alma Books Ltd (**P0031**)

Types: Fiction; Nonfiction; Poetry; Scripts
Formats: Theatre Scripts
Subjects: Autobiography; Drama; Fantasy; Literary; Literary Criticism; Music; Politics; Sociology
Markets: Adult

Closed to approaches.

Publishes a wide range of material, with a reputation for being controversial. Not accepting any new material.

P0141 Campbell
Publishing Imprint

Book Publisher: Pan Macmillan (**P0659**)

P0142 Candlemark & Gleam
Book Publisher
United States

eloi@candlemarkandgleam.com

https://www.candlemarkandgleam.com

Types: Fiction
Subjects: Fantasy; Science Fiction
Markets: Adult

Publishes mainly science fiction, but also speculative fiction, broadly defined. Cross-genre/interstitial and SF/F hybrid works are fine; ones with mythic/historical echoes even better. Send query by email with one-page synopsis and 10 pages (or, for medium works (12-42K), the complete ms) as attachments. See website for full guidelines.

P0143 Candy Jar Books
Book Publisher
Mackintosh House, 136 Newport Road, Cardiff, CF24 1DJ
United Kingdom
Tel: +44 (0) 29 2115 7202

shaun@candyjarbooks.co.uk

http://www.candyjarbooks.co.uk

Types: Fiction; Nonfiction
Markets: Adult; Young Adult

Send: Full text

Award-winning independent book publisher, publishing a wide variety of books, from nonfiction, general fiction and children's, through to a range of cult TV books. Submit by post or using online submission form. No children's picture books. See website for full guidelines.

Publishing Director: Shaun Russell

P0144 Canongate Books
Book Publisher
14 High Street, Edinburgh, EH1 1TE
United Kingdom
Tel: +44 (0) 1315 575111

info@canongate.co.uk

https://canongate.co.uk

Types: Fiction; Nonfiction; Translations
Subjects: Autobiography; Comedy / Humour; Culture; History; Literary; Politics; Science; Travel
Markets: Adult

How to send: Through a literary agent

Publisher of a wide range of literary fiction and nonfiction, with a traditionally Scottish slant but becoming increasingly international. Publishes fiction in translation under its international imprint. No children's books, poetry, or drama. Accepts submissions through literary agents only.

Publishing Imprints: Canongate Classics (*P0145*); Canongate International (*P0146*)

P0145 Canongate Classics
Publishing Imprint

Book Publisher: Canongate Books (**P0144**)

P0146 Canongate International
Publishing Imprint

Book Publisher: Canongate Books (**P0144**)

P0147 Canopus Publishing Ltd
Book Publisher
United Kingdom

robin@canopusbooks.com

http://www.canopusbooks.com

Types: Nonfiction
Subjects: Arts; Science; Technology
Markets: Academic; Adult

Publishes books spanning the arts and sciences, including physics, astronomy, and engineering.

Editor: Robin Rees

P0148 Career Press
Book Publisher
65 Parker Street, Suite 7, Newburyport, MA 01950
United States
Tel: +1 (978) 465-0504
Fax: +1 (978) 465-0243

mpye@rwwbooks.com

http://www.careerpress.com

Types: Nonfiction
Formats: Reference
Subjects: Business; Finance; How To; Leisure; Lifestyle; Self Help; Spirituality
Markets: Adult

Send: Full text

If available, send completed MS with SASE. Otherwise, submit outline, author bio, marketing plan, and one or two sample chapters with SASE. Publishes books of practical information and self improvement for adults, covering such topics as education, health, money matters, spiritual matters, business philosophy, etc. Author should familiarise themselves with the catalogue before submitting. No children's books, fiction, cookbooks, humour books, picture books, photography books, memoirs, gambling titles, or coffee-table publications.

Publishing Imprint: New Page Books (*P0615*)

P0149 Carina Press
Publishing Imprint
United States

Submissions@CarinaPress.com

https://www.carinapress.com

Book Publisher: Harlequin Enterprises (**P0362**)

Types: Fiction
Subjects: Contemporary; Erotic; Romance
Markets: Adult

Send: Full text

Digital-first adult fiction imprint. See website for details submission guidelines and to submit via online submission system.

Editors: Kerri Buckley; Stephanie Doig

P0150 Carolrhoda Lab
Publishing Imprint

Book Publisher: Lerner Publishing Group **(P0514)**

P0151 Cartwheel Books
Publishing Imprint

Book Publisher: Scholastic **(P0790)**

P0152 Castle Point Books
Publishing Imprint

Publishing Imprint: St Martin's Press **(P0834)**

P0153 The Catholic University of America Press
Book Publisher
240 Leahy Hall, 620 Michigan Avenue NE, Washington, DC 20064
United States
Tel: +1 (202) 319-5052

cua-press@cua.edu

https://www.cuapress.org

Types: Nonfiction
Subjects: History; Literature; Philosophy; Politics; Religion; Sociology
Markets: Academic; Professional

Send: Query
Don't send: Full text

Publishes books disseminating scholarship in the areas of theology, philosophy, church history, and medieval studies. Send query with outline, CV, sample chapter, and publishing history.

Company Director: Trevor Lipscombe

P0154 Catnip Publishing Ltd
Book Publisher
Hathaway House, Popes Drive, London, N3 1QF
United Kingdom

http://www.catnippublishing.co.uk
https://www.facebook.com/catnipbooks/

CHILDREN'S > **Fiction**
  Novels; *Picture Books*
TEEN > **Fiction** > *Novels*

YOUNG ADULT > **Fiction** > *Novels*

Publishes fiction for children of all ages, from picture books to teen.

Editor: Non Pratt

Publishing Imprints: Happy Cat; Happy Cat First Readers

P0155 Cedar Fort
Book Publisher
2373 W. 700, S. Springville, UT 84663
United States
Tel: +1 (801) 489-4084

http://www.cedarfort.com

Types: Fiction; Nonfiction
Formats: Short Fiction
Subjects: Adventure; Comedy / Humour; Fantasy; History; Mystery; Religion; Romance; Science Fiction; Self Help; Thrillers
Markets: Adult; Children's; Young Adult

Send: Full text

Publishes books with strong moral or religious values that inspire readers to be better people. No poetry, short stories, or erotica. See website for full submission guidelines, and to submit using online submission system.

Publishing Imprints: Bonneville Books *(P0117)*; CFI *(P0157)*; Council Press *(P0192)*; Front Table Books *(P0304)*; Hobble Creek Press *(P0410)*; Horizon Publishers *(P0418)*; King Dragon Press *(P0494)*; Pioneer Plus *(P0705)*; Plain Sight Publishing *(P0706)*; Sweetwater Books *(P0846)*

P0156 Cengage
Book Publisher
Cheriton House, North Way, Andover, SP10 5BE
United Kingdom
Tel: +44 (0)1264 332424
Fax: +44 (0)1264 342745

EMEAHEPublishing@cengage.com

http://www.cengage.co.uk

Types: Nonfiction
Markets: Academic

Send: Query
Don't send: Full text

Welcomes unsolicited material aimed at students. Send query by email in first instance. See website for full guidelines.

Book Publishers: Gale **(P0309)**; KidHaven Press; Zero to Ten Limited

P0157 CFI
Publishing Imprint

Book Publisher: Cedar Fort **(P0155)**

P0158 Changemakers
Book Publisher
Maryland
United States

office1@jhpbooks.net

https://www.johnhuntpublishing.com/changemakers-books/

Types: Nonfiction
Subjects: Adventure; Anthropology; Archaeology; Autobiography; Business;

Commercial; Current Affairs; Lifestyle; Men's Interests; Nature; Philosophy; Psychology; Self Help; Spirituality
Markets: Adult

Send: Full text

Transform your life, transform your world. We publish for individuals committed to transforming their lives and transforming the world. Our readers seek to become positive, powerful agents of change. We inform, inspire, and provide practical wisdom and skills to empower us to write the next chapter of humanity's future.

Authors: Mark Hawthorne; P T Mistleberger; Jayne Morris; Michelle Ray; Neil Richardson; Gleb Tsipursky; Nicholas Vesey; Tim Ward

P0159 Changemakers Books
Publishing Imprint

Book Publisher: John Hunt Publishing Ltd

P0160 The Charles Press, Publishers
Book Publisher
230 North 21st Street, Suite 312, Philadelphia, PA 19103
United States
Tel: +1 (215) 470-5977

submissions@charlespresspub.com

http://www.charlespresspub.com

Types: Nonfiction
Subjects: Crime; Health; How To; Lifestyle; Medicine; Psychology; Religion; Sociology
Markets: Adult

Send: Query
Don't send: Full text

Send proposal outlining your book, your purpose and rationale behind writing it, its market, competition, ideas for marketing, and author bio. Particularly interested in instructional (how-to) books, psychology, parenting, criminology, true crime and suicide. No fiction, poetry, children's books, short stories, science fiction, romance or humour. Consult website before submitting.

P0161 Charlesbridge Publishing
Book Publisher
9 Galen Street, Watertown, MA 02472
United States
Tel: +1 (617) 926-0329
Fax: +1 (800) 926-5775

tradeeditorial@charlesbridge.com

https://www.charlesbridge.com
https://twitter.com/charlesbridge
https://www.facebook.com/CharlesbridgePublishingInc
https://www.pinterest.com/charlesbridge/
https://www.instagram.com/

charlesbridgepublishing/
https://charlesbridgebooks.tumblr.com/
https://www.youtube.com/user/Charlesbridge1

CHILDREN'S
Fiction
Board Books; *Early Readers*; *Middle Grade*; *Picture Books*
Nonfiction
Board Books: General
Early Readers: General
Middle Grade: Arts; Biography; History; Mathematics; Nature; Science; Social Issues
Picture Books: General

Send: Full text
How to send: Word file email attachment; PDF file email attachment
How not to send: In the body of an email

Publishes books for children, with teen and adult imprints.

Publishing Imprints: Charlesbridge Teen (**P0162**); Imagine Publishing (**P0438**)

P0162 Charlesbridge Teen
Publishing Imprint
9 Galen Street, Watertown, MA 02472
United States
Tel: +1 (800) 225-3214
Fax: +1 (800) 926-5775

ya.submissions@charlesbridge.com

https://charlesbridgeteen.com
https://twitter.com/CharlesbridgeYA
https://www.facebook.com/
CharlesbridgePublishingInc/
https://www.pinterest.com/charlesbridge/
https://www.instagram.com/charlesbridgeteen/
http://charlesbridgebooks.tumblr.com/

Book Publisher: Charlesbridge Publishing (**P0161**)

YOUNG ADULT
Fiction > *Novels*
Nonfiction > *Nonfiction Books*

Send: Query; Synopsis; Writing sample; Proposal; Outline
How to send: Email attachment

Features storytelling that presents new ideas and an evolving world. Our carefully curated stories give voice to unforgettable characters with unique perspectives. We publish books that inspire teens to cheer or sigh, laugh or reflect, reread or share with a friend, and ultimately, pick up another book. Our mission – to make reading irresistible!

P0163 Chatto & Windus
Publishing Imprint
United Kingdom

Book Publisher: Vintage (**P0934**)

P0164 Chicago Review Press
Book Publisher
814 North Franklin Street, Chicago, Illinois 60610
United States
Tel: +1 (312) 337-0747
Fax: +1 (312) 337-5110

frontdesk@chicagoreviewpress.com

http://www.chicagoreviewpress.com

Types: Fiction; Nonfiction
Formats: Film Scripts
Subjects: Autobiography; Crafts; Culture; Gardening; History; Lifestyle; Music; Politics; Science; Sport; Travel; Women's Interests
Markets: Adult; Children's; Young Adult

Closed to fiction proposals as at January 2018. Check website for current status. Publishes nonfiction through all imprints, and fiction through specific imprint listed above. Also publishes children's and young adult titles, but no picture books. See website for full submission guidelines.

Publishing Imprints: Academy Chicago; Lawrence Hill Books (**P0507**)

P0165 Childswork / ChildsPLAY, LLC
Book Publisher
40 Aero Road, Unit #2, Bohemia, NY 11716
United States
Tel: +1 (800) 962-1141

https://childswork.com
https://www.facebook.com/
childsworkchildsplay/
https://twitter.com/childswork
https://www.pinterest.com/childswork/
https://www.instagram.com/
childsworkchildsplay/
https://www.youtube.com/
childsworkchildsplay
https://www.linkedin.com/company/
child%27s-work

PROFESSIONAL > **Nonfiction** > *Nonfiction Books*
Child Psychotherapy; Education; Psychology

How not to send: Post

A leading provider in child therapy resources, focusing on therapeutic tools used by counselors, teachers and therapists.

P0166 Choc Lit
Book Publisher
Penrose House, Camberley, Surrey, GU15 2AB
United Kingdom
Tel: +44 (0) 1276 586367

info@choc-lit.com

https://www.choc-lit.com
https://twitter.com/choclituk
https://www.facebook.com/Choc-Lit-

30680012481/
https://www.instagram.com/choclituk/
https://www.youtube.com/channel/
UCLZBZ2qeR5gtOyDoqEjMbQw

Fiction > *Novels*
Contemporary Romance; Fantasy Romance; Historical Romance; Romance; Romantic Suspense; Timeslip Romance

Send: Query; Synopsis
How to send: Online submission system

Publishes romance suitable for an adult audience, between 60,000 and 100,000 words in length.

Author: Juliet Archer

Publishing Imprint: Ruby Fiction (**P0770**)

P0167 Christian Alternative
Publishing Imprint

Book Publisher: John Hunt Publishing Ltd

P0168 Church House Publishing
Publishing Imprint

Book Publisher: Hymns Ancient & Modern Ltd (**P0428**)

P0169 Cinnamon Press
Book Publisher
Office 49019, PO Box 92, Cardiff, CF11 1NB
United Kingdom
Tel: +44 (0) 1766 832112

jan@cinnamonpress.com

https://www.cinnamonpress.com

Fiction > *Novels*

Nonfiction > *Nonfiction Books*

Poetry > *Poetry Collections*

Closed to approaches.

Small-press publisher of full length poetry collections, unique and imaginative novels, and practical and informative nonfiction with wide appeal. Willing to consider most genres as long as writing is thought-provoking, enjoyable, and accessible; but does not publish genre fiction (romantic, erotica, horror or crime), biography, autobiography, academic, technical or how-to. No unsolicited MSS. See website for submission details.

Editor: Jan Fortune

P0170 Circle Books
Publishing Imprint

Book Publisher: John Hunt Publishing Ltd

P0171 Cisco Press
Publishing Imprint

Book Publisher: Pearson (**P0670**)

P0172 Citadel Press
Publishing Imprint

Book Publisher: Kensington Publishing Corp.
(**P0488**)

P0173 City Limits Publishing
Book Publisher
8161 Hwy 100 Suite 280, Nashville, TN 37221
United States
Tel: +1 (615) 270-2088

publish@citylimitspublishing.com

https://citylimitspublishing.com
https://www.facebook.com/
CityLimitsPublishing/
https://www.instagram.com/citylimits_pub/
https://twitter.com/citylimits_pub
https://nl.pinterest.com/citylimitspublishing/

Fiction > *Novels*
Drama; Romance; Thrillers

Nonfiction > *Nonfiction Books*
Autobiography; Literature; Photography;
Travel

How to send: Online submission system

A Tennessee-based publishing company that
helps authors find voice, develop writing and
storytelling abilities, and publish works.

P0174 Clarity Press, Inc.
Book Publisher
2625 Piedmont Road NE, Suite 56, Atlanta,
GA 30324
United States
Tel: +1 (404) 647-6501

claritypress@usa.net

http://www.claritypress.com

Types: Nonfiction
Subjects: Current Affairs; Finance; History;
Legal; Politics; Sociology; Warfare
Markets: Adult

Send: Query
Don't send: Full text

Send query letter first, with CV, table of
contents and synopsis by email. No
submissions by post. Publishes books on
human rights issues and social justice. Visit
website before querying.

Editorial Director: Diana G. Collier

P0175 Clarkson Potter
Publishing Imprint
1745 Broadway, New York, NY 10019
United States
Tel: +1 (212) 782-9000

http://crownpublishing.com/archives/imprint/
clarkson-potter

Book Publishers: Penguin Random House
(**P0683**); The Crown Publishing Group

Types: Nonfiction
Subjects: Arts; Commercial; Cookery; Design;
Lifestyle; Literary
Markets: Adult

How to send: Through a literary agent

Imprint dedicated to lifestyle, publishing books
by chefs, cooks, designers, artists, and writers.
Accepts approaches via literary agents only.

P0176 Coaches Choice
Book Publisher
PO Box 1828, Monterey, CA 93942
United States
Tel: +1 (888) 229-5745

info@coacheschoice.com

http://www.coacheschoice.com

Types: Nonfiction
Subjects: How To; Sport
Markets: Adult; Professional

Send: Query
Don't send: Full text

Publishes books for sports coaches at all levels.
Send proposal package with outline, CV, and
two sample chapters.

P0177 Colin Smythe Ltd
Book Publisher
38 Mill Lane, Gerrards Cross,
Buckinghamshire, SL9 8BA
United Kingdom
Tel: +44 (0) 1753 886000
Fax: +44 (0) 1753 886469

info@colinsmythe.co.uk

http://www.colinsmythe.co.uk

Types: Fiction; Nonfiction; Poetry; Scripts
Formats: Theatre Scripts
Subjects: Biography; Drama; Fantasy; History;
Hobbies; Literary Criticism; Science Fiction
Markets: Adult

Publishes fiction, nonfiction, drama, and
poetry. Particular interest in Irish literature. No
unsolicited MSS.

Authors: Hugh Cook; Peter Bander van Duren;
James Joyce; Terry Pratchett; Oscar Wilde

Editor: Colin Smythe

P0178 College Press Publishing
Book Publisher
2111 N. Main Street, Suite C, Joplin, MO
64801, PO Box 1132, Joplin, MO 64801
United States
Tel: +1 (800) 289-3300

collpressbooks@gmail.com

https://collegepress.com

Types: Nonfiction
Subjects: Biography; History; Religion
Markets: Adult

Send: Query
Don't send: Full text

Publishes Bible studies, topical studies
(biblically based), apologetic studies, historical
biographies of Christians, Sunday/Bible School
curriculum (adult electives). No poetry, game
or puzzle books, books on prophecy from a
premillennial or dispensational viewpoint, or
any books that do not contain a Christian
message. Send query by email or by post with
SASE. See website for required contents.

Publishing Imprint: HeartSpring Publishing
(*P0399*)

P0179 Collins
Publishing Imprint
United Kingdom

Book Publisher: HarperCollins UK (**P0382**)

P0180 Colonsay Books
Publishing Imprint

Publishing Imprint: House of Lochar (**P0424**)

P0181 Colourpoint Educational
Book Publisher
Colourpoint House, Jubilee Business Park, 21
Jubilee Road, Newtownards, Northern Ireland,
BT23 4YH
United Kingdom
Tel: +44 (0) 28 9182 0505

sales@colourpoint.co.uk

https://colourpointeducational.com
https://twitter.com/ColourpointEdu

ACADEMIC > **Nonfiction** > *Nonfiction
Books*
Biology; Business; Chemistry; Design;
Digital Technology; English; French; Gaelic;
Geography; Health; History; Home
Economics / Domestic Science; Legal;
Lifestyle; Mathematics; Physical Education;
Physics; Politics; Religion; Technology

Send: Query
How to send: Email

Provides textbooks, ebooks and digital
resources for Northern Ireland students at Key
Stage 3 level, and the CCEA revised
specification at GCSE and AS/A2/A-level.

Editor: Wesley Johnston

P0182 Compass Books
Publishing Imprint

Book Publisher: John Hunt Publishing Ltd

P0183 Concord Theatricals Ltd
Book Publisher
Aldwych House, 71 – 91 Aldwych, London,
WC2B 4HN
United Kingdom
Tel: +44 (0) 20 7054 7200

acquisitions@concordtheatricals.co.uk

https://www.concordtheatricals.co.uk

Scripts > *Theatre Scripts*
   Drama; Musicals

Send: Full text

Publishes plays only. Send submissions by email only, following the guidelines on the website.

P0184 Constable & Robinson
Publishing Imprint

Publishing Imprint: Little, Brown Book Group (**P0532**)

P0185 Cool Springs Press
Publishing Imprint

Book Publisher: The Quarto Group, Inc. (**P0739**)

P0186 Corgi
Publishing Imprint

Book Publisher: Transworld Publishers (**P0875**)

P0187 Cork University Press
Book Publisher
Ireland
Tel: +353 (0) 21 490 2980

corkuniversitypress@ucc.ie

http://www.corkuniversitypress.com

Types: Nonfiction
Formats: Film Scripts
Subjects: Architecture; Arts; Cookery; Culture; Current Affairs; Drama; History; Legal; Literature; Music; Philosophy; Politics; Self Help; Sociology; Sport; Travel; Women's Interests
Markets: Academic

Publishes distinctive and distinguished scholarship in the broad field of Irish Cultural Studies.

Publishing Imprints: Atrium (*P0059*); Attic Press (*P0060*)

P0188 Cornell University Press
Book Publisher
Sage House, 512 East State Street, Ithaca, New York 14850
United States
Tel: +1 (607) 277-2239
Fax: +1 (607) 277-2374

msk55@cornell.edu

http://www.cornellpress.cornell.edu

Types: Nonfiction
Subjects: Anthropology; Biography; History; Literary Criticism; Nature; Philosophy;

Politics; Science; Women's Interests
Markets: Academic; Adult

Send: Query
Don't send: Full text

Particularly interested in anthropology, Asian studies, biological sciences, classics, history, industrial relations, literary criticism and theory, natural history, philosophy, politics and international relations, veterinary science, and women's studies. No poetry or fiction. Send proposal with table of contents, one sample chapter, author CV or resume, information about length, intended audience, plans for illustrations, and information on any other presses currently considering your proposal.

Editor: Mahinder Kingra

P0189 Cornerstone
Book Publisher

Book Publisher: Penguin Random House UK (**P0685**)

P0190 Corsair
Publishing Imprint

Publishing Imprint: Little, Brown Book Group (**P0532**)

P0191 Cosmic Egg Books
Publishing Imprint

Book Publisher: John Hunt Publishing Ltd

P0192 Council Press
Publishing Imprint

Book Publisher: Cedar Fort (**P0155**)

P0193 Countryside Books
Book Publisher
35 Kingfisher Court, Hambridge Road, Newbury, Berkshire, RG14 5SJ
United Kingdom
Tel: +44 (0) 1635 43816
Fax: +44 (0) 1635 551004

info@countrysidebooks.co.uk

http://www.countrysidebooks.co.uk

Types: Nonfiction
Subjects: Architecture; History; Leisure; Lifestyle; Photography; Travel; Warfare
Markets: Adult

Publishes nonfiction only, mostly regional books relating to specific English counties. Covers topics such as local history, walks, photography, dialect, genealogy, military and aviation, and some transport; but not interested in natural history books or personal memories. No fiction or poetry.

P0194 Crabtree Publishing
Book Publisher
347 Fifth Ave, Suite 1402-145, New York, NY 10016

United States
Tel: +1 (212) 496-5040
Fax: +1 (800) 355-7166

http://www.crabtreebooks.com

Types: Nonfiction
Subjects: History; Science; Sociology
Markets: Academic; Children's

Closed to approaches.

Publishes educational books for children. No unsolicited mss -- all material is generated in-house.

P0195 Craftsman Book Co.
Book Publisher
6058 Corte Del Cedro, Carlsbad, CA 92011
United States
Tel: +1 (800) 829-8123

http://craftsman-book.com

Types: Nonfiction
Subjects: Crafts; How To
Markets: Professional

Publishes books, software, manuals, videos, and other materials for professional builders. See website for submission details.

Editor: Laurence Jacobs

P0196 Creative Essentials
Publishing Imprint
United Kingdom

Book Publisher: Oldcastle Books Group (**P0635**)

P0197 Cressrelles Publishing Co. Ltd
Book Publisher
10 Station Road Industrial Estate, Colwall, Malvern, WR13 6RN
United Kingdom
Tel: +44 (0) 1684 540154
Fax: +44 (0) 1684 540154

simon@cressrelles.co.uk

http://www.cressrelles.co.uk

Types: Nonfiction; Scripts
Subjects: Drama
Markets: Academic; Adult

Send: Full text

Welcomes submissions. Publishes plays, theatre and drama textbooks, and local interest books. Accepts scripts by post or by email.

Book Publisher: New Playwrights' Network (NPN) (**P0617**)

Editor: Simon Smith

Publishing Imprints: Anchorage Press, Inc. (*P0037*); J. Garnet Miller (*P0460*); Kenyon-Deane (*P0491*); New Playwrights' Network (*P0616*)

P0198 Crime & Mystery Club
Publishing Imprint
United Kingdom

Book Publisher: Oldcastle Books Group
(**P0635**)

P0199 Crime Express
Publishing Imprint

Book Publisher: Five Leaves Publications
(**P0289**)

P0200 Croner-i Limited
Book Publisher
240 Blackfriars Road, London, SE1 8NW
United Kingdom
Tel: +44 (0) 800 231 5199

sales@croneri.co.uk

https://www.croneri.co.uk

Types: Nonfiction
Subjects: Business
Markets: Professional

Publishes books and resources for business professionals covering tax and acounting, human resources, health and safety, and compliance.

P0201 Crosley-Griffith
Publishing Imprint
United States

Book Publisher: C&T Publishing (**P0138**)

P0202 Crossway
Publishing Imprint
1300 Crescent Street, Wheaton, IL 60187
United States
Tel: +1 (630) 682-4300
Fax: +1 (630) 682-4785

info@crossway.org

http://www.crossway.org

Types: Nonfiction
Subjects: Religion
Markets: Adult

Send: Query
Don't send: Full text

Publishes books written from an evangelical Christian perspective. Send query by email in the first instance.

P0203 Crowerotica Fantasies
Publishing Imprint

Publishing Imprint: Emerentsia Publications
(**P0258**)

P0204 Crux Publishing
Book Publisher
United Kingdom

hello@cruxpublishing.co.uk

http://cruxpublishing.co.uk

Types: Fiction; Nonfiction
Markets: Adult

Send: Query
Don't send: Full text

Founded to help authors publish (or republish) nonfiction works of the highest quality. Will also consider fiction if truly unique. Pursues a digital-first approach. See website for submission guidelines and more information.

P0205 Currock Press
Book Publisher
United Kingdom

john.i.clarke@btinternet.com

https://www.currockpress.com

Poetry > *Poetry Collections*

Closed to approaches.

No current plans for any further publications.

Editor: John Clarke

P0206 Custom House
Publishing Imprint

Book Publisher: HarperCollins (**P0378**)

P0207 Da Capo Press
Publishing Imprint
Market Place Center, 53, State Street, Boston, MA 02109
United States

DaCapo.Info@hbgusa.com

https://www.dacapopress.com

Book Publisher: Perseus Books (**P0693**)

Types: Nonfiction
Subjects: Arts; Culture; History; Music; Sport
Markets: Adult

Closed to approaches.

Originally a music publisher in the sixties, diversified into general trade publishing in the seventies. Specialises in history, music, the performing arts, sports, and popular culture. No unsolicited mss or book proposals.

P0208 Dafina
Publishing Imprint

Book Publisher: Kensington Publishing Corp.
(**P0488**)

P0209 Dalesman Publishing Co. Ltd
Book Publisher; Magazine Publisher
The Gatehouse, Skipton Castle, Skipton, North Yorkshire, BD23 1AL
United Kingdom
Tel: +44 (0) 1756 693479

jon@dalesman.co.uk

https://www.dalesman.co.uk

Types: Nonfiction
Subjects: Comedy / Humour; Crafts; History; Hobbies; Travel

Publishes regional books covering Yorkshire, and the Lake and Peak districts. Considers unsolicited MSS on relevant topics.

Editor: Jon Stokoe

Magazine: Dalesman (**M0168**)

P0210 Dalkey Archive Press
Book Publisher
6271 E 535 North Road, McLean, IL 61754
United States

subeditor@dalkeyarchive.com

http://www.dalkeyarchive.com

Types: Fiction; Nonfiction; Poetry; Scripts
Subjects: Autobiography; Experimental; Literary; Literary Criticism
Markets: Adult

Publishes primarily literary fiction, with an emphasis on fiction that belongs to the experimental tradition of Sterne, Joyce, Rabelais, Flann O'Brien, Beckett, Gertrude Stein, and Djuna Barnes. Occasionally publishes poetry or nonfiction. Send submissions by email. See website for full guidelines.

P0211 Damaged Goods Press
Book Publisher
United States

editor@damagedgoodspress.com

http://www.damagedgoodspress.com

Types: Nonfiction; Poetry
Subjects: Autobiography
Markets: Adult

Small press specialising in books by queer and trans people. Publishes chapbooks and full-length manuscripts of poetry, micro-memoir, lyric essay, prose poetry, and hybrid nonfiction. Content does not need to be queer or trans related.

P0212 Dancing Girl Press
Book Publisher
United States

dancinggirlpress@yahoo.com

http://www.dancinggirlpress.com

Types: Poetry
Subjects: Literary; Women's Interests
Markets: Adult

Closed to approaches.

Publishes chapbooks by female poets between 12 and 32 pages. No payment, but free 10 copies and 40% discount on further copies.

P0213 Dancing Star Press

Book Publisher
United States

submissions@dancingstarpress.com

https://www.dancingstarpress.com

Types: Fiction
Subjects: Fantasy; Science Fiction
Markets: Adult

Send: Full text

Publishes speculative fiction novellas between 17,500 and 40,000 words in length. Accepts manuscripts by email between April 1 and June 30, and between October 1 and December 31.

P0214 Darby Creek

Publishing Imprint

Book Publisher: Lerner Publishing Group (**P0514**)

P0215 Darf Publishers

Book Publisher
277 West End Lane, London, NW6 1QS
United Kingdom
Tel: +44 (0) 20 7431 7009
Fax: +44 (0) 20 7431 7655

submissions@darfpublishers.co.uk

https://darfpublishers.co.uk

Types: Fiction; Nonfiction; Translations
Markets: Adult; Children's

Publisher of new and emerging writers from around the world, translated into English. Accepts submissions in any genre. Send query by email with synopsis, three sample chapters, and a brief outline of your background and what qualifies you to write your book.

P0216 Darton, Longman & Todd Ltd

Book Publisher
1 Spencer Court, 140-142 Wandsworth High Street, London, SW18 4JJ
United Kingdom

editorial@darton-longman-todd.co.uk

http://www.darton-longman-todd.co.uk

Types: Fiction; Nonfiction
Formats: Film Scripts; TV Scripts
Subjects: Arts; Autobiography; Comedy / Humour; Cookery; Literature; Religion; Self Help; Sport; Women's Interests
Markets: Adult; Young Adult

Send: Full text

Publishes spritual and theological books – mainly Christian. Send query by email with proposal and sample chapter. See website for full guidelines.

P0217 DAW

Publishing Imprint

Book Publisher: Penguin Publishing Group (**P0682**)

P0218 Dawn Publications

Publishing Imprint
United States

https://dawnpub.com

Book Publisher: Sourcebooks, Inc.

CHILDREN'S > **Nonfiction** > *Nonfiction Books*: Nature

Publishes creative nonfiction manuscripts for children that relate to nature and science.

P0219 dbS Productions

Book Publisher
PO Box 94, Charlottesville, VA 22902-0094
United States
Tel: +1 (800) 745-1581
Fax: +1 (434) 293-5502

info@dbs-sar.com

http://www.dbs-sar.com

PROFESSIONAL > **Nonfiction** > *Nonfiction Books*: Search and Rescue

Describes itself as the leader in research and education in behavioral profiles of lost subjects. Always looking for new and interesting publications related to the field of search and rescue. Authors are encouraged to make contact early in the development of their projects.

Editor: Bob Adams

P0220 DC Thomson

Book Publisher
2 Albert Square, Dundee, DD1 9QJ
United Kingdom

innovation@dcthomson.co.uk

http://www.dcthomson.co.uk

Types: Fiction; Nonfiction
Markets: Adult; Children's

Publisher of newspapers, magazines, comics, and books, with offices in Dundee, Aberdeen, Glasgow, and London. For fiction guidelines send large SAE marked for the attention of the Central Fiction Department.

P0221 De Montfort Literature

Book Publisher
20-22 Wenlock Road, London, N1 7GU
United Kingdom
Tel: +44 (0) 20 7205 2881

info@demontfortliterature.com

https://www.demontfortliterature.com

Types: Fiction
Markets: Adult; Children's; Young Adult

Publisher founded by a hedge fund that successfully used data to predict (amongst other things) the bottom of the market in 2002, the 2008 crash, and Brexit. Now seeks to apply the same scientific approach to a new model of publishing based on predicting an author's chances of success. Where they find likely candidates, they will invest in the author by paying them an annual salary to become a full-time novelist. Applicants do not need to have already written a novel. The application process includes a psychometric test, an opportunity to discuss ideas, and a final interview. See website for full details.

P0222 Del Rey

Publishing Imprint
United Kingdom

Book Publisher: Ebury (**P0243**)

P0223 Delancey Press Ltd

Book Publisher
United Kingdom

delanceypress@aol.com

http://www.delanceypress.co.uk

Types: Fiction
Markets: Adult; Children's

Publishes fiction for adults and children, including humour.

P0224 DeVorss & Company

Book Publisher
PO Box 1389, Camarillo, CA 93011-1389
United States

editorial@devorss.com

https://www.devorss.com

Nonfiction > *Nonfiction Books*
Alternative Health; Inspirational; Lifestyle; Mind, Body, Spirit; Religion; Self Help; Spirituality

Send: Query; Outline; Table of Contents; Market info; Author bio; Self-Addressed Stamped Envelope (SASE)
How to send: Email; Post

A book publisher and distributor of Metaphysical, Inspirational, Spiritual, Self-Help, and New Thought titles.

P0225 Dey Street Books

Publishing Imprint

Book Publisher: HarperCollins (**P0378**)

P0226 Dial Books for Young Readers

Publishing Imprint
United States

Book Publisher: Penguin Young Readers Group (**P0688**)

CHILDREN'S
  Fiction
    Chapter Books; *Early Readers*; *Middle Grade*; *Picture Books*

Nonfiction
Chapter Books; Early Readers; Middle Grade; Picture Books
YOUNG ADULT
Fiction > Novels
Nonfiction > Nonfiction Books

Closed to approaches.

Publishes books for children, from beginner readers and picture books, to fiction and nonfiction for middle-grade and young adults. No unsolicited MSS.

Publishing Imprint: Dial Easy-to-Read

P0227 Dialogue Books
Publishing Imprint

Publishing Imprint: Little, Brown Book Group **(P0532)**

P0228 Discovery Walking Guides Ltd
Book Publisher
United Kingdom

ask.discovery@ntlworld.com

http://www.dwgwalking.co.uk

Types: Nonfiction
Subjects: Travel
Markets: Adult

Send: Query
Don't send: Full text

Publishes walking guidebooks and maps. Welcomes proposals for new projects. Send query by email. No attachments.

P0229 DK Publishing
Book Publisher
1450 Broadway, Suite 801, New York, NY 10018
United States

ecustomerservice@randomhouse.com

http://www.dk.com

Types: Nonfiction
Subjects: Culture; History; Nature; Science; Travel
Markets: Children's

How to send: Through a literary agent

Publishes highly visual nonfiction for children. Assumes no responsibility for unsolicited mss. Approach through an established literary agent.

P0230 Dodo Ink
Book Publisher
United Kingdom

dodopublishingco@gmail.com

http://www.dodoink.com

Types: Fiction
Subjects: Literary
Markets: Adult

Closed to approaches.

Independent UK publisher aiming to publish three novels per year, in paperback and digital formats. Publishes risk-taking, imaginative novels, that don't fall into easy marketing categories. Closed to submissions as at June 2017.

Editor: Sam Mills

P0231 Dodona
Publishing Imprint

Publishing Imprint: O-Books

P0232 Dodona Books
Publishing Imprint

Book Publisher: John Hunt Publishing Ltd

P0233 Dollarbooks PTY LTD
Book Publisher
20 Langerman Avenue, Milnerton, 7441
South Africa

info@thedollarbooks.com

https://thedollarbooks.com

Types: Fiction; Nonfiction; Poetry; Scripts; Translations
Formats: Film Scripts; Radio Scripts; Reference; Short Fiction; TV Scripts; Theatre Scripts
Subjects: Adventure; Anthropology; Antiques; Archaeology; Architecture; Arts; Autobiography; Beauty; Business; Comedy / Humour; Commercial; Contemporary; Cookery; Crafts; Crime; Culture; Current Affairs; Design; Drama; Entertainment; Erotic; Experimental; Fantasy; Fashion; Finance; Gardening; Gothic; Health; History; How To; Legal; Leisure; Lifestyle; Literary; Literary Criticism; Media; Medicine; Men's Interests; Music; Mystery; Nature; New Age; Philosophy; Photography; Politics; Psychology; Religion; Romance; Satire; Science; Science Fiction; Self Help; Sociology; Sport; Suspense; Technology; Thrillers; Traditional; Travel; Warfare; Westerns; Women's Interests
Markets: Academic; Adult; Children's; Professional; Young Adult

Send: Full text

Revolutionising the publishing industry and this is how it works. You, as an author, simply upload your book content, your cover and your biography, and we sell your work to the world for one US Dollar. We take 30% and you take 70% in royalties. Nobody can sell for less or more than you. You may think that a dollar for a book is very cheap, and you are perfectly correct. This is all about giving and receiving. Would you not rather sell 10 000 copies of your book for 1$ each instead of only a 100 or so copies at $6?

Authors: Craig Anthony Ferreira; Bandana Ojha; Scott Skipper

Editor: Craig Ferreira

P0234 Doubleday
Publishing Imprint
United States

Book Publisher: Knopf Doubleday Publishing Group **(P0498)**

P0235 Dovecote Press
Book Publisher
Stanbridge, Wimborne Minster, Dorset, BH21 4JD
United Kingdom
Tel: +44 (0) 1258 840549

online@dovecotepress.com

http://www.dovecotepress.com

Types: Nonfiction
Subjects: Architecture; Biography; History; Nature
Markets: Adult

Publishes books on architecture, local history, and natural history.

Editor: David Burnett

P0236 Down East Books
Publishing Imprint
United States

Book Publisher: The Globe Pequot Press **(P0324)**

P0237 Duncan Petersen Publishing Limited
Book Publisher
Studio 6 82, Silverthorne Road, London, SW8 3HE
United Kingdom
Tel: +44 (0) 20 0147 8220

duncan.petersen@zen.co.uk

http://duncanpetersen.blogspot.com/

Types: Nonfiction
Subjects: Antiques; Travel

Travel publishing house based in London. Publishes Hotel Guides, along with a variety of walking and cycling guides for Britain.

P0238 Dutton
Publishing Imprint
United States

Book Publisher: Penguin Publishing Group **(P0682)**

P0239 Dutton Children's Books
Publishing Imprint
United States

Book Publisher: Penguin Young Readers Group (**P0688**)

P0240 Dynasty Press
Book Publisher
36 Ravensdon Street, Kennington, London, SE11 4AR
United Kingdom
Tel: +44 (0) 7970 066894

admin@dynastypress.co.uk

http://www.dynastypress.co.uk

Types: Nonfiction
Subjects: Biography; History
Markets: Adult

Publishes books connected to royalty, dynasties and people of influence.

P0241 Earth Books
Publishing Imprint

Book Publisher: John Hunt Publishing Ltd

P0242 Eastland Press
Book Publisher
PO Box 99749, Seattle, WA 98139
United States
Tel: +1 (206) 931-6957
Fax: +1 (206) 283-7084

info@eastlandpress.com

http://www.eastlandpress.com

Types: Nonfiction
Subjects: Health; Medicine
Markets: Professional

Send: Query
Don't send: Full text

Publishes textbooks for practitioners of Chinese medicine, osteopathy, and other forms of bodywork.

P0243 Ebury
Book Publisher
United Kingdom

Book Publisher: Penguin Random House UK (**P0685**)

Publishing Imprints: BBC Books (**P0085**); Del Rey (*P0222*); Ebury Enterprises (*P0244*); Ebury Press (*P0245*); Pop Press (*P0713*); Rider Books (*P0758*); Vermilion (*P0928*); Virgin Books (*P0939*); WH Allen (*P0965*)

P0244 Ebury Enterprises
Publishing Imprint
United Kingdom

Book Publisher: Ebury (**P0243**)

P0245 Ebury Press
Publishing Imprint
United Kingdom

Book Publisher: Ebury (**P0243**)

P0246 Ecco
Publishing Imprint

Book Publisher: HarperCollins (**P0378**)

P0247 Economist Books.
Publishing Imprint

Publishing Imprint: Profile Books (**P0721**)

P0248 EDGE Science Fiction and Fantasy Publishing
Publishing Imprint
Acquisitions Editor, EDGE Science Fiction and Fantasy Publishing, P.O. Box 1714, Calgary, AB, T2P 2L7
Canada
Tel: +1 (403) 254-0160
Fax: +1 (403) 254-0456

michelle@hadespublications.com

http://www.edgewebsite.com

Book Publisher: Hades Publications, Inc. (**P0351**)

Types: Fiction
Subjects: Fantasy; Science Fiction
Markets: Adult

Send: Query
Don't send: Full text

Currently seeking science fiction and fantasy submissions between 75,000 and 100,000 words. Occasional young adult. No horror, erotica, religious fiction, short stories, dark/gruesome fantasy, or poetry. See website for full submission guidelines.

P0249 Ediciones Lerner
Publishing Imprint

Book Publisher: Lerner Publishing Group (**P0514**)

P0250 The Educational Company of Ireland
Book Publisher
Ballymount Road, Walkinstown, Dublin 12
Ireland

amolumby@edco.ie

http://www.edco.ie

Types: Nonfiction
Markets: Academic; Adult; Children's; Professional

Send: Query
Don't send: Full text

Publishes textbooks and ancillary educational materials for the Primary and Post-Primary markets. Submit proposals by post or by email. See website for full guidelines.

Editor: Aoibheann Molumby

P0251 Educator's International Press
Book Publisher
756 Linderman Avenue, Kingston, NY 12401
United States
Tel: +1 (518) 334-0276
Fax: +1 (703) 661-1547

info@edint.com
submissions@edint.com

https://edint.presswarehouse.com

ACADEMIC > **Nonfiction** > *Nonfiction Books*

Send: Query; Synopsis; Author bio; Outline
How to send: Email

Main mission was initially to keep scholarly and educations content in print and to assist established educational authors in keeping their published books in print at a time when many publishers typically put out of print those books that had annual sales totalling less than 500 copies.

Publisher: William Clockel

P0252 Educe Press
Book Publisher
Butte, MT
United States

editor@educepress.com

https://educepress.com

Types: Fiction; Nonfiction; Poetry
Formats: Short Fiction
Subjects: Literary
Markets: Adult

Closed to approaches.

Publishes literary fiction, nonfiction, and poetry. Closed to submissions as at April 2019. Check website for current status.

Editors: Colin Cote; Carrie Seymour

Publisher: Matthew R. K. Haynes

P0253 Egmont Books
Publishing Imprint
United Kingdom

Book Publisher: HarperCollins UK (**P0382**)

P0254 Ekstasis Editions
Book Publisher
United States

ekstasis@islandnet.com

http://www.ekstasiseditions.com

Types: Fiction; Nonfiction; Poetry
Formats: Short Fiction
Subjects: Literary; Spirituality
Markets: Adult; Children's

Send: Query
Don't send: Full text

Usually accepts submissions from Canadian authors only. Send query by post with SAE with sufficient Canadian postage for return, with author bio, synopsis, and first three chapters up to a maximum of 50 pages.

P0255 Electio Publishing
Book Publisher
United States

info@electiopublishing.com

http://www.electiopublishing.com

Types: Fiction
Subjects: Adventure; Autobiography; Fantasy; History; Horror; Literary; Mystery; Religion; Romance; Science Fiction
Markets: Academic; Adult

Closed to approaches.

First and foremost a faith-based publisher, but will consider anything that is marketable to a wide audience, whether it is fiction or nonfiction.

P0256 Elektra Press
Book Publisher
United States

http://elektrapress.com

Types: Fiction; Nonfiction
Markets: Adult; Young Adult

Send: Query
Don't send: Full text

Describes itself as a conventional independent publishing house that thinks unconventionally. Willing to consider most genres of fiction and nonfiction, other than hate books and gratuitous pornography. Approach using submission form on website.

Editor: Don Bacue

P0257 Elsevier Ltd
Book Publisher
The Boulevard, Langford Lane, Kidlington, Oxford, OX5 1GB
United Kingdom
Tel: +44 (0) 1865 843000
Fax: +44 (0) 1865 843010

https://www.elsevier.com

Types: Nonfiction
Formats: Reference
Subjects: Health; Medicine; Science; Technology
Markets: Academic; Professional

Send: Query
Don't send: Full text

Publisher of medical, scientific, and technical books for the professional and academic markets.

Book Publishers: Morgan Kaufmann Publishers; Reed Business Information (RBI)

P0258 Emerentsia Publications
Publishing Imprint
Sweden

emerentsia.publications@gmail.com

http://www.emerentsiabooks.com

Publishing Imprint: Emerentsia Publications (**P0258**)

Types: Fiction; Nonfiction
Formats: Short Fiction
Subjects: Erotic; Fantasy; Mystery; Romance; Science Fiction; Self Help
Markets: Adult

Send: Full text

We write and publish primarily epic fantasy, science fiction, mystery fiction, urban fantasy and fairy retellings, but we're working on expanding our publications as we become more established.

Authors: Liz Crowe; N. Lee; Nathalie M.L. Romer

Publishing Imprints: Crowerotica Fantasies (*P0203*); Emerentsia Publications (**P0258**); Oh! With Dots (*P0631*)

P0259 Encounter Books
Book Publisher
900 Broadway, Suite 601, New York, NY 10003
United States
Tel: +1 (855) 203-7220

https://www.encounterbooks.com

Types: Nonfiction
Subjects: Autobiography; Culture; Current Affairs; History; Philosophy; Politics; Psychology; Religion; Science; Sociology
Markets: Adult

Publisher dedicated to advancing its love of liberty and the cultural achievements of the West.

Editor: Roger Kimball

P0260 Entangled digiTeen
Publishing Imprint

Publishing Imprint: Entangled Teen (**P0261**)

P0261 Entangled Teen
Publishing Imprint
United States

http://www.entangledteen.com

Book Publisher: Entangled Publishing, LLC

Types: Fiction
Subjects: Contemporary; Fantasy; History; Romance; Science Fiction; Thrillers
Markets: Young Adult

Send: Full text

Publishes young adult romances between 50,000 and 100,000 words, aimed at ages 16-19. Submit via website using online submission system.

Publishing Imprint: Entangled digiTeen (*P0260*)

P0262 Enthusiast Books
Book Publisher
PO Box 352, Pepin, WI 54759
United States
Tel: +1 (715) 381-9755

info@iconobooks.com

http://www.enthusiastbooks.com

Types: Nonfiction
Subjects: History; Hobbies; Travel; Warfare
Markets: Adult

Send: Query
Don't send: Full text

Publishes books for transportation enthusiasts. Send query with SASE and outline.

P0263 Entrepreneur Press
Book Publisher
United States

books@entrepreneur.com

https://www.entrepreneur.com/press

PROFESSIONAL > **Nonfiction** > *Nonfiction Books*
    Business; Entrepreneurship; Finance

Send: Outline; Table of Contents; Writing sample; Market info; Author bio
How to send: Online submission system

An independent publishing company that publishes titles focusing on starting and growing a business, personal finance, real estate and careers. Submit proposals online via online submission system.

Publisher: Justin Koenigsberger

P0264 Epic Ink
Publishing Imprint

Book Publisher: The Quarto Group, Inc. (**P0739**)

P0265 Essex Publications
Publishing Imprint
United Kingdom

http://www.uhpress.co.uk/subject-areas/essex-publications

Book Publisher: University of Hertfordshire Press (**P0906**)

ACADEMIC > **Nonfiction** > *Nonfiction Books*: Local History

This series aims to publish important scholarly studies on the historic county of Essex in attractive and well-illustrated volumes.

P0266 Everyman's Library
Publishing Imprint
United States

Book Publisher: Knopf Doubleday Publishing Group (**P0498**)

P0267 Everything With Words
Book Publisher
United Kingdom

info@everythingwithwords.com

http://www.everythingwithwords.com

ADULT > **Fiction**
Novels: Literary
Short Fiction: General

CHILDREN'S > **Fiction** > *Novels*

How to send: Email

Publishes fiction for adults and children, including short story anthologies. No picture books or stories in rhyme for young children. Looks for good stories rather than didactic tales. No crime or fantasy.

P0268 Exley Publications
Book Publisher
16 Chalk Hill, Watford, WD19 4BG
United Kingdom
Tel: +44 (0) 1923 474480

https://www.helenexley.com

Types: Nonfiction
Markets: Adult

Publishes gift books.

P0269 F. Warne & Co.
Publishing Imprint
United States

Book Publisher: Penguin Young Readers Group (**P0688**)

P0270 Faculty of 1000 Ltd
Book Publisher
Middlesex House, 34-42 Cleveland Street, London W1T 4LB
United Kingdom

info@f1000.com

https://f1000.com

Types: Nonfiction
Subjects: Science
Markets: Academic

Aims to transform the way science is communicated, by providing innovative solutions to rethink how research is shared, used and reused.

P0271 Fahrenheit Press
Book Publisher
United States

submissions@fahrenheit-press.com

http://www.fahrenheit-press.com

Types: Fiction
Subjects: Commercial; Crime; Thrillers
Markets: Adult

Publishes crime and thriller print and ebooks. Send submissions by email.

P0272 Fair Winds Press
Publishing Imprint

Book Publisher: The Quarto Group, Inc. (**P0739**)

P0273 Falstaff Books
Book Publisher
United States

info@falstaffbooks.com

http://falstaffbooks.com

Types: Fiction
Subjects: Fantasy; Horror; Romance; Science Fiction
Markets: Adult

Closed to approaches.

Publishes novels and novellas in the following genres: Fantasy, Urban Fantasy, Science Fiction, Horror, Romance, Weird West, and misfit toys.

P0274 Familius
Book Publisher
1254 Commerce Way, Sanger, CA 93657
United States
Tel: +1 (559) 876-2170
Fax: +1 (559) 876-2180

bookideas@familius.com

https://www.familius.com

Types: Nonfiction
Subjects: Autobiography; Comedy / Humour; Cookery; Finance; Health; Hobbies; Lifestyle; Medicine; Self Help
Markets: Adult; Children's; Young Adult

Send: Query
Don't send: Full text

Publishes nonfiction for adults, young adults, and children, focused on family as the fundamental unit of society. Submit by email or if necessary by post.

P0275 Family Tree Books
Publishing Imprint
United States

Book Publisher: Penguin Publishing Group (**P0682**)

P0276 Fand Music Press
Book Publisher
Glenelg , 10 Avon Close , Petersfield , Hampshire , GU31 4LG
United Kingdom
Tel: +44 (0) 1730 267341

contact@fandmusic.com

https://fandmusic.com

Fiction > *Short Fiction*: Music

Nonfiction > *Nonfiction Books*: Music

Poetry > *Any Poetic Form*: Music

Publisher of sheet music, now also publishing books about music, CD recordings, and poetry and short stories.

Managing Editor: Peter Thompson

P0277 Farcountry Press
Book Publisher
Acquisitions, Farcountry Press, PO Box 5630, Helena, MT 59604
United States
Tel: +1 (800) 821-3874

editor@farcountrypress.com

http://www.farcountrypress.com

Types: Nonfiction
Subjects: Cookery; History; Nature; Photography
Markets: Adult; Children's

Send: Query
Don't send: Full text

Publishes photography, nature, and history books for adults and children, as well as guidebooks and cookery titles. No fiction or poetry. Send query with SASE, sample chapters, and sample table of contents. See website for full submission guidelines.

P0278 Farrar, Straus & Giroux, Inc.
Book Publisher
120 Broadway, New York, NY 10271
United States
Tel: +1 (212) 741-6900

sales@fsgbooks.com

https://us.macmillan.com/fsg

Types: Fiction; Nonfiction; Poetry
Markets: Adult; Children's; Young Adult

Closed to approaches.

Not accepting submissions.

Publishing Imprint: Hill and Wang

P0279 Farrar, Straus and Giroux Books for Younger Readers
Book Publisher
175 Fifth Avenue, New York, NY 10010
United States

childrens.editorial@fsgbooks.com

http://us.macmillan.com/publishers/farrar-straus-giroux#FYR

Types: Fiction; Nonfiction
Markets: Children's; Young Adult

Closed to approaches.

Publishes fiction, nonfiction, and picture books for children and teenagers. No unsolicited mss.

P0280 Favorite World Press

Book Publisher
United States

info@favoriteworldpress.com

https://www.favoriteworldpress.com

ADULT
Fiction > *Novels*
Animals; Environment; Nature; Sustainable Living

Nonfiction > *Nonfiction Books*
Animals; Environment; Nature; Sustainable Living

Poetry > *Any Poetic Form*
Animals; Environment; Nature; Sustainable Living

CHILDREN'S
Fiction
Middle Grade: Nature
Picture Books: Nature

Nonfiction > *Nonfiction Books*: Nature

YOUNG ADULT
Fiction > *Novels*
Animals; Environment; Nature; Sustainable Living

Nonfiction > *Nonfiction Books*
Animals; Environment; Nature; Sustainable Living

Send: Query; Author bio; Synopsis; Writing sample
How to send: Online contact form

An independent publisher based in New York City. We believe that one of the best ways to help change the world is to start small. Our primary mission is to educate, entertain, and inspire young readers with books that focus on nature, wildlife, green living, and compassionate action. Our titles are specifically chosen to encourage creativity, critical thinking, and the confidence to show caring. By fostering an appreciation for the wild and the wondrous and an understanding of the importance of being kind towards both people and the planet, we aim to help shape the next generation of brave, big-hearted, planetary stewards. We help shape them – they help shape the world!

We also focus on young adult and adult fiction and nonfiction books for a general audience that illuminate and celebrate the splendor of nature, demystify the functioning of the environment, and promote biodiversity conservation and sustainable living.

We globally distribute high-quality hardcover, paperback, and electronic books through all major outlets, including Amazon, Barnes & Noble, WHSmith, and Booktopia.

For a complete list of genres and submission guidelines please see our website.

P0281 Fernwood Publishing

Book Publisher
32 Oceanvista Lane, Site 2A, Box 5, Black Point, NS B0J 1B0
Canada
Tel: +1 (902) 857-1388
Fax: +1 (902) 857-1328

editorial@fernpub.ca

http://www.fernwoodbooks.ca

Types: Nonfiction; Translations
Formats: Reference
Subjects: Anthropology; Archaeology; Business; Culture; Current Affairs; Finance; Health; History; Literary Criticism; Medicine; Nature; Philosophy; Politics; Sociology; Sport; Women's Interests
Markets: Academic; Adult

Send: Query
Don't send: Full text

Social justice publisher. Publishes both for a general and academic audience, including reference books, for use in college and university courses. Concentrates on social sciences, humanities, gender studies, literary criticism, politics, and cultural studies. Send 5-8 page proposal including tentative table of contents; the theoretical framework of the book, and how it relates to the subject matter; market analysis; level (college / university); and estimated length and completion date. See website for full details.

Editor: Wayne Antony

Publisher: Errol Sharpe

P0282 Fidra Books

Book Publisher
United Kingdom

info@fidrabooks.co.uk

http://www.fidrabooks.co.uk

Types: Fiction
Markets: Children's

Ssmall independent publisher specialising in reprinting children's books that have been unfairly neglected and deserve to be back in print. Books range from 1930s adventure stories to iconic 1960s fantasy novels and from pony books by Carnegie medal winning authors to contemporary boarding school stories.

Editors: Malcolm Robertson; Vanessa Robertson

P0283 Fircone Books Ltd

Publishing Imprint
The Holme, Church Road, Eardisley, Herefordshire, HR3 6NJ

United Kingdom
Tel: +44 (0) 1544 327182

info@logastonpress.co.uk

https://logastonpress.co.uk/product-category/firconebooks/

Book Publisher: Logaston Press

Nonfiction > *Nonfiction Books*
Church Architecture; Church Art

Publishes books on church art and architecture, and children's illustrated books.

P0284 Firebird

Publishing Imprint
United States

Book Publisher: Penguin Young Readers Group (**P0688**)

P0285 Firefly

Book Publisher
D.20, Cardiff Metropolitan University, Cyncoed Road, Cyncoed, Cardiff, CF23 6XD
United Kingdom

submissions@fireflypress.co.uk
hello@fireflypress.co.uk

https://fireflypress.co.uk
https://www.facebook.com/FireflyPress/
https://twitter.com/FireflyPress
https://www.instagram.com/fireflypress/
https://www.youtube.com/channel/UCqzaLmXCoGJEQuaooZcnb4Q

CHILDREN'S > **Fiction**
Early Readers; *Middle Grade*
TEEN > **Fiction** > *Novels*

YOUNG ADULT > **Fiction** > *Novels*

How to send: Through a literary agent

Publishes fiction and nonfiction for children and young adults aged 5-19. Not currently accepting nonfiction submissions. Fiction submissions through agents only. Not currently publishing any picture books or colour illustrated book for any age group.

Editor: Janet Thomas

P0286 Fiscal Publications

Book Publisher
Unit 100, The Guildhall, Edgbaston Park Road, Birmingham, B15 2TU
United Kingdom
Tel: +44 (0) 800 678 5934

info@fiscalpublications.com

https://www.fiscalpublications.com

ACADEMIC > **Nonfiction** > *Nonfiction Books*
Economics; Finance; Taxation

PROFESSIONAL > **Nonfiction** > *Nonfiction Books*
Economics; Finance; Taxation

Send: Query
How to send: Email

Publishes academic and professional books specialising in taxation, public finance and public economics. Materials are relevant worldwide to policy-makers, administrators, lecturers and students of the economics, politics, law and practice of taxation.

Editor: Andy Lymer

P0287 Fisherton Press

Book Publisher
United Kingdom

general@fishertonpress.co.uk

http://fishertonpress.co.uk

Types: Fiction
Markets: Children's

Closed to approaches.

Closed to submissions as at April 2018. Check website for current status. Aims to publish books for children that adults will also enjoy reading, whether for the first time or the hundredth. Send query with ideas or fully written or illustrated texts with short bio, by email.

Editor: Eleanor Levenson

P0288 Five Leaves Bookshop

Publishing Imprint

Book Publisher: Five Leaves Publications (**P0289**)

P0289 Five Leaves Publications

Book Publisher
14a Long Row, Nottingham, NG1 2DH
United Kingdom
Tel: +44 (0) 1158 373097

info@fiveleaves.co.uk

https://fiveleaves.co.uk/

Types: Fiction; Nonfiction; Poetry; Scripts
Formats: Short Fiction
Subjects: Arts; Biography; Crime; History; Literature; Politics; Religion; Sociology
Markets: Adult; Young Adult

Closed to approaches.

Small publisher with interests including social history, Jewish culture, politics, poetry, and fiction. Publishes both commercial and non-commercial work. No unsolicited mss.

Editor: Ross Bradshaw

Publishing Imprints: Bromley House Editions (*P0131*); Crime Express (*P0199*); Five Leaves Bookshop (*P0288*); More Shoots More Leaves (*P0592*); New London Editions (*P0614*); Richard Hollis (*P0757*)

P0290 Flame Tree Publishing

Book Publisher
6 Melbray Mews, London, SW6 3NS
United Kingdom
Tel: +44 (0) 20 7751 9650
Fax: +44 (0) 20 7751 9651

info@flametreepublishing.com

http://www.flametreepublishing.com

Types: Nonfiction
Subjects: Cookery; Culture; Lifestyle; Music
Markets: Adult

Publihses practical cookbooks, music, popular culture and lifestyle books. Very rarely accepts unsolicited mss or book proposals.

P0291 Flashlight Press

Book Publisher
527 Empire Blvd., Brooklyn, NY 11225
United States
Tel: +1 (718) 288-8300

submissions@flashlightpress.com

http://www.flashlightpress.com

Types: Fiction
Markets: Children's

Send: Full text

Publishes picture books for children aged 4-8, with universal themes dealing with family/social situations, of around 1,000 words. Send queries by email including completed form from submissions page of website, and attach your manuscript. Response within three months. No submissions by post.

Editor: Shari Dash Greenspan

P0292 Fleet

Publishing Imprint

Publishing Imprint: Little, Brown Book Group (**P0532**)

P0293 Floris Books

Book Publisher
Canal Court, 40 Craiglockhart Avenue,
Edinburgh, EH14 1LT
United Kingdom
Tel: +44 (0) 1313 372372

floris@florisbooks.co.uk

https://www.florisbooks.co.uk
http://www.facebook.com/FlorisBooks
https://twitter.com/FlorisBooks
http://www.youtube.com/user/FlorisBooks
http://pinterest.com/florisbooks/

ADULT > **Nonfiction** > *Nonfiction Books*
Arts; Astrology; Health; Holistic Health; Literature; Mind, Body, Spirit; Parenting; Philosophy; Religion; Space; Spirituality

CHILDREN'S
Fiction

Board Books; *Early Readers*; *Middle Grade*; *Novels*; *Picture Books*; *Short Fiction*
Nonfiction > *Nonfiction Books*
Activities; Crafts

Send: Synopsis; Writing sample; Table of Contents; Author bio
How to send: Online submission system; Post

Publishes a wide range of books including adult nonfiction, picture books and children's novels. No poetry or verse, fiction for people over the age of 14, or autobiography, unless it specifically relates to a relevant nonfiction subject area. No submissions by email. Send by post or via online form. See website for full details of areas covered and submission guidelines.

Publishing Imprint: Kelpies (**P0484**)

P0294 Focal Press

Book Publisher
Taylor & Francis Books, 711 3rd Avenue, New York, NY 10017
United States
Tel: +1 (212) 216-7800
Fax: +1 (212) 564-7854

simon.jacobs@taylorandfrancis.com

http://www.focalpress.com

Book Publisher: Taylor & Francis Books

Types: Nonfiction
Formats: Film Scripts; Theatre Scripts
Subjects: Media; Music; Photography; Technology
Markets: Academic; Professional

Send: Query
Don't send: Full text

Publishes media technology books for students and professionals in the fields of photography, digital imaging, graphics, animation, new media, film and digital video production, broadcast and media distribution technologies, music recording / production, mass communications, and theatre technology. Submit proposal by email.

P0295 Folens Ltd

Book Publisher
Hibernian Industrial Estate, Greenhills Road, Tallaght, Dublin 24, D24 DH05
Ireland

proposals@folens.ie

https://www.folens.ie

Types: Nonfiction
Markets: Academic

Send: Full text

Publishes educational books and digital content for Primary and Post-Primary teachers and students in Ireland.

P0296 Footprint Handbooks
Book Publisher
5 Riverside Court, Lower Bristol Road, Bath,
BA2 3DZ
United Kingdom
Tel: +44 (0) 1225 469141

contactus@morriscontentalliance.com

http://www.footprinttravelguides.com

Types: Nonfiction
Formats: Reference
Subjects: Travel
Markets: Adult

Publishes travel guides written by a small team
of experts. See careers section of website for
any opportunities.

P0297 Forever
Publishing Imprint

Book Publisher: Grand Central Publishing
(**P0335**)

P0298 Forge
Publishing Imprint

Publishing Imprint: Tor/Forge (**P0870**)

P0299 The Foundry Publishing
Company
Book Publisher
PO Box 419527, Kansas City, MO 64141
United States

customercare@thefoundrypublishing.com

https://www.thefoundrypublishing.com

Types: Nonfiction
Subjects: Religion
Markets: Adult

Publishes Christian books. Send submissions
by post.

P0300 Fox Book Press
Publishing Imprint

Book Publisher: Beacon Publishing Group
(**P0088**)

P0301 Frances Lincoln
Children's Books
Publishing Imprint
74-77 White Lion Street, London, N1 9PF
United Kingdom
Tel: +44 (0) 20 7284 9300
Fax: +44 (0) 20 7485 0490

QuartoKidsSubmissions@Quarto.com

http://www.quartoknows.com/Frances-
Lincoln-Childrens-Books

Book Publisher: The Quarto Group, Inc.
(**P0739**)

Types: Fiction; Nonfiction; Poetry
Subjects: Culture
Markets: Children's

Publishes picture books, multicultural books,
poetry, picture books and information books.
Submit by email. See website for full
guidelines.

Editor: Katie Cotton

Publishers: Janetta Otter-Barry; Rachel
Williams

P0302 Free Association Books
Ltd
Book Publisher
1 Angel Cottages, Milespit Hill, London, NW7
1RD
United Kingdom

contact@freeassociationpublishing.com

https://freeassociationpublishing.com

Types: Nonfiction
Subjects: Health; History; Politics;
Psychology; Sociology
Markets: Adult

Send: Query
Don't send: Full text

Send submissions by post or by email.
Publishes books on a wide range of topics
including psychotherapy, social work, health
studies, history, public policy and more.

P0303 Free Spirit Publishing
Book Publisher
6325 Sandburg Road, Suite 100, Minneapolis,
MN 55427-3674
United States
Tel: +1 (612) 338-2068
Fax: +1 (612) 337-5050

help4kids@freespirit.com

http://www.freespirit.com

Types: Fiction; Nonfiction
Subjects: How To; Lifestyle; Self Help;
Sociology
Markets: Academic; Adult; Children's; Young
Adult

Send: Query
Don't send: Full text

Publishes nonfiction books and learning
materials for children and teens, parents,
educators, counselors, and others who live and
work with young people. Also publishes fiction
relevant to the mission of providing children
and teens with the tools they need to succeed in
life, e.g.: self-esteem; conflict resolution; etc.
No general fiction or storybooks; books with
animal or mythical characters; books with
religious or New Age content; or single
biographies, autobiographies, or memoirs.
Submit by proposals by post or through online
submission system. No submissions by fax or

email. See website for full submission
guidelines.

P0304 Front Table Books
Publishing Imprint

Book Publisher: Cedar Fort (**P0155**)

P0305 FT Prentice Hall
Publishing Imprint

Book Publisher: Pearson (**P0670**)

P0306 FunStitch Studio
Publishing Imprint
United States

Book Publisher: C&T Publishing (**P0138**)

P0307 G.P. Putnam's Sons
Publishing Imprint
United States

Book Publisher: Penguin Publishing Group
(**P0682**)

P0308 G.P. Putnam's Sons
Books for Young Readers
Publishing Imprint
United States

consumerservices@penguinrandomhouse.com

https://www.penguin.com/publishers/
gpputnamssonsbooksforyoungread/

Book Publisher: Penguin Young Readers
Group (**P0688**)

CHILDREN'S > Fiction
  Novels; *Picture Books*

How to send: Through a literary agent

Publishes approximately fifty trade hardcover
books a year for children, including lively,
accessible picture books and some of today's
strongest voices in fiction.

P0309 Gale
Book Publisher
27500 Drake Road, Farmington Hills, MI
48331
United States
Tel: +1 (800) 877-4253
Fax: +1 (877) 363-4253

gale.customerservice@cengage.com

https://www.gale.com
https://www.facebook.com/GaleCengage/
https://www.linkedin.com/company/gale
https://twitter.com/galecengage
https://www.youtube.com/user/GaleCengage

Book Publisher: Cengage (**P0156**)

ACADEMIC > Nonfiction
  Nonfiction Books: Business; Education;
  Finance; Health; History; Legal; Literature;
  Medicine; Science; Sociology; Technology
  Reference: General

ADULT > Nonfiction
Nonfiction Books: Business; Education;
Finance; Health; History; Hobbies; Legal;
Literature; Medicine; Science; Sociology;
Technology
Reference: General

PROFESSIONAL > Nonfiction
Nonfiction Books: Business; Education;
Finance; Health; Legal; Medicine; Science;
Technology
Reference: General

Supplies businesses, schools, and libraries with
books and electronic reference materials.

Book Publisher: KidHaven Press

Publishing Imprints: The Taft Group;
Blackbird Press; Charles Scribner & Sons;
Five Star; G.K. Hall & Co.; Graham &
Whiteside Ltd; Greenhaven Publishing; KG
Saur Verlag GmbH & Co. KG; Lucent Books;
Macmillan Reference USA; Primary Source
Media; Schirmer Reference; St James Press;
Thorndike Press; Twayne Publishers; UXL;
Wheeler Publishing

P0310 Galley Beggar Press
Book Publisher
United Kingdom

submissions@galleybeggar.co.uk

http://galleybeggar.co.uk

Types: Fiction; Nonfiction
Formats: Short Fiction
Subjects: Literary
Markets: Adult

Closed to approaches.

Publishes adult literary fiction (novels and
short story collections) and narrative nonfiction
only. Open to submissions by email during
specific submission windows. See website for
full details.

P0311 Gambit Books
Publishing Imprint

Publishing Imprint: Harvard Common Press
(**P0391**)

P0312 Garden-Door Press
Book Publisher
Ithaca, NY
United States

gardendoorpress@gmail.com

http://www.garden-doorpress.com

Types: Poetry
Subjects: Experimental; Literary
Markets: Adult

Closed to approaches.

Micro-press based in Ithaca, New York.
Publishes poetry chapbooks. Closed to
submissions as at April 2019. Check website
for current status.

P0313 Gazing Grain Press
Book Publisher
United States

gazinggrainpress@gmail.com

https://www.gazinggrainpress.com

Types: Fiction; Nonfiction; Poetry
Subjects: Women's Interests
Markets: Adult

Inclusive feminist literary press. Publishes
poetry, fiction, and nonfiction chapbook
contests, and book reviews. Accepts
submissions for chapbooks through annual
contest only ($15 entry fee). See website for
details.

P0314 Geddes & Grosset
Book Publisher
Gresham Publishing Company Limited,
Academy Park, Building 4000, Glasgow, G51
1PR
United Kingdom

http://www.geddesandgrosset.co.uk

Book Publisher: Gresham Books Ltd

Types: Fiction; Nonfiction
Formats: Reference
Subjects: Comedy / Humour; Cookery; Health;
History; Self Help; Spirituality
Markets: Adult; Children's

Publishes dictionaries, bilingual books, English
grammar and usage texts, Self-Help, Diet and
Health, and Mind, Body and Spirit. Imprint
focuses on Scottish titles.

Publishing Imprint: Waverley Books

P0315 Gemstone Publishing
Book Publisher
1940 Greenspring Drive, Suite I-L, Timonium,
MD 21093
United States
Tel: +1 (443) 318-8467
Fax: +1 (443) 318-8411

humark@gemstonepub.com

https://www.gemstonepub.com

Types: Nonfiction
Formats: Reference
Subjects: Hobbies
Markets: Adult

Publishes nonfiction and reference works such
as price guides relating to comics and other
collectables.

**P0316 Genealogical
Publishing Company**
Book Publisher
3600 Clipper Mill Road, Suite 260, Baltimore,
Maryland 21211
United States
Tel: +1 (410) 837-8271
Fax: +1 (410) 752-8492

web@genealogical.com

https://genealogical.com

Types: Nonfiction
Subjects: History; Hobbies; How To
Markets: Adult

Publishes books for amateur genealogists.

**P0317 The Geological Society
Publishing House**
Book Publisher; Magazine Publisher
Unit 7, Brassmill Enterprise Centre, Brassmill
Lane, Bath, BA1 3JN
United Kingdom
Tel: +44 (0) 1225 445046

https://www.geolsoc.org.uk/publications

ACADEMIC > Nonfiction
Articles: Earth Science; Geology
Nonfiction Books: Earth Science; Geology;
Memoir

Publishes postgraduate books and journals on
the earth sciences.

: Angharad Hills

Magazines: Geochemistry: Exploration,
Environment, Analysis (*M0245*); Journal of the
Geological Society (*M0308*); Petroleum
Geoscience (*M0413*); Proceedings of the
Yorkshire Geological Society (*M0440*);
Quarterly Journal of Engineering Geology and
Hydrogeology (*M0452*); Scottish Journal of
Geology (*M0496*)

**P0318 George Ronald
Publisher**
Book Publisher
3 Rosecroft Lane, Welwyn, Herts, AL6 0UB
United Kingdom
Tel: +44 (0) 1438 716062

sales@grbooks.com

http://grbooks.com
http://www.facebook.com/pages/George-
Ronald-Books/25850856123

Nonfiction > *Nonfiction Books*: Religion

Send: Query
How to send: Email

Religious publisher, concentrating solely on
books of interest to Baha'is. Send email for
copy of submission guidelines.

P0319 Gertrude Press
Book Publisher
United States

editor@gertrudepress.org

https://www.gertrudepress.org

Types: Fiction; Nonfiction; Poetry
Formats: Short Fiction
Subjects: Literary
Markets: Adult

Send: Full text

Publishes work by writers identifying as LGBTQ, both in online journal form and as chapbooks. Considers work for chapbook publication through its annual contests only. See website for details.

P0320 **Gifted Unlimited, LLC**
Book Publisher
12340 U.S. Highway 42, No. 453, Goshen, KY 40026
United States
Tel: +1 (502) 715-6306

info@giftedunlimitedllc.com

https://www.giftedunlimitedllc.com

Types: Nonfiction
Markets: Academic; Adult; Children's

Send: Query
Don't send: Full text

Publishes books that support the academic, social, or emotional needs of gifted children and adults. No fiction, poetry, or K-12 classroom materials. Approach via proposal submission form on website.

P0321 **Gingko Library**
Book Publisher
4 Molasses Row, Plantation Wharf, London, SW11 3UX
United Kingdom
Tel: +44 (0) 20 3637 9730

gingko@gingkolibrary.com

http://www.gingkolibrary.com

Types: Nonfiction
Subjects: Architecture; Arts; Biography; Finance; History; Literature; Music; Philosophy; Politics; Religion; Science; Technology
Markets: Academic; Adult

Send: Full text

Welcomes proposals for new, learned books that deal with topics pertaining to the Middle East and North Africa, or the Islamic world in general, whether they are academic monographs, edited volumes, or general interest (nonfiction) books. Send query by email.

P0322 **GL Assessment**
Book Publisher
1st Floor Vantage London, Great West Road, Brentford, TW8 9AG
United Kingdom
Tel: +44 (0) 20 8996 3333
Fax: +44 (0) 20 8742 8767

info@gl-assessment.co.uk

https://www.gl-assessment.co.uk

ACADEMIC > **Nonfiction** > *Nonfiction Books*

Publishes educational testing and assessment material.

P0323 **Glass Poetry Press**
Book Publisher
United States

editor@glass-poetry.com

http://www.glass-poetry.com/submissions.html

Types: Poetry
Markets: Adult

Closed to approaches.

Publishes poetry manuscripts between 15 and 25 pages. Currently closed to submissions.

P0324 **The Globe Pequot Press**
Book Publisher
246 Goose Lane, 2nd Floor, Guilford, CT 06437
United States

GPSubmissions@rowman.com

http://www.globepequot.com
https://rowman.com/Page/GlobePequot
https://www.facebook.com/globepequot/
https://twitter.com/globepequot

Book Publisher: Rowman & Littlefield Publishing Group

Nonfiction > *Nonfiction Books*
Biography; Business; Cookery; Gardening; History; Mind, Body, Spirit; Nature; Travel

Send: Outline; Table of Contents; Writing sample; Author bio; Market info
How to send: Email; Post

Publishes books about iconic brands and people, regional interest, history, lifestyle, cooking and food culture, and folklore – books that hit the intersection of a reader's interest in a specific place and their passion for a specific topic.

Publishing Imprints: Applause (*P0044*); Astragal Press; Backbeat (*P0072*); Down East Books (*P0236*); FalconGuides; Lyons Press (*P0549*); Mcbooks Press (*P0576*); Muddy Boots (*P0597*); Pineapple Press (*P0703*); Prometheus (*P0722*); Skip Jack Press (*P0815*); Stackpole Books (*P0836*); TwoDot (*P0887*); Union Park Press (*P0897*)

P0325 **Gnome On Pig Productions Incorporated**
Book Publisher
Canada

booksubmissions@ gnomeonpigproductions.com

https://www.gnomeonpigproductions.com

Types: Fiction; Nonfiction
Subjects: Drama; Erotic; Fantasy; Horror;

Science Fiction
Markets: Adult; Children's; Young Adult

Closed to approaches.

Publishes fiction for children, teens, new adults, and adults. Also occasional nonfiction. Closed to submissions as at February 2020. Check website for current status.

P0326 **Godstow Press**
Book Publisher
60 Godstow Road, Wolvercote, Oxford, OX2 8NY
United Kingdom
Tel: +44 (0) 1865 556215

info@godstowpress.co.uk

http://www.godstowpress.co.uk

Fiction > *Novels*
Historical Fiction; Philosophy; Spirituality

Poetry > *Any Poetic Form*
Philosophy; Spirituality

Small publisher of creative work with a spiritual / philosophical content, particularly historical fiction.

Editors: David Smith; Linda Smith

P0327 **Goldsmiths Press**
Book Publisher
Room 2, 33 Laurie Grove, New Cross, London, SE14 6NW
United Kingdom

goldsmithspress@gold.ac.uk

https://www.gold.ac.uk/goldsmiths-press

Types: Fiction; Nonfiction; Poetry
Markets: Academic; Adult

Send: Query
Don't send: Full text

University press aiming to cut across disciplinary boundaries and blur the distinctions between theory, practice, fiction and nonfiction. See website for proposal forms and submit by email.

Editors: Adrian Driscoll; Sarah Kember; Ellen Parnavelas; Guy Sewell

P0328 **Gollancz**
Publishing Imprint

Book Publisher: The Orion Publishing Group Limited (**P0647**)

P0329 **Gomer**
Publishing Imprint

Book Publisher: Gomer Press (**P0330**)

P0330 **Gomer Press**
Book Publisher
Llandysul Enterprise Park, Llandysul, Ceredigion, SA44 4JL
United Kingdom

Tel: +44 (0) 1559 363092
Fax: +44 (0) 1559 363758

gwasg@gomer.co.uk

http://www.gomer.co.uk

Types: Fiction; Nonfiction; Poetry; Scripts
Formats: Reference; Theatre Scripts
Subjects: Arts; Autobiography; Culture;
Drama; History; Leisure; Literature; Music;
Nature; Religion; Sport; Travel
Markets: Academic; Adult; Children's; Young
Adult

Send: Query
Don't send: Full text

Publishes fiction, nonfiction, plays, poetry,
language books, and educational material, for
adults and children, in English and in Welsh.
Query before making a submission.

Publishing Imprints: Gomer (*P0329*); Pont
Books. (*P0711*)

P0331 Goop Press
Publishing Imprint

Book Publisher: Grand Central Publishing
(**P0335**)

P0332 Government Publications
Book Publisher
Ireland

publications@opw.ie

https://www.opw.ie/en/
governmentpublications/

Types: Nonfiction
Formats: Reference
Subjects: Architecture; Legal
Markets: Adult; Professional

Publishes Irish government publications.

P0333 GPC Books
Publishing Imprint

Publishing Imprint: University of Wales Press
(**P0917**)

P0334 Grand Central Life & Style
Publishing Imprint

Book Publisher: Grand Central Publishing
(**P0335**)

P0335 Grand Central Publishing
Book Publisher
United States

https://www.grandcentralpublishing.com

Book Publisher: Hachette Book Group (**P0346**)

Types: Fiction; Nonfiction
Subjects: Beauty; Comedy / Humour; Culture;

Fashion; Lifestyle; Mystery; Romance;
Thrillers
Markets: Adult

How to send: Through a literary agent

Publishes a wide variety of fiction, nonfiction,
humour, beauty, fashion, romance, lifestyle,
mystery/thrillers, and pop culture books.
Approaches from literary agents only.

Publishing Imprints: Forever (*P0297*); Goop
Press (*P0331*); Grand Central Life & Style
(*P0334*); Twelve (*P0882*)

P0336 Granta Books
Book Publisher
12 Addison Avenue, London, W11 4QR
United Kingdom
Tel: +44 (0) 20 7605 1360
Fax: +44 (0) 20 7605 1361

info@granta.com

https://granta.com/books/

Types: Fiction; Nonfiction
Subjects: Autobiography; Culture; History;
Literary; Literary Criticism; Nature; Politics;
Sociology; Travel
Markets: Adult

Closed to approaches.

Publishes around 70% nonfiction / 30% fiction.
In nonfiction publishes serious cultural,
political and social history, narrative history, or
memoir. Rarely publishes straightforward
biographies. No genre fiction. Not accepting
unsolicited submissions.

P0337 Graphic Universe
Publishing Imprint

Book Publisher: Lerner Publishing Group
(**P0514**)

P0338 Graphix
Publishing Imprint

Book Publisher: Scholastic (**P0790**)

P0339 Great Source Education Group
Book Publisher

Book Publisher: Houghton Mifflin Harcourt
(**P0421**)

P0340 Greenway Music Press
Publishing Imprint
United States

https://www.areditions.com/gmp/shop.html

Book Publisher: A-R Editions (**P0013**)

Nonfiction > *Nonfiction Books:* Music

Brings important but under-appreciated
compositions to a larger audience. Focuses on
music for standard chamber ensembles, solo
instruments and voices, and keyboard.

P0341 Greenwillow Books
Publishing Imprint

Book Publisher: HarperCollins (**P0378**)

P0342 Griffin
Publishing Imprint

Publishing Imprint: St Martin's Press (**P0834**)

P0343 Grub Street Publishing
Book Publisher
4 Rainham Close, London, SW11 6SS
United Kingdom
Tel: +44 (0) 20 7924 3966
Fax: +44 (0) 20 7738 1008

post@grubstreet.co.uk

http://www.grubstreet.co.uk

Types: Nonfiction
Formats: Reference
Subjects: Cookery; History; Warfare
Markets: Adult

Send: Full text

Publishes books on cookery and military
aviation history only. No fiction or poetry.
Accepts synopses and sample material by
email. See website for full submission
guidelines and specific email addresses for
different topics.

P0344 Gryphon House, Inc.
Book Publisher
PO Box 10, 6848 Leon's Way, Lewisville, NC
27023
United States
Tel: +1 (336) 712-3490
Fax: +1 (877) 638-7576

info@ghbooks.com

http://www.gryphonhouse.com

Types: Nonfiction
Subjects: How To
Markets: Adult; Children's; Professional

Send: Query
Don't send: Full text

Publishes books intended to help teachers and
parents enrich the lives of children from birth
to age eight. See website for proposal
submission guidelines.

P0345 Gwasg Prifysgol Cymru
Publishing Imprint

Publishing Imprint: University of Wales Press
(**P0917**)

P0346 Hachette Book Group
Book Publisher
United States

https://www.hachettebookgroup.com

Book Publisher: Hachette Livre (**P0350**)

Types: Fiction; Nonfiction
Subjects: Contemporary; Literary
Markets: Adult

Includes 24 imprints covering the entire array of contemporary fiction and nonfiction, from the most popular to the most literary.

Book Publishers: Grand Central Publishing (**P0335**); Little, Brown and Company (**P0531**); Perseus Books (**P0693**); Piatkus Books

P0347 Hachette Books
Publishing Imprint
United States

Book Publisher: Perseus Books (**P0693**)

P0348 Hachette Digital
Publishing Imprint

Publishing Imprint: Little, Brown Book Group (**P0532**)

P0349 Hachette Go!
Publishing Imprint
United States

Book Publisher: Perseus Books (**P0693**)

P0350 Hachette Livre
Book Publisher
France

https://www.hachette.com

Types: Fiction; Nonfiction
Markets: Academic; Adult; Children's

International publishing group with operations in all English speaking markets.

Book Publishers: Hachette Book Group (**P0346**); Quercus Books (**P0742**)

Publishing Imprint: Headline Publishing Group

P0351 Hades Publications, Inc.
Book Publisher

Publishing Imprint: EDGE Science Fiction and Fantasy Publishing (**P0248**)

P0352 Hal Leonard Performing Arts Publishing Group
Book Publisher
33 Plymouth Street, Suite 302, Montclair, NJ 07042
United States

submissions@halleonardbooks.com

https://www.halleonardbooks.com

Types: Nonfiction
Subjects: Arts; Music
Markets: Adult

Send: Query
Don't send: Full text

Welcomes submissions pertaining to music and the performing arts. Send proposal by email as a Word or PDF attachment. See website for full guidelines.

Book Publisher: Amadeus Press

P0353 Halban Publishers
Book Publisher
United Kingdom
Tel: +44 (0) 20 7692 5541

books@halbanpublishers.com

http://www.halbanpublishers.com

Types: Fiction; Nonfiction
Subjects: Autobiography; History; Literary Criticism; Philosophy; Politics; Religion
Markets: Adult

Closed to approaches.

Closed to submissions as at March 30, 2019. Check website for current status. Independent publisher of fiction, memoirs, history, biography, and books of Jewish interest. Send query with synopsis by email only. No unsolicited MSS.

Editors: Martine Halban; Peter Halban

P0354 Half Mystic Press
Book Publisher
United States

press@halfmystic.com

https://www.halfmystic.com

Types: Fiction; Nonfiction; Poetry; Scripts
Formats: Short Fiction
Subjects: Autobiography; Music
Markets: Adult

Publishes poetry, essay, and short story collections; drama; memoirs; novellas; full-length novels; experimental work. See website for full submission guidelines. $3 fee per submission.

P0355 Halsgrove
Book Publisher
Halsgrove House, Ryelands Business Park, Bagley Road, Wellington, Somerset, TA21 9PZ
United Kingdom
Tel: +44 (0) 1823 653777
Fax: +44 (0) 1823 216796

sales@halsgrove.com

http://www.halsgrove.com

Types: Nonfiction
Subjects: Arts; Biography; History; Photography
Markets: Adult

Send: Full text

Publishes regional material covering various regions in the areas of history, biography, photography, and art. No fiction or poetry.

Send query by email with brief synopsis in first instance.

P0356 Hampton Roads Publishing
Publishing Imprint
65 Parker Street, Suite 7, Newburyport, MA 01950
United States
Tel: +1 (978) 465-0504
Fax: +1 (978) 465-0243

submissions@rwwbooks.com

http://redwheelweiser.com

Publishing Imprint: Red Wheel

Types: Nonfiction
Subjects: Health; Spirituality
Markets: Adult

Send: Query
Don't send: Full text

Publishes books on metaphysics, spirituality, and health. Send query by email with author info and proposal. See website for full guidelines.

P0357 Handtype Press
Book Publisher
United States

handtype@gmail.com

http://handtype.com

Types: Fiction; Nonfiction; Translations
Subjects: Autobiography
Markets: Adult

Send: Query
Don't send: Full text

Showcases literature and art created by signers (both deaf and hearing) or about the deaf or signing experience. Will consider fiction, essays, memoirs, and translations into English of signed and written works in other languages. Send query with a brief summary of your project, your publishing history, and a sample of your work (preferably the first 20 pages of prose) in a Word file.

P0358 HappenStance Press
Book Publisher
21 Hatton Green, Glenrothes, Fife, KY7 4SD
United Kingdom

https://www.happenstancepress.com
https://twitter.com/Nell_Nelson
https://www.facebook.com/HappenStance-Press-114680661902101/

Poetry > *Any Poetic Form*

Closed to approaches.

Small publisher of poetry chapbooks by both new and established poets. Unlikely to publish poets with no track record.

Editor: Helena Nelson

P0359 **Harcourt**
Publishing Imprint

Book Publisher: Pearson (**P0670**)

P0360 **Harlequin Dare**
Publishing Imprint
Canada

CustomerService@Harlequin.com

https://www.harlequin.com

Book Publisher: Harlequin Enterprises (**P0362**)

Types: Fiction
Subjects: Contemporary; Romance; Women's Interests
Markets: Adult

Send: Full text

Imprint which aims to push the boundaries of sexual explicitness while keeping the focus on the developing romantic relationship. Submit novels up to 50,000 words via online submission system available on website.

Editor: Kathleen Scheibling

P0361 **Harlequin Desire**
Book Publisher
195 Broadway, 24th floor, New York, NY 10007
United States
Tel: +1 (212) 207-7000

submissions@harlequin.com

https://www.harlequin.com

Types: Fiction
Subjects: Contemporary; Romance
Markets: Adult

Send: Full text

Publishes contemporary romances up to 50,000 words, featuring strong-but-vulnerable alpha heroes and dynamic, successful heroines, set in a world of wealth and glamour. See website for more details and to submit via online submission system.

Editor: Stacy Boyd

P0362 **Harlequin Enterprises**
Book Publisher
Bay Adelaide Centre, East Tower, 22 Adelaide Street West, 41st Floor, Toronto, ON M5H 4E3
Canada
Tel: +1 (888) 432-4879

https://www.harlequin.com
https://harlequin.submittable.com/submit
https://www.facebook.com/HarlequinBooks
https://twitter.com/HarlequinBooks
https://www.pinterest.com/harlequinbooks/
https://www.youtube.com/user/harlequinbooks
https://www.instagram.com/harlequinbooks/

Book Publisher: HarperCollins (**P0378**)

ADULT > **Fiction** > *Novels*: Romance

YOUNG ADULT > **Fiction** > *Novels*: Romance

How to send: Submittable

International publisher of romance fiction. See website for current needs, and appropriate imprints or series to submit to. Also offers manuscript critiquing service.

Book Publisher: Harlequin American Romance

Publishing Imprints: Carina Press (**P0149**); HQN Books; Harlequin Books; Harlequin Dare (**P0360**); Luna; MIRA; Mills & Boon; Red Dress Ink; Silhouette; Steeple Hill Books; Steeple Hill Café

P0363 **Harlequin Heartwarming**
Book Publisher
22 Adelaide Street West, 41st Floor, Toronto, ON M5H 4E3
Canada
Tel: +1 (888) 432-4879

submissions@harlequin.com

https://www.harlequin.com

Types: Fiction
Subjects: Contemporary; Romance
Markets: Adult

Send: Full text

Publishes wholesome contemporary romances set in small towns and close-knit communities. Interested in feel-good stories with happy endings. No explicit or behind-closed-doors sex, nudity, pre-marital sex, graphic violence, religious, paranormal, or heavy suspense. Submit via online submission system.

Editor: Kathleen Scheibling

P0364 **Harmony Ink Press**
Book Publisher
5032 Capital Circle SW, Ste 2 PMB 279, Tallahassee, FL 32305-7886
United States
Tel: +1 (800) 970-3759
Fax: +1 (888) 308-3739

submissions@harmonyinkpress.com

https://www.harmonyinkpress.com

Types: Fiction
Subjects: Fantasy; Mystery; Romance; Science Fiction
Markets: Young Adult

Closed to approaches.

Publishes Teen and New Adult fiction featuring significant personal growth of unforgettable characters across the LGBTQ+ spectrum. Closed to general submissions as at November 2019.

P0365 **Harper Audio (UK)**
Publishing Imprint
United Kingdom

Book Publisher: HarperCollins UK (**P0382**)

P0366 **Harper Books**
Publishing Imprint

Book Publisher: HarperCollins (**P0378**)

P0367 **Harper Business**
Publishing Imprint
195 Broadway, New York, NY 10007
United States
Tel: +1 (212) 207-7000

http://www.harperbusiness.com

Book Publisher: HarperCollins (**P0378**)

Types: Nonfiction
Subjects: Business
Markets: Adult; Professional

How to send: Through a literary agent

Publishes innovative, authoritative, and creative business books from world-class thinkers. Accepts approaches through literary agents only.

P0368 **Harper Design**
Publishing Imprint

Book Publisher: HarperCollins (**P0378**)

P0369 **Harper Inspire**
Publishing Imprint
United Kingdom

Book Publisher: HarperCollins UK (**P0382**)

P0370 **Harper Luxe**
Publishing Imprint

Book Publisher: HarperCollins (**P0378**)

P0371 **Harper North**
Publishing Imprint
United Kingdom

Book Publisher: HarperCollins UK (**P0382**)

P0372 **Harper Perennial**
Publishing Imprint

Book Publisher: HarperCollins (**P0378**)

P0373 **Harper Voyager**
Publishing Imprint
United Kingdom

Book Publishers: HarperCollins (**P0378**); HarperCollins UK (**P0382**)

P0374 **Harper Wave**
Publishing Imprint

Book Publisher: HarperCollins (**P0378**)

P0375 **Harper360**
Publishing Imprint
United Kingdom

Book Publisher: HarperCollins UK (**P0382**)

P0376 HarperAudio
Publishing Imprint

Book Publisher: HarperCollins (**P0378**)

P0377 HarperChildren's Audio
Publishing Imprint

Book Publisher: HarperCollins (**P0378**)

P0378 HarperCollins
Book Publisher
195 Broadway, New York, NY 10007
United States
Tel: +1 (212) 207-7000

https://www.harpercollins.com

Types: Fiction; Nonfiction
Formats: Reference
Subjects: Adventure; Autobiography;
Business; Commercial; Contemporary;
Cookery; Fantasy; Finance; Gothic; History;
Literary; Mystery; Religion; Romance; Science
Fiction; Self Help; Suspense; Travel; Westerns
Markets: Adult; Children's; Young Adult

Send: Query
Don't send: Full text

One of the world's largest publishers, almost
all imprints are open to agented submissions
only. Of the two imprints that accept
approaches direct from authors the first seeks
romance, and the second seeks visionary and
transformational fiction for digital first format.
See submission section of website for further
details.

Book Publishers: Harlequin Enterprises
(**P0362**); HarperCollins UK (**P0382**);
HarperImpulse; Zondervan Publishing House

Publishing Imprints: Amistad (*P0035*);
Anthony Bourdain Books (*P0041*); Avon
Books (**P0067**); Balzer + Bray (*P0076*);
Broadside Books (*P0129*); Custom House
(*P0206*); Dey Street Books (*P0225*); Ecco
(*P0246*); Greenwillow Books (*P0341*); Harper
Books (*P0366*); Harper Business (**P0367**);
Harper Design (*P0368*); Harper Luxe (*P0370*);
Harper Perennial (*P0372*); Harper Voyager
(*P0373*); Harper Wave (*P0374*); HarperAudio
(*P0376*); HarperChildren's Audio (*P0377*);
HarperCollins 360 (*P0379*); HarperCollins
Children's Books (*P0380*); HarperFestival
(*P0383*); HarperOne (*P0386*); HarperTeen
(*P0387*); HarperTeen Impulse (*P0388*);
HarperVia (*P0389*); Katherine Tegen Books
(*P0481*); Morrow Gift (*P0593*); Nelson Books
(*P0611*); Shelf Stuff (*P0809*); Thomas Nelson
(*P0859*); Tommy Nelson (*P0865*); W
Publishing Group (*P0941*); Walden Pond Press
(*P0943*); WestBow Press (*P0964*); William
Morrow (*P0975*); Witness (*P0978*);
Zonderkidz (*P0994*); Zondervan (*P0995*);
Zondervan Academic (*P0996*)

P0379 HarperCollins 360
Publishing Imprint

Book Publisher: HarperCollins (**P0378**)

P0380 HarperCollins Children's Books
Publishing Imprint
United Kingdom

Book Publishers: HarperCollins (**P0378**);
HarperCollins UK (**P0382**)

P0381 HarperCollins Ireland
Publishing Imprint
United Kingdom

Book Publisher: HarperCollins UK (**P0382**)

P0382 HarperCollins UK
Book Publisher
The News Building, 1 London Bridge Street,
London, SE1 9GF, GLASGOW OFFICE:, 103
Westerhill Road, Bishopbriggs, Glasgow, G64
2QT
United Kingdom
Tel: +44 (0) 20 8741 7070
Fax: +44 (0) 20 8307 4440

enquiries@harpercollins.co.uk

https://www.harpercollins.co.uk

Book Publisher: HarperCollins (**P0378**)

Types: Fiction; Nonfiction
Formats: Film Scripts; Reference
Subjects: Autobiography; Cookery; Crafts;
Crime; Entertainment; Fantasy; Gardening;
Health; History; Leisure; Lifestyle; Literary;
Media; Science; Science Fiction; Sport;
Thrillers; Warfare
Markets: Adult; Children's

How to send: Through a literary agent

One of the UK's three largest publishers, with
one of the broadest ranges of material
published. All approaches must come through
an agent. No unsolicited MSS.

Authors: Cecelia Ahern; Agatha Christie;
Patricia Cornwell; Lindsey Kelk; Derek Landy

Book Publisher: HarperPress

Publishing Imprints: 4th Estate (**P0009**); Avon
(*P0066*); The Borough Press (*P0122*); Collins
(*P0179*); Egmont Books (*P0253*); HQ
(*P0425*); HQ Digital (*P0426*); Harper Audio
(UK) (*P0365*); Harper Inspire (*P0369*); Harper
North (*P0371*); Harper Voyager (*P0373*);
Harper360 (*P0375*); HarperCollins Children's
Books (*P0380*); HarperCollins Ireland
(*P0381*); HarperFiction (*P0384*);
HarperNonFiction (*P0385*); Mills & Boon;
Mudlark (*P0598*); One More Chapter (*P0638*);
Times Books (*P0862*); William Collins
(*P0974*)

P0383 HarperFestival
Publishing Imprint

Book Publisher: HarperCollins (**P0378**)

P0384 HarperFiction
Publishing Imprint
United Kingdom

Book Publisher: HarperCollins UK (**P0382**)

P0385 HarperNonFiction
Publishing Imprint
United Kingdom

Book Publisher: HarperCollins UK (**P0382**)

P0386 HarperOne
Publishing Imprint

Book Publisher: HarperCollins (**P0378**)

P0387 HarperTeen
Publishing Imprint

Book Publisher: HarperCollins (**P0378**)

P0388 HarperTeen Impulse
Publishing Imprint

Book Publisher: HarperCollins (**P0378**)

P0389 HarperVia
Publishing Imprint

Book Publisher: HarperCollins (**P0378**)

P0390 Harvard Business Publishing
Book Publisher
United States
Tel: +1 (800) 545-7685
Fax: +1 (617) 783-7666

custserv@hbsp.harvard.edu

https://hbsp.harvard.edu
https://www.facebook.com/HarvardBizEdu/
https://twitter.com/HarvardBizEdu
https://www.linkedin.com/company/
harvardbizedu
https://www.youtube.com/channel/UCRp-
04NDMZh_61j-HszFbSg

ACADEMIC > **Nonfiction** > *Nonfiction
Books*
   Business; Management

PROFESSIONAL > **Nonfiction** > *Nonfiction
Books*
   Business; Management

Publishes business books for the professional
and academic markets.

Editor: Astrid Sandoval

P0391 Harvard Common Press
Publishing Imprint
100 Cummings Center, Suite 253C, Beverly,
MA 01915

United States
Tel: +1 (978) 282-9590
Fax: +1 (978) 282-7765

dan.rosenberg@quarto.com

http://www.harvardcommonpress.com

Book Publisher: The Quarto Group, Inc.
(P0739)

Types: Nonfiction
Subjects: Cookery; Lifestyle
Markets: Adult

Send: Query
Don't send: Full text

Publishes books on cookery and parenting. See website for full guidelines.

Editorial Director: Dan Rosenberg

Publishing Imprint: Gambit Books (*P0311*)

P0392 Harvard Square Editions (HSE)
Book Publisher
United States

https://harvardsquareeditions.org

Types: Fiction
Subjects: Literary; Nature; Sociology
Markets: Adult

Accepts novel and novella submissions with environmental and social themes. Send query with brief synopsis, first chapter, author's name and contact info and a one-paragraph bio in third person via online form on website.

P0393 Harvest House Publishers
Book Publisher
PO Box 41210, Eugene, OR 97404-0322
United States
Tel: +1 (800) 547-8979
Fax: +1 (888) 501-6012

http://harvesthousepublishers.com

Types: Fiction; Nonfiction
Subjects: Comedy / Humour; Contemporary; Cookery; Health; History; Lifestyle; Men's Interests; Mystery; Religion; Romance; Suspense; Westerns; Women's Interests
Markets: Adult; Children's; Young Adult

Publisher of Christian literature. Does not accept submissions directly, but is a member of an association which accepts proposals to share with their members. See website for full details.

P0394 Harvill Secker
Publishing Imprint
United Kingdom

Book Publisher: Vintage (**P0934**)

P0395 Hawthorn Press
Book Publisher
1 Lansdown Lane, Stroud, Gloucestershire, GL5 1BJ
United Kingdom
Tel: +44 (0) 1453 757040
Fax: +44 (0) 1453 751138

info@hawthornpress.com

http://www.hawthornpress.com

Types: Nonfiction
Subjects: Lifestyle; Self Help
Markets: Adult

Send: Query
Don't send: Full text

Publisher aiming to contribute to a more creative, peaceful and sustainable world through its publishing. Publishes mainly commissioned work, but will consider approaches. Send first two chapters with introduction, full table of contents/book plan, brief author biography and/or CV. Allow at least 2–4 months for response. Send submissions by email.

P0396 Hay House Publishers
Book Publisher
The Sixth Floor, Watson House, 54 Baker Street, London, W1U 7BU
United Kingdom
Tel: +44 (0) 20 3675 2450
Fax: +44 (0) 20 3675 2451

submissions@hayhouse.co.uk

http://www.hayhouse.co.uk

Types: Nonfiction
Subjects: Biography; Business; Current Affairs; Finance; Health; Lifestyle; Medicine; Men's Interests; Nature; Philosophy; Psychology; Religion; Self Help; Sociology; Women's Interests
Markets: Adult

Send: Query
Don't send: Full text

Describes itself as the world's leading mind body and spirit publisher. Approach via form on website. See website for full submission guidelines.

P0397 Haynes Publishing
Book Publisher
Sparkford, Near Yeovil, Somerset, BA22 7JJ
United Kingdom
Tel: +44 (0) 1963 440635

bookseditorial@haynes.co.uk

http://www.haynes.co.uk

Types: Nonfiction
Formats: Reference
Subjects: How To; Leisure; Sport; Technology
Markets: Adult

Mostly publishes motoring and transport titles, including DIY service and repair manuals for cars and motorbikes, motoring in general (including Motor Sports), but also home, DIY, and leisure titles. Unsolicited MSS welcome, if on one of the above areas of interest.

P0398 Health Professions Press
Book Publisher
Acquisitions Department, Health Professions Press, P.O. Box 10624, Baltimore, MD 21285-0624
United States
Tel: +1 (410) 337-9585
Fax: +1 (410) 337-8539

mmagnus@healthpropress.com

http://www.healthpropress.com

Types: Nonfiction
Formats: Reference
Subjects: Health; How To; Medicine; Psychology; Self Help
Markets: Academic; Adult; Professional

Send: Query
Don't send: Full text

Publishes health books aimed primarily at professionals, students, and educated consumers interested in topics related to ageing and eldercare. See website for submission guidelines and to download Publication Questionnaire.

P0399 HeartSpring Publishing
Publishing Imprint

Book Publisher: College Press Publishing (**P0178**)

P0400 Hellgate Press
Book Publisher
United States
Tel: +1 (800) 795-4059

harley@hellgatepress.com

http://www.hellgatepress.com

Types: Fiction; Nonfiction
Subjects: Adventure; Autobiography; History; Travel; Warfare
Markets: Adult; Children's; Young Adult

Send: Query
Don't send: Full text

Publishes nonfiction titles on military history and experiences, and fast-paced Historical or Adventure Fiction Books for Children, Teens and Young Adults. Primarily interested in American soldiers and their battles, but will also consider books on other armies (including the ancient world) and travel/adventure books. Send query with synopsis by email or post.

P0401 Hendrick-Long Publishing Co.

Book Publisher
10635 Tower Oaks, Suite D, Houston, Texas 77070
United States
Tel: +1 (281) 635-0583

hendrick-long@att.net

http://hendricklongpublishing.com

Types: Fiction; Nonfiction
Subjects: Arts; Biography; Cookery; Culture; History; Science; Warfare; Westerns
Markets: Children's; Young Adult

Send: Query
Don't send: Full text

Publishes Texas-related fiction and nonfiction for children and young adults. Send query with SASE, outline, synopsis, and two sample chapters.

Editors: Caroline Ingrid Long; Joann Taylor Long; Michael Long; Vilma Long

P0402 Henry Holt and Company

Book Publisher
175 Fifth Avenue, New York, NY 10010
United States

http://www.henryholt.com

Book Publisher: Macmillan

Types: Fiction; Nonfiction
Markets: Adult

Closed to approaches.

No submissions. Any material submitted will be recycled or discarded unread.

Book Publisher: Henry Holt and Company Books for Young Readers

P0403 Heritage House

Book Publisher
103 – 1075 Pendergast Street, Victoria, BC, V8V 0A1
Canada
Tel: +1 (250) 360-0829 ext. 103

books@heritagehouse.ca

http://www.heritagehouse.ca

Types: Nonfiction
Subjects: Adventure; Anthropology; Arts; Biography; Business; Comedy / Humour; Contemporary; Crime; Culture; History; Nature; Politics; Sport; Warfare; Women's Interests
Markets: Adult

Send: Full text

Publishes books on the heritage and historical and contemporary culture of Canada. Submit query by email only with one-page synopsis and one or two sample chapters. See website for full guidelines.

P0404 Heroic Books

Book Publisher; Editorial Service
United Kingdom

info@heroicbooks.com

http://www.heroicbooks.com
https://www.facebook.com/HeroicBooks/
https://twitter.com/HeroicBooks
https://www.instagram.com/heroicbooks/

ADULT > **Fiction** > *Novels*
Fantasy; Science Fiction

YOUNG ADULT > **Fiction** > *Novels*
Fantasy; Science Fiction

How to send: Online submission system

Costs: Offers services that writers have to pay for.

We are an innovative publisher across the fantasy and science fiction genre. We are committed to finding the most exciting authors and publishing their work to the highest possible quality. Experienced in media and business beyond the traditional, we are committed to breaking new ground for our authors. Working with illustrators, narrators, and other creatives, we aim to make sure every novel reaches its full potential. So, if you are an author, an artist, a narrator, a reader – please join us.

Author: Davis Ashura

Book: A Testament of Steel

Editor: Zoe George

P0405 Hertfordshire Publications

Publishing Imprint
United Kingdom

http://www.uhpress.co.uk/subject-areas/hertfordshire-publications

Book Publisher: University of Hertfordshire Press (**P0906**)

ACADEMIC > **Nonfiction** > *Nonfiction Books:* Local History

P0406 HiddenSpring

Publishing Imprint

Book Publisher: Paulist Press (**P0665**)

P0407 High Plains Press

Book Publisher
PO Box 123, Glendo, WY 82213
United States
Tel: +1 (800) 552-7819
Fax: +1 (307) 735-4590

editor@highplainspress.com

http://www.highplainspress.com

Types: Nonfiction; Poetry
Subjects: Autobiography; History; Nature
Markets: Adult

Send: Query
Don't send: Full text

Regional publisher specialising in books on the American West. Publishes nonfiction and one book of poetry with a strong sense of place (the West) per year. For nonfiction send query with 2-3 page summary and first two chapters by post with SASE. For poetry send sample of ten poems. No fiction or children's material.

P0408 Hippocrene Books, Inc.

Book Publisher
171 Madison Avenue, New York NY 10016
United States
Tel: +1 (212) 685-4371
Fax: +1 (718) 228-6355

editorial@hippocrenebooks.com

https://www.hippocrenebooks.com

Types: Nonfiction
Formats: Reference
Subjects: Cookery; History
Markets: Adult

Publishes general nonfiction, particularly foreign language reference books and ethnic cookbooks. No fiction. Send submissions by email.

P0409 The History Press

Book Publisher
97 St George's Place, Cheltenham, Gloucestershire, GL50 3QB
United Kingdom
Tel: +44 (0) 1242 895310
Fax: +44 (0) 1453 883233

web@thehistorypress.co.uk

https://www.thehistorypress.co.uk
https://www.facebook.com/thehistorypressuk/
https://twitter.com/TheHistoryPress/
https://www.pinterest.com/thehistorypress/

Nonfiction > *Nonfiction Books:* History

Send: Query; Synopsis; Author bio; Market info; Proposal
Don't send: Full text
How to send: Email

Publishes books on history, from local to international. Welcomes submissions from both new and established authors. Send query by email. No unsolicited mss. See website for full guidelines.

Publishing Imprint: Phillimore (**P0697**)

P0410 Hobble Creek Press

Publishing Imprint

Book Publisher: Cedar Fort (**P0155**)

P0411 Hodder & Stoughton Ltd

Book Publisher
Carmelite House, 50 Victoria Embankment, London, EC4Y 0DZ

United Kingdom
Tel: +44 (0) 20 3122 6000

enquiries@hachette.co.uk

https://www.hodder.co.uk

Types: Fiction; Nonfiction
Subjects: Autobiography; Comedy / Humour; Commercial; Cookery; History; Lifestyle; Literary; Spirituality; Travel
Markets: Adult

How to send: Through a literary agent

Large London-based publisher of nonfiction and commercial and literary fiction.

Book Publishers: Hodder Faith; John Murray (Publishers) Ltd (**P0470**)

Publishing Imprint: Nicholas Brealey Publishing (**P0620**)

P0412 Hodder Education
Book Publisher
Carmelite House, 50 Victoria Embankment, London, EC4Y 0DZ
United Kingdom
Tel: +44 (0) 1235 827720
Fax: +44 (0) 1235 400450

educationenquiries@hodder.co.uk

http://www.hoddereducation.co.uk

Types: Nonfiction
Formats: Reference
Subjects: Health; Medicine; Science; Self Help
Markets: Academic; Adult

Send: Query
Don't send: Full text

Publishes educational and reference books including home learning and school textbooks. See website for more details and for specific submission addresses for different types of books.

Book Publisher: Rising Stars (**P0759**)

P0413 Hodder Gibson
Book Publisher
211 St Vincent Street, Glasgow, G2 5QY
United Kingdom
Tel: +44 (0) 1413 334650

hoddergibson@hodder.co.uk

http://hoddergibson.co.uk

Types: Nonfiction
Markets: Academic

Send: Query
Don't send: Full text

Publishes Scottish school textbooks and learning materials. Make initial approach through form on website.

P0414 Hogarth Press
Publishing Imprint
United Kingdom

Book Publisher: Vintage (**P0934**)

P0415 Holiday House, Inc.
Book Publisher
50 Broad Street #301, New York, NY 10004
United States
Tel: +1 (212) 688-0085
Fax: +1 (212) 421-6134

submissions@holidayhouse.com

http://www.holidayhouse.com

Types: Fiction; Nonfiction
Markets: Children's; Young Adult

Send: Full text

Independent publisher of children's books, from picture books to young adult fiction and nonfiction. Send complete ms by post or by email. No need to include SASE.

P0416 Holloway House
Publishing Imprint

Book Publisher: Kensington Publishing Corp. (**P0488**)

P0417 Honno Welsh Women's Press
Book Publisher
Honno, Unit 14, Creative Units, Aberystwyth Arts Centre, Aberystwyth, Ceredigion, SY23 3GL
United Kingdom
Tel: +44 (0) 1970 623150
Fax: +44 (0) 1970 623150

post@honno.co.uk

http://www.honno.co.uk

Types: Fiction; Nonfiction; Poetry
Formats: Short Fiction
Subjects: Autobiography; Commercial; Crime; Fantasy; Literary; Science Fiction; Thrillers; Women's Interests
Markets: Adult; Children's; Young Adult

Send: Query
Don't send: Full text

Feminist Welsh publisher. Publishes work from women born in, living in, or significantly connected to Wales, only. Publishes fiction, autobiographical writing and reprints of classic titles in English and Welsh, as well as anthologies of poetry and short stories. Particularly looking for literary fiction, crime/thriller, commercial women's fiction, science fiction and fantasy. All submissions must be sent as hard copy; no email submissions. Send query with synopsis and first 50 pages. Not currently accepting children's, novellas, poetry, or short story collections by a single author.

Editor: Caroline Oakley

P0418 Horizon Publishers
Publishing Imprint

Book Publisher: Cedar Fort (**P0155**)

P0419 Hot Key Books
Book Publisher
535 King's Road, London, SW10 0SZ
United Kingdom
Tel: +44 (0) 20 7490 3875

hello@bonnierbooks.co.uk

http://hotkeybooks.com

Book Publisher: Bonnier Books (UK) (**P0118**)

Types: Fiction; Nonfiction
Markets: Children's; Young Adult

How to send: Through a literary agent

Publishes fiction and nonfiction for teens and young adults. Accepts approaches through literary agents only.

P0420 Houghton Mifflin College Division
Book Publisher

Book Publisher: Houghton Mifflin Harcourt (**P0421**)

P0421 Houghton Mifflin Harcourt
Book Publisher
125 High Street, Boston, MA 02110
United States
Tel: +1 (617) 351-5000

corporate.communications@hmhco.com

http://www.hmco.com

Types: Fiction; Nonfiction
Formats: Reference
Subjects: Autobiography; History; Literature
Markets: Academic; Children's

Educational publisher publishing nonfiction and early readers for children.

Book Publishers: Great Source Education Group (*P0339*); Houghton Mifflin College Division (*P0420*); Houghton Mifflin School Division (*P0422*); Houghton Mifflin Trade & Reference Division (*P0423*); McDougal Littell Inc. (*P0577*); Promissor Inc. (*P0723*); The Riverside Publishing Co. (*P0761*)

Publishing Imprint: Clarion Books

P0422 Houghton Mifflin School Division
Book Publisher

Book Publisher: Houghton Mifflin Harcourt (**P0421**)

P0423 Houghton Mifflin Trade & Reference Division
Book Publisher

Book Publisher: Houghton Mifflin Harcourt (**P0421**)

P0424 House of Lochar

Publishing Imprint
Isle of Colonsay, PA61 7YR
United Kingdom
Tel: +44 (0) 1951 200232
Fax: +44 (0) 1951 200232

sales@houseoflochar.com

http://www.houseoflochar.com

Publishing Imprint: House of Lochar (**P0424**)

Types: Fiction; Nonfiction
Subjects: Biography; History; Literary;
Literature; Travel
Markets: Adult; Children's

Publishes fiction and nonfiction related to
Scotland and / or Celtic themes, including
history, fiction, transport, maritime, genealogy,
Gaelic, and books for children. No poetry or
books unrelated to Scottish or Celtic themes.

Publishing Imprints: Colonsay Books (*P0180*);
House of Lochar (**P0424**); West Highland
Series. (*P0962*)

P0425 HQ

Publishing Imprint
United Kingdom

Book Publisher: HarperCollins UK (**P0382**)

P0426 HQ Digital

Publishing Imprint
United Kingdom

Book Publisher: HarperCollins UK (**P0382**)

P0427 Human Kinetics

Book Publisher
1607 N Market Street, Champaign, Illinois
61825
United States
Tel: +1 (800) 747-4457
Fax: +1 (217) 351-1549

acquisitions@hkusa.com

https://us.humankinetics.com
https://www.facebook.com/HumanKinetics

ACADEMIC > **Nonfiction** > *Nonfiction*
Books
  Fitness; Health; Nutrition; Sport

ADULT > **Nonfiction** > *Nonfiction Books*
  Fitness; Health; Nutrition; Sport

PROFESSIONAL > **Nonfiction** > *Nonfiction*
Books
  Fitness; Health; Nutrition; Sport

Send: Query; Table of Contents
How to send: Post; Email

Publishes books on health, fitness, and sport,
aimed at the academic market, professionals in
the field, and the general public. Send query by
post or email.

P0428 Hymns Ancient & Modern Ltd

Book Publisher
13a Hellesdon Park Road, Norwich, NR6 5DR
United Kingdom

https://www.hymnsam.co.uk

Types: Nonfiction
Formats: Reference
Subjects: Biography; Comedy / Humour;
Music; Religion
Markets: Academic; Adult

Send: Query
Don't send: Full text

Publishes religious books including hymn
books, liturgical material, and schoolbooks.

Publishing Imprints: Canterbury Press; Church
House Publishing (**P0168**); SCM Press; Saint
Andrew Press (**P0776**)

P0429 Ian Allan Publishing Ltd

Book Publisher
Terminal House, Shepperton, TW17 8AS
United Kingdom

https://www.ianallanpublishing.com

Types: Nonfiction
Formats: Reference
Subjects: History; Hobbies; Travel; Warfare
Markets: Adult

Former publisher of nonfiction and reference
books relating to transport, now publishes
Masonic books and magazine.

Publishing Imprints: Lewis Masonic (*P0517*);
Midland Publishing

P0430 Ibbetson Street Press

Book Publisher
25 School Street, Somerville, MA 02143
United States
Tel: +1 (617) 628-2313

tapestryofvoices@yahoo.com

http://ibbetsonpress.com

Types: Poetry
Subjects: Literary
Markets: Adult

Send: Full text

Poetry press publishing a regular journal and
poetry books. Send query by email with brief
bio and 3-5 poems in the body of the email. No
attachments.

Editors: Harris Gardner; Lawrence Kessenich;
Emily Pineau

P0431 Icon Books Ltd

Book Publisher
Omnibus Business Centre, 39-41 North Road,
London, N7 9DP
United Kingdom

Tel: +44 (0) 20 7697 9695
Fax: +44 (0) 20 7697 9501

submissions@iconbooks.com

http://www.iconbooks.co.uk

Types: Nonfiction
Subjects: Arts; Comedy / Humour; History;
Philosophy; Politics; Psychology; Religion;
Science; Sport
Markets: Adult

Send: Query
Don't send: Full text

Submit by email only. See website for full
guidelines. Has in the past tended to publish
series of books, including an ongoing series of
graphic introductions to key figure and ideas in
history, science, psychology, philosophy,
religion, and the arts, but increasingly
publishing individual nonfiction titles in such
areas as politics, popular philosophy and
psychology, history, sport, humour and,
especially, popular science.

P0432 ICSA Publishing

Book Publisher
Saffron House, 6–10 Kirby Street, London,
EC1N 8TS
United Kingdom
Tel: +44 (0) 20 7580 4741

publishing@icsa.co.uk

https://www.icsa.org.uk/shop

Types: Nonfiction
Formats: Reference
Subjects: Legal
Markets: Professional

Publishes books aimed at secretaries and
administrators, providing guidance on legal
and regulatory compliance.

P0433 IDW Publishing

Book Publisher
2765 Truxtun Road, San Diego, CA 92106
United States

letters@idwpublishing.com

http://www.idwpublishing.com

Types: Fiction
Subjects: Adventure; Science Fiction
Markets: Adult; Children's; Young Adult

Publisher of comic books and graphic novels
based on well known intellectual properties,
for both children and adults.

P0434 Idyll Arbor

Book Publisher
39129 264th Ave SE, Enumclaw, WA 98022
United States
Tel: +1 (360) 825-7797
Fax: +1 (360) 825-5670

sales@idyllarbor.com

http://www.idyllarbor.com

Types: Nonfiction
Subjects: Health; How To; Leisure; Medicine; Psychology
Markets: Adult; Professional

Send: Full text

Publishes practical books on healthcare and therapies aimed at people or families dealing with a condition and activity directors. Will accept completed mss or queries, but prefers to receive query with outline and sample chapter by email.

P0435 Iff Books
Publishing Imprint

Book Publisher: John Hunt Publishing Ltd

P0436 Ig Publishing
Book Publisher
PO Box 2547, New York, NY 10163
United States
Tel: +1 (718) 797-0676
Fax: +1 (718) 797-0676

robert@igpub.com

http://igpub.com

Types: Fiction; Nonfiction
Subjects: Culture; Literary
Markets: Adult; Young Adult

Send: Query
Don't send: Full text

Publishes original literary fiction from writers who are perceived to have been overlooked by the mainstream publishing establishment, plus political and cultural nonfiction. Young adult imprint is devoted to bringing back young adult literature from as far back as the '30s and '40s and as recently as the '70s and '80s. No unsolicited mss. Send query by email only.

Editor-in-Chief: Robert Lasner

P0437 Igloo Books Limited
Book Publisher
Cottage Farm, Mears Ashby Road, Sywell, Northants, NN6 0BJ
United Kingdom
Tel: +44 (0) 1604 741116
Fax: +44 (0) 1604 670495

customerservice@igloobooks.com

http://igloobooks.com

Types: Fiction; Nonfiction
Formats: Reference
Subjects: Cookery; Hobbies; Lifestyle
Markets: Adult; Children's

Publishes nonfiction and gift and puzzle books for adults, and fiction, nonfiction, and novelty books for children.

P0438 Imagine Publishing
Publishing Imprint
United States

adult.submissions@charlesbridge.com

https://www.imaginebooks.net
https://twitter.com/Imagine_CB
https://www.facebook.com/ImaginePress/
https://www.pinterest.com/charlesbridge/adult-books-from-imagine-publishing/
https://www.instagram.com/imagine_cb/

Book Publisher: Charlesbridge Publishing (**P0161**)

Nonfiction
  Coffee Table Books: General
  Nonfiction Books: Arts; Comedy / Humour; Cookery; History; Nature; Politics; Women's Studies
  Puzzle Books: General

Send: Full text; Writing sample
How to send: Email

Publishes 8-10 titles a year, primarily focused on history, politics, women's studies, and nature.

P0439 Imagine That Publishing
Book Publisher
Marine House, Tide Mill Way, Woodbridge, Suffolk, IP12 1AP
United Kingdom
Tel: +44 (0) 1394 386651

customerservice@topthatpublishing.com

https://www.imaginethat.com
https://www.facebook.com/ImagineThatPublishing/
https://twitter.com/imaginethatbook
https://www.instagram.com/imaginethatbook/

CHILDREN'S
  Fiction > *Novels*
  Nonfiction > *Nonfiction Books*

Closed to approaches.

Publishes Activity Books, Board Books, Fiction, Magnetic Books, Novelty Books, Picture Storybooks, Press Out & Play, and Sticker Books. Does not currently publish "regular" children's or adults fiction. See online book catalogue for the kinds of books published. If suitable for the list, send submissions by email (preferred), ideally under 1MB, or by post (mss not returned). See website for full guidelines. Responds within 8 weeks if interested. No simultaneous submissions.

Editors: Dan Graham; Josh Simpkin-Betts

P0440 Imbrifex Books
Book Publisher
8275 South Eastern Avenue, Suite 200, Las Vegas, Nevada 89123
United States
Tel: +1 (702) 309-0130

acquisitions@imbrifex.com

https://imbrifex.com

Types: Fiction; Nonfiction
Subjects: Autobiography; Travel
Markets: Adult

Send: Query
Don't send: Full text

Publishes fiction, travel and memoir. Welcomes book proposals and queries from both authors and agents. See website for full guidelines.

Editors: Megan Edwards; Mark Sedenquist

P0441 Immanion Press
Book Publisher
United Kingdom

editorial@immanion-press.com

https://www.immanion-press.com/

Types: Fiction; Nonfiction
Subjects: Comedy / Humour; Fantasy; Horror; Literary; Science Fiction; Spirituality
Markets: Adult

Send: Query
Don't send: Full text

Closed to fiction submissions as at April 2020. Publishes innovative and intelligent dark fantasy, literary fantasy, science fiction, horror, slipstream, magic realism, and black comedies. Also publishes nonfiction on magic, qabala, Tarot and associated thematic subjects. No derivative or "twee" high fantasy, overly technical, non-character driven science fiction, or visceral gore horror. Send synopsis with first 30 pages and author bio by post or by email as Word, PDF, or plain text attachment. Full submission details on website.

P0442 Impact
Publishing Imprint
United States

http://www.impact-books.com

Book Publisher: Penguin Publishing Group (**P0682**)

Types: Nonfiction
Formats: Reference
Subjects: Arts; How To
Markets: Adult

Publishes books to assist artists drawing comics, superheroes, Japanese-style manga, fantasy, creatures, action, caricature, anime, etc.

: Pamela Wissman

P0443 Impress Books Limited
Book Publisher
13-14 Crook Business Centre, New Road, Crook, County Durham, DL15 8QX
United Kingdom

contact@impress-books.co.uk

http://www.impress-books.co.uk
http://instagram.com/impress_books

https://twitter.com/impressBooks1
https://www.facebook.com/Impress-Books-1623623654535795/

Fiction > *Novels*
Crime; Historical Fiction; Literary

Nonfiction > *Nonfiction Books*

Send: Full text; Writing sample; Synopsis
How to send: Word file email attachment;
Online contact form

Interested in quality, thought-provoking titles for the enquiring general reader. Specialises in discovering and nurturing fresh voices in crime, historical and literary fiction.

P0444 Indiana Historical Society Press

Book Publisher
450 West Ohio Street, Indianapolis, IN 46202
United States
Tel: +1 (317) 232-1882

ihspress@indianahistory.org

https://indianahistory.org

Types: Nonfiction
Subjects: History
Markets: Adult; Children's

Send: Query
Don't send: Full text

Publishes books on the history of Indiana.
Send query with SASE.

P0445 Indiana University Press

Book Publisher
IU Office of Scholarly Publishing, Herman B
Wells Library E350, 1320 E 10th Street E4,
Bloomington, IN 47405-3907
United States
Tel: +1 (812) 855-8817
Fax: +1 (812) 855-7931

iupress@indiana.edu

http://www.iupress.indiana.edu

Types: Nonfiction
Formats: Film Scripts
Subjects: Anthropology; History; Media;
Music; Philosophy; Religion; Travel; Warfare
Markets: Academic

Send: Query
Don't send: Full text

Submit proposals via online proposal submission form.

P0446 Indie Authors Press

Book Publisher
United Kingdom

https://www.salgado-reyes.com

Types: Fiction
Subjects: Fantasy; Horror; Science Fiction
Markets: Adult

A family-run hybrid publisher for independent authors, based in the UK. Publishes Science fiction, Cyberpunk, Fantasy fiction, Dark fantasy, Horror. See website for open submission calls.

P0447 Indigo Dreams Publishing

Book Publisher
24 Forest Houses, Halwill, Beaworthy, Devon,
EX21 5UU
United Kingdom

publishing@indigodreams.co.uk

http://www.indigodreams.co.uk

Types: Poetry
Subjects: Literary
Markets: Adult

Closed to approaches.

**Closed to submissions as at November 2018.
Will re-open late 2019.** Publishes poetry collections up to 60/70 pages and poetry pamphlets up to 36 pages. See website for submission guidelines.

Authors: Roselle Angwin; Frances
Galleymore; Paula Rae Gibson; Seema Gill;
Charlie Hill; James Lawless; Robert Leach;
Dennis Loccoriere; Angela Locke; Char
March; Ann Pilling; Cyril Tawney

Editor: Ronnie Goodyer

P0448 Information Today, Inc.

Book Publisher
143 Old Marlton Pike, Medford, NJ 08055-8750,
United States
Tel: +1 (609) 654-6266
Fax: +1 (609) 654-4309

custserv@infotoday.com

http://www.infotoday.com

Types: Nonfiction
Subjects: Technology
Markets: Adult

Publishes books and magazines on information technology.

P0449 Ink Road

Publishing Imprint

Book Publisher: Black & White Publishing Ltd
(**P0098**)

P0450 Insomniac Press

Book Publisher
520 Princess Avenue, London, ON N6B 2B8
Canada
Tel: +1 (519) 266-3556

http://www.insomniacpress.com

Types: Fiction; Nonfiction; Poetry
Formats: Reference; Short Fiction
Subjects: Business; Comedy / Humour;

Commercial; Crime; Culture; Experimental;
Finance; Gardening; Health; Legal; Lifestyle;
Literary; Literary Criticism; Medicine; Music;
Mystery; Politics; Religion; Self Help; Sport;
Suspense; Travel
Markets: Adult

Send: Query
Don't send: Full text

Particularly interested in creative nonfiction on business / personal finance; gay and lesbian studies; black Canadian studies and others. No science fiction, cookbooks, romance, or children's books. Send query by email or post in first instance. Approaches by authors who have had work published elsewhere (e.g. short stories in magazines) will receive closer attention.

P0451 International Publishers

Book Publisher
235 W 23rd Street, New York, NY 10011-2302
United States
Tel: +1 (212) 366-9816
Fax: +1 (212) 366-9820

service@intpubnyc.com

https://www.intpubnyc.com

Nonfiction > *Nonfiction Books*
Culture; Gender Issues; History; Marxism;
Philosophy; Politics; Social Issues

Marxist publishers of books on labour rights, race and gender issues, Marxist science, etc.

P0452 InterVarsity Press (IVP)

Book Publisher
36 Causton Street, London, SW1P 4ST
United Kingdom
Tel: +44 (0) 20 7592 3900

submissions@ivpbooks.com

https://ivpbooks.com
https://www.facebook.com/ivpbooks
https://www.instagram.com/ivpbooks/
https://twitter.com/IVPbookcentre

ACADEMIC > **Nonfiction** > *Nonfiction
Books*: Religion

ADULT > **Nonfiction** > *Nonfiction Books*
Biography; Christian Living; Church
History; Contemporary Culture; Religion

Send: Query
How to send: Online contact form

Aims to produce quality, Evangelical books for the digital age. Send query through form on website.

P0453 Interweave

Publishing Imprint
United States

Book Publisher: Penguin Publishing Group
(**P0682**)

Types: Nonfiction
Subjects: Crafts; Hobbies
Markets: Adult

Editor: Kerry Bogert

P0454 IOP Publishing
Book Publisher
Temple Circus, Temple Way, Bristol, BS1 6HG
United Kingdom
Tel: +44 (0) 1179 297481
Fax: +44 (0) 1179 294318

ebooks@ioppublishing.org

https://ioppublishing.org

Types: Nonfiction
Subjects: Science
Markets: Academic; Professional

Send: Query
Don't send: Full text

Publishes books in physics and related areas such as mathematical physics, medical physics, astronomy, materials science, nanoscience, electronic materials and instrumentation. Continually looking to add new high-quality books. If you have an idea for an advanced textbook, monograph, review or handbook submit according to guidelines on website.

P0455 Iqon Editions
Publishing Imprint

Book Publisher: The Quarto Group, Inc. **(P0739)**

P0456 Italica Press
Book Publisher
99 Wall Street, Suite 650, New York, NY 10005
United States
Tel: +1 (917) 371-0563

inquiries@ItalicaPress.com

http://www.italicapress.com

Types: Fiction; Nonfiction; Poetry; Scripts; Translations
Subjects: Arts; Drama; History; Travel
Markets: Adult

Publishes English translations of medieval, Renaissance and early-modern texts, historical travel, English translations of modern Italian fiction, dual-language poetry, drama, and a series of studies in art and history.

P0457 Itchy Coo
Publishing Imprint

Book Publisher: Black & White Publishing Ltd **(P0098)**

P0458 Ivy Kids
Publishing Imprint

Book Publisher: The Quarto Group, Inc. **(P0739)**

P0459 Ivy Press
Publishing Imprint

Book Publisher: The Quarto Group, Inc. **(P0739)**

P0460 J. Garnet Miller
Publishing Imprint

Book Publisher: Cressrelles Publishing Co. Ltd **(P0197)**

P0461 J.A. Allen
Publishing Imprint
The Stable Block, Crowood Lane, Ramsbury, Wiltshire, SN8 2HR
United Kingdom
Tel: +44 (0) 1672 520280

enquiries@crowood.com

http://www.crowood.com

Book Publishers: The Crowood Press; Robert Hale Publishers

Types: Nonfiction
Subjects: How To
Markets: Adult

Send: Query
Don't send: Full text

Publishes books on horses and horsemanship. Send query by post, fax, or email. No unsolicited mss.

Editor: Lesley Gowers

P0462 Jacar Press
Book Publisher
6617 Deerview Trl, Durham, NC 27712
United States
Tel: +1 (919) 810-2863

jacarassist@gmail.com

http://jacarpress.com

Types: Poetry
Subjects: Literary
Markets: Adult

Send: Full text

Publisher of full-length and chapbook collections of poetry. Accepts submissions through annual competitions only ($15 submission fee). Also publishes online magazine.

P0463 Jacaranda Books Art Music Ltd
Book Publisher
27 Old Gloucester Street, London, WC1N 3AX
United Kingdom

office@jacarandabooksartmusic.co.uk

https://www.jacarandabooksartmusic.co.uk

Types: Fiction
Subjects: Arts; Autobiography; Beauty; Commercial; Crime; Fashion; History; Literary; Music; Photography; Science Fiction; Women's Interests
Markets: Adult

Send: Query
Don't send: Full text

Publishes adult fiction and nonfiction, including crime, romance, illustrated books, biography, memoir, and autobiography. Particularly interested in books where the central character or theme relates to minority groups and/or has strong female protagonists. Also interested in original works from or about African, African-American, Caribbean and black British artists working in the fields of photography, fine art, fashion, and contemporary and modern art, and artists of calibre from the soul, blues, R&B and reggae traditions. Send query with writer CV, detailed synopsis, and 20-30 pages of consecutive text. See website for full submission guidelines.

Publisher: Valerie Brandes

P0464 James Clarke & Co.
Book Publisher
PO Box 60, Cambridge, CB1 2NT
United Kingdom
Tel: +44 (0) 1223 366951
Fax: +44 (0) 1223 366951

publishing@jamesclarke.co.uk

http://www.jamesclarke.co

Types: Nonfiction
Formats: Reference
Subjects: Religion
Markets: Academic

Send: Query
Don't send: Full text

Publishes nonfiction and reference for the academic market on mainly theological subject matter. Download new book proposal form from website and return by post, fax, or email. See website for full guidelines.

Publishing Imprint: The Lutterworth Press

P0465 Jamii Publishing
Book Publisher
United States

submissions@jamiipublishing.com

http://www.jamiipublishing.com

Types: Fiction; Nonfiction; Poetry
Formats: Short Fiction
Subjects: Literary
Markets: Adult; Children's

Closed to approaches.

Publishes literary poetry, including slipstream, hybrid, children's poetry, multiple authors, short story, lyric essay, visual/textual.

Manuscripts must be a part of a larger community based project. No royalties.

Editor: Nikia Chaney

P0466 Jane's Information Group
Book Publisher
Sentinel House, 163 Brighton Road, Coulsdon, Surrey, CR5 2YH
United Kingdom

https://www.janes.com

Types: Nonfiction
Formats: Reference
Subjects: Warfare
Markets: Adult

Publisher of magazines, books, reference works, online material, and yearbooks related to defence, aerospace, security, and transport topics.

P0467 Jewish Lights Publishing
Publishing Imprint
4507 Charlotte Ave, Suite 100, Nashville, TN 37209
United States
Tel: +1 (615) 255-2665
Fax: +1 (615) 255-5081

submissions@turnerpublishing.com

http://jewishlights.com

Book Publisher: Turner Publishing (**P0879**)

Types: Fiction; Nonfiction
Subjects: Crime; History; Men's Interests; Mystery; Philosophy; Religion; Science Fiction; Women's Interests
Markets: Adult; Children's; Young Adult

Publishes work about the unity and community of the Jewish People and the relevance of Judaism to everyday life. Send submissions by email.

P0468 Joffe Books Ltd
Book Publisher
United Kingdom

submissions@joffebooks.com

http://www.joffebooks.com

Types: Fiction
Subjects: Crime; Mystery; Suspense; Thrillers
Markets: Adult

Send: Full text

Publishes full-length crime fiction, mysteries, and thrillers. No kids books, sci-fi, nonfiction, conspiracy theories, or erotic. Send query by email with complete ms as an attachment, a synopsis in the body of the email, and 100 words about yourself. Include "submission" in the subject line. Reply not guaranteed unless interested. See website for full guidelines.

Editor: Jasper Joffe

P0469 John Blake Publishing
Book Publisher
United Kingdom
Tel: +44 (0) 20 3770 8888

hello@blake.co.uk

https://johnblakebooks.com

Types: Fiction; Nonfiction
Formats: Film Scripts; TV Scripts
Subjects: Autobiography; Business; Comedy / Humour; Commercial; Cookery; Crime; Entertainment; Health; History; Legal; Music; Nature; Politics; Science; Self Help; Sport; Travel; Warfare
Markets: Adult

How to send: Through a literary agent

Considers submissions via a literary agent only.

Publishing Imprint: Dino Books

P0470 John Murray (Publishers) Ltd
Book Publisher
Carmelite House, 50 Victoria Embankment, London, EC4Y 0DZ
United Kingdom
Tel: +44 (0) 20 3122 6777

https://www.hodder.co.uk

Book Publisher: Hodder & Stoughton Ltd (**P0411**)

Types: Fiction; Nonfiction
Markets: Adult

How to send: Through a literary agent

Accepts approaches through literary agents only.

P0471 John Scognamiglio Books
Publishing Imprint

Book Publisher: Kensington Publishing Corp. (**P0488**)

P0472 Jonathan Cape
Publishing Imprint
United Kingdom

https://www.penguin.co.uk/company/publishers/vintage/jonathan-cape.html

Book Publisher: Vintage (**P0934**)

Types: Fiction; Nonfiction; Poetry
Markets: Adult

Send: Query
Don't send: Full text

Renowned for its prizewinning fiction, nonfiction, poetry and graphic novels.

P0473 Jordan Publishing
Book Publisher
21 St Thomas Street, Bristol, BS1 6JS
United Kingdom

http://www.lexisnexis.co.uk/products/jordan-publishing.html

Book Publisher: LexisNexis (**P0518**)

Types: Nonfiction
Subjects: Legal
Markets: Professional

Legal publisher specialising in family law, company and commercial, insolvency, private client, civil litigation and personal injury.

P0474 Josef Weinberger Ltd
Book Publisher
12-14 Mortimer Street, London, W1T 3JJ
United Kingdom
Tel: +44 (0) 20 7580 2827
Fax: +44 (0) 20 7436 9616

general.info@jwmail.co.uk

http://www.josef-weinberger.com

Types: Scripts
Formats: Theatre Scripts
Markets: Adult

Publishes theatre scripts for musicals, plays, pantomimes, operas, and operettas.

P0475 JournalStone Publishing
Book Publisher
United States

journalstone.submissions@gmail.com

https://journalstone.com

Types: Fiction
Subjects: Commercial; Gothic; Literary
Markets: Adult

Closed to approaches.

Publishes horror in all its forms – from literary to weird, Gothic to psychological, and (almost) everything in between.

P0476 JourneyForth
Book Publisher
1430 Wade Hampton Boulevard, Greenville, SC 29609-5046
United States
Tel: +1 (800) 845-5731

journeyforth@bjupress.com

http://www.bjupress.com

Types: Fiction; Nonfiction
Subjects: Adventure; Biography; History; Mystery; Nature; Religion; Sport; Westerns
Markets: Adult; Children's; Young Adult

Publishes adult nonfiction and children's and youth fiction, all from a conservative Christian worldview.

Editor: Nancy Lohr

P0477 Judson Press
Book Publisher
1075 First Avenue, King of Prussia, PA 19406
United States
Tel: +1 (800) 458-3766
Fax: +1 (610) 768-2107

acquisitions@judsonpress.com

https://www.judsonpress.com

Types: Nonfiction
Subjects: Religion
Markets: Adult

Publishes adult nonfiction for Christians.

P0478 Kamera Books
Publishing Imprint
United Kingdom

Book Publisher: Oldcastle Books Group
(**P0635**)

P0479 Karnak House
Book Publisher
United Kingdom

karnakhouse@aol.com

https://www.karnakhouse.co.uk

Types: Fiction; Nonfiction; Poetry
Subjects: Anthropology; Culture; History;
Literary Criticism; Music; Philosophy;
Politics; Religion; Science; Women's Interests
Markets: Adult; Children's

Publisher of books on the culture and history
of African civilisations and cultures
worldwide.

P0480 The Kates Hill Press
Book Publisher
39 Cowley Drive, Dudley, West Midlands,
DY1 2SS
United Kingdom
Tel: +44 (0) 1384 254719

kateshillpress1992@gmail.com

https://kateshillpress.com

Types: Fiction; Nonfiction; Poetry
Formats: Short Fiction
Subjects: Autobiography; Comedy / Humour;
Crime; History; Sociology; Sport
Markets: Adult

Small independent publisher producing short
runs of fiction and social history books with a
west midlands theme or by a west midlands
writer. Also publishes booklets of poetry and
dialect verse by Black Country/West Midlands
poets.

P0481 Katherine Tegen Books
Publishing Imprint

Book Publisher: HarperCollins (**P0378**)

P0482 Kathy Dawson Books
Publishing Imprint
Penguin Group, 375 Hudson Street, New York,
NY 10014
United States

http://kathydawsonbooks.tumblr.com

Book Publishers: Penguin Group (USA);
Penguin Young Readers Group (**P0688**)

Types: Fiction
Markets: Children's; Young Adult

Send: Query
Don't send: Full text

Publishes middle grade and young adult
fiction. Submit query by post only, with first
10 pages and details of any relevant publishing
history. Do not include SASE – all
submissions are recycled. Response only if
interested.

P0483 Kaya Press
Book Publisher
c/o USC ASE, 3620 S. Vermont Ave KAP
462, Los Angeles, CA 90089
United States

acquisitions@kaya.com

http://www.kaya.com

Types: Fiction; Nonfiction; Poetry
Subjects: Arts; Culture; Literary Criticism
Markets: Adult

Send: Full text

Independent not-for-profit publisher of Asian
and Pacific Islander diasporic literature,
publishing fiction, poetry, critical essays, art,
and culture. Send complete MS by email as
Word or PDF attachment, with contact info,
description of project, why you feel this
publisher is appropriate, and list of any
previous publications / awards. See website for
full details.

P0484 Kelpies
Publishing Imprint
United Kingdom

floris@florisbooks.co.uk

https://discoverkelpies.co.uk
https://www.facebook.com/DiscoverKelpies/
https://twitter.com/DiscoverKelpies

Book Publisher: Floris Books (**P0293**)

CHILDREN'S
Fiction
　Novels: Adventure; Comedy / Humour;
　Fantasy; Ghost Stories; Magic; Romance;
　Science Fiction; Scotland; Thrillers;
　Traditional
　Picture Books: General, and in
　particular: Scotland
Nonfiction
　Nonfiction Books: Education; History;
　Scotland; Sport

　Picture Books: General, and in
　particular: Animals; Scotland

Publishes Scottish books for children
everywhere. Does not accept unsolicited
submissions direct from authors, unless they
are from under-represented communities.
Welcomes submissions from literary agents.

P0485 Kenilworth Press
Publishing Imprint
Quiller Publishing, Wykey House, Wykey,
Shrewsbury, Shropshire, SY4 1JA
United Kingdom
Tel: +44 (0) 1939 261616

info@quillerbooks.com

https://www.quillerpublishing.com/product-
category/equestrian-kenilworth-press

Book Publisher: Quiller Publishing Ltd

Nonfiction > *Nonfiction Books*
　Equestrian; Horses

Send: Synopsis; Writing sample; Market info;
Author bio; Self-Addressed Stamped Envelope
(SASE)
How to send: Email; Post

Equestrian publisher publishing nonfiction.
Not accepting poetry or novels.

Editor: John Beaton

P0486 Kensington Hardcover
Publishing Imprint

Book Publisher: Kensington Publishing Corp.
(**P0488**)

P0487 Kensington Mass-Market
Publishing Imprint

Book Publisher: Kensington Publishing Corp.
(**P0488**)

P0488 Kensington Publishing Corp.
Book Publisher
119 West 40th Street, New York, NY 10018
United States
Tel: +1 (800) 221-2647

jscognamiglio@kensingtonbooks.com

http://www.kensingtonbooks.com

Types: Fiction; Nonfiction
Subjects: Autobiography; Business;
Commercial; Contemporary; Crime; Fantasy;
Health; History; Lifestyle; Literary; Mystery;
Romance; Science Fiction; Self Help;
Suspense; Thrillers; Warfare; Women's
Interests
Markets: Adult

Send: Query
Don't send: Full text

No children's, young adult, or poetry. Send query only, in the body of the email. No attachments. See website for full guidelines.

Editor: John Scognamiglio

Publishing Imprints: Aphrodisia (*P0043*); Brava (*P0123*); Citadel Press (*P0172*); Dafina (*P0208*); Holloway House (*P0416*); John Scognamiglio Books (*P0471*); KTeen (*P0503*); KTeen Dafina (*P0504*); Kensington Hardcover (*P0486*); Kensington Mass-Market (*P0487*); Kensington Trade Paperback (*P0489*); Lyle Stuart Books (*P0548*); Lyrical Caress (*P0550*); Lyrical Liaison (*P0551*); Lyrical Press (**P0552**); Lyrical Shine (*P0553*); Lyrical Underground (*P0554*); Pinnacle (*P0704*); Rebel Base Books (*P0752*); Zebra; Zebra Shout (*P0989*)

P0489 Kensington Trade Paperback
Publishing Imprint

Book Publisher: Kensington Publishing Corp. (**P0488**)

P0490 Kent State University Press
Book Publisher
1118 Library, PO Box 5190, Kent, OH 44242
United States
Tel: +1 (330) 672-7913
Fax: +1 (330) 672-3104

ksupress@kent.edu

http://www.kentstateuniversitypress.com

Types: Nonfiction
Subjects: Arts; Biography; History; Literary Criticism
Markets: Academic

Publishes general nonfiction, but particularly scholarly works in the fields of American studies, biography, history, and literary studies.

P0491 Kenyon-Deane
Publishing Imprint

Book Publisher: Cressrelles Publishing Co. Ltd (**P0197**)

P0492 Kernpunkt Press
Book Publisher
United States

http://www.kernpunktpress.com

Types: Fiction; Nonfiction
Formats: Short Fiction
Subjects: History; Literary; Science Fiction
Markets: Adult

Send: Query
Don't send: Full text

Independent publisher of literary fiction. Values art over entertainment. Send

submission through online submission system. $10 submission fee.

Editor-in-Chief: Jesi Buell

P0493 Kettillonia
Book Publisher
Sidlaw House, South Street, NEWTYLE, Angus, PH12 8UQ
United Kingdom
Tel: +44 (0) 1828 650615

james@kettillonia.co.uk

http://www.kettillonia.co.uk

Types: Fiction; Nonfiction; Poetry
Formats: Short Fiction
Subjects: Comedy / Humour; History; Literary; Literature
Markets: Adult

Publisher of pamphlets containing original, adventurous, neglected and rare Scottish writing.

Editor: James Robertson

P0494 King Dragon Press
Publishing Imprint

Book Publisher: Cedar Fort (**P0155**)

P0495 Kirkbride Bible Company
Book Publisher
1102 Deloss Street, Indianapolis, IN 46203
United States
Tel: +1 (800) 428-4385
Fax: +1 (317) 633-1444

info@kirkbride.com

http://www.kirkbride.com

Types: Nonfiction
Formats: Reference
Subjects: Religion
Markets: Adult

Publisher of bible reference titles.

P0496 Klutz
Publishing Imprint

Book Publisher: Scholastic (**P0790**)

P0497 Kluwer Law International
Book Publisher
250 Waterloo Road, First Floor, London, SE1 8RD
United Kingdom

https://kluwerlawonline.com

Book Publisher: Wolters Kluwer (**P0979**)

Types: Nonfiction
Subjects: Legal
Markets: Professional

Send: Query
Don't send: Full text

Publisher of international law titles, including looseleafs and journals. Welcomes unsolicited synopses and ideas on relevant topics.

P0498 Knopf Doubleday Publishing Group
Book Publisher
United States

http://knopfdoubleday.com

Book Publisher: Penguin Random House (**P0683**)

Fiction > *Novels*

Nonfiction > *Nonfiction Books*

Publishing Imprints: Alfred A. Knopf (*P0027*); Anchor Books (*P0036*); Black Lizard (*P0102*); Doubleday (*P0234*); Everyman's Library (*P0266*); Nan A. Talese (**P0601**); Pantheon (*P0661*); Schocken Books (*P0789*); Vintage Books (*P0935*)

P0499 Kogan Page Ltd
Book Publisher
45 Gee Street, 2nd Floor, London, EC1V 3RS
United Kingdom
Tel: +44 (0) 20 7278 0433

kpinfo@koganpage.com

https://www.koganpage.com

Types: Nonfiction
Formats: Reference
Subjects: Business; Finance; How To; Technology
Markets: Adult; Professional

Publisher of business management books on training, finance, personnel, small business, industrial relations, etc.

P0500 Kokila
Publishing Imprint
United States

Book Publisher: Penguin Young Readers Group (**P0688**)

P0501 Kore Press
Book Publisher
4207 E. Waverly Street, Tucson, AZ 85712
United States
Tel: +1 (520) 261-2438

https://korepress.org

Types: Fiction; Nonfiction; Poetry
Subjects: Autobiography; Culture; Literary; Literary Criticism
Markets: Adult

Closed to approaches.

Publishes fiction, poetry, nonfiction, hybrid, and cultural criticism. Accepts submissions both through open submission windows and competitions.

Managing Editor: Ann Dernier

P0502 Krause Publications
Publishing Imprint
United States

Book Publisher: Penguin Publishing Group
(P0682)

Types: Nonfiction
Formats: Reference
Subjects: Antiques; Hobbies; How To; Sport
Markets: Adult

Largest publisher of material on hobbies and collectibles in the world. Send query with outline, sample chapter, and description of how your book will make a unique contribution.

P0503 KTeen
Publishing Imprint

Book Publisher: Kensington Publishing Corp.
(P0488)

P0504 KTeen Dafina
Publishing Imprint

Book Publisher: Kensington Publishing Corp.
(P0488)

P0505 Lantana Publishing
Book Publisher
The Oxford Foundry, 3-5 Hythe Bridge Street, Oxford, OX1 2EW
United Kingdom

submissions@lantanapublishing.com

http://www.lantanapublishing.com

Types: Fiction; Nonfiction
Subjects: Contemporary; Culture
Markets: Children's

Send: Full text

Publishes picture books and narrative nonfiction focused on diversity for 4 to 8 year olds up to 500 words (prefers 200-400 words). Particularly interested in contemporary writing with modern-day settings, especially if they feature Black, Asian and Minority Ethnic families. Publishes almost exclusively authors of Black, Asian and Minority Ethnic backgrounds.

P0506 Laurence King Publishing Ltd
Book Publisher
361-373 City Road, London, EC1V 1LR
United Kingdom
Tel: +44 (0) 20 7841 6900
Fax: +44 (0) 20 7841 6910

commissioning@laurenceking.com

https://www.laurenceking.com
https://twitter.com/LaurenceKingPub

https://www.instagram.com/LaurenceKingPub/
https://www.facebook.com/
LaurenceKingPublishing
https://www.pinterest.co.uk/LaurenceKingPub/
https://vimeo.com/laurencekingpublishing
https://www.youtube.com/user/
laurencekingpub

Book Publisher: Hachette UK

ACADEMIC > **Nonfiction** > *Nonfiction Books*
Architecture; Arts; Beauty; Design; Fashion; Films; Music; Nature; Photography; Popular Culture; Popular Science

ADULT > **Nonfiction** > *Nonfiction Books*
Architecture; Arts; Beauty; Design; Fashion; Films; Music; Nature; Photography; Popular Culture; Popular Science

CHILDREN'S > **Nonfiction** > *Illustrated Books*

Send: Query; Synopsis; Market info; Author bio
How to send: Email

Publisher of books on the creative arts. Send proposal by email.

P0507 Lawrence Hill Books
Publishing Imprint
Chicago Review Press, 814 North Franklin Street, Chicago, Illinois 60610
United States
Tel: +1 (312) 337-0747

ytaylor@chicagoreviewpress.com

http://www.chicagoreviewpress.com

Book Publisher: Chicago Review Press
(P0164)

Types: Nonfiction
Subjects: Politics; Women's Interests
Markets: Adult

Send: Query
Don't send: Full text

Publishes nonfiction on progressive politics, civil and human rights, feminism, and topics of interest to African Americans and other underrepresented groups. Send query by email.

Editor: Yuval Taylor

P0508 Leapfrog Press
Book Publisher
PO Box 505, Fredonia, NY 14063
United States

acquisitions@leapfrogpress.com

http://www.leapfrogpress.com

Types: Fiction; Nonfiction; Poetry
Formats: Short Fiction
Subjects: Literary
Markets: Adult; Children's; Young Adult

Send: Query
Don't send: Full text

Publisher with an eclectic list of fiction, poetry, and nonfiction, including paperback originals of adult and middle-grade fiction and nonfiction. Closed to general submissions between January 15 and around June 15 each year, but accepts adult, young adult (YA) and middle grade (MG) novels, novellas, and short story collections through its annual fiction contest until May 1. Submit online through online submission system.

P0509 Leaping Dog Press
Book Publisher
United States

editor@leapingdogpress.com

http://www.leapingdogpress.com

Types: Fiction; Poetry; Translations
Subjects: Comedy / Humour; Literary
Markets: Adult

Closed to approaches.

Publishes accessible, edgy, witty, and challenging contemporary poetry, fiction, and works in translation. Not accepting submissions as at September 2019. Check website for current status.

P0510 Leaping Hare Press
Publishing Imprint

Book Publisher: The Quarto Group, Inc.
(P0739)

P0511 Legend Press
Book Publisher
107-111 Fleet Street, London, EC4A 2AB
United Kingdom
Tel: +44 (0) 20 7936 9941

submissions@legend-paperbooks.co.uk

http://www.legendpress.co.uk

Types: Fiction
Subjects: Commercial; Contemporary; Crime; History
Markets: Adult

Send: Query
Don't send: Full text

Publishes a diverse list of contemporary adult novels. No children's books, poetry or travel writing. See website for full submission guidelines and online submission system.

Editor: Tom Chalmers

P0512 Leo Cooper
Publishing Imprint

Book Publisher: Pen & Sword Books Ltd
(P0674)

P0513 Lerner Digital
Publishing Imprint

Book Publisher: Lerner Publishing Group
(P0514)

P0514 Lerner Publishing Group

Book Publisher
241 First Avenue North, Minneapolis, MN
55401-1607
United States
Tel: +1 (800) 328-4929
Fax: +1 (800) 332-1132

custserve@lernerbooks.com

https://lernerbooks.com
https://www.facebook.com/lernerbooks
https://twitter.com/lernerbooks

CHILDREN'S
  Fiction
    Audiobooks; *Ebooks*; *Graphic Novels*;
    Middle Grade; *Novels*; *Picture Books*
  Nonfiction
    Audiobooks; *Ebooks*; *Nonfiction Books*
YOUNG ADULT
  Fiction
    Audiobooks; *Ebooks*; *Novels*
  Nonfiction
    Audiobooks; *Ebooks*; *Nonfiction Books*

How to send: Through a literary agent; By referral

Publishes fiction and nonfiction for children and young adults. No submissions or queries from unagented or unreferred authors.

: Zelda Wagner

Publishing Imprints: Carolrhoda Books; Carolrhoda Lab (*P0150*); Darby Creek (*P0214*); Ediciones Lerner (*P0249*); First Avenue Editions; Graphic Universe (*P0337*); Kar-Ben Publishing; Lerner Digital (*P0513*); Lerner Publications; LernerClassroom (*P0515*); Millbrook Press (*P0588*); Twenty-First Century Books (*P0883*); Zest Books (*P0992*)

P0515 LernerClassroom

Publishing Imprint

Book Publisher: Lerner Publishing Group (**P0514**)

P0516 Les Figues Press

Book Publisher
6671 Sunset Blvd., Suite 1521, Los Angeles, CA 90028
United States
Tel: +1 (323) 734-4732

info@lesfigues.com

http://www.lesfigues.com

Types: Fiction; Poetry
Formats: Short Fiction
Markets: Adult

Send: Full text

Publishes fiction and poetry. Accepts submissions through its annual contest only ($25 entry fee). Accepts poetry, novellas, innovative novels, anti-novels, short story

collections, lyric essays, hybrids, and all forms not otherwise specified. Submit via form on website.

P0517 Lewis Masonic

Publishing Imprint

Book Publisher: Ian Allan Publishing Ltd (**P0429**)

P0518 LexisNexis

Book Publisher
Lexis House, 30 Farringdon Street, EC4A 4HH
United Kingdom
Tel: +44 (0) 330 161 1234

customer.services@lexisnexis.co.uk

http://www.lexisnexis.co.uk

Types: Nonfiction
Formats: Reference
Subjects: Legal
Markets: Professional

Publishes books, looseleafs, journals etc. for legal professionals.

Book Publisher: Jordan Publishing (**P0473**)

P0519 LexisNexis Canada

Book Publisher
111 Gordon Baker Road, Suite 900, Toronto, ON, M2H 3R1
Canada
Tel: +1 (800) 668-6481

productdevelopment@lexisnexis.ca

https://www.lexisnexis.ca

Types: Nonfiction
Formats: Reference
Subjects: Business; Finance; Legal
Markets: Professional

Send: Query
Don't send: Full text

Publishes books for the professional legal, business, and accountancy markets. Send query by email. See website for full guidelines on submitting a proposal.

P0520 Liberalis

Publishing Imprint

Book Publisher: John Hunt Publishing Ltd

P0521 Libraries Unlimited

Publishing Imprint
United States

Book Publisher: ABC-CLIO (**P0016**)

P0522 Lillenas Music

Book Publisher
25 Music Square West, Nashville, TN 37203
United States
Tel: +1 (615) 687-6780
Fax: +1 (615) 252-4831

info@lillenas.com

https://lillenas.com

Types: Nonfiction
Subjects: Music; Religion
Markets: Adult; Children's; Young Adult

Publishes religious music books.

P0523 The Lilliput Press

Book Publisher
62-63 Sitric Road, Arbour Hill, Dublin 7
Ireland

editorial@lilliputpress.ie
contact@lilliputpress.ie

http://www.lilliputpress.ie

Fiction > *Novels*: Ireland

Nonfiction
  Nonfiction Books: Architecture; Arts; Biography; Cultural Criticism; Environment; Food; Genealogy; History; Ireland; Literary Criticism; Literature; Local History; Memoir; Mind, Body, Spirit; Music; Nature; Philosophy; Photography; Travel
  Reference: Ireland

Poetry > *Any Poetic Form*: Ireland

Closed to approaches.

Publishes books broadly focused on Irish themes. Send query by email with one-page synopsis and complete ms or three sample chapters. See website for full guidelines.

P0524 Limitless Publishing

Book Publisher
United States

submissions@limitlesspublishing.com

http://www.limitlesspublishing.net

Types: Fiction; Nonfiction
Subjects: Fantasy; Mystery; Romance; Science Fiction; Suspense; Thrillers; Warfare
Markets: Adult; Young Adult

Send: Query
Don't send: Full text

Send submissions by email with brief bio, writing background and publishing history, social networks used, decsription of your book, and the first four chapters as a Microsoft Word attachment.

P0525 Lincoln First Editions

Publishing Imprint

Book Publisher: The Quarto Group, Inc. (**P0739**)

P0526 Liquid Light Press

Book Publisher
United States

editor@liquidlightpress.com

http://www.liquidlightpress.com

Types: Poetry
Subjects: Literary
Markets: Adult

Publishes poetry chapbooks. Send submissions by email. $25 reading fee per submission.

Editor: Markiah Friedman

P0527 Little Tiger Group
Book Publisher

Publishing Imprint: Little Tiger Press (**P0528**)

P0528 Little Tiger Press
Publishing Imprint
1 The Coda Centre, 189 Munster Road,
London, SW6 6AW
United Kingdom
Tel: +44 (0) 20 7385 6333
Fax: +44 (0) 20 7385 7333

info@littletiger.co.uk

http://www.littletigerpress.com

Book Publisher: Little Tiger Group (**P0527**)

Types: Fiction
Markets: Children's

Closed to approaches.

**Not accepting submissions as at May 2018.
Check website for current status.** Accepts unsolicited MSS up to 750 words. If inside UK include SAE for response (no postage vouchers/coupons); if from outside the UK include email address for response (no material returned). See website for full guidelines. No submissions by email or on disc.

P0529 Little Wing
Publishing Imprint
United Kingdom

https://mangobooks.co.uk/pages/about-mango-books

Book Publisher: Mango Books (**P0562**)

Nonfiction > *Nonfiction Books:* Entertainment

Publishes titles in the entertainment genre.

P0530 Little, Brown
Publishing Imprint

Publishing Imprint: Little, Brown Book Group (**P0532**)

P0531 Little, Brown and Company
Book Publisher
1290 Avenue of the Americas, New York, NY 10104
United States

https://www.littlebrown.com

Book Publisher: Hachette Book Group (**P0346**)

Types: Fiction; Nonfiction
Markets: Adult; Children's

How to send: Through a literary agent

Publishes general fiction and nonfiction for the adult and children's markets. No unsolicited MSS or approaches direct from authors – will only consider approaches from literary agents.

P0532 Little, Brown Book Group
Publishing Imprint
Carmelite House, 50 Victoria Embankment,
LONDON, EC4Y 0DZ
United Kingdom
Tel: +44 (0) 20 3122 7000

info@littlebrown.co.uk

http://www.littlebrown.co.uk

Book Publisher: Hachette UK

Types: Fiction; Nonfiction
Subjects: Autobiography; Comedy / Humour;
Crime; Entertainment; Fantasy; History; How
To; Literary; Literature; Science Fiction;
Thrillers
Markets: Adult; Young Adult

How to send: Through a literary agent

Accepts submissions via agents only.

Book Publisher: Virago Press

Publishing Imprints: Abacus (*P0015*); Atom
(*P0058*); Blackfriars (*P0104*); Constable &
Robinson (*P0184*); Corsair (*P0190*); Dialogue
Books (*P0227*); Fleet (*P0292*); Hachette
Digital (*P0348*); Little, Brown (*P0530*); Orbit;
Piatkus Constable & Robinson (*P0700*);
Sphere (*P0829*); Virago (*P0938*)

P0533 Liverpool University Press
Book Publisher
4 Cambridge Street, Liverpool, L69 7ZU
United Kingdom
Tel: +44 (0) 1517 942233

lup@liv.ac.uk

https://www.liverpooluniversitypress.co.uk

Types: Nonfiction
Subjects: Archaeology; Architecture; Arts;
Culture; History; Literature; Politics; Science
Fiction; Sociology
Markets: Academic

Send: Query
Don't send: Full text

Publishes books and journals, specialising in
Modern Languages, Postcolonial, Slavery and
Migration Studies, Irish History, Labour
History, Science Fiction Studies and Art
History. Download proposal submission form
from website.

Editors: Anthony Cond; Alison Welsby

P0534 Lodestone Books
Publishing Imprint

Book Publisher: John Hunt Publishing Ltd

P0535 LOM ART
Book Publisher
16 Lion Yard, Tremadoc Road, London
United Kingdom

lom.art@mombooks.com

https://www.mombooks.com/lom/

Book Publisher: Michael O'Mara Books Ltd
(**P0586**)

Types: Nonfiction
Markets: Adult; Children's

Send: Query
Don't send: Full text

Publishes illustrated nonfiction for children
and adults. Send query with overview and
synopsis in the body of your email, or by post
with SASE.

Editor: Imogen Williams

P0536 Lonely Planet
Book Publisher
302 DLF City Court, Sikanderpur|Gurgaon
122002
India

https://www.lonelyplanet.com

Types: Nonfiction
Formats: Reference
Subjects: Travel
Markets: Adult

Publishes travel guides.

P0537 Longman
Publishing Imprint

Book Publisher: Pearson (**P0670**)

P0538 Lorenz Books
Publishing Imprint

Book Publisher: Anness Publishing Ltd
(**P0040**)

P0539 Lost Horse Press
Book Publisher
105 Lost Horse Lane, Sandpoint, ID 83864
United States
Tel: +1 (208) 255-4410

losthorsepress@mindspring.com

http://www.losthorsepress.org

Types: Fiction; Poetry
Formats: Short Fiction
Subjects: Literary
Markets: Adult

Send: Full text

Publishes collections of poetry and short
stories, submitted through their annual
competitions (reading fee applies). No general
submissions.

P0540 Lost Lake Folk Art
Publishing Imprint

Book Publisher: Shipwreckt Books Publishing Company (**P0811**)

P0541 Lost Tower Publications
Book Publisher
United Kingdom

http://losttowerpublications.jigsy.com

Types: Fiction; Poetry
Subjects: Adventure; Autobiography; Contemporary; Crime; Experimental; Fantasy; Gothic; Leisure; Lifestyle; Mystery; Science Fiction; Spirituality; Suspense; Thrillers; Women's Interests
Markets: Adult; Children's; Young Adult

Formed in 2011 as part of a poetry book publishing campaign to promote poetry world wide as an attractive and entertaining art form for the twenty first century. We print 3-4 books a year collecting the best photographs and poetry from around the world, to produce high quality books for people to enjoy. Our books are available to buy worldwide either from Amazon or to order through your local bookshop. In March 2013 we published a journey of hope through poems and photographs which have been collected from around the world. The work in this anthology has been collected from every continent of our planet and illustrates ideas of hope from many of the world religions; looks at the different forms hope can take and how hope can always be found if you look carefully into the world which surrounds you.

Author: Rainbow Reed

Editor: Harry Yang

P0542 Louisiana State University Press
Book Publisher
338 Johnston Hall, Louisiana State University, Baton Rouge, LA 7080
United States

https://lsupress.org
https://blog.lsupress.org/
https://www.facebook.com/pages/LSU-Press/38236386996
https://twitter.com/lsupress
https://soundcloud.com/lsupress_and_tsr

ACADEMIC > **Nonfiction** > *Nonfiction Books*
    African American; American Civil War; American History; Archaeology; Architecture; Caribbean History; Culture; Environment; History; Literature; Louisiana; Media; Poetry as a Subject; Roots Music; Social Justice; US Southern States; World War II

ADULT

Nonfiction > *Nonfiction Books*
    Louisiana; US Southern States

Poetry > *Any Poetic Form*

Send: Query; Writing sample; Outline; Author bio; Table of Contents; Market info
How to send: Email attachment

Publishes scholarly monographs and general interest books about Louisiana and the South.

Poetry proposals should include a cover letter, a one-page summary of the work, few sample poems from the work, and a current resume or curriculum vitae.

Proposals for everything except poetry should include a cover letter, working title, table of contents, sample chapters, information about competitive titles, and a resume or curriculum vitae.

P0543 Loyola Classics
Publishing Imprint

Book Publisher: Loyola Press (**P0544**)

P0544 Loyola Press
Book Publisher
3441 North Ashland Avenue, Chicago, IL 60657
United States
Tel: +1 (773) 281-1818
Fax: +1 (773) 281-0152

submissions@loyolapress.com

http://www.loyolapress.org

Types: Nonfiction
Subjects: Religion
Markets: Adult

Send: Query
Don't send: Full text

Catholic publisher of books on Catholic tradition, prayer, and spirituality. Send one-page query email or by post. See website for full guidelines.

Publishing Imprint: Loyola Classics (*P0543*)

P0545 Luath Press Ltd
Book Publisher
543/2 Castlehill, The Royal Mile, Edinburgh, EH1 2ND
United Kingdom
Tel: +44 (0) 131 225 4326

sales@luath.co.uk

http://www.luath.co.uk

Types: Fiction; Nonfiction; Poetry
Subjects: Arts; Beauty; Biography; Crime; Current Affairs; Drama; Fashion; History; Leisure; Lifestyle; Nature; Photography; Politics; Sociology; Sport; Thrillers; Travel
Markets: Adult; Children's; Young Adult

Send: Query
Don't send: Full text

Publishes a range of books, usually with a Scottish connection. Check upcoming publishing schedule on website, and – if you think your book fits – send query with SAE, synopsis up to 250 words, manuscript or sample chapters, author bio, and any other relevant material. See website for full submission guidelines. Approaches by email will not be considered.

Managing Editor: G.H. MacDougall

P0546 Luna Bisonte Prods
Book Publisher
137 Leland Avenue, Columbus OH 43214-7505
United States

bennettjohnm@gmail.com

http://www.johnmbennett.net

Types: Poetry
Subjects: Experimental
Markets: Adult

Publisher of poetry chapbooks. Avant-garde and experimental work only. Send query with brief bio, publishing history, and a few sample poems.

P0547 Luna Press Publishing
Book Publisher
149/4 Morrison Street, Edinburgh, EH3 8AG
United Kingdom

lunapress@outlook.com

http://www.lunapresspublishing.com

Types: Fiction; Nonfiction
Formats: Short Fiction
Subjects: Fantasy; Science Fiction
Markets: Academic; Adult

Send: Query
Don't send: Full text

Publishes Science Fiction, Fantasy, and Dark Fantasy (including their sub-genres). Will consider short stories, novelettes, novellas, novels, graphic novels, academic material. See website for submission guidelines.

P0548 Lyle Stuart Books
Publishing Imprint

Book Publisher: Kensington Publishing Corp. (**P0488**)

P0549 Lyons Press
Publishing Imprint
United Kingdom

Book Publisher: The Globe Pequot Press (**P0324**)

P0550 Lyrical Caress
Publishing Imprint

Book Publisher: Kensington Publishing Corp. (**P0488**)

P0551 Lyrical Liaison
Publishing Imprint

Book Publisher: Kensington Publishing Corp.
(**P0488**)

P0552 Lyrical Press
Publishing Imprint
Kensington Publishing Corp., 119 West 40th
Street, New York, NY 10018
United States

jscognamiglio@kensingtonbooks.com

https://www.kensingtonbooks.com

Book Publisher: Kensington Publishing Corp.
(**P0488**)

Types: Fiction
Subjects: Mystery; Romance; Suspense;
Thrillers; Women's Interests
Markets: Adult

Send: Query
Don't send: Full text

Send query by email with synopsis as
attachment. See website for full list of editors'
emails and interests and approach one editor
only.

Editor: John Scognamiglio

P0553 Lyrical Shine
Publishing Imprint

Book Publisher: Kensington Publishing Corp.
(**P0488**)

P0554 Lyrical Underground
Publishing Imprint

Book Publisher: Kensington Publishing Corp.
(**P0488**)

P0555 Mabecron Books Ltd
Book Publisher
3 Briston Orchard, St Mellion, Saltash,
Cornwall, PL12 6RQ
United Kingdom

sales@mabecronbooks.co.uk

https://mabecronbooks.co.uk

Types: Fiction; Nonfiction
Subjects: Cookery
Markets: Adult; Children's

Send: Full text

Welcomes submissions of books with quality,
style, and saleability. Favours books with a
Cornish theme. Absence of a Cornish theme
will not mean a book is necessarily rejected,
but makes the decision more difficult.
Particularly interested in children's picture
books, cookery, and children's fiction. Send
submissions by post only, with SAE.

P0556 Macmillan Children's Books
Publishing Imprint

Book Publisher: Pan Macmillan (**P0659**)

P0557 Macmillan Collector's Library
Publishing Imprint

Book Publisher: Pan Macmillan (**P0659**)

P0558 Macmillan Education
Book Publisher
United Kingdom

https://www.springernature.com/gp/
macmillaneducation

Book Publisher: Springer Nature (**P0831**)

ACADEMIC > **Nonfiction** > *Nonfiction
Books*: Education

Publishes a wide range of educational
materials for the international market.

P0559 Macmillan Publishers
Book Publisher
175 Fifth Avenue, New York, NY 10010
United States

press.inquiries@macmillan.com

https://us.macmillan.com

Types: Fiction; Nonfiction
Markets: Adult; Children's; Young Adult

How to send: Through a literary agent

US office of international publisher of
hardcover, trade paperback, and paperback
books for adults, children, and teens.

Book Publisher: Macmillan New Writing

Publishing Imprint: St Martin's Press (**P0834**)

P0560 Mad Gleam Press
Book Publisher
482 Alvarado St, Monterey, CA 93940
United States

madgleampress@gmail.com

https://www.madgleampress.com

Types: Fiction; Poetry
Subjects: Literary
Markets: Adult

Closed to approaches.

**Closed to submissions as at June 2019.
Check website for current status.** Publishes
fiction and poetry collections. Particularly
interested in collaborative / transmedia pieces.
Send submissions by email with author bio /
resume.

P0561 Mandrake of Oxford
Book Publisher
PO Box 250, Oxford, OX1 1AP
United Kingdom

mandrake@mandrake.uk.net

http://mandrake.uk.net

Types: Fiction; Nonfiction
Subjects: Arts; Crime; Culture; Erotic; Health;
Horror; Lifestyle; Mystery; Philosophy;
Science Fiction; Self Help; Spirituality
Markets: Adult

Send: Query
Don't send: Full text

Send query by post or by email. May also
include synopsis. See website for full
guidelines, and for examples of the kind of
material published.

P0562 Mango Books
Book Publisher
United Kingdom

https://mangobooks.co.uk

Nonfiction > *Nonfiction Books*
Crime; Mystery

How to send: Email

Publishes nonfiction on crime, detection, and
mystery. Welcomes submissions.

Publishing Imprints: Blue Lamp Books
(**P0110**); Little Wing (**P0529**)

P0563 Manic D Press
Book Publisher
PO Box 410804, San Francisco, CA 94141
United States

mss@manicdpress.com

https://www.manicdpress.com

Types: Fiction; Poetry
Formats: Short Fiction
Markets: Adult; Children's

Send: Query
Don't send: Full text

Before submitting, you must have read at least
one of the publisher's books. You do not need
to have bought one -- they can be borrowed
from libraries -- but you need to have read one.
Prefers email submissions. Send 5-10 poems,
3-5 short stories, a synopsis and one chapter
for novels, a representative sample for graphic
novels, visual art, or children's books.

P0564 Manor House Publishing
Book Publisher
452 Cottingham Crescent, Ancaster ON L9G
3V6
Canada

mbdavie@manor-house.biz

https://manor-house-publishing.com

Types: Fiction; Nonfiction; Poetry
Formats: Short Fiction
Subjects: Biography; Business; Fantasy; New Age; Politics
Markets: Adult; Young Adult

Send: Query
Don't send: Full text

Send query by email only. See website for full guidelines. Response only if interested.

P0565 Mantle
Publishing Imprint

Book Publisher: Pan Macmillan (**P0659**)

P0566 Mantra
Publishing Imprint

Publishing Imprint: O-Books

P0567 Mantra Books
Publishing Imprint

Book Publisher: John Hunt Publishing Ltd

P0568 Mantra Lingua Ltd
Book Publisher
Global House, 303 Ballards Lane, London, N12 8NP
United Kingdom
Tel: +44 (0) 20 8445 5123
Fax: +44 (0) 20 8446 7745

info@mantralingua.com

http://www.mantralingua.com

Types: Fiction; Nonfiction; Translations
Markets: Children's

Send: Full text

Multilingual educational publishers of nonfiction and picture books for children up to 12 years. 1,400 words maximum (800 for children up to 7). All books are print products which are sound enabled, playing back audio narrations or music, etc. Send submissions by email. See website for more details.

P0569 Margaret River Press
Book Publisher
PO Box 47, Witchcliffe, WA 6286
Australia
Tel: +61 (0) 8 9757 6009

info@margaretriverpress.com

https://margaretriverpress.com

Types: Fiction; Nonfiction; Poetry
Formats: Short Fiction
Subjects: Autobiography; Leisure; Lifestyle
Markets: Adult

Closed to approaches.

Small press based in Australia. Closed to submissions as at December 2019.

P0570 Marion Boyars Publishers
Book Publisher
26 Parke Road, London, SW13 9NG
United Kingdom

catheryn@marionboyars.com

http://www.marionboyars.co.uk

Types: Fiction; Nonfiction
Formats: Film Scripts; Theatre Scripts
Subjects: Anthropology; Autobiography; Culture; Drama; Literary Criticism; Music; Philosophy; Psychology; Sociology; Women's Interests
Markets: Adult; Children's

Not accepting new submissions as at March 2020. Check website for current status.

Editor: Catheryn Kilgarriff

P0571 Marsh Hawk Press
Book Publisher
PO Box 206, East Rockway, NY 11518-0206
United States

https://marshhawkpress.org

Types: Poetry
Subjects: Literary
Markets: Adult

Send: Full text

Publishes poetry chapbooks submitted through its three national poetry prizes (submission fees apply).

P0572 Martin Books
Book Publisher

Book Publisher: Simon & Schuster UK Limited (**P0813**)

P0573 Martin Sisters Publishing
Book Publisher
United States

submissions@martinsisterspublishing.com

http://www.martinsisterspublishing.com

Types: Fiction; Nonfiction
Formats: Short Fiction
Subjects: Fantasy; Religion; Science Fiction; Self Help
Markets: Adult; Children's; Young Adult

Send: Query
Don't send: Full text

Accepts queries for all genres of fiction, including science fiction and fantasy, and nonfiction, including self-help. Submissions may include Christian fiction, inspirational, collections of stories. No poetry, torrid or any books containing extreme violence. Send query by email with marketing plan and (for fiction) 5-10 pages in the body of the email. No attachments. See website for full guidelines.

P0574 Marvel Comics
Book Publisher
1290 Avenue of the Americas, New York, NY 10104
United States
Tel: +1 (212) 576-4000

https://www.marvel.com

Types: Fiction
Subjects: Adventure; Comedy / Humour; Fantasy; Horror; Science Fiction
Markets: Adult; Children's; Young Adult

Publisher of action comics.

P0575 MC Press
Book Publisher
3695 W. Quail Heights Court, Boise, ID 83703-3861
United States
Tel: +1 (208) 629-7275 Ext. 502

agrubb@mcpressonline.com

http://www.mcpressonline.com

Types: Nonfiction
Subjects: How To; Technology
Markets: Professional

Send: Query
Don't send: Full text

Publisher of computer books (IBM technologies) aimed at midrange IT professionals. Send proposals by email.

Editor: Anne Grub

P0576 Mcbooks Press
Publishing Imprint
United States

Book Publisher: The Globe Pequot Press (**P0324**)

P0577 McDougal Littell Inc.
Book Publisher

Book Publisher: Houghton Mifflin Harcourt (**P0421**)

P0578 McGraw-Hill Education
Book Publisher
PO Box 182605, Columbus, OH 43218
United States
Tel: +1 (800) 338-3987
Fax: +1 (800) 953-8691

https://www.mheducation.com

Types: Nonfiction
Formats: Film Scripts; Theatre Scripts
Subjects: Arts; Business; Health; History; Legal; Music; Politics; Psychology; Science; Sociology; Technology
Markets: Academic

Publishes a wide range of nonfiction educational books.

Book Publisher: Open University Press
(**P0641**)

P0579 McSweeney's McMullens
Publishing Imprint

Book Publisher: McSweeney's Publishing
(**P0580**)

P0580 McSweeney's Publishing
Book Publisher
849 Valencia St., San Francisco, CA 94110
United States
Tel: +1 (415) 642-5609

custservice@mcsweeneys.net

https://www.mcsweeneys.net

Types: Fiction; Nonfiction; Poetry
Subjects: Arts; Comedy / Humour; Cookery
Markets: Adult; Children's

Send: Full text

Accepts electronic submissions of complete manuscripts only (except in the case of cookbooks, which may be submitted as complete mss or proposals). Not currently accepting poetry submissions. See website for full details.

Publishing Imprint: McSweeney's McMullens
(**P0579**)

P0581 Melbourne University Publishing Ltd
Book Publisher
Level 1, 715 Swanston Street, Carlton, Victoria, 3053
Australia
Tel: +61 (0) 3 9035 3333
Fax: +61 (0) 3 9342 0399

mup-submissions@unimelb.edu.au

https://www.mup.com.au

Types: Nonfiction
Subjects: Arts; Autobiography; Crime; Design; History; Lifestyle; Literature; Politics; Science; Sociology; Sport
Markets: Academic; Adult

Publishes nonfiction only. No fiction, children's literature, or poetry. Send submissions by email only. See website for full submission guidelines.

P0582 Mentor Books
Book Publisher
43 Furze Road, Sandyford Industrial Estate, Dublin 18
Ireland
Tel: 01 2952112
Fax: 01 295 2114

admin@mentorbooks.ie

http://www.mentorbooks.ie

Types: Nonfiction
Subjects: Biography; Business; Comedy / Humour; Crime; History; Politics; Science; Sport
Markets: Academic; Adult

Publishes educational books and general nonfiction of Irish interest.

P0583 Merlin Unwin Books
Book Publisher
Palmers House, 7 Corve Street, Ludlow, Shropshire, SY8 1DB
United Kingdom
Tel: +44 (0) 1584 877456

books@merlinunwin.co.uk

http://www.merlinunwin.co.uk

Types: Nonfiction
Subjects: Autobiography; Comedy / Humour; Cookery; Leisure; Nature; Sport
Markets: Adult

Publishes books on the countryside and countryside pursuits, covering such topics as nature, fishing, shooting, etc.

P0584 Messianic Jewish Publishers
Book Publisher
6120 Day Long Lane, Clarksville, MD 21029
United States
Tel: +1 (410) 531-6644

Lisa@MessianicJewish.net

http://www.messianicjewish.net

Types: Fiction; Nonfiction
Subjects: Religion
Markets: Adult

Send: Query
Don't send: Full text

Publishes books which address Jewish evangelism; the Jewish roots of Christianity; Messianic Judaism; Israel; the Jewish People. Publishes mainly nonfiction, but some fiction. See website for full submission guidelines.

P0585 Michael Joseph
Book Publisher
80 Strand, London, WC2R 0RL
United Kingdom
Tel: +44 (0) 20 7139 3000

https://www.penguin.co.uk/company/publishers/michael-joseph.html

Book Publishers: Penguin Random House
(**P0683**); Penguin Random House UK (**P0685**)
Types: Fiction; Nonfiction
Subjects: Autobiography; Commercial; Cookery; Crime; Lifestyle; Thrillers; Women's Interests
Markets: Adult

How to send: Through a literary agent

Publishes women's fiction, crime, thrillers, cookery, memoirs and lifestyle books. Accepts submissions through literary agents only.

P0586 Michael O'Mara Books Ltd
Book Publisher
16 Lion Yard, Tremadoc Road, London, SW4 7NQ
United Kingdom
Tel: +44 (0) 20 7720 8643
Fax: +44 (0) 20 7627 3041

enquiries@mombooks.com

https://www.mombooks.com

Types: Nonfiction
Subjects: Biography; Comedy / Humour; History
Markets: Adult; Children's

Send: Full text

Independent publisher dealing in general nonfiction, royal and celebrity biographies, humour, and anthologies, and books for children through its imprint (including quirky nonfiction, humour, novelty, picture, and board books). Welcomes ideas, and prefers synopses and sample text to unsolicited mss. No fiction. See website for full details.

Book Publisher: LOM ART (**P0535**)

Publishing Imprint: Buster Books (**P0137**)

P0587 Michelin Maps and Guides
Book Publisher
The Dairy, Munden Estate, Watford, Hertfordshire, WD25 8PZ
United Kingdom
Tel: +44 (0) 1923 205247

themichelinguide-gbirl@michelin.com

https://travel.michelin.co.uk

Types: Nonfiction
Formats: Reference
Subjects: Travel
Markets: Adult

Publishes travel guides; maps; atlases; and hotel and restaurant guides.

P0588 Millbrook Press
Publishing Imprint

Book Publisher: Lerner Publishing Group
(**P0514**)

P0589 Minotaur
Publishing Imprint

Publishing Imprint: St Martin's Press (**P0834**)

P0590 Mirror Books
Book Publisher
Northern & Shell Building, 10 Lower Thames Street, London, EC3R 6EN

United Kingdom
Tel: +44 (0) 20 7293 3740

submissions@mirrorbooks.co.uk

https://mirrorbooks.co.uk

Types: Fiction; Nonfiction
Subjects: Autobiography; Crime; Drama
Markets: Adult

Closed to approaches.

Accepts submissions from new and existing
authors for fiction and nonfiction. Interested in
real life, memoir, crime, passion, and human
drama. Approach by email or by post,
including three draft chapters, the genre of
your book, and your target market. See website
for more details.

P0591 Moon Books
Publishing Imprint
Worthing, UK
United Kingdom

office1@jhpbooks.net

https://www.johnhuntpublishing.com/moon-
books/

Book Publisher: John Hunt Publishing Ltd

Types: Nonfiction
Subjects: Religion
Markets: Adult

Send: Full text

What is Paganism? A religion, a spirituality, an
alternative belief system, nature worship? You
can find support for all these definitions (and
many more) in dictionaries, encyclopedias, and
text books of religion, but subscribe to any one
and the truth will evade you. Above all
Paganism is a creative pursuit, an encounter
with reality, an exploration of meaning and an
expression of the soul. Druids, Heathens,
Wiccans and others, all contribute their
insights and literary riches to the Pagan
tradition. We invite you to begin or to deepen
your own encounter, right here, right now.

Authors: Cyndi Brannen; Morgan Daimler;
Melusine Draco; Jane Meredith; Rachel
Patterson; Emma Restall-Orr; Llyn Roberts;
Elen Sentier

P0592 More Shoots More Leaves
Publishing Imprint

Book Publisher: Five Leaves Publications
(**P0289**)

P0593 Morrow Gift
Publishing Imprint

Book Publisher: HarperCollins (**P0378**)

P0594 Motorbooks
Publishing Imprint

Book Publisher: The Quarto Group, Inc.
(**P0739**)

P0595 Mountaineers Books
Book Publisher
1001 SW Klickitat Way, Suite 201, Seattle,
WA 98134
United States
Tel: +1 (206) 223-6303
Fax: +1 (206) 223-6306

submissions@mountaineersbooks.org

https://www.mountaineers.org

Types: Nonfiction
Subjects: Adventure; Leisure; Nature; Travel
Markets: Adult

Send: Query
Don't send: Full text

Publishes books on adventure travel, biking,
camping, climbing, conservation,
environment/nature, hiking, mountaineering,
mountaineering literature, natural history,
outdoor adventure, paddle sports (canoeing,
kayaking, SUP), safety/first aid, skiing (alpine,
Nordic, boarding), snowshoeing, surfing,
walking, and wilderness skills. Imprint
publishes books on sustainable foods, urban
and wilderness foraging, organic/sustainable
gardening, wildlife gardening, urban farming,
general wildlife, natural living, and general
outdoor-related gift topics. No fiction,
children's books, general tourist/travel guides,
or guides dealing with hunting, fishing,
snowmobiling, horseback riding, or organised
spectator sports. Send proposal or complete ms
by email. See website for full guidelines.

Publishing Imprint: Skipstone (*P0816*)

P0596 Mud Pie Books
Book Publisher
43 Leckford Road, Oxford, OX2 6HY
United Kingdom
Tel: +44 (0) 7985 935320

info@mudpiebooks.com

http://mudpiebooks.com

Types: Nonfiction
Subjects: Religion
Markets: Adult

Publishes books about Buddhism, and books
for Buddhists.

P0597 Muddy Boots
Publishing Imprint
United States

Book Publisher: The Globe Pequot Press
(**P0324**)

P0598 Mudlark
Publishing Imprint
United Kingdom

Book Publisher: HarperCollins UK (**P0382**)

P0599 Murdoch Books UK Ltd
Book Publisher
United Kingdom
Tel: +44 (0) 20 8785 5995
Fax: +44 (0) 20 8785 5985

http://www.murdochbooks.co.uk

Book Publisher: Murdoch Books Pty Limited
Australia

Types: Nonfiction
Subjects: Cookery; Crafts; Design; Gardening;
Lifestyle
Markets: Adult

Publishers of full-colour nonfiction.

P0600 Myriad Editions
Book Publisher
New Internationalist Publications, The Old
Music Hall, 106-108 Cowley Rd, Oxford, OX4
1JE
United Kingdom
Tel: +44 (0) 1865 403345

submissions@myriadeditions.com

https://myriadeditions.com

Types: Fiction; Nonfiction
Subjects: Autobiography; Contemporary;
Crime; History; Literary; Medicine; Politics;
Thrillers
Markets: Adult

Closed to approaches.

Publishes literary fiction: contemporary and
historical; crime fiction: psychological and
political thrillers with strong female characters;
graphic novels: documentary comics, graphic
reportage, fiction, memoir and life writing,
graphic medicine; and literary or political
nonfiction: feminist, literary nonfiction,
memoir. No young adult fiction, children's
books, horror, science fiction, fantasy, plays or
poetry, or books that have been previously
published or self-published (in print or as
ebooks) unless you are a graphic novelist. Do
not send proposals – send complete manuscript
by email. See website for full guidelines.

P0601 Nan A. Talese
Publishing Imprint
1745 Broadway, 22nd floor, New York, NY
10019
United States
Tel: +1 (212) 782-8918
Fax: +1 (212) 782-8448

ntalese@randomhouse.com

http://www.randomhouse.com/nanatalese

Book Publisher: Knopf Doubleday Publishing
Group (**P0498**)

Types: Fiction; Nonfiction
Subjects: Culture; History; Literary;
Philosophy; Sociology
Markets: Adult

How to send: Through a literary agent

Publishes nonfiction and literary fiction with a compelling storyline, good characterisation and use of language. Accepts approaches via a literary agent only.

Editorial Director / Publisher: Nan Talese

P0602 Nancy Paulsen Books
Publishing Imprint
United States

Book Publisher: Penguin Young Readers Group (**P0688**)

P0603 National Museum Wales
Book Publisher
Cathays Park, Cardiff, CF10 3NP
United Kingdom
Tel: +44 (0) 300 111 2 333

post@museumwales.ac.uk

http://www.museumwales.ac.uk

Types: Nonfiction
Subjects: Archaeology; Arts; History; Nature; Sociology
Markets: Academic; Adult; Children's

Publishes books based on the collections and research of the museum, aimed at adults, children, and schools. Publishes in both Welsh and English.

P0604 National Museums Scotland Enterprises
Book Publisher
National Museums of Scotland, Chambers Street, Edinburgh, EH1 1JF
United Kingdom
Tel: +44 (0) 1312 474026
Fax: +44 (0) 1312 474012

publishing@nms.ac.uk

https://www.nms.ac.uk/about-us/our-organisation/nms-enterprises/

Types: Nonfiction
Subjects: Archaeology; Arts; Culture; History; Literature; Nature
Markets: Academic; Adult; Children's

Publishes books reflecting the range and international importance of the museum's collections., from catalogues to children's books, academic monographs, biographies, and souvenir booklets.

P0605 National Trust
Publishing Imprint

Book Publisher: Pavilion Books Group Limited (**P0666**)

P0606 Natural History Museum Publishing
Book Publisher
The Natural History Museum, Cromwell Road,

London, SW7 5BD
United Kingdom
Tel: +44 (0) 20 7942 5336

publishing@nhm.ac.uk

http://www.nhm.ac.uk/business-services/publishing.html

Types: Nonfiction
Subjects: Arts; Nature; Science
Markets: Adult

Publishes accessible, fully illustrated books about the natural world.

P0607 Naughty Nights Press
Book Publisher
Canada

submissions@naughtynightspress.com

http://naughtynightspress.blogspot.com

Types: Fiction
Subjects: Erotic; Fantasy; Romance
Markets: Adult

Publishes erotic and paranormal romance ebooks. See website for full submission guidelines.

P0608 NBM Publishing
Book Publisher
160 Broadway, Suite 700 East Wing, New York, NY 10038
United States

tnantier@nbmpub.com

http://nbmpub.com

Types: Fiction
Subjects: Comedy / Humour; Fantasy; Horror; Mystery; Satire; Science Fiction
Markets: Adult; Young Adult

Send: Query
Don't send: Full text

Publisher of graphic novels, interested in general fiction, humour, satire of fantasy and horror, and mystery. No superheroes. Accepting approaches from previously published authors only (including those with proven success in online comics). No submissions from authors outside North America. See website for full submission guidelines.

Editor: Terry Nantier

P0609 Necro Publications
Book Publisher
United States

https://necropublications.com

Types: Fiction
Subjects: Horror
Markets: Adult

Closed to approaches.

Small press publishing hardcore horror. Closed to submissions as at December 2019. Check website for current status.

P0610 Negative Capability Press
Book Publisher
United States

swalker@negativecapabilitypress.org

http://www.negativecapabilitypress.org

Types: Fiction; Nonfiction; Poetry
Subjects: Literary
Markets: Adult

Send: Full text

Publishes books of literary fiction, nonfiction, and poetry. Accepts submissions through competitions and open submissions ($25 submission fee) via online submission system.

P0611 Nelson Books
Publishing Imprint

Book Publisher: HarperCollins (**P0378**)

P0612 New Holland Publishers (UK) Ltd
Book Publisher
Bentinck House, 3-8 Bolsover Street, London, W1W 6AB
United Kingdom
Tel: +44 (0) 20 3473 3220

enquiries@nhpub.co.uk

http://www.newhollandpublishers.com

Types: Nonfiction
Formats: Reference
Subjects: Arts; Biography; Comedy / Humour; Cookery; Crafts; Design; Gardening; Health; History; How To; Lifestyle; Nature; Photography; Self Help; Spirituality; Sport; Travel
Markets: Adult

Send: Full text

International publisher of nonfiction and reference. Send query with SAE, synopsis and short bio of about 300 words each, current comparison titles (and how yours is different), proposed target market and methods of promotion. Include first three chapters or complete ms. See website for full details.

P0613 New Island
Book Publisher
16 Priory Office Park, Stillorgan, County Dublin
Ireland
Tel: + 353 1 278 42 25

editor@newisland.ie

http://www.newisland.ie

Types: Fiction; Nonfiction; Poetry; Scripts
Formats: Short Fiction

Subjects: Autobiography; Comedy / Humour; Cookery; Crime; Current Affairs; Drama; History; Literary; Literary Criticism; Politics; Sociology; Travel; Women's Interests
Markets: Adult

Closed to approaches.

Closed to submissions as at December 2018. Aims to re-open in spring 2019. Check website for current status. Committed to literature and literary publishing. Publishes in all literary areas, from fiction to drama to poetry. Also publishes nonfiction of Irish interest, especially social affairs and biographies. No children's books. Not currently accepting drama and poetry. Seeking submissions of literary fiction, general fiction, crime fiction, short stories, history, biography, memoir, autobiography, and food and drink. Accepts submissions by email only. Send query with one-page synopsis and full manuscript or poetry collection as Word .doc or .docx attachments. Include details of any previous publications. No submissions by post. See website for full details.

Publishing Imprint: Brookside (*P0132*)

P0614 New London Editions
Publishing Imprint

Book Publisher: Five Leaves Publications (**P0289**)

P0615 New Page Books
Publishing Imprint

Book Publisher: Career Press (**P0148**)

P0616 New Playwrights' Network
Publishing Imprint

Book Publisher: Cressrelles Publishing Co. Ltd (**P0197**)

P0617 New Playwrights' Network (NPN)
Book Publisher
10 Station Road Industrial Estate, Colwall, Herefordshire, WR13 6RN
United Kingdom
Tel: +44 (0) 1684 540154

simon@cressrelles.co.uk

http://www.cressrelles.co.uk

Book Publisher: Cressrelles Publishing Co. Ltd (**P0197**)

Types: Scripts
Formats: Theatre Scripts
Subjects: Drama
Markets: Adult

Send: Full text

Established in the 1970s to promote scripts by new writers. Send scripts by email or by post.

Editor: Simon Smith

P0618 New Riders
Publishing Imprint

Book Publisher: Pearson (**P0670**)

P0619 New Walk Editions
Book Publisher
c/o Nick Everett, School of English, Leicester University, University Road, Leicester, LE1 7RH
United Kingdom

newwalkmagazine@gmail.com

https://newwalkmagazine.com

Poetry > *Poetry Collections*

Send: Full text; Author bio
How to send: Word file email attachment; Post

A small press specialising in extremely high quality poetry pamphlets. Interested in poetic plurality: equally interested in established and new poets, and a broad church stylistically and thematically. Send 12-20 pages of poems by email or by post.

Editor: Nick Everett

P0620 Nicholas Brealey Publishing
Publishing Imprint
Hodder & Stoughton Ltd., Carmelite House, 50 Victoria Embankment, London, EC4Y 0DZ
United Kingdom
Tel: +44 (0) 20 3122 6777

educationenquiries@hodder.co.uk

https://www.hodder.co.uk

Book Publisher: Hodder & Stoughton Ltd (**P0411**)

Types: Nonfiction
Subjects: Business; Culture; Finance; Psychology; Self Help; Travel
Markets: Adult; Professional

Closed to approaches.

Not accepting submissions as at March 2018.

P0621 Nick Hern Books Ltd
Book Publisher
The Glasshouse, 49a Goldhawk Road, London, W12 8QP
United Kingdom
Tel: +44 (0) 20 8749 4953
Fax: +44 (0) 20 8735 0250

submissions@nickhernbooks.co.uk

http://www.nickhernbooks.co.uk

Types: Nonfiction; Scripts
Formats: Film Scripts; Theatre Scripts
Markets: Adult; Professional

Send: Query
Don't send: Full text

Publishes plays attached to significant professional productions in major theatres only. No unsolicited scripts. Also publishes books by theatre practitioners and for theatre practitioners. No critical, analytical or historical studies. Send proposals by email or by post.

P0622 No Starch Press, Inc.
Book Publisher
245 8th Street, San Francisco, CA 94103
United States
Tel: +1 (415) 863-9900
Fax: +1 (415) 863-9950

editors@nostarch.com

https://nostarch.com

Types: Nonfiction
Subjects: Technology
Markets: Adult; Children's; Young Adult

Send: Query
Don't send: Full text

Publishes unique books on technology, with a focus on open source, security, hacking, programming, alternative operating systems, LEGO®, science, and maths. See website for full guidelines.

P0623 North Light Books
Publishing Imprint
United States

Book Publisher: Penguin Publishing Group (**P0682**)

P0624 NorthSouth Books
Book Publisher
600 Third Avenue, 2nd Floor, NY, NY 10016
United States
Tel: +1 (917) 210-5868

submissionsnsb@gmail.com

https://northsouth.com

Types: Fiction
Markets: Children's

Send: Full text

Publishes picture books for children up to 1,000 words. Seeks fresh, original fiction on universal themes that would appeal to children aged 3-8. Generally does not acquire rhyming texts, as must also be translated into German. Send submissions by email as Word document or pasted directly into the body of the email. Authors do not need to include illustrations, but if the author is also an illustrator sample sketches can be included in PDF or JPEG form.

P0625 Nourish Books
Book Publisher
Unit 11, Shepperton House, 89 Shepperton Road, London, N1 3DF

United Kingdom
Tel: +44 (0) 20 3813 6940

enquiries@watkinspublishing.com

https://nourishbooks.com

Types: Nonfiction
Subjects: Cookery
Markets: Adult

Send: Query
Don't send: Full text

Publishes books on food and drink. Send query by email with short bio, proposal, and sample chapter (10 pages max). See website for full guidelines.

P0626 The O'Brien Press
Book Publisher
12 Terenure Road East, Rathgar, Dublin 6, D06 HD27
Ireland
Tel: +353-1-4923333
Fax: +353-1-4922777

books@obrien.ie

http://www.obrien.ie

Types: Fiction; Nonfiction
Formats: Reference
Subjects: Architecture; Arts; Autobiography; Business; Comedy / Humour; Cookery; Crafts; Crime; Drama; History; Lifestyle; Literature; Music; Nature; Photography; Politics; Religion; Sport; Travel
Markets: Adult; Children's; Young Adult

Mainly publishes children's fiction, children's nonfiction and adult nonfiction. Generally doesn't publish poetry, academic works or adult fiction. Send synopsis and two or three sample chapters. If fewer than 1,000 words, send complete ms. See website for full guidelines.

P0627 Oak Tree Press
Book Publisher
33 Rochestown Rise, Rochestown, Cork
Ireland
Tel: +353 86 244 1633
Fax: +353 86 330 7694

info@oaktreepress.com

https://oaktreepress.eu

Types: Nonfiction
Subjects: Business; Finance; Legal
Markets: Professional

Publishes books on business, particularly for small business owners and managers.

P0628 Oberon Books
Book Publisher
521 Caledonian Road, London, N7 9RH
United Kingdom
Tel: +44 (0) 20 7607 3637
Fax: +44 (0) 20 7607 3629

george@oberonbooks.com

http://www.oberonbooks.com

Types: Nonfiction; Scripts
Formats: Theatre Scripts
Subjects: Drama
Markets: Adult; Professional

Publishes play texts, and books on dance and theatre. Specialises in translations of European classics and contemporary plays, though also publishes edited performance versions of classics including Shakespeare. Play texts are usually published in conjunction with a production. Play scripts may be submitted by post or by email. Book proposals for trade and professional titles should include summary, table of contents, estimate word count, and sample chapter.

Publishing Imprint: Absolute Classics (*P0019*)

Senior Editor: George Spender

P0629 Oberon Press
Book Publisher
205–145 Spruce Street, Ottawa, Ontario, K1R 6P1
Canada
Tel: +1 (613) 238-3275
Fax: +1 (613) 238-3275

oberon@sympatico.ca

http://www.oberonpress.ca

Types: Fiction; Nonfiction; Poetry
Markets: Adult

Closed to approaches.

No longer accepting new manuscript submissions.

P0630 Octopus Books
Book Publisher
United States

octopusbooks@gmail.com

http://www.octopusbooks.net

Types: Poetry
Subjects: Contemporary; Literary
Markets: Adult

Closed to approaches.

Publishes contemporary poetry. Accepts submissions during April only, via online submission system.

Editors: Hajara Quinn; Zachary Schomburg; Mathias Svalina

P0631 Oh! With Dots
Publishing Imprint

Publishing Imprint: Emerentsia Publications (**P0258**)

P0632 The Ohio State University Press
Book Publisher
180 Pressey Hall, 1070 Carmack Road, Columbus, OH 43210-1002
United States
Tel: +1 (614) 292-8256
Fax: +1 (614) 292-2065

info@osupress.org

https://ohiostatepress.org

Types: Fiction; Nonfiction; Poetry
Formats: Film Scripts
Subjects: Business; Crime; Culture; Finance; Health; History; Literary Criticism; Media; Politics; Sociology; Women's Interests
Markets: Academic

Send: Query
Don't send: Full text

Publishes mainly academic nonfiction. Check website for appropriate editor to submit your work to and details of the appropriate material to submit.

Editors: Becca Bostock-Holtzman; Tara Cyphers; Ana Jimenez-Moreno; Kristen Elias Rowley; Tony Sanfilippo

P0633 Ohio University Press
Book Publisher
30 Park Place, Suite 101, Athens, OH 45701-2909
United States

huard@ohio.edu

https://www.ohioswallow.com

ACADEMIC > **Nonfiction** > *Nonfiction Books*
Africa; American History; American Midwest; Anthropology; Appalachia; Art History; Arts; Asia; Central America; Environment; Europe; Films; Food; Gender; Health; History; Journalism; Legal; Literature; Media; North America; Ohio; Performing Arts; Philosophy; Politics; Religion; South America; Sport; TV; Women

Send: Query; Table of Contents; Writing sample; Author bio
Don't send: Full text

Publishes primarily nonfiction. See website for full guidelines.

Editor: Ricky S. Huard

Publishing Imprint: Swallow Press (*P0844*)

P0634 Oldcastle Books
Publishing Imprint
United Kingdom

Book Publisher: Oldcastle Books Group (**P0635**)

P0635 Oldcastle Books Group
Book Publisher
18 Coleswood Road, Harpenden,
Hertfordshire, AL5 1EQ
United Kingdom
Tel: +44 (0) 1582 766348

publicity@oldcastlebooks.com

http://www.oldcastlebooks.co.uk

Fiction > *Novels*

Nonfiction > *Nonfiction Books*

How to send: Through a literary agent

Accepts submissions through literary agents only.

Managing Director: Ion S. Mills

Publishing Imprints: Creative Essentials (*P0196*); Crime & Mystery Club (*P0198*); High Stakes Publishing; Kamera Books (*P0478*); No Exit Press; Oldcastle Books (*P0634*); Pocketessentials; Pulp! The Classics (*P0729*)

P0636 Oleander Press
Book Publisher
16 Orchard Street, Cambridge, CB1 1JT
United Kingdom

editor@oleanderpress.com

http://www.oleanderpress.com

Types: Fiction; Nonfiction; Poetry
Formats: Reference
Subjects: Biography; History; Horror;
Literature; Travel
Markets: Adult; Children's

Closed to approaches.

Closed to submissions as at June 2020.

Publishes biography, Cambridge / local, children's, classic horror, language and literature, fiction, games and pastimes, modern poets, Arabia, and Libya. Looking for nonfiction – in particular children's nonfiction. Send submissions by email or by post.

Editor: Jon Gifford

P0637 Omnibus Press
Book Publisher
14/15 Berners Street, London, W1T 3LJ
United Kingdom
Tel: +44 (0) 20 7612 7400

omniinfo@wisemusic.com

https://omnibuspress.com

Book Publisher: Wise Music Group (**P0976**)

Types: Nonfiction
Subjects: Biography; Music
Markets: Adult

Publisher of music books, including song sheets and rock and pop biographies.

P0638 One More Chapter
Publishing Imprint
United Kingdom

Book Publisher: HarperCollins UK (**P0382**)

P0639 Oneworld Publications
Book Publisher
10 Bloomsbury Street, London, WC1B 3SR
United Kingdom
Tel: +44 (0) 20 7307 8900

submissions@oneworld-publications.com

http://www.oneworld-publications.com

Types: Fiction; Nonfiction; Translations
Subjects: Anthropology; Arts; Biography;
Business; Commercial; Current Affairs;
History; Literary; Literature; Nature;
Philosophy; Politics; Psychology; Religion;
Science; Self Help
Markets: Adult

Send: Query
Don't send: Full text

Not accepting fiction submissions as at August 2018, but hopes this will change in the near future. Check website for current status. Nonfiction authors must be academics and/or experts in their field. Approaches for fiction must provide a clear and concise synopsis, outlining the novel's main themes. See website for full submission guidelines, and forms for fiction and nonfiction, which may be submitted by email.

P0640 Ooligan Press
Book Publisher
PO Box 751, Portland, OR 97207
United States
Tel: +1 (503) 725-9748
Fax: +1 (503) 725-3561

https://ooligan.pdx.edu

Types: Fiction; Nonfiction; Poetry
Subjects: Autobiography; History; Literary;
Sociology
Markets: Adult; Young Adult

Send: Query
Don't send: Full text

Publishes works of historical and social value, or significance to the Pacific Northwest region (Northern California, Oregon, Idaho, Washington, British Columbia, and Alaska). Accepts queries by email and proposals via onlnie submission system. See website for full details.

P0641 Open University Press
Book Publisher
United Kingdom

Laura.Pacey@mheducation.com

https://www.mheducation.co.uk/professionals/open-university-press

Book Publisher: McGraw-Hill Education (**P0578**)

Types: Nonfiction
Subjects: Health; Psychology; Sociology
Markets: Academic; Professional

Publishes books on social sciences only.

P0642 Orb
Publishing Imprint

Publishing Imprint: Tor/Forge (**P0870**)

P0643 Orchard Books
Publishing Imprint
United States

Book Publisher: Scholastic (**P0790**)

P0644 Orenda Books
Book Publisher
16 Carson Road, West Dulwich, London, SE21 8HU
United Kingdom

westcamel@orendabooks.co.uk

http://orendabooks.co.uk

Types: Fiction
Subjects: Crime; Literary; Thrillers
Markets: Adult

Closed to approaches.

Closed to submissions until February 2019. Check website for current status. Publishes literary fiction and upmarket genre fiction only. No nonfiction, screenplays, children's books, or young adult. Send one-page synopsis and full ms (or three-chapter sample) by email.

P0645 Orion Children's Books
Book Publisher

Book Publisher: The Orion Publishing Group Limited (**P0647**)

P0646 Orion Paperbacks
Book Publisher

Book Publisher: The Orion Publishing Group Limited (**P0647**)

P0647 The Orion Publishing Group Limited
Book Publisher
Carmelite House, 50 Victoria Embankment, London, EC4Y 0DZ
United Kingdom
Tel: +44 (0) 20 3122 6444

http://www.orionbooks.co.uk

Types: Fiction; Nonfiction
Formats: Reference
Subjects: Adventure; Archaeology; Arts;
Autobiography; Beauty; Commercial;
Cookery; Culture; Current Affairs; Design;
Fantasy; Fashion; Gardening; Health; History;
Lifestyle; Literature; Nature; Science Fiction;

Sport; Travel; Warfare
Markets: Adult; Children's; Young Adult

How to send: Through a literary agent

One of the UK's leading commercial publishers. Accepts approaches through agents only.

Authors: Linwood Barclay; Maeve Binchy; Michael Connelly; Gillian Flynn; Cathy Kelly; Ian Rankin

Book Publishers: Orion Children's Books (*P0645*); Orion Paperbacks (*P0646*); Orion Trade (*P0648*); Weidenfeld & Nicholson (*P0956*); Weidenfeld & Nicolson

Publishing Imprint: Gollancz (*P0328*)

P0648 Orion Trade
Book Publisher

Book Publisher: The Orion Publishing Group Limited (**P0647**)

P0649 Osprey Publishing Ltd
Book Publisher
Commissioning Editor, Editorial Department, Osprey Publishing, Kemp House, Chawley Park, Cumnor Hill, Oxford, OX2 9PH
United Kingdom
Tel: +44 (0) 1865 757022
Fax: +44 (0) 1865 242009

editorial@ospreypublishing.com

http://www.ospreypublishing.com

Types: Nonfiction
Subjects: History; Warfare
Markets: Adult

Send: Query
Don't send: Full text

Publishes illustrated books on military history and aviation. Welcomes synopses and ideas for books by post or by email, but no unsolicited MSS. See website for full guidelines.

P0650 Our Street Books
Publishing Imprint

Book Publisher: John Hunt Publishing Ltd

P0651 Oversteps Books
Book Publisher
6 Halwell House, South Pool, Nr Kingsbridge, Devon, TQ7 2RX
United Kingdom

alwynmarriage@overstepsbooks.com

http://www.overstepsbooks.com

Types: Poetry
Markets: Adult

Closed to approaches.

Closed to submissions as at September 2018. Check website for current status. Poetry publisher. Send email with copies of six poems that have been published in magazines or won

competitions, along with details of dates or issue numbers and email addresses of the editors. Include poems and information in the body of your email. No submissions by post.

P0652 Oxbow Books
Book Publisher
The Old Music Hall, 106-108 Cowley Road, OX4 1JE
United Kingdom
Tel: +44 (0) 1865 241249
Fax: +44 (0) 1865 794449

orders@oxbowbooks.com

https://www.oxbowbooks.com
https://www.facebook.com/oxbowbooks
https://www.twitter.com/oxbowbooks
https://www.linkedin.com/company/oxbow-books

ACADEMIC > **Nonfiction** > *Nonfiction*
Books: Archaeology

Publisher of academic books on archaeology.

Editor: Richard Purslow

Publishing Imprint: Aris & Phillips

P0653 Oxford University Press
Book Publisher
Great Clarendon Street, Oxford, OX2 6DP
United Kingdom
Tel: +44 (0) 1865 556767
Fax: +44 (0) 1865 556646

onlinequeries.uk@oup.com

https://global.oup.com

Types: Fiction; Nonfiction
Formats: Reference
Subjects: Current Affairs; Drama; Finance; History; Legal; Literature; Medicine; Music; Philosophy; Politics; Religion; Science; Sociology
Markets: Academic; Adult; Children's; Professional

Publishes academic works including journals, schoolbooks, dictionaries, reference works, classics, and children's fiction, and nonfiction.

Book Publisher: Nelson Thornes Limited

P0654 P8tech
Book Publisher
6 Woodside, Churnet View Road, Oakamoor, Staffordshire, ST10 3AE
United Kingdom

info@P8tech.com

https://www.p8tech.com

Types: Nonfiction
Subjects: Technology
Markets: Professional

Publishes IT books and ebooks for technology professionals. Current emphasis on Java and Oracle technologies. Books are heavy on the practical and full of code and screenshots.

P0655 Pace Press
Book Publisher
2006 S Mary St, Fresno, CA 93721
United States
Tel: +1 (800) 345-4447

kent@lindenpub.com

https://quilldriverbooks.com/pace-press/

Types: Fiction
Subjects: Fantasy; History; Horror; Mystery; Romance; Science Fiction; Thrillers; Westerns
Markets: Adult

Closed to approaches.

Closed to submissions as at January 2020. Check website for current status. Send query by post or email with synopsis, author bio, and first three or four chapters / 50 pages of your manuscript. See website for full guidelines.

P0656 Pact Press
Book Publisher
Raleigh, NC
United States

info@regalhousepublishing.com

http://pactpress.com

Types: Fiction; Nonfiction; Poetry
Formats: Short Fiction
Subjects: Literary
Markets: Adult

Publishes short stories, poetry, nonfiction, and literary fiction on themes such as social justice, racism, discrimination, gender equality, LGBTQ concerns, immigration, poverty and homelessness. Submit via online submission system. $5 submission fee.

P0657 Pale Fire Press
Book Publisher
United States
Tel: +1 (520) 477-7909

http://palefirepress.com

Types: Fiction
Subjects: Literary
Markets: Adult

Closed to approaches.

Closed to submissions as at January 2020. Check website for current status.

P0658 Palgrave Macmillan
Book Publisher
United Kingdom

https://www.palgrave.com

Book Publisher: Springer Nature (**P0831**)

ACADEMIC > **Nonfiction**
Nonfiction Books: Business; Culture; Economics; Environment; Films; Geography; Health; History; International; Journalism; Language; Literature; Media; Neuroscience;

Philosophy; Politics; Psychology; Sociology; TV; Theatre
Reference: Business; Philosophy
PROFESSIONAL > **Nonfiction** > *Nonfiction Books*
Business; Management

Send: Query; Submission Form; Author bio; Writing sample

Download proposal form from website and submit by email to relevant editorial contact.

Book Publisher: BFI Publishing

P0659 Pan Macmillan

Book Publisher
20 New Wharf Road, Kings Cross, London, N1 9RR
United Kingdom
Tel: +44 (0) 20 7014 6000

webqueries@macmillan.co.uk

https://www.panmacmillan.com

Types: Fiction; Nonfiction; Poetry
Subjects: Adventure; Biography; Commercial; Contemporary; Crime; Fantasy; History; Literary; Nature; Politics; Romance; Science; Science Fiction; Self Help; Thrillers
Markets: Children's; Young Adult

Accepts submissions for science fiction and fantasy direct from authors. Submissions in all other areas must come via a literary agent.

Book Publisher: Pan Macmillan Australia **(P0660)**

Publishing Imprints: Bello (*P0091*); Bluebird (*P0112*); Campbell (*P0141*); Macmillan Children's Books (*P0556*); Macmillan Collector's Library (*P0557*); Mantle (*P0565*); Picador; Tor (*P0868*); Two Hoots (*P0884*)

P0660 Pan Macmillan Australia

Book Publisher
Australia

pan.reception@macmillan.com.au

https://www.panmacmillan.com.au

Book Publisher: Pan Macmillan **(P0659)**

ADULT
 Fiction > *Novels*
 Contemporary; Crime; Drama; Historical Fiction; Literary; Psychological Suspense; Saga; Thrillers

 Nonfiction > *Nonfiction Books*
 Contemporary; Crime; Health; History; Lifestyle; Memoir; Mind, Body, Spirit; Narrative Nonfiction

CHILDREN'S > **Fiction** > *Middle Grade*

YOUNG ADULT > **Fiction** > *Novels*

Send: Query; Author bio; Market info; Synopsis; Proposal; Writing sample
How to send: Online submission system

Accepts submissions via online submission system.

P0661 Pantheon

Publishing Imprint
United States

Book Publisher: Knopf Doubleday Publishing Group **(P0498)**

P0662 Parthian Books

Book Publisher
The Old Surgery, Napier Street, Cardigan, SA43 1ED
United Kingdom
Tel: +44 (0) 7890 968246

info@parthianbooks.com

https://www.parthianbooks.com

Fiction
 Novels: Literary
 Short Fiction: Literary

Nonfiction > *Nonfiction Books*

Poetry > *Poetry Collections*

Closed to approaches.

Publisher of poetry, fiction, and creative nonfiction, of Welsh origin, in the English language. Also publishes English language translations of Welsh language work. Send query with SAE, and (for fiction) a one-page synopsis and first 30 pages, or (for poetry) a sample of 15-20 poems. No email submissions, genre fiction of any kind, or children's / teenage fiction. See website for full submission guidelines.

P0663 PassKey Publications

Book Publisher
5348 Vegas Drive PMB 1670, Las Vegas, NV 89108
United States

support@passkeyonline.com

https://www.passkeypublications.com

Types: Nonfiction
Subjects: Business; Finance
Markets: Adult

Publishes taxation and accountancy textbooks.

P0664 Patrician Press

Book Publisher
United Kingdom
Tel: +44 (0) 7968 288651

patricia@patricianpress.com

https://patricianpress.com

Types: Fiction; Nonfiction; Poetry
Formats: Short Fiction
Markets: Adult; Children's

Small and independent non-profit press, with the aim of encouraging and promoting writers of high quality fiction and poetry. Imprint

publishes books for children. Contact by email only.

Publishing Imprint: Pudding Press (*P0727*)

P0665 Paulist Press

Book Publisher
997 Macarthur Boulevard, Mahwah, NJ 07430
United States
Tel: +1 (201) 825-7300
Fax: +1 (201) 825-8345

submissions@paulistpress.com

http://www.paulistpress.com

Types: Fiction; Nonfiction
Subjects: Culture; Philosophy; Religion; Self Help
Markets: Adult; Children's

Send: Query
Don't send: Full text

Catholic publishing house, publishing mainly religious and spiritual nonfiction for adults, as well as a small but growing number of religious fiction books for children. Send proposal by email or by post the SASE. See website for full guidelines.

: Rev. Lawrence Boadt

Publishing Imprint: HiddenSpring (*P0406*)

P0666 Pavilion Books Group Limited

Book Publisher
43 Great Ormond Street, London, WC1N 3HZ
United Kingdom
Tel: +44 (0) 20 7462 1500

info@pavilionbooks.com

https://www.pavilionbooks.com

Types: Fiction; Nonfiction
Subjects: Arts; Beauty; Comedy / Humour; Cookery; Crafts; Culture; Design; Fashion; Gardening; History; Lifestyle
Markets: Adult; Children's

Send: Query
Don't send: Full text

Publishes nonfiction for adults and fiction and nonfiction for children (including picture books and colouring books). Send query with SAE, outline, and sample chapter, by post. Due to high volume of submissions, no acknowledgement of receipt is provided.

Publishing Imprints: Batsford (*P0083*); Collins & Brown; National Trust (*P0605*); Pavilion; Pavilion Children's (*P0667*); Portico (*P0716*)

P0667 Pavilion Children's

Publishing Imprint

Book Publisher: Pavilion Books Group Limited **(P0666)**

P0668 Pavilion Publishing

Book Publisher
Blue Sky Offices Shoreham, 25 Cecil Pashley
Way, Shoreham-by-Sea, West Sussex, BN43
5FF
United Kingdom
Tel: +44 (0) 1273 434943

info@pavpub.com

http://www.pavpub.com

Types: Nonfiction
Formats: Reference
Subjects: Health; Sociology
Markets: Professional

Publishes books and resources for public,
private and voluntary workers in the health,
social care, education and community safety
sectors. Welcomes submissions from both new
and established authors, and organisations that
are developing training materials.

P0669 Peachpit Press

Publishing Imprint

Book Publisher: Pearson (**P0670**)

P0670 Pearson

Book Publisher
Edinburgh Gate, Harlow, CM20 2JE
United Kingdom
Tel: +44 (0) 845 313 6666
Fax: +44 (0) 845 313 7777

eloise.cook@pearson.com

http://www.pearsoned.co.uk

Types: Nonfiction
Markets: Academic; Professional

World's largest publisher of educational
material, including books for primary school
pupils through to professionals. See website for
appropriate imprint to approach, and specific
submission guidelines.

Book Publishers: Pearson Scott Foresman; Que
Publishing

Publisher: Eloise Cook

Publishing Imprints: Addison Wesley (**P0022**);
Allyn & Bacon (*P0030*); BBC Active (*P0084*);
Benjamin Cummings; Cisco Press (*P0171*); FT
Prentice Hall (*P0305*); Harcourt (*P0359*);
Longman (*P0537*); New Riders (*P0618*);
Peachpit Press (*P0669*); Penguin Longman
(*P0679*); Prentice Hall (*P0718*); SAMS
Publishing (*P0783*); Wharton (*P0966*); York
Notes (*P0988*)

P0671 Peepal Tree Press

Book Publisher
17 King's Avenue, Leeds, LS6 1QS
United Kingdom
Tel: +44 (0) 113 245 1703

contact@peepaltreepress.com

https://www.peepaltreepress.com

Types: Fiction; Nonfiction; Poetry
Formats: Short Fiction
Subjects: Arts; Autobiography; Culture;
Drama; Literary; Literature
Markets: Adult

Publishes international Caribbean, Black
British, and south Asian writing. Submit
through online submission system.

P0672 Pelican Publishing Company

Book Publisher
990 N. Corporate Drive, Suite 100, New
Orleans, LA 70123
United States

editorial@pelicanpub.com

https://www.pelicanpub.com

Book Publisher: Arcadia Publishing

ADULT > **Nonfiction** > *Nonfiction Books*
Comedy / Humour; Music; Sport

CHILDREN'S
 Fiction
  Middle Grade: Adventure
  Picture Books: Adventure; Holidays
 Nonfiction
  Middle Grade: Biography; Cookery;
Regional History
  Picture Books: Biography; Holidays;
Regional History
YOUNG ADULT
 Fiction > *Novels:* Adventure

 Nonfiction > *Nonfiction Books*
  Biography; Regional History

Send: Query; Author bio; Synopsis; Table of
Contents; Writing sample
How to send: Email

Publishes nonfiction for all ages and fiction for
children and young adults only. No adult
fiction. Send query by email. See website for
full guidelines.

Editor: Nina Kooij

P0673 Pen & Sword Aviation

Publishing Imprint

Book Publisher: Pen & Sword Books Ltd
(**P0674**)

P0674 Pen & Sword Books Ltd

Book Publisher
47 Church Street, Barnsley, South Yorkshire,
S70 2AS
United Kingdom
Tel: +44 (0) 1226 734222
Fax: +44 (0) 1226 734438

editorialoffice@pen-and-sword.co.uk

https://www.pen-and-sword.co.uk

Types: Nonfiction
Subjects: Antiques; Archaeology; Arts;
Autobiography; Crafts; Crime; Gardening;

Health; History; Lifestyle; Nature;
Photography; Science; Sociology; Sport;
Travel; Warfare
Markets: Adult

Send: Query
Don't send: Full text

Publishes across a number of areas including
military history, naval and maritime history,
aviation, local history, family history,
transport, discovery and exploration,
collectables and antiques, nostalgia and true
crime. In 2017, launched a new lifestyle
imprint which publishes books on areas such as
health and diet, hobbies and sport, gardening
and wildlife and space. Submit proposal using
form on website.

Editor: Lisa Hooson

Publishing Imprints: Leo Cooper (*P0512*); Pen
& Sword Aviation (*P0673*); Pen & Sword
Maritime (*P0675*); Remember When;
Wharncliffe Books; White Owl (*P0968*)

P0675 Pen & Sword Maritime

Publishing Imprint

Book Publisher: Pen & Sword Books Ltd
(**P0674**)

P0676 Penguin Books

Publishing Imprint
United States

Book Publisher: Penguin Publishing Group
(**P0682**)

P0677 Penguin Classics

Publishing Imprint
United States

Book Publisher: Penguin Publishing Group
(**P0682**)

P0678 Penguin General

Book Publisher

Book Publisher: Penguin Random House UK
(**P0685**)

P0679 Penguin Longman

Publishing Imprint

Book Publisher: Pearson (**P0670**)

P0680 Penguin Press

Book Publisher

Book Publisher: Penguin Random House UK
(**P0685**)

P0681 The Penguin Press

Publishing Imprint
United States

Book Publisher: Penguin Publishing Group
(**P0682**)

P0682 Penguin Publishing Group
Book Publisher
United States

Book Publisher: Penguin Group (USA)

Publishing Imprints: Avery (*P0065*); Berkley (*P0092*); Blue Rider Press (*P0111*); DAW (*P0217*); Dutton (*P0238*); Family Tree Books (*P0275*); G.P. Putnam's Sons (*P0307*); Impact (**P0442**); Interweave (**P0453**); Krause Publications (**P0502**); North Light Books (*P0623*); Penguin Books (*P0676*); Penguin Classics (*P0677*); The Penguin Press (*P0681*); Plume (*P0708*); Popular Woodworking Books (**P0714**); Portfolio Penguin (*P0715*); Riverhead Books (**P0760**); Sentinel (*P0802*); TarcherPerigee (*P0851*); Viking (*P0929*); Writer's Digest Books (*P0981*)

P0683 Penguin Random House
Book Publisher
1745 Broadway, New York, NY 10019
United States
Tel: +1 (212) 366-2000

https://www.penguinrandomhouse.com

Types: Fiction; Nonfiction; Poetry
Formats: Reference
Subjects: Arts; Autobiography; Comedy / Humour; Cookery; Entertainment; Fantasy; History; Mystery; Politics; Romance; Science; Science Fiction; Suspense; Travel
Markets: Adult; Children's; Young Adult

How to send: Through a literary agent

One of the world's largest publishing houses. Accepts approaches via literary agents only.

Book Publishers: The Crown Publishing Group; Knopf Doubleday Publishing Group (**P0498**); Michael Joseph (**P0585**); Penguin Random House UK (**P0685**)

Publishing Imprint: Clarkson Potter (**P0175**)

P0684 Penguin Random House Children's
Book Publisher

Book Publisher: Penguin Random House UK (**P0685**)

P0685 Penguin Random House UK
Book Publisher
One Embassy Gardens, 8 Viaduct Gardens, London, SW11 7BW, 20 Vauxhall Bridge Road, London, SW1V 2SA
United Kingdom
Tel: +44 (0) 20 7010 3000

https://www.penguin.co.uk
https://www.facebook.com/penguinbooks
https://www.instagram.com/penguinukbooks/

https://twitter.com/PenguinUKBooks
https://www.youtube.com/user/penguinbooks

Book Publisher: Penguin Random House (**P0683**)

ADULT
Fiction > *Novels*
Nonfiction > *Nonfiction Books*

CHILDREN'S
Fiction
   Chapter Books; *Early Readers*; *Middle Grade*; *Novels*; *Picture Books*
Nonfiction > *Nonfiction Books*

How to send: Through a literary agent

Publishes a wide range of fiction, nonfiction, poetry, and reference, for children and adults. No queries or unsolicited MSS, other than through a literary agent.

Audio Book Publisher: Penguin Random House UK Audio

Book Publishers: Cornerstone (*P0189*); Ebury (**P0243**); Michael Joseph (**P0585**); Penguin General (*P0678*); Penguin Press (*P0680*); Penguin Random House Children's (*P0684*); Transworld Publishers (**P0875**); Vintage (**P0934**)

P0686 Penguin Workshop
Publishing Imprint
United States

Book Publisher: Penguin Young Readers Group (**P0688**)

P0687 Penguin Young Readers
Publishing Imprint
United States

Book Publisher: Penguin Young Readers Group (**P0688**)

P0688 Penguin Young Readers Group
Book Publisher
United States

https://www.penguin.com/publishers/penguin-young-readers-group/

Book Publisher: Penguin Group (USA)

Publishing Imprints: Dial Books for Young Readers (**P0226**); Dutton Children's Books (*P0239*); F. Warne & Co. (*P0269*); Firebird (*P0284*); G.P. Putnam's Sons Books for Young Readers (**P0308**); Kathy Dawson Books (**P0482**); Kokila (*P0500*); Nancy Paulsen Books (*P0602*); Penguin Workshop (*P0686*); Penguin Young Readers (*P0687*); Penguin Young Readers Licenses (*P0689*); Philomel (*P0698*); Puffin (*P0728*); Razorbill (**P0749**); Speak (*P0827*); Viking Children's Books (*P0930*)

P0689 Penguin Young Readers Licenses
Publishing Imprint
United States

Book Publisher: Penguin Young Readers Group (**P0688**)

P0690 Peony Press
Publishing Imprint

Book Publisher: Anness Publishing Ltd (**P0040**)

P0691 Percy Publishing
Book Publisher
United Kingdom

enquiries@percy-publishing.com

https://www.percy-publishing.com

Types: Fiction
Markets: Adult

How to send: Through a literary agent

Founded in 2014 and awarded "Best Publisher" in 2016. Due to high level of submissions can now only accept submissions via a literary agent.

P0692 Perfect Edge
Publishing Imprint

Book Publisher: John Hunt Publishing Ltd

P0693 Perseus Books
Book Publisher
United States

https://www.perseusbooks.com
https://www.facebook.com/pages/Perseus-Books-Group/108204045874204
https://twitter.com/PerseusBooks
https://www.instagram.com/perseus_books/

Book Publisher: Hachette Book Group (**P0346**)

Nonfiction > *Nonfiction Books*

How to send: Through a literary agent

Independent publishing division acquired in 2016.

Publishing Imprints: Avalon Travel (*P0064*); Basic Books; Black Dog & Leventhal (*P0100*); Counterpoint Press; Da Capo Press (**P0207**); Hachette Books (*P0347*); Hachette Go! (*P0349*); PublicAffairs (*P0726*); Running Press (*P0771*); Seal Press; Westview Press

P0694 Peter Lang Oxford
Book Publisher
United Kingdom

editorial@peterlang.com

https://www.peterlang.com
https://www.facebook.com/pages/Peter-Lang-Oxford/260315267419469

https://twitter.com/peterlangoxford
http://peterlangoxford.wordpress.com/

ACADEMIC > **Nonfiction** > *Nonfiction Books*
Art History; Culture; Films; History; Ireland; Language; Literature; Media; Religion; Scotland; Sociology; South-East Asia; Sport; United Kingdom

Send: Query
How to send: Email

Select appropriate editor from website and query by email.

Editor: Na Li

Publishing Director: Lucy Melville

Senior Editors: Tony Mason; Dr Laurel Plapp

P0695 Peter Owen Publishers
Book Publisher
Conway Hall, 25 Red Lion Square, London, WC1R 4RL
United Kingdom

info@peterowen.com

https://www.peterowen.com
https://twitter.com/PeterOwenPubs
https://www.facebook.com/peter.owen.publishers
https://www.instagram.com/peterowenpublishing

Fiction > *Novels*
International; Literary

Nonfiction > *Nonfiction Books*

Does not want:

> **Nonfiction** > *Nonfiction Books*
> Memoir; Self Help; Spirituality; Sport

Send: Query
How to send: Email

Publishes general nonfiction and international literary fiction. No first novels, short stories, poetry, plays, sport, spirituality, self-help, or children's or genre fiction. Accepts query by email only, including cover letter, synopsis, and one or two sample chapters. No submissions by post. Prefers fiction to come from an agent or translator as appropriate.

Editorial Director: Antonia Owen

P0696 Phaidon Press Limited
Book Publisher
2 Cooperage Yard, London, E15 2QR
United Kingdom
Tel: +44 (0) 20 7843 1000
Fax: +44 (0) 20 7843 1010

submissions@phaidon.com

http://www.phaidon.com

Types: Nonfiction
Formats: Film Scripts

Subjects: Architecture; Arts; Beauty; Cookery; Culture; Design; Fashion; History; Music; Photography; Travel
Markets: Academic; Adult; Children's

Send: Full text

Publishes books in the areas of art, architecture, design, photography, film, fashion, contemporary culture, decorative arts, music, performing arts, cultural history, food and cookery, travel and books for children. No fiction or approaches by post. Send query by email only, with CV and short description of the project. Response only if interested.

P0697 Phillimore
Publishing Imprint
United Kingdom

https://www.thehistorypress.co.uk

Book Publisher: The History Press (**P0409**)

Types: Nonfiction
Subjects: History
Markets: Adult

P0698 Philomel
Publishing Imprint
United States

Book Publisher: Penguin Young Readers Group (**P0688**)

P0699 Philosophy Documentation Center
Book Publisher
PO Box 7147, Charlottesville, VA 22906-7147
United States
Tel: +1 (434) 220-3300

leaman@pdcnet.org

https://www.pdcnet.org

Types: Nonfiction
Formats: Reference
Subjects: Philosophy
Markets: Academic

Publishes books, journals, and reference materials on philosophy and related fields.

Company Director: George Leaman

P0700 Piatkus Constable & Robinson
Publishing Imprint

Publishing Imprint: Little, Brown Book Group (**P0532**)

P0701 Piccadilly Press
Book Publisher
80-81 Wimpole Street, London, W1G 9RE
United Kingdom
Tel: +44 (0) 20 7490 3875

hello@bonnierbooks.co.uk

http://www.piccadillypress.co.uk

Types: Fiction; Nonfiction
Subjects: Comedy / Humour; Contemporary
Markets: Children's; Young Adult

How to send: Through a literary agent

No longer accepts unsolicited submissions. Approach through a literary agent.

P0702 Pimpernel Press
Book Publisher
22 Marylands Road, London, W9 2DY
United Kingdom
Tel: +44 (0) 7976 047767

info@pimpernelpress.com

http://www.pimpernelpress.com

Types: Nonfiction
Subjects: Arts; Design; Gardening
Markets: Adult

Publishes books on art, design, houses, and gardens. Send submissions by post.

P0703 Pineapple Press
Publishing Imprint
United States

Book Publisher: The Globe Pequot Press (**P0324**)

P0704 Pinnacle
Publishing Imprint

Book Publisher: Kensington Publishing Corp. (**P0488**)

P0705 Pioneer Plus
Publishing Imprint

Book Publisher: Cedar Fort (**P0155**)

P0706 Plain Sight Publishing
Publishing Imprint

Book Publisher: Cedar Fort (**P0155**)

P0707 Plexus Publishing Limited
Book Publisher
26 Dafforne Road, London, SW17 8TZ
United Kingdom

plexus@plexusuk.demon.co.uk

http://www.plexusbooks.com

Types: Nonfiction
Formats: Film Scripts
Subjects: Biography; Culture; Music
Markets: Adult

Publishes illustrated nonfiction books specialising in biography, popular culture, movies and music.

P0708 Plume
Publishing Imprint
United States

Book Publisher: Penguin Publishing Group
(**P0682**)

P0709 Pocol Press
Book Publisher
3911 Prosperity Avenue, Fairfax, VA 22031
United States
Tel: +1 (703) 870-9611

http://www.pocolpress.com

Types: Fiction; Nonfiction
Formats: Short Fiction
Subjects: Commercial; Contemporary; Horror;
Literary
Markets: Adult

Send: Query
Don't send: Full text

Send query with SASE, author bio, publishing
credits, audience details, and synopsis. No
unsolicited MSS, queries by email, or self-
published books.

P0710 Policy Press
Publishing Imprint

Book Publisher: Bristol University Press
(**P0126**)

P0711 Pont Books.
Publishing Imprint

Book Publisher: Gomer Press (**P0330**)

P0712 Poolbeg
Book Publisher
123 Grange Hill, Baldoyle Industrial Estate,
Baldoyle, Dublin 13
Ireland
Tel: +353 1 806 3825

info@poolbeg.com

http://www.poolbeg.com

Types: Fiction; Nonfiction
Subjects: Cookery; Gardening; Travel;
Women's Interests
Markets: Adult; Children's

Send: Full text

Publishes mainly women's and children's
fiction, but also some nonfiction. Send query
with synopsis, bio, and three chapters, both in
hard copy and on a USB stick. If no response
after three months assume rejection. See
website for full guidelines.

Editors: Paula Campbell; publisher

Publishing Imprint: Ward River Press (*P0947*)

P0713 Pop Press
Publishing Imprint
United Kingdom

Book Publisher: Ebury (**P0243**)

P0714 Popular Woodworking Books
Publishing Imprint
United States

Book Publisher: Penguin Publishing Group
(**P0682**)

Types: Nonfiction
Subjects: Crafts; Hobbies
Markets: Adult

Publishes books for woodwork enthusiasts.

P0715 Portfolio Penguin
Publishing Imprint
United States

Book Publisher: Penguin Publishing Group
(**P0682**)

P0716 Portico
Publishing Imprint

Book Publisher: Pavilion Books Group
Limited (**P0666**)

P0717 Praeger
Publishing Imprint
United States

Book Publisher: ABC-CLIO (**P0016**)

P0718 Prentice Hall
Publishing Imprint

Book Publisher: Pearson (**P0670**)

P0719 Press 53
Book Publisher
560 N. Trade Street, Suite 103, Winston-
Salem, NC 27101
United States
Tel: +1 (336) 770-5353

editor@press53.com

http://www.press53.com

Types: Fiction; Poetry
Formats: Short Fiction
Subjects: Literary
Markets: Adult

Publishes collections of poetry and short
stories. No novels or book length fiction. Finds
authors through its competitions, and through
writers being active in the literary community
and literary magazines.

Editor: Kevin Morgan Watson

P0720 Princeton Architectural Press
Book Publisher
202 Warren Street, Hudson, NY 12534
United States
Tel: +1 (518) 671-6100

submissions@papress.com

http://www.papress.com

Types: Nonfiction
Subjects: Architecture; Design
Markets: Adult

Send: Query
Don't send: Full text

Download submission guidelines from website
and submit by post.

P0721 Profile Books
Publishing Imprint
29 Cloth Fair, London, EC1A 7JQ
United Kingdom
Tel: +44 (0) 20 7841 6300
Fax: +44 (0) 20 7833 3969

info@profilebooks.com

https://profilebooks.com

Publishing Imprint: Profile Books (**P0721**)

Types: Nonfiction
Subjects: Biography; Business; Comedy /
Humour; Culture; Current Affairs; Finance;
History; Politics; Psychology; Science
Markets: Adult

Closed to approaches.

Award-winning small publisher noted for
author-friendly relations. Published the
number-one Christmas bestseller in 2003.
Accepts direct queries by email (up to 250
words) with first 10 pages, with QUERY and
the title of your work in the subject line. No
attachments. See website for full guidelines.

Authors: Alan Bennett; Francis Fukuyama;
Peter Nichols; Sue Unerman

Publishing Imprints: Economist Books.
(*P0247*); Profile Books (**P0721**); Serpent's Tail
(**P0805**)

P0722 Prometheus
Publishing Imprint
United States

Book Publisher: The Globe Pequot Press
(**P0324**)

P0723 Promissor Inc.
Book Publisher

Book Publisher: Houghton Mifflin Harcourt
(**P0421**)

P0724 Psyche
Publishing Imprint

Publishing Imprint: O-Books

P0725 Psyche Books
Publishing Imprint

Book Publisher: John Hunt Publishing Ltd

P0726 PublicAffairs
Publishing Imprint
United States

Book Publisher: Perseus Books (**P0693**)

P0727 Pudding Press
Publishing Imprint

Book Publisher: Patrician Press (**P0664**)

P0728 Puffin
Publishing Imprint
United States

Book Publisher: Penguin Young Readers Group (**P0688**)

P0729 Pulp! The Classics
Publishing Imprint
United Kingdom

Book Publisher: Oldcastle Books Group (**P0635**)

P0730 Purdue University Press
Book Publisher
504 West State Street, West Lafayette, IN 47907-2058
United States

pupress@purdue.edu

http://www.thepress.purdue.edu

ACADEMIC > **Nonfiction** > *Nonfiction Books*
Agriculture; Anthropology; Business; Education; Engineering; Health; History; Indiana; Judaism; Language; Leadership; Literature; Philosophy; Politics; Science; Technology

PROFESSIONAL > **Nonfiction** > *Nonfiction Books*
Agriculture; Business; Education; Engineering; Health; Leadership; Science; Technology

Send: Query; Author bio; Table of Contents; Proposal; Writing sample

Publishes scholarly and professional information. Welcomes proposals in its core subjects, which should be emailed to the Director.

Editorial Director: Justine Race

Managing Editor: Margaret Hunt

Publishing Imprint: PuP

P0731 Pure Indigo Limited
Book Publisher
Publishing Department, 17 The Herons, Cottenham, Cambridge, CB24 8XX
United Kingdom
Tel: +44 (0) 7981 395258

submissions@pureindigo.co.uk

http://www.pureindigo.co.uk/publishing

Types: Fiction; Nonfiction
Subjects: Fantasy; Science Fiction
Markets: Children's

Send: Query
Don't send: Full text

Publishes books for children, including single-player role-playing gamebooks and books designed to support early readers. Prefers submissions by email. See website for guidelines.

P0732 PUSH
Publishing Imprint

Book Publisher: Scholastic (**P0790**)

P0733 Pushkin Children's Books
Publishing Imprint

Book Publisher: Pushkin Press (**P0734**)

P0734 Pushkin Press
Book Publisher
71-75 Shelton Street, London, WC2H 9JQ
United Kingdom
Tel: +44 (0) 20 3735 9078

books@pushkinpress.com

http://pushkinpress.com

Types: Fiction; Nonfiction
Subjects: Autobiography; Contemporary; Traditional
Markets: Adult; Children's

Publishes novels, essays, memoirs, children's books, including timeless classics and contemporary.

Publishing Imprint: Pushkin Children's Books (*P0733*)

P0735 QED Publishing
Publishing Imprint
The Old Brewery, 6 Blundell Street, London, N7 9BH
United Kingdom
Tel: +44 (0) 20 7812 8633

QuartoHomesSubmissions@Quarto.com

https://www.quartoknows.com/QED-Publishing

Book Publisher: The Quarto Group, Inc. (**P0739**)

CHILDREN'S
    Fiction > *Picture Books*
    Nonfiction > *Illustrated Books*

Send: Query; Proposal
How to send: Email

Publishes fresh, informative, high-quality books that will appeal to children, parents and teachers alike, from entertaining, innovative facts for the classroom to beautifully illustrated

fiction that kids will want to take home. Always on the lookout for authors and artists with creative ideas that enhance and broaden their publishing list of children's books.

Publisher: Steve Evans

P0736 Quadrille Publishing Ltd
Book Publisher
5th & 6th Floors, 52-54 Southwark Street, London, SE1 1UN
United Kingdom
Tel: +44 (0) 20 7601 7500

editorial@quadrille.co.uk

http://www.quadrille.co.uk

Types: Nonfiction
Subjects: Beauty; Comedy / Humour; Cookery; Crafts; Design; Fashion; Gardening; Health
Markets: Adult

Send: Query
Don't send: Full text

Publishes quality illustrated nonfiction. No fiction or books for children. Prefers to receive submissions by email. See website for full details.

P0737 Quarry
Publishing Imprint

Book Publisher: The Quarto Group, Inc. (**P0739**)

P0738 Quarto Children's Books
Publishing Imprint

Book Publisher: The Quarto Group, Inc. (**P0739**)

P0739 The Quarto Group, Inc.
Book Publisher
The Old Brewery, 6 Blundell Street, London, N7 9BH
United Kingdom
Tel: +44 (0) 20 7700 6700
Fax: +44 (0) 20 7700 8066

http://www.quarto.com

ADULT > **Nonfiction** > *Nonfiction Books*

CHILDREN'S > **Nonfiction** > *Nonfiction Books*

Publisher of illustrated nonfiction books for adults and children.

Publishing Imprints: Apple Press; Aurum Press; Book Sales (*P0120*); Bright Press; Burgess Lea Press (*P0134*); Cool Springs Press (*P0185*); Epic Ink (*P0264*); Fair Winds Press (*P0272*); Frances Lincoln; Frances Lincoln Children's Books (**P0301**); Harvard Common Press (**P0391**); Iqon Editions (*P0455*); Ivy Kids (*P0458*); Ivy Press (*P0459*); Jacqui Small; Leaping Hare Press

(*P0510*); Lincoln First Editions (*P0525*); Motorbooks (*P0594*); QED Publishing (**P0735**); Quarry (*P0737*); Quarto Children's Books (*P0738*); Quarto Publishing (*P0740*); Race Point Publishing (*P0745*); Rock Point Gift & Stationery (*P0763*); Rockport Publishing (*P0765*); SmartLab Toys (*P0819*); Union Books; Voyageur Press (**P0940**); Walter Foster Jr. (*P0945*); Walter Foster Publishing (**P0946**); Wellfleet Press (*P0958*); White Lion Publishing (*P0967*); Wide-Eyed Editions (**P0970**); Words & Pictures (**P0980**); becker&mayer! books (**P0089**); becker&mayer! kids (*P0090*); small world creations (*P0818*)

P0740 Quarto Publishing
Publishing Imprint

Book Publisher: The Quarto Group, Inc. (**P0739**)

P0741 Quattro Books
Book Publisher
12 Concord Ave, 2nd Floor, Toronto, Ontario, M6H 2P1
Canada
Tel: +1 (416) 893-7979

info@quattrobooks.ca

http://quattrobooks.ca

Types: Fiction; Poetry
Subjects: Literary
Markets: Adult

Publishes novellas of literary fiction, and poetry. Accepts work from Canadian citizens residing in Canada only. Novellas should be between 20,000 and 40,000 words. No genre fiction. Not accepting poetry manuscripts as at June 2019. No electronic submissions.

P0742 Quercus Books
Book Publisher
Carmelite House, 50 Victoria Embankment, London, EC4Y 0DZ
United Kingdom
Tel: +44 (0) 20 3122 6000

enquiries@quercusbooks.co.uk

https://www.quercusbooks.co.uk

Book Publisher: Hachette Livre (**P0350**)

Types: Fiction; Nonfiction
Subjects: Crime; Fantasy; Science Fiction
Markets: Adult; Children's

How to send: Through a literary agent

Publishes fiction and nonfiction. Accepts submissions only via a literary agent.

Publishing Imprint: Jo Fletcher Books

P0743 Quill Driver Books
Publishing Imprint
2006 South Mary Street, Fresno, CA 93721
United States

Tel: +1 (800) 345-4447
Fax: +1 (559) 233-6933

kent@lindenpub.com

https://quilldriverbooks.com

Book Publisher: Linden Publishing

Types: Nonfiction
Subjects: Architecture; Arts; Biography; Business; Comedy / Humour; Crime; Health; Hobbies; Lifestyle; Self Help; Spirituality; Technology; Travel
Markets: Adult

Send: Query
Don't send: Full text

Publishes nonfiction only. Send a book proposal including synopsis; commercial info; author platform; and sample chapters or supporting materials. See website for full guidelines.

Editor: Kent Sorsky

P0744 Quintet Publishing
Book Publisher
Ovest House, 58 West Street, Brighton, BN1 2RA
United Kingdom
Tel: +44 (0) 1273 716 000

mark.searle@quarto.com

https://www.quartoknows.com/Quintet-Publishing

Types: Nonfiction
Subjects: Cookery; Crafts; Culture; Lifestyle; Photography
Markets: Adult

Publishes illustrated nonfiction on a co-edition basis with partners around the world.

P0745 Race Point Publishing
Publishing Imprint

Book Publisher: The Quarto Group, Inc. (**P0739**)

P0746 Radioactive Cloud
Book Publisher
United States

https://radioactivecloud.weebly.com

Types: Poetry
Subjects: Literary
Markets: Adult

Send: Full text

Publishes poetry chapbooks between 15 and 30 pages in length. Submit via online submission system during submission window (December 1 – January 15).

P0747 Ransom Note Press
Book Publisher
P.O. Box 419, Ridgewood, NJ 07451
United States

editorial@ransomnotepress.com

http://www.ransomnotepress.com

Types: Fiction
Subjects: Mystery; Suspense
Markets: Adult

Send: Query
Don't send: Full text

Publishes mystery and suspense novels only. Accepts approaches via post or email. See website for full submission guidelines.

P0748 Ransom Publishing Ltd
Book Publisher
Unit 7, Brocklands Farm, West Meon, Hampshire, GU32 1JN
United Kingdom
Tel: +44 (0) 1730 829091

steve@ransom.co.uk

http://www.ransom.co.uk

Types: Fiction; Nonfiction
Markets: Adult; Children's; Professional; Young Adult

Closed to approaches.

An independent specialist publisher of high quality, inspirational books that encourage and help children, young adults, and adults to develop their reading skills. Books are intended to have content which is age appropriate and engaging, but reading levels that would normally be appropriate for younger readers. Also publishes resources for both the library and classroom. No picture books or early years books. Will consider unsolicited mss. Email with synopsis and sample (up to three chapters) in first instance, or full ms if under thousand words.

Editor: Steve Rickard

P0749 Razorbill
Publishing Imprint
345 Hudson Street, New York, NY 10014
United States

http://www.razorbillbooks.com

Book Publisher: Penguin Young Readers Group (**P0688**)

Types: Fiction; Nonfiction
Subjects: Adventure; Comedy / Humour; Contemporary; Culture; Fantasy; Literary; Romance; Science Fiction; Suspense
Markets: Children's; Young Adult

Send: Query
Don't send: Full text

Publishes mainly fiction for middle grade and young adult. Send query with SASE, outline, target group, publishing credits (if any), and up to 30 pages. No picture books. Response only if interested.

P0750 REaDLips Press
Book Publisher
United States

readlipspress@gmail.com

https://readlipspress.com

Types: Fiction
Subjects: Literary
Markets: Adult

Send: Query
Don't send: Full text

Publishes literary fiction novellas between 20,000 and 60,000 words. Send blurb, bio, and summary by email. See website for full guidelines.

P0751 REAL LIFE PRESS/Biography REAL LIFE PRESS/Fiction FLASHfacts
Publishing Imprint

Book Publisher: Real Life Press

P0752 Rebel Base Books
Publishing Imprint

Book Publisher: Kensington Publishing Corp. **(P0488)**

P0753 Red Moon Press
Book Publisher
P.0. Box 2461, Winchester, VA 22604-1661
United States
Tel: +1 (540) 722-2156

jim.kacian@redmoonpress.com

http://www.redmoonpress.com

Types: Fiction; Nonfiction; Poetry; Translations
Subjects: Biography; Literary Criticism
Markets: Adult

Send: Query
Don't send: Full text

Publishes anthologies of haiku, Haibun, and related forms, plus relevant works of fiction, collections of essays, translations, criticism, etc. Send query in first instance.

P0754 Red Rattle Books
Book Publisher
United Kingdom

editor@redrattlebooks.co.uk

http://www.redrattlebooks.co.uk

Types: Fiction; Nonfiction
Subjects: Crime; Horror
Markets: Adult

Closed to approaches.

Not accepting submissions as at January 2019. Check website for current status. Independent, family run company, publishing new crime, horror and nonfiction

books. Submit via website using online submission form.

P0755 Regency House Publishing Limited
Book Publisher
The Manor House, High Street, Buntingford, Hertfordshire, SG9 9AB
United Kingdom

https://beta.companieshouse.gov.uk/company/02673368

Nonfiction > *Nonfiction Books*

Publishes and packages mass-market nonfiction. Does not accept fiction or unsolicited MSS.

Chair: Brian Trodd

Managing Director: Nicolette Trodd

P0756 Repeater Books
Book Publisher
United Kingdom

https://repeaterbooks.com

Types: Fiction; Nonfiction; Poetry
Subjects: Arts; Culture; Current Affairs; Literature; Music; Philosophy; Politics
Markets: Adult

Send: Full text

Aims to publish in every sphere and genre, "combining vigorous dissent and a pragmatic willingness to succeed". Submit complete ms via online submission system.

P0757 Richard Hollis
Publishing Imprint

Book Publisher: Five Leaves Publications **(P0289)**

P0758 Rider Books
Publishing Imprint
United Kingdom

Book Publisher: Ebury **(P0243)**

P0759 Rising Stars
Book Publisher
Carmelite House, 50 Victoria Embankment, London, EC4Y 0DZ
United Kingdom
Tel: +44 (0) 20 3122 6000

primary@bookpoint.co.uk

https://www.risingstars-uk.com
https://www.youtube.com/channel/UCTO7hZc1TrfzBKFEo4i8qkQ
https://twitter.com/risingstarsedu
https://www.facebook.com/Rising-Stars-547479242046479/timeline/
https://www.instagram.com/risingstarsedu

Book Publisher: Hodder Education **(P0412)**

ACADEMIC > **Nonfiction** > *Nonfiction Books*: Education

Send: Query
How to send: Online submission system

Publisher of educational books and software for children aged 3-18. Always looking for people bursting with ideas and imagination and a view of primary education. Complete survey online in first instance.

Publishing Director: Ben Barton

P0760 Riverhead Books
Publishing Imprint
United States

Book Publisher: Penguin Publishing Group **(P0682)**

Types: Fiction; Nonfiction
Subjects: Commercial; Contemporary; Literary
Markets: Adult

Publisher of bestselling literary fiction and quality nonfiction.

Editor: Megan Lynch

P0761 The Riverside Publishing Co.
Book Publisher

Book Publisher: Houghton Mifflin Harcourt **(P0421)**

P0762 Robert D. Reed Publishers
Book Publisher
POB 1992, Bandon, OR 97411
United States
Tel: +1 (541) 347-9882
Fax: +1 (541) 347-9883

bob@rdrpublishers.com

http://www.rdrpublishers.com

Types: Nonfiction
Subjects: Autobiography; Business; Comedy / Humour; Finance; Health; History; Lifestyle; Psychology; Self Help; Spirituality
Markets: Adult; Children's

Send: Query
Don't send: Full text

Publishes nonfiction by authors with a platform to sell their books. Manuscripts must have been professionally edited. Send query through contact form on website. No longer publishes fiction.

P0763 Rock Point Gift & Stationery
Publishing Imprint

Book Publisher: The Quarto Group, Inc. **(P0739)**

P0764 Rocket Science Press
Publishing Imprint

Book Publisher: Shipwreckt Books Publishing Company (**P0811**)

P0765 Rockport Publishing
Publishing Imprint

Book Publisher: The Quarto Group, Inc. (**P0739**)

P0766 Romance Publications
Book Publisher
United States

romancepublications@gmail.com

https://www.facebook.com/romance.publications/

Fiction
Novelette: Romance
Novellas: Romance
Novels: Romance
Short Fiction: Romance

How to send: Email

Publishes romantic stories that include a central love story and emotionally satisfying and optimistic ending. In addition to novels, we publish novellas, novelettes, and short stories. We are currently accepting short stores (450-550) words to be published in our monthly newsletters and anthologies of short stories. Anthologies will be sold for a profit, and the authors will receive a portion of the royalties that is typically given to a single author, which is 25%.

P0767 Roundfire
Publishing Imprint

Book Publisher: John Hunt Publishing Ltd

P0768 Route Publishing
Book Publisher
PO Box 167, Pontefract, WF8 4WW
United Kingdom
Tel: +44 (0) 1977 793442

info@route-online.com

http://www.route-online.com

Types: Fiction; Nonfiction
Formats: Film Scripts
Subjects: Autobiography; Contemporary; Culture; Music
Markets: Adult

Publisher of nonfiction (particularly music books) and occasional fiction. Only accept a handful of titles a year. Response no guaranteed. If submitting by post, include SAE if return of work required.

Editors: Ian Daley; Isabel Galan

P0769 Routledge
Book Publisher
United Kingdom

https://www.routledge.com

Book Publisher: Taylor & Francis Books

Types: Nonfiction
Subjects: Anthropology; Archaeology; Architecture; Business; Crime; Finance; Health; Legal; Nature; Politics; Psychology; Science; Technology
Markets: Academic; Adult; Professional

Send: Query
Don't send: Full text

International academic imprint. Send proposal with sample chapters and author CV (see website for detailed guidelines). No fiction, poetry, travel, or astrology.

Book Publisher: David Fulton (Publishers) Ltd

P0770 Ruby Fiction
Publishing Imprint
Penrose House, Crawley Drive, Camberley, Surrey, GU15 2AB
United Kingdom
Tel: +44 (0)1276 586367

info@rubyfiction.com

https://www.rubyfiction.com
https://twitter.com/rubyfiction
https://www.facebook.com/pages/RubyFiction

Book Publisher: Choc Lit (**P0166**)

Fiction > *Novels*
Romance; Thrillers; Women's Fiction

Send: Author bio; Synopsis
How to send: Online submission system

Publishes thrillers, women's fiction and romances without the hero's point of view, between 60,000 and 100,000 words, suitable for a female adult audience.

P0771 Running Press
Publishing Imprint
United States

Book Publisher: Perseus Books (**P0693**)

P0772 RYA (Royal Yachting Association)
Book Publisher
RYA House, Ensign Way, Hamble, Southampton, Hampshire, SO31 4YA
United Kingdom
Tel: +44 (0) 23 8060 4100
Fax: +44 (0) 23 8060 4299

enquiries@rya.org.uk

https://www.rya.org.uk/

Nonfiction > *Nonfiction Books*
Boats; Sailing; Yachts

Publisher of books on boating and sailing.

Editor: Phil Williams-Ellis

P0773 Saddle Road Press
Book Publisher
1483 Wailuku Drive, Hilo, HI 96720
United States

info@saddleroadpress.com

http://saddleroadpress.com

Types: Fiction; Poetry
Formats: Short Fiction
Subjects: Autobiography; Literary
Markets: Adult

Closed to approaches.

Closed to submissions as at September 2019. Check website for current status. Small literary press publishing full-length poetry collections, poetry chapbooks, literary fiction, essays, memoir, and hybrid forms, in both print and eBook editions. Currently looking for collections of poetry and hybrid poetry/prose, and collections of short fiction and lyric essays. Submit through online submission system. $20 submission fee.

P0774 Saffron Books
Book Publisher
EAPGROUP, PO Box 13666, London, SW14 8WF
United Kingdom
Tel: +44 (0) 20 8392 1122
Fax: +44 (0) 20 8392 1122

info@eapgroup.com

http://www.saffronbooks.com

Types: Fiction; Nonfiction
Subjects: Archaeology; Arts; Business; Culture; Current Affairs; Finance; History; Sociology
Markets: Adult

Send: Query
Don't send: Full text

Publishes books on art, archaeology and architecture, art history, current affairs and linguistics, with a particular emphasis on Asia, Africa, and the Middle East. Also publishes fiction. Welcomes proposals for books and monographs from new or established authors. Send query by email, post, or fax (not preferred for long documents). See website for full guidelines.

P0775 Sage Publications
Book Publisher
1 Oliver's Yard, 55 City Road, London, EC1Y 1SP
United Kingdom
Tel: +44 (0) 20 7324 8500
Fax: +44 (0) 20 7324 8600

info@sagepub.co.uk

https://uk.sagepub.com

Types: Nonfiction
Subjects: Anthropology; Archaeology; Arts; Business; Crime; Finance; Health; History; Media; Medicine; Politics; Psychology; Religion; Science; Sociology; Technology
Markets: Academic; Professional

Publishes academic books and journals. See website for guides for authors and making submissions, etc.

Book Publisher: CQ Press

P0776 Saint Andrew Press
Publishing Imprint
Norwich Books and Music, 13a Hellesdon Park Road, Norwich, NR6 5DR
United Kingdom
Tel: +44 (0) 1603 785925
Fax: +44 (0) 1603 785915

admin@norwichbooksandmusic.co.uk

https://standrewpress.hymnsam.co.uk

Book Publisher: Hymns Ancient & Modern Ltd (**P0428**)

Types: Nonfiction
Formats: Reference
Subjects: Religion
Markets: Adult; Children's

Send: Query
Don't send: Full text

Publisher of religious books for the UK and international Christian retail and trade markets, including general reference and children's books. See website for full submission guidelines.

P0777 Saint Julian Press
Book Publisher
2053 Cortlandt, Suite 200, Houston, TX 77008
United States
Tel: +1 (281) 734-8721

ronstarbuck@saintjulianpress.com

http://www.saintjulianpress.com

Types: Poetry
Subjects: Literary
Markets: Adult

Closed to approaches.

Literary poetry publisher. Charges reading fees of between $50 and $80 depending on manuscript length. Closed to submissions until late 2019 / early 2020. Check website for current status.

Editor: Ron Starbuck

P0778 The Salariya Book Company
Book Publisher
25 Marlborough Place, Brighton, East Sussex, BN1 1UB
United Kingdom

Tel: +44 (0) 1273 603306
Fax: +44 (0) 1273 621619

salariya@salariya.com

http://www.salariya.com

Types: Fiction; Nonfiction
Subjects: Adventure; Fantasy; History; Nature; Science
Markets: Children's

Closed to approaches.

Not accepting submissions as at February 2019. Check website for current status. Publishes books of fiction and nonfiction for children.

Publishing Imprints: Book House (*P0119*); Scribblers (*P0798*); Scribo (*P0799*)

P0779 Salo Press
Book Publisher
United Kingdom

editorsalopress@gmail.com

https://salopress.weebly.com

Types: Poetry
Subjects: Experimental; Literary
Markets: Adult

An independent micro publisher focusing on poetry of an experimental / weird / surreal / cerebral nature. See website for current submission opportunities.

Editor: Sophie Essex

P0780 Salt Publishing Ltd
Book Publisher
12 Norwich Road, CROMER, Norfolk, NR27 0AX
United Kingdom
Tel: +44 (0) 1263 511011

submissions@saltpublishing.com

http://www.saltpublishing.com

Types: Fiction; Nonfiction; Poetry
Formats: Short Fiction
Subjects: Biography; Crime; Gothic; Literary Criticism; Mystery; Thrillers
Markets: Adult; Children's

Currently accepting submissions of contemporary adult poetry and nonfiction by British residents. See website for full submission guidelines.

P0781 Salvo Press
Publishing Imprint
221 River St, 9th Floor, Hoboken, NJ 07030
United States
Tel: +1 (212) 431-5455

info@salvopress.com

http://salvopress.com

Book Publisher: Start Publishing (**P0838**)

Types: Fiction
Subjects: Literary; Mystery; Thrillers
Markets: Adult

Publishes quality mysteries, thrillers, and literary books in eBook and audiobook formats.

P0782 Samosir Books
Book Publisher
United Kingdom

https://samosirbooksltd.blogspot.com

Types: Nonfiction
Subjects: Adventure; Comedy / Humour; Culture; Travel
Markets: Adult

Dedicated to publishing and distributing travel related literature worldwide.

Authors: Chris Raven; Simon Raven

P0783 SAMS Publishing
Publishing Imprint

Book Publisher: Pearson (**P0670**)

P0784 Sandstone Press Ltd
Book Publisher
Suite 1, Willow House, Stoneyfield Business Park, Inverness, IV2 7PA
United Kingdom
Tel: +44 (0) 1349 865484

submissions@sandstonepress.com
info@sandstonepress.com

https://sandstonepress.com
https://www.youtube.com/channel/UC_36jtKtY2dy8roy5jQMQHg
https://www.facebook.com/SandstonePress
https://twitter.com/sandstonepress

Fiction > *Novels*

Nonfiction > *Nonfiction Books*

Send: Query; Submission Form; Synopsis; Writing sample
How to send: Word file email attachment; Through a literary agent

Accepts submissions of nonfiction from agents and authors all year. Accepts submissions of fiction from agents all year, but accepts submissions of fiction from authors during specific windows only. Check website for status regarding fiction submissions from authors. Accepts approaches via email only. See website for full guidelines.

P0785 Santa Monica Press
Book Publisher
P.O. Box 850, Solana Beach, CA 92075
United States
Tel: +1 (800) 784-9553

acquisitions@santamonicapress.com

http://www.santamonicapress.com

Types: Nonfiction
Formats: Film Scripts; Reference
Subjects: Architecture; Arts; Biography; Comedy / Humour; Culture; Entertainment; History; Literature; Photography; Sport; Travel
Markets: Adult

Send: Query
Don't send: Full text

Accepts proposals from agents and directly from authors, but post or by email. See website for full submission guidelines.

P0786 Saqi Books
Book Publisher
26 Westbourne Grove, London, W2 5RH
United Kingdom
Tel: +44 (0) 20 7221 9347
Fax: +44 (0) 20 7229 7492

elizabeth@saqibooks.com

http://www.saqibooks.com

Types: Fiction; Nonfiction
Subjects: Architecture; Arts; Cookery; History; Literary; Politics
Markets: Academic; Adult

Send: Query
Don't send: Full text

Publisher of books related to the Arab world and the Middle East (initially), but now also covering South and Central Asia. Also publishes European fiction. Not accepting fiction submissions as at September 2019. See website for full submission guidelines.

Publishing Imprint: Telegram Books (**P0853**)

P0787 Sarabande Books, Inc.
Book Publisher
822 E. Market St., Louisville, KY 40206
United States
Tel: +1 (502) 458-4028

info@sarabandebooks.org

http://www.sarabandebooks.org

Types: Fiction; Nonfiction; Poetry
Subjects: Literary
Markets: Adult

Send: Full text

Nonprofit literary press championing poetry, fiction, and essays. Accepts submissions through its annual competitions, for which an entry fee must be paid.

P0788 Sawday's
Book Publisher
Merchants House, Wapping Road, Bristol, BS1 4RW
United Kingdom
Tel: +44 (0) 1172 047810

hello@sawdays.co.uk

https://www.sawdays.co.uk

Types: Nonfiction
Subjects: Nature; Travel
Markets: Adult

Publishes guidebooks and books on environmental topics.

P0789 Schocken Books
Publishing Imprint
United States

Book Publisher: Knopf Doubleday Publishing Group (**P0498**)

P0790 Scholastic
Book Publisher
557 Broadway, New York, NY 10012
United States

TeachingResources@Scholastic.com

https://www.scholastic.com
https://scholastic.force.com/scholasticfaqs/s/article/How-do-I-submit-a-manuscript-for-teaching-ideas

CHILDREN'S
  Fiction
    Chapter Books; *Early Readers*; *Middle Grade*; *Novels*; *Picture Books*
  Nonfiction
    Chapter Books; *Early Readers*; *Illustrated Books*; *Middle Grade*
PROFESSIONAL > **Nonfiction** > *Nonfiction Books*: Education

Send: Query; Table of Contents; Writing sample

The world's largest publisher and distributor of children's books. Provides professional services, classroom magazines, and produces educational and popular children's media.

Book Publishers: Arthur A. Levine Books; Chicken House Publishing; Scholastic UK (**P0797**)

Publishing Imprints: AFK (*P0024*); Cartwheel Books (*P0151*); Graphix (*P0338*); Klutz (*P0496*); Orchard Books (*P0643*); PUSH (*P0732*); Scholastic Audio (*P0791*); Scholastic Focus (*P0793*); Scholastic Inc. (*P0794*); Scholastic Press (*P0795*); Scholastic Reference (*P0796*)

P0791 Scholastic Audio
Publishing Imprint

Book Publisher: Scholastic (**P0790**)

P0792 Scholastic Children's Books
Book Publisher

Book Publisher: Scholastic UK (**P0797**)

P0793 Scholastic Focus
Publishing Imprint

Book Publisher: Scholastic (**P0790**)

P0794 Scholastic Inc.
Publishing Imprint

Book Publisher: Scholastic (**P0790**)

P0795 Scholastic Press
Publishing Imprint

Book Publisher: Scholastic (**P0790**)

P0796 Scholastic Reference
Publishing Imprint

Book Publisher: Scholastic (**P0790**)

P0797 Scholastic UK
Book Publisher
Euston House, 24 Eversholt Street, London, NW1 1DB, WITNEY:, Windrush Park, Range Road, Witney, OXON, OX29 0YD, SOUTHAM:, Westfield Road, Southam, Warwickshire, CV47 0RA
United Kingdom
Tel: +44 (0) 1926 887799
Fax: +44 (0) 1926 883331

enquiries@scholastic.co.uk

https://www.scholastic.co.uk

Book Publisher: Scholastic (**P0790**)

Types: Fiction; Nonfiction
Markets: Children's

Publisher of fiction and nonfiction for children, as well as educational material for primary schools.

Book Publisher: Scholastic Children's Books (*P0792*)

P0798 Scribblers
Publishing Imprint

Book Publisher: The Salariya Book Company (**P0778**)

P0799 Scribo
Publishing Imprint

Book Publisher: The Salariya Book Company (**P0778**)

P0800 Seaworthy Publications
Book Publisher
6300 N Wickham Road, Unit #130-416, Melbourne, FL 32940
United States
Tel: +1 (321) 610-3634
Fax: +1 (321) 259-6872

queries@seaworthy.com

http://www.seaworthy.com

Types: Nonfiction
Subjects: Hobbies; Leisure; Travel
Markets: Adult

Send: Full text

Nautical book publisher specialising in recreational boating. Send query by email outlining your work and attaching sample table of contents and two or three sample chapters. See website for full submission guidelines.

P0801 SelfMadeHero
Book Publisher
139 Pancras Road, London, NW1 1UN
United Kingdom

submissions@selfmadehero.com

https://selfmadehero.com

Types: Fiction; Nonfiction
Subjects: Biography; Crime; Horror; Science Fiction
Markets: Adult

Publishes fiction and nonfiction graphic novels. Send query by email or by post with one-page synopsis and at least eight pages of sequential art (up to 5MB if sending by email). See website for full guidelines.

P0802 Sentinel
Publishing Imprint
United States

Book Publisher: Penguin Publishing Group (**P0682**)

P0803 September Publishing
Book Publisher
United Kingdom
Tel: +44 (0) 20 3637 0116

info@septemberpublishing.org

https://www.septemberpublishing.org

Types: Nonfiction
Subjects: Arts; Autobiography; Comedy / Humour; Politics; Travel
Markets: Adult

Publishes extraordinary lives and expert insight. Welcomes submissions from both authors and agents via form on website.

P0804 Seren Books
Book Publisher
Suite 6, 4 Derwen Road, Bridgend, CF31 1LH
United Kingdom
Tel: +44 (0) 1656 663018

Seren@SerenBooks.com

https://www.serenbooks.com
https://www.facebook.com/SerenBooks
http://www.twitter.com/SerenBooks
http://www.pinterest.com/SerenBooks

Fiction
  Novels: Literary
  Short Fiction: Literary

Nonfiction > *Nonfiction Books*
  Arts; Biography; Current Affairs; Drama; History; Literary Criticism; Memoir; Music; Photography; Sport; Travel

Poetry > *Poetry Collections*

Send: Full text

Publishes fiction, nonfiction, and poetry. Specialises in English-language writing from Wales and aims to bring Welsh culture, art, literature, and politics to a wider audience. Accepts nonfiction submissions by post or by email. Accepts poetry submissions by post only. Accepts fiction only from authors with whom there is an existing publishing relationship.

Poetry Editor: Amy Wack

Publisher: Mick Felton

P0805 Serpent's Tail
Publishing Imprint
3 Holford Yard, Bevin Way, London, WC1X 9HD
United Kingdom
Tel: +44 (0) 20 7841 6300

info@profilebooks.com

http://www.serpentstail.com

Publishing Imprint: Profile Books (**P0721**)

Types: Fiction; Nonfiction
Subjects: Autobiography; Crime; Culture; Current Affairs; Music; Politics
Markets: Adult

Accepts queries by email (up to 250 words) with sample text (10 pages or the first chapter only). See website for full submission guidelines. No poetry, Young Adult, Fantasy, Science Fiction, children's picture books, or screenplays.

P0806 Severn House Publishers
Book Publisher
Eardley House, 4 Uxbridge Street, London, W8 7SY
United Kingdom
Tel: +44 (0) 20 3011 0525

sales@severnhouse.com

http://severnhouse.com

Types: Fiction
Subjects: Crime; History; Horror; Mystery; Romance; Science Fiction; Thrillers
Markets: Adult

How to send: Through a literary agent

Accepts submissions via literary agents only. Targets the UK and US fiction library markets, and considers only authors with a significant background in these markets.

P0807 Shearsman Books
Book Publisher
PO Box 4239, Swindon, SN3 9FN
United Kingdom
Tel: +44 (0) 1179 572957

editor@shearsman.com

https://www.shearsman.com

Types: Nonfiction; Poetry; Translations
Subjects: Autobiography; Literary Criticism
Markets: Adult

Send: Query
Don't send: Full text

Publishes poetry books of at least 60 A5 pages. Publishes mainly poetry by British, Irish, North American and Australian/New Zealand poets, plus poetry in translation from any language—although particular interest in German, Spanish and Latin American poetry. Submit only if MS is of appropriate length and most of it has already appeared in UK or US magazines of some repute. Send selection of 6-10 pages by post with SASE or by email with material embedded in the text or as PDF attachment. No other kind of attachments accepted. Also sometimes publishes literary criticism on poetry, and essays or memoirs by poets.

Editor: Tony Frazer

P0808 Sheldrake Press
Book Publisher
PO Box 74852, London, SW12 2DX
United Kingdom
Tel: +44 (0) 20 8675 1767
Fax: +44 (0) 20 8675 7736

enquiries@sheldrakepress.co.uk

http://www.sheldrakepress.co.uk

Types: Nonfiction
Subjects: Architecture; Comedy / Humour; Cookery; History; Music; Travel
Markets: Adult

Publisher of illustrated nonfiction titles covering travel, history, cookery, music, humour, and stationery. No fiction.

Publisher: Simon Rigge

P0809 Shelf Stuff
Publishing Imprint

Book Publisher: HarperCollins (**P0378**)

P0810 Shepheard-Walwyn (Publishers) Ltd
Book Publisher
107 Parkway House, Sheen Lane, London, SW14 8LS
United Kingdom
Tel: +44 (0) 20 8241 5927

books@shepheard-walwyn.co.uk

https://shepheard-walwyn.co.uk

Types: Nonfiction; Poetry
Subjects: Biography; Finance; History; Philosophy; Politics
Markets: Adult

Publishes mainly nonfiction, particularly the areas listed above and also books of Scottish interest, and gift books in calligraphy and / or illustrated. Also some poetry.

P0811 Shipwreckt Books Publishing Company

Book Publisher
Ruchford, MN
United States

contact@shipwrecktbooks.com

http://www.shipwrecktbooks.com

Types: Fiction; Nonfiction; Poetry
Subjects: Autobiography; Comedy / Humour; Culture; Current Affairs; Fantasy; Gardening; Health; History; Legal; Leisure; Lifestyle; Literary; Medicine; Mystery; Nature; Politics; Science Fiction; Spirituality; Sport; Suspense; Warfare; Women's Interests
Markets: Adult; Children's; Young Adult

Closed to approaches.

Not accepting submissions as at May 2020. Publishes books and literary magazine. Submit brief bio, synopsis, and first ten pages (or a couple of poems) using form on website.

Publishing Imprints: Lost Lake Folk Art (*P0540*); Rocket Science Press (*P0764*); Up On Big Rock Poetry (*P0922*)

P0812 Silvertail Books

Book Publisher
United Kingdom

editor@silvertailbooks.com

http://www.silvertailbooks.com

Types: Fiction; Nonfiction
Subjects: Commercial
Markets: Adult

Welcomes submissions for commercial fiction and nonfiction, either through an agent or direct from authors. Submit by email only. No postal submissions. Response not guaranteed.

Author / Literary Agent / Publisher: Humfrey Hunter (**L0676**)

P0813 Simon & Schuster UK Limited

Book Publisher
1st Floor, 222 Gray's Inn Road, London, WC1X 8HB
United Kingdom
Tel: +44 (0) 20 7316 1900
Fax: +44 (0) 20 7316 0332

enquiries@simonandschuster.co.uk

https://www.simonandschuster.co.uk

Types: Fiction; Nonfiction
Subjects: Autobiography; Business; Comedy / Humour; Commercial; Cookery; Health; History; Literary; Politics; Science; Spirituality; Sport; Travel
Markets: Adult; Children's; Young Adult

How to send: Through a literary agent

Publisher of commercial and literary fiction and nonfiction for adults and children, including children's fiction and picture books. No unsolicited MSS.

Book Publishers: Martin Books (*P0572*); Simon & Schuster Children's Publishing

Publishing Imprints: The Free Press; Pocket Books; Scribner; Simon & Schuster

P0814 SisterShip Press Pty Ltd

Book Publisher
Australia

sistershippress@gmail.com

https://sistershippress.com

Types: Fiction; Nonfiction; Poetry
Formats: Film Scripts; Reference; Short Fiction
Subjects: Adventure; Autobiography; Business; Comedy / Humour; Commercial; Contemporary; Cookery; Crafts; Crime; Entertainment; Fantasy; Health; Hobbies; How To; Leisure; Lifestyle; Literary; Mystery; Nature; Psychology; Romance; Satire; Science; Self Help; Technology; Thrillers; Traditional; Women's Interests
Markets: Academic; Adult; Children's; Professional; Young Adult

Send: Full text

We are passionate about writing. We are excited about books. We (initially) are here for women; women with finished manuscripts. A nautical theme is our favourite but we are keen to read any adventure/travel/inspirational story – fiction or nonfiction. Technical books are also invited. We have a team with vast experience in all aspects of boating – professionally and recreationally. Read our FAQ on our website.

Editor: Jackie Parry and Shelley Wright

P0815 Skip Jack Press

Publishing Imprint
United States

Book Publisher: The Globe Pequot Press (**P0324**)

P0816 Skipstone

Publishing Imprint

Book Publisher: Mountaineers Books (**P0595**)

P0817 Skyhorse Publishing, Inc.

Book Publisher

Book Publisher: Allworth Press (**P0029**)

Publishing Imprints: Arcade Publishing; Sky Pony Press

P0818 small world creations

Publishing Imprint

Book Publisher: The Quarto Group, Inc. (**P0739**)

P0819 SmartLab Toys

Publishing Imprint

Book Publisher: The Quarto Group, Inc. (**P0739**)

P0820 Smith/Doorstop Books

Book Publisher
The Poetry Business, Campo House, 54 Campo Lane, Sheffield, S1 2EG
United Kingdom
Tel: +44 (0) 1484 434840
Fax: +44 (0) 1484 426566

office@poetrybusiness.co.uk

https://poetrybusiness.co.uk

Types: Nonfiction; Poetry
Subjects: Arts; Autobiography; Crime; Culture; Literary; Literary Criticism
Markets: Adult; Children's

Resolves to discover new and exciting poetry to showcase and publish. Accepts unsolicited mss only during open calls for submissions to guest-edited anthologies. See website for upcoming anthology publication opportunities. Also publishes winners of annual competitions.

P0821 Smithsonian Institution

Magazine Publisher; Book Publisher
PO Box 37012, MRC 513, Washington, DC 20013-7012
United States

info@si.edu

https://www.si.edu
https://www.facebook.com/Smithsonian
https://instagram.com/smithsonian
https://www.pinterest.com/smithsonian/
https://smithsonian.tumblr.com/
https://twitter.com/smithsonian
https://www.youtube.com/c/smithsonian

Magazines: Air & Space Magazine (**M0020**); Smithsonian Magazine (**M0513**)

P0822 Snowbooks

Book Publisher
55 North Street, Thame, OXON, OX9 3BH
United Kingdom

submissions@snowbooks.com

http://www.snowbooks.com

Types: Fiction; Nonfiction
Subjects: Crafts; Crime; Fantasy; History; Horror; Leisure; Science Fiction; Sport; Thrillers
Markets: Adult

Send: Full text

Open to submissions of horror, science fiction, and fantasy novels over 70,000 words. Named joint Small Publisher of the Year at the 2006 British book Trade Awards. Friendly attitude towards authors and unsolicited approaches. See website for guidelines. Approach via email only – postal submissions will neither be read nor returned, even if sent through an agent.

Managing Director: Emma Barnes

P0823   Soho Press
Book Publisher
United States
Tel: +1 (212) 260-1900

soho@sohopress.com

https://sohopress.com

Types: Fiction
Subjects: Crime; Literary
Markets: Adult; Young Adult

Publishes bold literary voices, award-winning international crime fiction, and groundbreaking young adult fiction.

P0824   Somerville Press
Book Publisher
Dromore, Bantry, Co. Cork
Ireland
Tel: 353 (0) 28 32873

somervillepress@eircom.net

http://www.somervillepress.com

Types: Fiction; Nonfiction
Markets: Adult

Publishes fiction and nonfiction, mainly of Irish interest.

P0825   Soul Rocks
Publishing Imprint

Book Publisher: John Hunt Publishing Ltd

P0826   Southwater.
Publishing Imprint

Book Publisher: Anness Publishing Ltd **(P0040)**

P0827   Speak
Publishing Imprint
United States

Book Publisher: Penguin Young Readers Group **(P0688)**

P0828   Special Interest Model Books Ltd
Book Publisher
50a Willis Way, Poole, Dorset, BH15 3SY
United Kingdom
Tel: +44 (0) 1202 649930
Fax: +44 (0) 1202 649950

orders@specialinterestmodelbooks.co.uk

https://www.specialinterestmodelbooks.co.uk

Nonfiction > *Nonfiction Books*
Amateur Radio; Amateur Winemaking; Hobbies; Model Aircraft; Model Making; Model Ships and Boats; Radio Control

Publishes practical manuals for hobbyists in the fields of model engineering, scale modelling, radio-controlled models and home winemaking and brewing.

Editor: Chris Lloyd

P0829   Sphere
Publishing Imprint

Publishing Imprint: Little, Brown Book Group **(P0532)**

P0830   SportsBooks Limited
Book Publisher
9 St Aubyns Place, York, YO24 1EQ
United Kingdom
Tel: +44 (0) 1904 613475

info@sportsbooks.ltd.uk

http://www.sportsbooks.ltd.uk

Types: Nonfiction
Subjects: Biography; Sport
Markets: Adult

Publishes sports nonfiction.

Publishing Imprint: BMM *(P0114)*

P0831   Springer Nature
Book Publisher

Book Publishers: Macmillan Education **(P0558)**; Palgrave Macmillan **(P0658)**; Springer-Verlag London Ltd

P0832   Square Peg
Publishing Imprint
United Kingdom

Book Publisher: Vintage **(P0934)**

P0833   St Martin's Paperbacks
Publishing Imprint

Publishing Imprint: St Martin's Press **(P0834)**

P0834   St Martin's Press
Publishing Imprint
United States

publicity@stmartins.com

https://us.macmillan.com/smp

Book Publishers: Macmillan Publishers **(P0559)**; Macmillan

Types: Fiction; Nonfiction
Formats: Reference
Subjects: Biography; Crime; History; Mystery; Politics; Self Help; Travel
Markets: Academic; Adult

How to send: Through a literary agent

Approach via literary agent only. Began by importing UK authors to the States and continues to buy heavily in the United Kingdom. No unsolicited MSS or unagented queries.

Publishing Imprints: Castle Point Books *(P0152)*; Griffin *(P0342)*; Minotaur *(P0589)*; St Martin's Paperbacks *(P0833)*; Thomas Dunne Books **(P0858)**; Wednesday Books *(P0955)*

P0835   St Pauls
Book Publisher
2187 Victory Boulevard, Staten Island, NY 10314
United States
Tel: +1 (800) 343-2522
Fax: +1 (718) 698-8390

sales@stpauls.us

http://www.stpaulsusa.com

Types: Nonfiction
Subjects: Biography; Religion; Self Help
Markets: Adult

Send: Full text

Publishes books for a Roman Catholic readership.

P0836   Stackpole Books
Publishing Imprint
United States

Book Publisher: The Globe Pequot Press **(P0324)**

P0837   Star Bright Books
Book Publisher
13 Landsdowne Street, Cambridge, MA 02139
United States
Tel: +1 (617) 354-1300
Fax: +1 (617) 354-1399

info@starbrightbooks.com

https://starbrightbooks.org

CHILDREN'S
Fiction
Chapter Books; *Picture Books*
Nonfiction
Chapter Books: General
Picture Books: General, and in particular: Biography; Diversity

How to send: Post
How not to send: Email

Publishes books that are entertaining, meaningful and sensitive to the needs of all children. Welcomes submissions for picture books and longer works, both fiction and nonfiction. See website for full submission guidelines.

P0838   Start Publishing
Book Publisher

Publishing Imprint: Salvo Press (**P0781**)

P0839 Stash Books

Publishing Imprint
United States

Book Publisher: C&T Publishing (**P0138**)

P0840 Stone Bridge Press

Book Publisher
1393 Solano Avenue, Suite C, Albany, CA
94706
United States
Tel: +1 (510) 524-8732

sbpedit@stonebridge.com

https://www.stonebridge.com

Types: Fiction; Nonfiction; Poetry;
Translations
Formats: Film Scripts; Reference
Subjects: Arts; Business; Crafts; Culture;
Design; Lifestyle; Literature; Spirituality;
Travel
Markets: Adult; Children's

Send: Query
Don't send: Full text

Publishes books about Asia and in particular
Japan and China. Send brief query by email in
the first instance.

P0841 Stonewood Press

Book Publisher
Submissions, Stonewood Press, Diversity
House, 72 Nottingham Road, Arnold,
Nottingham, NG5 6LF
United Kingdom

stonewoodpress@gmail.com

http://www.stonewoodpress.co.uk

Types: Fiction; Poetry
Formats: Short Fiction
Subjects: Contemporary
Markets: Adult

**Note: Current submission status is unclear.
The publisher's website states it is closed to
new submissions, but that submissions re-
open from the start of 2017.** Independent
publisher dedicated to promoting new writing,
with an emphasis on contemporary short
stories and poetry. Send query with biography,
publishing history, and either one story and a
brief outline of the others in the collection, or
up to 10 poems and details of how many other
poems are in the collection. Submit by post
only. No children's books, creative nonfiction,
novels, or drama.

Editor: Martin Parker

P0842 Sunrise River Press

Book Publisher
838 Lake St S, Forest Lake, MN 55025
United States
Fax: +1 (800) 895-4585

submissions@sunriserverpress.com

https://www.sunriserverpress.com

Types: Nonfiction
Subjects: Health; Medicine; Self Help
Markets: Adult; Professional

Send: Full text

An award-winning publisher and part of a
three-company publishing house with more
than 33 years in specialty book publishing.
Since the early 1990s, this publisher has
published books exclusively for the
professional healthcare market. The company
is now transitioning its healthcare publishing
efforts to the serious end of the consumer
market, focusing on subjects such as weight
loss, nutrition, diet, food and recipes, family
health, fitness and specific diseases such as
cancer, anorexia, Alzheimer's, autism and
depression – especially as they relate to the
baby boomer generation. We are actively
seeking proposals from potential authors on
these and related topics. Our publishing house
currently publishes close to 30 consumer titles
per calendar year (through our two sister
companies). Our books consistently receive
national and international publicity in
enthusiast magazines.

P0843 Sunstone Press

Book Publisher
Box 2321, Santa Fe, NM 87504-2321
United States
Tel: +1 (505) 988-4418
Fax: +1 (505) 988-1025

http://www.sunstonepress.com

Types: Fiction; Nonfiction; Poetry
Formats: Reference; Short Fiction; Theatre
Scripts
Subjects: Adventure; Archaeology;
Architecture; Arts; Autobiography; Business;
Comedy / Humour; Cookery; Crafts; Crime;
Fantasy; Gardening; Health; History; How To;
Legal; Music; Mystery; Nature; Photography;
Politics; Religion; Romance; Science Fiction;
Sport; Travel; Warfare; Westerns; Women's
Interests
Markets: Adult; Children's

Send: Query
Don't send: Full text

Began in the 1970s with a focus on nonfiction
about the American Southwest, but has since
expanded its focus to include mainstream
themes and categories in both fiction and
nonfiction. Send query by post only with short
summary, author bio, one sample chapter, table
of contents, marketing plan, and statement on
why this is the right publisher for your book.

P0844 Swallow Press

Publishing Imprint

Book Publisher: Ohio University Press
(**P0633**)

P0845 Sweet Cherry
Publishing

Book Publisher
Unit 36, Vulcan House, Vulcan Road,
Leicester, LE5 3EF
United Kingdom

submissions@sweetcherrypublishing.com

https://www.sweetcherrypublishing.com

CHILDREN'S > Fiction
  Middle Grade; Picture Books

Send: Query; Writing sample; Synopsis;
Author bio
How to send: Email
How not to send: Post

Publishes books for children of all ages.
Specialises in sets and series, so unlikely to
take on a stand-alone title. Send submissions
by email only. No postal submissions. See
website for full submission guidelines.

Editor: Abdul Thadha

P0846 Sweetwater Books

Publishing Imprint

Book Publisher: Cedar Fort (**P0155**)

P0847 Tailwinds Press

Book Publisher
PO Box 2283, Radio City Station, New York,
NY 10101-2283
United States

submissions@tailwindspress.com

http://www.tailwindspress.com

Types: Fiction; Nonfiction
Subjects: Literary
Markets: Adult

Send: Full text

New York City-based independent press
specialising in high-quality literary fiction and
nonfiction. Send submissions by post or email.
See website for full guidelines.

P0848 Tammy Chapbooks

Book Publisher
United States

thetjournal@gmail.com

http://www.tammyjournal.com

Types: Fiction; Poetry
Subjects: Literary
Markets: Adult

Send: Full text

Publishes a literary journal and chapbooks. For
chapbook submissions, send up to 30 pages of
writing via online submission system ($12
submission fee).

Editors: Thomas Cook; Tyler Flynn Dorholt;
JoAnna Novak

P0849 Tango Books Ltd
Book Publisher
PO Box 32595, London, W4 5YD
United Kingdom
Tel: +44 (0) 20 8996 9970

info@tangobooks.co.uk

https://www.tangobooks.co.uk

Types: Fiction; Nonfiction
Markets: Children's

Closed to approaches.

**Closed to submissions as at June 2019.
Check website for current status.** Publisher
of children's fiction (ages 1-8), nonfiction
(ages 1-15), and novelty books, up to 1,000
words. Send query by email or by post with
complete text, bio, and SAE. No poetry or
verse, or texts that are very British in content
or style. See website for complete guidelines.

P0850 TANSTAAFL Press
Book Publisher
United States

submissions@tanstaaflpress.com

https://tanstaaflpress.com

Types: Fiction
Formats: Short Fiction
Subjects: Fantasy; Science Fiction
Markets: Adult

Send: Query
Don't send: Full text

Publishes science fiction, cyberpunk,
alternative histories, post apocalyptic and
fantasy of novel length. Will consider
exceptional works in other genres of fiction, or
short story compilations of the above topics.
Send query by email with 300-500 word
summary and first 1,000 words as a text
attachment. See website for full guidelines.

P0851 TarcherPerigee
Publishing Imprint
United States

Book Publisher: Penguin Publishing Group
(P0682)

P0852 Tate Publishing
Book Publisher
Millbank, London, SW1P 4RG
United Kingdom

submissions@tate.org.uk

https://www.tate.org.uk/publishing

Types: Nonfiction
Subjects: Arts; History
Markets: Adult; Children's

Send: Query
Don't send: Full text

Publishes exhibition-related and art-history
titles, as well as books for children. Accepts

proposals by post or by email. See website for
guidelines.

P0853 Telegram Books
Publishing Imprint
26 Westbourne Grove, London, W2 5RH
United Kingdom
Tel: +44 (0) 20 7221 9347
Fax: +44 (0) 20 7229 7492

elizabeth@saqibooks.com

https://saqibooks.com/imprint/telegram/

Book Publisher: Saqi Books **(P0786)**

Fiction > *Novels*

Closed to approaches.

Publishes fiction from around the world. Not
accepting submissions as at November 2020.

P0854 The Templar Company Limited
Book Publisher
2.08 The Plaza, The Plaza, 535 King's Road,
London, SW10 0SZ
United Kingdom
Tel: +44 (0) 20 3770 8888

hello@templarco.co.uk

https://www.templarco.co.uk

Book Publisher: Bonnier Books (UK) **(P0118)**

Types: Fiction; Nonfiction
Markets: Children's

How to send: Through a literary agent

Publishes children's fiction and picture and
novelty books. Encourage anybody who
wishes to have their work considered by one of
their imprints to seek representation by an
agent. No unsolicited mss or proposals.

P0855 Temple Lodge Publishing
Book Publisher
Hillside House, The Square, Forest Row,
RH18 5ES
United Kingdom

office@templelodge.com

https://www.templelodge.com

Types: Nonfiction
Subjects: Science; Spirituality
Markets: Adult

Send: Query
Don't send: Full text

Originally founded to develop the work of
Rudolf Steiner. Publishes nonfiction from a a
spiritual-scientific perspective. Send a
summary with list of chapters and sample
chapters by email or by post with SAE.

P0856 Thames & Hudson Inc.
Book Publisher
500 Fifth Avenue, New York, NY 10110
United States
Tel: +1 (212) 354-3763
Fax: +1 (212) 398-1252

bookinfo@thames.wwnorton.com

https://www.thamesandhudsonusa.com

Types: Fiction; Nonfiction; Poetry
Formats: Film Scripts; TV Scripts; Theatre
Scripts
Subjects: Anthropology; Antiques;
Archaeology; Architecture; Arts; Beauty;
Biography; Business; Comedy / Humour;
Crafts; Design; Fashion; Gardening; Health;
History; Literary Criticism; Medicine; Music;
Nature; Philosophy; Photography; Religion;
Science; Sport; Travel; Warfare
Markets: Adult

Send: Query
Don't send: Full text

Send proposals up to six pages by email. No
attachments or unsolicited mss.

P0857 Thames and Hudson Ltd
Book Publisher
181A High Holborn, London, WC1V 7QX
United Kingdom
Tel: +44 (0) 20 7845 5000

submissions@thameshudson.co.uk

http://www.thamesandhudson.com

Types: Nonfiction
Formats: Reference
Subjects: Archaeology; Architecture; Arts;
Beauty; Biography; Crafts; Culture; Design;
Fashion; Gardening; History; Lifestyle;
Literature; Nature; Philosophy; Photography;
Religion; Science; Travel
Markets: Adult; Children's

Send: Query
Don't send: Full text

Publishes illustrated nonfiction only. No
fiction. Prefers to receive submissions by
email, but will accept submissions by post. See
website for full details.

P0858 Thomas Dunne Books
Publishing Imprint
St Martin's Press, 175 5th Avenue, New York,
NY 10010
United States

thomasdunnebooks@stmartins.com

https://us.macmillan.com/thomasdunne

Publishing Imprint: St Martin's Press **(P0834)**

Types: Fiction; Nonfiction
Subjects: History; Mystery; Politics; Sport;
Suspense; Thrillers; Women's Interests
Markets: Adult

How to send: Through a literary agent

Publishes popular trade fiction and nonfiction. Accepts approaches via literary agents only.

P0859 **Thomas Nelson**
Publishing Imprint

Book Publisher: HarperCollins (**P0378**)

P0860 **Thomson Reuters Round Hall**
Book Publisher
13 Exchange Place, International Financial Services Centre, Dublin 1
Ireland
Tel: 01 602 4832

pamela.moran@thomsonreuters.com

http://www.roundhall.ie

Book Publisher: Thomson Reuters

Types: Nonfiction
Formats: Reference
Subjects: Legal
Markets: Academic; Professional

Send: Query
Don't send: Full text

Publishes information on Irish law in the form of books, journals, periodicals, looseleaf services, CD-ROMs and online services. See website for submission guidelines.

Editor: Pamela Moran

P0861 **Three Hares Publishing**
Book Publisher
United Kingdom

submissions@threeharespublishing.com

https://threeharespublishing.com

Types: Fiction; Nonfiction
Subjects: Crime; Psychology; Thrillers
Markets: Adult; Children's

Closed to approaches.

Closed to submissions as at July 2019. Check website for current status. Will consider all kinds of fiction and nonfiction, except picture books. Particularly interested in crime/psychological thrillers and Middle Grade fiction. Send query by email with one-page synopsis and first three chapters. See website for full guidelines.

P0862 **Times Books**
Publishing Imprint
United Kingdom

Book Publishers: HarperCollins UK (**P0382**); Henry Holt & Company Inc.

P0863 **Tiny Owl**
Book Publisher
7 Peacock Yard, Iliffe Street, London, SE17

3LH
United Kingdom

info@tinyowl.co.uk

http://tinyowl.co.uk

Types: Fiction
Markets: Children's

Publisher of books for children.

P0864 **Titan Books**
Book Publisher
Titan House, 144 Southwark Street, London, SE1 0UP
United Kingdom

https://www.titanbooks.com

Types: Fiction; Nonfiction
Formats: Film Scripts; Short Fiction; TV Scripts
Subjects: Comedy / Humour; Entertainment; Science Fiction
Markets: Adult; Young Adult

Send: Query
Don't send: Full text

Publisher of graphic novels, particularly with film or television tie-ins, and books related to film and TV. No unsolicited fiction or books for children, but will consider ideas for licensed projects they have already contracted. Send query with synopsis by post only. No email submissions.

P0865 **Tommy Nelson**
Publishing Imprint

Book Publisher: HarperCollins (**P0378**)

P0866 **Top Hat Books**
Publishing Imprint

Book Publisher: John Hunt Publishing Ltd

P0867 **Top Publications, Ltd**
Book Publisher
3100 Independence Parkway, Suite 311-359, Plano, TX 75075
United States
Tel: +1 (972) 490-9686
Fax: +1 (972) 233-0713

submissions@toppub.com

http://www.toppub.com

Types: Fiction
Formats: Short Fiction
Subjects: Adventure; Commercial; Contemporary; History; Horror; Mystery; Romance; Science Fiction; Suspense; Warfare
Markets: Adult; Young Adult

Send: Query
Don't send: Full text

Small press publisher of mainstream fiction. Authors should be willing to invest large amounts of time promoting their book and attending book-signings, etc. Send query letter

by email only, giving information about yourself, your book, and your marketing ideas for it. No queries or submissions by post. Email approaches only. Any queries or submissions sent through the post will not be responded to.

Editor: Victoria Lam

P0868 **Tor**
Publishing Imprint

Publishing Imprint: Tor/Forge (**P0870**)
Book Publisher: Pan Macmillan (**P0659**)

P0869 **Tor Teen/Starscape**
Publishing Imprint

Publishing Imprint: Tor/Forge (**P0870**)

P0870 **Tor/Forge**
Publishing Imprint
Tom Doherty Associates, LLC, 175 Fifth Avenue, New York, NY 10010
United States

https://www.torforgeblog.com

Book Publisher: Macmillan

Types: Fiction; Nonfiction
Subjects: Fantasy; History; Horror; Mystery; Science Fiction; Suspense; Women's Interests
Markets: Adult; Children's

Send: Query
Don't send: Full text

Particular emphasis on science fiction, fantasy, and horror. Open submissions policy. Send query with synopsis, first three chapters (or 40-60 pages), and SASE for response. See website for full submission guidelines.

Publishing Imprints: Forge (*P0298*); Orb (*P0642*); Tor (*P0868*); Tor Teen/Starscape (*P0869*); Tor/Seven Seas (*P0871*)

P0871 **Tor/Seven Seas**
Publishing Imprint

Publishing Imprint: Tor/Forge (**P0870**)

P0872 **Torrey House Press, LLC**
Book Publisher
150 S. State St. Suite 100, Salt Lake City, UT 84111
United States
Tel: +1 (801) 209-1657

mail@torreyhouse.com

http://torreyhouse.com

Types: Fiction; Nonfiction
Subjects: Culture; History; Literary; Nature
Markets: Adult

Send: Query
Don't send: Full text

Publishes narrative nonfiction and literary fiction with a natural history, environmental, or a natural landscape theme, or about the politics and practice of sustainable living. Submit using online submission manager on website.

Editors: Kirsten Johanna Allen; Mark Bailey

P0873 TouchWood Editions
Book Publisher
Canada
Tel: +1 (250) 360-0829
Fax: +1 (250) 386-0829

submissions@touchwoodeditions.com

http://www.touchwoodeditions.com

Types: Fiction; Nonfiction
Subjects: Arts; Autobiography; Cookery; Culture; Gardening; History; Lifestyle; Literary; Nature; Photography; Suspense; Travel
Markets: Adult

Send: Full text

Accepts submissions by email only. Response only if interested. Publishes Canadian authors only. See website for full guidelines.

P0874 Transworld Ireland
Publishing Imprint

Book Publisher: Transworld Publishers (**P0875**)

P0875 Transworld Publishers
Book Publisher
61-63 Uxbridge Road, Ealing, London, W5 5SA
United Kingdom
Tel: +44 (0) 20 8579 2652

info@transworld-publishers.co.uk

https://www.penguin.co.uk/company/publishers/transworld.html

Book Publisher: Penguin Random House UK (**P0685**)

Types: Fiction; Nonfiction
Subjects: Biography; Comedy / Humour; Cookery; Crime; Fantasy; Health; History; Literary; Literature; Music; Romance; Science; Science Fiction; Spirituality; Sport; Thrillers; Travel
Markets: Adult; Children's

How to send: Through a literary agent

Large publisher publishing a wide range of fiction and nonfiction for children and adults. No unsolicited MSS. Approach via a literary agent only.

Publishing Imprints: Bantam Books (*P0078*); Bantam Press (*P0079*); Black Swan (*P0103*); Corgi (*P0186*); Transworld Ireland (*P0874*)

P0876 Trentham Books
Publishing Imprint
United Kingdom

p.gordon-smith@ucl.ac.uk

https://www.ucl.ac.uk/ucl-press

Book Publisher: UCL Press (**P0889**)

Types: Nonfiction
Subjects: Design; Science; Sociology; Technology; Women's Interests
Markets: Academic

Send: Query
Don't send: Full text

Open access publisher of edited volumes, scholarly editions, textbooks and journals. Welcomes proposals.

Editor: Pat Gordon-Smith

P0877 Trotman & Co. Ltd
Book Publisher
21d Charles Street, Bath, BA1 1HX
United Kingdom
Tel: +44 (0) 01225 584950

dellao@trotman.co.uk

http://www.trotman.co.uk

Types: Nonfiction
Formats: Reference
Markets: Academic; Professional

Send: Full text

Publishes books on careers, employment and training resources, higher education guides, teacher support material, etc. Send query by email with brief summary, details of target audience, and list of chapters / sections.

P0878 TTA Press
Magazine Publisher; Book Publisher
5 Martins Lane, Witcham, Ely, Cambs, CB6 2LB
United Kingdom

http://www.ttapress.com

Magazine: Crimewave (**M0158**)

P0879 Turner Publishing
Book Publisher

Publishing Imprint: Jewish Lights Publishing (**P0467**)

P0880 Turnstone Press
Book Publisher
Artspace Building, 206-100 Arthur Street, Winnipeg, Manitoba, Canada R3B 1H3
Canada
Tel: +1 (204) 947-1555
Fax: +1 (204) 947-1556

editor@turnstonepress.com

http://www.turnstonepress.com

Types: Fiction; Nonfiction; Poetry
Formats: Short Fiction
Subjects: Fantasy; Literary; Literary Criticism; Mystery; Thrillers
Markets: Adult

Literary publisher publishing the work of Canadian authors or landed immigrants only. Publishes literary fiction, literary non-fiction – including literary criticism – and poetry. Publishes literary mysteries, thrillers, noir, speculative fiction, and fantasy under imprint. No contact by email. All submissions must be by post with SASE. Mss without SASE will be recycled without response, as will submissions requesting response by email. See website for full guidelines.

Publishing Imprint: Ravenstone

P0881 Turtle Books
Book Publisher
866 United Nations Plaza, Suite #525, New York, NY 10017
United States
Tel: +1 (212) 644-2020
Fax: +1 (212) 223-4387

http://www.turtlebooks.com

Types: Fiction; Nonfiction; Poetry
Subjects: Adventure; Culture; Fantasy; History; Literature; Nature; Sociology; Sport; Westerns
Markets: Children's

Send: Full text

Publishes children's illustrated books, often in both English and Spanish. Submit complete MS rather than sending a query.

Editor: John Whitman

P0882 Twelve
Publishing Imprint

Book Publisher: Grand Central Publishing (**P0335**)

P0883 Twenty-First Century Books
Publishing Imprint

Book Publisher: Lerner Publishing Group (**P0514**)

P0884 Two Hoots
Publishing Imprint

Book Publisher: Pan Macmillan (**P0659**)

P0885 Two Rivers Press
Book Publisher
7 Denmark Road, Reading, RG1 5PA
United Kingdom

anne@tworiverspress.com

https://tworiverspress.com

Types: Nonfiction; Poetry
Subjects: Arts; Culture; Literary
Markets: Adult

Publishes poetry, art, culture, and local interest books, focusing on Reading and the surrounding area.

P0886 Two Sylvias Press
Book Publisher
PO Box 1524, Kingston, WA 98346
United States

twosylviaspress@gmail.com

http://twosylviaspress.com

Types: Nonfiction; Poetry
Subjects: Autobiography
Markets: Adult

Publishes poetry, memoirs, essays, and books on the craft of writing. Runs two poetry prizes.

P0887 TwoDot
Publishing Imprint
United States

Book Publisher: The Globe Pequot Press
(**P0324**)

P0888 Tyndale House Publishers, Inc.
Book Publisher
351 Executive Drive, Carol Stream, IL 60188
United States
Tel: +1 (855) 277-9400
Fax: +1 (866) 622-9474

https://www.tyndale.com
https://facebook.com/TyndaleHouse
https://twitter.com/TyndaleHouse
https://pinterest.com/TyndaleHouse/
https://instagram.com/tyndalehouse/
https://youtube.com/user/TyndaleHP/

ADULT
  Fiction > *Novels*
    Allegory; Christianity; Contemporary Romance; Contemporary; Historical Fiction; Historical Romance; Mystery; Romantic Suspense; Suspense; Thrillers

  Nonfiction
    Nonfiction Books: Arts; Autobiography; Biography; Business; Christian Living; Christianity; Comedy / Humour; Culture; Current Affairs; Education; Finance; Health; History; Leadership; Leisure; Memoir; Personal Development; Politics; Psychology; Sport
    Reference: Christianity

CHILDREN'S
  Fiction
    Chapbook: Christianity
    Picture Books: Christianity

  Nonfiction > *Nonfiction Books*
    Christian Living; Christianity

TEEN

Fiction > *Novels*: Christianity

Nonfiction > *Nonfiction Books*
  Christian Living; Christianity; Relationships; Sex

How to send: Through a literary agent

Christian publisher, publishing bibles, nonfiction, fiction, and books for kids and teens.

P0889 UCL Press
Book Publisher
United Kingdom

c.penfold@ucl.ac.uk

https://www.ucl.ac.uk/ucl-press

Types: Nonfiction
Markets: Academic

Send: Query
Don't send: Full text

Open access publisher of scholarly monographs, edited volumes, scholarly editions, textbooks and journals in all subject areas. Welcomes proposals.

Publishing Imprint: Trentham Books (**P0876**)

P0890 Ugly Duckling Presse
Book Publisher
The Old American Can Factory, 232 Third Street, #E303 (corner Third Avenue), Brooklyn, NY 11215
United States
Tel: +1 (347) 948-5170

office@uglyducklingpresse.org

https://uglyducklingpresse.org

Types: Nonfiction; Poetry; Translations
Subjects: Experimental; Literary
Markets: Adult

Closed to approaches.

Closed to submissions as at June 2019. Check website for current status. Nonprofit publisher of poetry, translation, experimental nonfiction, performance texts, and books by artists. Check website for specific calls for submissions.

P0891 UKA Press
Book Publisher
United Kingdom

andrea@ukapress.com

http://www.ukapress.com

Fiction > *Novels*

Nonfiction > *Nonfiction Books*

Poetry > *Poetry Collections*

Send: Query
How to send: Through a literary agent

This publisher was created to publish fresh, exciting work by talented writers from around the world.

We're looking for originality, sparkle and the promise of something unexpected. Genre and style aren't important; quality is.

Accepts submissions through literary agents only.

P0892 Ulverscroft Ltd
Book Publisher
The Green, Bradgate Road, Anstey, Leicester, LE7 7FU
United Kingdom
Tel: +44 (0) 1162 364325

m.merrill@ulverscroft.co.uk

https://www.ulverscroft.com

Types: Fiction; Nonfiction
Markets: Adult

Publishes a wide variety of large print titles in hard and soft cover formats, as well as abridged and unabridged audio books. Many titles are written by the world's favourite authors.

Book Publisher: F.A. Thorpe (Publishing)

Editor: Mark Merrill

P0893 Unbound Press
Book Publisher
Unit 18, Waterside, 44-48 Wharf Road, London, N1 7UX
United Kingdom
Tel: +44 (0) 20 3997 6790

support@unbound.com

https://unbound.com
https://facebook.com/unbound
https://twitter.com/unbounders
https://instagram.com/unbounders

Fiction > *Novels*

Nonfiction > *Nonfiction Books*

Send: Full text

Crowdfunding publisher. Submit manuscripts via form on website.

P0894 Unicorn
Publishing Imprint

Book Publisher: Unicorn Publishing Group
(**P0895**)

P0895 Unicorn Publishing Group
Book Publisher
Charleston Studio, Meadow Business Centre, Ringmer, Lewes, East Sussex, BN8 5RW
United Kingdom
Tel: +44 (0) 1273 812066

ian@unicornpublishing.org

http://www.unicornpublishing.org

Types: Fiction; Nonfiction
Formats: Reference
Subjects: Arts; Biography; Culture; History;
Warfare
Markets: Adult

Publishes books on the visual arts and cultural
history, military history, and historical fiction.
Approach by email or by post.

Editor: Lucy Duckworth

Publishing Imprints: Unicorn (*P0894*);
Uniform (*P0896*); Universe (*P0899*)

P0896 Uniform
Publishing Imprint

Book Publisher: Unicorn Publishing Group
(**P0895**)

P0897 Union Park Press
Publishing Imprint
United States

Book Publisher: The Globe Pequot Press
(**P0324**)

P0898 Unity
Book Publisher
Integrated Marketing Department, Attention:
Product Manager, 1901 NW Blue Parkway,
Unity Village, Missouri 64065-0001
United States
Tel: +1 (816) 524-3550

acquisitions@unityonline.org

https://www.unity.org

Types: Nonfiction
Subjects: Philosophy; Self Help; Spirituality
Markets: Adult

Send: Full text

Publisher of books on Spirituality, New
Thought, personal growth, spiritual leadership,
mind-body-spirit, and spiritual self-help. Send
query by email as PDF attachment. See
website for full guidelines.

P0899 Universe
Publishing Imprint

Book Publisher: Unicorn Publishing Group
(**P0895**)

P0900 University College
Dublin (UCD) Press
Book Publisher
UCD Humanities Institute Room H103,
Belfield, Dublin 4,
Ireland
Tel: + 353 1 4716 4680

ucdpress@ucd.ie

http://www.ucdpress.ie

Types: Nonfiction
Subjects: Drama; History; Literary Criticism;
Music; Nature; Politics; Religion; Science;
Sociology; Warfare
Markets: Academic

Send: Query
Don't send: Full text

Peer-reviewed publisher of contemporary
scholarship with a reputation for publications
relating to historic and contemporary Ireland.
Send synopsis with market description, a
paragraph about the career and publications of
the author(s), and two specimen chapters in
hard copy (not email attachments). Will accept
proposals up to 8 pages by email, but unlikely
to consider a proposal without specimen
material. See website for full guidelines.

Executive Editor: Noelle Moran

P0901 The University of Akron
Press
Book Publisher
120 E. Mill Street, Suite 415, Akron, OH
44308
United States

uapress@uakron.edu

https://www.uakron.edu/uapress/

Types: Nonfiction; Poetry
Subjects: Cookery; Culture; History; Sport
Markets: Adult

Send: Query
Don't send: Full text

For nonfiction, complete and submit form on
website. Also publishes books of poetry,
mainly through its annual competition.

P0902 University of Alaska
Press
Book Publisher
Editorial Department, University of Alaska
Press, PO Box 756240, 104 Eielson Building,
Fairbanks, AK 99775-6240
United States
Tel: +1 (907) 474-5831
Fax: +1 (907) 474-5502

UA-acquisitions@alaska.edu

http://www.alaska.edu/uapress/

Types: Fiction; Nonfiction; Poetry;
Translations
Subjects: Autobiography; Culture; History;
Nature; Politics; Science; Sport
Markets: Academic; Adult

Closed to approaches.

Publisher based in Alaska, publishing
academic and general trade books on an
expanding range of subject areas, including
politics and history, Native languages and
cultures, science and natural history, biography
and memoir, poetry, fiction and anthologies,

and original translations. Send proposals by
post. No unsolicited mss.

P0903 University of Arkansas
Press
Book Publisher
McIlroy House, 105 N. McIlroy Avenue,
Fayetteville, AR 72701
United States
Tel: +1 (479) 575-7544

mbieker@uark.edu

https://www.uapress.com

Types: Nonfiction; Poetry
Markets: Academic; Adult

Accepts unsolicited proposals for scholarly
books in the social sciences and humanities as
well as nonfiction works of local or regional
interest. Also publishes poetry books through
its poetry competitions, for which there is a
standard entry fee. Submit via online
submission system.

Editors: Mike Bieker; David Scott
Cunningham

P0904 University of California
Press
Book Publisher
United States

krobinson@ucpress.edu

https://www.ucpress.edu

Types: Nonfiction
Formats: Film Scripts
Subjects: Anthropology; Arts; Crime; Culture;
History; Media; Music; Psychology; Religion;
Sociology
Markets: Academic

Scholarly publisher based in California.

: Maura Roessner

Editorial Director: Kim Robinson

P0905 University of Exeter
Press
Book Publisher
Reed Hall, Streatham Drive, Exeter, EX4 4QR
United Kingdom
Tel: +44 (0) 1392 263066
Fax: +44 (0) 1392 263064

n.massen@exeterpress.co.uk

http://www.exeterpress.co.uk

Types: Nonfiction
Formats: Film Scripts; Reference
Subjects: Archaeology; Culture; History;
Literature; Philosophy; Religion; Sociology
Markets: Academic

Send: Query
Don't send: Full text

Publisher of academic books. See website for
guidelines on submitting a proposal.

Editors: Anna Henderson; Hetty Marx; Nigel Massen

P0906 University of Hertfordshire Press

Book Publisher
College Lane, Hatfield, Hertfordshire, AL10 9AB
United Kingdom
Tel: +44 (0) 1707 284681

uhpress@herts.ac.uk

http://www.herts.ac.uk/UHPress

ACADEMIC > **Nonfiction** > *Nonfiction Books*
    History; Literature; Local History; Mathematics; Psychology; Theatre

Send: Query; Submission Form
How to send: Email

Publisher of academic books on local history, including imprints for Essex, West Midlands, and Hertfordshire.

Editor: Jane Housham

Publishing Imprints: Essex Publications (**P0265**); Hertfordshire Publications (**P0405**); West Midlands Publications (**P0963**)

P0907 University of Iowa Press

Book Publisher
119 West Park Road, 100 Kuhl House, Iowa City IA 52242-1000
United States
Tel: +1 (319) 335-2000
Fax: +1 (319) 335-2055

uipress@uiowa.edu

http://www.uiowapress.org

Types: Fiction; Nonfiction; Poetry
Formats: Short Fiction; Theatre Scripts
Subjects: Anthropology; Archaeology; Arts; Biography; Culture; History; Literary; Literature; Nature; Warfare
Markets: Academic; Adult

Send proposals for nonfiction by email. Accepts fiction and poetry through annual competitions only.

P0908 University of Massachusetts Press

Book Publisher
New Africa House, 180 Infirmary Way, 4th Floor, Amherst, MA 01003-9289
United States
Fax: +1 (413) 545-1226

cdougan@umpress.umass.edu

http://www.umass.edu/umpress

Types: Fiction; Nonfiction; Poetry
Subjects: Culture; History; Nature; Politics
Markets: Academic; Adult

Focuses primarily on books in the field of American studies, including books that explore the history, politics, literature, culture, and environment of the United States – as well as works with a transnational perspective. In addition to publishing works of scholarship, the Press produces books of more general interest for a wider readership. Also publishes poetry and fiction via its annual competitions only.

Editor-in-Chief: Matt Becker

P0909 University of Missouri Press

Book Publisher
113 Heinkel Building, 201 S 7th Street, Columbia, MO 65211
United States
Tel: +1 (573) 882-7641
Fax: +1 (573) 884-4498

upress@missouri.edu

https://upress.missouri.edu

Types: Nonfiction
Subjects: History; Literary Criticism; Politics; Warfare
Markets: Academic

Send: Query
Don't send: Full text

Scholarly publisher of a range of subject lists, with a focus on American History (esp. US Military, African American, Political), Journalism, Political Science, Missouri History and Regional Studies, and Literary Criticism (gen. American and British). Also happy to consider enquiries regarding work in any area of the humanities or natural history. No fiction or poetry. See website for full guidelines.

Editor-in-Chief: Andrew J. Davidson

P0910 University of Nevada Press

Book Publisher
University of Nevada Press, Morrill Hall Mail Stop 0166, Reno NV 89557-0166
United States
Tel: +1 (775) 784-6573

jbanducci@unpress.nevada.edu

https://www.unpress.nevada.edu

Types: Fiction; Nonfiction
Subjects: Anthropology; Arts; Culture; Current Affairs; Finance; History; Literature; Nature; Politics; Science; Sociology
Markets: Academic; Adult

Send: Query
Don't send: Full text

Publishes scholarly books in the humanities and social sciences in the fields of environmental studies, public health, mining studies, Native American studies, urban studies, Basque studies, gambling and

commercial gaming, and select fiction. Will also publish books on any topic which contribute to our understanding of Nevada, the Great Basin, and American West. See website for full submission guidelines and submit proposals by email.

Editor: JoAnne Banducci

P0911 University of New Mexico Press

Book Publisher
1717 Roma Ave. NE, Albuquerque, NM 87106
United States
Tel: +1 (505) 277-3343

custserv@unm.edu

https://www.unmpress.com/

Types: Nonfiction
Formats: Film Scripts
Subjects: Anthropology; Archaeology; Architecture; Arts; Culture; History; Literary Criticism; Nature; Photography; Warfare
Markets: Adult

Send: Query
Don't send: Full text

Send query by email to relevant editor. See website for details.

P0912 University of North Texas Press

Book Publisher
1155 Union Circle #311336, Denton, TX 76203-5017
United States
Tel: +1 (940) 565-2142
Fax: +1 (940) 369-8760

Ronald.Chrisman@unt.edu

https://untpress.unt.edu

Types: Fiction; Nonfiction; Poetry
Formats: Theatre Scripts
Subjects: Antiques; Architecture; Arts; Biography; Business; Comedy / Humour; Cookery; Crime; Finance; History; Legal; Literary Criticism; Medicine; Nature; Photography; Politics; Religion; Science; Sociology; Sport; Technology; Travel; Warfare; Women's Interests
Markets: Academic

Publishes titles on Texas, its history, military history, and social issues. Also covers women's interests and multicultural issues. Also publishes fiction and poetry through its annual competitions. See website for more details.

P0913 University of Pennsylvania Press

Book Publisher
3905 Spruce Street, Philadelphia, PA 19104-4112
United States

Tel: +1 (215) 898-6261
Fax: +1 (215) 898-0404

custserv@pobox.upenn.edu

https://www.upenn.edu/pennpress

ACADEMIC > **Nonfiction** > *Nonfiction Books*
African Diaspora; Atlantic; Culture; History; Intellectual History; Judaism; Literary Criticism; Medieval; North America; Political History; Renaissance; South America

Send: Query
How to send: Email

Send query by email to appropriate editor.

Associate Editor: Jenny Tan

Company Director: Eric Halpern

Editor-in-Chief: Walter Biggins

Senior Editors: Robert Lockhart; Jerome Singerman

P0914 **University of Pittsburgh Press**
Book Publisher
7500 Thomas Boulevard, Pittsburgh, PA 15260
United States
Tel: +1 (412) 383-2456
Fax: +1 (412) 383-2466

scrooms@upress.pitt.edu

https://upittpress.org

Types: Nonfiction; Poetry
Subjects: Architecture; History; Philosophy; Science
Markets: Academic

Send: Query
Don't send: Full text

Publishes books on Latin American studies, Russian and East European studies, international relations, poetry, Pittsburgh and Western Pennsylvania regional studies, environmental studies, architecture and landscape history, urban studies, composition and literacy, the history of science, and the philosophy of science. No hard sciences, memoirs, or fiction. Only considers poetry manuscripts from poets who have already published full-length collections of at least 48 pages. Poets who have not may submit to the first-book competition run by the press. See website for full guidelines.

Editorial Director: Sandy Crooms

P0915 **University of Texas Press**
Book Publisher
3001 Lake Austin Blvd, 2.200, Stop E4800, Austin, TX 78703-4206
United States
Tel: +1 (800) 252-3206
Fax: +1 (512) 232-7178

info@utpress.utexas.edu

https://utpress.utexas.edu

Types: Nonfiction
Formats: Film Scripts
Subjects: Anthropology; Archaeology; Architecture; Arts; Cookery; Culture; Current Affairs; History; Media; Music; Nature; Photography
Markets: Academic; Adult

Send: Query
Don't send: Full text

Send query with proposal, table of contents, sample chapter, and CV. Brief email queries are also acceptable. Publishes scholarly books and journals on the above subject areas, as well as regional books and some general readership nonfiction. See website for full details.

P0916 **University of Virginia Press**
Book Publisher
University of Virginia Press, P.O. Box 400318 (Postal), 210 Sprigg Lane (Courier), Charlottesville, VA 22904-4318
United States
Tel: +1 (434) 924-3468
Fax: +1 (434) 982-2655

vapress@virginia.edu

https://www.upress.virginia.edu/

Types: Nonfiction
Subjects: Architecture; History; Literary Criticism; Sociology
Markets: Academic

Considers academic books in areas including humanities, social sciences, American history, African-American studies, architecture, Victorian literature, Caribbean literature and ecocriticism.

P0917 **University of Wales Press**
Publishing Imprint
University Registry, King Edward VII Avenue, Cathays Park, Cardiff, CF10 3NS
United Kingdom
Tel: +44 (0) 29 2037 6999

press@press.wales.ac.uk

http://www.uwp.co.uk

Publishing Imprint: University of Wales Press (**P0917**)

Types: Nonfiction
Subjects: Culture; History; Literature; Media; Nature; Philosophy; Politics; Religion; Sociology
Markets: Academic

Send: Query
Don't send: Full text

Make contact by phone or by email at an early stage – preferably before book is written.

Publishing Imprints: GPC Books (*P0333*); Gwasg Prifysgol Cymru (*P0345*); University of Wales Press (**P0917**)

P0918 **The University of Wisconsin Press**
Book Publisher
728 State Street, Suite 443, Madison, WI 53706
United States
Tel: +1 (608) 263-1101
Fax: +1 (608) 263-1173

uwiscpress@uwpress.wisc.edu

http://www.wisc.edu/wisconsinpress

Types: Fiction; Nonfiction; Poetry
Formats: Film Scripts; Short Fiction
Subjects: Anthropology; Autobiography; Culture; History; Media; Nature; Politics; Travel
Markets: Academic

Send: Query
Don't send: Full text

Publishes scholarly, general interest nonfiction books and books featuring the American mid-west, along with a limited number of novels and short story collections. Publishes poetry via its annual competition only, for which there is an entry fee.

P0919 **University Press**
Publishing Imprint

Book Publisher: Beacon Publishing Group (**P0088**)

P0920 **University Press of Kansas**
Book Publisher
2502 Westbrooke Circle, Lawrence, KS 66045-4444
United States
Tel: +1 (785) 864-4154
Fax: +1 (785) 864-4586

upress@ku.edu

http://www.kansaspress.ku.edu

Types: Nonfiction
Subjects: History; Legal; Nature; Philosophy; Politics; Warfare
Markets: Academic

Send: Query
Don't send: Full text

See website for list of acquisitions editors and their interests, and send appropriate editor an email including: 1. Overview: Subject, argument, research 2. Core Contribution: what's unique, significant, exciting? 3. Comparison to other works in the field 4. Intended audience 5. Length of work (preferably in words) and number and type of illustrations 6. Annotated table of contents 7. Status of proposed work and timeline for completion 8. Bio or CV Proposals may be sent by email but do not attach partial or complete manuscripts.

Editors: David Congdon; Joyce Harrison; Kim Hogeland

P0921 University Press of Mississippi
Book Publisher
United States

press@ihl.state.ms.us

https://www.upress.state.ms.us

Types: Nonfiction
Formats: Film Scripts; TV Scripts
Subjects: Architecture; Arts; Autobiography; History; Literature; Media; Music; Nature; Photography; Women's Interests
Markets: Academic; Adult

Non-profit publisher of scholarly and trade titles on subjects such as American, Southern, African-American and popular culture; literature, performace, art, photography and the liberal arts; history, folklore, ethnic, and women's studies.

P0922 Up On Big Rock Poetry
Publishing Imprint

Book Publisher: Shipwreckt Books Publishing Company (**P0811**)

P0923 Usborne Publishing
Book Publisher
83-85 Saffron Hill, London, EC1N 8RT
United Kingdom
Tel: +44 (0) 20 7430 2800
Fax: +44 (0) 20 7430 1562

https://usborne.com

Types: Fiction; Nonfiction
Formats: Reference
Markets: Children's

How to send: Through a literary agent

Publisher of children's reference now expanding into children's fiction. All nonfiction written in-house and fiction submissions accepted via literary agents only.

P0924 Vallentine Mitchell
Publishing Imprint
Catalyst House, 720 Centennial Court, Centennial Park, Elstree, Herts, WD6 3SY
United Kingdom
Tel: +44 (0) 20 8292 5637

editor@vmbooks.com

https://www.vmbooksuk.com

Types: Nonfiction
Subjects: Culture; History; Philosophy; Religion
Markets: Academic; Adult

Send: Query
Don't send: Full text

Publishes books on Jewish history, culture and heritage, Jewish thought, Middle Eastern history, politics and culture and the Holocaust, for both academic and general readerships. Offices in Hertfordshire and Chicago, Illinois. Send proposals by email.

P0925 VanderWyk & Burnham
Book Publisher
1610 Long Leaf Circle, St. Louis, MO 63146
United States
Tel: +1 (314) 432-3435
Fax: +1 (314) 993-4485

quickpublishing@sbcglobal.net

http://www.vandb.com

Types: Nonfiction
Subjects: Lifestyle; Psychology; Self Help
Markets: Adult

Closed to approaches.

Not accepting unsolicited proposals or submissions as at May 2020.

P0926 Vegetarian Alcoholic Press
Book Publisher
United States

vegalpress@gmail.com

http://www.vegetarianalcoholicpress.com

Types: Fiction; Poetry
Formats: Short Fiction
Subjects: Literary
Markets: Adult

Send: Full text

Publishes poetry and short story collections. Send submissions by email.

P0927 VerbalEyze Press
Book Publisher
United States

submissions@verbaleyze.org

https://verbaleyze.org/press

Types: Fiction; Nonfiction; Poetry; Scripts
Formats: Short Fiction
Markets: Adult; Children's; Young Adult

Send: Query
Don't send: Full text

Publishes work by young writers aged 13-22, including novels, memoirs, graphic novels, poetry collections, short stories, and one-act plays. See website for full guidelines.

P0928 Vermilion
Publishing Imprint
United Kingdom

Book Publisher: Ebury (**P0243**)

P0929 Viking
Publishing Imprint
United States

Book Publisher: Penguin Publishing Group (**P0682**)

P0930 Viking Children's Books
Publishing Imprint
United States

Book Publisher: Penguin Young Readers Group (**P0688**)

P0931 Viking Dog
Book Publisher
United States

contact@viking-dog.com

https://www.viking-dog.com
https://www.instagram.com/vikingdogent/
https://www.facebook.com/vikingdogent/
http://twitter.com/vikingdogent
https://www.youtube.com/channel/UCmZtTxwsFYEKNa-eBrtHxhg?view_as=subscriber
https://vimeo.com/user70568100

Fiction > *Novels*
Adventure; Fantasy; Science Fiction; Thrillers; Westerns

Scripts
Film Scripts: Adventure; Fantasy; Science Fiction; Thrillers; Westerns
TV Scripts: Adventure; Fantasy; Science Fiction; Thrillers; Westerns

Send: Query
How to send: Email

A content company based in Los Angeles that creates, publishes and distributes film and book projects.

P0932 Vine Leaves Press
Book Publisher
Australia

submissions@vineleavespress.com

https://www.vineleavespress.com

Types: Fiction; Nonfiction
Formats: Reference; Short Fiction
Subjects: Autobiography; Literary
Markets: Adult

Send: Query
Don't send: Full text

Publishes novels (all genres accepted, but with a literary bent), memoirs / biographies / autobiographies, creative nonfiction, and writing / publishing reference books, and short story collections. Send query by email with first ten pages and author bio.

P0933 Vinspire Publishing
Book Publisher
PO Box 1165, Ladson, SC 29456-1165

United States
Tel: +1 (843) 695-7530

vinspirepublishingeic@gmail.com

https://www.vinspirepublishing.com

Types: Fiction
Subjects: Comedy / Humour; History; Mystery; Romance; Thrillers; Westerns
Markets: Adult; Young Adult

Closed to approaches.

Accepts agented approaches only, except during open submission calls, which are announced on the website and via social media.

P0934 Vintage
Book Publisher
United Kingdom

Book Publisher: Penguin Random House UK (**P0685**)

Publishing Imprints: The Bodley Head (*P0116*); Chatto & Windus (*P0163*); Harvill Secker (*P0394*); Hogarth Press (*P0414*); Jonathan Cape (**P0472**); Square Peg (*P0832*); Vintage Classics (*P0936*); Vintage Paperbacks (*P0937*); Yellow Jersey (*P0985*)

P0935 Vintage Books
Publishing Imprint
United States

Book Publisher: Knopf Doubleday Publishing Group (**P0498**)

P0936 Vintage Classics
Publishing Imprint
United Kingdom

Book Publisher: Vintage (**P0934**)

P0937 Vintage Paperbacks
Publishing Imprint
United Kingdom

Book Publisher: Vintage (**P0934**)

P0938 Virago
Publishing Imprint

Publishing Imprint: Little, Brown Book Group (**P0532**)

P0939 Virgin Books
Publishing Imprint
United Kingdom

Book Publisher: Ebury (**P0243**)

P0940 Voyageur Press
Publishing Imprint
Book Proposals, Voyageur Press, Quayside Publishing Group, 400 First Avenue North, Suite 300, Minneapolis, MN 55401
United States

Tel: +1 (800) 458-0454
Fax: +1 (612) 344-8691

customerservice@quaysidepub.com

http://www.voyageurpress.com

Book Publisher: The Quarto Group, Inc. (**P0739**)

Types: Nonfiction
Subjects: Culture; History; Lifestyle; Music; Nature; Photography; Travel
Markets: Adult

Send: Query
Don't send: Full text

Publishes books on nature and the

environment; country living and farming heritage; regional and cultural history; music;

travel and photography. See website for full submission guidelines.

P0941 W Publishing Group
Publishing Imprint

Book Publisher: HarperCollins (**P0378**)

P0942 W.W. Norton & Company Ltd
Book Publisher
15 Carlisle Street, London, W1D 3BS
United Kingdom
Tel: +44 (0) 20 7323 1579

office@wwnorton.co.uk

http://wwnorton.co.uk

Types: Fiction; Nonfiction; Poetry
Formats: Film Scripts
Subjects: Adventure; Anthropology; Archaeology; Architecture; Autobiography; Business; Comedy / Humour; Crafts; Crime; Current Affairs; Design; Drama; Finance; Health; History; Hobbies; Legal; Leisure; Lifestyle; Literature; Medicine; Music; Nature; Philosophy; Politics; Psychology; Religion; Science; Self Help; Sociology; Sport; Technology; Travel; Women's Interests
Markets: Academic; Adult; Professional

UK branch of a US publisher. No editorial office in the UK – contact the main office in New York (see separate listing).

P0943 Walden Pond Press
Publishing Imprint

Book Publisher: HarperCollins (**P0378**)

P0944 Walker Books Ltd
Book Publisher
87 Vauxhall Walk, London, SE11 5HJ
United Kingdom
Tel: +44 (0) 20 7793 0909

editorial@walker.co.uk

http://www.walkerbooks.co.uk

Types: Fiction; Nonfiction
Markets: Children's

Publishes fiction and nonfiction for children, including illustrated books. Not accepting unsolicited fiction or picture books as at September 2019.

P0945 Walter Foster Jr.
Publishing Imprint

Book Publisher: The Quarto Group, Inc. (**P0739**)

P0946 Walter Foster Publishing
Publishing Imprint
Suite A, Irvine, CA 92618
United States
Tel: +1 (800) 426-0099
Fax: +1 (949) 380-7575

info@walterfoster.com

http://www.walterfoster.com

Book Publisher: The Quarto Group, Inc. (**P0739**)

Types: Nonfiction
Subjects: Crafts; How To
Markets: Adult; Children's; Young Adult

Publishes how-to craft books and kits for children and adults.

P0947 Ward River Press
Publishing Imprint

Book Publisher: Poolbeg (**P0712**)

P0948 Washington State University Press
Book Publisher
Cooper Publications Building, PO Box 645910, Pullman, WA 99164-5910
United States
Tel: +1 (509) 335-8821
Fax: +1 (509) 335-8568

wsupress@wsu.edu

https://wsupress.wsu.edu

Types: Nonfiction
Subjects: Biography; Cookery; Culture; History; Nature; Politics; Westerns
Markets: Academic; Adult

Send: Query
Don't send: Full text

Send query by post or by email (preferred) with author CV, summary of proposed work, sample bio, and one or two sample chapters. Specialises in the American West, particularly the prehistory, history, environment, politics, and culture of the greater Northwest region. No fiction, poetry, or literary criticism. See website for full guidelines.

Editor-in-Chief: Linda Bathgate

P0949 **Watkins Media**
Book Publisher

Book Publishers: Angry Robot (**P0039**);
Watkins Publishing (**P0950**)

P0950 **Watkins Publishing**
Book Publisher
Unit 11, Shepperton House, 89 Shepperton
Road, London, N1 3DF
United Kingdom
Tel: +44 (0) 20 3813 6940

enquiries@watkinspublishing.com

https://www.watkinspublishing.com

Book Publisher: Watkins Media (**P0949**)

Types: Nonfiction
Subjects: History; Lifestyle; Religion; Self
Help
Markets: Adult

Publishes books in the field of Mind, Body and
Spirit. Not accepting submissions as at April
2019. Check website for current status.

P0951 **Watson-Guptill Publications**
Publishing Imprint
United States

http://crownpublishing.com/archives/imprint/
watson-guptill

Book Publisher: The Crown Publishing Group

Types: Nonfiction
Formats: Reference; Theatre Scripts
Subjects: Architecture; Arts; Crafts; Culture;
Design; How To; Lifestyle; Music;
Photography
Markets: Adult; Children's

Send: Query
Don't send: Full text

Publishes art and art instruction books.

P0952 **Wayne State University Press**
Book Publisher
4809 Woodward Avenue, Detroit, Michigan
48201-1309
United States

annie.martin@wayne.edu

https://www.wsupress.wayne.edu

Types: Nonfiction
Subjects: Culture; Media; Religion
Markets: Academic

Send: Query
Don't send: Full text

Actively acquiring books in African American
studies, media studies, fairy-tale studies,
Jewish studies, citizenship studies, and
regional studies: books about the state of
Michigan, the city of Detroit, and the Great
Lakes region. Send query by post or by email

to appropriate acquisitions editor (see website
for details and individual contact details).

P0953 **We Are One Body Audio Theatre**
Book Publisher
1100 Ligonier Street, Latrobe, PA 16063
United States
Tel: +1 (844) 392-6228 ext. 5

grettelyndarkey@waob.org

https://waobaudiotheatre.org

Types: Fiction; Poetry; Scripts
Formats: Short Fiction; Theatre Scripts
Subjects: Adventure; Comedy / Humour;
Crime; Drama; Experimental; Fantasy; Gothic;
History; Literary; Literature; Mystery;
Religion; Romance; Satire; Science Fiction;
Suspense; Thrillers; Westerns
Markets: Academic; Adult; Children's;
Professional; Young Adult

Send: Full text

Seeks to build a creative haven for writers,
artists, and actors who wish to express truth,
beauty, and goodness in their work. To this
end, the members of the audio theatre try to
create a friendly environment where all are
welcome to participate as part of Christ's body,
whether as contributors or as listeners. We
believe with J. R. R. Tolkien that "we have
come from God, and inevitably the myths
woven by us, though they [may] contain error,
will also reflect a splintered fragment of the
true light, the eternal truth that is with God.
Indeed only by myth-making, only by
becoming 'sub-creator' and inventing stories,
can Man aspire to the state of perfection that he
knew before the Fall." We believe that
storytelling — as a creative act — is one
example of how God created us in his image.
By crafting stories that utilize our God-given
creative energy, we believe that we join with
him in bringing truth, beauty, and goodness to
the earth. In engaging in our work as sub-
creators under the great Creator, we use our
imaginations and the talents that we have been
given to craft works of art that we hope will
inspire others to create. We know that the
imagination is key to our efforts, and is a great
gift from God. Therefore, we strive to create
inventive stories that help our listeners to
engage with their imaginations, in the hope
that their willingness to experience invisible
things might help them to a better
understanding of the invisible God.

Authors: James G. Bruen; Joe Campbell; Sean
Dailey; Grettelyn Darkey; Sean Fitzpatrick;
Paul Fox; Megan Gannon; Nicholas Hannon;
Richard Infante; Julianne Leonard; Kelsey
McIntyre; Joe Potts; Christopher Reibold;
Elizabeth Saenz; Michael Thimons; Nathan B.
Turner

Editor: Grettelyn Darkey

P0954 **Weasel Press**
Book Publisher
United States

thedude@weaselpress.com

https://www.weaselpress.com

Types: Fiction; Nonfiction; Poetry
Formats: Short Fiction
Subjects: Experimental; Literary
Markets: Adult

From autumn 2020 will only accept work from
authors of colour, or who identify as LGBTQ+,
or who are disabled. Submit through online
submission system.

P0955 **Wednesday Books**
Publishing Imprint

Publishing Imprint: St Martin's Press (**P0834**)

P0956 **Weidenfeld & Nicholson**
Book Publisher

Book Publisher: The Orion Publishing Group
Limited (**P0647**)

P0957 **Welbeck Publishing Group**
Book Publisher
20 Mortimer Street, London, W1T 3JW
United Kingdom
Tel: +44 (0) 20 7612 0400
Fax: +44 (0) 20 7612 0401

submissions@welbeckpublishing.com

https://www.welbeckpublishing.com/

Types: Fiction; Nonfiction
Formats: Reference
Subjects: Commercial; Entertainment; History;
Sport
Markets: Adult; Children's

Send: Query
Don't send: Full text

Publishes illustrated reference, sport,
entertainment, commercial fiction and
children's nonfiction. Synopses and ideas for
suitable books are welcomed, but no
unsolicited MSS, academic, or poetry. Send
query by email only with short synopsis,
author bio, market info, and up to two chapters
up to a maximum of 20 pages. See website for
full guidelines.

P0958 **Wellfleet Press**
Publishing Imprint

Book Publisher: The Quarto Group, Inc.
(**P0739**)

P0959 **Wells College Press**
Book Publisher
170 Main St, Aurora, NY 13026
United States
Tel: +1 (315) 364-3420

bookartscenter@wells.edu

https://wellsbookartscenter.org/wells-college-press/

Types: Nonfiction; Poetry
Subjects: Arts; Design
Markets: Adult

Publishes poetry chapbooks and books on art, design, and typography.

P0960 Welsh Academic Press
Publishing Imprint
PO Box 733, Caerdydd, Cardiff, CF14 7ZY
United Kingdom
Tel: +44 (0) 29 2021 8187

post@welsh-academic-press.com

http://www.welsh-academic-press.com

Book Publisher: Ashley Drake Publishing Ltd
(**P0055**)

Types: Nonfiction
Subjects: History; Politics
Markets: Academic

Send: Query
Don't send: Full text

Publishes academic monographs, reference works, text books and popular scholarly titles in the fields of education, history, political studies, Scandinavian and Baltic studies, contemporary work and employment, and medieval Wales. Complete questionnaire available on website.

Publishing Imprint: St David's Press

P0961 Wesleyan University Press
Book Publisher
215 Long Lane, Middletown, CT 06459
United States
Tel: +1 (860) 685-7730
Fax: +1 (860) 685-7712

stamminen@wesleyan.edu

http://www.wesleyan.edu/wespress

Types: Nonfiction
Subjects: Music
Markets: Academic

Send: Query
Don't send: Full text

Accepting proposals in the areas of dance and music. See website for submission guidelines.

P0962 West Highland Series.
Publishing Imprint

Publishing Imprint: House of Lochar (**P0424**)

P0963 West Midlands Publications
Publishing Imprint
United Kingdom

http://www.uhpress.co.uk/subject-areas/west-midlands-publications

Book Publisher: University of Hertfordshire Press (**P0906**)

ACADEMIC > **Nonfiction** > *Nonfiction*
Books: Local History

This series aims to publish scholarly, attractive, well-illustrated and accessible studies on the history of the English West Midlands, a region which broadly encompasses the historic counties of Derbyshire, Herefordshire, Shropshire, Staffordshire, Warwickshire and Worcestershire.

P0964 WestBow Press
Publishing Imprint

Book Publisher: HarperCollins (**P0378**)

P0965 WH Allen
Publishing Imprint
United Kingdom

Book Publisher: Ebury (**P0243**)

P0966 Wharton
Publishing Imprint

Book Publisher: Pearson (**P0670**)

P0967 White Lion Publishing
Publishing Imprint

Book Publisher: The Quarto Group, Inc.
(**P0739**)

P0968 White Owl
Publishing Imprint

Book Publisher: Pen & Sword Books Ltd
(**P0674**)

P0969 Whitecap Books Ltd
Book Publisher
Suite 209, 314 West Cordova Street,
Vancouver, BC, V6B 1E8
Canada

bookinfo@whitecap.ca

https://www.whitecap.ca

Types: Nonfiction
Subjects: Cookery; History; Nature
Markets: Adult

Closed to approaches.

Publishes visually appealing books on food, wine, health and well-being, regional history, and regional guidebooks.

P0970 Wide-Eyed Editions
Publishing Imprint
The Old Brewery, 6 Blundell Street, London,
N7 9BH
United Kingdom

Tel: +44 (0) 20 7700 6700
Fax: +44 (0) 20 7700 8066

QuartoExploresSubmissions@Quartous.com

https://www.quartoknows.com/Wide-Eyed-Editions

Book Publisher: The Quarto Group, Inc.
(**P0739**)

Types: Nonfiction
Subjects: Arts; Nature; Travel
Markets: Children's

Send: Query
Don't send: Full text

Publishes books on the arts, natural history and armchair travel. Send query with proposal by email. See website for full guidelines.

P0971 Wild Goose Publications
Book Publisher
The Iona Community, 21 Carlton Court,
Glasgow, G5 9JP
United Kingdom
Tel: +44 (0) 1414 297281

admin@iona.org.uk

http://www.ionabooks.com

Types: Nonfiction; Poetry
Subjects: Health; Politics; Religion; Sociology
Markets: Adult

Send: Query
Don't send: Full text

Publishes books on Holistic Spirituality, Social Justice, Political and Peace Issues, Healing – Innovative Approaches to worship, Song and Material for Meditation and Reflection. Send query with synopsis and two or three sample chapters. Not a poetry publisher, but will sometimes include poems in its books. Samples of suitable poems may be sent to be held on file in case they are suitable for use in a future book.

P0972 Wilderness Press
Book Publisher
c/o Keen Communications, 2204 First Avenue
South, Suite 102, Birmingham, AL 35233
United States
Tel: +1 (800) 443-7227
Fax: +1 (205) 326-1012

https://www.wildernesspress.com/

Types: Nonfiction
Subjects: How To; Leisure; Nature; Travel
Markets: Adult

Publisher of books on the outdoors, travel, and outdoor activities.

P0973 Wiley-Blackwell
Publishing Imprint
9600 Garsington Road, Oxford, OX4 2DQ
United Kingdom

Tel: +44 (0) 1865 776868
Fax: +44 (0) 1865 714591

https://www.wiley.com/WileyCDA/Brand/id-35.html

Book Publisher: John Wiley & Sons, Inc.

PROFESSIONAL > Nonfiction
Nonfiction Books; Reference

A global provider of content-enabled solutions to improve outcomes in research, education and professional practice with online tools, journals, books, databases, reference works and laboratory protocols. Has strengths in every major academic, scientific and professional field. Partners with over 800 prestigious societies representing two million members.

P0974 **William Collins**
Publishing Imprint
United Kingdom

Book Publisher: HarperCollins UK (**P0382**)

P0975 **William Morrow**
Publishing Imprint

Book Publisher: HarperCollins (**P0378**)

P0976 **Wise Music Group**
Book Publisher

Book Publisher: Omnibus Press (**P0637**)

P0977 **Wisteria Publishing**
Book Publisher
United Kingdom
Tel: +44 (0) 07368 338693

wisteriasubmission@outlook.com

https://wisteriasubmission.wixsite.com/wisteriapublishing

Types: Fiction; Nonfiction; Poetry
Formats: Short Fiction
Subjects: Arts; Beauty; Biography; Comedy / Humour; Commercial; Contemporary; Crafts; Entertainment; Fantasy; Fashion; Gothic; Health; How To; Lifestyle; Literary; Romance; Self Help; Thrillers; Women's Interests
Markets: Adult; Children's

Send: Full text

A small, independent publishing house created by a writer who wanted to make an easier and more friendly experience for the author. Bigger royalties, more involvement from the author and simpler contracts.

Authors: Lisa Gourley; Jennifer Marston; Taylor Martin; Petra Quelch

P0978 **Witness**
Publishing Imprint

Book Publisher: HarperCollins (**P0378**)

P0979 **Wolters Kluwer**
Book Publisher

Book Publishers: Kluwer Law International (**P0497**); Wolters Kluwer (UK) Ltd

P0980 **Words & Pictures**
Publishing Imprint
The Old Brewery, 6 Blundell Street, London, N7 9BH
United Kingdom
Tel: +44 (0) 20 770 6700

maxime.boucknooghe@quarto.com

https://www.quartoknows.com/words-pictures

Book Publisher: The Quarto Group, Inc. (**P0739**)

Types: Fiction
Markets: Children's

Always on the lookout for authors and artists with creative ideas to enhance and broaden their list of children's books. See website for submission guidelines.

Editor: Maxime Boucknooghe

P0981 **Writer's Digest Books**
Publishing Imprint
United States

Book Publisher: Penguin Publishing Group (**P0682**)

P0982 **Wyldblood Press**
Book Publisher; Magazine Publisher; Online Publisher
Thicket View, Bakers Row, Bakers Lane, Maidenhead, SL6 6PX
United Kingdom
Tel: +44 (0) 7961 323023

admin@wyldblood.com

https://wyldblood.com
https://www.facebook.com/Wyldblood-Press-115385210261475/

ADULT > Fiction
Novels: Fantasy; Science Fiction
Short Fiction: Fantasy; Science Fiction
YOUNG ADULT > Fiction
Novels: Fantasy; Science Fiction
Short Fiction: Fantasy; Science Fiction

Send: Query; Synopsis; Full text
How to send: Email attachment
How not to send: PDF file email attachment

We're a publisher of speculative and literary fiction. We're based in England but sell all over the world both online and in print. We believe there's always room for high quality writing and never enough spaces to find it, so we're working hard to create a new home for inspiring new work. By speculative we mean science fiction and fantasy but that reflects our tastes and not our limits. Good writing breaks through boundaries and knows no genre limits.

We will be publishing novels, anthology collections, a bimonthly magazine (from Jan 2021) (ebook and print) and flash fiction (online only).

P0983 **Yale University Press (London)**
Book Publisher
47 Bedford Square, London, WC1B 3DP
United Kingdom
Tel: +44 (0) 20 7079 4900

trade@yaleup.co.uk

https://www.yalebooks.co.uk

ADULT > Nonfiction
Nonfiction Books: Architecture; Arts; Biography; Business; Computers; Current Affairs; Economics; Fashion; Health; History; Language; Legal; Literature; Mathematics; Medicine; Memoir; Music; Philosophy; Politics; Religion; Science; Society; Sociology; Technology; Wellbeing
Reference: General

CHILDREN'S > Nonfiction > Nonfiction *Books:* Education

Send: Query; Author bio; Market info; Table of Contents; Writing sample
How to send: Post; Phone; Email

Publishes world class scholarship for a broad readership.

Editor: Sophie Neve

Editorial Directors: Mark Eastment; Julian Loose

Managing Director / Publisher: Heather McCallum

Senior Editor: Joanna Godfrey

P0984 **Yellow Flag Press**
Book Publisher
United States

https://www.yellowflagpress.com

Types: Poetry
Subjects: Literary
Markets: Adult

Publishes trade paperback books as well as handmade chapbooks and broadsides in limited edition printings. Free open reading period in April, but submissions can be made at other times of the year with a $5 discounted sample chapbook purchase.

Editor: J. Bruce Fuller

P0985 **Yellow Jersey**
Publishing Imprint
United Kingdom

Book Publisher: Vintage (**P0934**)

P0986 Yes Poetry
Book Publisher
United States

editor@yespoetry.com

https://www.yespoetry.com

Types: Poetry
Subjects: Literary
Markets: Adult

Closed to approaches.

Has published a poetry magazine since 2010, and since 2016 has also published poetry chapbooks. Closed to chapbook submissions as at October 2019. Check website for current status.

P0987 YesYes Books
Book Publisher
1614 NE Alberta Street, Portland, OR 97211
United States

info@yesyesbooks.com

https://www.yesyesbooks.com

Types: Fiction; Poetry
Subjects: Literary
Markets: Adult

Accepts submissions of fiction and poetry between April 1 and May 15, and via its two contests in autumn.

P0988 York Notes
Publishing Imprint

Book Publisher: Pearson (**P0670**)

P0989 Zebra Shout
Publishing Imprint

Book Publisher: Kensington Publishing Corp. (**P0488**)

P0990 ZED Press
Book Publisher
Canada

zedpresschapbook@gmail.com

https://zedpresswindsor.wordpress.com

Types: Poetry
Subjects: Experimental; Literary
Markets: Adult

Send: Full text

Publishes poetry chapbooks. Looks for experimental work and seeks to highlight voices that are underrepresented in literature. Accepts manuscripts up to 32 pages in length, by email. See website for full guidelines.

P0991 Zero Books
Publishing Imprint
Portland, OR
United States

https://www.johnhuntpublishing.com/zer0-books/

Book Publisher: John Hunt Publishing Ltd

Types: Nonfiction
Subjects: Culture; Philosophy; Politics
Markets: Adult

Send: Full text

The modern world is at an impasse. Disasters scroll across our smartphone screens and we're invited to like, follow or upvote, but critical thinking is harder and harder to find. Rather than connecting us in common struggle and debate, the internet has sped up and deepened a long-standing process of alienation and atomization. We want to work against this trend.

Authors: Ben Burgis; Mark Fisher; Graham Harman; Owen Hatherley; Angela Nagle; Laurie Penny; Nina Power; Eugene Thacker

P0992 Zest Books
Publishing Imprint

Book Publisher: Lerner Publishing Group (**P0514**)

P0993 ZigZag Education
Book Publisher
Unit 3, Greenway Business Centre, Doncaster Road, Bristol, BS10 5PY
United Kingdom
Tel: +44 (0) 1179 503199
Fax: +44 (0) 1179 591695

support@ZigZagEducation.co.uk

http://www.zigzageducation.co.uk

Types: Nonfiction
Subjects: Arts; Business; Design; Drama; Finance; Health; History; Legal; Leisure; Media; Music; Philosophy; Politics; Psychology; Religion; Science; Sociology; Sport; Technology; Travel
Markets: Academic; Children's; Professional; Young Adult

Educational publisher publishing photocopiable and digital teaching resources for schools and colleges. Register on publisher's author support website if interested in writing or contributing to resources.

P0994 Zonderkidz
Publishing Imprint

Book Publisher: HarperCollins (**P0378**)

P0995 Zondervan
Publishing Imprint

Book Publisher: HarperCollins (**P0378**)

P0996 Zondervan Academic
Publishing Imprint

Book Publisher: HarperCollins (**P0378**)

Index

Comic Books

Coming of Age

Commentary

*See more specifically: Social Commentary;
    Cultural Commentary*

Commercial

*See more specifically: Upmarket Commercial
    Fiction; Commercial Women's Fiction*

Literary Criticism
See more broadly: Literature

Literary Horror
See more broadly: Literary; Horror

Literary Journalism
See more broadly: Literary; Journalism

Literary Memoir
See more broadly: Memoir

Literary Mystery
See more broadly: Literary; Mystery

Literary Thrillers
See more broadly: Literary; Thrillers

Medieval
See more broadly: History
University of Pennsylvania Press............P0913

Medieval Literature
See more broadly: Literature
Ashley Drake Publishing Ltd P0055

Memoir
See more broadly: Autobiography
See more specifically: Literary Memoir; Celebrity Memoir

Men's Fiction
Richter, Rick...L1147

Men's Interests

Mental Health
See more broadly: Health
Ekstrom, Rachel L0419
Finegan, Stevie.......................................L0469
Simpson, Cara Lee L1282

Methodism
See more broadly: Christianity
Light & Life M0322

Middle East
See more broadly: Regional
Chudney Agency, The.............................L0269
Davies, Sarah...L0342
Hakim, Serene L0596

Middle Grade

Midwifery
See more broadly: Nursing

Military
See more broadly: Warfare
*See more specifically: Special Forces; Military
    Aviation*

Military Aviation
See more broadly: Military; Aviation

Military History
See more broadly: History; Warfare

Millennial Fiction

Mind, Body, Spirit
See more broadly: Health

Model Aircraft
See more broadly: Model Making

Model Making
See more broadly: Crafts
*See more specifically: Model Aircraft; Model
    Ships and Boats*

Model Ships and Boats
See more broadly: Model Making

Modern History
See more broadly: History

Motherhood
See more broadly: Parenting

Motivational Self-Help
See more broadly: Self Help

Motor Boats
See more broadly: Boats

Motorbikes
See more broadly: Vehicles

Motorcycling
See more broadly: Hobbies

Motorhomes
See more broadly: Vehicles

Motorsports
See more broadly: Sport

Mountain Lifestyle
See more broadly: Lifestyle

Multicultural
See more broadly: Culture

Music
*See more specifically: Popular Music; Roots
    Music; Church Music*

Mysticism
See more broadly: Supernatural / Paranormal
See more specifically: Fortune Telling
Narrative Essays
See more broadly: Narrative Nonfiction
See more specifically: Personal Essays

Neuroscience

New Adult

New Age

New Zealand

News

Noir

Nonfiction

Popular
See more specifically: Popular Science; Popular History; Popular Culture; Popular Music; Popular Psychology

Popular Culture
See more broadly: Culture; Popular

Popular History
See more broadly: History; Popular

Popular Music
See more broadly: Music; Popular

Popular Psychology
See more broadly: Psychology; Popular

Popular Reference

Popular Science
See more broadly: Science; Popular

Post-Apocalyptic
See more broadly: Science Fiction

Postcolonialism
See more broadly: Culture; Society

Pregnancy
See more broadly: Parenting

Prehistoric Animals
See more broadly: Animals
See more specifically: Dinosaurs

Prescriptive Nonfiction

Claim your free access to www.firstwriter.com: See p.423

Time Travel

See more broadly: Science Fiction

Timeslip Romance

See more broadly: Romance

Trade

See more broadly: Business

Traditional

Translations

Transport

See more specifically: Aviation; Vehicles

Travel

*See more specifically: Road Trips; Sailing; Air
   Travel*

Claim your free access to **www.firstwriter.com**: See p.423

Get Free Access to the firstwriter.com Website

To claim your free access to the firstwriter.com website simply go to the website at https://www.firstwriter.com/subscribe and begin the subscription process as normal. On the second page, enter the required details (such as your name and address, etc.) then for "Voucher / coupon number" enter the following promotional code:

- **D34C-HAS9**

This will reduce the cost of creating a subscription by up to $15 / £10 / €15, making it free to create a monthly, quarterly, or combination subscription. Alternatively, you can use the discount to take out an annual or life subscription at a reduced rate.

Continue the process until your account is created. Please note that you will need to provide your payment details, even if there is no up-front payment. This is in case you choose to leave your subscription running after the free initial period, but there is no obligation for you to do so.

When you use this code to take out a free subscription you are under no obligation to make any payments whatsoever and you are free to cancel your account before you make any payments if you wish.

If you need any assistance, please email support@firstwriter.com.

If you have found this book useful, please consider leaving a review on the website where you bought it.

What you get

Once you have set up access to the site you will be able to benefit from all the following features:

Databases

All our databases are updated almost every day, and include powerful search facilities to help you find exactly what you need. Searches that used to take you hours or even days in print books or on search engines can now be done in seconds, and produce more accurate and up-to-date information. Our agents database also includes independent reports from at least three separate sources, showing you which are the top agencies and helping you avoid the scams that are all over the internet. You can try out any of our databases before you subscribe:

Search dozens of **current competitions**

Search **over 2,300 literary agents and agencies**

Search **over 2,400 magazines**

Search **over 2,800 book publishers** that **don't** charge fees

Plus advanced features to help you with your search:

- Save searches and save time – set multiple search parameters specific to your work, save them, and then access the search results with a single click whenever you log in. You can even save multiple different searches if you have different types of work you are looking to place.
- Add personal notes to listings, visible only to you and fully searchable – helping you to organise your actions.
- Set reminders on listings to notify you when to submit your work, when to follow up, when to expect a reply, or any other custom action.
- Track which listings you've viewed and when, to help you organise your search – any listings which have changed since you last viewed them will be highlighted for your attention!

Daily email updates

As a subscriber you will be able to take advantage of our email alert service, meaning you can specify your particular interests and we'll send you automatic email updates when we change or add a listing that matches them. So if you're interested in agents dealing in romantic fiction in the United States you can have us send you emails with the latest updates about them – keeping you up to date without even having to log in.

User feedback

Our agent, publisher, and magazine databases all include a user feedback feature that allows our subscribers to leave feedback on each listing – giving you not only the chance to have your say about the markets you contact, but giving a unique authors' perspective on the listings.

Save on copyright protection fees

If you're sending your work away to publishers, competitions, or literary agents, it's vital that you first protect your copyright. As a subscriber to firstwriter.com you can do this through our site and save 10% on the copyright registration fees normally payable for protecting your work internationally through the Intellectual Property Rights Office.

Monthly newsletter

When you subscribe to firstwriter.com you also receive our monthly email newsletter – described by one publishing company as "the best in the business" – including articles, news, and interviews for writers. And the best part is that you can continue to receive the newsletter even after you stop your paid subscription – at no cost!

Terms and conditions

The promotional code contained in this publication may be used by the owner of the book only to create one subscription to firstwriter.com at a reduced cost, or for free. It may not be used by or disseminated to third parties. Should the code be misused then the owner of the book will be liable for any costs incurred, including but not limited to payment in full at the standard rate for the subscription in question. The code may be used at any time until the end of the calendar year named in the title of the publication, after which time it will become invalid. The code may be redeemed against the creation of a new account only – it cannot be redeemed against the ongoing costs of keeping a subscription open. In order to create a subscription a method of payment must be provided, but there is no obligation to make any payment. Subscriptions may be cancelled at any time, and if an account is cancelled before any payment becomes due then no payment will be made. Once a subscription has been created, the normal schedule of payments will begin on a monthly, quarterly, or annual basis, unless a life Subscription is selected, or the subscription is cancelled prior to the first payment becoming due. Subscriptions may be cancelled at any time, but if they are left open beyond the date at which the first payment becomes due and is processed then payments will not be refundable.